to think about what is particular and what is universal about the descent of one of the world's most "civilized' nations into genocidal barbarism, then I believe it succeeds." —*Financial Times*

"Insightful . . . [Evans] strikes a reasoned balance between the need to understand societal context and building a convincing case for the importance of individual personalities. . . . This is a valuable work for readers interested in history or threats to democracy."
—*Shelf Awareness*

"Superb . . . Searching, humane scholarship."
—*The Washington Times*

PENGUIN BOOKS

HITLER'S PEOPLE

Richard J. Evans is one of the world's leading historians of modern Germany. He has served as Regius Professor of History at the University of Cambridge; president of Wolfson College, Cambridge; and provost of Gresham College in London. He has received the Hamburg Medal for Art and Science for cultural services to the city and the British Academy's Leverhulme Medal and Prize, awarded for a significant contribution to the humanities or social sciences. In 2000, he was the principal expert witness in the David Irving Holocaust denial libel trial at the High Court of Justice in London, subsequently the subject of the film *Denial*. His books include *Death in Hamburg* (winner of the Wolfson History Prize), *In Defence of History*, *The Coming of the Third Reich*, *The Third Reich in Power*, *The Third Reich at War*, and *The Pursuit of Power: Europe 1815–1914*, volume 7 of the Penguin History of Europe. His most recent books are *Eric Hobsbawm: A Life in History* and *The Hitler Conspiracies: The Third Reich and the Paranoid Imagination*. In 2012, he was knighted for services to scholarship.

RICHARD J. EVANS

Hitler's People
The Faces of the Third Reich

PENGUIN BOOKS

PENGUIN BOOKS
An imprint of Penguin Random House LLC
1745 Broadway, New York, NY 10019
penguinrandomhouse.com

Copyright © 2024, 2025 by Richard J. Evans

Penguin Random House values and supports copyright. Copyright fuels creativity, encourages diverse voices, promotes free speech and creates a vibrant culture. Thank you for buying an authorized edition of this book and for complying with copyright laws by not reproducing, scanning, or distributing any part of it in any form without permission. You are supporting writers and allowing Penguin Random House to continue to publish books for every reader. Please note that no part of this book may be used or reproduced in any manner for the purpose of training artificial intelligence technologies or systems.

Illustration credits appear on pages xiii-xiv.

ISBN 9780593296448 (paperback)

THE LIBRARY OF CONGRESS HAS CATALOGED THE HARDCOVER EDITION AS FOLLOWS:
Names: Evans, Richard J., author.
Title: Hitler's People : The Faces of the Third Reich / Richard J. Evans.
Other titles: Faces of the Third Reich
Description: New York : Penguin Press, 2024. | Includes bibliographical references and index.
Identifiers: LCCN 2024025047 (print) | LCCN 2024025048 (ebook) | ISBN 9780593296424 (hardcover) | ISBN 9780593296431 (ebook)
Subjects: LCSH: Nationalsozialistische Deutsche Arbeiter-Partei—Biography. | Nazis—Biography.
Classification: LCC DD244 .E83 2024(print) | LCC DD244(ebook) | DDC 943.086/0922—dc23/eng/20240604
LC record available at https://lccn.loc.gov/2024025047
LC ebook record available at https://lccn.loc.gov/2024025048

First published in Great Britain by Allen Lane publishing,
an imprint of Penguin Random House UK, in 2024.
Simultaneously published in the United States of America by
Penguin Press, an imprint of Penguin Random House LLC, in 2024.
This revised edition published by Penguin Books,
an imprint of Penguin Random House UK, in 2025.
Published by Penguin Books 2025.

Printed in the United States of America
1st Printing

The authorized representative in the EU for product safety and compliance is Penguin Random House Ireland, Morrison Chambers, 32 Nassau Street, Dublin D02 YH68, Ireland, https://eu-contact.penguin.ie.

*In memoriam John Dixon Walsh (1927–2022),
who taught me History*

Contents

List of Illustrations — xiii

Preface — xv

Prologue: The Lady at the Trial — xxi

PART I
The Leader

Introduction — 3

1 The Dictator: Adolf Hitler — 11

PART II
The Paladins

Introduction — 105

2 The 'Iron Man': Hermann Göring — 109
3 The Propagandist: Joseph Goebbels — 133
4 The Soldier: Ernst Röhm — 149
5 The Policeman: Heinrich Himmler — 163
6 The Diplomat: Joachim von Ribbentrop — 183
7 The Philosopher: Alfred Rosenberg — 203
8 The Architect: Albert Speer — 219

PART III
The Enforcers

Introduction — 235

9 The Deputy: Rudolf Hess — 239
10 The Collaborator: Franz von Papen — 255

11 The 'Worker': Robert Ley   275
12 The Schoolmaster: Julius Streicher   291
13 The Hangman: Reinhard Heydrich   303
14 The Bureaucrat: Adolf Eichmann   319
15 The Loudmouth: Hans Frank   335

PART IV
The Instruments

Introduction   355
16 The General: Wilhelm Ritter von Leeb   359
17 The Professional: Karl Brandt   375
18 The Killers: Paul Zapp and Egon Zill   387
19 The 'Witch' and the 'Beast': Ilse Koch and Irma Grese   399
20 The Mother: Gertrud Scholtz-Klink   413
21 The Star: Leni Riefenstahl   427
22 The Denunciator: Luise Solmitz   443

Conclusion   461
Epilogue: The Lady on the Train   471

Notes   475
Bibliography   547
Index   581

List of Illustrations

Photographic credits are shown in italics

p. 10: Hitler standing by the Baltic Sea in East Prussia, before 1932. *Ullstein Bild/Getty Images.*

p. 110: Hermann Göring, holding a lion cub at the miniature zoo on his Carinhall Estate, Berlin, c. 1935. *Bettmann/Getty Images.*

p. 132: Joseph Goebbels, 1930s. *Universal History Archive/Getty Images.*

p. 148: Ernst Röhm, c. 1930. *Hulton Archive/Getty Images.*

p. 164: Heinrich Himmler (*left*) with General Walter von Reichenau, watching the NSDAP Winter Games in Rottach-Egern, 1937. *Ullstein bild/Getty Images.*

p. 182: Joachim von Ribbentrop (*left*) with Benito Mussolini during negotiations in Mussolini's saloon car, 1940. *Heinrich Hoffmann/Ullstein Bild/Getty Images.*

p. 202: Alfred Rosenberg speaking at a festival to mark the composer Handel's 250th birthday, Halle, 1935. *Bettmann/Getty Images.*

p. 220: Albert Speer, 1933. *Ullstein Bild/Getty Images.*

p. 240: Rudolf Hess delivering a speech, c. 1935. *Gamma-Keystone/Getty Images.*

p. 256: Franz von Papen, 1934. *Imagno/Getty Images.*

p. 276: Robert Ley (*left*) during a factory visit in Berlin, with the Duke of Windsor, 1937. *FPG/Archive Photos/Getty Images.*

p. 290: Julius Streicher giving a speech at Berlin-Tempelhof Airport, 1935. *Ullstein Bild /Getty Images.*

p. 304: Reinhard Heydrich in a fencing suit, 1943. *Ullstein Bild /Getty Images.*

p. 320: Adolf Eichmann, undated photograph. *Ullstein Bild/Getty Images.*

p. 334: Hans Frank, 1935. *Bettmann/Getty Images.*

p. 360: Wilhelm Ritter von Leeb, 1941. *Heinrich Hoffmann/Ullstein Bild/Getty Images.*

LIST OF ILLUSTRATIONS

p. 374: Karl Brandt during his trial, Nuremberg, 1947. *Gamma-Keystone/Getty Images*.

p. 389: Paul Zapp (*above*) during his trial, Munich, 1970. *Keystone/Hulton Archive/Getty Images*. Egon Zill (*below*) with Bosnian volunteers of the Waffen-SS, 1943. *Bundesarchiv (Bild 146-1974-059-40)*.

p. 400: (*above*) Ilse Koch, 1940. *Universal History Archive/UIG/Getty Images*. (*below*) Irma Grese, awaiting trial at Celle, 1945. *Apic/Getty Images*.

p. 414: Gertrud Scholtz-Klink delivering a speech, Stuttgart, 1938. *Heinrich Hoffmann/UIllstein Bild/Getty Images*.

p. 429: Leni Riefenstahl witnessing a massacre of Jews in Końskie, Poland, 1939. *Instytut Pamieci Narodowej, Warsaw (GK-5-1-237-5-1)*.

p. 444: Luise Solmitz with her husband, Friedrich Solmitz, and daughter Gisela. *Staatsarchiv Hamburg (Solmitz-Nachlass, Bestand 622-1/140 Solmitz, Akte 16)*.

Preface

Who were the Nazis? What motivated the leaders and functionaries of the Nazi movement and those who put their project into action? What had happened to their moral compass? Were they in some sense deviant, or deranged, or degenerate? Were they gangsters acting with criminal intent? Or were they 'ordinary men' (and a few women), or perhaps, more precisely, 'ordinary Germans'? Did they come from the margins of society, were they outsiders, or were they in some sense part of German society's mainstream? And how do we explain Hitler's drive to achieve dictatorial power? Was he a kind of empty shell, devoid of personal qualities and without a personal life, into which Germans poured their deepest political ambitions and desires? What made otherwise normal people carry out, or approve, terrible and murderous atrocities against Nazism's real and supposed enemies? Or were they perhaps not normal at all? Beyond this, why did so many leading Germans in responsible positions, in the key institutions of society, go along with dictatorship, war and genocide? And what did those of them who survived the war think about their conduct under the Third Reich? Did they gain a moral perspective on it, did they repent, did they come to an understanding of what they had done?

These questions are at the heart of the present book. And in the past few years, they have gained new urgency and importance. For, since shortly after the beginning of the twenty-first century, democratic institutions have been under threat in many countries across the world. Strongmen and would-be dictators are emerging, often with considerable popular support, to undermine democracy, muzzle the media, control the judiciary, stifle opposition, and undermine basic human rights. Political corruption, lies, dishonesty and deceit are becoming the new currency of politics, with fatal results for our fundamental freedoms. Hatred and persecution of minorities are on the increase, stoked by unscrupulous politicians. The future is bleak, the prospects for freedom and democracy uncertain.

How do we explain the rise and triumph of tyrants and charlatans? What causes someone to be gripped by a lust for power and domination? Why do such men – and they are almost always men – manage to gather round them disciples and supporters willing to carry out their commands? Is society's set of moral values so weak, or so warped, that their willingness to violate the conventional precepts of human decency comes to know no bounds? In this troubling situation, many people look to the past for answers to these questions. The paradigm of democracy's collapse and dictatorship's triumph remains the fate of Germany's Weimar Republic and the rise of the Nazis. Hitler and his circle have been understood in many different ways: as a group of psychopaths, a gang of criminals, a collection of outsiders, even a modern version of the most deranged and destructive Emperors of Ancient Rome and their courts. Not infrequently, they have been described as insane, or at least psychologically disturbed in some way. This book takes a close look at the people who overthrew the fragile democracy of the Weimar Republic, set up the Third Reich, kept it in power for over a decade, and drove it into war, genocide and self-destruction. Only by examining individual personalities and their stories can we reach an understanding of the perverted morality that made and sustained the Nazi regime, and, by doing so, perhaps learn some lessons for the troubled era in which we live.

Yet in the half-century after the war, the biographical approach was unfashionable, especially in Germany, for the obvious reason that the cult of 'great men' reached its disastrous climax under Nazism and turned out to be a dangerously undemocratic way of understanding human society. Leading historians of Nazism, such as the late Hans Mommsen, emphasized instead structural factors, institutions and processes. Mommsen even thought it would be easier to understand Nazism and the Third Reich if one left out individuals from the story altogether.[1] In Germany, more generally, an emphasis on the importance of individuals in the Nazi movement and the Third Reich too easily seemed to distract attention from the involvement of German institutions and traditions and, more generally, the German people themselves, in this darkest of all chapters of modern history. Pinning everything on

Hitler, or even on his immediate underlings as well, looked too much like a kind of exculpation of the great mass of Germans.

In the last few decades, a vast amount of research has been carried out into the social and institutional history of Germany and the Germans in the first half of the twentieth century. Paradoxically perhaps, it has redirected historians' attention once more, in a different and more sophisticated form, onto the leaders and servants of the Nazi movement and the Nazi regime, posing the questions of who they were, what they were like, how much power they wielded, and in what ways they worked together to create and run the most murderous and most destructive regime in human history. They were, after all, individuals, often with sharply delineated personalities, whose thoughts and actions had a material effect, especially under a dictatorship that imposed few restrictions on their appetites, their desires, their ideas, their actions or their lust for power.

In recent years, therefore, major, deeply researched biographies have been published of virtually all the major Nazi leaders, and a great many studies have appeared of individuals lower down the ladder of power. Our knowledge of men like Goebbels, Speer, Himmler, Rosenberg, and indeed Hitler himself has been transformed by the publication of diaries, letters and memoirs, of annotated scholarly editions of documents, and of numerous previously unavailable sources of many kinds. We also know vastly more than we did half a century ago about the ordinary Germans of the Nazi era, including lower-level perpetrators, what motivated them and why they served the regime with such a lack of scruple. Here too, there have been publications of letters, diaries and memoirs, often of very humble individuals, that have yielded a rich and complex harvest of new material with which to deepen our understanding of the problems facing people in Hitler's Germany and the ways in which they tried to deal with them. The transformation of our knowledge of the Nazi movement and the Nazi dictatorship goes far down the scale of responsibility and complicity, and the biographical approach, often based on evidence presented in post-war trials, has emerged as a mainstay of 'perpetrator research' (*Täterforschung*) since around the turn of the century. The basis for an attempt at answering the questions with which this book began is now available to a far greater extent than it was even twenty years ago.[2]

The individuals who stand at the centre of this book range from top to bottom, from Hitler himself all the way down to the lowest ranks of the Nazi Party and beyond. The present work consciously takes as its model the classic study by the late German historian, journalist and broadcaster Joachim C. Fest, *The Face of the Third Reich*, first published in 1963 and reprinted many times since. Fest's book became an instant bestseller and was translated into many foreign languages. More than sixty years after its first publication, it is still well worth reading. Yet, as a book written several decades ago, *The Face of the Third Reich* has been overtaken by historical research in many matters of detail. Moreover, our overall understanding of Nazi Germany has also changed dramatically since the 1960s. Writing at the height of the Cold War, Fest saw the Third Reich as a 'totalitarian' society comparable to Stalin's dictatorship in the Soviet Union. The end of the Cold War in Europe has led to changes in perspective that have been backed by developments in the discipline of history itself. Our view of the Nazi regime has grown more sophisticated, and questions of what made people become 'perpetrators', 'bystanders' and 'victims' – to adopt categories which themselves need to be interrogated and applied in a nuanced and discriminating way – have to be understood within a wider context of coercion and consent; people did not, in other words, make decisions as morally autonomous individuals, acting in a vacuum unconstrained by their historical context, but neither were they automata deprived of the power of judgement and just doing what they were told. The reasons for the decisions they made have to be sought not simply in their psychological makeup as individuals, but also in their reaction to the situations in which they found themselves, and their relation to the wider society around them.[3]

Two decades ago or so, I tried to explain Nazism through a large-scale narrative history of the Third Reich. After the publication of the third and final volume in 2008, I moved on to other projects.[4] When I returned to working on Nazi Germany, I found that much had changed: new research, new archival discoveries, new, previously unpublished documents, had become available, new work had developed fresh perspectives and novel interpretations. The emergence in our own time of a class of unscrupulous populist politicians who do not care whether what they are saying is true, and the massive growth of the internet and social media, have fostered a much more widespread uncertainty about truth, coupled with a disdain for evidence-based statements and the work of scholars and experts. All of this has prompted reflections on my earlier work, and preparing the present book has provided the opportunity to revisit and in some cases reconsider the conclusions I reached in it. Coming back to the history of Nazi Germany from a different angle – the biographical – has been a fascinating and rewarding experience.

The book is structured in four parts. The first looks again at the career and ideas of Adolf Hitler, the Leader; in the second part, we turn to his immediate circle of subordinates; the third part tells the stories of the enablers and executors of Nazi ideology; and the fourth and final part surveys a variety of lower-level perpetrators and instruments of the regime. This is not a biographical dictionary, however; rather, it is a collection of interlinked biographical essays and reflections on individual personalities. Obviously, there is a certain arbitrariness about the selection; Joachim Fest, for example, included a chapter on Martin Bormann, but relatively little is known about this largely behind-the-scenes figure, who achieved importance only towards the end of the regime, so I have chosen to omit him. While Fest included a chapter on 'intellectuals' – mainly literary figures – I have included one on professionals – focusing in particular on medical practitioners. I have included coverage of ordinary perpetrators, who did not emerge clearly from Fest's survey either as a group or as individuals. Fest included a general chapter on women, but it is one of the weakest in his book, and I have focused instead on a series of particular women, ranging from fanatical supporters of the regime to 'fellow travellers' and profiteers from Nazi rule. Each chapter can be read on its own, independently of what precedes it, though this necessitates some repetition, which I have tried to keep to a minimum. The opening chapter, on Hitler, as well as being an exploration of the key figure in the whole story, presents a background narrative against which the following chapters have to be read, thus, I hope, avoiding going over the same ground time after time.

I began writing this book out of a sense of curiosity: over many years of teaching about and researching the Third Reich, I felt I knew far more about the bigger historical processes and impacts of the Nazis than I did about their individual leaders and followers, whose character in many instances I realized I did not fully understand. This volume is my attempt to explore the personalities of perpetrators, set in their social and political contexts; but I hope that at least some patterns and

PREFACE

commonalities emerge as well. During my explorations I have received help from many individuals and institutions. I could not have even begun this enterprise without drawing on the vast resources of Cambridge University Library, whose holdings on modern German history are second to none. Many people have listened patiently to me as I tried to explain my approach, and I have benefited hugely from their encouragement. Working with Ella Wright, Helen Sage and the rest of the 72 Films team on *Rise of the Nazis* for BBC 2, and, across the Atlantic, Rachael Profiloski, Axel Gerdau and the team at Spectacle Films, was an instructive and rewarding experience that taught me a lot. A number of friends and colleagues have read the typescript, and I am deeply indebted to Joanna Bourke, Niamh Gallagher, Jan Rueger, Rosie Schellenberg and Nik Wachsmann for their encouragement and their suggestions and corrections. Simon Winder at Allen Lane in London and Scott Moyers and Helen Rouner at the Penguin Press in New York have been exemplary editors, while Richard Duguid has been a pleasure to work with on the production of this book. Richard Mason has been a meticulous copy-editor and Cecilia Mackay an indefatigable picture researcher. Christine L. Corton has sustained me throughout the process of research, writing and production, as well as turning a professional eye on the proofs. I am deeply indebted to them all. As always, I alone am responsible for any errors.

The dedication to my tutor at Oxford reflects my gratitude for a wonderful introduction to the discipline of history that has lasted a life time.

Barkway, Hertfordshire, January 2024

Prologue: The Lady at the Trial

The photojournalist Marie-Claude Vaillant-Couturier (1912–1996) was arrested in February 1942 for Resistance activities in France and sent to Auschwitz, where she was interned until her transfer to Ravensbrück concentration camp in August 1944. She gave the following evidence about what she had witnessed in Auschwitz to the Nuremberg War Crimes Tribunal, under examination by the French prosecutor, Charles Dubost, on 28 January 1946.

> MME. VAILLANT-COUTURIER: ... [W]e saw the unsealing of the cars and the soldiers letting men, women, and children out of them. We then witnessed heart-rending scenes; old couples forced to part from each other, mothers made to abandon their young [adolescent] daughters, since the latter were sent to the camp, whereas mothers and [small] children were sent to the gas chambers. All these people were unaware of the fate awaiting them. They were merely upset at being separated, but they did not know that they were going to their death. To render their welcome more pleasant at this time – June to July 1944 – an orchestra composed of internees, all young and pretty girls dressed in little white blouses and navy blue skirts, played [...] at the arrival of the trains, gay tunes such as "The Merry Widow," the "Barcarolle" from "The Tales of Hoffman," and so forth. They were then informed that this was a labor camp and since they were not brought into the camp they saw only the small platform surrounded by flowering plants. Naturally, they could not realize what was in store for them. Those selected for the gas chamber, that is, the old people, mothers, and children, were escorted to a red-brick building.
> DUBOST: These were not given an identification number?

VAILLANT-COUTURIER: No.
DUBOST: They were not tattooed?
VAILLANT-COUTURIER: No. They were not even counted.
DUBOST: You were tattooed?
VAILLANT-COUTURIER: Yes, look. [The witness showed her arm.] They were taken to a red-brick building, which bore the letters "Baden," that is to say "Baths." There, to begin with, they were made to undress [...] before they went into the so-called shower room. Later on, at the time of the large convoys from Hungary, they had no more time left to play-act or to pretend; they were brutally undressed, and I know these details as I knew a little Jewess from France who lived with her family at the "Republique" district.
DUBOST: In Paris?
VAILLANT-COUTURIER: In Paris. She was called "little Marie" and she was the only one, the sole survivor of a family of nine. Her mother and her seven brothers and sisters had been gassed on arrival. When I met her she was employed to undress the babies before they were taken into the gas chamber. Once the people were undressed they took them into a room, which was somewhat like a shower room, and gas capsules were thrown through an opening in the ceiling. An SS man would watch the effect produced through a porthole. At the end of 5 or 7 minutes, when the gas had completed its work, he gave the signal to open the doors; and men with gas masks – they too were internees – went into the room and removed the corpses. They told us that the internees must have suffered before dying, because they were closely clinging to one another and it was very difficult to separate them.

After that a special squad would come to pull out gold teeth and dentures; and again, when the bodies had been reduced to ashes, they would sift them in an attempt to recover the gold.

At Auschwitz there were eight [*actually, four*] crematories but, as from 1944, these proved insufficient. The SS had large pits dug by the internees, where they put branches, sprinkled with gasoline, which they set on fire. Then they threw the corpses into the pits. From our block we could see after about three-quarters of an hour or an hour after the arrival of a convoy, large flames coming from the crematory, and the sky was lighted up by the burning pits ...
DUBOST: Can you tell us about the selections that were made at the beginning of winter?

PROLOGUE: THE LADY AT THE TRIAL

VAILLANT-COUTURIER: ... During Christmas 1944 – no, 1943, Christmas 1943 – when we were in quarantine, we saw, since we lived opposite Block 25, women brought to Block 25 stripped naked. Uncovered trucks were then driven up and on them the naked women were piled, as many as the trucks could hold. Each time a truck started, the infamous Hössler ... ran after the truck and with his bludgeon repeatedly struck the naked women going to their death. They knew they were going to the gas chamber and tried to escape. They were massacred. They attempted to jump from the truck and we, from our own block, watched the trucks pass by and heard the grievous wailing of all those women who knew they were going to be gassed. Many of them could very well have lived on, since they were suffering only from scabies and were, perhaps, a little too undernourished ...

Since the Jewesses were sent to Auschwitz with their entire families and since they had been told that this was a sort of ghetto and were advised to bring all their goods and chattels along, they consequently brought considerable riches with them. As for the Jewesses from Salonika, I remember that on their arrival they were given picture postcards bearing the post office address of "Waldsee," a place which did not exist; and a printed text to be sent to their families, stating, "We are doing very well here; we have work and we are well treated. We await your arrival." I myself saw the cards in question; and the *Schreiberinnen*, that is, the secretaries of the block, were instructed to distribute them among the internees in order to post them to their families. I know that whole families arrived as a result of these postcards.

[Cross-examination by Dr Hanns Marx, attorney for Julius Streicher]

MARX: ... You said before that the German people must have known of the happenings in Auschwitz. What are your grounds for this statement?
VAILLANT-COUTURIER: I have already told you: To begin with there was the fact that when we left, the Lorraine soldiers of the Wehrmacht who were taking us to Auschwitz said to us, "If you knew where you were going, you would not be in such a hurry to get there." Then there was the fact that the German women who came out of quarantine to go to work in German factories knew of these events, and they all said that they would speak about them outside. Further, the fact that in all the factories where the prisoners worked they were in contact with the German

civilians, as also were the female guards, who were in touch with their friends and families and often told them what they had seen.

(International Military Tribunal, Trial Proceedings, vol. 6, Forty-Fourth Day, Monday 28 January 1946, Morning Session)

PART I

The Leader

Introduction

There is no way of beginning this book except with a biographical essay on Hitler. Without Hitler, there would have been no Third Reich, no World War II, and no Holocaust, or at least not in the form that these calamitous events took. Yet Hitler has often been described as an enigma. We all know he was the dictator who started World War II and ordered the extermination of six million European Jews before committing suicide in the Berlin bunker on 30 April 1945. If we want a more detailed answer to the questions that surround him, however, we can turn to the series of biographies that have been published at intervals since the 1930s. Leaving aside the thousands of derivative potboilers, speculative fantasies, politically exploitative narratives, sensational but dubious 'revelations' and obsessive but unprovable theorizings that continue to flood the book market, the press, the internet and the media, we still have a number of serious, deeply researched, and carefully assembled lives of the Nazi leader. The first was penned during Hitler's lifetime by the liberal German journalist Konrad Heiden, a contemporary who witnessed Hitler's rise to prominence from Munich in the 1920s and early 1930s and, after he had fled Germany in January 1933, wrote a well-informed life linking Hitler's rise to power to the wishes and anxieties of the German people.[1]

It was not until after Hitler's death and the defeat of the Third Reich, however, that a fuller picture could be painted of the Nazi dictator's life. The first serious post-war biography was by the British historian Alan Bullock, a prominent intellectual in the Labour Party and well known to the British public through his contributions to BBC radio's *The Brains Trust*. His biography *Hitler: A Study in Tyranny* depicted Hitler as a political opportunist, driven not by ideology or belief but by an untrammelled 'will to power'. Bullock was heavily influenced in this view by the disillusioned German conservative Hermann Rauschning, who saw Hitler's seizure of power as a 'revolution of nihilism', to quote the title of his penetrating analysis of the rise of Nazism. But Bullock's interpretation was quickly challenged by his fellow Oxford don Hugh Trevor-Roper, author of the classic investigative report *The Last Days of Hitler* (1947), who in his essay 'The Mind of Adolf Hitler' argued that Hitler was in fact driven by a coherent set of purposes.[2]

Despite the massive public success of Bullock's biography, it was Trevor-Roper's view that eventually prevailed. In 1969, as serious academic research into Nazism and its origins was just getting under way in Germany, the Stuttgart historian Eberhard Jäckel published a short book arguing that Hitler was dominated, not by a lust for power, but by two core beliefs: antisemitism, an exterminatory hatred of all Jews; and *Lebensraum*, 'living-space', the idea that Germany and the Germans needed to conquer East-Central and Eastern Europe in order to survive.[3] In the light of such arguments, Bullock eventually changed his mind and in his later work admitted to a strong degree of ideology in Hitler's mental make-up.[4] All subsequent biographies have indeed portrayed Hitler as an ideologue. But they have varied widely in approach and interpretation. The conservative German journalist Joachim Fest, an accomplished and knowledgeable historian, was first in the field, with a massive biography first published in English in 1974.[5] Like Rauschning, Fest also saw Hitler as a revolutionary, though one who incorporated reactionary elements into his world view. More than anyone else, however, it was Albert Speer whose picture of the Nazi leader exerted the most influence on Fest, who collaborated with the former arms minister on his memoir *Inside the Third Reich* and took up many of Speer's often-misleading interpretations in his biography. Fest was widely praised at the time for his psychological insights into Hitler's character, but today many of these seem vague and unsubstantiated. In linking Hitler's career to its wider historical context, Fest relied too much on sweeping psychological generalizations about 'the German people', the 'pathology' of the times, and the 'disorientation' of ordinary Germans that supposedly followed the defeat of 1918. Reviewers also charged that he underplayed the role of conservative elites in bringing Hitler to power and supporting him thereafter.[6]

It was not until the very end of the 1990s, however, that Fest's biography was superseded by another, even more voluminous one, in two volumes, by the British historian Ian Kershaw. Originally a medievalist, Kershaw had retrained as a historian of Nazi Germany at the Institute for Contemporary History in Munich. Here his mentor was the Institute's Director Martin Broszat, who focused above all on impersonal structures of power in Nazi Germany. Applying the Weberian concept of charisma to the German dictator's life, Kershaw portrayed Hitler as in part the creation of a 'charismatic community' of enthusiastic disciples whose adulation pushed the Nazi leader into an ever-stronger belief in himself during the 1920s. Initially sceptical about his own ability to lead Germany out of the chaos of the early post-war years, Hitler had become convinced by the mid-1920s of what his immediate supporters unceasingly assured him was his historic mission. He did not, therefore, as many commentators had implied, seduce people into following him: it was his followers who inspired him to lead them. After the 'seizure of power', Hitler's ideological drive began to be translated into policies, but, given his irregular work habits, his subordinates often had to guess at how this was to be done, 'working towards the Führer', as the phrase coined by one senior civil servant put it. Since they usually imagined that the policy he would have favoured was the most 'National Socialist', or in other words, the most extreme one, this generated a self-perpetuating process of radicalization to which Hitler generally felt obliged to conform.[7]

Precisely the opposite line was taken by the German historian Peter Longerich, author of a number of important biographies of leading Nazis including Joseph Goebbels and Heinrich Himmler.[8] Longerich declared that it was time to abandon the idea of Hitler as 'a man who stood in the shadow of his own charisma', the creation of 'social forces and the determinative structure of the Nazi system of rule'.[9] Instead, he argued, 'whether in foreign policy and waging war, terror and mass murder, church policy, cultural questions or the everyday life of the Germans, everywhere Hitler determined the policy of the regime in detail.'[10] Yet a reading of Longerich's book reveals numerous instances where his determination to ascribe everything to the workings of Hitler's will is something of an overreaction to previous attempts to depict Hitler as a 'weak dictator', the plaything of impersonal structural forces, reacting to rather than shaping events. And as the author of the latest major biography, the German journalist Volker Ullrich, an academically trained historian with a string of important books to his credit, points out, the claim that Kershaw's biography presented readers with a dictator who was 'basically interchangeable, redundant, at best weak' is unfair.[11] In fact, Kershaw avoided the twin pitfalls of 'intentionalism', ascribing everything that happened to Hitler's will, and 'functionalism', ascribing it all more or less exclusively to impersonal, structural factors, and focused instead on the interaction between the two, thus transcending this long-running debate.[12]

This indeed is the line taken by Ullrich himself in his biography of the Nazi leader.[13] But Ullrich also presented a more human Hitler than either Kershaw or Longerich had done. It is striking, beyond all the marked differences between the approach of his various biographers, how there seems to be a general agreement that Hitler was a man without a personal life, devoid of normal human feeling, who threw himself into politics not least as a way of escaping his inner emptiness. Such a view goes as far back as Konrad Heiden, who wrote that he 'lacked the courage for a private life'.[14] Kershaw wrote of Hitler's 'disturbed sexuality, his recoiling from physical contact, his fear of women, his inability to forge genuine friendship and emptiness in human relations'.[15] Longerich declared that 'a private Hitler outside his public role simply did not exist'.[16] Fest had also concluded that 'Hitler did not have a private life.'[17] Ullrich wrote in similar terms of Hitler's 'lack of an inner emotional compass'.[18] In reaching these conclusions, Hitler's biographers were, perhaps unconsciously, echoing Hitler himself, who insisted repeatedly that he had sacrificed his private life and happiness for Germany: single, and, as far as the public was concerned, without a life-partner, he was 'married to Germany'. In fact, however, both Ullrich and Longerich provided plenty of detail about Hitler's close friendships with other people throughout his life, his loyalty to staff with whom he had built a close relationship over many years, and the private life he led with his entourage, especially in his mountain retreat on the Obersalzberg. As for his sexuality, the fact that his medical records indicate that he took a sexual stimulant made from bull's testicles when he was with Eva Braun would seem to be convincing enough evidence for its existence.[19] Historians and others are sometimes criticized for 'humanizing' Hitler, but, as Ullrich argues, that is precisely what needs to be done. Hitler was a human being, and his life and career therefore raise difficult and troubling questions about what it means to be human.[20]

INTRODUCTION

Over the years, biographers of Hitler have had access to an ever-increasing quantity of information and documentation about him. If Konrad Heiden based his contemporary account of the Nazi leader on newspaper reports, interviews and personal observation, Alan Bullock was able to use the post-war transcripts and documents of the Nuremberg War Crimes Tribunal, while the publication from 1962 onwards of Hitler's speeches between 1932 and 1945 in a compendious four-volume collection by the German publicist and writer Max Domarus, and an edition of his earlier writings from 1905 to 1924, published in 1980, provided an important basis for the studies by Fest and Kershaw.[21] The years since 1990 have seen a scholarly edition of Hitler's speeches and proclamations covering the period 1925 to 1933, an annotated reprint of his autobiographical tract *Mein Kampf*, the voluminous diaries of Propaganda Minister Joseph Goebbels, the office diaries of the SS chief Heinrich Himmler, the full journals of the Nazi ideologue Alfred Rosenberg, and much more besides.[22]

One particularly controversial source is the so-called 'table-talk' in which the monologues to which Hitler subjected his lunch and dinner companions in 1941–42 are reported. In July 1941 Martin Bormann came up with the idea of recording these for posterity. Bormann entrusted the task to his adjutant Heinrich Heim, a Nazi lawyer. Hitler did not engage in casual conversation but treated his audience to monologues in which he expounded his ideas on a vast range of topics, and at the height of his power these words of wisdom surely demanded to be preserved, in the view of his acolytes. Heim accompanied Bormann to these meals and listened attentively to what Hitler said, immediately dictating notes to a secretary after the meal was over, sometimes revising them later. Bormann read the resulting documents shortly afterwards, and made a few additions and corrections based on his own memory of the respective monologue, then Heim corrected the typed-up version before the fair copy was produced and archived. During a break between 12 March and 1 August 1942 while Heim was away, his duties were carried out by Henry Picker, another legally trained Nazi official. Heim continued to write up the monologues until 7 September 1942. A few, less detailed, notes were taken on occasion in 1943–44, but they are a good deal less interesting. It was Picker who, after the war, first published an edition of what he called 'Hitler's Table-Talk', which also included the Heim records, together with a variety of testimonies confirming their authenticity and explanatory notes by Picker himself.[23]

These were, then, not based on shorthand transcripts taken by Hitler's secretaries, as has sometimes been assumed, but written up after the event. How reliable are they? Obviously, they are not an exact record, and indeed Heim prefaced each of them with a phrase such as 'The boss expressed himself among other things, in effect, as follows.' Moreover, while Bormann was satisfied with Heim's reports, he was far more critical of Picker's, which contained numerous minor slips and even misdatings and mistranscriptions. However, there is no evidence that anyone, including Bormann, interpolated new material or inserted tendentious amendments in order to give readers a false impression of Hitler's views. After all, by 1941 Hitler was regarded, not least by his staff and by Nazi fanatics like Martin Bormann, as a kind of God, and the actual reason for recording the 'table-talk' was to put down his thoughts as a kind of sacred text, a guide to the imagined Nazi future. Altering the record in any significant way would have been tantamount to sacrilege. Of course, Hitler can hardly have expected his listeners not to repeat what he said to others, so his remarks were far from being private or confidential. But nothing in the 'table-talk' went in any way counter to Hitler's known views as expounded in his speeches and directives, and the frequent repetitions and revisits to previously discussed topics reveal complete consistency in what Hitler said during the period of time covered. They add details to what is already known but contain no startling revelations.[24] It does not follow from the fact that they were written up from memory that they did not more or less faithfully reproduce anything Hitler said, or distorted or misrepresented his thoughts.[25]

Many of the leading Nazis who survived the war, along with those who knew them, published memoirs, some of which have appeared only relatively recently. All this material has its problems, but taken together it provides an indispensable basis for assessing and reassessing Hitler's life and his part in the Nazi movement and the Third Reich. In addition, our knowledge of the wider context of Nazism and the Third Reich has been transformed by a veritable flood of scholarly articles and monographs in the past thirty or more years. The Nazi movement, and still more the Nazi regime, left behind an almost insurmountable mass of bureaucratically generated documentation, only a fraction of which has

INTRODUCTION

been published. So there is no lack of material with which to study the Nazi leader. And yet, despite all this, opinion among historians and biographers remains deeply divided. Understanding what motivated Hitler, and why he was able to exert such power and fascination over so many people, continues to pose real challenges to the historian.[26] The first chapter in this book addresses these challenges and tries to provide answers to them.

I
The Dictator: Adolf Hitler

I

For the first thirty years of his life, Adolf Hitler was a nobody. He was born into obscurity in Braunau, Austria, on 20 April 1889, the son of a minor Austrian civil servant. The absence of information has been filled by speculation, most of it without any firm basis in the evidence, much of it driven by a misguided desire to find explanations for his later career in a supposedly warped individual pathology rooted in the experiences of his early years.[1] Nor can Hitler's own account in his autobiographical political tract *Mein Kampf* be relied on. He did not, as he suggested, grow up in poverty; nor does his father Alois seem to have been an alcoholic. Nevertheless, the use of corporal punishment by his father to keep him in line does appear to have been greater than was normal in late nineteenth-century Austria, and no doubt Hitler was telling the truth when he said he feared his father more than he loved him.[2] Still, his father was supportive of his desire to be an artist, contrary to the impression left in *Mein Kampf*. In 1900, recognizing his talent for drawing, his father enrolled him, not in the humanistic high school which would have qualified him for a career in the professions, but in a technical high school (*Realschule*).[3] Noticeably undisciplined at his school in Linz, the young Hitler spent much of his time drawing and painting, but when, in 1907, he applied to the Academy of Fine Arts in Vienna, he was rejected on the grounds that he could not draw the human head. The Director told him to study architecture instead, but Hitler lacked the qualifications for entry. Still, he continued to think of himself as an artist above anything else.[4]

By this time, Hitler's parents had died, his father in 1903 and his mother, Klara, to whom he was much closer, in 1907. In February 1908 he moved to Vienna, where he stayed for the next five years. Living off his mother's modest legacy, an orphan's pension and subsidies from his wider family, he did not feel it necessary to find a job. Instead he frittered his time away, drawing and sketching, reading – particularly Germanic legends, along with the Wild West stories of Karl May, with their curious atmosphere of doom, decline and redemption through violence – and going to the opera, above all to the music-dramas of Richard Wagner, based largely on medieval myth and sagas of knightly heroism, love and death. His later assertion that he became a follower of the extreme nationalist and antisemite Austrian politician Georg Ritter von Schönerer must be treated with scepticism. Similarly, his claim in *Mein Kampf* to have become a radical antisemite in Vienna was belied by the fact that he was on good terms with a number of Jews during his years there.[5] There is, in fact, no reliable evidence for his having been interested in politics or imbued with a hatred of Jews at this time. Hitler's best friend during his teenage years, the music student August Kubizek, who later became a professional violinist and theatre conductor, left a vivid impression of his character. Passionate, articulate and energetic, Hitler, he remembered, loved to talk, his conversation ranging across many subjects. What he required, however, was not an interlocutor but a listener. The two teenagers became friends because they were regular visitors to the Linz opera, and shared lodgings for a time. A serious young man, Hitler, remembered Kubizek, had little sense of humour, though he was fond of mocking people he knew. He kept his innermost feelings to himself, though Kubizek reported that he fell in love with a girl called Stefanie, but was too shy to do anything about it. Still, Kubizek gave it as his opinion that Hitler's sexuality was 'absolutely normal'. His strict bourgeois moral opinions, however, kept him away from the brothels and street-walkers that were so attractive to so many of his young male contemporaries. Obsessed with art and architecture, he spent a good deal of time in the imaginary redesigning of towns and cities, above all Linz, an occupation that stayed with him until the end of his life.[6]

By September 1909 Hitler had spent his savings and was getting into serious financial difficulties, not least because he was spending so much on going to the opera. He was forced to live in a men's asylum for the homeless for many months, and a second attempt to gain entry to the Academy of Fine Arts was brusquely rejected. Firmly convinced that he would become a great artist, he refused to compromise or settle for an ordinary life. At the suggestion of a friend in the asylum he prepared and sold paintings copied from picture postcards, earning him a small income, but it was not until his twenty-fourth birthday in April 1913 that he was able to come into a solid inheritance from a relative. With a modest but sufficient income assured, he moved to Munich, on 25 May 1913, abandoning the multicultural milieu in which he had recently been living in Vienna for a Germany that he clearly admired and to which he must have thought German-speakers such as himself truly belonged. He remained an Austrian citizen, however, and was ordered by the Bavarian police to return to Austria in order to begin his obligatory military service. When he turned up for enrolment, his medical examination certified him as physically 'too weak', and he was able to return to Munich. Here he continued his aimless existence for the next several months, sitting in the coffee houses in Schwabing, a district known as the haunt of artists and bohemians, selling his copies of postcards. Nothing about his life up to this point indicated a future career in politics. His life had been a failure, his ambitions unfulfilled, and his early social position, growing up in a solidly bourgeois family, had sunk about as low as it could get. Of all the Nazi leaders, he was the most déclassé, his social decline the most precipitous.

The outbreak of World War I at the end of July 1914 seemed to solve all Hitler's problems. He claimed in *Mein Kampf* that it was the greatest time of his life, and there is no reason to disbelieve him. Filled with the overwhelming German patriotism shown on his face in the famous photograph that caught him in the crowds gathering on Munich's Odeonsplatz on 2 August 1914 to cheer Germany's entry into the war, he enlisted in the Bavarian army on 16 August, following an initial rejection. In the chaotic rush of mass recruitment, no one seems to have noticed that he was still an Austrian citizen, or that he was physically not really fitted for combat. After undergoing some rudimentary training, he was sent with his regiment to the Western Front. He survived his baptism of fire in a fierce encounter with British troops, was promoted to the rank known as *Gefreiter*, and assigned duties as a messenger taking orders from field headquarters to the front. His promotion did not entitle him to order other soldiers about, like a real corporal did; he would best be described as a 'senior private'. The award to him of an Iron Cross, First Class, is often taken as evidence of exceptional bravery, but while his actual position as dispatch-runner for regimental headquarters did involve some exposure to danger, it mainly involved activities behind the front line. Serving at HQ brought soldiers like Hitler into close contact with officers who had the power to award medals, and such soldiers were greatly over-represented among those who won the Iron Cross.[7]

His fellow soldiers remembered him as neither outstandingly brave nor notably cowardly: he was said to have performed his duties calmly and efficiently. Something of a loner, he was regarded by his comrades as an oddity, 'the artist' as they called him. While they chatted and joked, smoked, drank, or visited brothels, Hitler did none of these things, but sat on his own, reading. Where they were cynical about the war, Hitler repeatedly reaffirmed his commitment to total victory, though he generally did this in private, as his surviving correspondence testifies. When members of his regiment took part in the spontaneous, football-playing 'Christmas truce' of December 1914, Hitler refused to join in. Like other soldiers, he was quickly disabused of the romantic, heroic illusions that had inspired him to enlist. In their place, Hitler learned to be hard and ruthless and to be indifferent to suffering and death. Military hierarchy and discipline gave a sense of order and structure to his life, though he did not seek promotion, nor was he considered suitable for a higher rank by his superiors. On 5 October 1916 he sustained a shrapnel wound in his thigh, but it turned out not to be life-threatening. He took part in the ultimately unsuccessful 1918 Spring offensive on the Western Front. A few months later, he was temporarily blinded in a mustard-gas attack and sent for treatment and recovery to a hospital behind the lines, in the Pomeranian town of Pasewalk. It was here that he learned on 10 November 1918 of the final German defeat, the overthrow of the Kaiser, and the outbreak of revolution, spearheaded by left-wing workers' and soldiers' councils.[8]

II

The workers' and soldiers' councils soon yielded to the established opposition to the Kaiser, the Social Democratic Party, which took over the leadership of the country and, backed by the liberals and the Catholic Centre Party, established a new political order, far more progressive than the authoritarian polity of Bismarck and the Kaiser. The republican constitution voted through at a constitutive National Assembly held in the cultural centre of Weimar, the city of the classical German poets Goethe and Schiller in the late eighteenth century, was a thoroughly democratic one, giving women the vote for the first time, and making governments answerable to the legislature and the electorate. The Weimar Republic, as it came to be called, had to contend with many difficulties. The Treaty of Versailles, which sealed the Allied victory in the war, took away around 13 per cent of German territory and population on the eastern and western borders, removed overseas colonies from German control, and restricted Germany's army to 100,000 men while also banning combat aircraft and ships. Germany had to pay large financial reparations, in gold, for the damage caused by its forces' occupation of Belgium and north-east France. Political stability was made very difficult by the fact that there were no fewer than six major political parties, reflecting deep-seated and long-standing divisions of class, region and religion in the electorate – the Social Democrats, the Communists, the Catholic Centre, the Nationalists, the right-wing Liberals and the left-wing Liberals. Many conservative, nationalist and far-right political groups refused to accept the legitimacy of the new Republic and yearned for the Kaiser's return. On the left, the Communists damned the Republic as 'capitalist' and worked for a revolution that would bring in a regime along Soviet lines. Under the new constitution, the proportion of the vote won by any given party translated directly into the proportion of seats it won in the legislature. All governments had perforce to be coalitions of different parties, but this was less the consequence of proportional representation than of the multi-party system the Republic had inherited from the Kaiser's reign.

Hitler's later claim that it was the 1918 revolution that made him decide to enter politics was a drastic oversimplification. His entry into the political world was a more gradual process. There is no reason to doubt his shock at learning of Germany's defeat and the terms of the Armistice, but it was many months before he began to take political action. Initially he rejoined the army, in the absence of any other kind of employment. He remained inactive after the Bavarian revolutionary workers' and soldiers' council leader Kurt Eisner was assassinated in Munich by a nationalist fanatic in 1919, to be succeeded by a short-lived anarchist regime and then a council of hard-line Communists, whose rule in Munich, the Bavarian capital, was ended in a bloodbath by volunteer 'Free Corps' troops sent by the elected, moderate Social

Democratic government of Bavaria led by Johannes Hoffmann. Like many right-wingers in Bavaria, Hitler probably saw in Hoffmann the only immediate hope for the restoration of order; hence his willingness initially to support the Social Democrats. Elected by his fellow soldiers to represent them, he was chosen by the officers to investigate the conduct of the troops during the revolutionary events, and then to assist in counter-revolutionary 'education' courses for soldiers. Soon he was attracting attention with what one listener called his 'fanaticism' and his obvious popularity with his audiences. He had probably taken on these roles as a way of staying in the army, since he lacked any viable alternative way of supporting himself, but the result was that his identity as a soldier was giving way to a new self-consciousness as a politician. However, in many ways he continued to carry his military persona with him: for Hitler, politics was warfare by other means. In his self-presentation for the rest of his life, he always laid emphasis on his years as an ordinary front-line soldier, a man of the people in military uniform.[9]

Central to the thirty-one-year-old Hitler's emerging political world view after the war was a rabid antisemitism. The extreme right-wing nationalists who triumphed with the entry of the Free Corps into Munich regarded the revolution as the work of a Jewish conspiracy and the council regimes as the creation of Jewish subversives. Several of the revolutionaries, from Kurt Eisner to Ernst Toller and Eugen Leviné, were of Jewish origin, though almost all of them, as radical socialists, had repudiated their Jewish identity. But this gave a superficial plausibility to claims that the city had been living under 'Jewish rule' until the Free Corps arrived. Hitler's first expression of his newly extreme and obsessive hatred of Jews, in a letter to one of the students on his course, Adolf Gemlich, gave vent to his belief that for thousands of years the Jewish race had by its inner nature been characterized by subversion, cultural destruction and materialist greed. Rather than respond with violent pogroms, however, Hitler declared that a 'rational' antisemitism was more effective, meaning the removal of the Jews from the country by one means or another. It was important to realize, he told Gemlich, that 'Jewry [is] definitely a community of race and not religion.' The Jews were carriers of a 'racial tuberculosis of peoples'. All they wanted was money and power. Their ultimate aim was 'to rule the world': that was why they alone were 'international' in character. The governments that replaced the Kaiser and the German princes were mere tools of the

Jews. So was the press. So were the banks. In speech after speech in the early 1920s, Hitler obsessively repeated these fantastical claims. There was nothing particularly original about them. They were a more extreme version of a generalized feeling among German nationalists and conservatives that Germany had somehow been cheated of victory in World War I, and that malign forces, mainly located on the left, were responsible. What was unusual was the vehemence and effectiveness with which Hitler now began to propagate these views.[10]

In the decade that followed the end of World War I, political campaigning was still dominated by public speaking in mass assemblies, either in a meeting-hall of some kind (beer cellars were a favoured location in Bavaria) or in the open air. Radio was still in its infancy, television in its early stages of development. Hitler discovered he had a talent for rabble-rousing with which no other political figure of the day could compete. Until 1928 he spoke without a microphone or loudspeaker. Even before they had the resources of the state at their disposal, the Nazis made sure Hitler's speeches were encased in a wide range of rituals, including music, uniformed Nazi activists' banners and flags; the audience's sense of anticipation was deliberately heightened by keeping them waiting until Hitler arrived, inevitably late in launching into his speech. His deep, resonant voice would first capture his audience as he began quietly, with long pauses, getting his listeners to focus on his words, before he expounded his views in short, simple sentences, building to a climax as he neared his peroration, his face shining, his arms and fists underlining his words in carefully prepared gestures. At the end, he would take his audience with him in a frenzy of emotion into a quasi-religious apotheosis. He reduced the complexities of politics to a series of simple formulae. Everything was a matter of good or evil, right or wrong, everything was absolute, all solutions final. He knew how to speak to ordinary people in their own language, learning from observing his audiences while he spoke what worked and what did not. Sometimes he would use quasi-religious language to project himself, promising for example an 'empire of strength, of greatness, and of glory' when he came to power, and confessing in pseudo-Christian terms: 'Yes, indeed, I will take on the suffering of my people.'[11]

Sarcasm helped reduce the political objects of his contempt to mere objects of ridicule: his friend Ernst 'Putzi' Hanfstaengl 'detected the language of Vienna writers' café jokes', 'a mocking humour that hit home without seeming fiery or rude'.¹² At the same time, Hitler developed during the 1920s an ability to go far beyond mere sloganizing and to impress audiences with his considerable command of detail. He prepared and rehearsed his own speeches, and spoke without a script, though with the aid of a few jotted notes, so that his words seemed to his audiences to come spontaneously from the heart. He had, he claimed, learned from the Austrian Socialist Party how to direct propaganda to the masses, whose limited intellectual capacities made them receptive to an emotional appeal. To capture them it was necessary to deploy simple slogans, repeat them endlessly, never qualify or deviate from the main message. The masses were feminine and needed to be dominated. As he began to engage in public speaking, Hitler quickly came to realize the extraordinary nature of his talent, and rapidly gained confidence in the new political world he was entering.¹³

This was the world of small far-right nationalist groups in Munich, flourishing and multiplying in the counter-revolutionary atmosphere of the early 1920s. Aiming to succeed where the Kaiser had failed, they saw the Social Democrats and Communists as the Jewish-dominated enemies of Germany and sought to win over the working classes from them with a mixture of pseudo-socialist, ultra-nationalist and antisemitic policies and slogans. One of these groups, led by the locksmith Anton Drexler and calling itself the German Workers' Party (the key to its far-right character being the word 'German', deliberately pointing up a contrast with the avowed internationalism of the Left), seemed to Hitler's army superiors to be suitable for serving their counter-revolutionary purposes, so they sent him to a meeting on 12 September 1919 to see what could be done. Unable to resist raising his objections to some of the views expressed, he attracted the attention of the party's leaders, who soon began using him as a speaker. Before long, his success had enabled him to brush them aside, transforming the German Workers' Party from a tiny, conspiratorial sect into a public political movement, renaming it the National Socialist German Workers' Party (NSDAP). 'Socialist' in this context, as he was keen to explain, had nothing to do with Marxism because it valued private property and the individual, only demanding that National Socialist values should be maintained in consonance with those of the community.¹⁴

He drew up a 25-point Party programme which included the removal of citizenship rights from Jews and the confiscation of 'war profits', or in other words their economic annihilation. Parliamentary democracy was damned as corrupt, and the 'strengthening of the central power' pointed to the establishment of a dictatorship. The programme was declared 'unalterable', because Hitler did not want the kind of endless disputes that plagued normal political parties; it was soon afterwards largely put on ice, and the National Socialists ('Nazis' for short, analogous to 'Sozis' for Social Democrats) never put forward the kind of manifesto common to other political parties at election time. Hitler approved a design for the Party flag that cleverly combined the old Imperial colours of black, white and red, to appeal to traditional conservatives and monarchists, with the red background suggesting socialism, and the black hooked cross or swastika in a white circle denoting racism, ultra-nationalism and antisemitism. And from 7 August 1920 Hitler underlined the revolutionary character of the Party by addressing his audiences not, in the traditional bourgeois style, as *'Meine Damen und Herren'* ('Ladies and gentlemen'), but as *'Volksgenossen und -genossinnen'* ('Racial comrades, men and women'), deliberately playing on the use of 'comrade' by the left.'[15]

By the spring of 1920, the advent of a strongly right-wing government in Bavaria under Gustav Ritter von Kahr helped create more favourable conditions for the Nazis and other far-right groups. With a reactionary coup in Berlin only narrowly defeated by a general strike led by Social Democratic trade unions, and a series of assassinations of leading liberal and left-wing politicians by the young fanatics of the clandestine terrorist group the 'Organization Consul', the Weimar Republic seemed unable to overcome the troubles of its early months. Hitler's self-confidence grew with the ever-increasing size of the audiences he was attracting, and when others in the Party leadership proposed a merger with another far-right group, he resigned in protest. They knew he was indispensable, and caved in, admitting him back with dictatorial powers over the Party. As his growing prominence on the far right began to attract a circle of lieutenants around him – including Rudolf Hess, Hermann Göring, Heinrich Himmler, Ernst Röhm, Alfred Rosenberg and Julius Streicher, alongside some of his original sponsors such as Anton Drexler, Dietrich Eckart and Gottfried Feder – their undisguised admiration bolstered his confidence even further and finally convinced him that he would end Germany's humiliation and lead the country to a glorious future. By the end of 1922 party members were referring to him as the Leader (*Der Führer*) and were starting to use the greeting *Heil Hitler!*, which became compulsory within the Party in 1926.[16]

As soon as Hitler took charge of the Nazi movement, a new physical violence entered its political repertoire. The party already used bouncers at its public meetings, but in the course of 1921 they started to be more organized, becoming known informally as the *Sturmabteilungen* or 'Storm Divisions', led by Hans Ulrich Klintzsch, a young ex-member of the extreme right-wing assassination squad, the Organization Consul. They beat up and expelled protesters at Hitler's rallies, and, joined by ex-members of the Free Corps, armed themselves with knives, rubber truncheons, knuckle-dusters and even handguns and grenades to engage in pitched battles with the paramilitary units of other political parties, especially the Social Democrats. After leading one particularly bloody meeting-room brawl, Hitler and other Nazis were arrested, put on trial, and sentenced to three months' imprisonment for disturbing the peace. But the Nazis were by no means alone in their use of organized political violence. The militarization of politics was a consequence of four years of warfare, followed by a period of armed conflict in many parts of Europe, from Ireland to Silesia. The emergence of Communism, born in the violence of the Bolshevik Revolution and dedicated to the overthrow of 'bourgeois' democracy and the existing social order, further radicalized political antagonisms. In Italy, the former socialist Benito Mussolini led his *squadristi* in the violent takeover of northern towns and cities, culminating in a threatened 'March on Rome' that effectively blackmailed the political Establishment into conceding his appointment as Prime Minister in 1922.[17]

Mussolini's success left a deep impression on Hitler and the Nazis, who were strongly influenced by his style in a number of ways, including the adoption of the term 'Leader', the pseudo-Roman salute (right arm rigidly outstretched to be greeted by the Leader with the latter's right arm raised but bent backwards with open palm), and the carrying of standards at parades. The success of the 'March on Rome' seemed to Hitler and other leading figures on the far right in Germany an obvious model to follow as the country descended into chaos in 1923, with hyperinflation destroying the economy, French troops seizing assets in the industrial region of the Ruhr because of unpaid war reparations, and far-left parties threatening to take over in Saxony and Thuringia.

There was another important influence on the Nazis as well, in the shape of the Turkish military leader and nationalist politician Mustafa Kemal Pasha, later known as Kemal Atatürk. His success in wars against the Greeks and Armenians between 1919 and 1922, and the preservation of a united Turkey in defiance of Allied attempts to dismember the country, led to the abolition of the Ottoman Empire, the acceptance of Turkish sovereignty in the Treaty of Lausanne, signed on 24 July 1923, and the official establishment of the Turkish Republic on 29 October 1923. The Nazis were strongly influenced by Atatürk's decision to move the country's capital away from Constantinople, which he regarded as hopelessly corrupt, into the cleaner, purer environment (as he saw it) of Ankara. For Hitler, Munich was Germany's Ankara, Berlin its Constantinople.[18]

The trigger for action was the installation on 13 August 1923 of the moderate liberal Gustav Stresemann as Chancellor of a broad coalition of parties tasked with bringing Germany's multiple crises to an end. Over the following weeks, he introduced a policy of 'fulfilment' of the Treaty of Versailles, resuming payments of reparations and thereby getting the French to vacate the Ruhr. This was anathema to the Nazis, who secured the participation of the former World War I general, now a far-right enemy of the Weimar Republic, Erich Ludendorff, in an armed uprising in Munich on 9 November 1923. Hitler announced that he would march on Berlin after taking over the Bavarian capital, and establish a new national government with himself as its head. With overweening self-confidence he issued a public 'proclamation to all Germans', declaring the formation of a 'nationalist government' led by Ludendorff and himself, both with dictatorial powers. But the attempted *putsch*, launched in a beer cellar just outside the city centre, was dispersed in a hail of bullets as the Nazis, led by Hitler, tried to storm the Field Marshals' Hall on the Odeonsplatz. Fourteen Nazis were shot, and four policemen fell victim to Nazi fire. Hitler dislocated his shoulder in the mêlée, but escaped with the help of accomplices, only to be tracked down and arrested two days later, charged with treason. The dream of emulating Benito Mussolini and Atatürk and establishing a fascist-style regime in Germany was over – at least, for the time being. Inexperienced, full of illusions, and wildly over-optimistic, Hitler had failed to prepare the coup attempt properly, and neglected to secure the support, whether active or passive, of the ruling elite, the army, the civil service and the police. He would not make the same mistakes again.[19]

III

Hitler had now discovered an aim in life, one to which it soon became clear that his talents were ideally suited. But in the immediate aftermath of the failed uprising he was deeply depressed. For the first time, though not the last, he was recorded as considering suicide. Soon, however, he began to realize that his impending trial would present an opportunity to vindicate himself. The Bavarian government managed to get the court proceedings moved to Munich, and to appoint a politically sympathetic judge. This was Georg Neithardt, who had already shown remarkable leniency in presiding over the trial of Kurt Eisner's assassin, Count Arco-Valley, to whose supposedly patriotic motives he had paid homage. At the trial, which began on 26 February 1924, Neithardt allowed the Nazi leader to speak at enormous length in defence of his actions, which were, Hitler said, driven 'by a fanatically extreme nationalism of the highest ethics and morality'. The courts, Hitler declared, would not decide whether his actions had been justified: German history would decide. Among the numerous defendants, Ludendorff was acquitted, and the rest were given extremely lenient sentences. Hitler was condemned to the minimum sentence allowed, five years of 'fortress incarceration' (*Festungshaft*) in Landsberg Prison, 65 kilometres from Munich, with conditional release on parole allowed after six months. His actions in attempting the *putsch* were, the court declared, inspired 'by a pure patriotic spirit'.[20] Hitler repaid the judge by continuing his appointment after he came to power and laying a wreath on Neithardt's grave after his death in 1941. Meanwhile, the Nazis mythologized the *putsch* and instituted a cult of martyrdom around their fallen comrades. The elements of the later myth of sacrifice were already being assembled in the Munich courtroom.[21]

Recently published research has cast new light on the conditions under which Hitler served his sentence. Landsberg was a modern prison, built shortly before World War I, but besides ordinary inmates it also had a special section for those condemned to 'fortress incarceration'. Offenders sentenced in this category did not lose their civil rights, such as the right to vote, nor did they have to wear prison uniforms or carry out forced-labour duties. They could keep their own clothing, receive visitors, accept gifts, drink alcohol and smoke tobacco, and mingle with other prisoners in the same class. They had access to a garden and enjoyed many other privileges. Previously reserved for officers, aristocrats and men who had killed or injured their opponent in a duel, 'fortress incarceration' was frequently considered appropriate by the Weimar Republic's conservative judges for offenders who had in their view acted out of laudable motives and so did not deserve any form of punishment that dishonoured them. Hitler was one such. His prison files show that while he was in Landsberg, Hitler received no fewer than 345 visitors, on a total of 524 occasions. Erich Ludendorff came nine times, and Ernst Röhm seven, though most people, such as Hermann Göring, came only once. Many brought Hitler presents such as flowers, wine, cakes and books, or supplies he had purchased from outside, ranging from eggs, butter, coffee and noodles to crockery and saucepans. Conditions in the fortress were more like those of a hotel than a prison. Hitler's cell was referred to by some of his visitors as 'the delicatessen'. His fellow prisoners in 'fortress incarceration' included other participants in the beer-hall *putsch* such as Rudolf Hess; on 28 April 1924 a further forty members of the Nazi 'storm troop' were admitted. Most of their cells were decorated with swastikas and other political symbols, smoking and drinking were almost universal among the inmates (Hitler, a teetotal non-smoker, was an exception), writing facilities including typewriters and desks were available, and the prisoners could play games, correspond freely with the outside world, and arrange their day as they pleased. The prison became for several months the informal headquarters of the Nazi Party. However, Hitler kept his distance from all the communal sports, games and other activities on offer. 'A leader,' he said, 'cannot afford to be beaten by members of his retinue.'[22]

In the meantime, as letters of support for his stance during the trial came pouring in, and visitor after visitor expressed their admiration for his courage in launching the *putsch*, Hitler realized that the events of 1923–24 had catapulted him into a position of virtually undisputed leadership in the ultra-nationalist circles of the far right. Every visitor to Landsberg, every piece of fan mail, reinforced his self-belief and sense of mission. With several months of enforced leisure at his disposal, Hitler decided to work up the speech he had delivered at his trial, along with other writings, to compose a full-scale vindication. He had a typewriter and several reams of paper delivered to his cell, supplied from outside, and over the next few months put together an elaborate narrative of his life and justification of his actions and beliefs, often working late into the night. Gradually the project's scale grew until it also became an elaborate political manifesto, designed not least to underline his continuing claim to lead the Nazi Party, which was disintegrating into a mass of rival factions in his absence. After his release on 24 December 1924, having spent a mere nine months in Landsberg Prison, Hitler retreated to a boarding-house on the Obersalzberg, in the Bavarian Alps, which he had visited the previous year, and continued composing what became known as *Mein Kampf*, 'My Struggle' or 'My Battle'. A recently published scholarly edition has enabled us to learn more about the conditions of its composition, and take a fresh, critical view of its contents. It shows how, shifting parts of the text around, Hitler decided to split the book into two volumes, completing the first in time for publication on 18 July 1925. Hitler wrote only slowly, and volume two took a little longer, but in the later stages of composition he had the assistance of a secretary, who took down his drafts from dictation, speeding up the process and allowing it to be published on 10 December 1926. A one-volume popular edition appeared in 1930. Hitler's amanuensis and fellow prisoner Rudolf Hess and his wife Ilse, who had already carried out editorial work on the first volume, spent several months in total, together with Josef Stolzing-Cerny, a staff member of the Nazi daily newspaper the *Völkischer Beobachter*, correcting Hitler's untutored German and improving where possible his clumsy style. But the text itself was all Hitler's own work.[23]

For Hitler, who was legally banned from public speaking in these years, *Mein Kampf* was to a large extent a substitute for the speeches he would otherwise have delivered, and it was written very much in their style, with innumerable repetitions and exaggerations, appealing more to the emotions than to the intellect. His language was full of absolutes: decisions were 'unalterable', enemies would be 'annihilated', policies were 'unconditional'. Everything was reduced to simple dichotomies: good or evil, success or failure, triumph or disaster. All this reflected among other things the militarization of politics in 1920s Germany, beginning with the book's title and going on in the text to turn normally negative concepts like 'brutal', 'fanatical', 'ruthless' and 'barbaric' into positives. As in his speeches, Hitler called on religious expressions, popular proverbs and brief quotations from the classics to lend weight to his declarations. Particularly notable was his employment of the phrase *Sein oder Nichtsein* ('To be or not to be') from Shakespeare's *Hamlet* no fewer than six times in the book, to underline his 'all or nothing' approach to what he thought was at stake for Germany in World War I. Jews are reduced to a single collective ('the Jew', rather than 'the Jews') and described in dehumanizing terms as 'plague bacilli', or 'vermin', revealing the exterminatory core of Hitler's antisemitism from the very beginning.[24] Diatribes against their supposed degeneracy and subversiveness occupied a large part of the book.[25] Notoriously, towards the end of the second volume, he wrote of Germany's Jews: 'If one had on some occasion at the start of the war and during the war held twelve or fifteen thousand of these Hebrew polluters of the people down under poison gas, like hundreds of thousands of our best German workers from all classes and professions in the army at the front had to suffer, then the millionfold sacrifices of the front would not have been in vain.'[26]

By the end of the book, Hitler has made it clear that he already sees himself as Germany's future leader, guided to historical greatness by 'fate' and 'providence'. Although he avoids going into too much detail about the policies he wants to implement if and when he comes to power, their broad contours are already apparent: suppression of all opposition, destruction of democracy, creation of a dictatorship (though he tends to avoid the word), military conquest of 'living-space', particularly in Eastern Europe, removal of citizenship from Germany's Jews, prevention of the eugenically 'unfit' from breeding, ruthless use of the death penalty to crush political resistance. Some of the more readable passages in the book are devoted to propaganda, where, in a projection of what Hitler thought were the unscrupulous methods of the Socialists in pre-war Austria and the British and their allies during the war, the masses are regarded with contempt as 'feminine', passive, easily swayed by repeated appeals to the emotions. The masses, he wrote, wanted the 'victory of the stronger and the annihilation of the weak or his unconditional submission'. 'The nationalization of our masses will only succeed if . . . their international poisoners are exterminated.' Winning over the people was necessary if Hitler was ever to achieve power, but, at the same time, it was necessary to employ exterminatory violence against the Social Democrats and Communists and the Jewish conspiracy he thought was steering them.[27]

The ecstatic descriptions in *Mein Kampf* of the bloody victories of Nazi stormtroopers in meeting-hall brawls with their 'Marxist' opponents and their provocative violence in a march through Coburg in October 1922 made it clear that mass violence would continue to be an essential part of Nazi tactics alongside the appeal to the masses to vote for them in elections and the behind-the-scenes wooing of German elites. The book breathes an overpowering spirit of hatred and resentment, a murderous extremism, a ruthless disregard for ordinary human decency, and a cynical contempt for the conventions of political life. Hitler reveals fully for the first time here the real core of his political persona – the dog-eat-dog principles of the gutter imported into the world of mainstream politics.[28]

Volume One of *Mein Kampf* sold reasonably well: the first printing of 10,000 copies was almost sold out by the end of 1925. The second volume was not nearly so successful, but the single-volume popular edition, published at a time in 1930 when Hitler was becoming nationally known, had sold 228,000 copies by the end of 1932. Nevertheless, the book did not have a major political impact before 1933, and was not widely read or understood. After Hitler came to power it was virtually compulsory to possess a copy; every newlywed couple was also presented with one by the government free of charge. Altogether, the book sold a total of 12,450,000 copies between its first publication in 1925 and the death of its author twenty years later.[29] It had already brought Hitler significant income before 1933 and it would help make him a wealthy man afterwards.[30]

Anyone looking for detailed plans and programmes in *Mein Kampf* will be disappointed. Many of its more programmatic statements, from the need to raise real wages and protect the workers from exploitation, to the desirability of defending the rights of the federated states against the encroachments of the central authority, or, in foreign policy, the intention to forge an alliance with Great Britain, were to be ignored or unfulfilled after Hitler came to power. What comes through nonetheless are Hitler's character and beliefs, and these are expressed in a manner so unambiguous that a careful reader would surely have realized in broad terms what he would do and how he would rule if he ever came to power. Early post-war claims in Germany that although huge numbers of people had purchased the book, hardly any of them had bothered to read it, were patently self-exculpatory: in fact it was not only repeatedly and extensively quoted by Nazi propagandists but also, while there was still a free press in Germany before 1933, frequently discussed in the mainstream newspapers, often at length.[31]

One of the many functions of *Mein Kampf* at the time of its publication was to establish Hitler's claim to lead the nationalist ultra-right in Germany by projecting an image of himself as a thinker as well as a man of action. During his enforced absence from politics from 1924 to 1926, he made no attempt to reconcile the warring factions that filled the gap; on the contrary, he encouraged the competition for power in the expectation that no single group on the far right would be strong enough to resist him on his return – a technique he was to use among his leadership cadre to great effect during the Third Reich.[32] In the two years after his release, however, he pulled the Party together, formally refounding it at the beginning of 1925. He did not scruple to use his stormtroopers to assault and intimidate his rivals on the far right, break up their meetings, and pressure them into joining him.[33] And he disposed of other real and potential rivals by sidelining them – most notably Ludendorff, whom he encouraged to stand in the elections for Reich President in 1925, in the knowledge that the general would fail to win more than a handful of votes, thus condemning him to political irrelevance. More than this, Hitler now worked hard to extend the Nazi Party from its Bavarian base across to the north of the country. Here he encountered a rather different kind of 'national socialism' from his own – more left-wing, more anti-capitalist. In a personal charm offensive, he won over its main proponents, Joseph Goebbels and Gregor Strasser, to his side. Recognizing Goebbels's abilities as a propagandist, and Strasser's as an organizer, he gave them responsibility for these aspects of the Party's activities. They did not wholly abandon their original views – nor did Gottfried Feder, also a member of the 'Nazi left', who was mainly responsible for the economic clauses of the 1920 Party Programme – but these became far less influential, the more so since Hitler was now redoubling his efforts to win over the business community to his cause.[34]

Yet one of the most striking features of *Mein Kampf* was its lack of political realism. The limitless self-confidence with which Hitler portrayed himself as Germany's future leader was an expression of willpower rather than the product of political observation. Its blithe disregard for the realities of the situation in which he found himself was to be repeated in the final months of World War II. He was still living in a fantasy-world, but one in which he was now a great leader rather than a great artist, or rather, perhaps, a great artist who had turned his attention now to remoulding and reshaping German politics. The book was written just as the Weimar Republic was beginning to stabilize itself. Hitler remained on the outer right-wing fringes of politics. In the Reichstag elections of 20 May 1928 the Nazis won a risible 2.6 per cent of the national vote, an even lower figure than they had managed four years previously. The elections brought a 'grand coalition' of centrist parties to power under the Social Democrat Hermann Müller. The Republic seemed finally to be entering the calm waters of political stability, economic prosperity and social peace. But all this was about to change, and more dramatically than anyone could have imagined.[35]

IV

In October 1929, share prices on Wall Street, long overvalued, began to plummet to unprecedented depths. 'Black Thursday' was followed by 'Black Monday'; and then 'Black Tuesday', as billions of dollars were wiped from the value of stocks and shares. Within three years, these had lost nearly 90 per cent of their value. Over 4,000 banks and other lending institutions were put out of business as investors withdrew their funds to try and make ends meet. For Germany, the effects of the Wall Street crash were particularly devastating, as the economic recovery following the end of the inflation in 1924 had been financed mainly by short-term American loans, which were now called in, leaving German banks exposed. They in turn called in loans to industry, while fearful investors rushed to withdraw their endangered funds. Tariff barriers went up everywhere, including in the United States, making things more difficult for exporters. On 13 July 1931 the Danatbank, a major German financial institution, was forced to declare bankruptcy. These events plunged the German economy into a deepening depression, with unemployment eventually affecting over a third of the entire workforce. Hermann Müller's 'grand coalition' government disintegrated as its partners disagreed on how to cope with the crisis.[36]

The 'grand coalition' was succeeded by a conservative 'cabinet of experts' under Heinrich Brüning, a Catholic conservative appointed by the President, Field Marshal Paul von Hindenburg. Brüning's aim, supported by Hindenburg and his clique, was to sideline the Reichstag, rule by emergency decree, and pave the way for a restoration of the monarchy. He managed to get Germany off the Gold Standard, but, with the intention of demonstrating to the international community the injustice of reparations, he also made savage cuts in government expenditure, reduced benefits and raised taxes, causing further misery. The crisis was deeper, and lasted longer, even than the hyperinflation of the early 1920s. For many Germans, it proved the last straw. The unemployed, disillusioned with the Social Democratic Party's toleration of the Brüning government and its failure to do anything to protect them against the hammer-blows of Brüning's austerity measures, flocked to the Communist Party, which increased its vote in election after election, until in November 1932 it won 100 seats in the Reichstag. The Communists struck fear into the middle classes with their virtually daily demonstrations in the big cities, often accompanied by the violence of the paramilitary 'Red Front-Fighters' League', with their promise to create a 'Soviet Germany' and with their prediction of the imminent fall of capitalism. The October Revolution in Russia, followed by a campaign of terror, murder and dispossession against the aristocracy and bourgeoisie, was too recent to be ignored. Hitler believed this too, and he stoked these fears by focusing in his speeches on Communist acts of violence and murder. At the same time, he stressed his belief that Communism and Social Democracy were two sides of the same coin, subversive and dangerous, internationalist movements ('*Gesamtmarxismus*' or 'Marxism as a whole'), steered from behind by Jews, who were set on undermining Germany.[37]

But it was the Nazis who profited most from the economic crisis. They began to shift their efforts away from winning over the urban working class, an aim that had failed dismally to bring any results, and towards Protestant voters in the countryside, where they had done a good deal better than they had elsewhere without, so far, putting in any special effort. Downplaying the 'socialist' elements in their programme, and explaining their 'socialism' as no more than safeguarding the individual in a national community, they also started to woo the middle-class vote. This change in tactics quickly began to pay dividends.[38] Already at the beginning of 1930, regional state elections in Thuringia saw their support jump to over 11 per cent of the vote. In the summer of 1930 the Nazis' chance came when the Reichstag rejected Brüning's latest austerity measures. The Reich Chancellor promptly (and rather unwisely) called a general election, which was held on 14 September.[39] Sensationally, the Nazis increased their representation in the Reichstag from 12 seats to 107, voted in by 6.4 million electors.[40] This brought the Party into the centre of politics and made Hitler a major national political figure. In a series of regional elections, the Nazi vote also increased by leaps and bounds. The highest proportion of Nazi votes occurred in rural Protestant states such as Oldenburg, where they scored 48 per cent on 29 May 1932; Hesse, where they won 44 per cent on 19 June 1932; and in the similarly structured state of Mecklenburg-Schwerin, where they claimed a stunning 49 per cent on 5 June 1932. The Nazi vote was much lower in states with a strong Catholic element in the population, such as Württemberg (26.4 per cent of the vote on 24 April 1932). With the state having control over domestic affairs, from policing and security to culture and education, these were important results. By early 1933, the Nazis were already in power in five of the federated states, and starting to give a foretaste of how they would govern if and when they came to power on a national level.[41]

The kick-off for the election year of 1932 was provided by the constitutional requirement for Reich President Hindenburg to demit office when his seven-year tenure ended. First elected to the post in 1925 to the acclaim of conservatives who wanted a return to the days of Imperial Germany, Hindenburg, the leading German general of World War I, though deeply reactionary, had in the following years disappointed many of his followers by refusing to use his power to overturn the republican order. Unlike in present-day Germany, where the President is a mere figurehead, elected by the legislature, in the Weimar Republic the President was directly elected by the people and possessed very wide-ranging powers indeed, including the appointment and dismissal of the Reich Chancellor, the ability to dissolve the parliament and the right to rule by decree. These were to prove fatal for the Republic. Hitler noted the widespread disillusion of conservatives with the aged field marshal (eighty-four at the time) and put himself forward as the anti-Weimar candidate of the right. By the same token, the pro-Republic parties, most importantly the Social Democrats, reluctantly backed Hindenburg as the only viable way of stopping Hitler, who exulted in having driven them over to support of the arch-conservative field marshal. This gave Hindenburg nearly 50 per cent of the vote in the first round, but this was not quite enough to win outright, so a second round was held on 10 April. Although Hitler increased his support from 30.1 per cent to 36.8 per cent, Hindenburg managed to push his over the line, from 49.5 to 53 per cent, and was re-elected President. Hitler's repeated charge that the field marshal, despite his earlier achievements, was now too old to lead Germany into the future, had failed to have the desired effect.[42]

Upset by Brüning's failure to secure him an overall majority in the first round, thus necessitating a humiliating second subjection to the will of the electorate, and resenting the fact that he was the candidate of the centre and left when he had actually wanted to be the candidate of the right, Hindenburg forced Brüning to resign on 1 June 1932. He replaced him, on the advice of the army's key spokesman, General Kurt von Schleicher, with the conservative aristocrat Franz von Papen, who then proceeded to call an election with the idea of gaining more legitimacy from it. The result was a disaster for the conservatives. Held on 31 July, the election saw the Nazis win some 230 seats out of 608, and become for the first time the largest party in the Reichstag. With 13.7 million votes, or just over 37 per cent, they now eclipsed the pro-Weimar Social Democrats (22 per cent, or 8 million votes) and the Catholic Centre Party (12 per cent, or 4.5 million votes). Both of these parties more or less held their own, but the Communists continued to improve their position, winning 14 per cent, or 5.3 million votes. All the other parties were virtually annihilated. The bourgeois liberal and conservative parties lost almost all their support.[43]

Three key questions arise from these results. First, who voted for Hitler, and why? His campaigns centred on speeches delivered across the country, attended by huge crowds: on 27 July 1932, in the town of Eberswalde, for example, he spoke before an audience of 40,000, going on to speak to 20,000 in the town of Brandenburg and finally, in the evening, a packed Grunewald Stadium in Berlin, capacity 64,000. Within a few days he could deliver his message to half a million voters or more.[44] Hitler even flew from one meeting place to the next by aeroplane, enabling him to speak in several different venues in a single day, or was driven quickly from place to place in a particular region. He delivered no fewer than 150 speeches in the course of 1932. He even had a speech recorded so that it could be played at venues where he was unable to attend in person. No other politician could match this. His speeches presented the Nazi Party as the representative of the nation as a whole, whereas the other parties all stood for special interests. The Nazis were a movement, not a party in the old sense; they came from outside the political world, indeed in a sense they were anti-political.[45] They would end Germany's division into two camps, the 'Marxists' and the 'nationalists', and bring a decisive government to power that would take firm action to solve the multiple crises of the Republic. While the other parties dithered and temporized, the Nazis promised radical action.[46] The unrestrained extremism of Hitler's rhetoric appealed to the desperation of many voters. He made no secret of his determination to destroy the 'Marxist' Social Democrats and the 'Bolshevik' Communists, portraying them both as the tools of Jewish subversion, though overall he now tended to downplay his ingrained antisemitism because it had cut little ice with the German electorate in 1928. In speeches to Nazi Party members, duly reported in the press, he openly promised a geographical expansion of Germany that could only be achieved by war, asserting 'that the stronger, the better race, must expand its living-space'.[47]

And if he attacked big business, he was careful to insist that it was only Jewish big business he was criticizing. Hitler had always courted rich supporters, and been rewarded with the sponsorship of wealthy people like Helene, wife of the piano manufacturer Edwin Bechstein, the publisher Hugo Bruckmann and his wife Elsa, and the German-American art publisher, gifted pianist, composer of songs and socialite Ernst Hanfstaengl, known to his friends as 'Putzi'. Hitler went out of his way to reassure the overwhelmingly right-wing nationalist members of the business community that the Nazi Party had no intention of socializing private property, delivering no fewer than five speeches to business representatives in the Ruhr area in 1926–27, though with limited success. A speech to the exclusive Hamburg National Club on 28 February 1926 played down the antisemitism that permeated many of his other speeches, since he was aware that the Jewish business community in the city was closely integrated into the world of the mercantile and financial elite there. He took a similar line when he addressed an audience of industrialists in Düsseldorf on 26 January 1932, stressing his determination to eradicate 'Marxism' and promising a regeneration of German society. Normally in the early to mid-1920s wearing quasi-military dress and jackboots and carrying a whip, sometimes also with a pistol tucked into his belt, Hitler was on these occasions prepared to dress in bourgeois clothing, even, if required, in a dinner suit. He did succeed in winning over the steel magnate Fritz Thyssen, whose supposed memoirs – actually written by the American journalist Elmer Reeves from memories of conversations with the businessman – appeared under the sensational title *I Paid Hitler* (1941) and did much to underpin the claim that Hitler was financed primarily by big business. Originating in Communist propaganda, this was in fact a myth: most of the Nazis' financial support before 1933 came from membership subscriptions, sales and modest donations from small business, while big business continued to support bourgeois parties, notably the German National People's Party, which more or less collapsed in the face of the Nazis' electoral onslaught.[48]

Hitler's appeal was far broader than anything the capitalists could hope to achieve. With parades, razzamatazz and ceaseless activism, the Nazis projected an image of youthful dynamism and determination, contrasting favourably with the more sedate tactics of their colourless middle-aged rivals. More generally Nazi propaganda targeted specific groups of the population – women, workers, veterans, state employees, and so on – with promises to get Germany back to work, improve living standards, and end the chaos and humiliations of the Weimar Republic. The Nazis' use of visual media, posters and images carrying simple, strong messages to the public, was particularly powerful. The Party's unscrupulous propaganda, its barefaced lies and mendacious allegations against Hitler's opponents, frequently incurred libel suits by those it targeted; but this does not seem to have lost it significant support.[49]

All of this struck a particular chord with large parts of the electorate, especially the Protestant middle classes and rural workers in northern Germany, but the Nazis also won some support from unorganized industrial labourers, especially in small enterprises and small towns where the trade unions were not strong. Well over half of the Nazi Party's voters were from the middle classes, broadly defined. From their perspective, the Nazis might be violent, but they were also patriotic. They might be against democracy, but democracy had failed. They might not promise a return to the days of Bismarck and the Kaiser, but the Kaiser's son, 'Crown Prince' Wilhelm, had told them to vote for Hitler in the second round of the Presidential election because he thought Hitler might restore the authoritarian structures of the Empire. The 'Crown Prince' even claimed most of the credit for boosting Hitler's vote by two million between the two rounds. A new respectability was lent the Nazis by their co-optation into a campaign against the Young Plan, a scheme, fiercely debated in 1929–30 and eventually passed, to reduce the burden of reparations, anathema both to the conservative nationalists led by the press baron Alfred Hugenberg, and to the Nazis, who wanted reparations abolished altogether.[50]

Beyond this, millions of first-time voters flocked to the polls in support of the Nazi Party, above all women – the majority of the electorate by some margin, and far less likely to have voted previously than men – and the young. The Nazis gave them hope amid the gloom and despair engendered by Brüning's austerity cuts and promised to stem the rising threat of Communism. Of course, the prominence they gave to Hitler as their charismatic leader meant that millions voted for him personally, above all in the 1932 Presidential elections. But they also voted for the youthful dynamism of his Party, its determination to end the economic and political paralysis of the Republic, and its promise to restore Germany to what they felt was its rightful place in the world. Still, a vote for the Nazis was by no means a vote for all their policies. It was not even a vote for antisemitism. Hitler repeated *ad nauseam* his claim that the choice was simple: Nazism or 'Marxism': 'Either-or! *Germany is Germany or it will become Bolshevist.*' A vote for him was as much a negative vote as a positive one. The Nazi Party, as has often been observed, was a catch-all party of protest. To be sure, it ensnared some groups in society more than others, but its claim to unite all parts of German society behind it was by no means wholly false, and lent some plausibility to Hitler's oft-repeated promise to reconcile the country's warring parties in a new-found national unity.[51]

The second issue arising from the rapid growth in support for the Nazis in the early 1930s was the effect it had on the Nazi Party itself. Hitler's followers were now growing rapidly in number, until there were nearly 850,000 party members by the beginning of 1933. But the Party's rapid growth could not conceal the fact that there were serious internal stresses and strains that Hitler needed to resolve quickly. The first of these was the continuing problem of the 'Nazi left', now led by Gregor Strasser's brother Otto, who was committed to the nationalization of a wide range of businesses. Hitler was acutely conscious of the need to keep the business community onside, along with the country's social, military and administrative elites. Otto Strasser was forced to admit defeat and resigned from the Party on 4 July 1930, narrowly pre-empting his expulsion.⁵² Beyond this, Hitler's twin-track approach of boosting the Party's electoral support while at the same time attacking its opponents by the use of ruthless violence on the streets threatened at many points to get out of hand. The threat was made unmistakably clear at the opening of the Reichstag on 13 October 1930, when the newly elected Nazi deputies appeared in uniform, while stormtroopers roamed the streets of central Berlin smashing the windows of Jewish-owned department stores. Incidents of brutal behaviour by Nazi thugs multiplied. In the autumn of 1930 some young army officers in the south German town of Ulm were put on trial for breaching a general order not to engage in politics by joining the Nazi Party. Hitler swore on the witness stand that he intended to come to power legally and declared that he had tried to stop his followers from forming a quasi-military organization. Rightly, the court refused to believe him, declaring bluntly: 'The aim of the NSDAP is the violent overthrow of the existing form of the state.'⁵³ Further evidence to back up this judgement was provided by the police seizure and publication in the autumn of 1931 of the 'Boxheim documents', named after the Hessian inn where they were discovered: written by Werner Best, a young Nazi lawyer, they contained draft announcements to be issued after a violent seizure of power, including liberal use of the death penalty for anyone found resisting the Nazis. Hitler tried to distance himself by dismissing the documents as the expression of Best's private fantasies, but, he admitted, Best's plans might be necessary in the event of a Communist uprising. Hitler stated his real intentions from the witness stand at the Ulm officers' trial: 'When our movement is victorious in our legal struggle, there will be a German State Court and November 1918 will find its expiation, and heads will also roll.'⁵⁴

Hitler's statements were disregarded by a good many of his followers. His uniformed paramilitaries – stormtroopers or Brownshirts – in Berlin, for example, led by Walter Stennes, repeatedly pushed for more power, better pay, and greater freedom to carry out acts of violence, at one point occupying the city's Nazi Party headquarters in protest. Hitler managed to bring them to heel, since they endangered party discipline, but he did nothing to curb the everyday violence of the stormtroopers:

300 people were killed in street fighting in the year to March 1931, while in 1932, 155 people were killed in political clashes, most of them in June and July. Shootings, knifings, beatings with knuckle-dusters and rubber truncheons were a daily occurrence. Brüning barred the stormtroopers from wearing uniforms in December 1931, but they carried on marching anyway, dressed in civilian clothing. On 13 April 1932 he got Hindenburg to ban them altogether, but Brüning's successor as Chancellor from 1 June, Franz von Papen, lifted the prohibition.[55] Often largely unnoticed by the wider public, and not at all by the middle classes, the stormtroopers engaged in a ceaseless daily round of intimidation against their opponents, above all the Communists, whom they drove, stage by stage, out of their bases in the pubs and bars of working-class districts in Germany's cities. In December 1931 Hitler told the London *Times* of 'the bitterness and determination of the rank and file of his movement caused by the constant guerrilla warfare with the Communists, in which the Nazis had had 5,000 wounded and many killed in the first 11 months of this year'.[56]

On 17 July 1932 an intimidatory march by a large column of Brownshirts through a working-class district of the Hamburg conurbation was attacked by members of the Communist Red Front-Fighters' League; shots were fired, and the police responded by shooting wildly at the crowds: eighteen people were killed and over a hundred injured. Hitler backed the marchers and blamed the Communists. Papen used the events of this 'bloody Sunday' to remove the Social Democratic minority government in Prussia by a military coup, destroying the last bastion of democracy in Germany. Meanwhile the violence continued. On 10 August 1932 a gang of drunken Brownshirts murdered a Polish Communist in the village of Potempa in Upper Silesia; when five of them were found guilty in the subsequent trial in the nearby town of Beuthen and condemned to death, the Brownshirts rampaged through the streets, trashing Jewish shops and attacking newspaper offices. Hitler publicly condemned the verdict – subsequently commuted – and ostentatiously declared his support for the murderers. He had already made a cult of Nazi 'martyrs', notably Horst Wessel, a young Brownshirt responsible for leading a vicious attack on a group of Communists, shot dead by a Communist in retaliation in February 1930. 'Horst Wessel,' Hitler proclaimed to a huge demonstration that accompanied the inauguration of Wessel's gravestone in Berlin at the beginning of 1933, '*is not dead!*' He made no secret of his support for the use of extreme physical measures against his enemies. If he sometimes issued appeals for moderation, aimed at reassuring his middle-class supporters, they were always hedged about with qualifications that made it clear between the lines that he did not really want the violence to stop.[57]

The third question arising from the Nazis' stunning electoral successes in the early 1930s, and the fact that they were now the largest party in the Reichstag, was whether they should form a government. A vote of 37 per cent is often a strong enough basis for forming a government in a democratic political system. Hitler knew this, and he complained bitterly that the custom of asking the leader of the largest party to form a government had now been abandoned.[58] But even had it been honoured by Hindenburg, the Nazis would still have had to enter a coalition with another party or parties to form a majority with which to push legislation through the Reichstag. And therein lay the problem facing Hitler and other politicians in 1932. Hitler's declared intent was to destroy the Weimar Republic and create a dictatorship with himself at the helm. His was not the only right-wing party that wanted to dismantle the Weimar Republic; the conservative nationalists of the DNVP, the German National People's Party, nostalgic for the old days of the Kaiser, antisemitic and anti-democratic like the Nazis, shared this desire. In October 1931 the DNVP joined with the Nazis in a short-lived pact of right-wing associations known as the Harzburg Front. But the DNVP lost seats in July 1932 and could only attract just under 6 per cent of the vote, which together with the Nazis' 37 per cent still failed to make a majority. No other party was likely to go into a coalition with the Nazis. When the new Reichstag convened, the extremist parties cancelled each other out. Serried ranks of uniformed, chanting and singing Nazis and Communists confronted each other across the chamber, drowning out the voices of the remaining moderate democratic parties, notably the Social Democrats and the Catholic Centre. Walkouts of either the Nazi or the Communist deputies were common. It was obviously pointless even convening the Reichstag. In the six months following the July 1932 elections, it met for a total of only three days.[59]

Coming in the middle of an economic crisis of unprecedented severity, this stalemate was obviously untenable. While it continued, the Reich government carried on ruling by decree, so that the paralysis of the parliamentary system funnelled power up towards President Hindenburg and his coterie, which included his son Oskar, as well as Reich Chancellor von Papen, Schleicher and the head of the Presidential Office, State Secretary Otto Meissner, who had held the post since 1920. Led by Hindenburg, this group was determined to shift the political landscape sharply to the right by introducing an authoritarian regime, suppressing the left, and emasculating the legislature. But it needed a two-thirds majority in the Reichstag to be able to do this. And for this, the support of the Nazis was essential, in order to lend pseudo-democratic legitimacy to the continuing flow of Presidential decrees and provide the basis for the planned revision of the constitution. The manoeuvrings and secret meetings over the following months all centred on the question of how to do this. Initially at least, Hindenburg rejected the idea of appointing Hitler to head a national government. He could not accept his intolerance or his vulgarity or the violence of his supporters. Hitler's position was clear and simple. His self-confidence had been boosted by his election victories, and he declared that as the 'Leader', first of the Nazi Party and then potentially of all Germany, he would not enter a coalition government except in the position of Reich Chancellor. Not only did he reject Papen's offer to appoint him as Vice-Chancellor, he also sternly rejected a similar offer of a post in government to Gregor Strasser, the Nazi Party's chief organizer. Dismayed by his stubbornness, Strasser resigned from his party posts on 8 December 1932. Hitler quickly rallied his supporters in condemnation of this act of 'treachery', emphasizing yet again the need for unconditional loyalty to himself as Leader.[60]

By this time, a further national election had taken place, on 6 November 1932, in another attempt by Hindenburg, Papen and their circle to generate more support for the conservatives. The results came as a surprise. The Nazis lost two million votes, their share falling from 37.4 per cent to 33.1 per cent. The Communists' vote by contrast jumped from 14.5 per cent to 16.9 per cent, giving them 100 seats in the Reichstag. When combined with the vote for the Social Democrats, this gave the Left 37.3 per cent of the vote, more than the Nazis. The Nationalist DNVP improved its vote, winning just over 8 per cent.[61] But the Nazis' position was even worse than their losses suggested. They had recklessly overspent on the campaign and were now in deep financial trouble. The internal rows that culminated in Strasser's resignation were causing, or revealing, major divisions within the Party leadership. Hitler's intransigence was beginning to cause widespread dismay. On top of this, Papen, having failed again to deliver, was ousted by Kurt von Schleicher, the spokesman of the army, another right-wing political figure, who became Reich Chancellor on 3 December 1932. More clandestine meetings continued as the search for a solution to the political stalemate began again with fresh energy. But Schleicher fatally alienated Hindenburg, who owned a landed estate himself, with a plan for agrarian reform, while his repeal of benefit and wage cuts ordered by Papen alarmed influential business interests.[62]

The Nazis' weakness made this in the eyes of Hindenburg and his coterie the right moment to strike. It was particularly urgent because if the modest economic recovery that had evidently led to the decline in the Nazis' popularity continued, the Nazis might lose so many votes at the next election that they would no longer be able to provide the popular backing for an authoritarian revision of the Weimar Constitution. The solution mooted by Papen and Hindenburg was to concede Hitler's demand to be head of a new government, but to surround him with so many people of their own that he would be left with no room for manoeuvre. Frustrated by his own lack of support, Schleicher asked Hindenburg in effect to grant him dictatorial powers, but the aged President refused and instead continued negotiations – led by Papen, joined by Meissner from the civil service, and, significantly, Baron Kurt von Schröder, a banker and former army officer, who had already raised funds for the Nazi Party – to bring Hitler into government. On 30 January 1933 the Nazi leader was duly appointed Reich Chancellor in a coalition cabinet in which Papen was Vice-Chancellor, and all other posts went to members of his and Hindenburg's circle, except for the Ministry of the Interior, to which one of the leading Nazis, Wilhelm Frick, was appointed, and the Prussian Ministry of the Interior, held by Hermann Göring in an acting capacity while the legal issues around Papen's Prussian coup of the previous summer were still unresolved. From Hitler's point of view, these two posts were the crucial ones, since they opened the way to the pseudo-legal legitimation of the violence he was already unleashing on the streets. Everybody else involved in the negotiations felt a warm glow of satisfaction. Schleicher thought the army would now have a free hand to rule as a state within a state. Papen and Hindenburg thought they had got Hitler into a position where they could use his mass support to help put their own plans into effect. All of them were wrong. It quickly became clear that they had all fatally underestimated the Nazi leader. They were neither the first nor the last to make this mistake.[63]

V

By this time, in his early forties, Hitler had at last achieved something like a stable personal life. Far from being the cold, unemotional, asexual person imagined by many historians, he had always been susceptible to feminine charm. He was clearly close to a number of older, usually wealthy and well-situated women such as Helene Bechstein or Winifred Wagner, the English-born wife of the composer Richard Wagner's son Siegfried, a woman who ran the annual Bayreuth Festival after her husband's death in 1930 and allowed Hitler to turn it into something of a Nazi event. But there are also credible accounts of his admiration for younger, indeed much younger, women, such as Maria Reiter, who worked in a hotel where he was staying in the mid-1920s, or Henriette Hoffmann, daughter of his personal photographer Heinrich Hoffmann, and of his clumsy attempts to seduce them, which they seem uniformly to have rejected. More serious was his relationship with Angela ('Geli') Raubal, daughter of his half-sister of the same name. Just twenty years of age, Geli was his regular companion from 1928, accompanying him on trips and at political events. In October 1929 she moved into Hitler's apartment in Munich. But the jealous restrictions he imposed on her independence eventually became unbearable for her. On 19 September 1931 she was found dead on the floor of the apartment, blood streaming from a fatal gunshot wound to her lung, with a pistol next to her right hand. The autopsy left no doubt that she had committed suicide. Wild rumours about her relationship with Hitler began to circulate, encouraged by his political enemies, but Hitler and his entourage managed largely to keep them out of the media, claiming that she had accidentally shot herself while playing with the weapon (an unlikely story, since she seems to have been familiar enough with it). The damage-limitation worked. Hitler himself was briefly upset, but not suicidal: a few days later he was speaking to an audience of 10,000 supporters in Hamburg, before going secretly to lay flowers on Geli's grave, after which he barely mentioned her again.[64]

From this point onwards, Hitler insisted that he had sacrificed his private life for his country, a claim too many historians have subsequently believed. The truth was very different. In the spring of 1931 he met and fell in love with Magda Quandt, the elegant, divorced wife of an industrialist. Magda was flattered, but she was already in a relationship with the Nazi propaganda chief Joseph Goebbels; indeed, the couple married on 19 December 1931. After an awkward discussion, the three of them agreed that Hitler would content himself with being a family friend, and use Magda as a kind of official companion on public occasions. Already by this time, however, Hitler had made the acquaintance of Eva Braun, a young woman (born in 1912) from a petty-bourgeois family who worked in the studio of Hitler's photographer Heinrich Hoffmann. After the death of Geli Raubal, they began an affair early in 1932, though not before Hitler had her ancestry checked out to make sure it was 'Aryan'. There can be little doubt that it was a sexual relationship. However, Hitler did not allow Eva to be seen with him on public occasions. Feeling both hemmed in and neglected, she twice tried to commit suicide, threatening another scandal. Hitler gave in, and began to allow her to appear with him in public, though as a 'secretary' or 'staff member', settled her into a flat in Munich near his own, and eventually provided her with accommodation in the Reich Chancellery in Berlin. Over time, she also came to play the role of hostess in his rural retreat in the Bavarian Alps, on the Obersalzberg, where she filmed home movies in colour showing him relaxing with his entourage. But her role, indeed her entire existence, remained carefully concealed from the public until the very end, and there was no question of marriage or children. He was, as he continued to insist, 'married to Germany'.[65]

Even before he was appointed Reich Chancellor, Hitler had established around him an aura of unquestioning obedience and unchallenged leadership. His growing staff, consisting of men such as Julius Schaub, who acted as a kind of personal factotum, his chauffeurs, valets, and others, often had military, Brownshirt and ultra-nationalist backgrounds, but they had neither personal nor political influence over him. His earlier political rivals had been sidelined or dismissed. Only men who regarded him as a genius were allowed to come close; critics were not tolerated. The constant identification in his speeches of his own life with Germany's – 'Hitler *is* Germany', as Rudolf Hess declared in his ecstatic paean of praise in Leni Riefenstahl's film of the 1934 Nazi Party

Rally, *Triumph of the Will* – imbued him in the eyes of those who met him with a superhuman quality, reinforced by his emphatic and unqualified assertion of his own rightness, a confidence that was absolute and would brook no dissent. As his personal architect and later Munitions Minister Albert Speer wrote immediately after the end of the war, people who came into his presence, himself included, almost invariably found themselves overwhelmed; already convinced of his greatness, or at least persuaded of his mission, they hung on his every word, impressed by his apparent calmness and self-control. It was not only Speer who idolized him: many others who survived the war still confessed their faith in him under Allied interrogation despite all the devastation and collapse they saw around them. It was obviously in the detainees' interest to emphasize Hitler's responsibility for everything, but their repeated insistence on his greatness, and their oft-asserted belief in him and his legacy for Germany's future, were quite clearly genuinely heartfelt.[66]

Much of this effect came simply from the highly personal nature of his leadership, which imbued his person with enormous power and prestige. He possessed an ability to adapt himself to the people to whom he was speaking, whether to a crowd or to an individual, and he could display emotion as circumstances required, even, for example, appearing to weep with emotion as he implored rebellious stormtroopers to pledge their loyalty in August 1930. Many of his followers spoke with some awe of his blue eyes, which he had a disconcerting habit of fixing on them with a stare, sometimes warm, sometimes cold, always hypnotic. He had an autodidact's patchy and unsystematic knowledge of things, but also impressed with his powers of recall and command of detail. Within his inner circle and especially with his substitute families (Joseph and Magda Goebbels and their family, Winifred Wagner and hers, the photographer Heinrich Hoffmann and his), he could relax, show a caring side when (as Goebbels confessed more than once in his diaries) they got into personal difficulties; but the more he cultivated his charismatic, supra-historical image, the more he concealed his feelings behind the mask of the 'great man'. His burning, uncompromising belief in himself and his ideas often disarmed initially sceptical people. His private enthusiasms, for the cinema, for Wagner, for fast cars, for planning great public buildings, sometimes found their way into policy, but he kept his vegetarianism and his teetotalism to himself, except as an aspect of his self-projection as a man who gave up private pleasures for his political work. This did not stop him from indulging his love for cream cakes, while on the other hand his dislike of tobacco smoke, in an era when almost every adult German was addicted to cigarettes, found expression in a ban on smoking in Nazi buildings.[67]

Hitler was not popularly elected Reich Chancellor on 30 January 1933, since the immediate past election had been held more than two months before, in November 1932, and he had not won an overall majority, indeed had actually lost votes; but on the other hand he was the leader of the largest party, so he was not simply appointed to the office by a backstairs political intrigue as had been the case with Papen, who was almost entirely lacking in electoral support. Hitler's appointment was the result of both these factors working together. But although the Nazis celebrated Hitler's appointment with torchlit marches and parades across the country as the moment when the 'Third Reich' began, the real 'seizure of power' had yet to get under way. It owed a great deal to his ability to capitalize swiftly on lucky chances. One such was provided on the night of 27 February, when the Reichstag building was burned down by a young Dutch extreme (but non-Communist) leftist, Marinus van der Lubbe, as an act of protest against what he saw as the German political establishment's callous treatment of the unemployed. Hitler and Göring arrived on the scene when the building was still ablaze. The only news reporter present, the Berlin correspondent for the London *Daily Express*, Sefton Delmer, an English journalist who had somehow managed to inveigle himself into Hitler's inner circle, described them as surprised and panicky, an impression later confirmed by the head of the Prussian political police, Rudolf Diels. They clearly saw this as the first act in a Communist revolution, a plausible enough assumption given the Communists' record of mounting violent revolutions in Europe since 1917. Göring even claimed they were about to blow up public buildings including electricity generating stations, poison 'public kitchens', and kidnap the families of government ministers, although there was no evidence, either real or manufactured, to substantiate any of these wild and panicky allegations.

The following morning, Hitler persuaded the Cabinet and the President to share these alarmist views, and procured a decree that suspended civil liberties and allowed the police to arrest known Communists, beat up and intimidate their opponents, including many well-known politicians, and prevent the other parties from campaigning. Some 4,000

Communists were taken into custody. Gangs of stormtroopers drove in open lorries through the streets, arresting anyone who tried to distribute leaflets or campaign for the Communists and Social Democrats. Hitler's speeches blared out through loudspeakers set up in town squares. He had made the holding of fresh Reichstag elections a condition of his appointment as Reich Chancellor, and they duly took place on 5 March 1933. They were held under conditions that were neither free nor fair. That this was the case owed a great deal to Hitler's continuing use of street violence and intimidation, which now escalated dramatically as the stormtroopers were enrolled as auxiliary policemen on 22 February by Hermann Göring, acting as Prussian Minister of the Interior. Even with these restrictions, however, the Nazis only won just 44 per cent of the vote. They were carried over the 50 per cent threshold by their conservative Nationalist coalition partners, who gained another 8 per cent. Five million voters even cast their ballots for the Communists, who won over 12 per cent of the vote, with the Social Democrats polling a remarkable 18.3 per cent; Hitler had allowed the Communists to put up candidates in case their voters might switch to the Social Democrats if they were banned. The fact that the Left won nearly a third of the vote at a time when the stormtroopers were already arresting their candidates, beating them up, torturing them or driving them into exile, is an indication of the fact that Hitler and the Nazis still had a considerable amount of opposition to overcome.[68]

A tsunami of terror now engulfed the country. Armed stormtroopers rampaged through the streets, trashing and looting Social Democratic and Communist Party offices, arresting, humiliating, beating up, torturing and in some cases shooting dead the officials, administrators and public representatives of the two parties. By 25 March 1933 such actions had been carried out in forty-five towns across Germany. Three days earlier Heinrich Himmler, now chief of police in Bavaria, opened the first concentration camp, at Dachau, packing it with Communists and Social Democrats who were brutally beaten and maltreated. More were to follow. The day before, the newly elected Reichstag was formally opened by President Hindenburg in an elaborate ceremony in the Prussian military town of Potsdam, with Hitler, dressed in a frock-coat, bowing to him in homage, as to the old order, and a throne left symbolically vacant for the former Kaiser, whose sons participated prominently in the spectacle. The charade reconciled Hindenburg to Hitler's assumption of power; indeed, the old man could be seen wiping a tear from his eye as the ritual proceeded. It was just as successful in reassuring many conservative and monarchist members of the public that the Nazis were respectable people who would join with representatives of the old order in creating a Germany that would destroy the failed democratic constitution, sweep aside the Socialists and Communists, and restore the safe, successful and orderly world they thought they had lived in under the Kaiser. So many hundreds of thousands of them rushed to join the Nazi Party that they were known ironically as the *Märzgefallenen*, 'March Fallen', an allusion to the victims of the 1848 Revolution, and the Nazi Party had to suspend the recruitment of new members altogether for a time. Meanwhile, however, the violence and bloodshed continued unabated, fulfilling Hitler's promise on the night of the Reichstag fire, that 'there will be no more mercy now: anyone who stands in our way will be cut down.'[69]

Hitler needed further support in the Reichstag if he was to secure the two-thirds majority needed for a revision of the Weimar Constitution. The smaller parties, especially his coalition partners, would support him, but the Social Democrats would clearly oppose any attempt to undermine democracy. A total of 94 out of their 120 deputies braved the cordons of uniformed stormtroopers who ringed the Kroll Opera House, where the session was held on 23 March 1933, and the armed Brownshirts who crowded and jostled them as they entered the swastika-bedecked debating chamber. The Social Democratic spokesman Otto Wels insisted that the dictatorship would never destroy the ideals of democracy in the long run. Despite the intimidation, the Social Democrats voted against the Enabling Act, which Hitler, also now in uniform, introduced with an inflammatory speech threatening open violence should the measure be rejected. The Law would allow him to introduce legislation without the consent of parliament. Armed with an advance copy of Wels's speech, he responded by contemptuously dismissing the Social Democrats as history's losers. The vote now took place. Hermann Göring, presiding over the session as the representative of the largest party, illegally reduced the quorum from 432 to 378 by refusing to count the legitimately elected Communist deputies. The required two-thirds majority was supplied by the votes of the seventy-three deputies of the Catholic Centre Party, whose leaders had been persuaded by two days of discussion with Hitler that the Catholic Church and its lay organizations would remain untouched by any measures the Nazis imposed on society. The Catholic Centre deputies had already been intimidated by arrests and beatings, and were cowed by Hitler's threat of civil war. The Vatican, which was pursuing a policy of backing authoritarian regimes across Europe in order to suppress the threat of atheist Communism, pushed the Centre Party deputies further towards voting for the Law. The votes of the Nationalists and liberals were enough to secure its passage. From now on, laws and decrees could be enacted by the Cabinet alone, without reference to the President or the Reichstag. Together with the Reichstag Fire Decree, the Enabling Act provided the quasi-legal fig leaf for the introduction of a dictatorship and its perpetuation all the way up to 1945.[70]

Hitler had outmanoeuvred his conservative coalition partners with these measures. Initially they had applauded his policies, above all the ending of parliamentary democracy and the suppression of the labour movement, and by the time they recognized that they too were in the firing-line and started to criticize their Nazi partners for their violence and disorder, it was too late. Their complaints were loudly rejected on 30 May 1933 by Hitler in an outburst of rage in which he threatened them with a 'bloodbath lasting three days' if they did not knuckle under.[71] Hitler had also begun to restructure the Reich Cabinet, appointing a series of Nazis to it, beginning with Joseph Goebbels, who on 13 March 1933 occupied the newly created post of Reich Minister of Public Enlightenment and Propaganda. In May 1933 Hermann Göring joined as Minister of Aviation, and at the end of June 1933 the Nationalist press baron Alfred Hugenberg, who had incautiously revealed some of Hitler's longer-term intentions at an international conference, was replaced by the Nazi Richard Walther Darré. There were further appointments in 1934. But in a sense this scarcely mattered, since Hitler now marginalized the Cabinet, arrogating its powers to himself alone. It met ever less frequently, until after 1938 it did not meet again at all. In the meantime, armed Brownshirts stormed town halls and regional seats of government across the country and evicted the incumbents, using the flimsy pretext of the Reichstag Fire Decree. By 9 March 1933 all the federated states, from Hamburg to Bavaria, were being ruled by appointed 'Reich Commissars' and the swastika was flying over administrative buildings across the land.[72]

There was nothing particularly subtle or sophisticated about the

Nazi seizure of power, which took place above all in the months of March, April, May and June 1933. With over two million armed and violent men in its ranks, the stormtrooper movement, egged on by Hitler, simply took over all non-Nazi political organizations, looting their premises, brutally beating their representatives, intimidating their officials and closing down their operations. At least 600 people were killed in the mayhem, and countless others were injured. Between 100,000 and 200,000 Social Democrats and Communists were arrested and put into makeshift torture centres and concentration camps, to be released only after promising not to engage in politics again. A sufficient number of Catholic Centre Party and other 'bourgeois' party officials were maltreated to force the other political parties to dissolve themselves, while the left-wing parties were abolished by decree. Hitler felt strong enough amid this mass violence to threaten his Nationalist coalition partners if they failed to follow suit, which, cowed into submission, they did. By the end of June, Germany was a one-party state. The takeover of Germany's vast civil service, which included teachers, university professors, and hundreds of thousands of other state employees, was effected by a decree issued on 7 April 1933, which dismissed known supporters of non-Nazi political parties. Local administrations followed suit. In a situation where unemployment rates were still very high because of the continuing economic Depression, these measures had serious consequences for those people and their families. Small wonder that thousands flocked to join the Nazi Party as a way of keeping their jobs.[73]

Propelled forward with astonishing rapidity on the crest of this wave of unrestrained violence and brutality, the 'national uprising', as it was called by the Nazis, prompted people to greet each other with the Nazi salute, and sign their correspondence with the 'German greeting', *Heil Hitler!* – compulsory for all civil servants from 13 July 1933. Already from 11 March 1933 the Nazi flag, flown side-by-side with the old Imperial flag, was raised on official buildings instead of the black-red-gold flag of the Weimar Republic, another sign that the old elites were collaborating in the creation of the Nazi dictatorship. The wishes of both were fulfilled by the crushing of the trade unions and looting of their assets, followed by a compulsory celebration of the traditionally socialist May Day as the 'day of national labour'. By the autumn of 1933, the professions had all been corralled into Nazi organizations, including even the creative arts, which fell under the umbrella of Goebbels's new 'Reich Culture Chamber' and its various subdivisions. Resistance of any kind was brutally put down: in Köpenick, on the edge of Berlin, an incident of armed resistance to a round-up of Social Democrats prompted the local stormtroopers to arrest 500 members of the party and subject them to prolonged torture over several days, directly causing the death of ninety-one of them. Prominent opposition figures like Felix Fechenbach, who had once been the secretary of Kurt Eisner, were 'shot while trying to escape'. A former Prime Minister of Mecklenburg-Schwerin, the Social Democrat Johannes Stelling, was tortured to death. Leading Catholic Centre politicians such as Eugen Bolz, State President of Württemberg, were also arrested and beaten up before being released. Hitler's visceral hatred of anyone who opposed him, his intolerance, his inner conviction that violence and murder inflicted on his enemies were necessary in the interests of the nation, all opened the way to the physical brutality that was the essential underpinning of the seizure of power.[74]

At the same time, Hitler's actions also met with the approval of a substantial part of the population. Most important in a political sense was the army and its leadership. Not least as a result of Kurt von Schleicher's veiled threats of an army takeover during the negotiations that had led to his appointment, Hitler knew he had to get the army onside. Already on 3 February he had spoken to a meeting of senior military commanders summoned by the Army Minister Werner von Blomberg, a senior officer himself, who had just been appointed directly by Hindenburg in the expectation that he would defend the army's autonomy. Hitler promised them a major programme of rearmament, the introduction of conscription, the overthrow of democracy and its replacement by an authoritarian government, the return of Germany to great-power status and the 'conquest of new living-space in the East and its ruthless Germanization'. The generals had opposed the Weimar Republic from the outset and regarded the Treaty of Versailles with horror. Hitler's speech was music to their ears.[75] In the coming months he could count fully on their support. At the same time, big industrial firms for the first time gave major donations to the Nazis to help them with the March 1933 elections, having been put under heavy pressure to do so at a meeting of industrial leaders with Hitler in Göring's residence on 20 February 1933.[76]

Germany's much-vaunted unity had by now been underpinned by the creation of a one-party state. Voters would from now on only be able to choose between Nazi candidates or policies and spoiling their ballot papers or abstaining, and a mixture of intimidation and manipulation soon ensured that Hitler obtained near-unanimous support in every election and plebiscite, giving the impression, not least to the outside world, of overwhelming endorsement of the Nazi Party. A raft of new treason laws made advocating constitutional change, wishing to replace Hitler's government, or even criticizing Hitler and other leading Nazis, treasonable offences punishable by death. The existing legal system had been co-opted into the Nazi dictatorship, and where it still showed some independence, as in the Supreme Court's acquittal of the alleged Communist co-conspirators with Marinus van der Lubbe in the burning of the Reichstag, Hitler swiftly established a parallel system of special courts that would have no hesitation in doing his will. With hardly any exceptions, the legal system would from now on serve the interests of the Nazi regime and, as he put it, the German people, not some independent concept of abstract justice. The Catholic Church had been won over by a Concordat with the Papacy that appeared to guarantee the continuing existence of its lay organizations, while the Protestant Evangelical Church was being rapidly taken over from within by the 'German Christians', who, among other things, denied that Jesus was Jewish. Hitler had already begun to talk in grandiose terms of a new Reich that would last for a thousand years.[77] No internal or external power would ever overcome it.[78] This was what he dubbed the 'national socialist revolution' or the 'national uprising'.[79]

What permeated the whole process and drove it on was the violence Hitler encouraged, a rage and hatred against Socialists and Communists and democrats and indeed virtually everybody who did not support him that also consumed his rank-and-file followers as well as his cheerleaders and acolytes such as Goebbels and Göring. There were, however, two more problems to solve before he could assume complete and unfettered power. The first of these was the semi-autonomy of the stormtroopers, who numbered more than four million following the incorporation of the nationalist veterans' paramilitary organization, the *Stahlhelm* (Steel Helmets). In sheer numbers they dwarfed the regular army, which was limited to 100,000 men by the Treaty of Versailles. They were a source of continual disorder and violence, and without an obvious purpose once they had smashed rival paramilitary movements in the first half of 1933. Recognizing this fact, in August 1933 Göring rescinded his earlier order enrolling them as auxiliary policemen. As they increased in number, the stormtroopers were seen as a growing threat by Germany's military leadership. Their leader, Ernst Röhm, a close associate of Hitler's since the early 1920s, wanted them to be organized into a kind of national militia.[80] The leading generals were becoming ever more insistent that Röhm be brought to heel. The pressure to act was becoming increasingly urgent. At the end of June 1934, Hitler yielded to it, and launched what he presented as a pre-emptive strike, preventing a 'second revolution' to be spearheaded by the stormtroopers (in fact this was just a product of his propaganda). He had the stormtroopers' leadership arrested, ordered Röhm and several of his lieutenants to be executed, and brought the unruly organization to heel in the so-called 'Night of the Long Knives'. At least eighty-five people were killed; the true figure may have been many times more. The problem was solved, and a compulsory universal call-up of young men into the army followed a few months later.[81]

A second, not unrelated problem confronting Hitler in the first half of 1934 was the obvious decline in health of the aged President Hindenburg, who was in his mid-eighties. Hitler's conservative allies, above all the Vice-Chancellor, Franz von Papen, began jockeying for position in the succession, stressing their ideological distance from the Nazis (such as it was) and criticizing the violence that the stormtroopers had been meting out to opponents of the 'national revolution'. Hitler had been forced to tolerate Hindenburg's continued presence as head of state, and therefore his superior, because the field marshal was a widely venerated figure. But, once Hindenburg was gone, Hitler was determined not to allow anyone else to take his place, except himself. He prepared the way for this move by using the 'Night of the Long Knives' at the end of June 1934 to curb the conservatives by having Papen's speechwriter shot and the Vice-Chancellor dispatched to Vienna as German ambassador to Austria. Other victims included people who knew too much about Hitler's early career or had angered him in some way, such as the Bavarian politician Gustav Ritter von Kahr, who had frustrated him during the beer-hall *putsch* in November 1923, or Gregor Strasser, who had deserted him at a key moment at the end of 1932, or General Kurt von Schleicher, who had got in his way by getting himself appointed Reich

Chancellor instead of Hitler towards the end of the same year.[82] This murderous coda to the 'seizure of power' completed Hitler's rise to the unchallenged position of dictator. After Hindenburg's death on 2 August 1934, Hitler declared the post of President abolished, since nobody else would be worthy of it, and became *de facto* Head of State. All civil servants and military officers and troops from now on had to swear their personal allegiance to him, instead of the Constitution, as had been the case previously.

Although the Constitution of the Weimar Republic was in most respects formally still in force, the novelty of the new regime was made clear from the outset. It was known as the Third Reich because it was supposed to follow the First (the Holy Roman Empire of the German Nation, founded by Charlemagne in the year 800 – the original 'Thousand-Year Reich') and the Second (founded by Bismarck in 1871). Before long, the personality cult around Hitler reached such grotesque proportions that even he attempted to curb it. He issued orders, for example, to halt the rapid renaming of town squares and streets after himself, and refused to accept honorary doctorates from universities. He also demonstratively abstained from taking his salary as Reich Chancellor (he did not need it anyway, because he received generous royalties from *Mein Kampf* and income from the use of his image on postage stamps). None of this stopped the unceasing public adulation of Hitler as German 'leader', cemented in every official letter and every formal or informal greeting between citizens on the street or in the café or pub by the endlessly repeated phrase '*Heil Hitler!*'[83]

VI

As dictator Hitler had control over every area of domestic policy, should he choose to exercise it. No one ever challenged him on any aspect of policy. But of course he focused more on some areas than on others. As someone who had always thought of himself as an artist, Hitler for example paid particular attention to artistic and cultural policy. Almost immediately he ordered the construction of a 'House of German Art' in Munich to replace an older exhibition centre, the 'Glass Palace', which had accidentally burned down two years before. It would display cultural works he considered properly German. Speaking at the foundation-stone laying on 15 October 1933, he declared that there would be no more 'incomprehensible eccentricity' in the art world. Argument and division would cease here as in other aspects of German life, and indeed on Goebbels's orders art criticism was soon abolished, since in a situation where everything on show was approved by the regime, any criticism of art would amount to criticism of the regime itself.[84] So-called modern art, Hitler declared, was sick, incompetent, so primitive it could have been produced in the Stone Age by 'cultural Neanderthals', a view expressed in the notorious 'degenerate art' exhibition put on by Goebbels with Hitler's approval in 1937. 'From now on,' Hitler declared, 'we shall wage a relentless war of purgation against the last elements of the undermining of our culture.' Modernist artworks were removed from galleries and museums, directors who had favoured abstract art, post-Impressionism, *neue Sachlichkeit* and other modern artistic movements were fired, and artists who produced them were blacklisted. This was Hitler's revenge for his rejection as an artist before 1914, at a time when his painstakingly representational sketches were scorned and modernist painters like Picasso and Matisse were making their reputations. Art, he said, had to express the innermost essence of the German people – in practice, traditional representational art, painting and sculpture celebrating its heroism in past, present and future. 'Modern' art followed changing fashions; German art was eternal, because the German people was eternal.[85]

In fact, none of the unimaginative, conventional and unoriginal works Hitler promoted has stood the test of time; what lasted were precisely the paintings and sculptures he ridiculed, by artists most of whom had fled into exile when he came to power. Hitler intervened in Germany's artistic life actively, and he spoke on art far more often than any other dictator of the age. His views, mixed in with *völkisch* ideology, expressed more than anything else the petty-bourgeois prejudices of the ignorant and narrow-minded. Equally unoriginal in everything except their gigantomania were the pseudo-Classical public buildings he envisaged for the future of German towns and cities. Already in November 1937 he began planning the reconstruction of Berlin, converting it from the Prussian capital 'to the eternal capital city of the first German people's Reich'. Over the following years, working with his architect Albert Speer, he drew up plans for a new city – 'Germania' – intersected by two huge boulevards, one east–west, the other north–south (with a huge new train station at each end), and new public buildings, including a vast hall of the people topped by a dome bigger than that of St Peter's in Rome, a triumphal arch larger than the Arc de Triomphe in Paris, and similar overblown constructions. All this would demonstrate 'that our task is to provide a millennial people with a thousand-year historical and cultural past, a city that will last for a thousand years and be appropriate for its never-ending future'.[86] For Hitler, buildings represented power, a lesson he had learned from the imposing edifices of Vienna's Ringstrasse before 1914. He repeatedly proclaimed that Germans were now living in a time of unsurpassed greatness, and looked forward to a bright future in which their lives would continue to improve. Every coming generation 'will be ever stronger, ever mightier, and ever healthier, and give living generations an ever greater hope for the future'. At the same time, however, he told members of the Hitler Youth that they would have to acknowledge their devotion to 'an eternal Reich and an eternal people', sacrificing themselves if needed for the future of the German race.[87]

Hitler even considered modernists to be suffering from a hereditary distortion of the sense of perception, and gave some consideration to sterilizing those who remained in Germany, though this never came to pass.[88] One of his earliest legislative acts as Reich Chancellor was to pass the Law for the Prevention of Hereditarily Diseased Offspring, which came into effect on 1 January 1934. This laid down the groundwork for the following campaign of compulsory sterilization of the 'unfit', which included not only the very small number of Germans who suffered from serious hereditary conditions such as Huntingdon's disease, but also the vastly greater number who were sterilized because they were social deviants, alcoholics, mentally handicapped or 'morally feeble-minded'. On 7 September 1937 Hitler publicly justified the policy of 'racial hygiene' that would keep 'German blood' 'pure and unpolluted'. Eventually some 400,000 Germans were compulsorily sterilized; from 1939 onwards, on Hitler's express, signed orders, they began to be murdered, by gassing or lethal injection, or by starvation and medical neglect: men, women and children, numbering in the end around 200,000.[89] Nazism, Hitler proclaimed in justification, was a scientific doctrine dedicated through the means of eugenic selection to the improvement of the German race.

By way of contrast, Hitler had relatively little to say about the economy. His speeches on the subject were short and lacking in detail.

Among other things, he proclaimed that Germany would soon become self-sufficient, above all through the manufacture of artificial chemicals, fertilizers, fuel and rubber. Any shortages people might be experiencing were only temporary.[90] Rather than go into detail about the economic situation, he preferred to congratulate himself for bringing strikes and disputes to an end and boosting construction schemes. Technical difficulties with problems such as international exchange rates he 'solved' simply by declaring them fixed for all time.[91] He appointed the economics wizard Hjalmar Schacht, President of the Reichsbank and, from 1934, Minister of Economics, to engineer the economic recovery, though full employment was only achieved through the introduction of conscription in 1935 and the headlong rush to rearm, a policy that Schacht increasingly felt introduced serious distortions into the economy.[92] As far as Hitler was concerned, the massive borrowings that had underpinned rearmament would be repaid by conquest and annexation. Determined to avoid the shortages that had, he believed, undermined morale in World War I, Hitler promoted a policy of 'autarky', making Germany as far as possible self-sufficient, replacing imported oil and rubber with synthetic products (which in the end proved a wholly unrealistic ambition), and promoting domestic agriculture.[93]

Communist propaganda, both in the 1930s and afterwards, portrayed the Nazi regime as the tool of big business, but the Third Reich is more accurately described as a 'command economy', in which big business had real difficulty in influencing Nazi policy, and in many ways went along only reluctantly with policies such as 'autarky', antisemitism, expropriation, 'Aryanization' and labour conscription. Nevertheless, business derived considerable benefits from Hitler's relentless drive to rearm (some parts of industry, of course, more than others). Once it became clear that there was no way round these policies, many employers and businessmen went along with them more or less willingly. A small minority colluded in the forced sale of Jewish-owned businesses at a fair price because they were on friendly terms with the owners, but the vast majority exploited the policy for their own gain.[94] During the war, industrialists were to use forced and slave labour on a vast scale, with the SS managing labour camps attached to industrial enterprises in conditions similar to those obtaining in concentration camps, leading to death rates among workers that were extremely high.[95]

While he showed little detailed interest in economic and financial issues, Hitler had rather more to say about his desire to 'motorize' Germany. Already on 11 February 1933, less than a fortnight after his appointment, he opened a long-planned international motor-vehicle exhibition in Berlin with a speech full of enthusiasm for what was still a relatively new form of transport. Here he was presenting himself as a serious statesman with ambitious plans for a technological future, promising tax breaks for the automobile industry along with a far-reaching programme of road construction.[96] A new, cheaply available 'People's Car' (*Volkswagen*), the famous 'beetle', designed by Ferdinand Porsche after sketches by Hitler himself, would bring travel opportunities to every family (though it did not go into production before the war, and the many ordinary Germans who invested in the car, hoping to obtain one in due course, never got their money back). The *Volkswagen* was one of a number of consumer goods promoted by the regime, taking advantage of the rapidly falling price of electricity as more power stations came online, including a People's Fridge and a People's Radio, augmented by an ambitious programme of motorway (*Autobahn*) construction whose extent, however, was hugely exaggerated by Goebbels's propaganda machine.[97]

Above all, as soon as the seizure of power got under way, Hitler, together with the ever-willing Goebbels, began to translate his visceral and obsessive hatred and fear of Jews into action, setting the political and ideological context for waves of seemingly spontaneous antisemitic violence. Physical assaults on Jews, or people who the Nazis thought looked like Jews, had already been part of the stormtroopers' repertoire of violence for years. With the appointment of Hitler as Reich Chancellor, antisemitism became official government policy. On 6 March 1933, squads of Brownshirts ran up and down the Kurfürstendamm, one of Berlin's main shopping streets, assaulting Jews and even hauling them out of their cars to beat them senseless. Elsewhere they stormed the offices of Jewish lawyers and other professionals and forced their way into Jewish-owned shops, firing shots and smashing windows.[98] Reacting to protests and demonstrations in America against the mounting anti-Jewish violence, Hitler and Goebbels staged a nation-wide boycott of Jewish businesses on 1 April 1933. Hitler launched the action with a violent denunciation of 'international world Jewry' and its agents in Germany, 'the enemies of the nation within'. Stormtroopers daubed slogans on shop windows warning customers against going in, and stood menacingly outside to enforce the ban. The boycott was extended to Jewish lawyers and doctors. Many customers insisted on entering Jewish-owned shops anyway, and the measure was not renewed after 4 April.[99] The decree of 7 April 1933, firing politically undesirable civil servants, also dismissed individuals of 'non-Aryan descent', or in other words, Jews. Only those who had fought at the front in 1914–18 were exempted, on the express order of Hindenburg, who still wielded considerable influence at this time. If these official measures were intended to send a message to stormtroopers that the campaign against the Jews had to be centrally coordinated, they were a miserable failure: uncoordinated boycotts against Jewish businesses and professionals continued to be staged in many localities in the following months.[100]

Hitler repeatedly portrayed Germany as the victim of an international Jewish conspiracy. On 12 February 1936, for example, he fulminated against 'the hate-filled power of our Jewish enemy, an enemy to whom we have done no harm, but who tried to subjugate our German people and make us its slaves, an enemy who is responsible for all the misfortunes visited upon Germany in November 1918 and in the following years!' They were responsible for 'an endless procession of National Socialists murdered, almost always from behind, or beaten or stabbed or shot', men who nonetheless still marched in spirit with the living members of the movement as inspiring martyrs for the cause.[101] In September 1938 he declared that 'the nation is no longer willing to let itself be sucked dry by these parasites', at a time when Jews in Germany were being expropriated, deprived of the economic basis of their lives, and driven out of the country in growing numbers. As in so many of his claims, he was standing the truth on its head, pushing a paranoid conspiracy theory that lacked any kind of basis in reality.[102]

On 30 January 1939, the sixth anniversary of his appointment as Reich Chancellor, Hitler devoted a substantial part of his opening address to the newly 'elected' one-party Reichstag to a tirade of hate against the 'lust for revenge and greed for profit' of 'international Jewry', whom he blamed for all the misfortunes he claimed had befallen Germany in the course of the century, from the Treaty of Versailles to the post-war hyperinflation. Germany had been 'ruled and controlled by a foreign race'. But no more, he thundered. The German people had reclaimed their art and culture. The 'infiltration [*Einnisten*] of a foreign race that knew how to grab all the leadership positions for itself' was over. Already in this paranoid fantasy-world of his, the Jews were being disqualified as human beings by the word '*Einnisten*', usually reserved for vermin, such as ants making their nest inside a house. The Jews had laughed at him in the 1920s when he had prophesied that he would one day come to power and 'bring the Jewish problem to a solution', he said – a reference to the liberal and leftist press which he falsely claimed had been, along with so much else in the Weimar Republic, no more than the tool of a global Jewish conspiracy to undermine German civilization. 'I want to be a prophet again today,' he said. 'If international Jewry in Europe and beyond should succeed in plunging the peoples once again into a world war, then the result will be, not the Bolshevization of the earth and with it the victory of Jewry, but the annihilation of the Jewish race in Europe.'[103] Hitler's belief that capitalism and Communism were both steered from behind by a global Jewish conspiracy to destroy Germany and Europe was in full view here, for all to see. For him, this was to become one of the principal aims of the war he was to launch in September 1939. He later identified it as such to the extent that he subsequently misdated his January 1939 speech to the opening day of the conflict in September.[104]

Hitler regarded the promulgation of the Nuremberg Laws at the Party Rally in 1935 as only a provisional measure. Rushed through in an attempt to channel and organize the widespread grassroots antisemitic actions that had been building up over the previous few months, they made marriage and sexual relations between Jews and non-Jews in Germany illegal and hastened the mass emigration of German Jews to other countries, mainly the USA; about half of Germany's tiny Jewish community (less than 1 per cent of the population) had left the country by the time emigration was made illegal, in 1941. Hitler continued to declare, however, that 'the fight against the nation's internal enemies', meaning in particular the Jews, 'will never fail because of formal bureaucracy and its inadequacy', because the Party itself would take it up. The state, he said, with its formal system of laws and courts, was no more than 'an organizational form of racial life, driven on and ruled by the direct expression of the people's will to life – the Party of the National Socialist movement'. Hitler believed that formal legislation and the cumbersome and rule-bound operations of the law were hindrances to the implementation of the people's will, which he increasingly identified with his own. It was not until 26 April 1942, however, that Hitler secured a declaration of the Reichstag that his word was law and he was entitled to dismiss judges if they showed any independence in their rulings. A few months later, he was to boast that criminals had been 'extirpated', though everyday crimes from theft to murder in fact continued, despite a drastic worsening of conditions in state prisons and penitentiaries and the extermination of some 20,000 repeat offenders in the camps.[105]

Well before this point had been reached, however, Hitler had presided over innumerable violations of the law in respect to antisemitic actions, most notably on 9 November 1938, when he met with Propaganda Minister Joseph Goebbels to authorize the nationwide orgy of violence against Jewish people and property known to posterity as the *Reichskristallnacht*, or 'Night of Broken Glass'. There is no doubt that, while the idea might have originated with Goebbels, the order to unleash the violence came directly from Hitler himself, who was described by the Propaganda Minister in his diary as 'totally radical' on the policy. Supposedly in retaliation for the shooting of a German Embassy official in Paris, the destruction of thousands of Jewish properties, the burning down of hundreds of synagogues, and the arrest on Hitler's direct orders of some 30,000 Jewish men and their incarceration in concentration camps until they agreed to emigrate, was followed by a series of measures taking away most of the income and property of Germany's Jewish community. Especially younger Germans took part enthusiastically in the looting and destruction. In Hitler's paranoid mind, such lawless violence was a necessary security measure in preparation for the coming war, removing what he considered an internal threat to the nation's ability to fight. No formal laws were necessary: his order was enough, though the wave of horror and revulsion he knew would sweep across the international community at the pogrom persuaded him to keep his personal authorization for the violence from the public.[106]

The purpose of the law, he declared, was to defend the interests of the race. 'The judge,' he was reported to have said later in the *Table-Talk*, 'is the bearer of the self-preservation of the race.' War caused the death of the best young men, so the legal system had to compensate by getting rid of the worst. The judicial system, Hitler believed, was soft. He would read newspaper reports of trials in which a sentence had been passed that he considered too lenient, and order the convicted offender to be shot. The legal system was already co-opted into the regime and during the war it grew harsher and more punitive. Already in 1933 a whole raft of new treason laws passed the task of repression from the SS and SA, the camps, and the Gestapo over to the courts, the regular police and the prisons, so that a decline in the number of camp inmates to under 4,000 by 1935 was more than balanced by an increase in the number of state prisoners, 23,000 of whom were officially classified as political offenders in the same year.[107] In the meantime, however, Hitler's pseudo-legal powers were used by Himmler, the SS and the Gestapo to arrest and incarcerate in concentration camps people who had not violated the letter of the law, including for example homosexuals who had been imprisoned under paragraph 175 of the Criminal Code (as sharpened by the Nazi regime) and had reached the end of their term of imprisonment only to find the Gestapo waiting for them outside the prison gates on their release.[108]

Hitler also turned his attention to religious policy. In October 1937 he told senior officials in the Propaganda Ministry: 'After difficult inner struggles he had freed himself from his childish religious beliefs.' 'I now feel myself as fresh as a foal in a meadow.'[109] In search of totalitarian perfection, he attempted to bring the Protestant Church into the Nazi orbit through the 'German Christian' movement, which rejected the Old Testament as 'Jewish' and claimed Jesus was 'Aryan'. Catholics, owing their allegiance to the Pope, were subjected to growing discrimination, as autonomous institutions such as Catholic schools and youth organizations were suppressed. They were supposedly protected by the 1933 Reich Concordat signed between the Vatican and the German government, according to which German priests and bishops agreed not to engage in politics. Nevertheless, they were brought under Nazi control, and priests who tried to defend Catholic institutions, or uttered public criticism of the regime, were put into concentration camps. The same fate would befall priests who publicly opposed 'racial health' measures such as the compulsory sterilization of the 'unfit'. Replying to criticism by what he called 'the international Jewish press and propaganda campaign' against his Church policy, Hitler pointed out in 1939 that the 'church tax' levied by law on a proportion of German citizens' income provided the Churches with generous financial support, which would be taken away if the Nazi state decided on a complete separation of Church and state. Clergymen who stuck to religion, he said, and did not interfere in politics, would not be harmed. But clergymen who openly opposed the regime would be annihilated. The Church hierarchy, both Catholic and Protestant, cowed by such threats and in any case disposed to tolerate or support Nazi rule because it effectively warded off the threat of Communism, gave its blessing to the Nazi regime.[110]

However, while he rejected Christianity as un-German, a 'centuries-long violation of the freedom of the soul', Hitler was also sceptical of the efforts of leading Nazis such as Alfred Rosenberg and Heinrich Himmler to replace it with supposedly ancient Germanic cults. In a speech delivered on 6 September 1938, he publicly rejected the idea of National Socialism as 'a cultic movement', insisting: 'National Socialism is a cool, reality-based doctrine of the sharpest scientific understanding... The infiltration of mystically inclined occultist researchers into the Beyond must therefore not be tolerated in the movement.' The natural order had, he conceded, been created by God, but it was to be approached in a spirit of openness and scientific realism, not worshipped in vague and irrational 'cultic sites'.[111] He believed in God, he said on 24 February 1940, but in the remaining four paragraphs of his speech God was replaced by 'Providence', mentioned no fewer than seven times.[112] As reported in the *Table-Talk*, in 1941–42, he underlined his belief that Nazism was not a cult but a scientific movement that would eventually replace Christianity.[113]

VII

Hitler had never concealed the limitless scope of his ambitions for Germany, at least when he spoke to his followers. What he wanted went much further than the mere re-establishment of Germany as a great power or the revision of the Treaty of Versailles to give back to Germany what it had lost. On 5 November 1930, speaking in Mannheim to his followers, he declared, referring to the 'Scramble for Africa' in the 1880s:

> No people had more right to the concept of ruling the world [*Weltherrschaft*] than the German people. We would have had this right, and no other nation [*Stormy applause*]. Not England and not Spain, not Holland, no other nation could have had an inborn right on the basis of its

energy and competence, and also its numerical strength, to claim the domination of the world. In the first division of the world, we fell short, but we stand now at the beginning of a new, great shake-up of this world. Today, some people claim that we are entering an age of peace, but I have to say to them: Gentlemen, you have a poor understanding of the horoscope of our times, which points as never before not to peace, but to war.[114]

Nowhere had he laid out so clearly and unambiguously the extreme, indeed limitless nature of his foreign-policy ambitions or his unqualified belief in the use of military force to attain them.

During the first months of 1933, Hitler was too preoccupied with the establishment of supreme power within Germany itself to think much about foreign policy. In any case, his Nationalist coalition partners, including Foreign Minister Konstantin von Neurath, shared his ambition of overturning the Treaty of Versailles, as did the overwhelming majority of the ambassadors and other mandarins in the Foreign Office.[115] Indeed, virtually the entire political world in Germany shared this view. During the debate on the Enabling Act, even the Social Democrats gave their support to Hitler's immediate foreign-policy programme, despite their opposition to the Act itself.[116] So, as soon as his power was established, he began to implement his long-held intention of breaking free from the constraints imposed on Germany by the peace settlement in 1918–19. In his first major foreign-policy speech as Reich Chancellor, delivered on 17 May 1933, in the presence of the remaining deputies from the Centre Party, the Nationalists and the Social Democrats, he condemned what he called the one-sided enforcement of disarmament on Germany, and prepared the ground for the country's withdrawal from the League of Nations, which was to follow in November. The League, as Hitler declared, was the creation of the victor powers of World War I, and existed to enforce the injustices of the peace settlement of 1919. Germany's departure was legitimized by a nationwide referendum held, however, as German elections now were, under conditions of severe coercion, intimidation and falsification.[117]

From this point on, his speeches on foreign policy no longer expressed his real aims and purposes, as outlined in his 1930 speech to party members, quoted above. They constituted, in the term used by the Hitler biographer Peter Longerich, a 'smokescreen' behind which his actual intentions were concealed.[118] Instead of rousing his followers with open declarations of his drive to achieve global hegemony, he now concealed these ambitions behind a façade of lies and deceptions designed to lull the international community into acquiescence.[119] In January 1934 he concluded a non-aggression pact with Poland, a holding operation while Germany secretly rearmed in preparation for an eventual attack on the country that lay across its eastern border.[120] On 25 January 1935 he told an American journalist 'Germany itself will never violate peace on its own accord', and described war as a catastrophe that could only bring 'deep suffering' to a people.[121] Still nervous at the possibility of Franco-British intervention, he said, as he was to reiterate over the next few years, that 'National Socialism knows no policy of the correction of borders at the cost of foreign peoples.'[122]

The inhabitants of Hitler's homeland, Austria, of course, were not a 'foreign people' in his view, and brushing aside the caution of his diplomats, he promoted a violent attempt by the Austrian SS to overthrow the government by a coup, resulting in the assassination of the clerico-fascist dictator Engelbert Dollfuss on 25 July 1934. The coup was a fiasco, not least because the Austrian Brownshirts, still resentful after the very recent 'Night of the Long Knives', and the murder of their leaders in Germany, failed to support it, but also because Mussolini, angry at not having been consulted about Hitler's coup attempt, moved troops up to the border and threatened to intervene.[123] Hitler soon mended fences with the *Duce*, however, a policy made easier after Italy's invasion of Ethiopia the following year and its consequent isolation from the disapproving international community. Most of Hitler's actions in the mid-1930s went unopposed by Britain and France, the two leading European powers: the reintegration of the Saarland into Germany, mandated to the League of Nations until 1935, through a plebiscite in which the great majority of Saarlanders opted to rejoin Germany; the reintroduction of military conscription and the repudiation of the military clauses of the Treaty of Versailles the same year; and the remilitarization of the Rhineland in 1936, from which the Treaty had banned German troops and weaponry. There followed the incorporation of Austria into the Reich on 12 March 1938, enforced by a German military invasion (the *Anschluss*) but backed by the majority of Austrians. None of this was opposed by Britain or France. There was a widespread feeling in the international community that such actions merely applied the principle of national self-determination to Germany, and that could only, surely, be fair.[124] At every stage, Hitler went to great lengths to assure Britain, France and the rest of the world that his aim was peace, he had no intention of aggressive actions against other countries, and he was only claiming what was rightfully Germany's.[125] Hitler repeatedly professed friendship in particular with 'England', which he portrayed as a 'Germanic' nation, while privately taking the failure of Britain and France to intervene to halt Germany's aggressive foreign policy as evidence of their weakness and degeneracy. Nevertheless, just in case, the governments of these nations began to rearm themselves as well, behind the scenes.[126]

Towards the end of 1937, Hitler's foreign policy began to lose its earlier caution and markedly increased its pace. He had overcome his enemies within Germany, he said, and now it was time to overcome them in the wider world.[127] On 31 October 1937, speaking in confidence to senior officials in the Propaganda Ministry, he was reported to have said that:

> He, Hitler, had, by human standards, not very long to live. People didn't get old in his family. His parents both died early too. So it was necessary to solve the problems that had to be solved (living-space!) as soon as possible, so that this happened during his lifetime. Later generations would no longer be able to do this. His person alone was in a position to do this.[128]

On 20 October 1937 he had told the visiting Muslim dignitary the Aga Khan that this meant solving the Austrian, Sudeten, Danzig and Polish Corridor problems, by incorporating them into Germany. He asked his guest to tell the government in London that 'England must give us a free hand on the Continent, and we won't meddle in its overseas interests' – an 'offer' that was repeated many times in the following years, even during the war. It was completely meaningless, given Hitler's attitude to international agreements in general; it is mainly interesting as an indication of the low priority he gave to the recovery of the overseas colonies taken away from Germany by the Treaty of Versailles.[129] On 10 November 1937 he met with senior generals to outline his intentions, declaring that he did not expect serious British objections when he invaded Czechoslovakia.[130] The top generals shared his longer-term aims, but were thoroughly alarmed by his impatience, believing that, despite the headlong pace of rearmament, Germany was not ready either in 1937 or in 1938 for a major European war. Some of them even started to plot Hitler's arrest should he overstep the bounds of caution and rationality and begin a conflict that Germany had no chance of winning.[131]

Hitler had become increasingly dissatisfied with the Foreign Ministry establishment, who shared his ambition to establish hegemony in East-Central Europe but were more dubious about the violent methods he was prepared to use in achieving this end. On 4 February 1938 he replaced his Foreign Minister, the conservative nationalist Konstantin von Neurath, with the more pliant Nazi activist Joachim von Ribbentrop, who had been gaining influence for some time.[132] This was the end point of a far-reaching purge of the men Hitler felt were trying to put the brakes on his onward rush to war. Acting on Göring's initiative, Hitler also dismissed the War Minister Werner von Blomberg after the general's new bride, the much younger Erna Gruhn, turned out to have posed for pornographic photographs. In addition to this, the head of the army, Werner von Fritsch, was removed on trumped-up charges of homosexuality. Hitler took the opportunity to fire a number of conservative generals and restructure the defence apparatus, replacing the War Ministry with a newly created Supreme Command of the Armed Forces.[133] The armed forces, he insisted, had to practise 'blind loyalty and blind obedience' to his orders.[134] Hjalmar Schacht, whose position as Economics Minister was being undermined by the introduction of a Four-Year Plan, presided over by Hermann Göring on Hitler's orders in 1936 with the aim of preparing the German economy for war, had already resigned in November 1937 because he was unwilling to take the massive financial risk involved in the huge rearmament programme Hitler was now pushing forward. Hitler simply expected to recoup the losses from conquered countries when the time came. There can be no doubt that he was now deliberately heading towards a general European war.[135]

From this point onwards, traditional diplomatic norms were thrown out of the window. For Hitler, international agreements were mere pieces of paper, to be torn up when no longer required, despite his declaration that 'Whatever we have signed we will carry out, blindly and loyally!'[136] Politicians like the British Prime Minister Stanley Baldwin and his successor Neville Chamberlain believed him: as far as they were concerned, he was a relatively conventional statesman who would observe the terms of the treaties he signed. They were mistaken. Baldwin approved of an Anglo-German Naval Agreement in June 1935 that regulated the relative sizes of the British and German navies; Hitler denounced it less than four years later. In July 1936 Hitler signed a formal agreement with the Austrian government that the country's leader, Kurt Schuschnigg, regarded as a definitive settlement of the outstanding issues between the two states; Hitler abrogated it unilaterally less than two years later. On 30 September 1938 Chamberlain concluded an agreement with Hitler that guaranteed, he said, 'peace for our time', persuading Hitler not to invade Czechoslovakia at the cost of forcing the Czechs to cede territory to Germany. Within six months, Hitler had torn up the agreement and invaded anyway. Securing Soviet Russia's backing for his invasion of Poland – itself a violation of a treaty he had signed with the Poles in 1934 and publicly confirmed in January 1939 – he concluded the Nazi–Soviet Pact in August 1939, but he broke this too when he invaded the Soviet Union in June 1941. On 31 May 1939 Foreign Minister Ribbentrop signed a non-aggression treaty with Denmark, an act followed in October by a public assurance from Hitler that German–Danish relations were 'thus directed at an unalterably loyal and friendly cooperation'; Germany broke the agreement less than a year later by invading the country and occupying it within a few hours. On 6 October 1939 he declared that 'Germany's decision [is] irrevocable, namely: to bring about in the East of our Reich peaceful, stable and thus acceptable conditions'; eighteen months later this 'irrevocable' decision was revoked by the German invasion of the Soviet Union.[137]

It would be a mistake to attribute every stage in the road to war to Hitler alone. Although for example he always intended to incorporate his homeland, German-speaking Austria, into the Third Reich, the failure of his attempted coup in 1934 had made him cautious about when to do so, and he repeatedly reined in the Austrian Nazis, who remained committed to violence. Keen to acquire Austria's industrial resources for the Four-Year Plan, Hermann Göring overcame his hesitancy, pressing the Austrian Nazi leader Arthur Seyss-Inquart to take action and telling Hitler he would look weak if he did not order an invasion.[138] Hitler had already begun planning the invasion of Czechoslovakia in

April 1938, and made no attempt to conceal his intention to invade, provoked, he claimed by the oppression of the substantial German ethnic minority in the country, which he had been busy encouraging to join the Nazi Party and enter on a campaign of obstruction and subversion against the country's democratic government.[139] The British and French, led by Prime Minister Neville Chamberlain, threatened to declare war, however, should Germany stage a military invasion of Czechoslovakia. Chamberlain thought that if the principle of national self-determination enshrined in the Treaty of Versailles was applied and the German-speaking borderlands of Czechoslovakia were ceded to the German Reich, then Hitler would be 'appeased' and war avoided. In a series of dramatic meetings, culminating in the Munich Agreement on 30 September 1938, concluded without the participation of the hapless Czechs, Hitler gave way to Chamberlain's pressure, with repeated assertions that all he wanted was European peace. The western borderlands of Czechoslovakia in the 'Sudetenland' were annexed to the Reich, leaving the rest of the country exposed to a German invasion at some future date.[140]

Far from being happy with this result, however, Hitler was furious. Once the British Premier had returned to London, Hitler poured scorn on his old-fashioned appearance, which, he said, reminded him of 'the umbrellas of our former bourgeois world of political parties'. The British were 'tiny little worms', incapable, he thought, of coming to a 'manly' decision (in other words to declare war). He ranted and raved against British politicians, offloading his frustration in tirades against critics of Appeasement such as the Conservative politician Winston Churchill.[141] But he also knew that the German people were by no means enthusiastic about a general war. The Germans had been too heavily influenced, he complained, by the 'defeatism' of the Weimar Republic, and it was taking him too long, he confessed in a confidential speech delivered on 10 November 1938, 'to illuminate for the German people certain foreign-policy occurrences, that the people's inner voice itself began slowly to cry out for the use of force'.[142] But he failed: the scenes of popular jubilation that had greeted the outbreak of war in 1914 were not to be repeated in 1939.[143]

By this time, Hitler was no longer fulminating against the 'November criminals' – the liberals and Social Democrats who had concluded the Armistice of November 1918 and ushered in the Weimar Republic. On the contrary, he now greeted the catastrophe of 1918 as a necessary step on Germany's path to greatness:

> How often do some of us not ponder the question of what would have become of Germany if Fate had granted us a quick, easy victory in 1914! ... This victory would probably have had lamentable consequences. For at home, we would have been denied that realization that allows us today to recoil in horror from the path on which Germany already found itself in those days ... The state based on and sustained only by superficial military might would have known nothing of the importance of the sources of popular strength that were rooted in blood, and sooner or later become the destroyer of its own existence and the basis of its life! ... Instead of being pulled back from the brink of disaster by a catastrophic shock, we would have slowly but all the more surely succumbed to the creeping poison of the decomposition of the people![144]

Only through the rise and triumph of Nazism, he continued, was it possible to recognize and overcome the Jewish subversion that had already threatened Germany during World War I. 'Jewish' Bolshevism was a universal threat of historic proportions. Jews had taken over Russia – 'a brutal dictatorship of a foreign race, that has completely seized control over the actual Russian people for itself and used it accordingly'. Jewish-led subversives were exercising their influence everywhere, most recently in Spain, he claimed (in fact the Spanish Civil War had begun in 1936 as an extreme right-wing military coup attempt). National Socialism, he trumpeted, 'has banished the Bolshevik world threat from inside Germany'.[145]

Hitler crossed a modern Rubicon on 15 March 1939 when, following a propaganda barrage that alleged Czech maltreatment of the remaining ethnic Germans in the rump state, he sent German armies into Prague. The breach of the Munich Agreement this involved he blamed, with breathtaking effrontery, on Britain and France.[146] The country was dismembered, as neighbouring states such as Hungary and Romania grabbed their part of the spoils, leaving the lion's share to Germany, which on 16 March turned what was left of it into the 'Reich Protectorate of Bohemia and Moravia'. The German takeover finally made it clear to Chamberlain and the western Allies that Hitler intended far more than a mere revision of the Treaty of Versailles in the interest of German national self-determination. As Hitler was to claim in his

New Year's message on 1 January 1940, Germany was launching 'the construction of a new Europe' that would replace the 'Jewish-capitalist world' of the past. The crescendo of German propaganda against the supposed maltreatment of the ethnic German minority in Poland made it clear that the Poles were next on the list, though they would surely not be the last. When Chamberlain issued a formal guarantee of Polish integrity, backed up by the threat of war should Germany invade, Hitler was incandescent with rage. The 'English' would pay for it with their blood, should it come to a war, he thundered. He had always sought a lasting understanding with them, he complained; now this hope was being destroyed by the 'delusions of the leaders of Great Britain'. The accusation of aggression they levelled at him, he declared, was a barefaced reversal of the facts: Poland, like Czechoslovakia before it, he said, turning, as so often, the real truth on its head, was the aggressor, through its persecution of the millions of ethnic Germans who lived within its borders.[147]

Hitler never intended the prolonged diplomatic exchanges with the British and French during the summer of 1939 over his obvious threat to Poland to lead anywhere.[148] This time, unlike in Munich the previous year, British intervention would not deter him from military action. Already on 23 May 1939 Hitler told his top military officers that 'further successes cannot be achieved without spilling blood'. Overseas colonies would not provide 'living-space'. 'What is important for us is the extension of living-space in the East and the securing of our food supplies.' Poland had to be isolated, then smashed. A declaration of war by Britain and France, allied with the Soviet Union, would 'cause me to attack England and France with some annihilatory blows. England regards in our development the foundation of a hegemony that will rob England of its power. Thus England is our enemy, and the confrontation with England is a matter of life and death.' If a war started, then Germany must mount a 'lightning attack on Holland' and occupy Belgium as well. Britain's main weakness was its dependence on overseas food imports. It would be forced to capitulate if these were cut off. Hitler ordered the setting-up of a range of planning groups to get to work on how to realize these policy goals, all of them to maintain the strictest secrecy.[149]

VIII

Hitler's invasion of Poland was thus prepared many months in advance, and included contingency plans for a general European war at the same time. A non-aggression treaty negotiated between the German Foreign Minister Ribbentrop and the Soviet Foreign Minister Vyacheslav Molotov on 23 August 1939 smoothed the way, ensuring Soviet support for the destruction of Poland by secretly arranging for the Soviet Union to occupy the eastern part of the country. For Hitler this was simply a temporary agreement, signed for merely tactical reasons, and to be torn up, like so many other international agreements, when the time came. For Stalin, it bought time to reconstruct his armed forces after the damage they had suffered from his own political purges during the second half of the 1930s. For many Germans, shocked and surprised by the announcement of the Pact, Hitler appeared in a new light, cynically concluding an alliance with a power he had spent many years publicly condemning as the tool of a world Jewish conspiracy.[150]

Hitler justified the invasion of Poland on 1 September 1939 rather implausibly to the German and international public by condemning Polish attacks on German installations at the border that were in fact entirely spurious, with German concentration-camp inmates dressed as Polish soldiers having been killed by lethal injection and their bodies left on the scene as 'evidence'.[151] As Britain and France declared war on Germany at the beginning of September, Hitler claimed that the general war now under way was the result of the 'British encirclement' that had been practised since 1933. He had offered the English people peace, but to no avail. They now had to bear the consequences.[152] Hitler presented the war as a rerun of World War I: this time, however, a successful one. 'Are not once more the old encirclement politicians active, in part people who already in 1914 only knew hatred [for Germany]?' he had already asked rhetorically in his May Day speech in 1939. 'It is the same international clique of warmongers who were already making their mischief then.' Germany's critics of course were mainly 'Jewish mental parasites', journalists and intellectuals. 'The British policy of encirclement' he blamed on foreign and in particular Jewish fear and jealousy of his achievements in Germany. This was a fantasy in 1939, just as its equivalent had been in 1914. It concealed Hitler's bitter disappointment at his failure to stop the British declaration of war. As late as 13 August 1939 he had told the Italian Foreign Minister Galeazzo Ciano that he was convinced neither Britain nor France would declare war. Now he had been proved disastrously wrong. Almost as bad, he had been unable to persuade his ally Mussolini to join the war on Germany's side. It would be several months before the Italians took the plunge, acting, as in World War I, mainly in the expectation that they were joining the winning side.[153] As he launched the war, Hitler demonstratively announced that he would dress in military uniform until it was won. He was now the 'first soldier of the Reich'.

On 8 November 1939, delivering his customary speech in the Bürgerbräukeller in Munich, the beer-cellar from which he had launched his ill-fated *putsch* attempt in November 1923, Hitler delivered yet another hate-filled diatribe against the British, condemning them as warmongers, annexationists and exploiters of their colonies, filled with envy and hatred of Germany and the Germans. The British were uncivilized and backward. Beethoven had achieved more in the field of music than all the British, past and present, put together. The war was solely their fault.[154] It was not surprising that when a large explosion was detonated in the cellar shortly after he left, Hitler blamed the British. In fact it was the work of a lone working-class carpenter, Georg Elser, a convinced socialist who was bitterly opposed to the Nazi dictatorship and had worked in secret overnight to install a bomb in a hollowed-out pillar in the hall, timed to go off during Hitler's speech. It was only because he left unexpectedly early to catch a train to Berlin that Hitler escaped unharmed. This was, he claimed when he heard the news of the explosion, yet another instance in which Providence had come to his aid. In reaction to the news, two British agents were arrested by SS men at the Dutch border town of Venlo on suspicion of having organized the assassination attempt. Elser, meanwhile, was apprehended on the Swiss border, and after prolonged interrogation convinced the Gestapo that he had acted alone by constructing a replica of the bomb.[155]

All he wanted was peace, Hitler insisted hypocritically in his public pronouncements. In the same breath, however, he declared: 'Securing German living-space is for us the highest commandment.' Germany's claims to 'living-space' were justified by the 'standard of life' of the German people, and by their energy and industriousness. Here, therefore, embedded in his very language, was the racist claim to remove

'Slav subhumans' from Eastern Europe and replace them with Germans.[156] Thus when he spoke to his top generals on the eve of the invasion of Poland, on 22 August 1939, he urged them: 'Close your hearts to pity! Proceed with brutality! 80 million people must have their right. Their existence has to be secured. The stronger has the right! The greatest severity!' The aim of the invasion, he told them, was not to reach a particular geographical position. It was to annihilate Poland. 'The aim is the removal of the living forces' of Polish existence, the destruction in other words of Poland's leading strata.[157] From the very beginning, the war against Poland was a genocidal war: a war that Germany would win if for no other reason than the racial superiority of its people.[158] In the *Table-Talk* he was reported as declaring his intention to keep the Slavs 'at the lowest possible cultural level', Germanizing those who were suitable and reducing the numbers of the rest by denying them medical treatment and keeping them ignorant and uneducated. They would eventually be replaced by 100 million Germans. New *Autobahn* highways and broad-gauge railways would link the new German settlements.[159] And indeed the first steps were already taken towards this end with the dispossession and resettlement measures that followed the invasion of Poland.[160]

Hitler was already beginning to lose patience as his generals repeatedly deferred the invasion of France and the Low Countries on which he had already decided the previous autumn. Implementing the decision was proving impracticable because of adverse weather conditions.[161] When the weather finally improved, German forces swiftly conquered Denmark (April 1940), Belgium and the Netherlands (May 1940), and Norway (June 1940), in operations justified by Hitler with the pretext of preventing Britain from using those countries to launch an attack on Germany.[162] The chance betrayal of the relatively conventional invasion plan for France ('Case Yellow') led two of the bolder generals, Erich von Manstein and Heinz Guderian, to persuade Hitler that, rather than send the invasion force across the Belgian flatlands, he should instead go for a push through the wooded hills of the Ardennes, bypassing French defences. Hitler, ever the gambler, was taken with the idea, not least because of its inherently risky nature. In May 1940, when the weather at last improved, German armoured columns moved slowly through the valleys of the Ardennes, open to aerial bombardment if the French spotted them. But they did not. Breaking out into the north-eastern

French plains, the German armour, backed up by aerial assaults on French military airfields and followed by massed infantry, took the French and the British Expeditionary Force by surprise and forced them back towards the Channel. The British troops were forced to evacuate at Dunkirk, saved from total annihilation when Hitler took the advice of Göring, who boasted that his aeroplanes could destroy the British troops on the beaches, and the leading generals, who pleaded for their exhausted troops to be given a short break. By mid-June the French had been comprehensively defeated. Hitler was ecstatic. He underlined the link with World War I by having the railway carriage in which the 1918 Armistice had been signed hauled out of a museum and taken to the same spot for the French to sign their surrender.[163]

This was the moment of Hitler's greatest triumph. The disastrous defeat of World War I, which had obsessed him for so long, had been avenged. Hitler's racism was no more apparent than in the contrast he drew with the Norwegians a month after the German invasion, when armed resistance was still continuing. While condemning what he called Polish brutality and duplicity towards German soldiers, Hitler praised the Norwegian troops for their open and honourable behaviour. Captured Norwegian soldiers were, he ordered, to be released on the country's surrender. A similar command went out to the German occupying forces in the Netherlands. Both nations he considered belonged to the 'Aryan' race, unlike the Poles, whose soldiers were simply to be exterminated whether they surrendered or not. Poland was to be wiped from the map, its culture annihilated, its leading citizens killed. Much of the western part of the country was annexed to Germany; the rest was formed into the 'General Government' ruled over by the leading Nazi lawyer Hans Frank.[164] The conquest of Poland also brought some 1.7 million Jews under the control of the Nazis (around 1.6 million found themselves in the eastern areas annexed by the Soviet Union in October 1939). This presented the Nazis with a fresh problem – or opportunity. More than half of Germany's Jews – some 304,000 – had emigrated by the outbreak of war, largely as a consequence of Nazi decrees confiscating their assets and banning them from most occupations. Hitler ordered the Polish Jews to be arrested and confined in 'ghettos' in the principal towns and cities, where they were systematically deprived of resources, including adequate food rations and medical care. SS Task Forces (*Einsatzgruppen*) beat, humiliated and murdered numerous Jews in the course of rounding them up. In the ghettos themselves, 'Jewish Councils' (*Judenräte*) were appointed to carry out the almost impossible task of keeping the inhabitants alive. Hitler had embarked upon a new stage of his war against the Jews; before long, it would escalate further into a war of outright extermination.[165]

Meanwhile, in the early months of the war, Hitler's vanity and narcissism reached new and ever more extraordinary heights. Long before the outbreak of hostilities, on 1 May 1935 he had told a crowd of well over a million people assembled on the Tempelhof Field in Berlin that his personal will was also Germany's national will. Willpower was, in the end, all that mattered. 'My will – that must be the confession of us all – is your faith! My faith is everything in the world to me, just as it is to you! But the highest thing that God has given to me in this world is my people! My faith rests in them, I serve them with my will and I give them my life!'[166] The German people, he claimed on 21 May 1935, had elected him as their 'only representative'. On 23 November 1939 he told leading officers of the armed forces that a series of factors, including the weakness and debility of the British and French, made it inevitable that Germany would be victorious. And, he added: 'As a last factor I must, in all modesty, name my own person: irreplaceable ... I am convinced of the strength of my brain and of my decisiveness ... The fate of the Reich depends on me alone ... I will shrink from nothing, and annihilate anyone who is against me.'[167]

Hitler's self-identification with Germany and the German people was now beginning to edit them out of the picture: he would never stumble, make mistakes, or fail in any way, and if there were reverses and defeats, they would not be his fault, but somebody else's, most notably the generals'. Hyperbole by now had become Hitler's rhetorical stock-in-trade; indeed, he was not above altering military dispatches to make their claims of victory more emphatic. He was, he told an American journalist, 'working on the greatest arms programme of the world'.[168] The invasion of France was 'the greatest battle of all time',[169] and following its stunning success ('the most glorious victory of all time'), and that of the conquest of Norway and the Low Countries (the 'mightiest series of battles in world history'), Hitler now regarded himself as the greatest military leader ever, greater even than Napoleon or Caesar; this claim, often repeated in the Nazi-controlled media, led to mockery once Germany started to lose battles instead of winning them, with soldiers calling him the *Gröfaz* (abbreviating *Größter Feldherr aller Zeiten*, 'greatest general of all time'), echoing the Berlin slang term *Fatzke*, meaning 'stuck-up twerp'.[170] On his private early-morning tour of Paris following the victory over France, in the company of his architect Albert Speer and the sculptor Arno Breker, he made a point of visiting the tomb of Napoleon, symbolically announcing that he had now surpassed the former Emperor.[171] On 6 July 1940 he formally entered Berlin in triumph, to the jubilation of ecstatic crowds. In retrospect, this was the high point of his popularity, not least because most Germans now expected peace to be concluded with the British. In reality, however, Hitler was plunging deeper into the world of illusions he had entered when he had launched the war against enemies he mistakenly regarded as easy prey because he considered them racially inferior.

After his visit to Paris, Hitler decided that an amphibious landing in Britain could only be undertaken if the Luftwaffe achieved superiority in the air.[172] But this never happened. In the 'Battle of Britain' the Royal Air Force maintained its control of the skies. Nor did the British government, now led by Winston Churchill (appointed Prime Minister on 10 May 1940), react positively to a much-publicized repeat of Hitler's customary 'peace offer' made at the end of a lengthy and boundlessly boastful victory speech to the Reichstag on 19 July 1940.[173] Not only was Hitler disappointed, so too were millions of ordinary Germans. His response was to hurl tirades of hate and contempt at Churchill, Eden and other British 'blatherers, liars, loudmouths, self-important old women', pour scorn on British claims of success against the Germans ('they have lied and lied'), threaten to 'eradicate' British cities with '1 million kilograms' of bombs, and 'prophesy' that 'whatever is to come, England will break down!' He knew all this was mere bluster; indeed, in the published version of the speech, Hitler replaced the words '1 million kilograms' with 'more kilos'.[174] On 6 September 1940 he launched a series of 'terror attacks' against British cities to try and break civilian morale. Five days of clear skies was all that was needed, he declared. But the air raids failed in their purpose. Hitler had hugely underestimated the strength and depth of British defensive resources. The planned amphibious invasion had to be postponed. It was becoming increasingly clear that a new initiative was required. Reacting to the stubbornness of the British, Hitler decided in a military conference held on 31 July 1940 that they could only be brought to heel by removing their last hope of finding an ally in Europe, the Soviet Union, which therefore had to be destroyed as soon as possible (that is, 'spring 41').[175] On 18 December 1940 he issued orders to prepare for the invasion, codenamed 'Operation Barbarossa'.[176]

In the early part of 1941, Hitler continued to fulminate against 'a certain Jewish-international capitalist clique' he believed was steering British policies from behind the scenes. The British people, he prophesied in a grotesque misreading of popular morale in London and the provinces, would surely rise up against them and join 'the front against the international Jewish exploitation and ruination of peoples'.[177] He was thrown off course, however, by the events in the Mediterranean. Seeking to establish a new 'Roman Empire' in the region, Hitler's ally Mussolini invaded British-controlled territory in North Africa in September 1941 from the Italian colony of Libya. The following month Italian forces entered Greece. But Mussolini had vastly overestimated his armies' military strength, and these campaigns soon got into trouble. To make matters worse, at the end of April 1941 the pro-German regime in the composite South Slav state of Yugoslavia was overthrown in a military coup that favoured the Allied side. Hitler felt he had no option but to send his armies in to rescue the situation. The Germans, aided by Hungary and Bulgaria, quickly established control over Greece and Yugoslavia, and in May 1941 drove the British out of Crete. In Africa, from early 1941 the Afrika Korps, led by Erwin Rommel, succeeded in stabilizing the military situation in Germany's favour. However, in a private conversation with the Finnish leader Marshal Mannerheim in June 1942, Hitler was to say that the months of delay in launching Barbarossa that followed these events were attributable to his enforced diversion of men and matériel early in 1941 to rescue the Italians and re-establish control over Yugoslavia.[178]

Eventually, on 22 June 1941 the long-planned invasion of Soviet-controlled Eastern Europe was launched, the largest land invasion in history, with well over three million men and a colossal quantity of armour crossing the border. Hitler now changed the target of his invective to 'the Jewish-Bolshevist rulers' in Moscow who, he charged, had provoked the *putsch* in Yugoslavia that had forced him to invade the country earlier in the year: 'Within and without, there developed the conspiracy that is familiar to us, between Jews and democrats, Bolsheviks and reactionaries, with the sole aim of preventing the creation of the new state of the German people and to plunge the Reich once more into poverty and impotence.' If this was a result of a 'new, hate-filled policy of encirclement against Germany', it was also a deadly threat to 'European culture and civilization'. In a lengthy justification of Operation Barbarossa issued on the day of the invasion, Hitler repeatedly gave vent to his bizarre, paranoid hatreds and his feeling of facing a world of enemies, just as Germany had, he thought, in World War I. It was time, he declared, 'to rise up against this conspiracy of the Jewish-Anglo-Saxon warmongers and the equally Jewish rulers of the Bolshevik Moscow Central'. Somehow, he managed to present the war as a defensive operation rather than the bid for world power that it really was.[179]

Such lengthy statements from Hitler were becoming increasingly rare, however. During the war, he no longer addressed audiences of tens of thousands: the Nuremberg Party Rallies, the election campaigns, the May Day parades, the commemorations of the beer-hall *putsch*, even the 'confidential' addresses to party members and officials, all fell into desuetude. Increasingly he talked only to military conferences and in strategic discussions, and if the audience was a larger one, it was still limited in size, reaching a maximum of no more than a few thousand, as with the officer cadets to whom he spoke on some eight occasions up to 1943. If he spoke in the Reichstag, a body that met only on very special occasions, usually to hear Hitler announce a victory, it was almost exclusively on foreign-policy issues, and in particular to lend maximum publicity to spurious and insincere 'peace offers' to the British. After 26 April 1942 the Reichstag never met again, reflecting his fear that it might one day vote to depose him. The rhetorical skills that had underpinned his rise to power were no longer in evidence, as he gradually withdrew from communication with the German public.[180] Such speeches as he gave were no longer interrupted by shouts of '*Heil Hitler!*' or frenzied applause from the audience. The future he had promised Germany and the Germans in his speeches, with its prosperity, its stability and its supposed artistic achievements, now narrowed in perspective to one thing: war. As he remarked in a speech delivered on 30 September 1942: 'I had had at this time to busy myself more with action and with deeds. Besides this, I naturally can't deliver a speech every week or every month. What has to be declared today must be declared by our soldiers!'[181]

Increasingly, Hitler became absorbed in the minutiae of military operations. When a leading general, Fedor von Bock, warned him in September 1941 that he was attacking Moscow too late in the year to be sure of success, Hitler shouted that the generals had always tried to hold him back ever since he came to power. They were not going to do so this time.[182] As one of his secretaries, Traudl Junge, recalled shortly after the war, time and again generals would go to see Hitler determined to make it clear to him that his orders were unrealistic; but as soon as their intentions became clear, he would interrupt them with arguments that quickly made them doubt their own, until they left his presence full of uncertainty, too tired to persist even though they knew inwardly that he was wrong. It was as if they had been hypnotized.[183] But Bock was right. At first, Hitler's confidence appeared to be justified. Along a thousand-mile front, the German and allied armies advanced at breakneck speed, encircling and capturing or killing hundreds of thousands of Red Army soldiers. Hitler and his generals were euphoric. 'It's really not saying too much,' Franz Halder, Chief of the Army General Staff, noted in his diary on 3 July 1941, 'if I claim that the campaign against Russia has been won in 14 days.'[184]

Hitler's euphoria opened the way to a decisive escalation of the war against the Jews, who he thought were the driving force behind his enemies, above all the British Empire and the Soviet Union, increasingly joined by the United States, which was now openly supplying them with military aid and, in the Atlantic Charter, signed on 14 August 1941, linking it to the democratic principles he detested. As his armies powered into eastern Poland, Ukraine and other parts of East-Central and Eastern Europe, motorized SS Task Forces (*Einsatzgruppen*) drove in behind them, ordered by Hitler to kill Soviet political commissars and Jews thought to be supporting the Bolshevik regime. Within a few weeks they were massacring not only Jewish men but also women and children, shooting them into pits that the victims were forced to dig for themselves. At the end of July 1941, the murder programme was formally put into the hands of Reinhard Heydrich, the top official in the Reich Security Head Office; by the late autumn, killing centres had been set up in occupied Poland, at Belzec and Chelmno, where Jewish prisoners were crammed into hermetically sealed vans into which the vans' poisonous exhaust fumes were poured until the victims were dead. Following a conference of different government institutions called by Heydrich in November 1941, postponed and eventually held in January

1942, at Wannsee, in Berlin, the programme was carried out at stationary killing centres in the 'Operation Reinhard' extermination camps, Belzec, Sobibór and Treblinka, all in operation by the spring of 1942. At the largest of all the death camps, Auschwitz-Birkenau, opened a short time afterwards, a special gas, Zyklon-B, was employed for the murders, resulting in over a million deaths, almost all of them Jews taken from across German-occupied Europe. In the 'Old Reich' itself, the remaining Jews were forced to wear a yellow star, crammed into 'Jew-houses', and forbidden to emigrate from October 1941 onwards. Hitler of course knew about all these developments and indeed drove them on. By the end of the war, some six million Jews had been killed in pursuit of his paranoid obsession with what he believed to be a 'world Jewish conspiracy' against Germany.[185]

The Holocaust, as it unfolded, was not the product of any economic calculation; although considerable quantities of money, property, housing and artworks were looted from deported Jews across the Continent, their value was seriously reduced by the resources that had to be devoted to the arrest, deportation and murder of the six million victims. Nor was it launched in revenge for the defeat to which some commentators consider Hitler felt he had been subjected on the Eastern Front in the autumn of 1941 (when in fact he still thought he was winning the war). It was the product above all of Hitler's overweening self-confidence, shared by most of his generals, and his sense that he could now go ahead and turn his hatred and fear of the Jews into reality.[186] But he had miscalculated. As Ukrainian peasants greeted the invading troops with the traditional welcome offerings of bread and salt, expecting liberation from the horrors of Stalin's rule, they were met with more horrors, as the Germans looted and burned their way through the countryside, reduced towns to rubble, and met even minor acts of resistance with mass executions and the torching of entire villages. Soon, heartened by Stalin's abandonment of Bolshevik rhetoric to call on people to fight the Germans in the spirit of Russian patriotism, partisan groups were springing up everywhere, as Stalin's generals mobilized military reserves and brought them to the front. By early August, General Halder was confessing in his diary that 'we have underestimated the Russian colossus'. The Soviets, unlike the Germans, seemed to have limitless reserves of men and equipment. Reinforcements kept on arriving to take the place on the battlefront of the hundreds of thousands captured or killed.

When the autumn rains arrived, the German armies became bogged down in oceans of mud. Soon, the Russian winter was beginning to bite, with temperatures plunging to 40 degrees below zero. Such was Hitler's overweening confidence, born of his continuing contempt for the 'Slavs', that he ignored all these problems. In one of his increasingly rare public speeches, delivered in the Sportpalast in Berlin on 3 October 1941 to launch the year's Winter Aid programme, he declared that Operation Barbarossa was going exactly according to plan.[187] 'Never,' he proclaimed on 8 November 1941, 'has such a vast empire been smashed and beaten down in a shorter time than on this occasion Soviet Russia.'[188]

But his troops were tired after months of continual advance, they were ill equipped for a winter campaign, and their numbers were depleted by repeated counter-attacks launched by the Red Army. Disaster now loomed.[189] When the Soviet general Georgy Zhukov, bringing fresh reserves across from the east, launched a counter-attack, the Germans were forced back. On 8 December 1941 Hitler was forced to concede the necessity of adopting a 'basically defensive campaign' in view of the 'surprisingly early and severe winter in the East'.[190] In the terrible winter conditions, the German troops began to freeze to death in their thin summer uniforms. Hitler's Propaganda Minister Joseph Goebbels launched a massive campaign to get German civilians back home to send winter clothing to the beleaguered army.[191] But it was too late. Under the strain of defeat, one senior German general after another suffered a heart attack or a collapse in health and resigned. Hitler regarded anything other than uncompromising resistance to the advancing Russians as cowardice in the face of the enemy. Any general who ordered a strategic withdrawal in the interests of preserving the lives of his troops was met with instant dismissal. Furious with his senior officers, Hitler took over as commander-in-chief of the army himself.[192] Eventually he agreed to the adjustment of the front line to more defensible positions. Moscow did not fall. Operation Barbarossa had failed.[193]

In early December 1941, however, Hitler believed he saw a new opportunity to win the war when Japanese aircraft bombed the US Pacific fleet at Pearl Harbor, Hawaii. This, he thought, would divert the Americans' attention and resources from the Atlantic, where their ships had for many months been ferrying supplies to Britain and the Soviet Union. The Atlantic Charter signed between the United States and Great Britain on 14 August 1941 had taken a major step towards American involvement in the war by issuing a formal declaration of the two countries' commitment to democracy, free trade and national self-determination. In a lengthy speech delivered to the Reichstag on 11 December 1941, Hitler announced a declaration of war on the USA, coupling it with a furious attack on President Roosevelt and his 'Jewish-plutocratic clique'.[194] The declaration of war on the USA has often been described as Hitler's biggest strategic error. But the fact was that the USA was already so heavily committed to supporting the British and Soviets that the move made perfect sense. It allowed German U-boats to sink American supply ships and take whatever further measures against the USA had been previously impossible in light of the Americans' formal neutrality. And although Hitler repeated in his speech of 11 December 1941 the boasts he had been making about the progress of Operation Barbarossa, he must have known that the situation of the German armies would be improved if he could cut off the supplies the Red Army was receiving from across the Atlantic.[195]

Outwardly at least, he remained optimistic: 1941, he declared in his New Year's message for 1942, with characteristic hyperbole, had been 'the year of the greatest victories of all time'. The coming year would see 'the concerted conspiracy of Jewish capitalists and Jewish Bolsheviks' completely destroyed, and their 'annihilatory will' broken. In more than one respect, the message was further evidence of his growing departure from reality. Germany was already fighting two great powers, the British Empire and the Soviet Union, each of which commanded economic and military resources that were far greater than its own; the addition of the USA, with its even greater resources, made defeat inevitable in the medium-to-long run.[196] As the advance of German forces on the Eastern Front and in North Africa, where they had been sent to relieve the retreating Italians, stalled in the course of 1942 and then went into sharp reverse, Hitler's contempt for his generals – men he considered hidebound, slow and lacking in willpower – steadily deepened. With increasing frequency over the course of the war, Hitler dismissed senior officers and replaced them with more pliant subordinates. When one officer dared to present him with the realities of the situation, giving facts and figures on Soviet war production, which was far outpacing its German counterpart, Hitler, according to Halder, 'with foam in the corner of his mouth', screamed that this was 'idiotic rubbish'.[197]

Military disaster finally struck towards the end of 1942, when Allied forces inflicted a heavy defeat on General Erwin Rommel's Afrika Korps at El Alamein, followed by further landings of Allied troops in North Africa, preparing the way for the invasion of Sicily in early July 1943, and causing the collapse of Mussolini's Fascist regime and the country's withdrawal from the war. Brilliant though he was as a military tactician, Rommel was unable to secure the supplies he needed to fuel his tanks and keep the Afrika Korps going. Hitler blamed the defeat on what he saw as Rommel's loss of willpower. He responded to the African catastrophe by ordering the occupation of Vichy France, the client state created following the German victory over the country in late June 1940; and then sent troops into Italy to bring the country back into the conflict. This required a substantial input of German troops and equipment, weakening the German armed forces on the Eastern Front. On 10 September 1943, after his conquest of Rome was complete, Hitler broadcast to the German people over the radio, putting the blame for the fall of Mussolini on his internal 'reactionary' enemies, spurred on by the British. In the end, he said, it did not make much difference. But the example of Italy, he also said, should serve as a warning to Germany, and he was putting extra security measures in place to ensure that Germany's interests were protected in Germany itself as well as in Italy.[198]

Tired of being shouted at by Hitler, Franz Halder resigned as Chief of the Army General Staff in September 1942, to be replaced by Kurt Zeitzler, who Hitler said was less likely than his predecessor to dispute his orders. Despite repeated claims to the contrary (most notably his own), Hitler was not a military genius; he lacked not only military expertise but also any degree of strategic or tactical subtlety. Nor did he possess any experience of command. For him, as always, it was all a matter of willpower. Any withdrawal or realignment of forces was a sign of weakness. Every position had to be fought for, however hopeless the situation. Surrender to a 'conspiracy of Jews, capitalists and Bolsheviks' was never an option. Had he been leader of Germany in 1918, Hitler boasted, instead of being led by 'a man who lacked the strength to resist these enemies', Germany would never have agreed to sue for peace. Hugely and absurdly over-confident, he declared that the war was practically won.[199] But Zeitzler was realistic enough to tell Hitler in November 1942 that it was necessary to withdraw the German forces from Stalingrad on the river Volga, a city whose symbolic significance led Hitler to focus obsessively on its capture, if they were to be saved. For Hitler, ignoring the increasingly dire supply situation of the German forces in

Stalingrad, Zeitzler's recommendation was simply an act of cowardice. Hitler refused to allow Friedrich Paulus, the inexperienced staff officer in charge of the German forces in the city, a man he had appointed chiefly for his subservience to himself, to retreat – until it was too late. Zeitzler's advice was rejected and Hitler was forced to look on as Paulus's Sixth Army was almost completely annihilated by a massive Red Army counter-offensive, while Paulus himself ignored Hitler's heavy hint, conveyed in a notice of his promotion to the rank of field marshal, that he should commit suicide; instead he surrendered along with what was left of his army. It was a catastrophic defeat. Hitler was disgusted at the failure of this 'characterless weakling', as he called Paulus in a military conference after the capitulation of the Sixth Army, a man who should have shot himself or died fighting to the last. In public, however, he made no mention of the surrender, praising the troops for their heroic resistance against a numerically superior enemy.[200] Privately he fulminated against the generals so frequently and with such force that even Goebbels found his tirades often unfair.[201] Hitler even praised Stalin for having had a leading general, Marshal Tukhachevsky, shot for 'treason' in 1937, an example he would clearly have liked to have followed himself.[202]

Eventually, Zeitzler suffered a serious nervous breakdown and resigned, unable to resist Hitler's increasingly unrealistic orders and still retain some self-respect. By this time, Hitler would not listen to the professional soldiers at all. He was surrounded by traitors and incompetents, he complained. The sensible advice of Zeitzler's replacement Heinz Guderian to withdraw troops from far-flung corners of the Nazi Empire, from Norway, Italy and the Balkans, to help in the defence of the German homeland, was dismissed as yet further evidence of weakness, defeatism and lack of faith in ultimate victory. Early in 1945, indeed, Hitler would issue a general order for all commanding officers to report any plans for a retreat so that he could countermand them. Military conferences became nightmare occasions for the generals, as Hitler berated them for their cowardice and lack of faith. For their part, the generals knuckled under; those who did not subordinate themselves entirely to his will soon found themselves without a job. Hitler saw Zeitzler's resignation as an act of treachery, and shortly before the end of the war had him dishonourably discharged from the army and banned from wearing a uniform.[203]

Despite all this, in the course of 1943 Hitler was forced to concede implicitly that the war was going badly. After the disaster of Stalingrad, he avoided addressing the Party faithful in person, issuing instead a proclamation reminding them that, although 'the National Socialist movement often found itself at a stage in which only its fanatical adherents still managed to believe in a victory', it had always been the case that 'nevertheless, the movement has always stood up again, has overcome every setback and emerged from every crisis stronger than it was before.' The party had always been determined 'under no circumstances to capitulate and in no case to abandon the struggle'. 'We shall smash and destroy the power of the Jewish world coalition,' he declared, despite its 'seeming successes'.[204] Repeatedly he railed against what he called the barbarous deeds of the Asiatic hordes now advancing on Germany from the East, driven on by the 'eternal hatred of that accursed race that has been chastising the peoples for centuries as a true scourge of God'.[205] The atrocities committed by Stalin's regime – a subject on which Hitler did not need to engage in his usual exaggerations – occupied an increasingly prominent place in his addresses, indicating once more that he had now gone on to the defensive despite his claim that Germany would triumph against a world of enemies. He was now repeatedly insisting that there was to be no capitulation, and that Germans must stick together even when times were hard, in defiance of 'the annihilatory plans of our enemies, dictated by Jewish hatred'. Providence was confronting the German people with 'tough tests', but they would pull through.[206]

By this stage, it was obvious to all but the most diehard Nazi fanatics that Hitler was leading Germany into the abyss. Full realization came with the Allied landings in Normandy on 6 June 1944. After establishing a series of beachheads, the Allied forces began to advance, beating the Germans back and liberating Paris in August 1944. Meanwhile, on the Eastern Front, Hitler was forced reluctantly to sanction a military withdrawal from the Caucasus; in the late summer of 1943 a final attempt to halt the Red Army's advance was defeated at the Battle of Kursk. Recognizing that defeat was now staring Germany in the face, a group of mostly middle-ranking army officers, motivated also by their horror at the ongoing mass murder of Europe's Jews, resolved to kill Hitler and instigate a military coup. Their hope of concluding a peace with the Allies was illusory, given the fact that the Allies were committed to securing unconditional surrender. As the plot gathered more participants, civilian politicians, civil servants and others from various parts of the political spectrum, the Gestapo began to get wind of it, and the net started to close round the conspirators, who were increasingly forced to see their main purpose as rescuing Germany's honour, or at least some of it, by showing the world that some Germans refused to go along with the Nazis' crimes.

Their best opportunity came in July 1944. Hitler had spent the first few months of 1944 at his mountain retreat in the Bavarian Alps, on the Obersalzberg, near Berchtesgaden. He had rented property here in the 1920s, and bought a house in 1933. By the time the war was under way, the area housed a large complex of buildings managed by the head of the Party Chancellery, Martin Bormann. It included chalets owned by many of the leading Nazis, as well as an increasingly elaborate network of tunnels and underground storage facilities, all of it ringed by a tight security cordon. As the months passed, Hitler and his entourage spent increasing amounts of time in these to avoid air raids. But on 14 July 1944 Hitler left the area for the last time, and travelled back to Berlin. From there he journeyed onward to his eastern field headquarters at Rastenburg, where just over a week later one of the conspirators, Colonel Claus von Stauffenberg, planted a bomb underneath a table in a hut where Hitler was conducting a small military conference.[207]

Leaning over the heavy wooden table, Hitler escaped the full force of the blast, whose force was dissipated through the flimsy wooden walls of the conference hut. His eardrums were perforated and he had cuts and abrasions. Others present were not so lucky; one was killed in the explosion. The plotters lacked the support of most of the army and were fatally undermined by Hitler's survival; they were arrested and later put on trial, or killed themselves in order to avoid apprehension. Some, including Stauffenberg himself, were shot after a hastily convened drumhead court martial. Hitler considered his survival a 'miraculous deliverance'. Goebbels arranged for him to make a brief speech over the radio to reassure the people he was still alive. It was his first public address for several months. He blamed the assassination attempt on 'an absolutely tiny clique of ambitious, unscrupulous, and at the same time criminal, stupid officers'. Only later, as the Gestapo pursued the conspirators, did the full breadth and depth of the plot become clear. Some 5,000 people were eventually arrested, including relatives of the core group. Hitler condemned the attack as an attempt to repeat the 'stab in the back' of 1918. 'I see in this the finger of Providence pointing at me to continue my work, and so I will continue it.' The incident confirmed Hitler once more in his self-belief. And it deepened still further his distrust of both the army and the aristocracy whose scions had provided so many of the conspirators.[208]

Meanwhile, in the course of 1941, Hitler had come to believe that the 'world war' about which he had 'warned' the Jews in January 1939 had arrived, not only with his own invasion of the Soviet Union on 22 June 1941, but also, and perhaps even more, with the growing support given by the United States to Britain and the Soviet Union. Here in its classic form was the conspiracy theory that both capitalists and Communists, whom an objective appraisal would regard as irreconcilable enemies of one another, were in fact both steered from behind the scenes by a secret Jewish conspiracy aimed at dividing Germany and the Germans and setting them at each other's throats. 'The peoples,' declared Hitler, 'don't want to die on the battlefield just so that this rootless international race makes money from the business of war'; but in the same breath he condemned 'the Jewish slogan "Workers of the World, Unite"', which was, of course, the slogan of the world Communist movement.[209] On 25 October 1941, according to the *Table-Talk*, Hitler referred again to his self-styled prophecy of 30 January 1939, and to an order issued by the head of the SS, Heinrich Himmler, to kill Jewish women and children by driving them into the Pripet marshes in present-day southern Belarus and northen Ukraine, where they would drown:

> In the Reichstag, I prophesied to Jewry, the Jew will disappear from Europe if war is not avoided. This race of criminals has the two million dead of the [First] world war on its conscience, now hundreds of thousands again. Nobody can tell me: But we can't send them into the morass! For who bothers about our people? It's good if the terror that we are exterminating Jewry goes before us.[210]

On 26 April 1942, Hitler, addressing the Reichstag for what turned out to be its last ever meeting, devoted a considerable part of his speech to yet another harangue directed against the Jews, whom he described as 'the hidden forces' that had propelled Britain into war in 1914 and had done so again in 1939. They had conspired to bring Germany to defeat in 1918 and unleashed the Revolution. 'Jews were the carriers of that Bolshevik infection that once threatened to annihilate Europe. But they were also simultaneously the warmongers in the ranks of the plutocracies in

America as well as in Europe.' They aimed to degrade every human society to the level of beasts: 'What is then still left over is the animal in human beings and a Jewish stratum that is brought to positions of leadership as a parasite in the end destroys the sustenance on which it flourishes.'[211] Hitler launched this tirade precisely at the time when the Holocaust was reaching its terrible climax.[212]

On 25 January 1942 the *Table-Talk* noted him voicing his approval of the rapid extermination of the Jews while at the same time admitting the mass murder of hundreds of thousands of Red Army prisoners of war since the beginning of Operation Barbarossa:

> The Jew must get out of Europe. Otherwise we won't get any European understanding. He's stirring things up everywhere more than anybody else. In the end: I don't know, I'm colossally humane. At the time of Papal rule in Rome, the Jews were mistreated. Up to 1830 eight Jews were driven through the city, with donkeys. I'm only saying, the Jew has to go. I can't help it if he is broken in the process, I only see one thing: absolute extermination, if they don't go of their own free will. Why should I look at a Jew in a different way from a Russian prisoner? Many die in the prison camp because we have been driven into this situation by the Jews. But what can I do about it? Why did the Jews unleash the war?[213]

On 30 September 1942, addressing 12,000 young junior officers of the armed forces in Berlin, he recalled the threat he had uttered on 30 January 1939, as usual misdating it to 1 September 1939, that 'if Jewry starts an international world war in order more or less to exterminate the Aryan peoples of Europe, then it won't be the Aryan people who are exterminated, but the Jewish.' 'I shall,' he added, 'also stand by these prophecies.'[214] Similar statements can be found throughout the *Table-Talk*: the Jews were like rats; Europe had to be 'Jew-free'; he had to 'eliminate' the Jews to restore Germany fully to its strength; and so on.[215] On 16–17 April 1943 Hitler made repeated efforts during a conference with the Hungarian dictator Miklós Horthy to persuade the ageing strongman to hand over Hungary's large Jewish population to him for killing. The Jews, he told him, 'should be dealt with like tuberculosis bacilli with which a healthy body could be infected. That wouldn't be terrible, when one considers that even innocent natural creatures like hares and deer must be killed to prevent damage. So why should one spare any longer the beasts who wanted to bring us

Bolshevism?'[216] Although he was no friend of the Jews himself, Horthy was too much of a Hungarian nationalist to allow hundreds of thousands of his citizens to be handed over to a foreign power, even if it was an ally. Hitler and Ribbentrop were forced to abandon their attempt, at least for the moment.

In his customary speech on the twentieth anniversary of the beer-hall *putsch*, delivered on 8 November 1943, Hitler showed that the threat from the East was becoming more important in his mind than the one from the West. He predicted that 'one day the Jewish-Bolshevik East will relieve Jewry of its task ... For sooner or later the Jewish democracy of the West will end in Bolshevism.'[217] In his mind, all of Germany's enemies were now potentially united, often unconsciously, in their promotion of Communism. It did not matter, he said in his broadcast address to the nation on 30 January 1944, whether the Jewish conspirators who aimed at the annihilation of Germany 'are sitting in England or in America or in their headquarters in Moscow'. These 'self-bred Jewish bacteria' were the same everywhere, all working towards the same end. This was to be his last speech on the anniversary of his appointment as Reich Chancellor (30 January 1933). He was to make very few broadcasts after this, driving Goebbels to despair. The Propaganda Minister was to be all the more surprised when the dictator went before the microphone again on 30 January 1945, railing once more against the supposed conspiracy of Jewish Bolshevism, but failing to mention the military disasters that were already overwhelming Germany.[218]

IX

Inevitably, perhaps, during the autumn and winter of 1944, the strain on Hitler's nerves was at last beginning to tell. On 28 September 1944 he suffered a collapse and had to take to his bed. He did not get up until 11 October. Over time, his personal physician Theo Morell came to prescribe a large range and quantity of drugs to the dictator. The (very detailed and entirely credible) daily entries in the medical notebook that Morell kept, in order to avoid being held responsible in the event of Hitler's death, show that the medication he supplied was conventional, though he did make sure it was manufactured in factories in which he had a strong financial interest. But there is no evidence that Hitler was a drug addict, nor that the medication he took impaired his judgement.²¹⁹ None of his doctors, however, could do anything to halt or even slow down the effects of the Parkinson's disease from which he had been suffering for some time, including a marked tremor, in his left hand, noted by observers as early as 1941, when it began in his right leg, as well as an increasingly shuffling gait and growing muscular rigidity in his face. Electrocardiogram tests began to show a hardening of the arteries, and Hitler's hair was turning grey. The bomb attempt of July 1944 had also had an impact on his health. Early in 1945, as Albert Speer later reported, he was 'shrivelling up like an old man. His limbs trembled; he walked stooped, with dragging footsteps. Even his voice became quavering and lost its old masterfulness. Its force had given way to a faltering, toneless manner of speaking.' Although he was only in his mid-fifties, photographs taken at this time show him bent with age. Hitler had been ill before, in 1941, with stomach problems, and had undergone two operations for the removal of a polyp on his vocal chords, the second as late as 22 November 1944; both operations were successful. His teeth were in bad shape, probably as a result of his penchant for sugary cream cakes – he had two teeth extracted in the autumn of 1944. His eyesight deteriorated and he increasingly read documents and maps with the help of a large magnifying glass, in order not to be seen wearing spectacles; even the special 'Hitler typewriter' with enlarged letters would not do the trick any more. One of his secretaries, Christa Schroeder, noted how his physical condition was clearly deteriorating: increasingly, he had to take to his bed for short periods in order to rest and recuperate. His conversation became repetitive and centred on an ever-narrower range of topics, above all his German Shepherd dog Blondi. His refusal openly to recognize the reality of inevitable defeat was transporting him slowly but surely into the kind of fantasy-world in which he had lived throughout the 1920s, where victory was preordained by Providence and reversals of fortune were always just around the corner.²²⁰

As Allied forces advanced steadily eastwards, crossing the German border on 11 September 1944, Hitler, predictably, ordered that every town and village that stood in the enemy's path should be defended to the last, inflicting unacceptably heavy losses on the attackers. When he was told of the mounting destruction caused in Germany's cities by Allied bombing raids, Hitler would change the subject.²²¹ A successful German counter-attack held off the Red Army near Warsaw as the Polish Home Army rose up against the German occupiers. In days of fierce fighting, the uprising was annihilated and the city destroyed, as Stalin ordered the Soviet forces to do nothing to help the nationalist Poles.[222] Soon the Red Army resumed its advance, prompting Germany's allies, from Finland in the north to Romania in the south, to begin searching for a separate peace. Hitler seized the opportunity and declared that the desperate military situation had come about 'as a result of the failure of all our European allies'. In March 1944 he had ordered the military takeover of Hungary, whose government was already negotiating with Stalin; and in October he removed its leader Admiral Miklós Horthy, who was taken off to fortress confinement in Germany while a radically antisemitic Hungarian fascist regime was installed. By this time, 440,000 Jews had already been deported to Auschwitz.[223]

Meanwhile, the manufacture of 'miracle weapons' was being trumpeted by Goebbels's propaganda apparatus, including nerve gases, flying bombs, ground-to-air missiles, rockets, air-conditioned submarines and even an atom bomb. Hitler placed particular faith in the effects of a jet-engine fighter plane, the Messerschmitt Me262, but it was never manufactured in sufficient quantities to make a difference. These projects dissipated resources too widely, and depended on supplies of raw materials that were drying up. Hitler ordered a concentration on the V-1 flying bomb and the V-2 rocket, but again, not enough of them could be manufactured to have a major impact on the war, though they did some appreciable damage when they fell on London.[224] Hitler's next measure, announced on 25 September 1944, was the creation of the 'People's Storm' (*Volkssturm*), a levy of men previously exempted from military service, above all either because they were too young or too old – a policy he had written off in 1937 as useless. The launch of the measure was backed by propaganda in which Goebbels called to mind supposed historical parallels, notably the legendary popular mobilization in Prussia against Napoleon in 1813; the official date for the launch of the *Volkssturm*, 18 October 1944, was the anniversary of Napoleon's defeat in the Battle of the Nations at Leipzig in 1813. Goebbels also commissioned and released a new colour movie, *Kolberg*, telling the fictionalized story of a decision by the people of a town besieged by Napoleon to fight on to the bitter end whatever the cost. It was an implicit invitation to the Germans of Hitler's day to sacrifice themselves in what was claimed to be the national interest. It had little impact, because of its very limited release; it also wasted precious resources of manpower for the military scenes, which involved tens of thousands of men who might otherwise have been fighting at the front.[225] The *Volkssturm* itself was largely pointless except as a propaganda exercise: 175,000 of the poorly trained and badly equipped men and boys were killed before the war came to an end.[226]

Hitler spent the summer of 1944 at his eastern field headquarters in Rastenburg, but, by 20 November, Soviet forces were threatening the area, so he was forced to return to Berlin. On 16 December he attempted a last throw of the dice, launching a fresh offensive in the west, where he believed that he could repeat the triumph of 1940 in the Ardennes. Some 200,000 troops and large quantities of armour and equipment were transferred from the Eastern Front. Told by his Chief of the Army General Staff, Heinz Guderian, that the situation on the Eastern Front was at breaking point, and advised by him that it was folly to divert troops to the west, Hitler screamed at him: 'You don't need to lecture me! I've been leading the German armies at the Front for five years ... I'm better informed than you are!'[227] The threatened Red Army attack in the east, he said, was mere bluff. Hitler moved his headquarters once more, this time to a bunker complex at Ziegenberg, in Hesse, to be near the new offensive. If the troops believed in victory, he told his adjutant Nicolaus von Below, then victory would be theirs. To begin with, the German armies scored some successes, infusing Hitler with fresh confidence, before the overwhelming superiority of the Allies brought them to a halt. The net effect in the end was simply to weaken the German defences in the east. Hitler's initial optimism was dissipated and early in the New Year he was forced to bring 'Operation Autumn Mist' to an end, returning to Berlin from his western headquarters on 15 January 1945. But in reality the offensive was no longer really about winning. It was yet another example of Hitler's 'all-or-nothing' approach. After the new Ardennes offensive was broken in the lengthy 'Battle of the Bulge' (16 December 1944–25 January 1945), he told Below: 'I know the war is lost. The [Allied military] superiority is too great.' He had been let down by the Luftwaffe and betrayed by traitors in the army. 'Most of all I'd like to shoot myself with a bullet through the head.' But he was determined that there should be no repeat of 1918. 'We'll never capitulate. We can go under. But we'll take a world with us.' Death and destruction were all he could think of in his hour of despair.[228]

Hitler soon recovered his self-confidence, or at least gave the appearance of doing so. But as one defeat followed another, he began to isolate himself from the German masses, ceasing his visits to the front and refusing to go to the cities to talk to the civilians who had been bombed out of their homes. When he travelled anywhere by train he had the blinds kept down, even in daylight, to avoid seeing and being seen. He ceased his social visits, even to the Goebbels family, stopped going to theatre, abandoned listening to records, and gave up watching films late into the night. He involved himself increasingly in military details he had previously left to others, worked longer hours and more intensively than he had done for many years.[229] By the end of the year, Hitler had not spoken over the radio to the German people since his brief announcement that he had survived the plot against him the previous July. Goebbels had been pleading with him for months to deliver an address, even more important when things were going badly, as they had been, than when they were going well, he said. Hitler had only given speeches in public on seven occasions in 1941, five in 1942, and three in 1943 (plus one radio address). There had been none in the last five months of 1944. Yet public speaking had been a major source of his popularity. Shortly after midnight on New Year's Day 1945, he finally obliged.[230]

As in July 1944, the main effect of his broadcast was to reassure his audience that he was still alive – his silence of more than five months had inevitably given rise to rumours that he was dead, or at the very least, seriously ill. Once more, he blamed everything that had, in his mind, gone wrong with Germany since World War I, on 'the Jewish-international world conspiracy'. The German people, he insisted, would endure. 'It will pull itself out of this furnace of trials stronger and firmer than ever before in its history. But the power to which alone we owe this, the Jewish-international world-enemy – that power will not just fail in this attempt to exterminate Europe and its peoples, it will also bring about its own annihilation.' The speech was too late to have a significant effect on morale. Only the most fanatical 'old fighters' had been inspired by it. Doubtless they were pleased when Hitler broadcast to the nation again on 30 January 1945 – his last radio address – when he once more blamed 'Jewry' for the 'inner disintegration of our people' that had begun in 1918, and railed against the 'inner Asiatic' Bolsheviks who were now threatening Europe. But instead of speaking, as usual, on 24 February, the anniversary of the Nazi Party's foundation, he issued a lengthy proclamation in which he once more condemned the 'devilish pact between democratic capitalism and Jewish Bolshevism' that was attempting to destroy Germany, urged the German people to resist it to the end, and boasted that he had achieved the 'removal of all the pests' who had failed to rally to the 'preservation of our race'.[231]

On the ground, the inexorable advance of the Allied troops from east and west steadily shrank the area over which Hitler ruled. Nevertheless he still insisted on uncompromising resistance, referring to 'setbacks' rather than defeats. Paris was liberated on 19 August 1944. On 23 March 1945, Allied forces crossed the Rhine and entered Germany itself. On the Eastern Front, German forces had already been compelled to lift the siege of Leningrad (St Petersburg) in January 1944; in June, Allied forces, advancing up the Italian peninsula after crossing the Mediterranean from North Africa, reached Rome; in August, Germany's ally Romania switched sides in the face of invading Soviet forces. The Western Allies were also advancing in the south. When Warsaw was evacuated by the retreating German army in September 1944, Hitler lost his temper and had the staff officers who had ordered the retreat arrested by the Gestapo. A crack SS division, the *Leibstandarte*, suffered heavy losses in its defence of the Hungarian oilfields, and was rewarded for its defeat by Hitler sending Himmler to strip its surviving soldiers of their armbands, a very public humiliation that caused some of the troops to shoot themselves. Hitler did not care. By insisting on fighting to the end, he sacrificed the lives of millions of his soldiers. More than a third of all German troops killed during the war were killed between January and May 1945, when it was clear to most Germans that the war was already lost.[232] But, as he was reported to have said in 1942: 'A race, like the individual human being, needs a bloodletting for its regeneration.'[233]

The destruction of German towns and cities from the air was turning more and more of them into heaps of rubble. Power cuts and water shortages became more frequent with the destruction of gas and electricity generating plants, power lines and underground pipes. More than half a million civilians were eventually killed in the air raids. Living conditions began to worsen. In the autumn of 1944, for the first time, the Nazi authorities began to make serious reductions of food and other rations. The supply situation steadily deteriorated from now on, and was not to recover until many months after the end of the war. On 19 March 1945, Hitler issued the infamous 'Nero order': all military supplies, communications, industrial and other facilities within the Reich that could be useful for the enemy were to be destroyed in a ruthless scorched-earth policy.[234] The order, however, was widely disobeyed, encouraged in some cases by Albert Speer. After reading a memorandum Speer had presented to him rejecting the order because the German people would need the basic necessities if they were to survive after the war, Hitler told him that it was not necessary to worry about the German people, 'for the nation has proved to be the weaker, and the future belongs solely to the stronger eastern nation. In any case only those who are inferior will remain after this struggle, for the good have already been killed.'[235]

In Berlin, the increasing frequency and severity of bombing raids meant Hitler had to spend more and more time in the bunker that had been constructed beneath the Reich Chancellery in the 1930s and substantially extended during the war. The main bunker, only completed in 1944, was located 28 feet below the Reich Chancellery garden, protected by a solid concrete roof almost 10 feet thick. With some thirty rooms, its own electricity generator, water pumps and supply, waste-disposal facilities and radio and telephone connections, it was entirely self-contained.[236] The bombing of the Reich Chancellery on 3 February 1945, including Hitler's private apartments, forced him to move permanently into the bunker. To begin with, he climbed the stairs to the garden quite frequently to walk his dog, Blondi, and on 20 March 1945 he went up to inspect and decorate a small detachment of Hitler Youth who had been defending the city. But as the Red Army moved into Berlin, even this became too dangerous. On 20 April, his fifty-sixth birthday, he went up for the last time; a further attempt to come out, a week later, was frustrated by Soviet shelling. Inside the bunker, the foul air and failing latrine system were beginning to make life unbearable. The celebration of Hitler's birthday in the bunker was muted, with Hitler himself participating only reluctantly.[237] Outside, on the surface, the dull thumps of Soviet artillery fire could already be heard, the noise penetrating through the thick concrete into the room. Meanwhile, many of those who had stayed in the bunker up to this point now made their way out, piling up their cars with suitcases and driving through the rubble-strewn streets to Gatow and Staaken aerodromes on the outskirts of the city, to join one of the twenty flights that left in the three days following Hitler's birthday.[238]

By this time, Hitler had almost wholly lost touch with reality. His plans for the mass-production of 'miracle weapons' completely ignored the insoluble problems of supply. Looking to history for inspiration, he had a large portrait of Frederick the Great displayed in the bunker, hoping for a repetition of the dramatic turnaround in the monarch's fortunes at the lowest point of the Seven Years War. The Prussian king had been rescued by the death of his arch-enemy Tsarina Elizabeth of Russia and the succession of a Tsar who was one of his most fervent admirers. The death of US President Franklin D. Roosevelt on 12 April 1945 seemed to some in the bunker, notably Joseph Goebbels, a sign of hope and a possible last-minute turnaround, but it had no effect on Allied policy, which was continued unchanged by Roosevelt's successor, Harry S. Truman. The break-up of the Allied coalition, in which Hitler and Goebbels had placed such hopes, never came to pass. On 15 April Hitler issued a proclamation to the German troops on the Eastern Front, declaring that 'the deadly Jewish-Bolshevik enemy' was seeking 'to destroy Germany and exterminate our people'. But Germany was prepared. 'Create a sworn community for the defence not of the empty idea of a Fatherland but for the defence of your home, your women, your children and with them our future.' Retreat was cowardice, and any officer who ordered it was to be shot. If they stood firm, 'the final Asian assault will break ... Berlin stays German, Vienna will be German again'.[239]

Hitler continued in his daily military conferences to move little flags representing army divisions around Berlin on a map, ordering a tank unit led by Felix Steiner, a senior SS officer, to launch a counter-attack, supported by aircraft and infantry, in which he expected in his customary hyperbolic fashion that 'the Russians will suffer the greatest defeat, the bloodiest defeat in their history before the gates of the city of Berlin'. But the troops and the tanks simply didn't exist. When told the attack had not taken place, Hitler completely lost all self-control, screaming that the army and now too the SS had betrayed him. Everything was lost, he cried, shaking with rage. The war was lost. Göring must negotiate a peace deal with the Allies. He would stay in the bunker and take his own life. Informed by telephone of Hitler's breakdown, Goebbels moved into the bunker with his wife and children, determined to stay with him until the end, then create a heroic myth, just as he had tried to do after Stalingrad, of self-sacrifice for posterity.[240] Speaking to Hitler's secretary Traudl Junge, Magda Goebbels said: 'My children will rather die than live in shame and mockery. Our children have no place in the Germany that will exist after the war.'[241]

Hitler's breakdown on 22 April 1945 inaugurated the final act in the squalid and pointless drama being played out in the bunker. At last, the spell broken, his lieutenants, with the exception of Goebbels, began to desert him. Told of Hitler's rant, Hermann Göring, in Berchtesgaden, sent a telegram to Berlin assuming his rights as his nominated successor unless he heard otherwise. Hitler had already lost faith in him because of the failure of the Luftwaffe, and now, encouraged by Bormann, he reacted by instructing the *Reichsmarschall* to resign all his offices and ordering his arrest. Within a few hours, Göring was confined to his house, an SS unit stationed outside. Worse than any of this, Hitler now also lost faith in Himmler. Earlier in the year, now completely convinced that the generals were betraying him, Hitler had ordered the SS chief to command the Army Group Vistula. Predictably enough, Himmler tried to restore discipline among the demoralized troops by terrorizing them, but he had no military training, and was still so much in awe of Hitler that all he could do was imitate the Leader's refusal to yield an inch of ground to the enemy, with predictably catastrophic results. Realizing Himmler's inability to deal competently with a military situation, Hitler had him replaced within a few weeks. Then, however, he discovered that Himmler had been negotiating with neutral Sweden behind his back for Germany's surrender to be conveyed to the Allies. Declaring this to be 'the most shameful betrayal in human history', Hitler dismissed him from all his offices. To underline his fury, he had Himmler's liaison officer Hermann Fegelein arrested for deserting his post in the bunker and being in possession of documents relating to his boss's negotiations with the Swedes. Fegelein had been discovered in his apartment in Berlin, drunk and in the company of an unknown young woman. He was dragged back to the bunker, and shot outside at midnight, on Hitler's direct orders. The fact that Fegelein was married to Eva Braun's sister did not seem to matter to him.[242]

On 29 April 1945, after being shown photographs of Mussolini's naked corpse, hanging upside down from a petrol-station gantry next to that of his mistress Clara Petacci, Hitler told his staff over dinner that he was determined to avoid a similar fate. His body was to be burned until no trace of it remained, he said. At the end of dinner, he handed a cyanide capsule to each of his staff. 'I am very sorry', he said, 'that I can't present you with any better leaving gift.'[243] Now that death was certain, there was nothing to lose in yielding to Eva Braun's long-standing wish that he should marry her. Summoning a local Berlin official to the bunker, he now underwent a formal, legal ceremony of marriage with Eva Braun, certifying first, as he was obliged to by his own laws, that he was of Aryan descent. Goebbels and Bormann acted as witnesses, and there was a brief champagne reception afterwards. Hitler then called Traudl Junge into the conference room, now without its situation maps, in order for her to record his words in shorthand, to be typed up as soon as possible. Instead of, as she expected, a long justification and explanation of his life, he merely dictated, in an almost mechanical monotone, the terms of his personal and political testaments. After arranging for the disposal of his personal effects, he turned to the political part of the document. Here he briefly ascribed the war and destruction he had caused to the conspiratorial machinations of 'world Jewry'. Blaming the bombing of German cities on the Jews who, he believed, were steering the Allies from behind, he expressed his satisfaction that 'the real guilty party must pay for his guilt, even by more humane means.' Such an admission expressed an entirely mistaken belief that the gas chambers of Auschwitz and other extermination camps were a 'humane' method of killing, as well as a feeling of triumph that he had exacted on the Jews what he imagined to be a justified revenge.[244]

The political testament included provisions for the appointment of a successor, Grand Admiral Karl Dönitz, and a new government, headed by Goebbels as Reich Chancellor and Bormann as Party Minister. One of the few reappointments was Count Lutz Schwerin von Krosigk, who had originally been appointed Minister of Finance by Franz von Papen in his 'cabinet of barons' in 1932 and continued in office throughout the Third Reich. Both Junge and Below found these provisions completely unrealistic and pointless. The secretary did not comment on the final sentence in the testament, which clearly did not appear to her at all objectionable or unusual: 'Above all, I charge the leadership of the nation and its followers to the precise observation of the racial laws and the pitiless resistance against the world-poisoner of all peoples, international Jewry.' Hitler had often declared that National Socialism would outlive him. The unity and sense of purpose of the German people would 'have a further effect into the most distant future'.²⁴⁵ But privately he admitted to Junge: 'National Socialism is dead. Perhaps a similar idea will emerge in a hundred years' time with the force of a religion that will spread across the entire world. But Germany is lost. It was obviously not mature enough and not strong enough for the task I envisaged for it.'²⁴⁶ Hitler's megalomania had turned into a grotesque mélange of self-pity and self-importance mingled with the contempt he had been displaying towards Germany and the Germans for the previous several weeks.

On 30 April 1945, after saying farewell once more to his secretaries, Hitler retired with Eva Braun to his study at half-past three in the afternoon. Sometime later, gingerly opening the door, Hitler's valet Heinz Linge, Bormann following him, saw Hitler's lifeless body slumped on the sofa, blood oozing from a gunshot wound in his right temple. Eva Braun (now Eva Hitler) was beside him, a strong smell of bitter almonds coming from her corpse: she had taken cyanide (it had previously been tested on the dog Blondi). The odour lingered even after Linge and Otto Günsche, Hitler's personal adjutant, had removed the bodies.²⁴⁷ The two men wrapped the bodies in blankets and carried them up to the garden, where they doused them with petrol and, watched by Bormann, Goebbels and two senior army officers, set them alight. So thoroughly were the bodies burned that only the teeth remained among the ashes, later to be identified by a technician who had worked for Hitler's dentist.²⁴⁸ Hitler was dead, 'and with him', noted Traudl Junge, 'there also vanished the hypnotic compulsion under which we lived'.²⁴⁹

While the Red Army completed its occupation of Berlin, the remaining occupants of the bunker either committed suicide, like Martin Bormann, or, like Traudl Junge, made their escape through the maze of tunnels connecting the bunker with the Reich Chancellery and the underground railway network. Most of them, including Junge, were eventually arrested by Allied troops. In the small town of Flensburg, near the Danish border, Hitler's designated successor, Grand Admiral Karl Dönitz, briefly gathered together surviving top Nazis in a phantom interim government before they too were arrested. They were eventually brought with other leading Nazis before an International Military Tribunal convened at Nuremberg that year. Many of them were sentenced to death for their crimes; some managed to commit suicide; a few received terms of imprisonment; and a handful were acquitted.[250]

X

Adolf Hitler left only death and destruction behind him. Ordinary Germans had gradually lost faith in the dictator and his regime as defeat followed defeat, and life in Germany's devastated cities had progressively become more difficult for them to sustain. Instead of being restored to greatness, as Hitler had proclaimed, the country lay in ruins. With Hitler gone, Germany was divided into Soviet, American, British and French zones of occupation, and the Allied military closely monitored the population for any signs of continuing Nazi fanaticism. The possibility of a resistance movement emerging on the lines of those that had arisen in the countries the Nazis had conquered, from Poland to France, was vanishingly small. And yet it took many years before Germans could come to terms with Hitler, his crimes and his legacies. After the war, many others besides the remaining Nazi leaders were put on trial for their crimes, while a vast operation of 'denazification' attempted to bring home to the great mass of Germans, with varying degrees of success, the extent of their own complicity in them. The question remained, however, of why so many had followed Hitler almost to the very end.

From 1933 to 1945 Hitler was 'the Leader', legitimated not by constitutional convention but by History and Destiny. He stood outside the normal structures of politics. 'With the authority of the Reich Chancellor behind him,' as Ian Kershaw has remarked, 'backed by adoring crowds, surrounded by the trappings of power, enveloped by the aura of great leadership trumpeted by unceasing propaganda', Hitler impressed millions beyond the fanatical, the cynical or the gullible.[251] The more he brought success, in his foreign policy up to 1939 and in war thereafter, the more his personal power was enhanced. Everything in the Third Reich was designed to emphasize this power: oaths, ceremonies, rituals, the media, the schools, the Party organizations, the daily greeting of '*Heil Hitler!*' and the obligatory signing of letters and written communications with the same phrase – all of this simply underscored the ubiquity and potency of the Leader, until he became one of the reasons why people in Nazi Germany thought of themselves as fighting a world of enemies whose defeat his genius would surely bring about. Indeed, the thousands upon thousands of gravestones erected in the nation's cemeteries in memory of soldiers killed at the battlefront recorded those who lay beneath them as *'gefallen für Führer und Vaterland'*, 'fallen for Leader and Fatherland'. Constant adulation further corrupted Hitler's already narcissistic mentality. His arrogance and overconfidence, based on crude racial stereotypes, led him into fatal misjudgements during the war. The Americans, he declared, were 'as stupid as chickens'. 'The Russian colossus is collapsing under its immobility.' The 'English' were 'decadent'. The Jews were behind everything, manipulating all Germany's enemies as part of their gigantic conspiracy aimed at world domination. From the very beginning, misled by the memory of World War I, Hitler grotesquely overestimated the ability of Germany, a medium-sized European power, to confront and defeat three vast empires, the British, American and Soviet, any one of which possessed resources that far exceeded its own. But for Hitler, economic statistics were irrelevant: what counted in his mind was strength of will, a reflection above all of what he supposed to be the Germans' racial superiority.[252]

Hitler was neither a political nor a military genius. He had the good fortune to enter politics at a time when public speaking, live and before vast crowds, enjoyed its greatest potency. Even as an orator, however, he depended for his success not least on the spectacle and ritual with which his appearances were surrounded. The abject failure of his attempted *putsch* in November 1923 showed that the expectations of a seizure of power by force alone, engendered by the example of Mussolini in Italy, were entirely illusory. As late as 1928 Hitler was still an obscure figure on the margins of politics, supported by only an infinitesimal minority of the German people. What brought him popularity was the economic calamity of the Depression, in which desperate people turned to the Nazis for desperate remedies. Even so, he never won much more than just over a third of the vote in any free national election. But this was enough to persuade resentful conservative-nationalist elites to attempt to lend themselves political legitimacy by co-opting the Nazis into power alongside them in the furtherance of their aim of destroying Weimar democracy and installing an updated version of Wilhelmine authoritarianism. Without their collaboration, Hitler would not have been able to get his hands on the levers of power. There was nothing particularly subtle or calculating about his insistence only on entering a government as its head; this was simply another example of his crude and uncompromising 'all or nothing' approach.

What brought Hitler to supreme power within a few months of being appointed Reich Chancellor was a combination of murderous political violence whose ruthlessness was beyond anything imagined by the world of conventional politics in Germany, and a propaganda offensive that violated every standard of truthfulness and decency. The extensive overlap between the aims of the anti-democratic elites, including business leaders and the military, and those of the Nazis, ensured that however great the distaste of elites for the violence of the Nazis, they were willing to go along with their destruction of democracy. The era in which Hitler came to power was one still reeling under the unprecedented impact of World War I. In Germany, and in other parts of Europe too, it was common to observe the streets of the country's towns and cities filled with men in uniform. Existing political structures – above all, the Russian, German, Austrian and Ottoman Empires – had collapsed, revolutionary or democratic regimes had replaced them across the Continent, brief armed civil conflicts had laid bare the advent of a brutalized and intolerant clash of ideologies in which the conditions for democratic stability were largely absent. Murderous social and racial hatreds took hold at the extremes of politics, from Lenin's 'red terror' in Russia to Horthy's 'white terror' in Hungary and beyond. Hitler was a product of this political atmosphere. At the core of his world view was a visceral race-hatred of what he called the 'Jewish world-enemy', which from 1919 onwards he held responsible for all of Germany's ills, indeed ultimately all of the world's ills. Germany's internal divisions would be healed, he proclaimed, not only by the creation of a national community shaped by a one-party state and the leadership of one man – himself – but also by the removal of Germany's Jewish minority and ultimately, as became clear during the war, all Jews wherever they could be found. This paranoid conspiracy theory, the most murderous in history, represented the kind of irrationality normally found only on the fringes of politics; with Hitler, tragically, it had reached the centre.[253]

By the mid-1930s Hitler's position as sole dictator of Nazi Germany was unchallenged. He could not, of course, control every aspect of policy, but in some key areas such as foreign policy, the visual arts and race, he drove it on, or, on occasion (as before and during the Berlin Olympics of

1936), held it back for tactical reasons. Overall, however, it was Hitler's ideological obsessions that provided the essential foundation for everything that happened in the Nazi movement and the Third Reich. He set the parameters; subordinates were left to fill in the details. When they acted on their own initiative, it was always within the bounds of the ideology he had created. In 1939–40 he could bask in the glory and popularity of military success, but from December 1941 and above all from 1943 onwards Hitler refused to compromise or abandon a struggle that for him could only end in total victory or total defeat.

From very early on in his political career, despite his projected image as the superhuman dictator, he depended in many ways on a close circle of immediate subordinates to sustain him, bolster his public image, boost his self-confidence, and carry out his ideological programme. It is time now, therefore, to ask who Hitler's people were, what their role was, how they came to cluster around their Leader, and why they stuck with him almost to the very end.

PART II

The Paladins

Introduction

'It would be interesting,' the historian Christoph Klessmann wrote in 1971, 'generally to pursue the question of the extent to which fascist systems are particularly and inherently liable to bring deracinated criminals or psychopaths into leadership positions.'[1] Psychologists tended to see the Nazi leaders as deeply disturbed individuals. Douglas M. Kelley, the prison psychiatrist whose job it was to assess whether the defendants in the International Military Tribunal at Nuremberg were fit to stand trial, called Rudolf Hess 'a self-perpetuated hysteric . . . definitely a deviate from normal . . . [a] paranoid and childish individual, with gross hysterical manifestations'. Julius Streicher too was 'paranoid'. Robert Ley had 'frontal lobe damage' and 'organic brain disease' and was 'definitely abnormal'. The psychiatrists who examined the most prominent surviving Nazis in jail after the end of the war tended, predictably enough, to ascribe their crimes to individual pathologies. Hess had a 'hysterical personality', Hans Frank was 'emotionally hypermanic', Göring was 'an egotistical extrovert . . . exhibitionistic . . . with pathological traits', Ribbentrop was 'suggestible', Rosenberg was a 'bigoted, philosophic dilettante', Baldur von Schirach 'narcissistic', Streicher 'had a rigid insensitive and obsessive mentality . . . [and] a personality structure which borders on the frankly abnormal'. They had 'some of the blackest souls on earth'.[2] But they were all fit to stand trial.

At the same time, the top echelon of the Third Reich and the Nazi Party has also been seen as more than a disparate collection of psychopaths. For many commentators, starting during the war itself, they formed a kind of criminal collective. The view that the top Nazis were a criminal gang was widespread among the leading politicians on the Allied side. Winston Churchill called them a 'gang', while the epithet was common currency among the propaganda organs of the Soviets: *Pravda* for instance referred to the 'criminal Hitlerite gang' in March 1945. An Allied Control Commission report issued in Summer 1945 described them in contemptuous terms: 'So grotesque and preposterous are the principal characters in this galaxy of clowns and crooks in Ashcan, Dustbin and the other centres of detention that none but a "thrice double ass" could have taken them for rulers.'[3] The idea of the Nazi leaders as a gang of crooks went together with their description, initially popular in parts of the British government, as outlaws or bandits, to be shot as soon as it became possible, without waiting for a trial.[4]

The Hitler Gang, a 1944 'documentary-propaganda' film directed for Paramount Studios by John Farrow, probably best known nowadays as the director of the 1957 version of *Around the World in 80 Days* starring David Niven, and as the father of the actress Mia Farrow, portrayed the rise and the early years of the Nazi regime in the style of a 1930s Hollywood gangster movie. Instead of using established stars, it employed a cast of unknowns chosen for their physical resemblance to the leading Nazis. A number of them were exiles from Nazi-occupied Europe. It was based on extensive research, and though crude in its portrayal of the leading figures, stayed reasonably close to the course of events. Its portrayal of the 1934 'Night of the Long Knives' was particularly noteworthy: hardly any other event in the history of Nazism was as close to the playbook of 1930s gangster films as this. As Bosley Crowther of the *New York Times* pointed out, however, 'the emphasis in this picture is so heavily upon the "Hitler gang" and upon the inside intrigues by which it gained and held its power, that the impression conveyed is that these leaders are entirely responsible for the Nazi state ... It means that the grave responsibility of the German citizens for what they have allowed has been neatly tossed onto the shoulders of a few ruffians, Army officers and industrialists.'[5]

More persuasive has been the conceptualization of the Nazi leadership as a kind of imperial court, with Hitler as the monarch and Göring, Goebbels and the other top Nazis as the courtiers. The historian Hugh Trevor-Roper, an officer in the British Intelligence Services during the war, wrote his post-war bestseller *The Last Days of Hitler* in the style of the eighteenth-century historian Edward Gibbon's classic *The History of the Decline and Fall of the Roman Empire*, portraying the Nazi dictator as one of the more disagreeable Roman Emperors and the leaders of the Third Reich as his courtiers, still vying for the Leader's favour even when all was obviously lost.[6] As in many authoritarian regimes, untrammelled power allowed the dictator to appoint individuals from outside the political class, often in a quite arbitrary manner, simply because they made an impression on him, or had done him a favour. But while it was no guarantee of competence, this served to underline his distance from normal power structures and the politics of the Weimar Republic. Of course, Hitler's government did start as a coalition with non-Nazi right-wing nationalists, and a number of these survived for a surprisingly long time: Franz Gürtner, the Minister of Justice, for instance, or – the classic example – Lutz Count Schwerin von Krosigk, who served as Minister of Finance from the ministry of Franz von Papen in 1932 all the way through the Third Reich and was reappointed as a minister by the first post-war Cabinet of Karl Dönitz in May 1945. But, one after another, almost all of the other conservative members of Hitler's coalition appointed in January 1933 were replaced by Nazis, or in other words, by men who owed their position to Hitler and kept it simply because he continued to show them his favour.

Hitler has often been described as a loner, a man who stood apart from the rest of society. Yet while he liked to project an image of splendid isolation and social untouchability, in fact behind the scenes he craved human company and created a kind of private court for himself. These were the people with whom, especially in the 1920s, he liked to sit around in restaurants and cafés, or socialize with at their homes. They included his chauffeurs and bodyguards like Erich Kempke, Emil Maurice and Julius Schaub, early political acquaintances such as Anton Drexler, Hermann Esser and Dietrich Eckart, who did not stay the distance with him for one reason or another, Heinrich Hoffmann, his photographer, his patrons and financial backers such as Winifred Wagner, Hugo and Elsa Bruckmann, or Helene Bechstein. This was his entourage, some of whom – such as Ernst 'Putzi' Hanfstaengl, his adjutants such as Fritz Wiedemann, his successors Gerhard Engel and Nicolaus von Below, his doctors Karl Brandt (and his wife, Anni Rehborn) and, later on, Theo Morell – played a similar role in providing an intimate social milieu when Hitler's private entourage moved to the Berghof. Some of the power elite also moved in this social circle, notably Joseph Goebbels and Albert Speer. Something like a family life was provided by Eva Braun, her friends and their children. Those who survived the war kept in close touch and shared the belief that they had been unpolitical figures who were unfairly treated by the victorious Allies and their agents. But none of them ever dissociated themselves from Hitler, his extremist ideology or his criminal actions while he was alive, and none of them ever disputed his views; on the contrary, by providing him with a stable and supportive milieu, they sustained him throughout by making available a private world where he could relax and not worry about how he came across in public.[7]

The following chapters examine each of the most powerful men in the Third Reich in turn, asking why and how they achieved their position and, with the exception of Ernst Röhm, held on to it as long as they did. They were not, of course, a 'power elite' in the sense coined by the term's originator, the American political scientist C. Wright Mills, who saw the leaders of the military, corporate business and politics as the real controllers of American life; still, it seems justified to study them as the elite who dominated the Nazi Party and, with it, the Third Reich. All of them understood power and how to use it. All of them, apart from Albert Speer, were with Hitler almost from the beginning and stayed with him almost to the end. None of them ever openly questioned his authority, nor, at least until the regime's dying hours, did he ever feel any reason to suspect they might have posed a threat to him – unlike Stalin, who had only gradually emerged from the collective leadership of the Soviet Union and the Bolshevik Party following the death of Lenin, and so treated his real or potential rivals with such profound suspicion that he eventually purged them and had them executed. What kind of men, then, were the leading Nazis? Were they marginal, outcasts from society, disturbed or deranged? We also need to strip away the myths that were already beginning to accumulate around them during their lifetime, cut them down to size and view them as human beings. A closer look at each of them, especially in the light of recent documentary discoveries and detailed biographical studies, should help answer these questions. We begin with Hermann Göring, the 'second man in the Third Reich'.[8]

2
The 'Iron Man': Hermann Göring

Visitors to Carinhall, Hermann Göring's country estate near Berlin, during the 1930s would often be startled by the approach of an African lion – not a fully grown one, of course, but a lion nonetheless. Göring obtained the lions as young cubs under an arrangement with Dr Lutz Heck, Director of Berlin Zoo since 1932. When any one of them grew too large to be safe with humans, at around ten months, Göring would return it to the zoo in exchange for a new one. In total, there were seven of them in succession. They were kept in a cage on the estate and cared for by keepers supplied by the zoo. But Göring also let them roam around freely in the daytime, and the cub of the time would often turn up at breakfast, especially when there were guests, who no doubt were suitably impressed and perhaps just a little scared. On one occasion at least, Göring had himself filmed playing with his favourite lion of the day. He even continued the arrangement after the birth of his young daughter in 1938, ending it only when the war broke out.[1]

All of this was part of a carefully cultivated public image. It went along with his well-publicized hunting activities. Taking the title of *Reichsjägermeister*, 'Reich Master of the Hunt', he had a 'Reich Hunting Lodge' constructed on the Rominten Heath, a long-established hunting ground in East Prussia, and was often to be seen dressed in hunting costume – an appearance that may seem absurd in the twenty-first century, but which in the 1930s and 1940s advertised his self-fashioned links with German landed society in particular and German country life in general. Göring's much-trumpeted passion for hunting was not entirely genuine, however: for him, it was quantity rather than quality that counted. At his first outing at Rominten, the gamekeeper later complained, he shot the wrong deer and then gave the trophy no more than a glance before asking to be taken to the next

target once he had been photographed. None of this mattered as far as his flamboyant public image was concerned: indeed, Carinhall was made to look like a hunting lodge though in fact it was a large complex with modern amenities including a telephone exchange. Here he developed a habit of receiving important visitors and showing them his booty. Sir Eric Phipps, the British ambassador in the mid-thirties, was not impressed with any of this. When Göring arrived late for a dinner at the British Embassy in Berlin at the time of the 'Night of the Long Knives', he excused himself by telling the ambassador he had been out hunting. 'Animals, I hope,' was Phipps's ironic reply.[2]

Yet Phipps also remarked on another occasion that 'Lunching with the Warden of New College, General Goering might pass as almost civilized.'[3] Göring's self-image and its public projection extended beyond all this to encompass the attempt to portray himself as a kind of Renaissance man, a keen collector not only of hunting trophies but also of *objets d'art*. (The saying 'When I hear the word "culture", I reach for my gun', often attributed to him, was in fact pronounced, in a slightly different form, by a character in *Schlageter*, a play by the Nazi dramatist Hanns Johst.) He had already begun collecting in a modest way in the 1920s, and more ambitiously in the mid-1930s, but the outbreak of World War II, the conquest of Poland, then France and other Western European countries, and finally a large swathe of the Soviet Union, opened up the possibility of almost limitless expansion. Göring knew little about art, and could not tell a good painting from a bad one, but, employing the services of professional art experts, he scoured Europe in search of paintings, sculptures, tapestries, jewellery, carpets, fragments of Roman buildings, and everything he could lay his hands on. With these he furnished his various houses and castles, most notably Carinhall, which, with Hitler's agreement, he intended to repurpose as an art museum once the war was over. His preferences, for female nudes, portraits and triptychs, played a role, but in the end his acquisitiveness knew no bounds, and by the end of the war, his collection included 1,375 paintings, 250 sculptures, 108 tapestries, 200 pieces of antique furniture, 75 stained-glass windows, 60 Persian or French rugs, and 175 other *objets d'art* of various kinds. Particularly prominent were a large number of works by Brueghel, Cranach, Rembrandt, Rubens, Ruysdael, Tintoretto, Titian and Van Dyck. Göring paid for almost all of them, though a considerable number were presented to him as gifts, and he went to great lengths to avoid the impression that he was a looter; but behind the scenes, he used currency manipulation and pressure of various kinds to effect purchases at the lowest possible prices, especially the purchase of collections confiscated from their Jewish owners.[4]

Hermann Göring's background was unusual in a number of ways. It was marked by a cosmopolitanism alien to the great majority of leading Nazis. His father, Heinrich Göring, was a career diplomat who had acted as the first Governor of German South-West Africa from 1885 to 1890. His tenure was not regarded as a success, and his next posting was as German Consul General in Haiti, not as much of a demotion as it might seem, since German South-West Africa was little more than a colony in name only at this time. It was in Haiti that Hermann was conceived. Fearing that the West Indies was not a healthy place in which to give birth, Heinrich Göring and his wife moved back to Germany, where the baby Hermann was born in a hospital in Rosenheim on 12 January 1893. Hermann's mother Franziska, a Bavarian of Austrian background, had married Heinrich Göring in 1885 and immediately gone to live with him in Africa. A widower of forty-five, Heinrich already had five children, but they had been brought up by relatives after his first wife's death, a common enough practice in the German Foreign Service. In 1893 the infant Hermann was left with a relative in Germany while his mother returned to Haiti with Heinrich and their three older children for the next three years. In 1896 the family went back to Berlin, where Hermann was reunited with his family. After a brief period working in the German Foreign Office, Heinrich retired to a modest house in Berlin-Friedenau put at their disposal by the doctor Hermann Eppenstein, who had attended Franziska at the birth of her oldest child in South-West Africa. Eppenstein, a bachelor, became Franziska's lover. Unusually, relationship was open; when the family visited Eppenstein, Franziska slept with him while Heinrich was accommodated separately. Eppenstein, a wealthy landowner as well as a prosperous physician, gave one of his homes, Burg Veldenstein, a medieval castle located near Nuremberg, to the family to live in. Eppenstein spent more than a million Marks on renovating the place to bring its facilities up to modern standards. He was Hermann's godfather, and he contributed substantially to the costs of the boy's education. A practising Catholic, Eppenstein was also half-Jewish.[5]

However tempting it might be to extrapolate from any one of these features of his early life, none of them seems to have had any identifiable influence on Hermann Göring's character. What was crucial, however, was his father's taste for all things military. In Berlin, Heinrich took him to watch military parades in nearby Potsdam, kitted him out with miniature uniforms, and bought him a set of lead model soldiers to play with. After a conventional elementary schooling in Fürth, near Burg Veldenstein, and a spell in a boarding school at Ansbach, he was sent at the age of twelve, by his father, in agreement with Eppenstein, to a military school in Karlsruhe, where he spent the next four years living, training, drilling, and learning to subject himself to army discipline. In 1909 he transferred to a Prussian Military Academy in Lichterfelde, near Berlin. After three years as a cadet, he graduated in March 1912, and entered the Prussian Army, which stationed him on the French border. From an early age, therefore, he was marked out for a military career, in contrast to many of the younger members of the Nazi leadership. With the outbreak of World War I in August 1914 he went into action, winning his spurs on the Western Front.[6]

Hermann Göring's military career now took an unusual turn. Hospitalized with a serious bout of rheumatism brought on by damp conditions in the trenches, he was persuaded by a fellow officer, Bruno Loerzer, to join him in the German Air Force, founded in 1913. Refused permission to transfer to an air training school, he went up with Loerzer as an aerial observer, photographing French defensive emplacements. The pair's work was deemed valuable enough for the army authorities to drop a prosecution they were bringing against him for desertion, and in 1915 he finally got their permission to train as a fighter pilot. Shot down by a British fighter plane in his first sortie, he was badly injured and forced to spend six months recuperating before he went back into action. He soon proved an effective combat pilot, winning a growing reputation for skill and bravery. He had claimed twenty-two 'kills' of enemy planes by the end of the war, though a number of them were suspiciously lacking in independent substantiation, and he garnered an impressive collection of military honours, including an Iron Cross, a Hohenzollern medal, and the rare distinction of the *Pour le Mérite*, the Prussian equivalent of the Victoria Cross.[7] From May 1917 he was put in command of a squadron on the Flanders Front, and in July the following year he was appointed to lead the celebrated Number 3 Air

Squadron Group (*Geschwader*) after its commander, the 'Red Baron' Manfred von Richthofen, had been shot down and killed in action.[8]

Air aces were a new breed of fighter, celebrated in the public media and state propaganda as 'knights of the air', their dogfights over the Western Front portrayed as the modern equivalent of knightly tournaments, pitching individual pilots against one another and awarding victory in the joust to the one whose skill and speed prevailed. Fuelled by enthusiastic letters home from front-line soldiers watching the dramas unfolding above them, aerial combat was presented to the German public as a paradigm of honour, chivalry and sportsmanship. On the ground, the squalor and monotony of trench warfare destroyed any expectations of the valour and derring-do with which the troops may have enlisted; in the air, these notions survived, giving fighter pilots a kind of mythic aura that did not disperse even when the war was over. As the 'Red Baron', Richthofen acquired legendary status among the British, who produced admiring biographies of him after the end of the conflict. The reality, however, was different. Richthofen notched up his impressive tally of 'kills' by using the element of surprise, appearing out of nowhere to shoot down enemy planes, but most of the aircraft that fell victim to aerial attacks were slow-moving bombers, and numbers shot down, whether or not they were just sitting ducks, counted for far more than individual skills displayed in aerial combat. Hermann Göring was appointed to succeed Richthofen not because he was a brilliant air ace like Ernst Udet, who often flew solo on his missions, but because he was recognized as someone who could fit into a team and lead it.[9]

Göring's period in charge of the Richthofen group lent him the aura of the air ace, along with his impressive collection of medals and 'kills', however dubiously acquired. But the final months of the war were, in fact, a period of retreat and defeat: new British and French planes were superior to their German counterparts, and losses were sufficiently heavy for the Richthofen group to be merged with another one after a few weeks. German supplies were running low, and German ground forces were falling back all along the Western Front, their morale shattered by the failure of the 1918 spring offensive and the constant arrival of fresh American troops on the battlefield. When the Armistice was signed, Göring led his fliers back to Germany, where their squadrons were disbanded. They landed at a difficult moment. The November 1918 Revolution had already broken out, and the Workers' and

Soldiers' Council in Mannheim had taken charge on the ground and disarmed the pilots. Göring flew there with some of his unit and forced the Council at gunpoint to return the weapons. Then the airmen retreated to the Bavarian town of Aschaffenburg, where they spent a week carousing in the local inns while Göring delivered impromptu speeches condemning the Revolution and prophesying the resurgence of Germany from the shame of defeat. At the age of twenty-five he was without a job, and without a pension or other means of supporting himself.[10]

So he made use of his flying skills and reputation to obtain employment in Denmark as a sales agent for the Dutch – formerly German – aeroplane manufacturer Fokker, demonstrating the company's planes by taking prospective purchasers on brief trips and putting on aerobatic displays to please the onlookers. The Treaty of Versailles, which decreed the destruction of the entire German combat fleet, came as another blow, and helped persuade him not to return to Germany. In the spring of 1920 he changed jobs and began working as a pilot for Svensk-Lufttrafik, a Swedish airline founded the previous year, advertising his skills by performing stunts with a small single-seater between flights. Passenger aircraft at this early time in the history of aviation were patronized exclusively by the wealthy, with whom Göring came into contact at social events, and it was at one of these that he met Carin, the estranged wife of Nils von Kantzow, an Olympic gold medal-winning gymnast. She came from a monied background and had close connections to the far right-wing family of Eric von Rosen, an explorer who had swastika signs carved into his suitcases. Hermann and Carin fell in love, and married on 3 February 1923, after her divorce had come through.[11]

By this time, Göring had returned to Germany and enrolled as a student of political science at Munich University. The extreme right-wing nationalist atmosphere combined with Carin's fascist tendencies to push him in the direction of the nascent Nazi Party. In November 1922 Göring heard Hitler speak in public for the first time. The experience prompted him to join the Party. It was not so much that he agreed with its programme – indeed, he later claimed he never read it – as that he had a general, emotional feeling that Hitler's extreme, violent hostility to the Versailles settlement corresponded to his own resentful nationalism and penchant for violent action.[12] In a way, belonging to the Nazi movement provided Göring with a kind of substitute for the Richthofen squadrons, built on 'comradeship', 'love of the Fatherland', and a quasi-military hierarchical structure bound together by ties of solidarity and obedience. The acquisition of a war hero and air ace – someone who would in the twenty-first century be called a 'celebrity' – was a major coup for a movement that was still tiny, unnoticed, confined to one part of the country, and eking out a precarious existence on the outer fringes of Bavarian nationalist politics. Like other political parties in the Weimar Republic, the National Socialist German Workers' Party was associated with a paramilitary organization – the Storm Division (*Sturmabteilung*, or SA). Numbering only a few hundred very young men, it was led by a more experienced figure – Hans Ulrich Klintzsch, an ex-naval officer, placed at Hitler's disposal by the Free Corps leader Hermann Ehrhardt. By early 1923, however, Hitler was trying to shake off Ehrhardt's influence and establish the SA as an independent paramilitary organization, armed and uniformed and prepared to assert itself in Bavarian politics. In March 1923 Hitler demoted Klintzsch and appointed Hermann Göring to lead the SA.[13]

It was as leader of the stormtroopers that Göring took part in the disastrous beer-hall *putsch* of 8–9 November 1923, marching in the front row next to Hitler. He persuaded one detachment of Bavarian police not to obstruct their progress, but at the next barrier, as we have seen, the police opened fire, wounding Göring in the thigh. He fled with Carin across the Austrian border to Innsbruck, where he remained in hospital until Christmas Eve. In May 1924 he made his way with Carin to Venice, using a false passport and later visiting Mussolini in Rome at Hitler's request. By this time they had run out of money, but Carin obtained financial support from Hitler ('a genius ... I worship him completely') and they returned to Sweden, where Carin's mother was seriously ill.[14] Already more than a little overweight – as is easy to see from photographs taken during the abortive 1923 *putsch* – Göring was also suffering from further health problems. The morphine he had been prescribed during his stay in hospital had turned into an addiction, and the ignominious failure of the *putsch*, combined with lack of money and the increasing ill health of his wife, who suffered from tuberculosis, plunged him into a deep depression. His behaviour became erratic, and Carin, afraid for her safety, went to stay with her father. On 1 September 1925, after a violent incident at the medical centre where Göring was receiving his drugs, he was arrested by Swedish police, placed in a straitjacket and admitted to the Langbro mental hospital. Medical reports described him as hysterical, deeply antisemitic, and suffering from hallucinations. After being weaned off the drugs, he was discharged at the end of the year, though he had to return briefly for further treatment. He insisted he was not mad; all he was suffering from were the effects of the drugs he was injecting himself with. And his addiction was now a thing of the past. This was untrue: he continued to be dependent to varying degrees on drugs, and every year he underwent a temporary detox administered by Professor Hubert Kahle, a specialist in addiction treatment.[15]

During his time outside Germany, Göring had lost contact with Hitler to such an extent that his Party membership was cancelled and his leadership of the SA passed over to Ernst Röhm. Taking advantage of an amnesty for political offenders passed by the Reichstag in 1926, Göring returned to Germany the following year, and, after a brief resumption of his business career, went back into politics, meeting Hitler and persuading him to place him high on the Party list of candidates for the 1928 Reichstag election. This enabled him to take a seat in the chamber and earn a welcome salary as a member of the legislature. His presence in Berlin had a number of advantages for Hitler. For one thing, he acted as a kind of agent for the Party leader there, somewhat to the irritation of Goebbels and other Party radicals in the capital city. Göring counted as a conservative nationalist rather than a revolutionary, and as a celebrated military man was able to build up a useful network of contacts in the worlds of business and finance. He established good relations with the high aristocracy, sparking rumours that he was a secret monarchist, a belief he seemed to confirm with visits to the ex-Kaiser in his Dutch exile in January 1931 and May 1932, and friendships with Wilhelm's Hitler-supporting sons. He did very little work for the Party, speaking in the Reichstag only once, and avoiding the kind of organizational, campaigning and propaganda activities into which Goebbels had plunged himself in Berlin. This hardly endeared Göring to the Party rank and file, who also resented his sometimes openly expressed contempt for those – the great majority – who were less celebrated, less socially polished and less experienced than he was. But the good relations he established with conservative nationalist circles, thanks not least to his *Pour le mérite*, were to prove vitally important to Hitler, who increasingly came to regard him as indispensable.[16]

Meanwhile, the Great Depression hit the German economy with a vengeance, destroying the cohesion of the multi-party coalition government led by the Social Democrat Heinrich Müller. The appointment of Heinrich Brüning, a conservative monarchist with a reputation for economic expertise, as Reich Chancellor, did nothing to solve the country's desperate economic crisis, least of all because Brüning now imposed a long series of emergency austerity measures. The 1930 Reichstag elections, in which the Nazis shot from the margins of politics into the mainstream, winning 107 seats and six million votes, radically changed the political situation. The Brüning government struggled on, imposing a ban on the Nazi stormtroopers in April 1932, but when it was dismissed by Reich President Hindenburg on 30 May 1932, its successor, led by Franz von Papen, lifted the ban, and on 30 July the Nazis won 13 million votes. As the largest party in the Reichstag, the Nazis had the right to nominate the Speaker or President of the legislature. Hitler chose Göring to fill this role. Göring used his power over procedural rules to manoeuvre Papen out of office in September and then worked behind the scenes to force out his successor, Kurt von Schleicher, using his contacts with bankers, generals, conservative Nationalist politicians and top civil servants to help lever Hitler into office.[17]

It was at this point that Göring took up the mantle of a man of action once more. Appointed Acting Minister of the Interior for Prussia – illegally, as it turned out, since the courts subsequently invalidated the coup by which Papen had removed the Social Democratic government of Prussia the previous summer – he expanded the police force by enrolling a further 50,000 men, mostly Brownshirts, and told them that they could shoot down if necessary those hostile to SA and SS personnel. Thrown into a panic by the unexpected torching of the Reichstag building on the evening of 27 February 1933, he issued orders for the arrest of thousands of Communists, on the basis that the arson attack had been the curtain-raiser for a left-wing coup d'état. 'My mission,' he announced, 'is to destroy and exterminate ... I shall use the power of the state and the police to the utmost, my dear Communists.' At the subsequent trial of the perpetrator, the young Dutchman Marinus van der Lubbe (who was subsequently executed), and four leading Communists (who were acquitted), Göring was repeatedly challenged by the Communist Georgii

Dimitrov, one of the accused. Göring lost his temper. 'Your party is a party of criminals and must be destroyed!' he shouted at him, shaking his fist: 'You are a criminal who should be sent to the gallows!'[18]

Shortly after being appointed, Göring had merged the various political police agencies in Prussia into a single new body, the Gestapo. Although he sat in the Reich Cabinet only by virtue of being Minister without Portfolio, the fact that Prussia covered the majority of Germany's land surface and included the majority of its population gave him immense power, which he used repeatedly in moments where crisis management was required. The last of these was the action he and Hitler took against Ernst Röhm and the Brownshirts in the 'Night of the Long Knives' on 30 June–1 July 1934. While Hitler moved against the SA leadership in Munich, Göring, by agreement, took charge of events in Berlin, where, together with Himmler and Heydrich, he shouted orders for people on the list that he and Hitler had compiled to be shot. A policeman present in Göring's office described the atmosphere as one of 'blatant bloodthirstiness', noting the raucous laughter that burst out with every report of a killing. Göring personally ordered the murder on 30 June of two close aides of Vice-Chancellor von Papen, along with former leading Nazi Gregor Strasser and Hitler's predecessor as Reich Chancellor, Kurt von Schleicher. Any idea that Göring was a moderating influence on Hitler dissipated as a result of this action, along with a good deal of Göring's favourable reputation abroad.[19]

Once he had helped establish the Third Reich on a secure footing through his actions as Hitler's troubleshooter, Göring handed over a number of his functions to others. With the centralization of powers that came with the new regime, the Prussian Interior Ministry was merged into the Reich Interior Ministry in May 1934, while the Gestapo was handed over to Himmler in November. Göring was known widely as 'the Second Man in the Third Reich', despite Rudolf Hess's position as Deputy Führer, and employed by Hitler as an emissary on special foreign missions, bypassing the Foreign Office in a way that was typical for the administrative chaos of Hitler's regime. Göring had visited Italy on Hitler's behalf before the Nazis came into government, and he went again several times, also travelling around south-east Europe conducting negotiations on economic issues. Appointed Reich Air Minister on 5 May 1933, he was given overall command of the German Air Force, the Luftwaffe, on 1 March 1935. Since the Treaty of Versailles had banned the construction of combat aircraft, the new body had to be created virtually from scratch. Supervising and driving on the procurement and construction aspects of building up the Luftwaffe brought him not only a military role independent of those of the army and navy but also increasingly important powers over the economy. On 4 April 1936 he secured from Hitler the post of Raw Material and Currency Commissioner to assist him in his task; on 18 October the same year, dissatisfied with what seemed to him the slow tempo of rearmament, Hitler named him Representative for the Implementation of the Four-Year Plan.[20] In November 1937, when the Economics Minister Hjalmar Schacht was dismissed by Hitler because he had criticized the headlong rush to rearm as financially irresponsible, Göring effectively absorbed the Economics Ministry into the Four-Year Plan.[21]

Göring was now in charge of a vast and growing economic empire. His task was to prepare the German economy for a major war, to bend the resources of German industry to an intensified pace of rearmament. When he failed to bully German heavy industry into the headlong expansion that was required, he had a number of steel mills constructed, all belonging to the *Hermann-Göring-Werke*, which already by 1937 had become the largest steel conglomerate in Europe.[22] It was largely down to Göring that the German armed forces commanded the resources with which they launched a major war in 1939. As part of his preparations for war, he also took steps to take over the resources of Germany's small and rapidly diminishing Jewish population. Up to this point, Göring had not been particularly prominent in the implementation of the Nazis' antisemitic policies. Indeed, he claimed in an interview with the psychiatrist Leon Goldensohn after the war that:

> Anti-Semitism played no part in my life. If it were on the basis of anti-Semitism I would never have been interested in the Nazi movement. The thing which attracted me to the party was the political programme. I mean the creating of a greater Germany and the abolition of the Treaty of Versailles. Of course, if one joined the Nazi Party one had to adopt all the points of the party, more or less, including anti-Semitism.[23]

Naturally, he knew that his interlocutor was Jewish; nevertheless, it is clear that he was motivated in his antisemitic policy primarily by economic considerations. The antisemitism he exhibited in his early writings was perfunctory and conventional.[24] Cynically opportunist, he simply disregarded the human impact of the discriminatory measures he now unfolded against the Jews.

In 1938 he began to issue a series of decrees organizing the expropriation of Jewish-owned property, beginning with the compulsory registration of Jewish assets. In the aftermath of the nationwide pogrom of 9–10 November 1938, ordered by Hitler, he chaired a conference with representatives of various ministries that gave him the green light to decree the complete exclusion of Jews from Germany's economic life, banning them from running shops and practising trades. Seizing Jewish assets would in his view help the economy to fund the accelerated re-armament programme. Another decree ordered the Jews to pay for the damage caused to their own property by the rampaging mobs of Brownshirts who had trashed and looted them during the pogrom. But Göring also took the opportunity to further the complete exclusion of Jews from German society. On 14 December 1938, as quarrels over the implementation of these decrees broke out, he issued another decree, approved in advance by Hitler, ordering that 'all decrees and other important orders touching upon Jewish matters be cleared through my office'. It was Göring who ordered the establishment of a Reich Central Office for Jewish Emigration, though he delegated the responsibility for organizing and running the office to Reinhard Heydrich and the SS. On 28 December 1938, after consulting Hitler, he issued a decree forcing Germany's Jews into 'Jew-houses', which Göring saw as a practical and more publicly acceptable alternative to the establishment of ghettos, and sharpened up policy towards mixed Jewish-'Aryan' marriages in the process.[25]

By this stage in his life, Göring had developed what seemed to be an insatiable appetite for power. He had risen to the position in effect of Hitler's deputy not least by avoiding getting bogged down in the minutiae of government and administration. His good relations with the conservative nationalists had been a major asset in the early years of Hitler's regime, when the Nazi Party depended to a large extent on their collaboration. His international contacts had proved useful in dealing with potential allies. His military background and credentials as an air ace had brought him a growing power over the direction of the economy and an independent role as leader of the Luftwaffe. His capacity for swift, decisive and sometimes brutal action had been crucial when Hitler hesitated, as happened in the 'Night of the Long Knives'. Moreover, Göring had achieved something like stability, allied to popularity, in his personal life. His first wife, Carin von Kantzow, had fallen ill with tuberculosis and died of heart failure, perhaps brought on by her mother's death, on 17 October 1931, aged only forty-two. Genuinely distressed, Göring cared for her in her final days and named his main country residence after her. Six months after her death, however, he met and began a relationship with Emmy Sonnemann, a divorced screen and stage actress the same age as he was. Their marriage on 10 April 1935 was a major state occasion, with Hitler as one of the witnesses, filmed and broadcast in the weekly newsreel. On 2 June 1938, at the age of forty-five, she gave birth to their only child, Edda, an event publicized even more widely than the wedding. Essentially non-political, tall, elegant, glamorous and blonde, Emmy Göring frequently acted as Hitler's official consort, much to the irritation of Magda Goebbels, to whom, however, Hitler was personally far closer.[26]

As things turned out, this was the high point of Göring's career. In the change of gear that characterized Hitler's policy in 1937–38, Göring was one of the losers. He lobbied for appointment as War Minister when Werner von Blomberg was ousted from the position, but Hitler took over the responsibilities of the post himself, fobbing Göring off by promoting him to Field Marshal on 4 February 1938, though he entirely lacked the active military experience that would normally have justified this promotion. While he still had enough influence to push a hesitant Hitler to take action against Austria the following month (the *Anschluss*), and played a significant role in the peaceful resolution of the Munich crisis and the annexation of the Sudetenland later in the year, his commitment to securing international approval for German annexations of foreign territory no longer corresponded to Hitler's growing drive towards a general European war. Ribbentrop, appointed Foreign Minister on the same day that Göring was given the title of Field Marshal, now took the lead in foreign-policy matters, deliberately pushing Göring to the margins of the decision-making process. Göring angrily dismissed Ribbentrop as an 'idiot', a 'criminal fool' and 'Germany's top parrot' (a reference to what he saw as the Foreign Minister's tendency just to repeat what the Führer said). But all his raging could not stop Göring's loss of power in the making of German foreign policy, not least because, while he had cooperated closely with the Foreign Office under Ribbentrop's predecessor Konstantin von Neurath, the new Foreign Minister had his own well-established personal staff whom Göring was unable to influence. When Hitler decided to invade what was left of Czechoslovakia in March 1939, Göring was barely consulted. 'The whole matter,' he complained, 'had been carried out for the most part over my head.' His efforts to secure British neutrality in the coming war were energetic but fruitless in the face of Ribbentrop's radically anti-British position.[27]

By this stage, Hitler no longer trusted Göring as a man of action. Believing him to be weak-willed, especially when it came to launching a European war, he stopped him from controlling the economic affairs of the newly created Protectorate of Bohemia and Moravia. But Göring himself also seemed to have lost interest in gaining more power. In the spring of 1939 he embarked on a series of Mediterranean cruises. Although he met Mussolini on more than one occasion during his travels, the political results of these journeys were minimal; by this time it was Ribbentrop who was calling the foreign-policy shots. Once back in Germany, Göring boarded his motor yacht *Carin II* and travelled slowly around the country's inland waterways, stopping off at factories and shipyards to enjoy the applause of the assembled workers. He did not return to Berlin until the beginning of August. Unable to persuade Hitler to take a course that would avoid a general European war, he had preferred to absent himself from the decision-making scene altogether. He knew that Hitler and warmongering radicals like Ribbentrop had now seized control of foreign policy. Although he still tried behind the scenes to persuade the British to launch a repeat of Chamberlain's intervention at Munich in 1938, only now with respect to Poland, even using a Swedish friend, Birger Dahlerus, to attempt mediation, it was a lost cause.[28]

Named as his successor by Hitler at the start of the war, Göring was now fobbed off with medals, decorations and empty titles, culminating in his naming as 'Reich Marshal' at a ceremony in which Hitler promoted a number of generals to the rank of Field Marshal following the fall of France in the summer of 1940. The title was meaningless in military terms but was designed by Hitler to reassure Göring that he was somehow above the rank of a mere Field Marshal. But Göring's aim of avoiding a general war while the economy was being consolidated was now revealed as unrealistic in the light of Hitler's insatiable drive for conflict and conquest. His disapproval of Hitler's planned strike against the West melted away, like his other reservations about the Führer's military aggression, when Hitler asserted himself, and above all after the initial, stunning success of German armies in the invasion of France.

No longer a member of the inner decision-making circle around Hitler, he attempted to recover his position by assuring the Führer, over the protests of the military and naval leaders, that the Luftwaffe alone would drive the British into the sea at Dunkirk in late May 1940. But he supplied insufficient numbers of bombers, and the British fighter planes destroyed more German aircraft than had been lost in the whole of the campaign to that date. Göring was never a man for detail, and his confidence in the superiority of the Luftwaffe over the British Royal Air Force was not based on any sober assessment of the strength of the opposing forces. His management style only encouraged chaos in decision-making as he constantly played off his subordinates against one another, in order to stop them making common front against him, and he quarrelled with the other armed services instead of organizing a rational division of labour and resources. As the failure of the Luftwaffe in the Battle of Britain became clear to Hitler, Göring's star began swiftly to wane. It was Hitler who switched the campaign from the destruction of British airfields to London and other cities, in an unrealistic expectation that this would break civilian morale in the country, and from this point on, Hitler increasingly took charge of the war in the air, issuing orders directly to Göring's subordinates without involving him.[29]

Soon Hitler was treating him with open contempt, shouting at him about the failure of the Luftwaffe and berating him in staff conferences in what Göring later called a 'cruel and hateful' manner.[30] But the Luftwaffe was not the only sphere in which Göring was running into difficulties. His appetite for power had led to an accumulation of offices, all of which were run on the classic Nazi *Führerprinzip*, where decisions rested ultimately on the man at the top. So vast were Göring's responsibilities that he proved unable to provide the strategic leadership that each of them required. Industrial and military production suffered from a growing chaos and lack of coordination. Unwilling to surrender any power to others, Göring was plagued with incessant demands for decisions on even the most minor issues. In taking them, he often had to contend with objections from military leaders, Nazi Party officials, Gauleiters, industrialists and many others. The territorial conquests of 1939–42 extended his economic empire still further, but also made it even more unmanageable. The French and other subject economies failed altogether to make the contribution to the war effort that Göring expected.[31]

Göring continued to lose power after Operation Barbarossa was brought to a halt by the Red Army in December 1941. At the same time Hitler declared war on the USA, a power that Göring consistently underestimated. Criticisms of the inefficiencies that had become apparent in war production multiplied, and Göring took a large part of the blame. The rapidly expanding military-production conglomerate known as the 'Organisation Todt' was already working behind Göring's back to introduce new rationalization measures, when its founder, the engineer Fritz Todt, Minister of Munitions, a senior Nazi, perished in a plane crash on 8 February 1942. The young architect Albert Speer was appointed to take his place, despite Göring's bid for the succession. Hitler had already assumed a far greater responsibility for the conduct of the war as a result of the failure of Operation Barbarossa, and Speer became his instrument for improving the management of the war economy. By using his closeness to Hitler and his good relations with the industrialists, Speer outmanoeuvred Göring and gradually extended his own power over the management of the economy. At the same time, the growing employment of slave and forced workers from concentration camps and occupied countries – seven million workers in the Reich by the middle of 1944 – gave Himmler's SS an ever-increasing role in the economic sphere, a role Göring was unable to restrict since as head of the Four-Year Plan he was himself dependent on the use of forced labour for war production. The result of all this was a gradual shrinkage of Göring's economic empire during the middle years of the war.'[32]

In the area of antisemitic policy, where Göring had taken charge in 1938, the SS, and especially its Security Service under Reinhard Heydrich, increasingly took over once the war had begun. Göring followed Hitler's paranoid belief that, if a war began, it would be the Jews' fault, prophesying in 1938 that in this case there would be a 'major reckoning with the Jews'. As Nazi policy moved over to one of deliberate mass extermination following the launching of Operation Barbarossa on 22 June 1941, Göring gave in to pressure from the SS for a free hand in implementing the murder programme. On 31 July he signed an order to Heydrich, the key passage of which read: 'I hereby charge you with making all necessary preparations with regard to organizational, technical and material matters for bringing about a complete solution of the Jewish question within the German sphere of influence in Europe.'[33] With this order, he passed over responsibility to Himmler and Heydrich.

Here too, therefore, he had effectively withdrawn from active involvement in policy and its implementation.

Göring's public standing fell even further as the Allies began to launch major bombing raids on German cities. Famously, he declared in a public speech delivered in July 1939 in the Rhineland: 'If an enemy bomber reaches the Ruhr, my name is not Hermann Göring. You can call me Meyer' (one of the commonest German surnames). As Allied raids on German towns began in 1940, ordinary Germans began to do just that. Ingrained notions inherited from World War I and the perverted influence of Nazi ideology led Göring to declare: 'The Luftwaffe must attack and not defend.' To do anything else would be dishonourable. Once the bombing offensive against Germany had begun in earnest, in 1942, he ordered that 'the reprisal raids on Britain ordered by the Führer must be agreed to and carried out.'[34] In reporting to Hitler on an Allied thousand-bomber raid on Cologne in May 1942, his clumsy attempts to minimize the damage done led to Hitler effectively taking over key decisions on air strategy and aircraft production. Göring's loss of influence and prestige were apparent to everyone in the Nazi leadership well before the end of the year. In December 1942 Albert Speer thought that he 'gave the impression of a worn-out man', already sensing that Germany was not going to win the war. Göring promised Hitler that the Luftwaffe could keep General Paulus's beleaguered 6th Army in Stalingrad supplied, although he knew it was already no longer in a position to do so. Its failure severely damaged what was left of his reputation as Air Minister.[35] Under increasing pressure, he spent more and more time on his art collection, and started to escape from the mounting stress of failure by upping his intake of paracodeine, an addictive morphine substitute, which he had been struggling to keep down, with medical help, ever since his treatment in Sweden for the thigh wound suffered during the *putsch* of November 1923.[36] By the end of the war, he was consuming huge quantities, carrying with him a suitcase filled with some 20,000 tablets, each with a small quantity of paracodeine, especially manufactured for his personal use. According to one report, this amounted to most of the world's supply of the drug.[37]

Eased aside from the centres of power, and losing his influence even over the economy, Göring spent increasing amounts of time at Carinhall, managing his growing collection of artworks and entertaining visitors. He became, as the British historian Hugh Trevor-Roper reported after the war, a 'voluptuary':

> ... dressed (says an eyewitness) now like some oriental maharaja, now in a light-blue uniform with a bejeweled baton of pure gold and ivory, now in white silk, like a Doge of Venice, only studded with jewels, with the emblematic stag of St Hubertus on his head, and a swastika of gleaming pearls set between the antlers. There, in scenes of Roman luxury, he feasted and hunted and entertained, and showed his distinguished guests round the architectural and artistic wonders of his house – a study like a medium-sized church, a domed library like the Vatican library, a desk twenty-six feet long, of mahogany inlaid with bronze swastikas, furnished with two big golden baroque candelabra, and an inkstand all of onyx, and a long ruler of green ivory studded with jewels.[38]

Other reports noted that Göring had taken to painting his fingernails red, sometimes wore lipstick, and liked to dress as a Roman Emperor, in a toga.[39]

By late April 1945, as the Allied forces were approaching their final victory, Göring had lost all influence, discredited by the failure of the Luftwaffe, a failure that had destroyed such popularity as he had once possessed. He was still Hitler's designated successor, however, a fact of which he was more than conscious. When Hitler, in a momentary fit of despair, told his immediate entourage that he would remain in Berlin until the end, and if they wanted orders they should apply to Göring, the Reich Marshal, who was at his house in Berchtesgaden, sent a telegram to Hitler announcing that he was taking over. Hitler was furious. He dismissed Göring from all his posts and ordered his arrest. An attempt by Martin Bormann to have him shot failed, however, and Göring remained in Berchtesgaden until he voluntarily surrendered to American troops on 8 May 1945, under the misapprehension that he would be negotiating Germany's terms of surrender (he had evidently forgotten that the agreed Allied policy had for some time been to demand unconditional surrender). The officer who arrested him was over-friendly, however: he shook Göring's hand, treated him to a meal, and allowed him to give a press conference. Göring made good use of his command of English, which he had learned in Sweden during his stay there after the First World War, to establish cordial relations with his captors. When this was reported to General Eisenhower, the Allied

Supreme Commander immediately had him transferred to a prison. Eisenhower suppressed the accounts of the interviews, except for one, in which Göring was told that he was on the official Allied list of war criminals, to which he replied that was a big surprise for him, and he had no idea why.[40]

On admission to the Palace Hotel of Mondorf-les-Bains in Luxembourg where the high-ranking prisoners were held, he was weighed – 120 kilos, or 264 pounds – and examined. Colonel Andrus, the famously strict American officer who ran the facility, was shocked when he arrived: 'Goering had brought with him sixteen matched, monogrammed suitcases, a red hatbox, and his valet, Robert Kropp. I glanced down at the Reichsmarshal's fingernails. They were varnished bright red.'[41] So too were his toenails. Once he had been weaned off his dependence on paracodeine – an easy task, according to the prison psychiatrist Douglas Kelley, who was in charge of the detoxification programme, because 'his addiction was not very severe' – and slimmed down by a crash-diet, also overseen by Kelley, Göring, his health restored, reverted to the bold and vigorous behaviour he had displayed in his early days, assuming a leadership role among the remaining Nazi leaders on the one hand, and doing his best to charm his interrogators on the other.[42] Colonel Andrus reported that he was 'repeatedly abrupt and rude to his guards', arrogant and self-important. He complained to General Eisenhower that his valet had been taken away from him: 'May I have my valet for my assistance?' he asked plaintively.[43] The British trial judge Lord Birkett was impressed by 'his immense ability and knowledge, and his thorough mastery and understanding of every detail'.[44]

Behind the scenes he condemned his fellow defendants as 'chickenhearted' and threatened Speer with assassination by the Weimar-style secret murder squads that he was certain would re-emerge in Germany before long, because the former Minister of Munitions had let the side down by admitting guilt. Franz von Papen considered Göring 'the outstanding personality of the whole trial', the only one who had tried to defend his beliefs. He was, Papen said, 'the same uninhibited and jovial character I had always known ... He was a man of open, masculine nature, with great personal charm.'[45] When Göring talked to Gustave Gilbert about the murders he had carried out on the 'Night of the Long Knives' in 1934, the psychologist observed, 'the ruthless-gangster side of his personality stood clearly revealed as the jovial mask fell completely away.' At the same time, he refashioned himself once more, projecting himself to his interlocutors as a man who had been anything but antisemitic ('Anti-Semitism played no part in my life'). The Nazis' hatred of Jews was not genuine, he claimed – it had just been an electoral ploy ('Hitler had to carry an anti-Semitic platform in order to be successful'). 'Whenever Jews applied to me for help, I did so,' he added. Göring dismissed the trial as victors' justice, denied knowledge of the Holocaust, waved away as fakes the atrocity films shown to the defendants, and claimed he had been a moderating influence on Hitler. Full of bluster, he dismissed racism as a peripheral aspect of the Nazi movement and continued to insist that Hitler was a genius.[46] It was Goebbels who was to blame for antisemitism. Piling falsehood upon falsehood, he remained unrepentant to the end. He was a true German hero, he boasted, a Renaissance man, an honourable soldier who had only served his country as a passionate nationalist and observed his oath of loyalty to Hitler despite everything. He had always been loved by the people. He had never been afraid of death. His main concern now, he said, still nurturing the delusion that Nazism would one day rule in Germany again, was to ensure his reputation for posterity.[47]

Göring was appalled not by the sentence of death imposed on him by the Tribunal for his crimes – he had expected it all along – but by the fact that it was to be carried out by hanging, which he considered dishonourable. His request for a military execution, by firing squad, was refused. Two cyanide capsules had been removed from his clothing and effects on his arrival, but on 15 October 1946, the night before he was due to be executed, he crushed another cyanide capsule between his teeth (Colonel Andrus thought he had taken it 'either from the toilet pan or from his anus'), and died instantly. An official inquiry suggested the capsule had been concealed in his navel, or in the toilet in his cell. In a suicide note, Göring himself said he had always carried it on him, hiding it in his cell or in his riding boots. None of the guards was to blame. His body was cremated, like those of other Nazi war criminals, in the oven at the Dachau concentration camp, set up in 1933, and scattered in a nearby stream.[48] His widow, the former actress Emmy Sonnemann, unsurprisingly in view of her public prominence in the years of the Third Reich, was found guilty by a denazification court of being an active and important member of the Party, served a year in prison, and was banned from acting for five years. A good deal of her property, most of it acquired through her relationship with Göring, was confiscated. She wrote a rather vapid biography entitled *An der Seite meines Mannes* (*At My Husband's Side*), published in 1967, and died in Munich on 8 June 1973 at the age of eighty, still convinced of her late husband's greatness and patriotism. Her daughter with Göring, Edda, lived with her mother after the war, and received a conventional education. She trained as a law clerk and later worked in a hospital. While she refused invitations to talk about her father or his politics, she did mix in far-right circles, and attended memorial events for recently deceased Nazis. In the 1970s she had a much-publicized affair with Gerd Heidemann, a journalist at *Stern* magazine who had purchased Hermann Göring's yacht, the *Carin II*. Heidemann later became notorious as the chief promoter and publisher of the spurious Hitler diaries in 1983. Lawsuits forced Edda Göring to relinquish artworks given by her father, and she was denied the pension normally due to the orphaned children of former government ministers. She died on 21 December 2018.[49]

A more interesting and more unexpected member of Hermann Göring's family was his younger brother Albert (born 1895), who was an engineer and businessman. Albert believed that his true father was the family patron, his godfather Hermann Eppenstein, but in fact he was conceived while Franziska Göring was in Haiti with her husband; perhaps he wanted to associate himself with his half-Jewish godfather in this way. There were many stories of Albert Göring's hostility to Nazism. As export director for the Skoda works in occupied Czechoslovakia, he encouraged workers to commit acts of sabotage during the war, and maintained contacts with the Czech resistance. He helped dissidents escape by forging his brother's signature on documents, and requisitioned forced labourers from concentration camps and then allowed them to escape. Albert too had served in the First World War, but as a signals engineer rather than a fighting soldier. He may have belonged to what has been called the 'generation of the unconditional', but his politics were very far indeed from those of most of the rest of his family. His career demonstrates that there was nothing inevitable about his older brother's commitment to the Nazi cause, or his insatiable ambition, or his amoral character.[50]

For a time, Hermann Göring's political career had indeed justified his description as 'the second man in the Third Reich'. Throughout the 1930s and well into the war, his energy and ambition ensured that he remained a key figure in Nazi politics. His brief resurgence during the Nuremberg trial revealed the strength of his personality once more. Of all the leaders of the Third Reich, he was the one individual who was capable, at least in the 1930s, of putting pressure on Hitler to take action when he was showing signs of hesitation. To an extent greater than almost any other Nazi leader, Göring established and maintained an independence from Hitler that time and again enabled him to act on his own initiative. He was never personally close to the Nazi leader nor a member of his inner social circle, and the two men always addressed each other formally, using the respectful second-person *Sie* rather than the intimate *Du*. Yet he was always dependent on Hitler's approval, and, like so many others, he gave in to the Nazi leader on crucial issues. He persisted in pursuing a foreign policy that was more akin to the national-conservative position taken by the generals and politicians whom Hitler so brusquely pushed aside when he quickened the drive to war in 1937–38.[51]

In most respects, however, it would be a mistake to characterize Göring as a conservative or 'old-fashioned nationalist', even if he had a 'radical personality'.[52] He had no respect for conservative values, taking a ruthlessly amoral approach to every political question that confronted him, both at home and abroad. He portrayed himself as an honourable soldier, but what his conduct and his language betrayed was a cynical perversion of soldierly values and behaviour. His brutality, revealed in moments such as the 'Night of the Long Knives', his self aggrandizement, his ruthless ambition, his vanity, his corruption, his indifference to human suffering, his contempt for the normal decencies of human behaviour – all this and much more prompted some, like the prison psychologist Gustave Gilbert, to brand him a psychopath. But putting everything down to individual pathology was too simple. It was only in the twisted moral universe of the Third Reich that such a man could rise almost to the very summit of power.[53]

3
The Propagandist: Joseph Goebbels

At six foot seven inches tall, Hugh Carleton Greene, Berlin correspondent for the London *Daily Telegraph*, cut a striking and instantly recognizable figure. But when he slipped into Anhalter station not long after half-past four on the afternoon of 2 May 1938, he somehow managed to evade the security guards. The Nazi leader Adolf Hitler and his Propaganda Minister Joseph Goebbels were about to embark with their entourage on two trains heading to Italy for a state visit. Foreign correspondents were not allowed to report on their departure, but, amazingly, Greene made his way unnoticed through the crowds. As he wrote later:

> There was a long staircase lined by members of the Hitler Youth, and Goebbels, with his staff around him, started limping up it. So I fell in immediately behind him. Goebbels was about 18 inches shorter than me, and as we climbed that interminable staircase the lines of Hitler Youth on both sides started roaring with laughter. This was not the sort of reception to which Goebbels was accustomed, and he kept turning his head in a puzzled sort of way. I kept right behind him and I do not think that he saw me.

Thanks to the presence of Fritz Wiedemann, Hitler's adjutant, with whom he was on friendly terms, Greene was allowed to stay on the platform, where Goebbels was chatting to some of his staff. Hitler and his Propaganda Minister were due to catch the second train, scheduled to depart at 4.54 p.m. But Goebbels evidently did not notice the train starting to move off. 'As it went by,' Greene observed, 'a large SS man leant out of a carriage window, caught Goebbels under the arms and hauled him into the train with his short little legs kicking in the air.' The undignified spectacle occasioned more laughter among the spectators. It also said a good deal about Goebbels's standing in the Third Reich.[1]

Joseph Goebbels was not one of the Third Reich's most popular or imposing leaders. Jokes about him were commonplace, particularly among formerly Social Democratic or Communist workers. His propaganda was widely mocked. 'Lies have short legs' was – and still is – a common phrase in German, but during the Nazi period it was also common to change it to 'Lies have one leg too short', just as Goebbels did. As he was saying, during a speech, that 'the German people is like the German eagle, the head is our Führer, the right wing the SS, the left wing the SA', a worker standing at the back of the hall is alleged to have added, 'and the arsehole, that's you!'[2] Among Party members and supporters, Goebbels did not inspire fear, like Himmler, or respect, like Göring early on in the Third Reich. His self-confidence in public struck too many as arrogance, while his sharp tongue and even sharper pen endeared him to few. 'Nobody likes me,' he complained self-pityingly to his diary on 28 April 1931, adding a few weeks later: 'I haven't got many friends in the Party. Practically no one apart from Hitler.' Without a secure basis in the Party membership, he occupied a rather precarious position in the Party leadership, depending far more on Hitler's support than most of his rivals did. Sensing his relative weakness, both Göring ('a lump of frozen shit') and Himmler ('that crafty swine') tried to muscle in on his position on more than one occasion, though he managed to ward off the threat by appealing directly to the Party leader. More generally, especially in the German middle classes, Goebbels was widely regarded as a dangerous radical. For much of the time, indeed, particularly in the early 1930s, he felt obliged to use left-wing rhetoric in order to keep up good relations with the rabidly revolutionary Brownshirt movement in Berlin, which more than once threatened to oust him from his position as head of the Nazi Party in the capital city.[3]

It is at least possible that there was an element of social snobbery on the part of Göring and Himmler in their dealings with their rival. For, unlike them, Goebbels came from a lower-middle-class background. His father Fritz was a clerk who worked in a factory; his mother Katharina, daughter of a farmhand, was of even more humble origin. Both were staunch Catholics, and Joseph, born on 29 October 1897, was the fourth of six children. He was frequently ill; a bout of osteomyelitis left him with a twisted right foot, a deformity that surgical treatment failed to correct. Throughout his life, he walked with a limp; he was unable to join in play with his school classmates and was thrown back on his own resources. He was a voracious reader, working his way through large swathes of Russian literature in translation as a teenager. He compensated for his physical weakness by studying conscientiously and graduating top of his class. Unable for medical reasons to serve in the armed forces, he entered university in 1917, completed a degree in literature, and graduated four years later with a doctorate (a dissertation at the time was a relatively short piece of work that could be completed in just a few months). Evidently proud of his academic achievements, he was ever after known as 'Dr Goebbels'.[4]

Goebbels's family background was conventionally conservative, but he was pulled to the right in his student years, as he passed through a series of universities – Bonn, Würzburg, Freiburg, Munich, Heidelberg; it was quite normal for students in Germany to move from one university to another several times during their undergraduate years. He must therefore have been affected by the extreme nationalist atmosphere of the student body at the time. Like others of his generation, he tried to make amends for his inability to fight for Germany during World War I, though the reason was not youth but physical weakness. The Rhineland was occupied during the 1920s by Allied forces, which stoked resentment in the local population. In 1923 Goebbels found work briefly as a bank clerk, but he was soon fired. He began to imbibe antisemitic views, blaming the weak, chaotic, disunited and impoverished state of Germany at this time on the unspecified but universally malign influence of 'the Jews'. He wrote continually: unpublished plays and novels and, increasingly, articles for the press. But he was still financially dependent on his father, and found himself adrift and without a clear future. The economic crisis affecting universities in the inflationary years of the early Weimar Republic made it impossible for him to build a career for himself. It was not surprising that he resented the established middle classes and the academic world which he was unable to join.[5]

Around this time, Goebbels read widely in socialist literature – Karl Marx, August Bebel, Rosa Luxemburg among others – but found it mostly tedious, though he admired its general tenor. 'Socialism', for him, meant a form of populist nationalism, and he did nothing to work out what it meant in terms of policy. He was still adrift, looking for an answer to his problems: and he found it in Adolf Hitler and the Nazi Party. Galvanized by reports of the Munich beer-hall *putsch* of November 1923 and by Hitler's nationalistic justification of his behaviour in his subsequent trial,

Goebbels started to read up on Nazism, and began to criticize the older generation of ultra-nationalists as stuffy and lacking in energy. Hitler, he enthused, was clearly a man of sincerity, a man with a 'German soul'. He would lead Germany out of the humiliation of foreign occupation.[6] 'Out of the despair and depressing scepticism of the last few years,' he wrote in his diary, 'has arisen once again my belief in the nation and in the German spirit.'[7] He read *Mein Kampf* on its first publication, and was bowled over: 'Who is this man? Half-plebeian, half-god!' Goebbels finally met Hitler in early November 1925, at a regional party meeting in Brunswick: 'A born people's tribune,' he enthused: 'The coming dictator.' On 20 November they met again: 'How I love him! What a fellow!' His devotion was immediately personal and unconditional.[8]

Yet there were potential differences. Goebbels and his allies had manoeuvred out the existing leadership of the regional party in north-western Germany, and created a new organization in which he functioned as 'business manager'. Hitler was understandably suspicious of this group, which had emerged during his enforced absence from the political scene. Specifically, Goebbels regarded the Soviet Union as a potential ally, while Hitler thought of it as a Jewish-run racket that had to be destroyed in order to clear the ground for the German colonization of Eastern Europe. On 14 February 1926, at a party conference in Bamberg, Goebbels's views were denounced in a two-hour speech by Hitler. The Nazi leader also shocked him by opposing the idea of a referendum on the confiscation of the extensive properties still held by the former German princes. Private property, the Führer insisted, must be respected. Was Hitler a reactionary, Goebbels wondered. 'One of the greatest disappointments of my life,' he wrote in his diary: 'I no longer totally believe in Hitler. That's the terrible thing. I've lost my inner conviction. I'm now just half the man I was.'[9]

Conscious of the threat the north-west German group posed to the unity of the Party, Hitler now launched a charm offensive, inviting Goebbels to Munich, putting a car at his disposal, sending him flowers, and winning him over in a series of meetings in the spring and early summer of 1926. This had the desired effect of dividing Goebbels from his colleagues, and deepening still further his subservience. 'He is a genius,' he wrote in his diary: 'The naturally creative instrument of divine destiny.' He was completely converted to Hitler's views on the subjects that had divided them. Building on his success, the Nazi leader now appointed Goebbels Gauleiter (Regional Leader) of Berlin. The troublesome north-western association was dissolved.[10]

On 9 November 1926 Goebbels travelled to Berlin to take up his new duties. Hitler had given him a substantial district to look after, stretching far beyond the limits of Germany's capital city. But all was not well with the Nazi Party there. It was riven by internal disputes and personal rivalries, and the Strasser brothers – Gregor and Otto – had a strong following there, dedicated to a 'left-wing' version of National Socialism. Goebbels immediately moved to stamp his authority on the Berlin party organization. At the same time, he launched an intensive propaganda campaign, through speeches, leaflets and posters, along with a newspaper, *Der Angriff (The Attack)*, edited by himself, which was frequently banned for its extremist language and its personal invective. Goebbels attracted a seemingly endless series of prosecutions. He was an accomplished speaker, practising and rehearsing his addresses, and varying his tone and inflexion skilfully to keep his audiences engaged. Unlike so many other Nazi orators, he neither ranted nor screamed, always keeping himself under control and carefully calculating the effect he intended his words to have. His propaganda methods were borrowed to a considerable extent from the commercial advertising industry, stressing simple messages clearly expressed in punchy slogans and striking images. They were supplemented by violent action on the streets, aimed at winning dominance over the Communist and Social Democratic paramilitaries who were so ubiquitous in the city's public spaces. Brawls, woundings and even gunfights ensued.[11]

Goebbels's unscrupulous, sensationalist methods soon attracted public attention; but they also attracted the attention of the police chief, the Social Democrat Karl Zörgiebel, who banned the Berlin Party on 5 May 1927. Goebbels himself was barred from public speaking at the end of August. In late February 1928 he was sentenced to six weeks in prison for inciting the beating-up of a heckler at a Nazi meeting some months before. Like many other political offenders, he benefited from an amnesty passed by the Reichstag and did not have to serve his sentence. Although there were further prosecutions against him, the ban on the Berlin party was lifted in the run-up to the 1928 Reichstag election, held on 20 May. The Party won only 2.6 per cent of the vote – 1.6 per cent in Berlin – but Hitler had put Goebbels high on the national list of candidates, so he was elected and became a Reichstag deputy, giving him immunity from prosecution. Over the following months, Brownshirt violence, openly encouraged by Goebbels, led to increasing numbers of armed clashes with Communist paramilitaries. In January 1930 a young Brownshirt leader, Horst Wessel, was shot by two Communists in his home, dying of his wounds some weeks later. Goebbels immediately built a quasi-religious cult around Wessel, portraying him as a martyr and declaring a song written by Wessel, 'Die Fahne hoch!' ('Raise the Flag!'), as the Nazi Party's official anthem.[12]

Goebbels played a key role in the propaganda that helped the Nazis to their electoral breakthrough in 1930, when they won 107 seats in the Reichstag. Building on this success, he expanded his role with Hitler's backing to become the propaganda supremo of the Nazi Party. Unlike other leading figures, however, he lacked a secure base in the Party and was almost completely dependent on Hitler's approval. Goebbels was not a 'narcissist', as some have claimed; he was not in love with himself, he was in love with Hitler. In the early 1930s the two men's relationship was very close. The catalyst was the woman who was to become Goebbels's wife: Magda Quandt. Born on 11 November 1901, Magda was well educated and from a well-off background, with pronounced rightwing nationalist opinions. In 1921 she had married a much older man, the industrialist Günther Quandt, with whom she had a son, Harald, but the couple divorced eight years later after she had an affair with a student. The settlement left Magda as a woman of substantial independent means. In 1930 she joined the Nazi Party in Berlin, where she met Goebbels towards the end of the year.[13]

Goebbels had a strong sex-drive and had conducted several affairs during the 1920s, some more serious than others, but in Magda he finally found a kindred spirit. When he introduced her to Hitler, however, it quickly became apparent that the Party leader was smitten by her as well. Goebbels was consumed by jealousy and suspicion. The situation clearly could not last, and Magda brought it to a head by moving the planned date of her wedding forward to 19 December 1931, informing Hitler personally of her intention. 'Hitler resigned,' reported Goebbels in his diary: 'He really is very lonely. Has no luck with women.' The three came to an arrangement: Magda, socially skilled, well turned out and at ease in high society, would remain married to Goebbels, but was to function platonically in public as Hitler's companion when it was felt that the occasion demanded one. 'We will all three be good to each other,' Goebbels wrote: 'He intends to be our most loyal friend . . . When he leaves us on that note, I have a bit of a bad conscience. But he wishes me the best of luck, and he has tears in his big, astonished eyes.' Hitler became a regular visitor to the Goebbels house following this agreement, while for their part Joseph and Magda signalled their closeness to the Nazi leader by giving every child subsequently born to them a name beginning with 'H' – Helga, Hildegard, Helmut, Holdine, Hedwig and Heidrun.[14]

In July 1932 national elections resulted in the Nazis becoming the largest party in the Reichstag. Goebbels's propaganda campaign for the November elections that year, however, focused on the person of Hitler, did not have the desired effect. The Party's acute shortage of funds also restricted the scope of its campaign. The Nazi vote fell by 4 per cent. Indeed, as we have seen, it was because they considered it weakened by these problems, and by the internal dissension that led to the resignation of Gregor Strasser, that the circle of conservatives around President Hindenburg engineered Hitler's appointment as Reich Chancellor on 30 January 1933 in a Cabinet where their representatives, headed by Franz von Papen, held the majority of seats. Goebbels portrayed this as a 'national revolution', symbolized in the long torchlit procession of Brownshirts and Nazi supporters through the Brandenburg gate and the centre of Berlin that evening.[15]

As the Nazis began to assert themselves in government, Goebbels was able to use their improved position and finances to unleash a massive propaganda campaign for the elections of 5 March 1933. Yet after the Reichstag Fire Decree of 28 February 1933, which seriously restricted the activities of the opposition parties, the Nazis were unable to score a significant victory, winning only 44 per cent of the vote. Still, with the 8 per cent chalked up by their conservative coalition parties, and a combination of threats, violence and promises, they were able on 23 March to secure the two-thirds of the Reichstag votes needed to alter the Constitution so that Hitler's Cabinet could pass decrees without requiring the approval of either the legislature or the President.[16]

Already by this time, Hitler had fulfilled a promise he had made to Goebbels before the election and appointed him head of a newly created Ministry for Popular Enlightenment and Propaganda on 14 March 1933. Goebbels grasped with enthusiasm the opportunities this gave him. Over the following months, proclaiming that the purpose of propaganda was to win over the 48 per cent of the German people who had not voted for the governing coalition on 5 March, he moved to 'co-ordinate' the media, partly through decrees, partly through the takeover of independent outlets by Party companies, partly through the threat of violence against those who showed any reluctance to comply. Not just administrators but also art gallery directors, orchestras and opera companies, theatres, newspapers and magazines, book publishers and much more besides were taken under the aegis of the Propaganda Ministry. Goebbels created a Reich Chamber of Culture, with numerous subdivisions (Chamber of Music, Chamber of Literature and so on), to which everyone who wished to exercise their profession was compelled by law to belong. Neither Jews nor known opponents of the regime were permitted to join.[17]

However, Goebbels's control over culture and the media was by no means complete. He failed in his attempt to wrest the major newspapers from Max Amann, who ran the Eher Verlag, the Nazi publishing house. He had to contend with the Nazi press chief Otto Dietrich, who sometimes pursued an independent line and issued press briefings of his own. Goebbels's attempts to close down the *Frankfurter Zeitung*, the formerly liberal daily, where journalists frequently engaged in veiled criticism of the Nazis, were rebuffed by Hitler, who valued the paper's international prestige and thought its survival helped the regime's image abroad. Goebbels was unable to take over Germany's museums, and had to contend with the Education Ministry, with 'Strength through Joy', the cultural organization of the Labour Front, and with many other institutions of the Nazi state. And then there was Alfred Rosenberg, whose Fighting League for German Culture was engaged in a relentless war against modernism, whereas Goebbels took a more relaxed attitude to it. Hitler, who shared Rosenberg's views, went to some lengths to persuade his Propaganda Minister of the 'degeneracy' of modern art, expressing himself appalled when he found a painting by the Expressionist artist Emil Nolde on the wall of Goebbels's house during a visit (though Nolde was himself a fully paid-up member of the Nazi Party). As elsewhere, Goebbels jumped promptly into line, even organizing a public exhibition of 'Degenerate Art' in Munich in 1937.[18]

Goebbels, following Hitler, ascribed 'degenerate' art and music to the 'Jewish' spirit of subversion. From the very beginning of the Third Reich, he implemented a variety of measures against Germany's Jewish population. On 1 April 1933 he organized a nationwide boycott of

Jewish-owned shops and businesses, carried out by Brownshirts pasting boycott notices on the windows and standing menacingly outside in front of the premises. It was not a great success: many customers, particularly regulars, went in anyway. On 10 May 1933, in the Third Reich's most notorious act of cultural vandalism, German students in nineteen university towns gathered pacifist, Marxist, liberal and other 'subversive' books, including especially those written by Jewish authors, from libraries and cast them onto bonfires in the main town squares. Goebbels attended the book-burning in Berlin to endorse this 'act against the un-German spirit', declaring: 'The era of extreme Jewish intellectualism is now at an end. The breakthrough of the German revolution has again cleared the way on the German path ... Here the intellectual foundation of the November Republic is sinking to the ground, but from this wreckage the phoenix of a new spirit will triumphantly rise.'[19]

By the 'un-German spirit' of course he meant 'Jewish', whether or not the individuals in question were actually Jewish. Nevertheless, at every juncture, Goebbels both justified the regime's antisemitic policies and repeatedly urged Hitler to drive them on. 'Again I make a massive advance in the Jewish question regarding Bolshevism,' he reported on 11 February 1937, for example: 'Leader enthusiastic,' he added. With Hitler's approval he instigated the violent anti-Jewish riots that erupted on the Kurfürstendamm, a prominent shopping street in Berlin, in June 1935. ('Jewry is once more trying to assert itself today on every street,' he complained in a regional Party rally on 30 June, adding further incitement in his paper *Der Angriff* on 15 July.) The disorder damaged the regime's reputation abroad at a delicate time, however, when the 1936 Berlin Olympics were less than a year away, so Hitler decided to put an end to it, introducing in September the infamous Nuremberg race laws which deprived German Jews of their citizenship.[20]

Although Goebbels, with his wife Magda, remained personally close to Hitler, he was not normally party to the regime's key decisions. He was left out of the conspiracy that led to the arrest and murder of the Brownshirt leader Ernst Röhm and up to 200 others on the night of 30 June–1 July 1934; indeed, he had focused wholly in the preceding weeks on the need to bring the conservative Vice-Chancellor Franz von Papen and the 'reactionaries' to heel. As always, Goebbels knuckled under and undertook a propaganda blitz to justify these events to the German people in the media, claiming they were legal simply by virtue of having been ordered by Hitler.²¹ In major foreign-policy issues such as the remilitarization of the Rhineland in 1936 or the annexation of Austria in 1938, Goebbels was excluded from the decision-making process and involved only when it came to justifying them to the German and international public. Even though he repeatedly discussed with Hitler the massive media campaign against the Czech government that he unrolled in the run-up to the dismemberment of Czechoslovakia with the Munich Agreement in the autumn of 1938, and against Poland in preparation for the invasion in September 1939, he was not involved in the details or timetabling of the actual policy decisions Hitler took.²²

Although Goebbels made a point of presenting an image of modesty and financial probity to the general public, he earned a substantial income from his ministerial position, as well as receiving a very generous expense allowance from Hitler. With these funds he amassed a collection of expensive cars and motorboats, and purchased two adjoining villas on the island of Schwanenwerder, in the Wannsee, a lake to the west of Berlin, one villa at a knock-down price from a Jewish banker forced to agree to the sale by the Berlin police chief, a friend of Goebbels. His residence in Berlin itself was renovated at a cost of 2.5 million Marks. In 1936 the city of Berlin granted him the cost-free use of another large villa, on the Bogensee, a lake to the north of the capital city, a villa which he rebuilt in the most lavish style. With thirty rooms, a service building with forty rooms, a garage for numerous cars, and a private cinema, the huge villa cost more than 2.3 million Reichsmarks, which Goebbels paid for in part by selling it to the state media company (even though he did not in fact own the villa).²³

But despite his worldly success, Goebbels did not enjoy a harmonious relationship with his wife Magda. Alienated by their frequent quarrels, the Propaganda Minister embarked on a passionate affair with the twenty-one-year-old Czech actress Lida Baarová, whom he met in June 1936, when he was thirty-nine. Dismayed by this turn of events, Magda told Hitler, who insisted that the affair come to an end. He was not prepared to lose Magda as his public female companion, but would have felt it necessary to dispense with her services in order to avoid speculation had the couple separated or divorced. This was, Goebbels confessed to his diary, 'the hardest time in my life'. As always, he gave in to Hitler, ending the relationship in the last days of October 1938, realizing perhaps that his position in the dictator's court depended almost entirely on the continuation of their triangular relationship.[24] When a young Polish Jew shot an official in the German Embassy in Paris in retaliation for the expulsion of his parents from Germany in the preceding weeks, along with 18,000 other Polish Jews, Goebbels, perhaps hoping to get back into Hitler's good books, whipped up antisemitic hatred in the media; and when the official succumbed to his wounds, Goebbels secured Hitler's approval for a nationwide pogrom in which 7,500 Jewish properties were trashed and over 1,000 synagogues burned to the ground. Some 30,000 Jewish men were taken to concentration camps on Hitler's personal orders, and at least ninety-one Jews, and in all probability many more, were murdered by the perpetrators of the pogrom – Brownshirts and SS men dressed in civilian clothing in order to lend support to Goebbels's propaganda line, that this was a 'spontaneous' outbreak of popular anger against the Jews. 'The whole nation is in uproar,' he reported with satisfaction the next morning.[25]

Goebbels's primary role throughout the following years was to provide the public justification for Hitler's wars of aggression, and then for the extermination of European Jews. He poured out false allegations of Polish maltreatment of ethnic Germans in a propaganda action that culminated in the fabrication of a Polish 'attack' on a radio station at Gleiwitz, near the German border, using concentration-camp prisoners who were dressed in Polish uniforms and then killed, their bodies left lying around as 'evidence' to be photographed by a propaganda team.[26] After the defeat of France in the summer of 1940, Goebbels issued detailed instructions for public celebrations in Berlin, with workers given the afternoon off and marched to their designated places along the processional route, which was decorated the night before by 8,000 people assigned to put up banners and bunting, while lorry-loads of flowers arrived to be strewn on the streets along which Hitler passed in his cavalcade. Overcome by the spectacle, and forgetting that it had been stage-managed by his own Ministry, Goebbels enthused: 'The Führer rides over nothing but flowers. Our people, our wonderful people!'[27]

Throughout the first half of the war, Goebbels did his utmost to strengthen the German people's faith in ultimate victory. He took a personal interest in the development of films, including the antisemitic *Jud Süss* (1940) and the anti-British *Ohm Kruger* (1941), both of which won praise for their high production values, and he spent a great deal of time reviewing raw cuts of *The Eternal Jew* (1940), a rabidly antisemitic documentary that showed footage from the Warsaw Ghetto alongside swarming rats. It proved too crude and extreme even for the German population under Nazism. After viewing it, Goebbels commented: 'These Jews must be annihilated.' Here too he was following Hitler's lead, after the dictator had privately criticized the German film industry for what he saw as its failure 'to touch the Jewish Bolsheviks'.[28]

Such propaganda had a direct bearing on policy towards German Jews. Still Gauleiter of Berlin, Goebbels was heavily involved in organizing the expulsion of German Jews from the capital city in the course of 1940–41. The Jewish people, he told a meeting of senior figures in the armed forces, the Labour Front, the Party and other institutions on 1 December 1941, were 'suffering a gradual process of annihilation that it intended for us ... Sympathy or even regret is wholly out of place.' He seems actually to have believed that a world Jewish conspiracy was orchestrating the actions of the British, and, from the middle of 1941, the Soviet Union and the United States of America, against Germany, and he framed his propaganda messages to portray Churchill, Roosevelt and Stalin as puppets of the Jews, hell-bent on exterminating the German race. Some 60 per cent of the Jews were being 'annihilated', he wrote in his diary on 27 March 1942, while the other 40 per cent were being worked to death. 'The Jews are being punished barbarically, to be sure, but they have fully deserved it.' His relentless war of words against them was intended not only to justify the extermination programme to the German people, but also to drive it forward.[29]

By early 1942, however, the German war effort was starting to falter. Brought to a halt by the Red Army and the deep snow of the Russian winter, the German armed forces, which Hitler and Goebbels had assumed would easily have brought the Soviet regime to collapse, were literally freezing to death. Goebbels organized a public rescue operation, with winter clothing being donated by German citizens to help maintain the fighting spirit of the troops. The year 1942 brought a resumption of the German advance in the East, but this too was halted as the winter came on, and a vast encircling movement by the Red Army cut off supplies to the Germans and their allies before the symbolically significant city of Stalingrad: the remnants surrendered at the beginning of 1943. From this point on, Goebbels's propaganda outpourings increasingly emphasized the self-sacrifice of the German soldier, along with portraying the war as a fight for the preservation of Western civilization against the Jewish-Bolshevik hordes. As the military situation deteriorated, he bombarded the German people at home with exhortations to redouble their efforts to win the war – most notoriously, in his stage-managed appearance before a vast crowd of fanatical supporters in Berlin's Sportpalast Palace on 18 February 1943, when, to cries of 'Yes!', accompanied by thunderous applause, he shouted 'Do you want total war ... more total and more radical than we can even imagine it today?'[30]

It was all fake, of course. The German war economy was already so stretched that there was hardly any room to tighten the rack still further, and ordinary Germans knew it. A few symbolic actions took place, such as the closure of cafés, many of which soon reopened under new names. Theatres, concert halls and opera houses were closed as part of 'total war' measures, but bomb damage brought cultural life in the towns and cities to an end in the course of 1944 anyway. As the Red Army advanced into Germany from the East, Goebbels broadcast atrocity propaganda to try and stiffen people's will to hold out. It had little effect. He poured resources into a lavishly produced movie, *Kolberg*, centred on the resistance of a German town and its people to the French during the Napoleonic Wars. Released on 30 January 1945, it came too late. Security Service reports recorded a growing mood of pessimism, even despair, after Stalingrad, deepened over the succeeding months by the increasingly effective bombing campaign being carried out by the Western Allies. After being appointed 'Plenipotentiary for Total War' by Hitler, Goebbels continued his efforts to replenish the rapidly diminishing armed forces with fresh recruits. But while he noted some successes in his diaries, it was in the end a hopeless task, limited partly by Goebbels's rivals in the field of labour mobilization, such as Speer, who had agendas of their own, and partly by Hitler's reluctance to go the whole way, for example by mobilizing women.[31]

During the war years, Goebbels went some way towards repairing the damage done to his relationship with the Nazi leader by his pre-war marital crisis. Something of the former closeness between Hitler and the Goebbels family was restored. 'When talking to Hitler,' he noted on 15 March 1945, 'one feels: "Yes, you're right. Everything you say is true."' He backed Hitler's infamous 'Nero order' for the destruction of Germany's economic resources in the face of the Allied invasion, and continued to share his leader's blind faith in eventual victory. When even this crumbled, Joseph and Magda Goebbels decided to join Hitler in the bunker beneath the Reich Chancellery despite his entreaties for them to seek safety elsewhere. After Hitler had committed suicide, naming Goebbels his successor as Reich Chancellor, the couple got the SS dentist Helmut Kunz to inject their six children with morphine, after which either Kunz, or Hitler's physician Ludwig Stumpfegger, put cyanide capsules into their mouths and crushed them, killing them instantaneously.[32]

As Magda Goebbels had already written to her adult son from her first marriage, Harald Quandt, an air-force officer languishing in a prisoner-of-war camp in Italy:

> The world after the Führer and National Socialism will not be worth living in, and therefore I have taken my children away. They are too dear to endure what is coming next, and a merciful God will understand my intentions in delivering them from it. We have now only one aim, loyalty unto death to the Führer. That we can end our lives with him is a mercy of fate that we never dared hope for.[33]

After murdering their children, the couple put on their coats and went up to the Reich Chancellery garden, where they bit on cyanide capsules. Acting on prior instructions, two SS men came up, shot them to make sure they were dead, poured petrol over them and set the bodies alight. There was not enough to burn the corpses properly, however, and they were easily recognized by Red Army soldiers when they entered the garden shortly afterwards.[34]

Since 1923 Goebbels had been keeping a detailed diary, at first mainly as a vehicle of self-expression in times of personal crisis, and then as a first draft of journalistic essays and reports. In due course he reworked sections for publication. *Kampf um Berlin* (*The Struggle for Berlin*, 1931) was followed by *Vom Kaiserhof zur Reichskanzlei* (*From the Kaiserhof [hotel] to the Reich Chancellery*, 1934), in which he logged the Nazi Party's progress into government. In 1936 he signed a lucrative contract with the Nazi Party's main publisher, Max Amann, for the diaries to be published twenty years after his death; and from 1941 onwards he dictated the daily diary entries to a secretary, making them less personal and more public; as far as his daily life was concerned, the diaries are mostly factually correct: they constitute a major source for the history of the Nazi movement and the Third Reich.[35]

In November 1944, realizing that the war was lost, but keen for the diaries to be preserved for posterity, he had them microfilmed and reproduced on glass plates, which he had buried in Potsdam, just outside Berlin. Here they were discovered after the war by the Soviets and shipped off to the Soviet secret-service archive in Moscow. There they were discovered after the fall of Communism by Elke Fröhlich, an historian from the Institute of Contemporary History in Munich, who undertook the heroic task of transcribing them and publishing them in twenty-nine volumes for the Institute: the last volume appeared in print as late as 2008. Thanks to these voluminous and extremely detailed journals, we now know more about Joseph Goebbels than we do about any other leading Nazi. They reveal him to have been unscrupulous, violent, murderous, self-absorbed, consumed by petty jealousies and rivalries, and above all deeply committed to the paranoid antisemitism that led to the extermination of European Jews.[36]

Goebbels's suicide illustrated, if illustration were needed, his total dependence on Hitler, indeed his complete identification with him. Early on in the Third Reich, he had defined the task of propaganda as listening to the German people's soul and then amplifying it back to them. He might equally have said that he was listening to Hitler's soul and amplifying it to the German people. Goebbels was, in other words, not merely subservient to the Nazi leader, he thought it important to divine his intentions and then strengthen them and prompt him to put them into effect. After all, as Rudolf Hess said, Hitler *was* Germany, and Germany *was* Hitler. Once his initial doubts had been quelled, Goebbels believed passionately in Hitler's greatness and destiny. There can be little doubt either that he was sincere in his belief that the Jews were engaged in a global conspiracy to destroy Germany. That provided the justification for the cascade of lies that Goebbels unleashed in his propaganda, and for his unprecedentedly unscrupulous deployment of disinformation both before and after Hitler's creation of the Third Reich. His propaganda tactics have been, and are being, widely imitated in the twenty-first century by populist politicians from Donald Trump to Viktor Orbán to discredit and ridicule their opponents and sweep aside opposition to their rule, though they are surely less ideologically fanatical in their motivation. By using derogatory nicknames for his critics, by denying the legitimacy of opposition to his cause, by cynically refusing to accept the truth when it turned out to be inconvenient, and by creating powerful but ultimately imaginary menaces to society that threaten to destroy it unless countered by the power of a supposedly great leader, Goebbels set an example that was to be followed long after his death.[37]

4
The Soldier: Ernst Röhm

On 5 January 1929 Ernst Röhm arrived in the Bolivian capital La Paz after a five-day train journey from Buenos Aires, accompanied by the Bolivian Army Chief of Staff General Hans Kundt, who had travelled with him on the long sea voyage from Hamburg. Kundt's appointment was part of a remarkable global diaspora of German military advisers that reached its apogee in the mid-1920s. Following the reduction of the German Army to a maximum of 100,000 soldiers by the Treaty of Versailles, many officers found themselves without employment in their home country, while, in other parts of the world, nationalist governments were looking to professionalize their armed forces. Despite their defeat in 1918, the German military enjoyed a high reputation across the globe, and German officers were available for hire in large numbers. They might also be able to secure much-needed supplies of weapons and munitions for their new masters. Perhaps the most celebrated example of this phenomenon was to be found in China, where the nationalist leader Chiang Kai-shek engaged Field Marshal Ludendorff's former Chief of Staff, Colonel Max Bauer, to head a military mission in 1928. But there was also a German military mission in Bolivia, where Kundt had in fact had already worked as head of an official military training programme supplied by the Kaiser's government from 1911 to the outbreak of the war.[1]

After military service in the First World War, Kundt went back to Bolivia, became a Bolivian citizen, and in 1921 was appointed Chief of the General Staff, heading a group of German officers who had also found positions in the military. Tensions were rising with the neighbouring state of Paraguay over the disputed border territory of the Gran Chaco, which was rumoured to contain rich deposits of oil. Exiled to Germany from 1926 to 1928 as a result of political intrigues in La Paz,

Kundt was recalled by President Hernando Siles to strengthen the army in the face of the looming conflict. It was in order to resume his position that Kundt returned to La Paz with Röhm at the beginning of 1929. Röhm learned Spanish quickly, aided by his prior command of Latin, and set to work training the troops. However, the two men fell out when Siles attempted to extend his term of office and the army staged a coup in order to restore democracy (an unusual move as far as military coups go, but, it seems, a genuine one). Although he had remained neutral in the conflicts that had led to the coup, Röhm was appointed chief adviser to the General Staff following the coup, but he then demanded to be made official Deputy to the Chief of the General Staff, and such was the unpopularity of Kundt and the Germans by this stage that the demand was rejected. By mid-October 1930, Röhm was on his way back to Germany. His advice to the coup leaders to seek an accommodation with Paraguay was rejected, war broke out in 1932, and the Bolivians were roundly defeated, losing a considerable amount of territory: clearly Kundt and Röhm's training programmes had not been very effective.[2]

Ernst Röhm later claimed he had agreed to serve in the Bolivian Army in the hope of taking part in the looming war with Paraguay. His reputation as a man of action had preceded him and given rise to rumours that he had had a hand in the military coup. But these were exaggerated, to say the least. He was in fact never really committed to Bolivian politics, and always envisaged returning to Germany, keeping up his contacts there throughout his stay on the South American continent. What the episode showed was that he was a military man through and through. No other career ever appealed to him. Born on 28 November 1887 in Munich, third child of a railway inspector, Julius Röhm, Ernst was well educated, attending the prestigious *Königliches Maximiliansgymnasium*, where he gained a solid grounding in the Classics and other humanistic disciplines, as well as becoming a proficient pianist. In his memoirs he cultivated a violent and undisciplined image, quoting a school report criticizing his 'inclination to disorder and unrest', but his school career was in fact a successful one, giving him a place in the upper middle class to which the great majority of the other pupils belonged. When he graduated, Röhm began officer training, where again he seemed to have experienced no problems with military discipline apart from a small number of very minor infringements. He received his commission in 1908, and settled into the privileged and ordered life of a junior officer in the Bavarian Army, based in Ingolstadt, a town in the centre of the kingdom. He shared in full the arrogance of the officer corps, its contempt for civilian life and in particular civilian politicians and bureaucrats, and its hope of engagement in war. In his memoirs, Röhm recalled this period with a good deal of nostalgia. His superiors at the time described him as 'a vigorous, cheerful, capable officer with a well-developed military spirit'.[3]

This comfortable life came to an abrupt end with the outbreak of the First World War in August 1914. Röhm's regiment was mobilized and deployed on the Western Front, where he was hit on 24 September by a shot that tore across his cheek and destroyed the upper part of his nose, disfiguring him for life. Ironically, he was hit while he was asleep on the front line. Plastic surgery reconstructed his face, though not very elegantly. He returned to active service in April 1915, now the bearer of the Iron Cross, Second Class, and the rank of First Lieutenant. Like many others, including Hitler, he found the regular life and camaraderie of the trenches deeply fulfilling. Differences of class and status sank into oblivion here. Conspicuous by his bravery, he was badly wounded at Verdun on 23 June 1916, shortly after being awarded the Iron Cross, First Class. When he returned to active service, in May 1917, it was as a staff officer concerned mainly with supplies and logistics.[4] In 1918, however, he caught influenza, as the 'Spanish flu' epidemic of that year swept across Europe. It was while he was recovering that the Bavarian monarchy was swept away in the November 1918 revolution, which brought the Workers' and Soldiers' Councils to power in Munich. When elections held in January 1919 revealed that the revolutionary regime had very little support outside Munich itself, Röhm wrote and distributed three pamphlets describing it as the creation of Jews and criminals and blaming Germany's military defeat on a 'stab in the back' by revolutionaries at home. As the council regime fell under the control of ultra-revolutionary socialists and anarchists, and then Communists, he joined the Free Corps unit led by Franz Ritter von Epp, a highly decorated army officer who had played a part in the genocidal massacres of the Herero and Nama in German South-West Africa before the war. The Free Corps put down the revolution in a welter of blood, with up to a thousand killed in a series of violent clashes. Röhm's entry into right-wing politics and paramilitary violence was prompted by his fury at the civilian councils' control over the military ('I boiled with rage,' he wrote later). He bitterly resented the destruction of the socially and politically privileged position that the army and its officers had enjoyed in Bavaria before the war. From now on he dedicated himself to its restoration.[5]

As the newly created Weimar Republic was replacing the Prussian, Bavarian and other armies with the much smaller Reichswehr, Röhm was working as Epp's Chief of Staff procuring arms and ammunition for him and passing on large quantities to the much larger Residents' Defence League (*Einwohnerwehr*), a counter-revolutionary organization that he himself had played a role in creating. By February 1920 it numbered some 224,000 men armed with more than 150,000 rifles and 1,000 machine guns. When Free Corps leaders and far-right politicians in Berlin attempted to depose the existing democratic government by force, in the so-called Kapp *putsch*, a general strike overcame the *putsch* but led to a widespread, Communist-led uprising in the Ruhr, aimed at defeating the backers of the *putsch* in Germany's most important industrial area. The government sent in the Free Corps of Epp, including Röhm, to defeat it, but once this was achieved, Allied pressure led the national government to order the dissolution of the Free Corps and the *Einwohnerwehr*. Driven underground, Röhm evaded attempts to bring him to heel, and used the many secret caches of illegal weapons under his control to build an independent position of influence on the nationalist ultra-right. By this time, he had joined, contacted, or assisted a number of organizations on this murky fringe of politics. One of them was the Nazi Party.[6]

Röhm and Hitler first met in May 1920, at one of the numerous small far-right groups that mushroomed in Munich at the time. They hit it off and became personal friends, calling each other by the intimate *Du* rather than the formal *Sie*. Hitler was a frequent visitor to Röhm's family home.[7] As the country descended into chaos in 1922–23, with hyperinflation spiralling out of control, the French occupying the Ruhr, and the economy in a state of almost complete collapse, Hitler considered the moment had come to launch a coup along the lines of Mussolini's 'March on Rome'. Gathering armed paramilitaries around him, Röhm supplied most of the muscle for the beer-hall *putsch* on 8–9 November 1923, taking over the Bavarian War Ministry in Munich while Hitler marched on the city centre. But confronted with the superior and better-organized and equipped forces of the Reichswehr, he was forced to surrender. Röhm went on trial with Hitler and other leading putschists and was found guilty of being an accessory to treason. He was handed down a short prison sentence that he had already served on remand, so he walked free when the trial ended. However, he was forced to resign his commission in the army. This was not unwelcome to him, however, since the prospects of promotion in the Reichswehr were minimal, given its restricted size, and it was clear he would do better outside it, despite the fact that in his own mind he was and always remained in the first place a soldier.[8]

While Hitler was serving out his sentence in Landsberg Prison, Röhm, with his approval, was rebuilding the shattered paramilitary movement, including the SA, nominally led by Hermann Göring. He also set up an independent organization, the *Frontbann*, built along quasi-military lines, and got himself elected as a Reichstag deputy, though he was not active in the national legislature and did not stand at the next election. Hitler, however, disapproved of all these moves, concerned that they were undermining his control over the Nazi movement, and realizing that Nazism had to focus more on the constitutional road to power after the failure of the *putsch*. Unwilling to persist without Hitler's support, Röhm resigned from all his positions on May Day 1925. The move left him struggling to support himself financially (he was unable to subsist on his meagre military pension), and he was forced to find work, first as a travelling salesman, then a factory worker, finally as a manual labourer. He began writing his autobiography, hoping to make some money from its sales. But things went from bad to worse as he was imprisoned again, though only for ten days, for failing to pay a fine for refusing to answer questions put to him by a Reichstag committee about his involvement in paramilitary violence and murders in the early 1920s. Röhm had hit a low point in his life. So in 1926 he made an attempt to pick up his military career by seeking a position in the Bolivian Army. Only when the threat of war with Paraguay began to look serious, however, in 1928, did his efforts meet with success.[9]

Although Röhm's departure for Bolivia was in effect an admission of his failure to adjust to civilian life in Germany, he did not abandon his political ties with his home country. For many years these ties had been in the first place with 'Crown Prince' Rupprecht, the claimant to the vacant Bavarian throne, with whom he corresponded regularly throughout his stay in South America. But Röhm's allegiance to Hitler became more important in the course of the 1920s, and in the months before his departure for Bolivia he resumed his activities in the murky world of the paramilitary associations with a view, once more, to providing the Nazis with the muscle he felt they needed to wage war against their opponents on the streets. Towards the end of 1930, Hitler recalled Röhm from Bolivia to the leadership of the SA in Germany in place of Franz Pfeffer von Salomon, who had led the Brownshirts successfully over the previous few years but failed to impose discipline on them. The ever-loyal Röhm, Hitler felt, could be trusted to restrain those of them who still favoured a violent *putsch*, and he appointed him SA Chief of Staff in January 1931. Röhm had not been involved in the internal disputes within the Nazi movement and the SA during his time in Bolivia, he had a strong reputation from the early 1920s as a paramilitary leader, he had retained his contacts with the armed forces, his rough image held an appeal to ordinary stormtroopers, and above all he had proven organizational and administrative abilities that Hitler needed to impose discipline on the rapidly growing but persistently disorderly Brownshirt movement.[10]

Dangerous conflicts within the SA nonetheless broke out in August 1930 and again the following year, above all in Berlin, where SA-men under Walther Stennes attacked the Nazi Party's offices on more than one occasion, and it was only with some difficulty that Hitler and Röhm, backed by Goebbels as the local Gauleiter, managed to restore order, purging refractory elements as far as they were able. Röhm brought old friends and army comrades from Bavaria into senior positions to assist in the task. This created a new elite leadership group, mostly with a higher, more educated social standing than the mass of the rank and file, with which he could tighten his grip on the SA.[11] As all this was going on, the SA was expanding almost exponentially, from 77,000 in January 1931 to 445,000 in August 1932.[12] With this growth in numbers, fuelled by mass unemployment that Röhm's organization promised to alleviate, came a radicalization of violence on the streets, as the quasi-military organizational structure he introduced and the violent propaganda pumped out by Goebbels, combined with the equally radical rhetoric and practice of the Communist Red Front-Fighters' League, taught the stormtroopers to regard their political opponents as enemies to be beaten, assaulted and killed. Hitler's repeated insistence on the Nazi Party's intention to stick to a legal route to power was intended mainly to curb the Brownshirts' lack of discipline, not to end their thuggery. Local urban SA units, each called a *Sturm* and based in a pub or bar, engaged in a constant war of attrition against Communist and socialist paramilitaries in an increasingly successful campaign to drive them out of their strongholds. 'Ordinary brawls,' remarked the Social Democratic police chief Albert Grzesinski, 'had given way to numerous attacks. Knives, blackjacks and revolvers had replaced political argument. Terror was rampant.'[13]

In the months following Hitler's appointment as Reich Chancellor on 30 January 1933, thousands upon thousands of young men flocked to join the SA, whose membership reached the staggering total of two million men by the middle of the year. Following the suspension of civil liberties by the Reichstag Fire Decree on 28 February 1933, the SA unleashed a campaign of unrestrained violence, intimidation and murder against the Nazis' opponents across the country, setting up makeshift torture centres and improvised concentration camps to beat them into submission. Local and regional governments were forced to abdicate and hand their powers over to Nazi functionaries. Röhm himself concentrated on ousting the Bavarian state government, a process that also involved a violent settling of scores with his personal enemies and critics. The SA was central to the 'seizure of power' between January and July of that year, as thousands of its members enrolled as auxiliary police and many of its leaders were placed in senior police positions in state after state. Its violence was essential to the process by which Hitler converted his post as head of a coalition government into dictator in a one-party state in the first half of the year. Röhm's contribution to this process was recognized by his appointment as Minister without Portfolio and membership in the Cabinet of the Reich government.[14]

By this time, however, the SA had largely lost its function as a blunt instrument with which the Nazis' opponents could be bludgeoned into submission, since these men had either fled the country or been imprisoned, cowed into silence or killed. Röhm organized its merger with the right-wing veterans' association, the *Stahlhelm* (Steel Helmets), boosting SA membership to over four million.[15] This created growing tensions with the army, whose numbers were restricted by the Treaty of Versailles to 100,000. While Röhm tried to keep the increasingly rowdy and disorderly rank and file occupied by drills and inspections, he developed the idea of turning the SA into a militia that would serve as a reservoir of trained troops for the army. His declaration in June 1933 that the SA 'will not tolerate the German Revolution going to sleep', and his threat to 'philistine souls' that the revolution would be carried further 'if need be, against them!', had already been countered publicly by Hitler (only 'fools', he told his Gauleiters in February 1934, could claim 'that the Revolution isn't over').[16] The idea of a mass militia based on the SA was completely unacceptable to the army, and Hitler backed the officers by proposing a massive increase in military strength, to be achieved, when the international situation allowed it, by the introduction of universal conscription (which eventually happened in March 1935). At the same time, he refused Röhm's request for the SA to be given adequate quantities of arms and ammunition. Hitler forced Röhm to sign an agreement with the Minister of Defence, General Werner von Blomberg, in February, that only the armed forces were entitled to bear arms.[17] Desperate for the backing of the conservative military leadership, which was threatening to get Hindenburg to sack Hitler, and concerned as well at the looming struggle over the succession to the clearly ailing old man, Hitler gave way to the army's entreaties to curb the SA and eliminate it as a possible rival. Backed by Himmler and Heydrich, who had been planning to curb the SA's excesses for some time, he finally decided to act. He sent the SA on leave and made his way with his entourage to Munich.[18]

In the notorious 'Night of the Long Knives', from 30 June to 1 July 1934, Hitler, accompanied by Goebbels and a squad of SS men, descended on the hotel at Bad Wiessee, in the Upper Bavarian hills, where Röhm and senior SA officers were preparing for a conference. Storming into Röhm's bedroom, whip in hand, Hitler declared he was arresting him for treason. Together with other leading Brownshirts, Röhm was transported to Munich's Stadelheim Prison. While Göring was overseeing a wave of arrests and murders in Berlin, including key conservatives, Hitler accused Röhm of preparing a *putsch* and thereby committing treason. Following shootings of SA men in a number of cities, including Munich, where six of them were executed in the prison courtyard, Hitler arranged for a loaded pistol to be placed at Röhm's disposal. If he had not used it to commit suicide after ten minutes, he was to be shot. Entering his cell after the ten minutes had passed, Theodor Eicke, Commandant of Dachau, and a fellow SS officer found the pistol still there, unused, and Röhm standing defiantly before them with his chest bared. To have committed suicide would have been an implicit admission of guilt. The two SS men aimed at his heart and fired. Röhm fell to the floor. Another SS officer came in and shot him again. The curbing of the Brownshirts was over. The vast majority of Germans were relieved, swallowing Goebbels's mendacious propaganda claim that the SA had been planning a coup in order to push through a 'second revolution' in Germany.[19]

Ernst Röhm has often been seen as a kind of modern *Landsknecht*, a thuggish soldier like the brutal mercenaries of the Thirty Years War, who gloried in mindless violence and perpetual conflict. 'He revelled,' it has been said, 'in the lawlessness of wartime life.'[20] Joachim Fest described him as a man dedicated to 'blind dynamism', an agent of a 'permanent revolution without any revolutionary idea of the future', a member of a 'lost generation' of front-line soldiers who 'wished to transmute their incapacity for civilian life into extremist adventurism and criminality masquerading as nationalism'.[21] Röhm himself did little to contradict this characterization. 'Because I'm an immature and bad person,' he wrote in his autobiography, 'war and unrest say more to me than well-behaved bourgeois order.'[22] He used words like 'intellectual', 'bourgeois', or 'prudent' in a pejorative sense, while 'ruthless' and 'daredevil' appear in his writings almost invariably as words of approbation. But historians have taken his own public self-assessment too much at face value, and have been over-influenced by the denunciations of the SA leader as a mindless revolutionary by Hitler and the rest of the Nazi leadership as they justified the 'Night of the Long Knives' to the mass of ordinary Germans.[23] The new information presented in Eleanor Hancock's 2008 biography points to a more complex character than is suggested by his carefully cultivated public image.

Röhm may not have been an astute or skilled politician, but he was far from being mindless or unideological in his approach to the problems of the day. He was in fact a monarchist. As noted, he maintained a close relationship and regular correspondence with 'Crown Prince' Rupprecht of Bavaria, though a degree of political realism caused both men to hold back from taking any action in support of the monarchist cause. Röhm regarded Fascist Italy, with its figurehead monarch King Viktor Emmanuel III and its dictator Benito Mussolini, as a model for a future Germany, along with Kemal Atatürk's Turkey.[24] Thus when Röhm spoke of the need to continue with the 'revolution' in the summer of 1933, he meant no more than the completion of the Nazi seizure of power and its cementing in the consciousness of the mass of ordinary Germans. Far from being an apostle of mindless violence and disorder, he was a strong advocate of military discipline and order. This is indeed what he was invited to Bolivia to impose on the nation's armed forces, and again charged with imposing on the SA when he returned to Germany in the early 1930s. When the situation threatened to get out of hand, he issued public appeals to cease 'excesses and acts of indiscipline', and denounced 'unscrupulous characters' within the organization, 'mainly Communist spies', who were creating havoc and bringing the Nazi movement into disrepute.[25] First and foremost Röhm was a soldier – his autobiography begins with the words: 'I am a soldier. I contemplate the world from my soldierly standpoint.'[26] War, he said, stimulated a people, peace sapped a nation's will. Only the soldier could rescue Germany. Politics and diplomacy had never really been part of the history of Germany: 'the sword has always determined the greatness of its history.'[27] He had already acquired this sense of soldierly identity before the war; it was not a product of an inability to adjust from wartime service to peacetime realities. Being a soldier meant discipline and order. Röhm was indeed an able and hard-working administrator, remembered after the war by a former friend as 'the most gifted general staff officer, an extraordinarily talented organizer and a man of clear judgement'.[28] It was not the camaraderie of life at the battlefront that he missed in the new social and political world of the Weimar Republic, but the order and stability of the world before August 1914, when he had enjoyed a settled and steadily improving place in society, backed by the solid bourgeois lifestyle of his family and the privileged world of the Bavarian officer corps. He was hardly a typical representative of a 'lost generation' of front-line soldiers, since the majority of the working-class rank and file were left wing in their political orientation. Rather, it was the conservative political and social identity of the overwhelmingly monarchist officer corps to which he belonged, which was lost when their life was shattered by the defeat of 1918 and the outbreak of the revolution.

In justifying the 'Night of the Long Knives', Hitler, along with Goebbels's propaganda apparatus, made veiled but unmistakable reference to the homosexuality of Röhm and some of the other leading Brownshirts.[29] Historians have tended to play down this aspect of their lives, not knowing, perhaps, how to relate it to their politics. The pioneering studies of fascism and sexuality by the late George L. Mosse have overcome this reticence, however, along with the emergence of the serious study of homosexuality and gender relations in the past.[30] The recent biography by Eleanor Hancock is the first to deal with Röhm's sexuality directly and in detail. Male homosexual practices were illegal in Germany according to Paragraph 175 of the Reich Criminal Code of 1871, still in force throughout both the Weimar Republic and the Third Reich, so they were perforce conducted in secret, though in the clubs and bars of 1920s Berlin it was very much an open secret. Hancock shows that it was not until 1924 that Röhm came to terms with his sexual orientation, but after this he was a regular customer in Berlin's gay bars and bathhouses, writing privately that 'The Turkish bath there is however in my opinion the summit of human happiness.'[31] When the British reporter Sefton Delmer, who had got to know many of the leading Nazis, went out for an evening with Röhm, who wrongly thought he was a British government agent, looking for the indiscretions for which the SA chief was well known, they ended up at the Eldorado, described by Delmer as:

> ... a drab dance bar of stale cigarette smoke and soap and sweat, where the much powdered and painted hostesses were all boys dressed up as girls with wigs and falsies and low-cut evening dresses. I was a trifle shocked when one of the 'girls', a huge creature with a very prominent Adam's apple and a distinctly blue chin under the layer of powder, sat down uninvited at our table and began to talk to Röhm about what appeared to have been a most enjoyable party they had been on together several nights earlier. 'Now there you have it, Herr Stabschef,' I said rashly, when 'she' had left us. 'No female tart would approach an ex-client like that and talk to him of their night together in the presence of a stranger.' Röhm, who normally was open and unashamed about his pick-ups and enjoyed joking about his 'weakness', was suddenly huffy. 'I am not his client. I am his commanding officer,' he said with complete seriousness. 'He is one of my stormtroopers!'[32]

Röhm's diatribes against the moral hypocrisy of German society derived from his belief that sexuality should be openly acknowledged rather than fearfully hidden. He saw no reason to feel guilty or ashamed about his own sexual orientation, and continued throughout his life to be a practising Protestant, another aspect of his life that underpinned his faith in openness and honesty. He did not conceal his homosexuality, except from his parents, and initially, at least, Hitler defended him from the rumours circulating about his gay lifestyle (the SA, he declared in 1931, 'is no moral institution for the education of young ladies, but an association of rough fighters'). But as Röhm became more prominent in the Nazi movement, his private life began to get him into trouble.[33]

While he was in Bolivia, Dr Karl-Günther Heimsoth, a physician who campaigned for homosexual rights, wrote to Röhm about a passage in his autobiography criticizing hypocrisy. Reading between the lines, Heimsoth correctly interpreted this as a plea for the legalization of male homosexuality, and the two men began a remarkably frank correspondence which, unluckily for Röhm, was seized during a police raid on Heimsoth's home in Berlin. The letters were leaked to the Social Democratic Party and published in March 1932 by the Social Democratic Reichstag deputy Helmuth Klotz. Characteristically, the Social Democrats took their stand on the same primly conservative moral basis as they had before the war on the occasion of another homosexual scandal, involving the Kaiser and his close friend Prince Philipp of Eulenburg.[34] Four Nazi Reichstag deputies responded to Klotz's revelations by physically assaulting him in the foyer of the Reichstag building.[35] Hitler ignored the scandal, commenting once more that he was not interested in Röhm's private life, though he did remove the Hitler Youth from Röhm's control by making its leadership directly responsible to himself. Shocked by the publicity given to the subsequent trial, Röhm abandoned the bathhouses of Berlin in favour of using one of his sexual partners, and then his manservant, to procure young men for him, and paying them for their services and their silence. Röhm managed in this way to keep himself out of the police files and the newspapers, but there is no doubt that the scandal of the Heimsoth letters did some damage to his reputation both within the Party and beyond. It was not surprising that Hitler's victims in the 'Night of the Long Knives' included Heimsoth himself as well as Röhm and other homosexuals in the top ranks of the SA, giving him the opportunity of presenting the murders as a morally justified operation against the entirely imaginary threat of a 'Röhm-*putsch*'.[36] Alfred Rosenberg, indeed, thought that the killings were undertaken mainly in order to root out homosexuals from the top ranks of the SA.[37]

Like Röhm, Heimsoth was a far right-wing nationalist, and both men were also influenced by *Sex and Character*, a large volume by the male supremacist and antisemitic writer Otto Weininger, published in 1903, and the German youth movement prophet Hans Blüher's *Die Rolle der Erotik in der männlichen Gesellschaft*, published in 1919. These works were part of a larger subculture of far-right and in part esoteric writers and publicists to which Heimsoth belonged – he was for example a keen student of astrology – and Röhm found the subculture's ideas congenial because he could unite its advocacy of the rule of a homoerotically charged 'band of brothers' with his belief in a world dominated by soldierly institutions and militaristic values. His murder, and the ensuing publicity, much of it damaging to the Nazi movement, which had apparently tolerated or even encouraged homosexuality in its ranks, provided Himmler with the opportunity to push the Nazis into a diametrically opposed position in which male homosexuality, quite wrongly as the example of Röhm shows, was seen as a sign of weakness and effeminacy. Before long, the law against homosexuality was toughened up, and homosexuals released from state prisons after completing their sentence for violating paragraph 175 of the Criminal Code found themselves taken off by the Gestapo to a concentration camp.[38]

None of this was relevant to the initiation of the 'Night of the Long Knives'. Leading a paramilitary movement that by 1934 was forty times larger than the official German Army, Röhm, searching for a new role for it after the Nazi seizure of power, came up with the idea of turning it into a kind of national militia, which by its very nature could only be a defensive organization. For Hitler and the armed forces, however, what was needed was an *offensive* organization, armed and drilled in preparation for the launch of a new European war that would reverse the disastrous outcome of the First World War. Röhm was murdered because his plans threatened to get in the way of Hitler's, not because, as Hitler claimed, he was plotting to plunge Germany into the chaos of permanent revolution, whatever that might mean (and there is no evidence that it really meant anything at all). Whatever else he was, Röhm was not a revolutionary.[39] The common portrayal of him in the literature as a mindless thug is also wide of the mark. As Hancock has noted:

> He collected engravings, read the German literary classics, and befriended artists like Carl Anton Reichel and opera singers like Hans Beer. He was an excellent piano player and frequently entertained his friends with

spontaneous piano recitals. Like Adolf Hitler, he was a passionate Wagnerian. In the period from 1926 to 1928, he was repeatedly the guest of Siegfried and Winifred Wagner in Haus Wahnfried at Bayreuth.[40]

He was well known for his lavish entertaining, and for the care he took over his dress and appearance, despite the disfiguring scar on his face. People who met him often commented on the strong scent of perfume that wafted into the room when he entered. For all this, however, he was still at heart a soldier, for whom, as for a number of other leading Nazis, politics was a continuation of war by other means. Enemies were to be treated as they would have been on the battlefield, with ruthless and unbridled violence. 'The Germans,' he explained, 'have forgotten how to hate.'[41] Röhm encouraged the torture and brutalization of Nazism's opponents, above all during the seizure of power in 1933, and felt no guilt about breaking the law in the process: they were the enemy, and deserved to suffer and die. At the same time, this essentially simplistic view of the world made it difficult for him to understand the compromises, deals and manoeuvres that were the principal currency of the political world, even under Hitler as Chancellor. Despite his personal closeness to Hitler, he was never part of the Nazi leader's inner decision-making circle and always maintained a degree of autonomy within the Nazi movement. 'A soldier,' he declared, 'knows no compromise.'[42] For all their differences, he was loyal to Hitler and put his faith in him. This was his undoing in the end.

5
The Policeman: Heinrich Himmler

On the evening of Friday 31 July 1942, the disillusioned Italian Fascist writer and newspaper reporter Curzio Malaparte found himself in the Lapland town of Rovaniemi, where there was a German military base. Late in the evening, after dinner, he was invited by General Eduard Dietl, the German commanding officer in northern Finland, to take part in a traditional sauna, an offer one does not lightly refuse when visiting the country. 'I thought,' wrote Malaparte, that

> I recognized one of the naked men seated on the lowest shelf. Sweat was streaming down his high-cheekboned face, in which nearsighted eyes, stripped of their glasses, glittered with a whitish, soft light, that is seen in the eyes of fish. He carried his head high with an air of arrogant insolence... He sat with his hands resting on his knees like a punished schoolboy. Between his forearms protruded a little rosy swollen drooping belly, the navel strangely in relief, so that it stood out against that tender rosiness like a delicate rosebud – a child's navel in an old man's belly... Large drops of sweat flowing down his chest glided over the skin of that soft belly and gathered in the hair like dew on a bush. The man seemed to be dissolving in water before our eyes... In a twinkling of an eye only a pool of perspiration on the floor would be left of him.

The man was Heinrich Himmler, head of the SS and chief architect of the Holocaust.[1]

Dietl led Malaparte into the room and raised his arm with a shout of '*Heil Hitler!*' Himmler rose to his feet and, still stark naked, returned the salute. His gesture was mistaken for the signal to begin the traditional ending to the sauna, in which the participants flog each other with small bunches of silver-birch twigs before rushing out into the snow. 'The other men,' Malaparte's narrative continued:

... raised their birch switches and began hitting each other first; then, by common consent, with ever-increasing energy, they applied their switches to Himmler's shoulders and back ... At first Himmler tried to fend them off, shielding his face with his arms, and laughed, but it was forced laughter revealing rage and fear ... Finally Himmler saw the door of the sauna open behind us, stretched out his arms to push his way through and ran out of the door, pursued by the naked men, who never ceased to hit him, and fled towards the river, into which he dived.

'Naked Germans,' Malaparte commented, 'are wonderfully defenceless ... They are no longer frightening.'

Malaparte's imagination often ran away with him, and this improbable story seems almost too absurd to be true.[2] Yet the publication in 1999 of Himmler's official diary provides corroboration. In any case, Himmler's visit to Finland was far more than recreational. During discussions with the government in Helsinki, he pressed the country's rulers to hand over foreign Jews living there, to be taken to the death camps. A mere 150 in number, they posed no more of a threat to Germany than did the Jews in other countries. Although the Finnish secret police began drawing up lists, word got out, and there were protests both within the government and in the general public. Eight Jews were deported to Auschwitz in the end, of whom only one survived.[3] The episode was a striking demonstration of the ideological obsessiveness of the head of the German SS, just as his behaviour in the sauna illustrated Himmler's personal cowardice and physical weakness.

Heinrich Himmler has attracted an unusual degree of social and intellectual snobbery from historians. Joachim Fest called him 'utterly mediocre', 'colourless', 'a romantically eccentric petty bourgeois'.[4] Hugh Trevor-Roper described him as an 'utterly insignificant man, common, pedantic, and mean'.[5] The German historian Karl Dietrich Bracher, in his classic study *The German Dictatorship*, called him a 'romantically overwrought petty-bourgeois with the hint of the pedantic bureaucrat ... colourlessly average and dependent, but devoid of feeling'.[6] His American biographer Richard Breitman characterized him as 'dull, pedantic and humourless – totally without flair'.[7] Contemporaries took a similar view. Hans-Georg Eismann, a military man who worked with him in the final phase of the war, described him as entirely ordinary-looking, with 'the face of the average citizen'.[8] Yet such dismissive judgements leave some key questions unanswered. How could a man so mediocre and so characterless attain such power in the Third Reich? What attracted him to Nazism in the first place? Only recently has the documentation become available to permit a reassessment of his character. The first fully researched and comprehensive biography, by Peter Longerich, based on a vast range of sources, including Himmler's office diary for 1941–42, came out in 2008, superseding all previous studies. But since then, fresh publications have further added to our knowledge, including an edition of his letters, which had been scattered across a number of different countries and brought together by his great-niece, the writer Katrin Himmler, and the historian Michael Wildt; and, not least, the second volume of his office diary, covering the years 1943–45.[9] These important publications allow us to paint a picture of Himmler that is rather different from the one that has been familiar since the 1960s.

Heinrich Himmler was not, to begin with, a 'petty bourgeois'. On the contrary, he was born, on 7 October 1900, into a respectable upper-middle-class family. His father, Gebhard Himmler, was not only a university graduate and a teacher at the prestigious Wilhelm Grammar School in Munich, but also served for three years in the 1890s as private tutor to a member of the Bavarian royal family, the Wittelsbachs. Gebhard and his family were solid members of the *Bildungsbürgertum*, the 'educated bourgeoisie', a prestigious and widely respected social stratum in Imperial Germany: economically well off, socially secure, and strongly identified with the nation and its mainstream cultural traditions, social institutions and ruling elites. As a state grammar school 'professor', Gebhard was also a state civil servant (*Beamte*), with all that implied in the hierarchical world of Wilhelmine Germany. Gebhard brought up his children – three sons, of whom Heinrich was the second oldest – with a good knowledge of Ancient Greek, Latin, Classics and History, and devoted himself conscientiously to their education and upbringing. He was in no sense a brutal, overbearing or authoritarian father. But the values he prized were not those of the typical 'humanist grammar school' as described, for instance, in Lion Feuchtwanger's great novel *The Oppermanns*, the values of a critical, questioning, independent mind: as the letters he wrote to his sons prior to his departure on a journey to Greece in 1910 stressed, they were instead obedience, hard work, devotion to duty, manly toughness and adoration of the Fatherland.[10] At school, Heinrich Himmler was not an isolated, unsuccessful or marginal figure: he seems to have had plenty of friends, and his school report for 1913–14 called him 'an apparently very able student who by tireless hard work, burning ambition and very lively participation achieved the best results in the class'.[11]

We know a great deal about Himmler's adolescence and young adulthood because he kept a diary throughout these years, instructed to do so by his father. It makes clear that the First World War, which broke out when Heinrich was thirteen, was a decisive event in his life. Instead of the academic career mapped out for him by his father, he decided he would be a soldier. But while, thanks to his father's influence in high places, he was enrolled in the army as an officer cadet and underwent military training, he never managed to experience any military action. Like many other young men of his generation, he saw this as a failure and tried to make up for it by a commitment to 'soldierly' values, a vision of politics as warfare, a readiness to use violence against whomever he identified as an enemy, and a lack of restraint in seeing through their political project that have led one historian to call them 'the generation of the unconditional'. This did not necessarily mean they were right-wing extremists – similar characteristics could be found in many young men of the same age, though working-class rather than bourgeois – who rejected the moderate traditions of Social Democracy and found their way into the Communist movement – but in Himmler's case it meant almost inevitably a gravitation towards the extreme right, given the conservative nationalist milieu in which he had grown up.[12] His self-identification as a soldier may also have been a kind of compensation for the fact that he was a sickly child, unathletic, frequently ill, and as an adolescent and young man, unable to withstand the physical rigours of military training; but it was also a reflection of a legitimation of violence in the war that carried over into the politics of the post-war era.

At the end of the war, he was discharged from the army, unable to continue because the peace settlement imposed a limit of 100,000 men on the strength of Germany's armed forces. After graduating from school, he enrolled in the agricultural faculty of the Technical University in Munich, where right-wing ex-officers pursued the anti-urban ideas of the *Artamanen*, a 'blood-and-soil' group, founded before the war, that advocated a 'return to the soil' for 'Aryan' nationalists. He joined a duelling fraternity and the army reserve: 'I'm just a soldier and I'm staying a soldier,' he wrote in his diary, adding that the uniform was 'always and again the dearest clothing for me'.[13] He went on to join two paramilitary organizations when the military reserve was disbanded at the insistence of the Allies. Crucial here was the fact that he was based in Munich, which after the revolutionary regimes of 1918–19 had been violently overthrown was a hotbed of ultra-right politics. His involvement, his growing political radicalism and his deepening antisemitism were not, as some have claimed, evidence of a rebellion against his father, but were an extension of his father's German-nationalist politics and earned with his full endorsement. Heinrich's elder brother Gebhard also entered with him into violent far-right paramilitary politics. Himmler's approval of the murder on 24 June 1922 of Foreign Minister Rathenau by right-wing extremists, who hated his politics of compromise and linked them to the fact that he was a Jew, was far from unusual in nationalist circles. Himmler's radicalism was deepened, however, by the economic crisis of inflation, then hyperinflation, that hit Germany just as he graduated. His parents were unable any longer to support him, and he was forced to earn a living by working in an artificial fertilizer factory for a year, from September 1922 to September 1923. Rudderless, his military ambitions thwarted, cut adrift from the bourgeois prosperity and security in which he had grown up, he was quite clearly downwardly socially mobile.

Searching for some kind of coherent ideological commitment, he read widely and deeply, imbibing ideas about Germanic heroism, racial purity, and the intrinsic evils of the Jews and the Jesuits. He also interested himself in the occult, in spiritualism and medieval mythology, and broke with the Catholicism of his youth as a result. These ideas led him to the fledgling Nazi Party; but, unusually, it was not Hitler who brought him into the movement – indeed, at this stage he did not even meet the Nazi leader. On 9 November he took part in the attempted coup of the Nazis, the beer-hall *putsch*, but not in the main action, when Hitler and his followers were dispersed by the police as they marched on the centre of Munich. Instead, he was photographed holding aloft the banner of an allied organization, the *Reichskriegsflagge* (Reich War Flag), a small paramilitary group led by the future head of the stormtroopers, Ernst Röhm, when it occupied the War Ministry building. He was joined by his elder brother Gebhard, who can be seen in the photograph standing by him. When the *putsch* failed, Himmler left the building with the rest of the group under a negotiated settlement and escaped without being charged.[14]

In the aftermath of this fiasco, Himmler plunged deeper into far-right politics. He started to work for Gregor Strasser, a leading Bavarian Nazi who had taken part in the *putsch* but was released from prison when he was elected to the Bavarian State Parliament and then to the Reichstag. Himmler engaged in organizational activities and began to give speeches, particularly on agrarian issues. When Strasser became the Party's propaganda chief, and then, in 1928, head of the Reich Party Organization, Himmler gained extensive new duties and responsibilities. He had found his career. The jobs he undertook for the Party did not pay well, however, and when he got married that same year, to Margarete (Marga) Boden, a nurse, seven years older than he was, the couple soon ran into financial difficulties. Setting up house in a village near Munich, they tried to supplement his income and the money she brought into the marriage with a small-scale agricultural enterprise, with chickens and turkeys and a pig for fattening. But the hens did not lay well and half the newborn chicks died. This brief and unsuccessful period of farming has given rise to the later and persistent legend that Himmler was a 'chicken breeder', and the claim that his experience with hens was later transferred to his attitude towards humans. But in fact it was entirely incidental to his life, and he continued to draw his main income from politics. More importantly, the relationship between Heinrich and Margarete was a close one, possessive and claustrophobic. When Heinrich was away, they exchanged daily letters, which are full of conventional, even cliché-ridden expressions of love, along with constant demands for the other's affection, and assurances of ideological conformity ('but we must share the same views, it can't be anything else'). The couple moved exclusively in Nazi and far-right circles, and showed little interest in, or sympathy for, people outside their immediate, highly politicized environment.[15]

Himmler's climb up the Party hierarchy was rapid. It owed a great deal to his relationship with Strasser, but he soon transferred his loyalty to his successor as propagandist-in-chief of the Nazi Party, Joseph Goebbels, much to his advantage. Initially he bore the responsibility for organizing events for leading Party speakers, and since this also involved providing security, he was made Deputy Reich Leader of the SS, Hitler's protection squad, set up in 1925. He applied himself to reforming the administration of the SS, and in January 1929 Hitler appointed him Reich Leader of the SS, leading to his resignation from the propaganda department after the Nazis' remarkable success in the 1930

Reichstag election. Encountering the turbulent and disorderly politics of the stormtroopers, a far larger organization to whose movement the SS was nominally subordinate, Himmler made unconditional loyalty to Hitler the central precept of the SS, using the motto provided by the Nazi leader: 'Your honour means loyalty' (*Deine Ehre heisst Treue*). He focused on trying, with mixed results, to turn the SS into an elite organization, disciplined, orderly and composed of fit young men from a solid social and above all racial background. He introduced a new set of ranks, designed smart new black uniforms, established a leadership corps consisting mostly of men born between 1890 and 1900 who had served as officers in the war, and sped up the recruitment process, building an organization of more than 40,000 men by the summer of 1932 – an impressive number, but still far smaller than Ernst Röhm's Brownshirt movement.[16]

Himmler's loyalty to Röhm, which continued during the latter's years in exile in Bolivia following the failure of the 1923 beer-hall *putsch*, smoothed relations between the SS and the Brownshirt movement when Röhm returned to lead it early in 1931. The SS was just as inclined to violence as its parent organization, and played a central role in a campaign of murder and terror in East Prussia in 1932, following 'the command of the Reich Leader of the SS to kill the Communist chieftains'. But it was a more targeted violence than that of the stormtroopers, whose numbers now swelled into the hundreds of thousands. Following Hitler's appointment as Reich Chancellor on 30 January 1933, and his effective assumption of dictatorial power with the Reichstag Fire Decree, the Nazis moved to take over the running of the federated states. The stormtroopers arrested Communists and Social Democrats all over Germany, along with a small number of real or suspected opponents of the Nazis, and incarcerated them in makeshift prisons and torture centres, beating and humiliating them, killing hundreds, and releasing the survivors only on their promise of abstaining from political activities thereafter. Himmler was appointed acting police chief in Munich, and then in Bavaria as a whole. He ordered the mass arrests of leftists, followed by leading figures in the conservative Bavarian People's Party, which soon dissolved itself. He set up a concentration camp in the town of Dachau to hold them. Staffed by SS men, it was at first so badly run, with unbridled violence and corruption, that the ensuing scandal obliged Himmler to fire the commandant and appoint a new one,

Theodor Eicke, who implemented a fresh set of camp rules that became standard across camps in Germany.[17]

By the middle of 1933, Himmler had enormously extended his power in the security apparatus of the Third Reich. Few comments about his personality have been as little heeded by historians as the attribution to him in his school report of 'burning ambition' and 'tireless hard work', and none has been as perceptive. Systematically using his wide network of colleagues and acquaintances, securing support from key regional Party figures by appointing them to high ranks in the SS, and building on the reputation for loyalty and orderliness he had established for the SS, he persuaded one state after another to appoint him head of its political police force. The greatest prize in this respect was Prussia, which covered more than half the country and contained over half its population. Here the political police were in the hands of Hermann Göring, but Himmler exploited the power struggles between Göring and Reich Interior Minister Wilhelm Frick, along with their mutual alarm at the indiscipline of the Brownshirts, to get himself appointed head of the Prussian political police (the Gestapo) in April 1934. The 'Night of the Long Knives', in which the SS played the central role, completed Himmler's rise to the top rank of Nazi leaders; though he had not played a significant part in its preparation, he was without doubt its principal beneficiary. The only downside of the affair for the SS was its over-confident staging of an abortive coup in Austria, frustrated by the refusal of the country's Nazi stormtroopers to take part.[18]

By 1936 Himmler had succeeded in outmanoeuvring his opponents in the Nazi regime to establish complete control over the Reich's police forces, including the Gestapo, even though this was still under the nominal control of Göring. Himmler justified the centralization of the repressive apparatus of the regime into an increasingly unified state-protection corps under his leadership by exaggerating the dangers of the Communist resistance. The task was above all preventive, the aim being to ensure 'that the Jewish-Bolshevik Revolution of the subhuman can never again be unfolded in Germany, the heart of Europe, from within or without by emissaries from outside'.[19] This aim, he believed, had not been pursued up to this point with the necessary ruthlessness. The concentration camps were merged and closed until only five were left, containing fewer than 4,000 political prisoners regarded as too dangerous to be released, such as the former German Communist leader Ernst

Thälmann. This did not mean, of course, that there was nothing left for the Gestapo to do. On the contrary, the decline in numbers was a result of the promulgation in 1933–34 of a whole raft of decrees that passed over the task of repression to the state police (including the Gestapo), the state courts (augmented by special political tribunals), and the regular state prisons and penitentiaries, where by 1935 official statistics revealed that 23,000 political prisoners were held. A gradual merger of the 'normative' and 'prerogative' state was taking place, sealed just after the outbreak of war by the unification of the SS and police forces in the Reich Security Head Office.[20]

In 1937–38 Himmler enforced an extension of the concentration camps' role to include the 'preventive detention' of 'asocials', petty criminals, vagrants, the 'work-shy' and homosexuals. Himmler was particularly concerned with homosexuality, which he considered a threat to the masculinity of the SS and the future of the nation. It is tempting to see in his personal horror of male homosexuality – which he ignored in the patron and protector of his early years, Ernst Röhm, for political reasons – an awareness of his own deficits in terms of masculine toughness and physical aggression. At any rate, in the close-knit groups of men who made up the SS, he was not going to allow homosexuality to take hold. In 1941, announcing a new edict from Hitler providing the death penalty for homosexual acts in the SS and police force, Himmler described these bodies as 'protagonists in the struggle for the extermination of homosexuality in the German people'. Male homosexuality, as we have seen, was an offence in Germany under the Criminal Law Code of 1871, so offenders were arrested by the police, tried in the courts, and sentenced to a state prison, but Himmler both sharpened the legal definition of a homosexual act and arranged for many homosexuals to be re-arrested on their release and transferred to a concentration camp. However, early on in the war he declared the battle had been won: 'On the whole, however, at least the broad mass of our young people have come away from this deviation.'[21] Indeed, fully half of the 50,000 men arrested for homosexuality under the Third Reich were arrested in the period 1937–39, and the campaign was scaled down thereafter.[22] Under the conditions of war, Himmler evidently concluded that he had more pressing matters to deal with.[23]

Himmler's obsession with combating homosexuality, above all in the SS itself, was only one of the increasing number of personal quirks that became more prominent the more power he accrued. As his biographer Peter Longerich has remarked: 'The organization and aims of the state protection corps were influenced by his phobias and prejudices, his fads and fancies, and his passions to an almost astonishing extent.'[24] These included a hatred of the Catholic Church in whose faith he had grown up. Himmler regarded Catholicism as 'Asiatic', a doctrine devised and propagated by Jews to preach a gospel of love and submission that would undermine everything that made the Germanic race great. Not only was the Catholic priesthood a 'homosexual male order' in itself, it also advocated a prudish, restrictive sexual morality that placed damaging restrictions on the Germanic race's drive to reproduce and strengthen itself. Since the early 1920s he had been an enthusiast for the pre-Christian Germanic religious cults idolized since before World War I by the ideologists of the racist ultra-right. He pressured SS officers and men to formally resign from the Church, and instituted pseudo-Germanic ceremonies for them to replace Christian ones, including celebrations of the summer and winter solstice (the latter to be named 'Yule' in place of Christmas), May Day, weddings and funerals. He set up a pseudo-scientific research institute, the *Ahnenerbe* ('Ancestral Heritage'), to dig up accounts of early medieval rituals and to pursue the imagined origins of the 'Aryan' race in Tibet, to where he dispatched SS officers to conduct measurements of the local inhabitants in order to establish their racial characteristics.[25] Himmler's foundation in 1935 of the *Lebensborn* ('Spring of Life') maternity homes for unmarried mothers, nominally run by a voluntary association, but in fact part of the SS, expressed his belief in a racial policy unrestricted by Christian morality; a woman would only be admitted after an examination of herself and the child's father. Indeed, theoretically at least, any man who sought admission to the SS had to pass a strict racial examination in order to qualify, though in practice the criteria became increasingly lax as the organization grew, above all during the war.[26]

Himmler's personal foibles emerge most strongly from his correspondence, in which he dispensed instructions and advice on an almost inconceivable variety of topics. Nothing seemed too trivial for his attention, all the way down to the quality of the porridge served in the *Lebensborn* homes. ('Boiling porridge with full-cream milk or skimmed milk', wrote his adjutant on 9 January 1944, 'does not correspond to the wishes of the *Reichsführer-SS*. Porridge must only be boiled with water.')[27] He told his officers to get married, or stop drinking, or deal more effectively with flies in their building. His correspondence for August and September 1938, just to take a random example, included instructions to individual SS officers to take a photograph of runes found on a sculpture in the Archaeological Museum in Florence, not to accept hunting invitations without his approval, to gather information about the history of the North Sea island of Heligoland, to abstain from smoking if they had been ill, and to begin a collection of the sayings of Adolf Hitler.[28] In all this, the influence of his father, the headmaster, can dimly be discerned: Professor Gebhard Himmler too concerned himself with his sons' conduct down to the last detail, issuing for instance a letter with elaborate instructions on the conduct of life before he travelled abroad in case he failed to return. A strong element of paternalism can be seen in Himmler's treatment of his underlings, concerning himself with their health and that of their families, sending congratulations and presents when a new baby was born to them, or disciplining them if they overstepped the mark or failed to follow his orders.[29]

The negative side of Himmler's micromanagement could easily degenerate into fantasies that had more than an element of sadism in them. In August 1944, for example, he announced his intention of setting up, 'after the war', a 'fly chamber' in which, while reading scientific literature about insects, SS leaders and members of the police force who had refused to take seriously the idea of dealing with the 'fly- and mosquito nuisance' were to be shut in with 'hundreds and thousands' of flies and mosquitoes and allow themselves to be 'caressed' by the insects.[30] Himmler took a particular interest in the medical experiments carried out on concentration-camp inmates, in violation of all ethical standards in medicine. Those who criticized the subjection of selected prisoners to research in which they were plunged into icy cold water, often with fatal results, to see how long a downed pilot could survive in the sea, he viewed as traitors and would report their names to their superiors.[31] Eccentricities such as these have led some historians to write off Himmler as an oddball and treat him as a pedantic administrator who simply carried out Hitler's orders like an automaton, without pausing to reflect on their morality, until he became almost by default the most deadly of the Third Reich's desktop murderers. Yet it was precisely his own ideas and his drive to implement them that propelled him forward.[32]

The core of Himmler's personal ideology was an unconditional belief in the principle that whatever served Germany's interests was morally justified. As he said on 4 October 1943, in a speech to leading SS officers in Posen (today Poznań in Poland):

> One principle must be absolutely basic for the SS man: we have to be honest, decent, loyal and comradely to those of our own blood, and to no one else. I'm totally indifferent to how the Russian is doing, or the Czech. We will get for ourselves whatever good blood is present in the peoples of our kind if necessary by stealing their children and bring them up amongst ourselves. Whether other peoples live in affluence or whether they perish from hunger interests me only insofar as we require them as slaves for our culture, otherwise it doesn't interest me. Whether 10,000 Russian women drop dead from exhaustion while they are digging a tank ditch, or whether they don't, interests me only insofar as the tank ditch is completed for Germany.[33]

This crude and vulgar declaration expressed among other things the thinking behind one of Himmler's most ambitious projects: the racial reordering of the whole of Europe. Securing an appointment to the newly created position of Reich Commissioner for the Strengthening of Ethnic Germandom, he set in motion a vast plan to bring ethnic Germans from the Soviet Union and other parts of Eastern Europe back into the Reich, with the agreement, at least during the period of their alliance, from 1939 to 1941, of Stalin and the Soviet authorities. As an inducement the migrants were offered free access to farms forcibly evacuated by dispossessed Polish peasants. In fact, the scheme did not get very far, since the process of screening the incoming ethnic Germans for ethnic purity and political reliability took too long. This was to be the curtain-raiser for a gigantic programme of ethnic restructuring in which, according to the 'General Plan for the East', which became official German government policy in 1942, between 30 and 45 million 'Slavs' were to perish from hunger and disease, making way in the medium to long term for 'Aryan' settlers all the way across East-Central Europe.[34]

When he spoke of 'decency', Himmler meant self-control, a virtue he valued above all in himself. Himmler was not personally corrupt, as so many other leading Nazis were; he lived comfortably but did not amass great stores of art objects or accumulate large collections of automobiles and the like. He worked long hours, travelling incessantly to inspect his fiefdoms, visiting concentration camps and observing murder actions, all without any outward display of emotion. He occasionally disciplined SS officers whose adherence to the basic principle of 'decency' he found lacking. The classic expression of his belief in 'decency' was in his notorious speech to senior SS officers in Posen on 6 October 1943:

> The sentence 'The Jews must be exterminated', with its few words, gentlemen, is easily spoken. For the man who has to carry it out, it is the absolute hardest and most difficult that there is ... We were confronted with the question: what about the women and children? – I decided to find an absolutely clear solution here too. So I did not regard myself as entitled to exterminate the men – in other words, to kill or have killed – and leave their children to grow up as avengers upon our sons and grandsons. The difficult decision had to be taken to let this people vanish from the earth. For the organization that had to carry out this task, it was the toughest that we had so far. It has been carried out, without – as I think I can say – our men and our leaders suffering damage in spirit and soul.

Himmler repeated these sentiments in speeches delivered to leading generals at Sonthofen the following year.[35]

Himmler was here consciously expressing his view that what he – and they – were doing was a historically necessary crime that would be regarded as such in the rest of the world. In this way, he was drawing them in to complicity and committing them to continue fighting for Germany in every way possible, including – as he saw it – ensuring its racial future by murdering Jewish women and children in their millions. In his speech of 4 October 1943, he referred directly to the extermination of the Jewish people: 'Most of you will know what it is like to see 100 corpses lying side by side or 500 or 1,000 of them. To have coped with this and – except for cases of human weakness – have remained decent, that has made us tough. This is an unwritten – never to be written – and yet glorious page in our history.'[36] Yet, unlike Hitler or Rosenberg, Himmler did not have a lifelong obsession with the imaginary threat posed to the 'Aryan' race by the Jews. Expressions of antisemitism are relatively rare in his letters, speeches and other writings, and insofar as they are present, they begin to appear relatively late in his career, growing out of his earlier anti-Bolshevism. His references to Jews are neutral and impersonal in tone, and often hidden behind euphemisms. But he was clear in his own mind that the task of murdering them in their millions had been entrusted to him. On 18 December 1941, following a discussion with Hitler, he noted in his office diary: 'Jew question/to be exterminated as Partisans.'[37] 'The occupied eastern territories will be free of Jews,' he wrote on 28 July 1942. 'The Leader has laid the execution of this very serious command upon my shoulders. No one can take it away from me.'[38] This was what Himmler called on 18 January 1943 'the final solution of the European Jewish Question'.[39]

Himmler carried out these terrible deeds in the closest consultation with Hitler, to whom he deferred on every issue while at the same time influencing him in a variety of ways. If Hitler explicitly disagreed with one of his policies, such as the propagation of a 'Germanic' neo-pagan religion, Himmler played it down rather than abandoning it altogether. On central issues such as the persecution of the Jews, they scarcely differed. The closeness of their relationship, especially during the war, can be read in the second volume of Himmler's office diary. From January 1943 to March 1945 he met with Hitler on no fewer than 168 occasions; on average, that is, six times a month. The frequency of their meetings fluctuated over this period; it was at its greatest in the late summer and autumn of 1943, when the two had twenty-one meetings in August alone, and sixty over the months August to November. Particularly important and pressing topics of conversation included the military crisis caused by the overthrow of Mussolini at the end of July 1943, which necessitated the dispatch of German forces to Italy, including senior SS officers tasked with rounding up Italian Jews for deportation to Auschwitz. They also discussed the extermination of European Jews in the death camps; and decided on Hitler's appointment of the SS chief to replace Wilhelm Frick as Reich Minister of the Interior on 20 August, an occasion that marked Himmler's final triumph in the long-running power struggle between the two men and the complete subordination of the Ministry to the SS. As soon as he took over, Himmler symbolized this by requiring his officials to address him as *Reichsführer-SS*, not as Minister. His power increased even further following the unsuccessful attempt on Hitler's life by Colonel Claus von Stauffenberg on 20 July 1944, when Hitler appointed Himmler head of the reserve army, giving him the command of nearly two million men on the home front, where some leading officers of the regular army had backed the attempted coup for which Hitler's assassination was to have provided the signal. It was Himmler who drove forward the arrest, trial and execution of the plotters, obtained Hitler's permission to take their families into custody in what he called *Sippenhaft* (clan detention), and used the opportunity to carry out the 'arrest of S.P.D.- u. K.P.D. bosses', former officials of the Social Democratic and Communist parties, 5,000 of them in all. 'Thälmann,' he noted in his office diary on 14 August, referring to the former Communist leader Ernst Thälmann, '– is to be executed.'[40]

In July 1944, indeed, the pattern of Himmler's meetings with Hitler became more intense, with eleven in all, but most of these took place before Stauffenberg's bomb went off, and focused on the military disaster on the Eastern Front, in which the Red Army had annihilated the German Army Group Centre in 'Operation Bagration', resulting in the loss of 400,000 German soldiers. Himmler made good the deficit, if only temporarily, with units of the SS and the Waffen-SS, enlarging his sphere of military competence still further.[41] By the final phase of the war, as Göring's star was fading, Himmler had accrued to himself a degree of power second only to that of Hitler himself. The SS was expanding into one area after another, building for example an economic empire of considerable dimensions, helped by the rapid expansion of the use of concentration-camp inmates as a reservoir of forced labour, distributed in a vast network of sub-camps attached to various munitions production facilities and factories, which by the end of the war held over 700,000 inmates.

Despite his closeness to the Nazi dictator, however, and his conscientiousness in carrying out his orders, Himmler was not tied to him emotionally in the way that many other Nazi leaders were. Indeed, in implementing the genocide of Europe's Jews, he was not only following Hitler's instructions, he was also advancing them in a constant dialogue with Hitler, encouraging him and pushing him on to extend the scope of the Holocaust ever further. Yet as Germany's military situation began to deteriorate, Himmler also began secretly to put out feelers to the Western Allies, offering to surrender small groups of Jewish prisoners to them. His estrangement from Hitler deepened in January 1945 after the dictator put him in command of Army Group Vistula, a task which Himmler proved entirely unfit to carry out. Following a series of military failures Hitler dismissed him from the post in mid-March. Himmler's command had one effect, however: it made him realize how hopeless the military situation had become. In other respects, he was drifting rapidly into a whole new world of illusions. He initiated secret negotiations with Count Folke Bernadotte, of the Swedish Red Cross, about the release of Swedish concentration-camp prisoners, and then others in addition, believing he could play the role of an honest broker in bringing the war to an end. He opened discussions with the World Jewish Congress, which he assured that the atrocity stories circulating about the camps were untrue. He confidentially promised General de Gaulle an alliance with a defeated Germany against the victorious 'Anglo-Saxons'. Fatally, he also proposed a partial surrender to the Allies, who immediately rejected the offer and publicized it in the press. Enraged by Himmler's conduct, which he regarded as treacherous, Hitler used his political testament, written on 29 April 1945, the day before his suicide, to dismiss him from all his offices and expel him from the Nazi Party.[42]

In the first days of May 1945, Himmler tried to offer his services to Hitler's designated successor, Grand Admiral Karl Dönitz, in the belief that the SS would have a significant role to play in the post-war order. Whether in doing this he was trying to keep up appearances, or prevent himself being overcome by despair, is uncertain. In any case, the offer was rejected. Recognizing the realities of the situation, and fearing arrest and trial by the Allies, he went on the run, adopting a false name and forged papers, removing his spectacles, and putting a patch over his right eye. Accompanied by a small group of followers, he tried to make his way to the Harz Mountains, perhaps with the idea of going into hiding and eventually emigrating; certainly he wrote no testament or message to posterity, looking to survive in obscure and inglorious anonymity. But he was stopped by British troops on 21 May and taken into custody. Brought before an officer, he removed his disguise and revealed himself to be the former head of the SS. From their experience with other senior SS men, the British realized he probably had a cyanide capsule concealed in his mouth, but when the doctor conducting his medical examination attempted to remove it, Himmler jerked his head to one side, bit on the capsule, and collapsed. He was dead within fifteen minutes. Unlike other leading Nazis, he had not had the resolve to commit suicide as soon as he knew the situation was hopeless. Nor had he gone out fighting against the enemy. During his final weeks he had sought to disclaim responsibility for his actions. His squalid death, a hasty and ill-considered decision taken in order to avoid being held to account by the Allies for all the crimes he had committed, merely underlined the fact that he had failed to live up to the ideals he had prescribed for his men. None of them made any attempt after the war to rescue his reputation from the contempt of posterity.[43]

Throughout his life, Himmler seems to have done his best to follow the stern admonitions of his father to remain loyal and faithful as well as tough and industrious. In one respect, however, he deviated from this precept, perhaps following another principle, this time of his own, that Christian morality should not interfere with a man's prime duty, to perpetuate the German race. In 1936 a young, blonde woman, Hedwig Potthast, was appointed his private secretary. Born into a middle-class family in 1912, she was generally regarded as pretty and charming; Himmler's deputy Reinhard Heydrich was reported to have said that 'one could warm one's hands and feet on her'.[44] Her letters revealed her as ambitious for a glamorous life, in search of which she moved from the Rhineland to Berlin and attached herself to the SS. By 1938 Potthast and Himmler had fallen in love. Although he visited her seldom in the comfortable home he provided for her, mostly speaking with her on the telephone, they had two children together. Himmler kept all of this secret. Potthast became friendly with a few people in leading Nazi circles, such as the wives of Martin Bormann and Oswald Pohl, but the relationship cannot have satisfied her ambition, and met with the strong disapproval of her conventionally Catholic parents. After the war, she lived quietly until her death in 1994. She never commented on Himmler's activities in the extermination of the Jews or in any other respect.[45]

Himmler refused to divorce his wife, citing the fact that it was not her fault that she could not have any more children. And indeed, despite his new relationship, he remained close to Marga right through the war, exchanging letters and presents, worrying about each other's health, and sharing responsibility for their daughter Gudrun. But he believed that monogamy was unnatural for men, and siring children was a national duty; and Marga agreed. Wife and daughter were proud of what they saw as his achievements, sympathized with his complaints about overwork, and never expressed the slightest doubt about the correctness of what he was doing. For his part, Himmler tried to bring up his daughter and the couple's adopted son Gerhard as good Nazis, punishing Gerhard in particular, when, as often happened, he failed to live up to the demands of obedience and cleanliness placed on him. There was, in other words, no contrast between Himmler's life as a Nazi and his life as a father.[46]

Himmler's personality was not the emotionless void of historical legend. On the contrary, he was capable of love, as his relationship with Hedwig Potthast showed, and his correspondence with his wife Margarete illustrated, even if this was expressed in conventional romantic clichés. At the same time, he practised the iron self-control he felt he needed in order to devote himself to what he conceived as his duty. That duty was to the future of the German race as he saw it, not in the first place to Hitler, who was merely the vehicle through which that future would be realized. In this pursuit, conventional morality and Christian precepts were irrelevant. Anything that got in the way had to be eliminated with a ruthless consequentiality that knew no bounds. At the same time, Himmler was also part of wider currents in German society. His life constituted a perverted version of the traditional virtues of the *Bildungsbürgertum*, the educated middle class, the social stratum from which he came. His 'burning ambition' propelled him towards thoughts and deeds that would have horrified them. Yet his own family never disowned them. Himmler's parents were proud of the achievements he registered before their deaths, respectively in 1936 and 1941. Himmler's brothers Gebhard and Ernst were drawn into his circle as he acquired more power. They joined the Nazi Party and built modest but successful careers under its wing: Gebhard, a qualified teacher, in the Reich Education Ministry; Ernst in the Reich radio service, where he distinguished himself with an antisemitic denunciation of a junior colleague. Neither of them raised any objections to anything their brother Heinrich did as head of the SS; both in fact joined the SS, Gebhard rising some way through the officer ranks. Ernst was killed in action in Berlin, serving in the hastily recruited and poorly trained and equipped *Volkssturm*, on 2 May 1945. Gebhard served in the Waffen-SS until he was captured by the British at the end of the war; he took a job in educational administration again, was dismissed because of his past, but readmitted on appeal; he died in 1982. According to Ernst's granddaughter Katrin, the surviving members of the family dealt with the notoriety of Heinrich by denying any involvement in the crimes of Nazism and presenting the enrolment of Gebhard and Ernst as an involuntary consequence of his unwanted patronage. It was not until Katrin, who married an Israeli, began researching the family's history that the full extent of their denial was revealed.[47]

6

The Diplomat: Joachim von Ribbentrop

Few leading Nazis have met with as much contempt from historians and contemporaries as Joachim von Ribbentrop, Foreign Minister of the Third Reich from 1938 until the end of the war. For Joachim Fest, he was a 'pothouse politician', whose 'inflated busybody arrogance' and 'lifelong intellectual helplessness' were the foundations of 'a career of astounding incompetence'.[1] More than one historian has dismissed him as a 'champagne salesman' or 'wine merchant'.[2] His secretary, Reinhard Spitzy, called him 'pompous, conceited, and none too intelligent'. The diplomats with whom he worked said he was 'lazy and worthless', 'vain and ambitious'. The Soviet ambassador in London, Ivan Maisky, wrote in his diary of Ribbentrop's 'gaucherie' and 'tactlessness'.[3] Hermann Göring told Hitler that Ribbentrop was a 'stupid ass', and when Hitler objected that 'he knows quite a lot of important people in England', Göring riposted by telling him, 'My Führer, that may be right, but the bad thing is, *they* know *him*.'[4] Franz von Papen, Hitler's Vice-Chancellor in 1933–34 and subsequently ambassador to Austria and then Turkey, said Ribbentrop was 'a husk with no kernel, and an empty façade for a mind'.[5] The British Prime Minister Neville Chamberlain found Ribbentrop 'so stupid, so shallow, so self-centred and so self-satisfied, so totally devoid of intellectual capacity, that he never seems to take in what is said to him'.[6] The Swedish diplomat Count Folke Bernadotte thought he was 'a man of very small mental stature, and, moreover, rather ridiculous'.[7] At the Nuremberg War Crimes Trials, the other defendants treated Ribbentrop with 'open contempt', according to the prison psychiatrist Gustave Gilbert. Hjalmar Schacht, the former Finance Minister, called him 'a good-for-nothing, stupid weakling!' The Nazi Governor of Poland, Hans Frank, described him as a 'poor simpleton' who 'did not know anything about foreign affairs'. Franz von Papen called him a 'fool'.[8] Another prison psychiatrist, Douglas Kelley, thought he was 'an individual who, without actual ability, achieved a high position'.[9]

How, then, did Ribbentrop come to be appointed German Foreign Minister under Hitler and stay in the job for seven years? Why was he one of the few leading Nazis who had access to him without a prior appointment? What motivated him, what drove him? Why, after living an apparently unpolitical life, did he suddenly join the Nazi Party at the age of almost forty and rise so rapidly up the hierarchy, to the irritation and dismay of so many Nazis of the first hour? And why was he so loyal to Hitler, and Hitler to him? The first important factor in his character formation was that – like Hermann Göring – he came from a military background. His father, Richard Ulrich Friedrich Joachim Ribbentrop, like his grandfather and a number of his forebears, was a career officer in the Prussian Army. Shortly after Joachim's birth on 30 April 1893 in the Rhenish garrison town of Wesel, where his father was an artillery lieutenant, the family moved to Wilhelmshöhe, near Kassel, following Richard Ribbentrop's promotion to major. Not long afterwards he was transferred again, this time as a staff officer, to Metz, in Lorraine, which had been annexed to Germany after the Franco-Prussian War of 1870–71. The garrison at Metz was one of the largest in Germany, not surprisingly given its location on the French border, and, as adjutant to a leading general, Richard Ribbentrop was regarded as an officer with a golden future before him.[10]

The Prussian officer corps before the First World War, and in many respects long after, was a whole world in itself, to a considerable extent cut off from the rest of German society. Hierarchical, authoritarian, tied to aristocratic values, deeply wedded to an extreme conservative and authoritarian view of politics and the nation, it was only made more isolated by the fact that its officers tended to live in military-dominated garrison towns rather than among ordinary citizens.[11] Its ideal mode of behaviour was what in German was called *Kadavergehorsam* ('corpse-like obedience'). Growing up in a family dominated by a paternal disciplinarian whose behaviour exhibited these characteristics in abundance must have exercised a huge influence on Joachim. Outspoken, gruff, stiff and unbending, Major Ribbentrop was a man, so his son confessed in his memoirs, 'more feared than loved' by his children.[12]

By contrast, Joachim's mother, Johanne Sophia Hertwig, who came from a well-off family of landowners, was (according to her son) gentle and loving. She was a fine pianist, and often played for her children for hours on end. Her husband was also musical, and the children were brought up to play instruments as well, in a manner more typical of a bourgeois civilian family than a military one. In a sense, they represented in a single family the 'two Germanies' – cultured and militaristic – identified by writers about the German national character, particularly after the Second World War: an amalgam dramatically illustrated by an incident recalled by Joachim long afterwards. When he entered the Lycée Fabert in Metz in 1904, at the age of eleven, his father promised to give him a violin for Christmas if he did well. But although Joachim boasted that he would be top of the class, the end-of-term examinations placed him only thirty-second out of the fifty pupils. On hearing of this disgrace, his father gave him a sound thrashing, and took the violin away as a punishment. Although Joachim improved his placing at Easter sufficiently for his father to relent and give him back the violin, the incident rankled for the rest of his life.[13]

Ribbentrop was a passionate violinist from this moment onwards, and even in his teenage years considered becoming a professional player. He found solace in music at many points of his life, most notably when his mother died from tuberculosis on 28 February 1902 after a long decline. His fiddle, he confessed in his memoirs, 'was always my faithful companion, it's never deserted me', something, he added bitterly, one could never say of human beings. He took it with him wherever he went. In Metz, he learned horse-riding and tennis, both of which would serve him well in the social circles in which he aspired to move. In addition, from 1904 to 1908, during his years at the Lycée, he took courses in French, achieving a high degree of fluency – an essential precondition, as he would discover later on, for success in the world of international diplomacy, where French was still the normal medium of conversation even after World War I.[14]

After his wife's death, his father remarried, this time to Olga-Margarete von Prittwitz und Gaffron, an aristocratic woman from another ultra-conservative military family. Clearly the remarriage strengthened the major's political views and emboldened him to be ever more outspoken in expressing them. A passionate admirer of Bismarck, the major had been shocked and dismayed by the Iron Chancellor's dismissal in 1890 at the hands of the new German Emperor, Wilhelm II. In

1907 the journalist Maximilian Harden began a press campaign exposing the widespread homosexuality in the Kaiser's inner circle of male friends, centred on the diplomat Prince Eulenburg and involving many prominent individuals. The affair escalated into a major public scandal, with suicides, libel actions, prosecutions for homosexuality (illegal at the time), blackmail, and much more.[15] Richard Ribbentrop, by now a lieutenant-colonel, made his disgust with these goings-on at the Imperial Court more than clear, and gave it as his opinion on numerous occasions that the Kaiser himself must also be guilty of homosexual acts. Reports of his robust and repeated condemnation of Wilhelm II reached Berlin. This was *lèse-majesté* of no small order, and could not be tolerated, least of all in the Prussian officer corps. The major was cashiered in disgrace from the army, losing the right to wear military uniform or use his military title. His career was over.[16]

This calamity changed everything for the family. They had lost their position in the military world and their status in society. It must have been a terrible blow to their self-esteem. The now ex-major could not bear to remain in Metz, or even in Germany, and emigrated to Arosa, a village situated in a remote, German-speaking part of the Swiss Alps, taking the children with him and forcing them to leave school. For the next year and a half the family lived modestly off a legacy from the major's first wife, spending much of their time on long hikes, mountaineering, and learning how to ski and ride a bobsleigh, with the help of English friends. Winter sports were only a relatively recent development in Switzerland, pursued mainly by British and Canadian holidaymakers. The children were given private lessons by English and French tutors and spent some time in a boarding school in Grenoble, subsidized by a wealthy relative, and Joachim considerably improved his command of both languages. The children made many friends in Arosa, both English and Canadian, and the boys were invited by an English family to stay in London with them for a year. Here they perfected their English, with a view to embarking on a career in commerce: their father's bitterness over his treatment by the army had dissuaded them from following in the family's military footsteps.[17]

In 1910 Ribbentrop took up an invitation from some Canadian friends, the Hamilton-Ewings, whom he had met in Switzerland, and sailed with his brother from London to Quebec, taking his violin with him, as always. He obtained employment as a trainee clerk in Molson's

Bank, on Montreal's Stanley Street, before getting a job with an engineering firm working on the rebuilding of the Quebec Bridge across the St Lawrence river after it had collapsed in 1907. Well before the project was completed (it was not finished until 1919, after it had collapsed again), Ribbentrop moved on to the National Transcontinental Railway, at that time still under construction. But 'the toughness and roughness of pioneering life in Canada' were too much for his constitution, even though he worked as a clerk and did not have to engage in physical labour, and in 1912 he came down with tuberculosis of the kidneys, probably passed on to him some years earlier by his mother. The disease led to a stay in hospital and the removal of a kidney. He returned to Germany to recuperate, then the following year sailed back across the Atlantic, to New York, where he worked for a time as a freelance newspaper reporter, before returning to Canada. This time he lived in Ottawa, where he used what was left of his mother's legacy to set up a modest business importing German wines.[18]

Apart from taking part in amateur musical events, Ribbentrop spent his spare time in sporting activities, competing for the famous Minto Skating Club in the national figure-skating championships. He found his way into high society and mingled with the rich, the aristocratic and the famous at parties, social events and musical evenings. But in the summer of 1914 all this came to a sudden end. As part of the British Empire, Canada was bound to follow the motherland into war with Germany, which it did on 9 September. Presciently, Ribbentrop left for New York to avoid being arrested as an enemy alien, leaving behind his business, his friends, his property, together with his ailing, tubercular elder brother, and abandoning Catherine Hamilton-Ewing, whom he had intended to marry (she later moved to England and joined the British Union of Fascists). It was another sharp break in his career. Since British ships – the vast majority – were refusing to take German passengers, he obtained a berth on board a small Dutch ocean liner, the *Potsdam*, bound for Rotterdam. The ship left Hoboken, New Jersey, on 15 August with several hundred German passengers on board. As it approached the other side of the Atlantic, however, the *Potsdam* was intercepted by a British warship and diverted to Falmouth. All German citizens on board were to be interned. Ribbentrop, who had already been denounced in the Canadian press as a German spy, bribed a steward to conceal him in the ship's coal-bunker, where an old friend from Metz was working. Here he remained in hiding for the rest of the voyage. On arriving in Rotterdam, Ribbentrop returned to his cabin, which had been left untouched, to have a bath and retrieve his belongings. The steward, who, according to Ribbentrop's memoirs, now revealed himself to be a German officer in disguise, returned the bribe and helped him disembark.[19]

After visiting his father and stepmother, Ribbentrop volunteered for military service in the 12th Hussars, a Prussian cavalry regiment. Despite only having one kidney, he passed the medical examination and underwent several weeks of training before being sent with the regiment to the Eastern Front. Now a first lieutenant, he was wounded several times, and in the summer of 1917 he was awarded the Iron Cross – originally only Second Class, but he successfully petitioned to have it upgraded to First Class. Transferred to the Western Front, where the regiment served out the rest of the war, Ribbentrop became seriously ill, and in April 1918 was sent after regaining his health to Istanbul as adjutant to the Military Plenipotentiary in charge of deliveries of war equipment to the Turks. Among the friends he made there was Franz von Papen, who was attached to the Ottoman Army. At the end of the war, he was briefly interned and then escaped, making his way back home via Italy. Like many other returning officers, he was shocked by the economic and political conditions obtaining in the Fatherland. 'Suddenly,' he noted in his memoirs, 'there were a great many Jews, who were busying themselves in many fields, politics, the economy, culture, and not always in a good way.' On his return to the War Ministry he was appointed to the staff of Major-General Ernst von Wrisberg, the man who in March 1919 originated the antisemitic version of the 'stab-in-the-back' myth, where he blamed the Jews for the German revolution and the overthrow of the Prussian officer class – 'no wonder, when this tribe is doing everything to annihilate a class that has long been a thorn in its eye'. It is not difficult to imagine how Wrisberg's antisemitic diatribes must have influenced the young and still impressionable Lieutenant Ribbentrop in his views.[20]

Like many demobilized soldiers, Ribbentrop found it difficult to get a job after the war. In the early summer of 1919, however, based on his knowledge of English and his experience in North America, he found employment in the Berlin branch of a firm importing cotton. He was soon promoted, and made enough money to support his brother, who had been moved, terminally ill, to a Swiss sanatorium. On the side,

Ribbentrop capitalized on his command of French to carry out a few private commissions to obtain French wines for wealthy Berliners, and towards the end of 1919 he registered this activity as a formally constituted business. Soon, however, his prospects were completely transformed. In the autumn of 1919, on a brief holiday in Bad Homburg, a resort in the Taunus Mountains, he entered a tennis tournament, where he met Annelies Henkell, whose father ran a well-known German firm selling sparkling wines. They married on 5 July 1920. Their first children were born successively in 1921 and 1922; eventually there would be five. It seems to have been a happy marriage. According to one of the prison psychiatrists at Nuremberg, Annelies, though three years younger than Ribbentrop, was a forceful and ambitious woman who completely dominated him, providing him with the maternal affection he had lacked as a child because of the illness and death of his mother. His secretary, somewhat melodramatically, compared her to Lady Macbeth.[21]

To begin with, Ribbentrop ran the Berlin branch of the Henkell firm, but his father-in-law procured him a partnership in a well-established wine-importing firm whose owner had appealed to him for financial support. The Schoeneberg and Ribbentrop company soon prospered, thanks not least to Ribbentrop's British and French connections and the lifting of legal restrictions on trade on 1 January 1924. So he quit the Henkell agency he had run to concentrate on the partnership. The epithet 'champagne salesman' has somewhat unfairly stuck to him ever since. It was his wife's money, however, that enabled them to build a substantial villa in the plush Berlin suburb of Dahlem, equipped with a swimming pool, a tennis court, and other impressive amenities. On 15 May 1925 their social ascent took an important step up, when he persuaded Gertrud von Ribbentrop, the elderly, unmarried cousin who had supported his stay at the boarding school in Grenoble, to adopt him legally in return for providing her with a pension of 450 Marks a month. The adoption enabled him from now on to add the noble prefix 'von' to his name. This was not necessarily the advantage he thought it would be: his mother-in-law complained that the move had made her family a laughing-stock. When his wartime friend Wolf-Heinrich Count von Helldorf (later a senior Nazi police official) proposed him as a member of the *Hererenklub*, an exclusive aristocratic gentleman's club in Berlin, he was blackballed on the grounds that only those who had inherited their title were acceptable. Nevertheless, Ribbentrop was accepted on a second attempt, backed by Franz von Papen, whom he had known in Istanbul during the war. With his wife, he began to run a social salon at their Dahlem home, where they entertained wealthy and prominent nationalist and conservative guests from the worlds of business and politics. Ribbentrop particularly enjoyed hobnobbing with members of the former Prussian and German royal family, the Hohenzollerns.[22]

Up to this point, Ribbentrop had not been politically active, although his views, like those of many other former army officers, were on the far right, and tinged, to put it no more strongly than that, with antisemitism. His business brought not only entry once more into high society but also contact with many men active in the political world. He was a supporter of the business-oriented German People's Party, but as the Great Depression broke on Germany in 1930 the Party collapsed, losing almost all its voters, most of whom went over to the Nazis. 'It became obvious,' he wrote later, 'that Germany would fall victim to communism . . . that Germany was steering towards the abyss.'[23] What was needed, he thought, was a coalition between the bourgeois and conservative parties on the one hand, and the rising popular force of the Nazis on the other. Influenced by his wife, and by Helldorf, who was already a member of the Nazi Party, Ribbentrop began to attend political dinners where such matters were discussed. At one of these, in 1930, he met Hitler, and was sufficiently impressed to write him out a cheque for 6,000 Marks. By 1931 he was being described by the Nazis as one of their supporters.[24]

In the spring of 1932 Hitler accepted an invitation to dinner at the Ribbentrops' villa in Dahlem, where Ribbentrop impressed the Nazi leader with his detailed knowledge of Britain and the British. 'Adolf Hitler,' Ribbentrop confessed many years later, at his Nuremberg trial:

> made a considerable impression on me even then. I noticed particularly the blue eyes . . . his detached nature . . . and the manner in which he expressed his thoughts. His statements always had something final and definite about them, and appeared to come from his innermost self. I had the impression that I was facing a man who knew what he wanted and had an unshakeable will and very strong personality . . . I [was] convinced that this man, if anyone, could save Germany . . .[25]

Then, by a stroke of good fortune for Ribbentrop, Papen was appointed Reich Chancellor in succession to Heinrich Brüning. Papen was desperate to win over the Nazis, now the largest party in the Reichstag, to his plan to introduce an authoritarian regime in Germany and destroy the Social Democrats, the Communists and the trade unions. In mid-August 1932 Ribbentrop travelled at Papen's behest to meet Hitler at Berchtesgaden to try and broker an agreement between the two men.[26] The attempt failed because of Hitler's insistence that he had to head the proposed coalition. But the two-hour harangue to which Hitler had treated him put Ribbentrop fully under his spell. At Helldorf's suggestion, he signed up as a member of the Nazi Party on 1 May 1932.[27]

As a confidant of Franz von Papen, Ribbentrop was involved in the efforts that took place over the following months to get Hitler to bring his Party – after the elections of 31 July 1932 by some distance the largest in the Reichstag – into line behind him. The situation was altered by Papen's overthrow and his replacement as Reich Chancellor by the military politician Kurt von Schleicher, whom Papen and other leading conservatives loathed and distrusted. At the request of Hitler's staff, Ribbentrop placed his house in Dahlem at the disposal of the various interested parties, who met there for dinner in conditions of great secrecy on 18 January 1933. Besides Hitler and Papen, Röhm and Himmler were also present. The discussions were inconclusive. At a second meeting in Dahlem, arranged by Papen on 22 January, Hitler and Papen were accompanied by Göring and two other Nazis, by State Secretary Otto Meissner, and by President Hindenburg's son Oskar. Papen offered to serve as Vice-Chancellor in a coalition government headed by Hitler. At further meetings in Ribbentrop's home, various members of Hindenburg's entourage met with leading Nazis to hammer out the idea of a 'national front', with which they eventually persuaded the President to approve Hitler's appointment as Reich Chancellor on 30 January.[28]

Hitler's gratitude for the role Ribbentrop had played in his appointment as Reich Chancellor was considerable.[29] For the moment, however, Ribbentrop received no official recognition from the Nazi leader. Instead, however, Hitler began to use him for particular, confidential foreign-policy missions, since he did not trust the Foreign Office, half of whose staff were aristocrats, led by Foreign Minister Konstantin von Neurath, a career diplomat and former ambassador in Rome. Ribbentrop may have rejoiced in his acquisition of the noble prefix 'von', but he was entirely outside the orbit of the Foreign Office, and he impressed Hitler with his command of foreign languages, his international business connections, and his experience of the world of high society. The Nazi dictator sent him to Paris in March 1933 and on subsequent occasions to try to improve relations with the French government, which he feared would be badly affected when, as intended, Germany withdrew from the League of Nations, as happened later in the year, and then began rearming.[30]

This was not at all to the liking of the German Foreign Office. On 5 February 1934 Neurath warned the British ambassador in Berlin, Sir Eric Phipps, that Ribbentrop was 'insufficiently acquainted with our policy to speak with authority'. In any case, the visits to Paris did not yield the hoped-for results, so Hitler turned his attention to London, where he again sent Ribbentrop on a series of informal missions. On all these occasions Ribbentrop was able to use his business contacts, and the support of Hitler, to meet with leading politicians and government ministers, and so become well known in the foreign-policy and political elites of Britain and France, although officials and politicians were at first uncertain about his role. On 20 April Ribbentrop was appointed 'Plenipotentiary for Matters of Disarmament', and then, ambassador-at-large, with an office situated in a building on Berlin's Wilhelmstrasse directly opposite the Foreign Office. Soon he had a substantial staff, funded by donations from the Nazi Party and from German industrialists: by 1936 it numbered 150 and was known as the Ribbentrop Office. Much to Neurath's irritation, this became in practice an alternative centre of power to the Foreign Office, gradually pushing aside another competing institution, Alfred Rosenberg's Foreign Policy Office of the Nazi Party.[31]

In June 1935 Ribbentrop, now equipped with the official title and rank of 'Ambassador Extraordinary of the German Reich on Special Mission', went to London to sign an Anglo-German Naval Agreement, fixing the total tonnage of the German Navy at 35 per cent of that of the Royal Navy. Although the details of the Agreement had been drawn up by the Naval Attaché at the German Embassy in London, Ribbentrop had offended the Foreign Office by ignoring diplomatic protocol and brusquely presenting his terms in a 'take-it-or-leave-it' manner. The Agreement undermined April's 'Stresa Front', in which Britain, France and Italy had condemned German rearmament. Hitler was ecstatic, inviting Ribbentrop to Berchtesgaden and improving the status and funding of his office. From this point on, Hitler considered him the leading German expert on British affairs. On 10 April 1936, when the German ambassador in London, Leopold von Hösch, had a fatal heart attack in his London residence, Hitler considered Ribbentrop the obvious choice as his successor and issued a formal appointment in August.[32]

Ribbentrop's mission was to win over the British to some kind of alliance with Germany, if possible as members of the Anti-Comintern Pact with Japan. He cultivated members of the social and political elite he considered sympathetic to this idea, especially the arch-appeaser Lord Londonderry, who entertained the Ribbentrops as his guest on his grand country estate in Ulster, at Mount Stewart.[33] But Ribbentrop's tenure of the London Embassy was not a success. A few weeks after his arrival, King Edward VIII, in whom he had placed great hopes since the young monarch was known to be pro-German and even to a degree pro-Nazi, was forced to abdicate because of his stubborn insistence on marrying Mrs Wallis Simpson, a twice-divorced American socialite. Ribbentrop earned a good deal of ridicule in Britain by furiously putting the royal abdication down to a plot hatched by Jews and Freemasons, and predicting the outbreak of civil war and 'shooting in the streets' over the issue.[34]

The brusque manner he affected in negotiations offended diplomats on both sides, while his own staff loathed and feared him because of the rudeness and ill-temper with which he treated them. The emphasis he placed on representing not Germany, but Nazi Germany, was thought inappropriate. When presented to King George VI he presented the stiff-arm Nazi salute as the shy and awkward monarch was approaching to shake his hand, and narrowly missed his chin. All embassy staff were ordered to render the salute on meeting heads of state, and heads of state were expected to reciprocate. (Hitler overruled this requirement when Neurath pointed out that if the Soviet ambassador gave the Communist clenched-fist salute to Hitler, the Nazi dictator would have to return it in like fashion.) Nazi flags were everywhere. SS men were posted at the Embassy door (Ribbentrop had for some time been an SS officer on top of his other appointments). Embassy women were ordered not to curtsey to British royalty as a sign of Germany's new assertiveness. Official communiqués now had to be in German instead of the conventional diplomatic language, French, which only had the effect of making other London embassies communicate with their German counterpart in their own language, forcing Ribbentrop's staff to hunt around the capital city for translators capable of deciphering Turkish, Finnish or Japanese.[35]

It soon became clear that Ribbentrop had become a laughing-stock in British society. So numerous were his gaffes that one newspaper referred to him as 'Von Brickendrop'. Anxious to keep close to Hitler, he returned to Germany on average once a month in 1937, which led to another epithet for him – 'the Wandering Aryan'. Increasingly offended by his treatment at the hands of the British, Ribbentrop began to turn against them. His attempts to persuade British politicians to back the return of Germany's overseas colonies, sequestrated at the Treaty of Versailles, fell on deaf ears, and, just as important, received no support from Berlin, since Hitler thought them a distraction from his long-term aim of conquering *Lebensraum* in Eastern Europe. But Hitler liked Ribbentrop's abrupt, undiplomatic style, and his refusal to conform to the polite conventions of the diplomatic world. Moreover, Ribbentrop learned that the best way to keep Hitler onside was to absorb what he said, then later repeat it back to him in a more radical form. As his secretary Reinhard Spitzy said:

> When Hitler said 'grey', Ribbentrop said 'Black, black, black'. He always said it three times more, and he was always more radical. I listened to what Hitler said one day when Ribbentrop wasn't present: 'With Ribbentrop it is so easy, he is always so radical. Meanwhile, all the other people I have, they come here, they have problems, they are afraid, they think we should take care and then I have to blow them up, to get strong. And Ribbentrop was blowing up the whole day and I had to do nothing.'[36]

Just as Ribbentrop's notorious snobbery and social climbing were rooted in an attempt to overcome the shame he must have felt as a teenager when his father was dishonourably dismissed from the army and forced to leave Germany, so his subservience to Hitler was surely the product of the quasi-military discipline to which he had been subjected by his father during his childhood.

These qualities now propelled Ribbentrop to the high point of his career. In 1937–38 Hitler, concerned about his own future health and encouraged by the feeling that Britain and France would not object to Germany's expansion into other European countries, began replacing cautious and conservative generals and Cabinet ministers with people he considered more radical and more loyal. His victims included Foreign

Minister Konstantin von Neurath, who was summarily dismissed on 4 February 1938 and replaced by Ribbentrop. While the cautious diplomat Neurath, like virtually everyone else in the Foreign Office, including all the ambassadors bar one, went along willingly with almost all of Hitler's policies at home and abroad, he nonetheless made it clear he had reservations about the aggressive turn they were taking in 1938 with the prospective invasion of Austria and then Czechoslovakia. Ribbentrop was not going to object to anything Hitler did. Nevertheless, he was kept on in London while Hitler sent in the German army to annex Austria, on 12 March.[37]

Initially, Ribbentrop did not transfer his staff from the Ribbentrop Office into the Foreign Office, though a number of them did come over later (the Ribbentrop Office itself soon dwindled into insignificance). But he did introduce a new style. Neurath's official residence had been a small house in the Foreign Office garden; Ribbentrop had it pulled down, and chose to live instead at Hindenburg's (and Bismarck's) former Presidential Palace at Wilhelmstrasse 73. This too, however, he had pulled down, getting Albert Speer to design a replacement so grand that it was not finished until 1940. The Ribbentrops also requisitioned a country retreat, a hunting lodge near Salzburg called Schloss Fuschl, forty minutes' drive from Berchtesgaden. When the owner, Gustav von Remnitz, who was a friend of the Henkells, protested, he was sent to the concentration camp at Dachau. Ribbentrop introduced diplomatic uniforms for officials, whom he addressed, according to one of them, 'in the language and brutal tone of a drill sergeant'. He spent an inordinate amount of time defending the sphere of influence of the Foreign Office against encroachments from other Nazi leaders. Herbert von Dirksen, the new ambassador in London, and his open enemy, said at the time that Ribbentrop's character was 'composed of an enormous ambition and at the same time a feeling that he is neither gifted nor strong enough to live up to his ambition. He suffers from a secret inferiority complex which he compensates for by haughty, dictatorial manners.'[38]

Hitler had chosen Ribbentrop as Foreign Minister because he would do as he was told. Nevertheless, Ribbentrop did exert some influence on him, pushing him in a more anti-British and pro-Soviet direction in the late 1930s. Following the German annexation of Prague in March 1939, and the Franco-British guarantee of Poland, obviously next on Hitler's list of countries to conquer, the Nazi leader realized the importance of guarding Germany's rear should war break out when he invaded Poland, and he came round to Ribbentrop's point of view. Officials began detailed talks that led to the conclusion of a German–Soviet trade agreement on 19 August 1939, and were then extended onto a more general level. Ribbentrop flew to Moscow to sign a pact with his counterpart Vyacheslav Molotov on 23 August, which included secret clauses intended to carve up Poland. It was Ribbentrop's hour of triumph. Lauded by Hitler as a 'second Bismarck', he received a standing ovation from his staff when he returned to the Foreign Office after his trip.[39]

Mostly, however, he continued to be noticed for his gaffes, his failures and his clumsy interventions. He wrecked Germany's carefully constructed good relations with China by publicly recognizing Japanese claims to Manchuko, and he offended the Italians by trying (unsuccessfully) to rush them into signing a formal treaty of alliance. Ribbentrop, an appalled Mussolini told his Foreign Minister Count Galeazzo Ciano, 'belongs to the category of Germans who are a disaster for their country'. The more they worked together, the more Ciano came to hate Ribbentrop, who was, he complained, 'always trying to impose his point of view' and 'behaved in a manner which I find very offensive'. During the Munich crisis, Ribbentrop more than once had a temper tantrum in front of the British ambassador Sir Nevile Henderson, because, he screamed, 'you have gone behind my back' in talking to the head of the German armed forces, General Wilhelm Keitel. This was the first in a series of shouting matches between the two men. At one meeting, Ribbentrop shouted at the ambassador: 'Britain is governed by Jews, a-ha-ha! Isn't it so?' Enraged, Henderson shouted at him in the typical British manner as he left: 'We, at least, are governed by gentlemen!'[40] Ribbentrop pressed as hard as he could for the invasion of Czechoslovakia, causing Göring, as head of the Luftwaffe, who, like many leading generals, did not think Germany was ready for a general war, to call him 'a criminal fool'. Ribbentrop threatened personally to shoot any of his officials who presumed to contradict his view that the British would not intervene. When the Munich Agreement was finally signed, without his participation, Ribbentrop called it 'a first-class stupidity'.[41]

In late August 1939, as the threat of a war with Britain over Poland loomed, he assured Hitler that – on the basis of his profound knowledge and experience of British politics – Chamberlain would renege on his guarantee to support Poland in the event of a German invasion: he was right, but he totally misread the state of opinion in Chamberlain's Cabinet, the Conservative Party and the House of Commons, which brushed aside the Prime Minister's desperate attempts to avoid war. Ribbentrop's assurances to Hitler that Mussolini would enter the war were equally mistaken – the Italians stood to one side in the crisis, saying they were not ready to join the conflict. When Sumner Welles, the American Assistant Secretary of State, met him in February 1940 on an exploratory peace mission, Ribbentrop subjected him to a two-hour harangue which Welles described as 'the most astonishing experience of my entire mission'. The Foreign Minister's meddling in the post-conquest political settlement in Norway only resulted in his sidelining by Hitler, while his backing of an abortive attempt to kidnap the former King Edward VIII, now Duke of Windsor, who was living in exile in Spain, then Portugal, was a fiasco. And so it continued.[42]

Hitler's conquest of many countries in 1939 and 1940 curtailed the role of the Foreign Office in most of them, as military governors and top SS officers moved in; France was perhaps the major exception, where Ambassador Otto Abetz aggrandized a good deal of power to himself. The German occupation raised the question of how the Jewish inhabitants of these countries were to be treated, a question that became far more urgent with the invasion of the Soviet Union (Operation Barbarossa) on 22 June 1941. The Foreign Office was necessarily involved, since a number of these countries were still, at least nominally, sovereign and independent foreign states. Initially, however, though Ribbentrop knew about the mass murder of Jews in Eastern Europe by late summer 1941, he avoided getting directly involved, leaving the details to his subordinate Martin Luther, originally an interior decorator whom he had hired to refurbish the London Embassy. Ribbentrop appointed him, first, to his own office and then took him into the Foreign Office with the nominal title of Under-Secretary. It was in this capacity that Luther attended the Wannsee Conference on 20 January 1942, held to coordinate the extermination of Europe's Jews. In August, however, Ribbentrop discovered that Luther was doing nothing to prevent the SS from taking over Jewish policy in south-eastern Europe. Enraged, he ordered Luther to stop concerning himself with this part of Europe.[43]

On 24 September 1942 Hitler discovered that the 'Final Solution' had more or less come to a stop in Romania and Dalmatia, and subjected Ribbentrop to a severe dressing-down. The Foreign Minister had already lost a good deal of power and influence, and clearly felt he could not afford to lose any more. In peacetime, he had ensured that his Ministry and its officials did their best to justify the antisemitic policies of the Third Reich to foreign countries, including the pogrom of 9–10 November 1938, though he was dismayed at the damage they did to Germany's reputation abroad. Keen to demonstrate his antisemitic zeal to those among his Nazi rivals who might have noticed the good relations he maintained with wealthy Jewish businessmen during his years as a wine merchant, he pressed for Jews emigrating from Germany to be banned from taking their capital with them, telling the French Foreign Minister in December 1938 that the Jews in Germany were without exception pickpockets, murderers and thieves. The property they possessed had been acquired illegally.[44] Now, upbraided by Hitler for his slackness in pushing forward the 'Final Solution', he sprang into action. 'The Foreign Minister,' Luther announced, 'has telephoned instructions to me to expedite as much as possible the evacuation of Jews from the various countries of Europe, because it is a known fact that the Jews stir up people against us everywhere.' In particular, the authorities in Slovakia, Croatia and Romania, and the governments of Bulgaria, Hungary and Denmark, were to be pressed to deliver up their Jews for 'evacuation', or in other words, murder.[45]

Early in 1943 a plot hatched within the Foreign Office to replace Ribbentrop with Luther was foiled by Himmler and the SS. Luther was sent to Sachsenhausen concentration camp just outside Berlin; he survived the experience but died of a heart attack on 13 May 1945 at the age of forty-nine, shortly after being liberated by Red Army troops. Like his fellow plotters, Luther had felt that Ribbentrop was incapable of negotiating terms with the foreign powers who were now clearly gaining the upper hand over Germany in the war. Ribbentrop now redoubled his efforts to demonstrate to Hitler his full commitment to the extermination of the Jews. When the German dictator and his Foreign Minister met with Admiral Miklós Horthy, the ruler of Germany's ally Hungary, on 16 and 17 April 1943, the two men put considerable pressure on him to deliver Hungary's Jews to the Germans. When Horthy asked what he should do with the Jews, 'the Reich Foreign Minister', according to the minutes of the meeting, 'replied that the Jews must either be annihilated or taken to concentration camps. There was no other way.' Hitler underlined this conclusion by saying that the Jews 'had to perish'.[46] The discussion had few tangible results, but in March 1944, when Horthy threatened to withdraw his troops from the Eastern Front in the face of the oncoming Red Army, Ribbentrop persuaded Hitler not to order an invasion, but to force the Hungarian leader to appoint a pro-German government. In the autumn of 1944 Ribbentrop completed the action by organizing a coup in Budapest that brought the rabidly antisemitic Arrow Cross Party to power. Altogether, more than 440,000 Hungarian Jews were deported under German orders to Auschwitz, with Ribbentrop being informed of the operation's progress at every stage.[47]

In the last, desperate months of the war, Ribbentrop pleaded with Hitler on a number of occasions to try to broker a separate peace with the Soviets, but Hitler always vetoed the idea, which in any case would have had no chance of success even had he gone along with it. The suggestion of turning to the West met with a similar response. He met with Hitler for a last time on 23 April 1945. The Nazi leader told him to approach the British, and Ribbentrop made his way out of Berlin, driving north-west to Schleswig-Holstein. After Hitler's death on 30 April, it became known that he had appointed the Austrian Nazi Arthur Seyss-Inquart as Foreign Minister in the new government of Admiral Karl Dönitz. When he learned that he had been dropped, Ribbentrop became 'almost hysterical', refused to believe at first that he had no place in the list of ministers compiled by Hitler, then 'ranted hysterically', complaining: 'This hurts me more than anything else he could have done.'[48]

Pulling himself together, he made for Flensburg, very near the Danish–German border, where Dönitz was setting up the new government, and tried to persuade him in vain to make him Foreign Minister. He wrote, as instructed earlier by Hitler, a long letter to 'Vincent' Churchill, but the rambling and incoherent document could not be delivered, because there was no postal service any more. Ribbentrop went into hiding amid the ruins of Hamburg, where he was betrayed by an acquaintance, a wine merchant's son, and arrested by the British on 14 June 1945. He was carrying a bag with 100,000 Marks in cash in it, which, he said, he needed to support himself until the fuss blew over and he could be treated with dignity as a former German Foreign Minister. He was taken to a holding prison and then to Nuremberg to face the International Military Tribunal. Throughout this period, guards and prison officials described him as deeply depressed, not troubling to clean his cell or make himself presentable: 'a tired old man awaiting death', as the prison psychiatrist Gustave Gilbert described him (he was in fact fifty-two years of age). 'We are only living shadows,' Ribbentrop told him, '– the remains of a dead era – an era that died with Hitler.' Another psychiatrist thought that 'Ribbentrop has the air at times of a ham actor taking the part of the great statesman . . . He is quite an affected fellow.'[49]

Ribbentrop's answers to questions put to him by his interrogators were evasive and dishonest. He denied having brought about a war, or knowing anything about military preparations for one, and said he could not understand why he was being called antisemitic. He had only been obeying Hitler's orders. Allied atrocities had been just as bad.[50] Hitler was a 'great personality', he said to another prison psychiatrist, who commented that 'he is assisting the building-up of an already well-on-its-way myth of the magnetism of Hitler'.[51] A similar line of defence occupied large parts of his mendacious memoirs, which he composed in his cell, along with a great deal of score-settling against his former rivals. He refused to criticize Hitler. Far from starting the war, the Nazi leader had only wanted to reverse the injustices of Versailles. The Jews had brought America into the war, and then Hitler had gone 'wild' with rage and launched the extermination programme. In any case, the first he had known about the Holocaust had been when the Red Army liberated the Majdanek concentration camp in July 1944.[52] His excuses and evasions did not convince the International Military Tribunal. Found guilty on all counts, he was hanged on 16 October 1946.[53]

His widow Annelies, seen by many as a dominant force in his life, remained committed to his memory, bringing out his memoirs (with comments and additions of her own) with a far-right publishing house in 1954. After a brief spell of imprisonment, and the sequestration of most of her property, she mixed in post-Nazi circles, published books blaming Britain for the war, and was awarded a medal by a neo-Nazi cultural foundation in 1973, not long before her death. Among her four children, the most notable was Rudolf, who had attended Westminster School during his father's time as ambassador in London (Ribbentrop was characteristically offended that he had been unable to get into Eton). Rudolf later signed up with the SS and served as a tank commander on the Eastern and Western Fronts. Stationed in Berlin in early 1945, he accompanied his father on his last visit to the bunker beneath the Reich Chancellery, and was shocked both by Hitler's physical condition and by his delusional attitude to the war. After three years in prison, Rudolf Ribbentrop was included in the Henkell family business as the result of a lawsuit brought by his mother against the managers, who considered his name would be a liability. He later became a banker, and died in 2019, at the age of ninety-eight. His lengthy memoir of his father, published in 2008, attempted to rescue Joachim von Ribbentrop's reputation, not least by claiming that he was not antisemitic, knew next to nothing about the extermination of the Jews, and always stood up to Hitler.[54]

7
The Philosopher: Alfred Rosenberg

Alfred Rosenberg was not originally a Reich German. He was a 'Baltic German'; that is, he was part of a privileged group of ethnically and linguistically German people who had lived in the Russian Empire, along the southern coast of the Baltic Sea, for many generations. Some of these were (mostly impoverished) landed nobility; others, like Rosenberg's family, were townspeople, merchants, craftsmen and professionals. Although the Baltic Germans lived in modest circumstances, they maintained a strong sense of racial superiority over native Latvians, Lithuanians, Estonians, Poles and other groups in the region, many if not most of whom had been serfs until very recently. The majority of them were Protestants. Their principal city was the old Hanseatic seaport of Reval (Tallinn), in what is now Estonia, numbering in the late nineteenth century some 66,000 inhabitants, around a quarter of whom were ethnic Germans, the rest mostly native Estonians. It was in Reval that Alfred Rosenberg was born on 12 January 1893. Brought up by two aunts, after his parents had both died before he had entered his teens, he lived in a culturally German milieu, and identified from the beginning with his German ethnicity.[1]

This would surely have been strengthened with the coming of the Bolshevik Revolution in 1917 and the consequent independence of Estonia, in which ethnic Germans were brusquely pushed to one side as members of a social stratum owing its allegiance to the Tsarist state. The Rosenberg family was modestly bourgeois, earning its income from trade, and sufficiently well off to send Alfred to a polytechnic in Riga, where he studied architecture. Here he joined the 'Rubonia' student duelling fraternity, which provided him with something like a second family. In 1915 the polytechnic relocated to Moscow, where Rosenberg completed his studies, returning to Reval to write his diploma dissertation and then going back to Moscow for graduation in January 1918, where he could observe the revolutionary regime at first hand. Back in Reval again after a short stay, he found himself in the new state of Estonia, where there was no place for him. The events of the previous months, particularly in Moscow, had implanted in him the convictions that were to last the rest of his life. On 30 November 1918 he delivered his first public speech. Its subject was 'Marxism and Jewry'. Revolution, he believed, was the expression of the Jews' inborn drive to subvert and destroy civilization.[2]

With armed conflicts raging across the region, Rosenberg, along with many other Baltic Germans, fled westwards to Germany, making his way first to Berlin in search of a job. Many were fleeing the Russian Revolution and he took with him the conviction that Bolshevism, and indeed beyond it, socialism and liberalism, were the creations of the Jews. Counter-revolutionary antisemitism was far from being a novelty in Russia at this time; violent pogroms had already swept across the country in the wake of the failed revolution of 1905. But the Revolution of 1917 filled it with a new virulence, which radical antisemites like Rosenberg brought with them to Germany.[3] Repelled by the left-wing atmosphere of Berlin in the last weeks of 1918, Rosenberg travelled south to Bavaria. Here he can only have been strengthened in his views by the series of revolutionary outbreaks that convulsed the city in the winter of 1918–19. By the end of May they were over, crushed in a bloodbath by heavily armed paramilitaries in the employ of the Social Democratic government. Rosenberg was not personally involved in these conflicts, but it was obvious which side he was on. Living a hand-to-mouth existence, he gravitated first towards the local community of Russian exiles, then the mass of small, extremist groups of racist and German-nationalist antisemites that emerged in Munich in the wake of the counter-revolution. Among these was the infant Nazi movement, whose meetings Rosenberg began to attend, along with those of other ultra-right associations. Listening to Hitler speaking, he wrote, he was won over within the first fifteen minutes as he saw 'a German front soldier' launching the struggle for Germany's recovery and developed for him a 'personal admiration' as he realized he was the man to follow.[4] Right at the beginning of his political career, therefore, Rosenberg conceived an attachment for Hitler not because he was won over by his views but because he recognized that Hitler was the person best equipped to put his own views into effect.

And those views were now propagated in an outpouring of words unequalled by any other member of the Nazi movement. From 1919 to 1923, Rosenberg turned out thirteen signed articles and seven books, bearing witness to his obsessive, monomaniacal antisemitism, with titles ranging from *Die Spur des Juden im Wandel der Zeiten* (*The Traces of the Jew across the Changing Times*), his first book, to 'The Russian-Jewish Revolution', his first article. Ironically, the Jews, or rather, as they saw themselves, ex-Jews, whom he listed as leading figures in the Russian Communist movement, would almost all fall victim to Stalin's purges in the 1930s, not that this would cause him in any way to change his opinion. Running through these publications is a drastically expressed paranoid fear of 'world Jewry', hell-bent on murder and destruction. The Germans, Rosenberg said, could only be protected by the deportation of all Jews from the country. The Weimar Republic marked the triumph of the Jewish will to power; the preservation of the German race demanded its overthrow.[5] To provide 'evidence' for these views, Rosenberg seized on the *Protocols of the Elders of Zion*, a document that made its way from Russia to Germany at the end of the war, purporting to be the minutes of an 1897 meeting of Jewish elders planning the takeover of the world. It mattered little that the pamphlet was exposed in 1921 as a tissue of falsifications; for Rosenberg, it expressed the larger truth about Jewish subversion which he repeated endlessly in his writings of these and later years.[6]

What Rosenberg did was to provide a systematic underpinning for the antisemitism of the Nazi Party. On the many other issues that concerned the leadership he had less to say. True, he did provide an elaborate commentary on the Nazi Party programme, but this was from the outset declared unalterable; what he offered was a kind of exegesis. Rosenberg's insistence that Communism was a tool of the Jews may have exercised some influence on Hitler, but in truth this idea was so commonplace on the extreme right in Germany after the First World War that it would be an exaggeration to say he actually gave the Führer the idea; Hitler could have got it anywhere. But the constant stream of anti-semitic writings that Rosenberg poured out was hard for anyone to ignore. He was not an effective public orator – his speeches sounded more like academic lectures than political propaganda – but he did have an enormous influence on the Nazi movement's ideas, above all through his editorship of the Party's daily paper, the *Völkischer Beobachter*

(*Racial Observer*), which he ran at first from behind the scenes, then from March 1923 onwards officially as the editor. In the day-to-day development of the Nazi Party, this was probably his most important activity at this time. Hitler himself later privately criticized Rosenberg's editorship of the *Völkischer Beobachter*, which, he said, at least at the beginning, 'stood on such a height that it was hard to understand even for me'. It only became a proper newspaper in the election campaigns of 1932, when Rosenberg had feared a landslide against the Party. 'His contempt for mankind,' Hitler is reported to have remarked, 'only increased when he made its style more popular because he feared the Nazi Party was losing support, in 1932.'[7] It took a long time for the *Völkischer Beobachter* to establish itself. But Hitler was underestimating its importance. Mixing general news mostly derived from press agencies, and Party propaganda (especially enthusiastic reports of Party events), it kept the Party in the public eye, and contributed further to building up the image of Hitler as the coming German dictator.

That image failed its first test in the misconceived beer-hall *putsch* of 8–9 November 1923, which Rosenberg, acting on Hitler's orders, had announced in his newspaper, and in which he took part. As we have seen, Hitler and some others were injured, and fourteen killed, but Rosenberg escaped without harm. Moreover, the state prosecutors decided not to bring charges against him, while Hitler was brought before a court and sentenced to a short period of incarceration in Landsberg Prison. Hitler knew that Rosenberg agreed with him on all significant ideological matters and was unconditionally loyal, so in his absence he named him acting leader of the Nazi Party, which was now banned as a result of its attempt to seize power by force. In this capacity, Rosenberg pushed the Party towards participation in parliamentary elections, and away from a continued, futile belief in seizing power by force alone, despite Hitler's own hesitations. But, still viewed as not quite German, Rosenberg was unable to hold the Nazi movement's warring factions together. Only when Hitler returned to politics after his release from prison did the Party unite again under his leadership. He was assisted in this task by Rosenberg, who in June 1924 founded a new magazine, *Der Weltkampf* (*The Global Struggle*), dedicated to 'the Jewish question of every country', which once again placed antisemitism at the ideological heart of the re-emerging movement. But Rosenberg was fundamentally a man of ideas, and the new phase the Party was entering was one of practical politics, of organization, of electoral campaigning, and finally of political manoeuvring, and here, as Hitler had learned from Rosenberg's period as acting Party leader, he would be of less use.[8]

For the next several years, therefore, Rosenberg focused on his ideological work, both as editor of the Party newspaper and as author of a continuing stream of books, pamphlets and articles. Racial hatreds, coupled with violent, bitter, obsessive loathing of the Jews, permeated his writings through the 1920s and beyond. The Weimar Republic was a 'swamp' created by the Jews, characterized by a 'lack of culture' and the 'insulting and defamation of the German character'. Rosenberg fulminated in the most violent, hate-filled terms against the 'racial undermining', the sexual libertinism, the 'protection of criminals' and the 'nigger culture' he saw all around him.[9] For him, race was less a matter of biology or inheritance than a question of values and beliefs, which he saw expressed in art and culture. The upright, manly Nordic-Germanic soul, he argued, was solidly rooted in reality, in struggle, in bravery, and in the drive for racial self-preservation. Opposed to this he saw the culture of modernity, relativism, abstraction, atonality, pacifism and cosmopolitanism, purveyed, as he saw it, by Jewish subversives across the globe. In 1930 Rosenberg summed up these ideas in the book that made his name: *Der Mythus des 20. Jahrhunderts. Eine Wertung der seelisch-geistigen Gestaltenkämpfe unserer Zeit* (*The Myth of the Twentieth Century: An Evaluation of the Psychological-Intellectual Structural Struggles of Our Time*).[10]

Post war writers, including Nazi autobiographers like Albert Speer, wrote off the book as absurd, confused and without importance, a view articulated most forcefully by Joachim Fest, who did much to shape historians' verdict on the Nazi ideologue. Fest saw Rosenberg as an outsider in the Nazi movement because he 'set faith above power'. His fanatical conviction meant that in the power struggles that raged within the movement and, later, the regime, he was 'again and again humiliated and passed over', 'rewarded with insultingly un-influential positions', 'a prophet without honour in his own country'.[11] It was not until the Nuremberg War Crimes Trials in 1946 that Rosenberg discovered that the Nazi leaders had never read *The Myth of the 20th Century*. In one of his mealtime monologues for instance, on 11 April 1942, Hitler was reported to have declared that Rosenberg's book was not to be regarded as an official Party publication because it was too mystical. Few 'Old Fighters' had read it. Only when it was publicly condemned by the

Catholic Church did it attract a wide readership. 'Just like many Gauleiters,' Hitler added in the *Table-Talk*, 'he too had only read a small part of it, since in his opinion it was written in a manner that was too hard to understand.'[12] The leader of the Hitler Youth, Baldur von Schirach, also claimed that officials of the movement had not read the book.[13]

Yet post-war judgements of Rosenberg should be treated with suspicion, since leading Nazis had every incentive to dissociate themselves from a man known to be a fanatical antisemite and an uncompromising ideologue.[14] Contemporary evidence indicates that at the time Rosenberg's ideas were taken with the utmost seriousness by Nazis and public alike. Hitler's reservations were more a matter of tactics than of principle. The book's militant anti-Christian position was politically inadvisable in the early 1930s, when Hitler was trying to win support in what was overwhelmingly a Christian country. The dictator was also recorded as saying that 'it was a great mistake that Rosenberg ever let himself be drawn into a battle of words with the Church', even though it was this that first made *The Myth of the 20th Century* popular, since it was bought by supporters of the Church to try to understand the roots of Nazi hostility. Rosenberg had nothing to gain from the struggle, which only led him to be condemned by the hierarchy.[15] Later on, however, as the Nazis' attempt to win over the Churches failed, and relations particularly with the Catholic community deteriorated, Rosenberg's anti-Christian position came to be shared by increasing numbers of Nazi Party members and officials, more and more of whom began formally to leave the Church.[16]

Rosenberg had the support of Himmler and Bormann, the SS and the Hitler Youth, and, in principle, the dictator himself, though, since he did not want to alienate the Churches and their congregations during the war, Hitler intimated that the 'reckoning' with Christianity would only come after the war was won. Rosenberg's support for a pseudo-Germanic neo-pagan religion, like Himmler's parallel efforts, won only limited backing from Hitler, who declared that National Socialism was in principle a scientific movement, not a religious one.[17] In fact, Hitler declared privately that *Der Mythus des 20. Jahrhunderts* was 'the most powerful of its kind', more powerful still than Houston Stewart Chamberlain's *Foundations of the Nineteenth Century*, the book to which Rosenberg intended his own to be a kind of sequel. It was universally understood to be the definitive theoretical statement of the Nazi Party's philosophy. Hitler never condemned the book in public; and it sold far beyond the circles of the Party's religious opponents, with sales reaching half a million by 1938 and a million four years later. After Hitler's *Mein Kampf*, it was undoubtedly the most important book produced by anyone in the leadership of the Nazi movement.[18] As Rosenberg noted proudly, when the book first appeared, Hitler had said to the Nazi publisher Max Amann: 'Indeed, when R.'s bones have long been bleached, people will still talk about this book.'[19] To his face, Hitler told Rosenberg 'that you are the deepest mind in the movement. You are the Church Father of National Socialism.' In the light of such praise, Rosenberg could not believe reports that Hitler had been saying to other people, that his work was 'nonsense and rubbish'.[20] At least some others in the Nazi leadership agreed: as Hermann Göring told him shortly after the outbreak of the war: 'You lay down our programme.'[21]

Rosenberg sought to implement his ideological agenda within the Nazi Party in a number of ways. In February 1934 Hitler placed him in charge of political education and censorship within the Nazi Party. His office soon spawned an elaborate bureaucratic structure. It unfolded a wide-ranging campaign of indoctrination, for example through mounting exhibitions – more than thirty of them in its first four years of existence – on topics ranging from motherhood to the German peasantry. However, like other offices in the Nazi system, it overlapped with many other institutions, from the Reich Ministry of Education to the Reich Chamber of Literature, headed by Joseph Goebbels, to which all authors, publishers and others in the book trade had to belong. Rosenberg's office successfully warded off attempts by Goebbels to absorb it into the Chamber, but in the ensuing power struggle it failed to obtain the ability to ban or censor books: it could only issue advice to the Chamber, which frequently turned it down. After years of bureaucratic infighting, Rosenberg managed to strengthen his position in March 1938 by persuading Hitler to appoint him to the rank of Reich Minister, with a seat in the Cabinet, but the Cabinet was scarcely meeting any more.[22]

In January 1940 Rosenberg secured from Hitler the commission to make preparations for the establishment after the war of a Nazi university, the *Hohe Schule der NSDAP*, which was to include institutes for the study of the Jewish Question (opened in Frankfurt in 1941), for racial studies, for research on the European East, for Germanic studies, and other similar subjects.[23] In order to create libraries and museums for the university, Rosenberg was authorized by Hitler in July 1940, against fierce competition from Goebbels in particular, to seize books, artworks and cultural objects from Jewish owners and institutions in occupied countries, which he proceeded to do on a vast scale. His *Einsatzstab Reichsleiter Rosenberg* (Action Staff of Reich Leader Rosenberg), created in order to implement this policy, ranged across Europe, looting manuscripts, books and cultural artefacts and transporting them for storage at the fantasy castle of Neuschwanstein, built for the eccentric Bavarian King Ludwig II in the nineteenth century. Altogether the plunder carried out by Rosenberg's staff numbered more than 21,000 cultural objects, more than two million books and manuscripts, and files covering several kilometres of shelf space. Rosenberg was not the only leading Nazi to engage in cultural looting, but the scale on which he engaged in it was considerably greater than anyone else's: Hitler's agents for example collected only a third as much, Göring's half as many. Rosenberg had no qualms about any of this, boasting in his diary in March 1941, for example: 'The things that my Action Staff have confiscated in Paris are undoubtedly unique . . . In addition the J. [Jewish] cultural treasures that have recently arrived at Neuschwanstein. The value estimated at 1 billion.'[24] Two years later he waxed even more lyrical when he visited 'a sorting store of my Action Staff. It is astonishing what valuables have been secured here from the whole of Europe.'[25]

Whereas Hitler focused on artworks for his planned museum in Linz, and Göring engaged in cultural spoliation mainly for his own personal profit and benefit, Rosenberg was led, as always, by ideological motives. In the scramble for loot, it was Rosenberg who asserted himself most successfully, fending off competition from other individuals and organizations, including the 'scientific' arm of Himmler's SS, the *Ahnenerbe*, and even Martin Bormann and Hitler's art agent Hans Posse. In this area, at least, Rosenberg could gather around him an active and energetic staff and win allies in the never-ending struggle for mastery within the Nazi power structure.[26] He gained considerably from the backing of Hitler, to whom he reported proudly in early September 1940 his theft of sixty-two boxes of loot hidden in a Rothschild palace in Paris.[27] And it was to Hitler's support that he owed the plans for his Institute for Research on the Jewish Question, which, he boasted in February 1941, 'already has the biggest library in the world: 350,000 volumes.

All from France, Belgium etc. Another 200,000 will likely be coming from Holland.'[28]

Rosenberg's activities in the cultural sphere also included the foundation in 1928 of the Fighting League for German Culture, which aimed to combat the 'cultural decline' of the Weimar Republic and encourage 'intrinsically' German culture instead. Many leading Nazis including Heinrich Himmler were among the members, who numbered around 300 in April 1929. The League put on lectures polemicizing against modern art and architecture, atonal music and left-wing drama. Rosenberg's League, despite the fact that its aims were closely aligned with Hitler's in this area, was outflanked by Goebbels's Reich Chamber of Culture, which provided the organizational structures and political direction Rosenberg was unable in the end to supply. It was almost predictable that Hans Hinkel, whose administrative abilities had prompted Rosenberg to appoint him as Reich Organization Leader of the Fighting League, went over to the Culture Chamber in 1933, becoming its chief administrator three years later.[29] Hitler indeed deliberately encouraged his subordinates in their rivalries, not least because this left him as the arbiter between them. Rosenberg found this frustrating, and vented his spleen against Goebbels on page after page of his diary. 'Everywhere I go, I hear unanimous complaints about the lack of direction of the Reich Chamber of Culture,' he wrote in 1934.[30] Yet Rosenberg's radical hostility to modernist art did in the end triumph over Goebbels's more relaxed approach, because it was shared by Hitler, as Rosenberg noted triumphantly in his diary on the occasion of the opening of the 'Great German Art Exhibition' in 1937.[31] And on a number of occasions Rosenberg managed to undermine Goebbels by sponsoring attacks on cultural figures backed by the Propaganda Minister, including the sculptor Ernst Barlach, the novelist Hans Fallada, and the composers Richard Strauss and Paul Hindemith, resulting in their demotion from positions in which Goebbels had sought to protect them.[32]

Rosenberg was also active in shaping Nazi foreign policy. In 1927 his tract *Der Zukunftsweg einer deutschen Aussenpolitik* (*The Future Course of a German Foreign Policy*) established him as the leading foreign-policy expert in the Party in its early years, not least because, as before, he systematized views that were also held by Hitler, who had discussed many of these ideas with him. Here Rosenberg was led once more by his racist ideology, advocating an alliance with 'England' because in his view it was racially pure and ethnicly closely aligned with Germany, and insisting that the Soviet Union was the main enemy, and not, as the Nazi left had claimed, Germany's most promising ally because it was, like Germany, an outsider in the diplomatic world of the 1920s. He thought Italy was a potential ally on strategic and ideological grounds, despite what he held to be the influence of the Jews over the country; partnership would even be worth the sacrifice of the disputed border region of South Tyrol. Globally, Germany's future lay in a colonial empire not overseas but in the European East, in a 'racial, national socialist, Germanic state in Central Europe'.[33] Above all, however, Rosenberg led everything back to what he viewed as the global struggle against the 'boundless world state' of the Jews, expressed through the 'Stock Exchange-Bolshevistic war of annihilation' they were waging against European civilization.[34]

Rosenberg's standing in the Party as its main foreign-policy expert led on 1 April 1933 to his appointment as head of a new institution, the Foreign Policy Office of the NSDAP. Just over two months after he had become Reich Chancellor, Hitler felt the need to create a Party rival to the conservative German Foreign Office, which was dominated by career diplomats. Following his appointment, Rosenberg offered his advice frequently to Hitler on many different aspects of foreign policy, including relations with Britain, Japan and other countries.[35] Most important in his view was his championing of an alliance with Britain. But the racial grounds on which he based his argument ('England' was a 'Germanic' nation) took a poor second place in Hitler's mind to strategic and power-political arguments. While Rosenberg devoted a good deal of time to cultivating sympathetic British interlocutors – none of them a major political figure – the German Foreign Office was briefing against him to the British press, and he soon had to abandon any idea of forging an alliance, above all after the increasingly anti-British Joachim von Ribbentrop, a man whom Rosenberg considered 'stupid and arrogant' in his dealings with Britain, had been appointed ambassador to London, and then Foreign Minister.[36] Typically, Hitler had also encouraged Ribbentrop's involvement in foreign policy for several years, allowing him in August 1934 to create his own alternative foreign office, in direct competition with Rosenberg's. Neither institution was able to counter the massive institutional weight of the German Foreign Office, virtually all of whose officials in practice accepted the new directions German foreign policy took under Hitler. Rosenberg proved unable to build up his own institution into an effective organization; indeed, a large proportion of its planned positions were left unfilled, and while it exerted some influence behind the scenes, it was in the end outmanoeuvred by other policymaking centres. Rosenberg was bypassed on key issues such as the Molotov–Ribbentrop Pact of 23 August 1939, which Rosenberg disliked on ideological grounds, considering that a deal with the United Kingdom would have been preferable.[37] He even tried to get the war postponed and negotiations begun with the British, all when it was too late. In the longer term, his consistent hostility to the Soviet Union and above all to Europe's Jews would have some effect. But on the major foreign-policy issues of the 1930s he failed to have much of an impact.[38]

His diary shows that his interventions were focused above all on policy towards Scandinavia, Romania and Afghanistan. Even here, however, he had little influence. His idea of a racially based alliance of the Scandinavian countries with Germany, pushed through the Nordic Society, founded in 1921 but taken over by the Nazis, with Rosenberg in the lead, after the seizure of power in January 1933, foundered on Hitler's assignment of Finland to the Soviet sphere of influence in the Molotov–Ribbentrop Pact in 1939 and the military conquest of Denmark and Norway in 1940.[39] The Romanian politician Octavian Goga, a client of Rosenberg's Foreign Office of the NSDAP, became Prime Minister in late December 1937 but was ousted by King Carol II in February 1939. The behind-the-scenes manoeuvres in Norway that brought Vidkun Quisling to power as part of the German invasion in 1940 were again sidelined by Hitler, who refused to give Quisling the freedom of action that Rosenberg desired for him.[40]

With the invasion of the Soviet Union on 22 June 1941, however, he moved into a far more important arena of policymaking and implementation. His diaries make clear that he was closely involved in planning for the order the Nazis intended to establish in Eastern Europe after the invasion.[41] 'Rosenberg,' Hitler said in the spring of 1941, 'now your time has come!' Hitler told him that he would be put in charge of the occupied East, after Rosenberg had handed him his plan for the area, including the total dismantling of the existing administrative structures, the resettlement of 'unwanted peoples', and much more besides. Rosenberg wrote triumphantly in his diary: 'Millions ... and the destiny of their lives will thus be placed in my hands. Germany can be freed for centuries from a pressure that has burdened it time and again in different forms!'[42] In July 1941 he was duly appointed Reich Minister for the Occupied Eastern Territories. In this capacity, Rosenberg believed it was his mission to carry out the historic task of destroying a centuries-old threat to Germany, the threat of the Slavs.[43] 'I had been allocated a huge task,' he wrote in his diary, 'indeed, the greatest the Reich had to offer – security for centuries, Europe's independence from abroad.' The area under his control, including Ukraine, the breadbasket of Europe, would guarantee food supplies for Germany for ever.[44]

Rosenberg busied himself with the details of establishing and staffing the Ministry, creating two 'Reich Commissariats' to carry out daily administrative tasks. But his plans did not go smoothly. His advocacy of 'the recognition of Ukrainian anti-Moscow views & thereby Ukrainian assistance in the securing of Ukrainian space' ran up against the opposition of Hitler, who told him that the Ukrainians should be treated like the Russians because they had shown their inferiority by allowing the latter to repress them for centuries. In Rosenberg's view, this would push them into supporting Stalin's idea of pan-Slavic unity in resisting the German invader.[45] His views were disregarded and the Ukrainians treated with the same murderous brutality as other occupied peoples in the East, not least because this was the policy pursued by Rosenberg's own subordinate Erich Koch, the Reich Commissioner for Ukraine. Bitterly, Rosenberg recalled in his diary a time in April 1941 when Hitler had still taken his advice.[46]

Further problems came with the usual turf wars within the Nazi leadership, and Rosenberg's diary is filled with complaints about Himmler and Ribbentrop muscling in on his territory. Speer also interfered in Rosenberg's business. Nevertheless, his Ministry was far more than an empty shell. Hitler appointed Rosenberg because he respected his knowledge of Eastern Europe, and backed him in his demarcation disputes with Himmler. Rosenberg did indeed mark up some successes with the Ministry, most notably the promulgation of a 'New Agricultural Order' on 15 February 1942, which reintroduced private ownership of land without splitting up the large collective farms introduced by the Soviets a decade before, leading to a rise in food production.[47] What really undermined Rosenberg's position, however, was a development over which he had no control at all – the steady shrinking of the area for which he was responsible from 1942 onwards, as the Red Army turned the tide and forced the German armies to retreat.[48] As a consequence, the Ministry was gradually slimmed down, with one area of competence after another disappearing and the responsible officials made redundant. 'Almost the entire Eastern territories are lost,' he admitted on 22 October 1944, and so he had begun dismantling the Eastern Ministry.[49] As the military situation deteriorated, Rosenberg saw the German retreat from the East as the consequence not of the superior resources, equipment and tactics of the Red Army, but of 'the reactionary rigidity of the generals, who had failed to understand 'the revolutionary course of this war'. Better ideological indoctrination would, he thought, have stiffened their resistance to the enemy.[50] The military-aristocratic attempt to kill Hitler on 20 July 1944 was 'a historically unique crime'.[51] Noting the fact that Colonel Claus von Stauffenberg, the man who planted the bomb, was a Catholic, Rosenberg wondered if the Vatican had been behind it.[52] The war, he had already noted in 1940, was an 'ideological struggle against a host of enemies who included our opponents in the Vatican'; later on, he spent time discussing with Himmler how the fight against the Catholic Church would be carried on once the war was over.[53]

But by this time Rosenberg's loss of influence was being compounded by the rise behind the scenes of the scheming Martin Bormann. By the late summer of 1943, Rosenberg was complaining about 'how much the old historical form of the court camarilla has completely unscrupulously and successfully begun to assert itself among us'.[54] Bormann never wrote tracts or delivered speeches, Rosenberg noted, but since he had succeeded Hess as head of the Party apparatus, he had gathered a lot of power. 'Nobody who receives instructions from him could decide whether he was confronted with a personal command of the Leader, or B[ormann]'s view.' Bormann was now instructing the Gauleiters, for instance, on the National Socialist attitude to Christianity, which was surely his, Rosenberg's, sphere. Although Rosenberg had objected, Bormann was now trying to undermine or bypass him in many of his functions,[55] 'an example of the most miserable waiting-room politics'.[56] By 1944 Bormann was successfully shutting him out from power simply by denying him access to Hitler; Rosenberg never managed to see the dictator again after 17 November 1943, and, failing to see how he had surrendered influence to other figures in the Nazi hierarchy such as Himmler, he put the blame squarely on Bormann for his sidelining.[57]

The primary struggle, however, was still in Rosenberg's mind the struggle against the Jews. Working through the malign, global forces of liberalism, democracy and above all Bolshevism, 'international Jewry', biologically programmed to commit treachery and subversion wherever it was located, was working to undermine civilization and destroy the German race.[58] His antisemitism was visceral, deeply emotional. 'Time and again,' he wrote in 1936, 'rage takes hold of me when I think what this Jewish people of parasites has done to Germany. Instinct and Plan have been at work here for many decades. Anyway, I'm satisfied to have done my bit to unmask this treachery.'[59] In the early stages of the war, he was a stubborn advocate of the idea, intensively discussed in SS and Foreign Office circles at the time, of deporting Europe's Jews to the French colony of Madagascar – a murderous plan, involving the brutal removal of a largely urban population from Europe and dumping it on a tropical island where it would have had extreme difficulty in surviving (the plan was abandoned because of Britain's continuing command of the seas).[60] Rosenberg rejoiced in reports of their mass murder. 'Now wherever Jews and Communists have been exterminated,' he noted during a visit to Latvia in September 1941, 'the people are reviving.'[61] Every blow against Germany or Germans was struck by Jews, he thought. When he learned in September 1941 that Stalin was forcibly deporting some 400,000 ethnic Germans from the Volga region, Rosenberg's immediate reaction was to suggest that 'if this mass murder is carried out, Germany would let the Jews of Central Europe pay for it', though they had of course absolutely nothing to do with the Soviet leader's decision. Rightly or wrongly, Stalin's brutal ethnic cleansing was perpetrated on security grounds following the German invasion, and the view, shared by Rosenberg and the Nazi leadership, that Stalin, a man whose own antisemitic prejudices and suspicions were growing year by year, was a tool of international Jewry was a paranoid fantasy.[62]

It was in the area run by Rosenberg and his Reich Commissioners that the mass shootings of hundreds of thousands of Jews, men, women and children, were carried out from the summer of 1941, a policy implemented by Himmler's SS but with the full support of Rosenberg's Reich Ministry for the Occupied Eastern Territories on every level of administration. Rosenberg had frequent discussions with Himmler in the autumn and early winter of 1941 about arrangements for the deportation and murder of Jews from Germany itself and in the region of Eastern Europe for which the Ministry was responsible. He also met several times with Hitler to discuss the same issue, noting of one such conversation held on 14 December 1941: 'I would take the view that we should not speak of the extermination of the Jews. The Leader approved of this position and said, they had saddled us with the war, and they had brought about the destruction, so it was no wonder that the consequences hit them first.'[63] Rosenberg's staff discussed the detailed arrangements for the mass murder with Himmler. In addition, Rosenberg's Ministry was well represented at the Wannsee Conference in January 1942, held to coordinate the extermination programme. Rosenberg himself continued to push the programme forward over the following months. On 4 May 1943 he told a meeting that it was necessary 'to exterminate the last remains of Jewish thought and existence. There must be no Jewish source of infection left.'[64] Rosenberg's antisemitism was thus far more than just theoretical: it had ended in his active participation in and justification of the killing of some six million Jews.

Arrested by the Allies shortly after the end of the war, Rosenberg was brought before the International Military Tribunal at Nuremberg, and charged on all four counts: of conspiracy to commit crimes against peace, crimes of aggression, war crimes and crimes against humanity. His defence was to portray himself as a mere theoretician, who had never imagined that these things would actually involve the physical annihilation of the Jews. Yet his views had changed relatively little. Interviewed by a prison psychiatrist at Nuremberg, he insisted that 'the cause of the Jewish question was, of course, the Jews themselves ... They spat on German culture.' It would have been better had they all been sent in the 1930s to Alaska or Madagascar.[65] But the court was in possession of far too much documentation for this excuse to be credible. He was found guilty on all four counts. The death sentence was carried out by hanging on 16 October 1946.

In his autobiography, written in prison, an unrepentant Rosenberg insisted on Germany's need for Hitler in the wake of the humiliation of World War I. He was great in every respect, Rosenberg insisted. 'I worshipped him, I stayed loyal to him to the end.'[66] National Socialism was a great idea whose time would come again. Hero-worship of Hitler was accompanied in Rosenberg by ambition and self-importance on the one hand, and a querulous resentment when he was frustrated or negated on the other. Hatred was probably the deepest emotion he felt.

Rosenberg's lack of human feeling came through in the manner in which he described his two marriages. First, he showed a real lack of sympathy during the last illness of his first wife, Hilda, a middle-class Baltic German woman whom he had married in 1915. Rather than eliciting his support, her suffering led to their separation in 1923, followed not long afterwards by her death. Two years later he married his second wife Hedwig, whom he had met in Munich, and who, he wrote in strikingly unemotional terms, 'always behaved towards me in a comradely manner'. On a less intimate scale, a diary entry written on 14 July 1942 described how, driving through Ukrain, he saw 'long lines of misery passing by, ragged people with a sack on their backs, pulling their miserable possessions on primitive carts from the countryside into the towns, or from the towns into the countryside'. He regarded them not as refugees from Nazism but as the product of Soviet rule, a rule that had brought 'a 25-years-long levelling-down of human instinct'.[67]

The following summer, after the most deadly Allied bombing raids of the war had devastated the port city of Hamburg, killing an estimated 40,000 people, Rosenberg did not waste any sympathy on the dead, the injured and the homeless survivors, but remarked merely: 'In view of this annihilation of the big cities there seems to me to be a chance to rediscover the rural as never before ... At any rate, I will engage myself in ensuring that world-cities with all their backyards never rise again.' At the very end of his life, Rosenberg had only 'a feeling of hatred ... when I think of the millions of murdered, hunted Germans', and a 'feeling of sympathy' with Hitler, who, he thought, had 'loved Germany so dearly', but was now 'dead, wrapped in a shroud, laid in a ditch, drenched in petrol, and burned'. He had not a single word of pity or remorse for the many millions, not only Jews but also Russians and other Europeans, to whom Hitler had brought death and destruction.[68] This striking lack of human feeling perhaps stemmed ultimately from the fact that so many of Rosenberg's close relatives had died, above all in his early life, so that he had learned very early to avoid committing himself emotionally to people.[69] He had, the prison psychiatrist Douglas R. Kelley concluded, a 'complete lack of consideration for human values and human rights'.[70]

8
The Architect: Albert Speer

No leading Nazi was more successful in rescuing his reputation after the war than Albert Speer. While Rudolf Hess managed to convince at least some people that he was mentally ill, and persuade a few that his 'peace mission' in May 1941 was something more than a mere harebrained escapade, Speer fooled almost everybody, including intelligent and informed historians such as Alan Bullock, Hugh Trevor-Roper, George L. Mosse, Gordon A. Craig and Alan Milward, into thinking that he was an unpolitical technocrat who never participated in the antisemitic obsessions, political ideologies and murderous activities of the Third Reich and its paladins. Even Gitta Sereny, an experienced and critical analyst of the Nazi regime, fell for his lies despite questioning him closely in a lengthy series of interviews conducted after his release from Spandau Prison in Berlin in 1966.[1] Hugh Trevor-Roper called Speer 'the real criminal of Nazi Germany', but this was something of a backhanded insult, since Trevor-Roper considered him an intelligent and cultured man, far removed from the vulgarity and fanaticism of the Nazi leaders, a man who did all he could to sustain Hitler's regime at a time when it was committing the most horrific crimes in human history. Unlike the others, he implied, Speer should have known better.[2]

Speer stuck to his story as long as he lived: he was an apolitical architect, seduced by the possibilities of technology that Nazism offered, bound to Hitler in a friendship created by their shared enthusiasm for urban design and architectural creativity, a man whose guilt lay not in taking part in the crimes of the Third Reich but in not knowing about them and making no attempt to find out. Both in his self-defence at the International War Crimes Tribunal held in Nuremberg after the war, where he was sentenced to twenty years in prison, and in his brilliantly perceptive and readable memoirs, composed in such close collaboration

with Joachim Fest and his publisher Wolf Jobst Siedler that they might almost be termed ghost-written, he succeeded in convincing the world that his guilt lay in his innocence.[3] The memoirs were an immediate best-seller. As Magnus Brechtken, his latest, most thorough and most critical biographer, has remarked, the memoirs mention 'no real persecution of the Jews, no crusades of annihilation, no violence, no wars of conquest. Instead, there's the hard-working Mr Speer, who somehow lived in the time after 1933, like most of his readers.'[4] Speer followed his memoirs with the publication of the secret diaries he had kept during his post-war imprisonment, revised and heavily augmented, again with the assistance of Fest and Siedler. Through these books, through the innumerable interviews he granted to researchers, and through television series such as the multi-episode *The World at War* (1973), which depended heavily on his participation, Speer succeeded in shaping a large part of the way in which not only he himself but also the Third Reich and its leading figures were understood and portrayed in the post-war years by historians and public alike. His interviews and his books seduced through the apparent reasonableness and intellectual acuity with which he presented himself, inviting reader and viewer to identify with him as a civilized, cultured and educated man, unlike the vast majority of leading Nazis, and to see the Third Reich from the point of view of an insider who was also an outsider.[5] Unpicking the lies and legends he wove around himself thus involves unpicking other parts of our understanding of Nazi Germany as well.

Albert Speer was the youngest of the men who formed the top echelon of Nazi leaders during the war. Born in Mannheim on 19 March 1905, he was the second of the three sons of an architect who was sufficiently well off to afford a house with fourteen rooms and an establishment consisting of no fewer than seven servants. In 1918 the family moved to the university town of Heidelberg, where Albert went to school, graduating in 1923 with fairly average grades. His family was able to continue supporting him through the inflation years thanks to a legacy they had converted into a dollar account at just the right time. As was normal for German students, he changed university twice, first from Mannheim to Munich, then from Munich to the Technical University in Berlin. He seems to have led a conventional student life, but besides the usual sports and amusements he won the approval of his professor, the architect

Heinrich Tessenow, and became his assistant on graduating in 1927, marrying his long-term girlfriend Margarete Weber the following year.[6]

Speer later claimed that he had been won over to Nazism on attending a rally addressed by Hitler in Berlin on 4 December 1930; the power of Hitler's rhetoric overwhelmed him, he wrote, bringing about a sudden, Damascene conversion. But in fact he had already joined the Nazi automobile club some months before, in the summer; as the owner of a car, he was a relatively rare phenomenon in the Party, and in this way he could put his services at its disposal. Well before he had heard Hitler speak in person, therefore, he must have become familiar with the Nazi Party and its programme. German universities at this time were hotbeds of extreme nationalism: student unions were the domain of the far right, duelling fraternities exercised a powerful influence, and conservative and nationalist professors dominated the teaching body. By the late 1920s, the National Socialist German Student League was becoming the leading political force in German higher education.[7]

It was not surprising, then, that Albert Speer became a convert to National Socialism. The speeches he heard by Hitler, then, later, Goebbels, were full of hatred against the Weimar Republic, against democracy, against 'subhuman' Communists, and for the creation of an exclusively 'Aryan' Germany, for the overcoming of social divisions in a 'people's community', and for the revival of Germany's fortunes in a political process in which violence would play a central role. After attending one rally addressed by Joseph Goebbels, Speer later claimed that he was shocked by the violence of the police against the participants as they left, but in fact the account of this meeting in the Nazi propagandist's diaries makes no mention of any such thing, enthusing instead about 'the masses' who, pumped up by his speech, streamed out onto the street 'as if mad ... Never had it been so wild.' Speer joined the Party on 1 March 1931, becoming a member of the Nazi stormtrooper organization at the same time, as well as the Fighting League of German Architects and Engineers. An intelligent and ambitious man, he surely knew what he was doing. The National Socialists were enjoying a massive rise in popularity in 1930, culminating in the national elections of 14 September, when they increased their representation in the German legislature from twelve to 107. Hitler was the coming man, and it seemed a natural step for an ambitious young professional from a bourgeois-nationalist background to join him.[8]

ALBERT SPEER

At the end of the winter semester 1931–32 Speer resigned from his university position, not because he was in financial difficulties (he was not, despite his later claim that he was), but because he had decided to work more intensively for the Nazi Party. He began to receive commissions from the Party for jobs like the conversion of buildings into Party offices, transmitted through his friend Karl Hanke, whom he had met in the summer of 1930 and who was subsequently Goebbels's personal adjutant. Spending increasing amounts of time in Berlin, Speer was drawn into close proximity to the Nazi elite by Hanke, and to signal this transition he resigned from the rowdy stormtrooper movement in the autumn of 1932, following the Nazi victory in the summer elections, and joined the motorized section of the SS. With the Nazi seizure of power in the first months of 1933, he started to receive further architectural commissions from Goebbels, notably the stage-set for the Nazi celebration of May Day as a 'Day of National Labour', in which workers were forced to participate – the day before the abolition of the trade unions. Speer presented this ideologically, as the expression of the Nazi revolution, with serried ranks of flag-carrying masses as its centre-point. Goebbels was so pleased with Speer's work that he offered him further commissions, culminating in the design and construction of a permanent site for the annual Nazi Party rally outside Nuremberg, and the creation of a 'cathedral of light' for the rally itself, consisting of rows of searchlights pointing vertically into the night sky. As Hitler himself put it, the effect of the whole presentation was to give 'the state of the German people the cultural endorsement of the Germanic race as for ever valid'.[9]

The financial and logistical organization of this gigantic project gave Speer valuable managerial experience. It also marked his rapid ascent through the Nazi hierarchy. He began to accumulate offices in the regime, including membership of the Senate of the Reich Chamber of Culture, Goebbels's organization of artists, writers, musicians and the like, to which no Jews were admitted and everyone in the culture industries had to belong in order to be allowed to work. The most important of these positions was the directorship of the programme *Schönheit der Arbeit* ('Beauty of Labour'), part of the Labour Front, the Nazi body, led by Robert Ley, that replaced the trade unions: its job was to compensate factory and other workers for the depressed wages, long hours, and lack of representation by unions that they had to endure under the Nazi regime by providing improved canteen and sporting facilities, free concerts and cultural events on the shop floor, and cleaner, tidier, more hygienic and better-ventilated working conditions. Needless to say, the workers were forced to carry out the improvements in their own spare time and at their own expense.[10]

It was during this period, 1933–34, that Speer first met Hitler, but contrary to the impression given in his memoirs, it was not until 1935 that he began to become close to him. Well into 1935, following the death the previous year of the Leader's favourite architect Paul Ludwig Troost, Hitler was commissioning other architects for buildings that would form part of his grandiose plans for the conversion of Berlin into a world capital (such as Tempelhof airport, the Olympic Stadium and the new Reich Air Ministry). But Speer quickly nosed ahead of the competition, and was soon accompanying the Nazi leader at meals and on his travels. His familiarity with the dictator won him ever more major contracts, which he steered through his rapidly expanding office, creaming off ever-greater profits for his private business. These included the German pavilion at the Paris World Exposition in 1937 and the new Reich Chancellery. He drew up an urban plan for Berlin that envisaged the demolition of large parts of the city to make way for gigantic buildings linked by boulevards and capped by four huge airports on the perimeter. All this led to his appointment as General Inspector of Buildings for the reconstitution of the Reich Capital, responsible to Hitler alone and thus bypassing the municipality and all the relevant ministries; Speer dealt with the objections of the mayor of Berlin at this usurpation of his power by eventually persuading Hitler to sack him.[11]

In 1938 Speer began preparations for the transformation of Berlin by securing the supply of building materials, in particular brick and stone on a huge scale (he estimated that two billion bricks a year would be required). This he achieved in collaboration with Heinrich Himmler, who set up an SS construction supply company, arrested some 12,000 'asocials' in April and June, and put them in concentration camps prior to using them as forced labour on these projects. Many of these prisoners were forced to work in degrading and murderous conditions in a gigantic brick factory situated close to Sachsenhausen concentration camp, just outside Berlin. Himmler had another concentration camp built in May 1938 at a granite quarry in Flossenbürg in a remote part of Bavaria. All of these facilities were constructed with the aim of providing materials for Speer's building projects, as was another quarry camp at Mauthausen, near Linz, in Austria. Petty criminals were prominent among the prisoners at these facilities; the heavy labour they were forced to carry out killed many of them in a process the SS termed 'annihilation through labour' (*Venichtung durch Arbeit*).[12] In addition, since Speer's construction plans required the demolition of a substantial number of houses and apartment blocks, he instigated enquiries as to how many were inhabited by Jews, who, he said, could be compulsorily evicted or dispossessed without compensation. Tens of thousands of Jewish families lost their homes as a result. In 1940 Speer sent a telegram to his staff in Berlin, asking about 'the eviction action of the 1,000 Jew-dwellings', which included a large house in the diplomatic quarter of the city that he purchased, at the state's expense, for conversion into an enormous office block for his ever-expanding private architectural practice. Speer also acquired a house cheaply from a member of the Rothschild family who had been forced to leave the country; it was located close to Goebbels's private house on the island of Schwanenwerder to the western side of Berlin, where Hitler was also for a time planning to live. However, when the Nazi leader lost interest in the area, preferring to escape to his retreat on the Obersalzberg, Speer sold the property, making a tidy profit in the process. Determined to be as close as possible to Hitler, Speer then set up a new branch of his office on the Obersalzberg itself, and made arrangements to live nearby with his family, purchasing a hunting lodge in the area for the purpose.[13]

With the beginning of the war, Speer began to move into construction projects for the armed forces, including an experimental rocket-propulsion site on the Baltic coast at Peenemünde, air-raid shelters, and some 200 armaments factories for Göring's Luftwaffe. After the invasion of Poland in September 1939 and the Soviet Union in June 1941, he extended the scope of his responsibilities to infrastructure and supply projects in the occupied European East. In the meantime, he had grown still closer to Hitler, and accompanied him on his private tour of Paris on 23 June 1940: two days later Hitler put him in charge of construction for a number of German cities, including Nuremberg. In occupied Alsace, another new concentration camp was now opened by the SS, at Natzweiler-Struthof, near where slave labourers were forced to work in quarries producing granite for the new German Stadium outside Nuremberg.[14] In Berlin itself, buildings began to be razed to make way for the planned Great Hall, after Speer had shown an enthusiastic Hitler a scale model of the reconstructed city, renamed *Germania*, intended to symbolize Germany's status as global hegemon after victory had been achieved in the war.[15]

Having reached the upper echelons of the Nazi leadership, Speer was now confronted with the task of asserting himself in the incessant power struggles waged at this level. Even in 1941, as plans were being laid for the reshaping of Berlin into a world capital, he clashed with a rival architect, Hermann Gieseler, whom Hitler had appointed his construction and design agent for Munich (the 'Capital of the Movement'), also commissioning him to turn the dictator's home town of Linz into a national cultural centre. With the support of Martin Bormann, Gieseler managed to stop Speer's attempt to take control of these functions. Shocked and frustrated, Speer petulantly resigned from his positions in the Labour Front, including the directorship of the 'Beauty of Labour' programme.[16] But on 8 February 1942 chance came to his aid in the form of the accidental death in a plane crash of the Minister of Munitions, the engineer Fritz Todt.[17] Speer, who happened to be on the spot, visiting Hitler at his field headquarters in Rastenburg (today Kętrzyn in Poland), was summoned to see the Nazi leader, who immediately appointed him to take Todt's place. The choice seemed an obvious one, as Goebbels noted in his diary: both men were regarded as technically competent, experienced managers of large-scale projects. Speer immediately secured from Hitler an official guarantee of complete control over armaments production, to ward off powerful figures like Göring who were circling around Todt's legacy like political vultures, and won the backing of his partner in the construction industry, Heinrich Himmler.[18]

At this moment, the German advance into Eastern Europe had run into difficulties, with the armies of Operation Barbarossa forced to a standstill before Moscow at the end of 1941. Dissatisfied with the performance of his generals, Hitler had removed a number of them from office and taken over the leadership of the army himself. Speer's appointment was made in parallel to this reorganization of the military effort, the product of a nascent sense of desperation about the future of the war that replaced the complacency of the early years of victory. Declaring 'the war must be won!' and constantly invoking the backing of Hitler, Speer took control over ever larger areas of the economy, reducing Göring, head of the Four-Year Plan, to little more than an economic figurehead, and later on pushing aside Economics Minister Walther Funk. Speer intensified cooperation with the SS above all in the requisitioning of forced labour; he put Fritz Sauckel, a regional Nazi leader appointed on 21 March 1942 as head of labour procurement, under continual pressure to provide ever greater numbers of foreign, overwhelmingly forced labourers, especially from the occupied territories in the East, along with concentration-camp inmates and prisoners of war, to feed the insatiable appetite of his Munitions Ministry. By the time the war came to an end, almost 14 million people had been dragooned into this service, working for minimal wages or no pay at all, and living in appalling conditions, overseen by brutal and murderous guards drawn from Himmler's SS. The number who perished is unclear, but certainly ran into the hundreds of thousands.[19]

Speer's collaboration with Himmler extended to supplying and financing materials for the extension of the concentration camp at Auschwitz, including the construction of a rail connection and crematoria for the 'special treatment' of prisoners, as the relevant file put it. Members of his staff visited the camp to check on the work. Speer carried out inspection tours of, among other sites, the concentration camp at Mauthausen, and tank factories employing slave labour. Always now dressed in uniform, he also toured munitions factories, handing out medals to German workers and managers, and urging an intensification of their efforts to secure a final victory. He betrayed no sense of awareness that the tide had turned in 1943 or the Allies were gaining the upper hand. In public he portrayed himself as a man of the people, a simple party comrade, a true member of the people's community, the *Volksgemeinschaft* that the Third Reich aimed to create among racially sound Germans. At the same time, he unfolded a major propaganda campaign that portrayed his command over the Nazi war economy as a triumph of energetic, politically committed management, implying that this qualified him, as the youngest of the Nazi leaders, to succeed Hitler when the time eventually came.[20]

In his memoirs, Speer boasted that 'within half a year of my taking office we had significantly increased production in all the areas within our scope'. Gun and tank manufacture was up by a quarter, while the entire armaments output almost doubled. By July 1944, despite increasingly intense Allied bombing raids, it had trebled, whereas the labour force had grown by only 30 per cent. Speer claimed that he had achieved the huge growth in efficiency in armaments output by applying 'the methods of democratic economic leadership', delegating responsibility and allowing increased individual initiative to businessmen and factory heads. Over-large numbers of variants of particular models of tanks or planes were reduced, increasing efficiency; unnecessary decorative flourishes, such as the lacquering of locomotives or the stylistic embellishment of weapons, were dispensed with, and everything was focused on the essentials; prices were fixed across the board, providing an incentive for manufacturers to cut costs; planning was streamlined and time-consuming alterations to projects were cut to a minimum, enabling more items to be turned out. What was striking about these boasts was that even long after the war was over, when he came to write his memoirs, Speer evidently had no consciousness that he was making a major contribution to a genocidal war started without provocation by the man he was now trying to help win it. He presented his management style as entirely politically neutral, even though he knew full well the purposes to which it was being put, with his full approval at the time. His irrational optimism, which ran counter to the gloomy realism of his predecessor Fritz Todt, was not least the product of his fanatical commitment to Hitler and the Nazi cause. Yet there was no way, even in 1941, that the war could have been won, whatever new efficiencies were introduced to the armaments industry. The failure of Operation Barbarossa should have been a warning. But Speer, blinded by his power, his achievements, and his belief in Hitler, could not see it.[21]

Subject to closer inspection, moreover, Speer's impressive claims turn out to be hollow. Many of the changes he boasted about had already been introduced before he took office, above all by Fritz Todt, who of course did not live to see them come to fruition, but also by Erhard Milch, who was in charge of aircraft production. On the other hand, repeated amendments to production programmes continued, slowing down production in the interest of what were often very minor technical improvements. This prompted a complaint by the head of the Planning Office in the Ministry of Munitions, Hans Kehrl, in March 1944, that 'nobody, not even our Minister, recognizes the importance of this matter'.[22] The improvement in productivity in the second half of the war was exaggerated by Speer, whose staff manipulated the statistics in order to impress Hitler and raise morale among the population. In a more limited way, it was real enough; but much of it came simply from manufacturers and workers learning from experience, rather from the measures the new Munitions Minister claimed to have introduced. Moreover, the simplification and rationalization of production was too often achieved at the cost of quality. The factories were churning out increasing quantities of planes, tanks and guns, but new tank models were rushed out before they were ready, so that the tanks frequently broke down, while combat aircraft were still too slow to match the speed of their Allied counterparts. Above all, no amount of rationalization could hope to bring German war production up to anywhere near the level required to match either British, American or Soviet production, let alone all three at the same time. Some 15,000 new combat planes were manufactured in Germany in 1942, 26,000 in 1943 and 40,000 in 1944, the increase reflecting among other things reforms introduced by Todt, Speer and Milch; but in 1944 this was still less than a fifth of the combined aircraft production of the three main Allied powers, and even had the improvements been able to continue, the total was never likely to be more.[23]

During this period, Speer was constantly travelling round Germany and occupied Europe, overseeing his ever-expanding empire; he only visited his family in Berchtesgaden when Hitler was there. In early October 1943 he was in Posen, where he spoke to the assembled Nazi Gauleiters about the war economy, threatening them with sanctions by the SS if they did not follow his line. There is conclusive evidence that he stayed there to listen to Himmler's notorious speech giving details of the genocidal 'Final Solution'. In December 1943 Speer carried out an inspection of the V-2 rocket production facility in the Harz Mountains, where slave labourers lived and toiled under conditions so appalling that a third of the 60,000-strong workforce died of hunger, disease and brutal mistreatment by the camp officers. His only action following the visit was to write to Hans Kammler, the SS officer in charge of the facility, congratulating him on his achievement. Yet at his trial before the Nuremberg War Crimes Tribunal, Speer denied ever having visited a labour camp of any kind and said he had not been in Posen to hear Himmler speak. Both these statements were lies.[24]

In the early months of 1944 Speer fell ill, initially with an inflammation of the knee, but then more generally with symptoms of serious physical exhaustion. He was in hospital, then convalescence, from mid-January till May. In his memoirs he insinuated that Himmler had used his absence from work to try and usurp his functions, but this was pure invention: in fact, he remained close to the SS leader, and continued to be regarded by the Nazi leadership as indispensable, as Goebbels's diaries show. His convalescence allowed Speer to spend time getting to know his five children (eventually there were six), whom he seldom otherwise saw.[25] When he eventually returned to work, it was to resume his futile drive to boost the war economy in what others, notably his predecessor Fritz Todt, had long recognized was a hopeless struggle against overwhelming odds. As late as December 1944, Speer was still boasting of 'decisive technical steps forward' that would demonstrate the 'superiority of our weapons' which 'the enemy' would come 'to feel to a constantly increasing degree'. Thus German workers could still expect what he called the 'final German victory'. While he was spurring the German people on to ever greater efforts, the numbers of Germans killed rose almost exponentially: over one and a quarter million German troops died in the last four and a half months of the war, making a total of a third of all German forces' deaths since September 1939. By April 1945 there were more than half a million sick and wounded German soldiers, airmen and sailors in hospital. More than 20,000 combat planes were lost in the second half of 1944 alone. A substantial part of the responsibility for this carnage lay with Speer, whose blind insistence on continuing the fight flew in the face of the hopeless and murderous reality.[26]

But by the end of January 1945 Speer was finally recognizing the inevitable, reporting to Hitler that the rapid advance of the Allies in East and West meant that the possibilities of supplying the German forces with weapons and ammunition were being reduced to almost zero. In mid-March he finally told Hitler that the economy was in a state of collapse. The dictator responded with his infamous 'Nero order', commanding the destruction of anything that could be of use to the oncoming enemy. Whereas Hitler, Goebbels and many others were determined to go down fighting, and Himmler sought to rescue the situation through negotiating independently with the Allies, Speer, who had just turned forty, began to look for a means of carrying on in a soon-to-be post-Nazi world. Germany's honour could be salvaged if the troops continued to resist the enemy as long as they could. But by ordering military production to continue and by frustrating Hitler's scorched-earth policy, he was himself forcing the Allies to attack and destroy production facilities, thus causing far more damage than the 'Nero order', which few Germans, looking to their own self-preservation, were prepared to follow. Speer's claim that he planned at this stage to assassinate Hitler has met with some scepticism, but has been independently corroborated; however, it came in the end to nothing. As for his own position, Speer sent his family into the countryside near the Baltic Sea, and rushed around collecting his valuables to use as a basis for the family's existence after the war. A final interview with Hitler, in which, if we are to believe Speer's account, the Armaments Minister confessed to his attempts to frustrate the implementation of the 'Nero order', led only to Speer's dismissal by the dictator shortly afterwards.[27]

Like other surviving Nazi leaders, including, for a short while, Himmler, Ley and Göring, Speer imagined he would be able to play a significant role in post-war Germany – a fantasy that, in all these cases, betrayed a continuing lack of comprehension of the depths of criminality to which they had all sunk. Incredibly, Speer made it known to several people in the final months of the war, and to fellow members of the shadowy post-Hitler Cabinet led by Karl Dönitz and based for a short while in Flensburg, in Schleswig-Holstein, that he expected to be asked by the victorious Allies to head the post-war operation to reconstruct Germany's bombed-out cities.[28] So his arrest, along with that of the other remaining Nazi leaders, came as a rude awakening. In their trial before the International War Crimes Tribunal in Nuremberg, from October 1945 to October 1946, Speer managed, however, to win over the sympathy of the court by demonstratively accepting its legitimacy, confessing to the crimes of the regime he had served so faithfully over the years, and providing the investigators with vast quantities of documents from his private practice and his Ministry. The other defendants, headed by Hermann Göring, were appalled by what they regarded as a betrayal of everything they had stood for. But they could do nothing to stop him.[29]

Speer distanced himself from the regime by claiming to have been a technocrat who had known nothing about Auschwitz. He denied ever having used slave labour, putting the blame on Fritz Sauckel, whose job it had been to organize and maximize the supply of slave labour that Speer had himself demanded. Somehow, Speer got away with it: nobody noticed the fact that key incriminating documents such as his official engagements diary were missing from the material he had supplied, and his most important partners in the regime – Hitler, Himmler, Goebbels – were no longer around to cast doubt on his denial of knowledge of the camps. The former Armaments Minister stated that the conditions in facilities he was known to have visited, such as the V-2 production centre at 'Camp Dora', had been just like those of a normal factory, even though he knew of the murderous conditions under which the forced labourers toiled, suffered and died there. His lies went unprobed by the prosecutors, who were largely unaware of the true nature of these facilities, and over-impressed by Speer's claim to have prepared a coup against Hitler early in 1945. In the end, he piled the blame on Hitler, excusing the German people who, like himself, he said, had fallen for the Führer's charismatic appeal.[30]

While many of the other defendants, including Sauckel, were sentenced to death and executed, Speer got away with a sentence of twenty years' imprisonment, most of it in Spandau Prison. He spent his time cultivating a garden, walking (in an imaginary journey around the world), and writing a secret diary. Frequent appeals were made by his sympathizers for his release, but all were in vain. After regaining his freedom in 1966, he became a best-selling author and much sought-after interviewee. By the time of his death at a hospital in London, on 1 September 1981, he was widely regarded as a 'good Nazi'. His wife Margarete and family had stood by him throughout his long incarceration; he rewarded them by beginning an affair with a married woman, a German who lived in London: it was his final betrayal. Only gradually was his elaborately exculpatory self-mythologization deconstructed. Despite his efforts to have them destroyed, his office diaries were made available in full to researchers not long after his death: the result was the young historian Matthias Schmidt's devastatingly revealing book, published in 1982, that exposed the omissions presented in Speer's own account of his role in the Nazi dictatorship and brought to public attention his part in the racial persecution and extermination of the Jews.[31] Schmidt's damning findings were ignored or explained away by historians and commentators as eminent as the Hitler specialist Eberhard Jäckel, the journalist Karl-Heinz Janssen, and, predictably enough, Joachim Fest and Wolf Jobst Siedler, who had co-written Speer's memoirs. Bit by bit, however, historians and journalists such as Volker Ullrich, of the weekly *Die Zeit*, laid bare Speer's lies and the role played by Fest and Siedler in propagating them. It was not until the release of the film director Heinrich Breloer's 2005 documentary *Speer und Er* (*Speer and Him*) that the demolition of Speer's account of himself reached a wider public. After Magnus Brechtken's critical biography, published in 2017, nothing of that account remains.[32]

PART III
The Enforcers

Introduction

While men like Goebbels, Göring, Himmler or, later on, Speer, to a greater or lesser extent helped shape the Third Reich and, under Hitler's leadership, played a significant role in its rise and fall, a second rank of leading figures outside the central locus of power played an important but ultimately subordinate part in its history. These included some who were with Hitler from the early years as well as some who rose to prominence later on. Some of them, like Rudolf Hess or Franz von Papen, occupied positions of public prominence not matched by any real political power; others, like Adolf Eichmann or, until his move to Prague, Reinhard Heydrich, worked mainly behind the scenes, largely shunning publicity and avoiding exposure by Goebbels's media machine. Still others, such as the antisemitic newspaper editor Julius Streicher, the Governor-General of occupied Poland Hans Frank, or the Labour Front leader Robert Ley, operated in their own particular sphere of influence largely separate from the overall direction of the regime as a whole. What united them was a shared loyalty to Hitler and the ideas that powered the Nazi Party.

There was no single personality type that could be described as 'Nazi'. The Marxist social scientists of the Frankfurt Institute for Social Research attempted shortly after the war to demonstrate that Nazis possessed an 'authoritarian personality' derived from a warped relationship with their authoritarian fathers, causing them unquestioningly to obey orders from above and abuse their power over people in positions subordinate to them. This led them to replicate this behaviour and project it onto the wider canvas of politics and society, transferring their fear and resentment of their fathers onto social and racial minorities, above all the Jews.

But this does not really explain very much. Why, when there were millions of people in the late nineteenth and early twentieth centuries who grew up in families dominated by an authoritarian father, did only some of them become Nazis? Individual psychopathology is of little use here. More important was the ultra-nationalist political culture that surrounded them. Individual murderers in all countries, whatever the political system that governs them, commit their crimes in violation of the norms imposed by ordinary society, which is why society imposes punishments on them, while Nazi murderers and fanatical supporters of Hitler were legitimated by the Nazi movement and the Third Reich. Nazism released people from the normal constraints that society imposes on the violent and abusive desires that exist to a degree among all of us, and actively encouraged people to act them out.[1] Ideological and historical context in the end was more important than individual psychology.

The range of explanations that historians have offered over the years for why people supported Hitler and implemented, or accepted, Nazi policies and ideas, is almost limitless. At a very basic level, some have suggested that the answer lies in human stupidity. Nazi ideology was a mishmash of half-baked concepts and simplistic slogans, designed to appeal to the semi-literate, the uneducated and the marginal. It seduced them through cheap rhetoric and mindless public display. Its appeal was above all to the gullible and the easily manipulated. Unfortunately for this view, however, many Nazis were neither stupid nor ignorant, but highly educated and well informed. University students in the 1920s were among the groups in society most susceptible to the blandishments of Hitler and his party. Many senior officers in the SS could brandish degree certificates and PhD dissertations in the face of those who questioned their intellectual ability or their professional qualifications. Ascribing to stupidity people's commitment to Nazism and their willingness to put its brutal and murderous ideas into practice, or to support or put up with them because they knew no better, simply will not wash.

Nazi perpetrators, mainly but not exclusively men, were not from one single generation; they transcended generational peer groups. Some of them had spent their formative years in the Empire, during the 1890s and 1900s; others had still been children at the time of the Nazi seizure of power. Studying them as age cohorts does not get one very far. More importantly, as the historian Alex J. Kay has observed:

INTRODUCTION

They were certainly united by a shared national trauma that cut across age groups and social backgrounds. Defeat in the First World War, the obliteration of German great-power ambitions (loss of colonies and substantial swathes of Reich territory; military and economic subjugation) and the tumultuous fallout of 1918–19 caused an individual and collective trauma in German society. This affected not merely those who consciously experienced these events but also – by means of intergenerational transmission – their progeny, who suffered a secondary traumatization. In this situation, ethnic-nationalist sentiments already present in the belated nation-state were radicalized further.[2]

These individuals were motivated among other things by a fervent conviction that absolutely radical measures were necessary to reverse the humiliation of 1918 and overcome this trauma. If ideology in its broadest sense was a common denominator, however, the central element of Nazism – antisemitism – was only one of the motivating factors in Nazi mass killing, since more than half the victims were not Jewish. Radical ethnic nationalism and biological racism were key factors in the Nazi murder of non-Jewish victims. Since the perpetrators included thousands of members of the German armed forces, who constituted a cross-section of German society, it seems reasonable to conclude that they represented not 'ordinary men' who might in a similar situation have been drawn from any national group, but 'ordinary Germans in extraordinary times'. The drive to kill Germany's supposed enemies was not innate in some imaginary German 'national character', but the consequence of Germany's unique situation in the quarter-century or so after the end of World War I.[3]

Like other prominent or influential Nazis, the men whose lives are examined in the following chapters had very often suffered a major setback in their career. Hitler's narrative of national crisis, disintegration and decline offered them a way to overcome the effects of this trauma by identifying their own lives with their country's. Germany's calamitous defeat and humiliation, like their own, could only be reversed by radical action. Blaming the Jews was an easy and simple way of avoiding a confrontation with the complex factors behind Germany's defeat in 1918. At the most basic level, it was impossible for them to admit that after four years of mass death and huge casualties on the battlefield, privation and even starvation at home, and stalemate followed by defeat on the front, Germany from 1914 to 1918 was not, in the end, capable of winning a war against a coalition of great powers, above all the British Empire and the United States. Defeat must have been the product of malign, hidden and conspiratorial forces, above all the global machinations of the Jews. Coming from a conservative, anti-democratic and antisemitic political milieu, men of widely differing backgrounds like Franz von Papen or Adolf Eichmann, Rudolf Hess or Robert Ley, Reinhard Heydrich, Julius Streicher or Hans Frank, could find fulfilment and compensation in committing themselves fully to the Nazi cause and carrying out its project without any kind of moral reservation.

9
The Deputy: Rudolf Hess

Early in 1914, Rudolf Hess, a nineteen-year-old commercial apprentice in Hamburg, decided to start wearing a monocle. It was not that he was poorly sighted in one of his eyes – indeed, his eyesight was near-perfect, good enough to allow him to train as a fighter pilot towards the end of the war; it was simply a social affectation, designed to impress his friends. Monocles were the height of fashion in the 1890s and 1900s. As J. Bryan Lowder notes of the monocle, which became a signifier of high social status in the 1890s:

> It was a symbol of wealth from the start.... Sporting one as a general part of one's attire was always something of a fashionable affectation. Like the lorgnette, spyglass, and, a direct ancestor, the quizzing glass, the monocle basically originated as a faddish accessory of those with the cash and the inclination to purchase such things. ... According to a 1950 article from *Optical Journal*, from the beginning the single lens carried with it 'an air of conscious elegance', making it ripe for ridicule: 'One had the feeling the wearer was being a trifle foolish, an attitude which resulted to some extent from the fact that monocles frequently did not fit and kept dropping out of place.'[1]

Rudolf Hess's mother Klara seems to have shared this feeling. After he had sent her a photograph of him wearing it, she replied: 'I'm absolutely delighted to make your acquaintance with your latest achievement, the monocle. It suits you tremendously, an orang-outang is scarcely more handsome.'[2] Still, the monocle, worn in conjunction with a top hat and frock coat, was a well-known symbol of capitalist wealth at the time, an obvious aspiration for a humble apprentice clerk such as Hess. It was also, however, favoured by army officers, including Hans von Seeckt,

Werner von Fritsch and Erich Ludendorff, conferring on the wearer a touch of the social cachet of the aristocratic Prussian officer.

The Hess family could not aspire personally to a social status as exalted as this. For several generations, beginning in the mid-eighteenth century, they were humble shoemakers in the Franconian town of Wunsiedel, in Protestant Franconia, before Rudolf's grandfather, Johann Christian Hess, staying with some distant relations in Livorno as a commercial trainee, met and married the daughter of the local Swiss consul, Johann Bühler. From here, in 1865, pursuing a career in commerce, he went to Alexandria, at that time a boom-town thanks to the Suez Canal project, the construction of a railway connection to Cairo, and the expansion of the harbour. There was a lively expatriate community of Europeans, mostly British and French, with a few Germans, Greeks, and others. Soon Johann Christian Hess had his own import–export company. He became sufficiently prosperous for his son Fritz to marry Klara Münch, the daughter of an industrialist from Hof, another town in Franconia. The couple moved into a substantial villa, located in the suburbs of Alexandria and equipped with a spacious garden. It was here that they brought up their three children, Rudolf (born 26 April 1894) and his younger brother and sister. Fritz was said later to have been a traditionally strict *paterfamilias*, neat, punctilious and something of a disciplinarian. This was not unusual in the German middle classes at the time, however, and historians such as Joachim C. Fest have laid too much stress on this, ascribing to the domination of his father Hess's own later slavish subservience to Hitler. Stories of his father's strictness all derive from much later, and Hess's relations with him seem in fact to have been cordial. Nor is there any contemporary evidence to support later stories that Rudolf Hess was prevented from going to university by his father's insistence on his preparing for a career in commerce. Hess himself had nothing but fond memories of his years in Egypt, his 'little paradise'.[3]

Rudolf's education in Alexandria was sporadic and unsatisfactory. Dissatisfied with the local schools, his father had secured the services of a private tutor, but the children's education was often interrupted by frequent stays in Germany, where Fritz had bought a plot of land in Reinholdsgrün, ten miles from Wunsiedel in north-eastern Bavaria, and built a small, two-storey villa where the family entertained guests, including hunting parties. So in March 1908 Rudolf was sent to a boarding school, the German House in Bad Godesberg, on the Rhine, an institution much favoured by expat families. Here he flourished, doing well in his studies, as he proudly reported in his letters to his parents. The only criticism the teachers levelled at him was that he was too shy and withdrawn, and needed to speak up more. The atmosphere in the school, as in Rudolf's home, was strongly patriotic and nationalistic, and it was hardly surprising that he joined the youth wing of the Navy League, a mass organization dedicated to supporting Germany's new battle fleet. All this was conventional enough for the son of a middle-class, Protestant family, as was the decision to enrol Rudolf in a commercial apprenticeship when he left school. Although the family was comfortably off, it belonged neither to the propertied nor to the educated middle class but was a step below them both. Acquiring a monocle was only one sign, if the most striking, of Rudolf Hess's social aspirations, his desire to rise in the world.[4]

We know about all this because Hess's letters to his parents survived, along with the replies, in the Hess family home for many decades, gathering dust in the attic until they were rediscovered by his son after his death in 1987. There is no indication in these letters he was unhappy in Hamburg, rather the contrary. Nor was he among the crowds that gathered to cheer the outbreak of war at the end of July 1914. On 27 July he reported to his parents:

> On Sunday I listened to the great war-cry in the cafés. Proper hurrah-patriotism! Among other things, half-drunk figures shouted out our most beautiful patriotic songs, and people regarded themselves as heroes when they threw out any Frenchmen, Russians or Serbs. Didn't impress me much. We should abandon the enthusiasm, or at least its physical expression, until the great moment is there for us; then I'll join in.[5]

Swept away by the heady enthusiasm for war that gripped the German middle classes at this moment, however, he went straight to Munich and enrolled in the Bavarian Army. The family's relatively modest social status was revealed by his automatic entry into the lowest rank, as a private, rather than being steered towards the officer class. His father was full of praise for his 'brave, dashing boy' and thought he would acquit himself bravely. Rudolf's letters home showed not only an enthusiasm for the war but also an aggressive hatred for the French 'barbarians' against whom it was being fought. After a period of training he finally fought them shortly before the end of the year, after which he moved rapidly up the ranks, becoming a non-commissioned officer in May 1915, and winning the Iron Cross, Second Class, along the way.[6]

Rudolf's letters to his parents betrayed a certain disappointment and impatience at the behaviour and attitudes of his fellow soldiers, many of whom were working-class men from the big cities. Their views were in many cases far removed from the patriotic enthusiasm of the German middle classes with whom he was familiar. On 1 August 1915, however, he escaped their company and enrolled for training as an officer. The course proved a disappointment: subjected to month after month of drill, gun practice and trench-digging, he envied contemporaries who were actively fighting at the front. The attitude of those who were already officers also irritated him: he wanted them to be his comrades but they behaved like his superiors. It was not until 8 October 1917 that he was finally promoted to lieutenant. Well before this time, however, Hess had seen action on the Western Front. On 12 June 1916 he was wounded in the upper arm and hand in an engagement north of Verdun; then, after recovering in a hospital behind the lines, he was ordered to the south-eastern front, where Romania had declared war on Austria-Hungary on 27 August 1916. Here he took part in an action against Russian troops who had come to relieve the Romanians, storming their lines and driving them back with heavy fire, as he enthusiastically reported to his parents. It was in Romania that Hess learned of the February 1917 Revolution in Russia and the overthrow of Tsar Nicholas II the next month. Coming across a propaganda pamphlet written in German by Russian revolutionaries, in which the Germans, the addressees, were told they would do better if they followed suit, he wrote a counter-blast in which he argued that the Russians needed a monarch like Kaiser Wilhelm II, and peace would surely come, though only 'when we are completely victorious!'[7]

A few months later he was wounded in the arm again, and then shortly afterwards in the left shoulder. Following his promotion to lieutenant, and feeling bored with life on the battlefront, Hess applied successfully for the Flying Corps, and began training once he had recovered from his wounds. It was not until early November, however, that he entered Fighter Squadron 35 as a pilot. As late as 1 November 1918 he still believed Germany would win the war.[8] The news of Ludendorff's dismissal from his post as First Quartermaster-General of the Great

General Staff in October 1918 had come as a terrible shock. Uncritically swallowing the propaganda line that the German armed forces were invincible, Hess blamed the defeat on the German masses, who always 'unfortunately picked on their great men for so long that they are overthrown'. His reverence for Ludendorff eerily prefigured his later hero-worship of Hitler: Ludendorff, he wrote, 'is of Bismarck's kind ... Despite the continual calumnies and antagonisms, Ludendorff has carried on serving the fatherland with his brilliant, powerful strength.'[9] The Allied Armistice terms, the overthrow of the Kaiser, and the Revolution of 1918 came to Hess as a series of further shocks:

> These are probably the most difficult moments of my life ... The ones who are to blame for everything are the Independents [Social Democrats]. For months they have agitated within the army, until the collapse came. Disguised as soldiers they came to the Front and stirred things up. As civilians they came into Belgian towns and stirred things up. – The enemy's conditions are indeed so terribly humiliating.[10]

Like Hitler, Hess was jolted into political activism by his outrage at Germany's – for him, unexpected – defeat. On 13 December 1918 he was discharged from the armed forces. His attempt to sign up as a pilot for a Free Corps unit to fight 'Spartacists' and 'irridentists' came to nothing. So he took advantage of a scheme pioneered by the Social Democratic government of Bavaria to allow veterans to enter university. The subject he chose to study was *Volkswirtschaft*, roughly, political economy. On occasion, too, he attended the lectures of Professor Karl Alexander von Müller, a right-wing nationalist who had once been a Rhodes Scholar at Oxford. The lectures were also attended by Hermann Göring, who, however, sat in the front row whereas Hess sat at the back.[11]

Like many students during the Weimar years, Hess had to support himself with a part-time job; he worked for a small furniture company, which his army friend Max Eduard Hofweber, a former colleague of the boss, had obtained for him. Hofweber was also deeply involved in ultra-right politics, and took Hess along to a meeting of the *Thule-Gesellschaft*, one of the many small ultra-nationalist, racist and antisemitic political groups that flourished in Munich after the end of the war. The group preached racial purity, linked to the idea that the 'Aryan' race was Nordic in origin (the word 'Thule' stood for a mythical country in the far north, sometimes identified with Iceland). Those who attended its meetings or associated with its members included early Nazis such as Anton Drexler, Dietrich Eckart, Gottfried Feder, Hans Frank, Ernst Röhm and Alfred Rosenberg. Its leading figure, Adam Glauer, was a convicted swindler who called himself Rudolf von Sebottendorff and dabbled in occultism, including astrology and alchemy.[12]

Hess absorbed all of these beliefs (from around this time, his letters began to make references to his horoscopes and to astrology, for example),[13] and was soon playing an active role in the society's affairs. His views were strengthened by the ultra-right political culture of the students he met while he was at Munich University. Like them, he applauded the assassination in February 1919 by a right-wing fanatic of Kurt Eisner, left-wing socialist Minister-President of Bavaria ('Eisner's removal was a blessing'), and when the murder opened the way for a radically revolutionary and then a Communist regime in Munich, he mounted sabotage actions against it, organized the supply of weapons to Thule Society members planning armed resistance, and ran a unit dedicated to forging documents such as rail tickets and official stamps. His unit also infiltrated the Communist Party in the city and supplied information on its members to the Free Corps units that crushed the revolutionary regime in a bloody invasion, sponsored by the legitimate Majority Socialist Bavarian government from its headquarters in northern Bavaria. Hess participated in the action, commanding a small artillery unit, and was lightly wounded in the fighting. His unit provided denunciations of many of the 'revolutionaries' who were summarily executed in the aftermath. He remained in the pay of the Free Corps, subsidized by the army, and took part in its brutal suppression of the 'Red Army' formed by striking Communist industrial workers in the Ruhr, who had helped defeat the anti-Republican 'Kapp *putsch*' in March–April 1920, a defeat that Hess described as 'sad'.[14]

His letters to his parents at this time breathe a strong spirit of hatred and violence against 'the Reds' and are filled with enthusiastic accounts of his part in the fighting in Munich. 'One mustn't think of peace. The only thing that keeps me going is hope for the day of revenge, even if it's still far off. Perhaps I'll still experience it.'[15] He fully shared the anti-semitism of the ultra-right, railing against the 'Jewish press', and the 'Jew-capitalists over there in the Entente'. 'But a strong German policy,' he complained in March 1920, 'doesn't suit our pack of Jews, so it exploits the power of its press correspondingly.' Reporting to his parents on his activities in the Bavarian capital, he described how 'in the past few days we have distributed many leaflets against All-Judah, and especially those that would open people's eyes to the Jewish workers' leaders'. The alleged seduction of the German working class by a (purely imaginary) Jewish clique of socialists was one of the stock beliefs of the ultra-right at this period and prompted the self-description of the Nazis (among other groups) as a nationalist workers' party. As his Free Corps battalion marched off to help quell the Ruhr uprising, reported Hess, each of them went with 'a wonderfully beautiful antisemitic swastika painted on the steel helmet', though they later had to remove them on orders from above. His letters at this time are full of antisemitic verbal abuse. There could be no doubt about the depth and strength of his prejudice against Jews; he had absorbed to the full the racial and conspiracist dogmas of the world in which he now moved: the unthinking milieu of ultra-nationalist violence and hatred characteristic of the Free Corps units of the early 1920s, later described in Klaus Theweleit's powerful psychohistorical study, *Männerphantasien* (*Male Fantasies*). Even the language that Hess used, with its fear-laden and dehumanizing description of an encounter he had, alone on a Munich street, with 'a rabble of Reds with women and children', mirrored that used in the novels and memoirs analysed by Theweleit.[16]

By this time, though he had almost completely neglected his studies (something that was far from being an exception among students in the notoriously tolerant German university system in the 1920s and for long afterwards), Hess had come under the influence of Karl Haushofer, a soldier who had served as adviser to the Japanese Army before the war. Like his friend Hofweber, Hess had served under Haushofer during the war, and by the end of January he had become a family friend of Haushofer, who was now an honorary professor at Munich University, having reached the rank of major-general and retired from military service. Haushofer had published a book holding up Japan's 'rejuvenating wars of expansion', including the invasion of Korea in 1910 and the war against Russia in 1904–5, as examples for the Germans to follow. A follower before the war of the antisemitic historian Heinrich von Treitschke, Haushofer was also a rabid antisemite, and an advocate of 'geopolitics', a doctrine he did much to develop, prescribing territorial expansion as the acid test of a race's viability in the global struggle for supremacy. *Lebensraum* – 'living space' – was the concept he adopted (from pre-war thinkers such as the geographer Friedrich Ratzel and the militarist Friedrich von Bernhardi) to justify his advocacy of the conquest of Eastern Europe, where the Germanic race, he thought, would expand by removing the region's Slavic inhabitants.[17]

At some time during this period, Rudolf Hess had his first encounter with Adolf Hitler, who like him was a war veteran still in the pay of the armed forces. This led Hess to take up with the fledgling Nazi Party early in 1920, although it was not until 1 July that he formally joined it, with the membership number 1,600. It was a natural step for him to take: many of those he knew and mixed with in the Thule Society were joining the Party, since Hitler was already by far the most effective public speaker on the far right. The Nazis seemed the best vehicle for publicizing the Society's ideas and eventually perhaps putting them into effect. Hess was not converted to the Nazi cause by hearing Hitler speak, or meeting him; he was already active in the milieu from which the cause emerged. He was what we would today call a right-wing terrorist, committed to the use of violence in furtherance of racism, antisemitism, and the overthrow of democracy. He dreamed of taking revenge on Germany's enemies: 'Then an ecstasy could once more overcome me, of a virtually senseless storm . . . as with the throwing of hand grenades following the enemy's explosions on Vimy Ridge.'[18] There was never any doubt about his commitment, but initially at least it was to the Party rather than to its leader. And his widespread contacts on the far right were of considerable use to the Party. It was Hess who put Hitler in touch with Ludendorff, for example, and Hess who pleaded Hitler's cause with the right-wing Bavarian Minister-President Gustav Ritter von Kahr. Soon, he was working closely with Hitler, helping him prepare his speeches and feeding him ideas derived from his reading of Haushofer. From Hitler's point of view, Hess had the inestimable advantage of possessing a wide range of useful skills he had acquired during his commercial apprenticeship, including shorthand and typing. Hitler made full use of these over the coming months and years, while the Nazi Party was still a small and underfunded organization. His closeness to Hitler inspired Hess with boundless enthusiasm for the Nazi leader. By April 1921 he was able to report of Hitler: 'He's become a dear friend to me. A splendid fellow!' He encouraged Hitler to believe in his mission to become Germany's leader, seeing in him a man who was close to the people and could speak as one of them. Socially disoriented, shot through with feelings of inferiority, not quite belonging to the solid middle class, and deeply affronted by the shock of Germany's defeat in 1918 and the following revolution, Hess had developed a fervent nationalist commitment. He found in Hitler and the Nazi movement a cause that would give his life meaning and purpose. It was not merely that beneath his hard, unyielding surface Hitler was kind to animals and got on well with children, he wrote: it was above all his iron determination to use any means necessary to bring Germany back to greatness. For Hess, too, the appeal of the Nazi Party lay not least in its promise to overcome the social divisions with which it had been so difficult for him to come to terms in his life. An essay Hess wrote at this time, in answer to a competition question asking for views on what kind of man was going to redeem Germany in the future from its humiliation in the present, breathed a violent spirit of hatred and revenge; the new leader, Hess wrote, had to be prepared to spill blood and throw aside all restraint in dealing with 'traitors'.[19]

From late 1921 onwards, Hess led a series of brutal attacks by a unit of the SA consisting entirely of university students, on Communists and Social Democrats, whose paramilitary formations had no hesitation in fighting back. On 4 November 1921, when fighting broke out at a major Nazi rally, he received a head wound that was serious enough to require stitches. At the same time, however, he returned to his studies, wrote essays and attended lectures. But Hitler soon summoned him to participate in the beer-hall *putsch*, where he appeared in his old army uniform alongside Hitler at the Bürgerbräukeller, like him brandishing a pistol, and then, acting on Hitler's orders, arrested several leading members of the conservative Bavarian government, keeping them hostage under guard while Hitler and the other leading Nazis mounted their coup attempt. On learning of its abject failure, and the escape of most of the hostages, Hess fled from Munich in a car with two of them, stopping several times in heavily wooded countryside to look, as he told them, for a suitable tree from which to hang them. Eventually however they drove off in the car, from which Hess had carelessly failed to remove the ignition key, while he was trying to find beds for the night in a villa some way off the road, and made their way back to Munich. Hess crossed the border into Austria, where he stayed briefly before returning to take refuge with Haushofer. Here he stayed in secret during Hitler's trial, but when he learned of the leniency of the sentences meted out to the putschists, he presented himself to the police, thinking this would be better for him than remaining on the run, 'with the sword of Damocles always hanging over me'. Charged with kidnapping members of the Bavarian government, he was sentenced to eighteen months of 'fortress arrest', and was allocated a pleasant room on the first floor at Landsberg Prison, where Hitler was also confined.[20]

Recent research has helped expose as a legend the oft-repeated claim that Hitler dictated his book *Mein Kampf* to Rudolf Hess in Landsberg: in fact, he wrote it all himself. Hess's role was confined mainly to the period after Hitler's release, when he corrected the proofs, supplying the column subtitles in the second volume, and helped prepare the two unwieldy volumes for publication. Hess's importance to Hitler in this period was rather different: it consisted of introducing him to his contacts, notably Haushofer, who visited him eight times and on more than one occasion had a lengthy conversation with Hitler, most likely firming up the Nazi leader's belief that Germany's long-term geopolitical aims should include the acquisition of *Lebensraum* in Eastern Europe. Hess told his father that his daily routine consisted of getting up at 5 o'clock and brewing a cup of tea for Hitler, reading or writing till 7.30 a.m., breakfasting, then chopping wood till 11 a.m., for a small wage. Then he enjoyed a hot bath, took an afternoon nap, had tea, read again, and ate supper, after which he played games outside or went for a walk with Hitler, conversing with him all the time, and ending the day with tea and cake once more. Hitler spent most of his time writing *Mein Kampf* and sometimes turned away visitors in order to be able to focus on his literary work. He frequently read aloud from his drafts, eliciting from Hess nothing but admiration, even awe. When it was published, Hess predicted on 23 July 1924, it would provoke 'a wave of astonishment, rage, admiration'.[21]

It was during this time that Hess became really close to Hitler, expounding his hero-worship to anyone who would listen. He was rewarded on their release from Landsberg on 2 January 1925 with appointment as Hitler's private secretary, turning down an offer to become Haushofer's assistant in order to do so. The job was far better paid than the university position, he explained to his parents, and still allowed him to continue his studies. He was allocated a female deputy secretary for the more humdrum aspects of the post, so that he could focus on accompanying Hitler on his travels, arranging his trips, booking meals and overnight stays, dealing with the press and handling his correspondence. Hess supported Hitler unconditionally in the various power struggles that took place within the Party in the last years of the Weimar Republic. Most of the time he stayed in the background, though he frequently appeared in the front row with Hitler on marches and demonstrations. This did not mean, however, that he was without personal ambition. Thanks to his academic experience, he said, 'I am suited to be a link between the mass movement and the educated class', and unlike many educated people he was happy to accept the rough and violent methods the Nazis employed.[22] Hess did a great deal to reinforce Hitler's authority within the Party and popularized the greeting '*Heil Hitler*' and the address '*Mein Führer*' when speaking to the Party leader.

Hess spent much of his spare time in physical activities, from Alpine skiing and hiking to participating in flying competitions with an aeroplane provided free of charge by the Nazi Party newspaper, the *Völkischer Beobachter*. He even used this to fly low over a Social Democratic open-air meeting in Hanover, drowning out the voice of the speaker. On 27 December 1927 he married his long-term girlfriend Ilse Pröhl, whom he had met seven years earlier as a fellow student in Munich. Born in 1900, she had joined the party in 1921 and again after it was unbanned in 1925. She was the daughter of a well-to-do doctor, and Hitler approved of the relationship sufficiently to act as a witness to the wedding, along with Haushofer. Hess revealed once more the fact that his views of women belonged in the world described by Klaus Theweleit. Fascist literature on women, argued Theweleit, divided them into 'angels' (nurses, mothers, etc.) or 'whores' (violent, uncontrollable, raging revolutionary nymphomaniac furies). Ilse, for Hess, clearly belonged in the former category. The couple went on walking tours and skiing trips together, and when they were apart, wrote each other frequent letters; Hess also addressed poems to her from time to time. Their only child, Wolf-Rüdiger, so called in part after Hitler's nickname of the time, 'Wolf', was born on 18 November 1937. Inspired by medieval sagas such as the *Nibelungenlied*, Hess prized loyalty above all else, in personal matters as well as political.[23]

It was this that gave Hess the chance to play a more public role than his previous one of Hitler's private secretary, when the electoral setback of November 1932 led to a serious crisis in the Nazi Party and the resignation of Gregor Strasser. Hitler made Hess head of a newly created Central Political Commission, which was intended to exercise a tighter control over the Party, its officials and its members, than had previously been the case. Independent actions that went against Hitler's own tactical intentions were no longer to be permitted. This was an almost impossible task to carry out in the first six months of 1933, after Hitler had been appointed Reich Chancellor – a process in which Hess had only been peripherally involved. In the chaos and violence of the Nazi seizure of power from February to July, the Party rapidly established its supremacy over the organs of the local, regional and national state, and it was neither necessary nor possible for Hess to oversee this process or drive it forward. In the course of the year, however, Hitler elevated Hess to a position of considerable prominence, making him for the first time a public figure: he was given a seat in the Cabinet, appointed Minister Without Portfolio, and finally nominated 'Deputy Leader' (*Stellvertreter des Führers*).[24]

His presence can be traced in various parts of the documentary record, from the drafting of the Nuremberg Laws in 1935 to the annexation of parts of Poland four years later. He delivered numerous antisemitic speeches, describing the League of Nations as 'a farce which functions primarily as the basis for the Jews to reach their own aims', and blaming the Jews once more for Germany's defeat in 1918.[25] He thoroughly approved of the policies adopted by the German conquerors in the occupation of Poland in 1939, including special laws discriminating against Poles. In public, Hess was a significant presence, introducing Hitler's speeches, presiding over major ceremonies, and accompanying Hitler on many of his travels. Hess's speeches helped maintain morale in the early part of the war. He had a reputation for being one of the few honest, upright and incorruptible leading figures in the Nazi regime. His self-identification as a soldier rather than a politician was widely applauded.[26] But the position of Deputy Führer was rather vaguely defined, and did not override those of other Nazi officials, such as, for example, the *Gauleiter* or regional leaders, who continued to enjoy direct personal access to Hitler. Hess was not without ambition: he reacted allergically to any perceived diminution of his status, but he was not really fitted for the constant power struggles within the Nazi regime, and had no real independent power base of his own. His title was in effect an empty one, and became even more so as time went on.

His functions were increasingly taken over by his chief of staff, the hard-working and hard-nosed Martin Bormann, who replaced him as Hitler's personal secretary in August 1935.[27]

Hess proved wholly incapable of dealing with the many complaints that were sent to him about the behaviour of leading Nazis; as 'Putzi' Hanfstaengl commented in a satirical Biblical allusion, 'Come to me, all who are struggling and burdened, and I will – do nothing.'[28] Hess was put in charge of the organization created to deal with Nazi Party members abroad, but did not really play a role in foreign policy; mostly he spent his time welcoming visiting delegations. He was not party to the major domestic and foreign-policy decisions within the regime. By 1939, Alfred Rosenberg was describing him in his diary as indecisive and depressed; he later noted that had let the Party apparatus slip from his grasp and was left without any really significant function.[29] His secretaries reported that he spent much of his time sitting at his desk, aimlessly shuffling papers or just staring into space. He often appeared confused when someone came in and spoke to him.[30]

By 1940 Hess was painfully conscious of his loss of power. Learning that Hitler intended to invade the Soviet Union, he cast his mind back to the 'geopolitical' doctrines of his mentor Karl Haushofer, and thought of Hitler's vague 'peace offer' to Britain made in the aftermath of the fall of France. The dangers of a war on two fronts were obvious. If he could bring about a separate peace with Britain, he would save Germany from this peril and get back into Hitler's good books. His intention was confirmed by one of his astrologers, who told him in late 1940 that he was ordained to bring about peace.[31] Advised by Haushofer's son Albrecht, he decided to contact the Duke of Hamilton, who, he believed, was a leading figure in a peace party within the British establishment. Hamilton, a flying ace like himself, had been a prominent member of the politically active, well-meaning and well-connected Anglo-German Fellowship, and was not entirely without influence, though far from being the key figure Hess thought he was. Although Hitler had banned Hess from flying because it was too dangerous, he took it up again in secret and in the autumn of 1940 began making preparations. At 5.45 p.m. on 10 May 1941, Hess clambered into the cockpit of a modified Messerschmitt Me110 heavy fighter plane parked on the apron of the manufacturer's airfield near Augsburg, started up the engine, and took off.[32]

Hess steered the plane towards the north-west, altering course a few times, and flew at a low altitude up the North Sea. Flying back and forth for a while to avoid detection by British radar, he eventually reached Northumberland on the north-east coast, from where he steered the aircraft across the Scottish lowlands towards Hamilton's estate. Failing to locate the duke's private airstrip, Hess parachuted to earth in a field nearby, allowing the plane to crash and burst into flames a little further on. The local Home Guard apprehended him, and he was eventually taken to meet the duke, to whom he revealed his true identity. The 'peace mission' he bore with him on the flight, which he had drafted himself, without assistance from anyone else, presented to the British government a fanciful set of proposals which boiled down to allowing the British to keep their global Empire if the British gave the Nazis a free hand on the European Continent – a repetition of a similar deal concocted by Hitler some time before. As Churchill realized when these terms were put to him, it was tantamount to a demand for surrender. Their acceptance would have left Britain as a Nazi client state. In Germany, an appalled Hitler vowed that Hess would be hanged if Britain fell to a Nazi invasion. Hess was jailed in the Tower of London, then moved, eventually, to a secure mental hospital in South Wales. After the war was over, he was tried at Nuremberg and sentenced to life imprisonment. On 17 August 1987 he committed suicide in Spandau Prison. To the end of his life, he never repented of his role in Nazi Germany or abandoned his admiration for Hitler. In this, he had the undeviating support of his wife Ilse and son Wolf-Rüdiger, who steadfastly maintained that he was a 'prisoner of peace' whose offer of a negotiated settlement with the British in 1941 had been both genuine and feasible.[33]

Although he presented himself as amnesiac and confused at the Nuremberg trials and pretended not to recognize people he had actually known well, such as his secretary, or Hermann Göring, and though Allied psychiatrists theorized endlessly about his state of mind, Rudolf Hess was not insane. His jailer at Nuremberg, Colonel Andrus, thought 'his madness was all a sham', and said as much in his reports.[34] Indeed, on 29 November 1945 Hess suddenly declared that his inability to remember anything had been 'tactical' and simulated: 'From now on my memory is once more available, also for outside.'[35] The abject failure of his quixotic 'peace mission', the death of Hitler and the defeat of Germany, the Nuremberg trials and the complete obliteration of the Third Reich and everything it stood for, must have turned his world upside-down, and it is scarcely surprising that he showed signs of disorientation. 'Hess's behaviour, both in court and in prison,' Franz von Papen thought, 'was not that of a normal person ... I am personally convinced that Hess was insane, although he may have had lucid moments.'[36] Nevertheless, he was judged sane enough to stand trial. He tried more than once to kill himself, but unlike so many other leading Nazis, he failed, at least until his final attempt, many years after the war was over. In his suicide note he apologized to his former secretary for pretending not to recognize her. He may even have felt guilt for the first time, as he read through the transcripts and evidence of the Nuremberg trials. In the end, Hess was an unthinking, instinctive man of action, driven by racism, antisemitism, violent nationalism, and animated by an uncritical, dog-like devotion to Hitler. His frustrated social ambitions were partly overlaid by war service, and then fulfilled in an unconventional way by his involvement with the Nazi Party. For all his fanatical commitment to Hitler, however, he was unable to make the transition into a bureaucratic role that the coming to power of the Nazis brought with it. His lack of comprehension of the new political world of the Third Reich led to his fateful flight to Scotland on 10 May 1941 and, ironically, doomed him to inaction and imprisonment for the rest of his life.

10
The Collaborator: Franz von Papen

The verdict of both contemporaries and historians on Franz von Papen has been almost uniformly contemptuous. A political dilettante, superficial and none too bright, politically naïve and inexperienced, he was, it is largely agreed, imbued with a sublime aristocratic self-confidence that blinded him to the danger posed by Hitler and the Nazis, men whose inferior social status would, he thought, make them easy to dominate and manipulate. In his memoirs, he portrayed himself as an honourable person motivated by a deep Catholic faith; not a Nazi or anything like it, but someone who was trying to do his best to keep the Nazis under control and mitigate the worst features of their rule. Both his own account of his life, however, and the dismissive verdict passed on him by so many of those who have written about him, seriously underestimate Papen in a variety of ways. 'The picture of a naïve, politically inexperienced and misled hobby politician,' one historian has remarked, 'contributes in the end to playing down' his crucial political role in the early 1930s, a judgement that cannot have been unwelcome even to Papen himself.[1]

Although he presented himself as a typical scion of the nobility, Franz von Papen was neither a conventional nor a traditional Prussian military aristocrat. His family had originally gained their wealth from the ownership and exploitation of salt mines in the Westphalian town of Werl. Since the late fifteenth century, however, the von Papens had owned a knightly estate at Köningen, certifying their noble prefix ('von') with the Habsburg Emperor in 1708. After the area was transferred to Prussia as part of the Vienna Settlement in 1815, the family did its best to assimilate into the Prussian nobility. But while the high aristocracy and the Prussian Junkers were Protestant, with a significant presence in the German Evangelical Church, the Lutheran-Calvinist institution

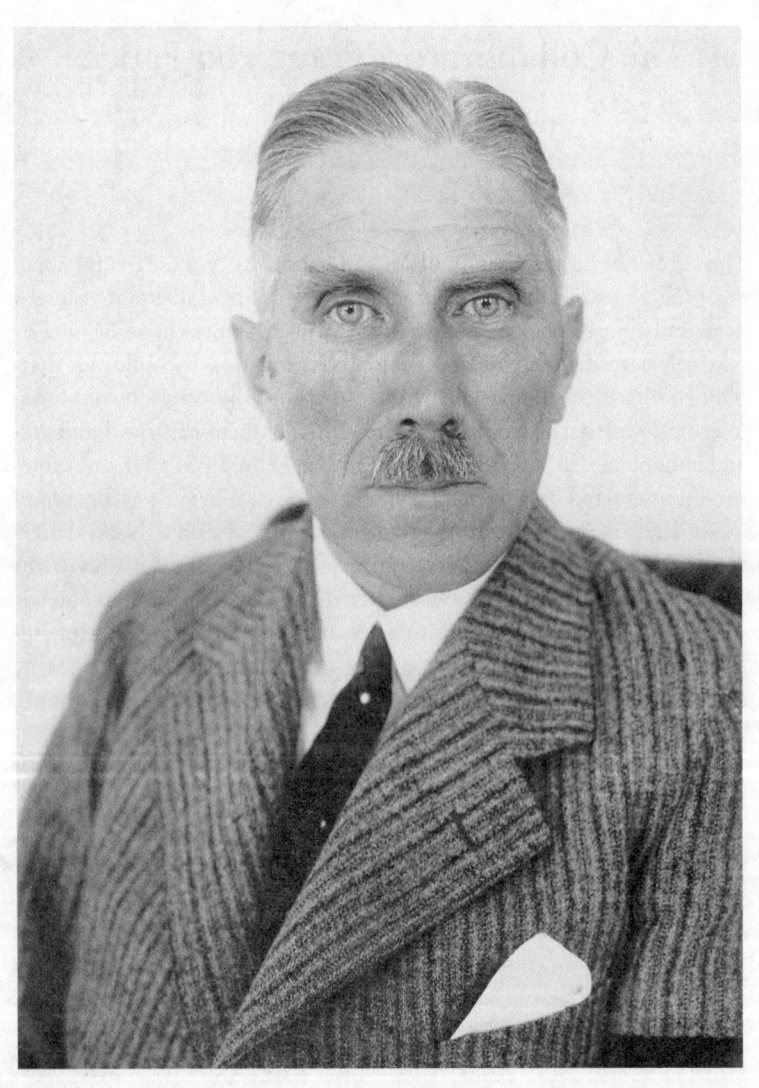

headed by the King of Prussia, the von Papens retained their deep Catholic faith and their high social position in the congregation of the Catholic archbishop of Cologne, who was an independent secular sovereign within the Holy Roman Empire, abolished in 1803.[2] They did not have a formal title – they were not dukes or barons of anywhere – so it was not surprising that Friedrich von Papen, Franz's father, entered the Prussian officer corps, serving in Bismarck's wars of German unification: an obvious way of confirming his place in the Prussian aristocracy. This tradition was continued by his son Franz. Born on 29 October 1879, and thus escaping the impact of the struggle between Bismarck's Reich and the Catholic Church known as the *Kulturkampf*, Franz von Papen was admitted at the age of eleven to an officer cadet school at Bensberg, in the environs of Cologne, and trained there from 1891 to 1895, living in Spartan conditions and experiencing the harsh discipline of the Prussian Army. Appointed as a non-commissioned officer, he was transferred to the Lichterfelde Barracks, just outside Berlin, to undergo further training. For a time he served in the Imperial Court as a page, attending Kaiser Wilhelm II on grand state occasions. 'I am thankful,' he wrote in his memoirs many years later, 'to have seen the German Empire in all its power and majesty.' If it had not been overthrown, he thought, 'there would never have been a Hitler'.[3]

A skilled horseman, he was commissioned on 15 March 1898 into the cavalry and was stationed in Düsseldorf. Here he spent much of his spare time as an amateur jockey, taking part in horse races in his spare time. 'Steeplechasing,' he wrote later, 'requires considerable self-discipline, endurance and powers of decision, as well as a fine contempt for broken bones – by no means a bad training for a politician.' He was transferred to another cavalry school, in Hanover, and obtained leave to go to England in order to go fox-hunting, where he encountered, he said, the best thoroughbred mounts he had ever ridden. On his return to Germany, he met, through relations, Martha von Boch-Galhau, youngest daughter of René von Boch-Galhau, who owned the ceramic-wares company Villeroy and Boch. The couple married on 3 May 1905 and stayed married for the rest of their lives. A pious and deeply conservative Catholic, Martha brought a substantial dowry into the marriage and then inherited a considerable fortune on her father's death in 1908, enabling Franz to live independently. The family firm was based in the Saarland, on the French border, and was part-French; Martha mostly spoke French at home, and, as something of a snob, she regarded her husband's alliance with the Nazis as a mistake, refusing to render the Nazi salute even in the presence of the dictator himself.[4]

It was partly in order to please his socially ambitious father-in-law that Franz von Papen applied to join the General Staff, passing the required examination in 1907. The course of training at the War Academy lasted three years, during which he attended lectures on 'military science', and spent a summer in France, not least to improve his command of the language. He was among only thirty out of 150 trainee officers co-opted to the General Staff itself on a trial basis. The work there was constant and demanding, he reported, but he came through this testing period and was attached permanently to the General Staff on 9 March 1913, with the rank of captain. At this point, however, Papen's career took an unusual and unexpected turn: in the autumn of 1913 he was appointed military attaché to the German Embassy in Washington DC and the German Legation in Mexico, probably, he thought, because he was generally regarded as an Anglophile.[5] He sailed for America on 6 January 1914, leaving behind his wife and growing family. The position of military attaché was undemanding, and he spent much of his time horse-riding and socializing. The only excitement was provided by a trip to Mexico, where a revolution was in full swing, and relations with the USA were extremely tense. Soon, however, Papen's situation was to change dramatically. On 1 August 1914, still in neutral Mexico, he was told that war had broken out in Europe. By the time he got to New York, it was well under way.[6]

A well-known part of the job of a military attaché was to gather information, a task that could all too easily slide over into espionage. In time of war, rumours were soon circulating about Papen, who was accused of organizing 'a widespread net of saboteurs, to have instigated strikes in the docks and munitions factories, to have employed squads of dynamiters, and to have been the master spy at the head of a veritable army corps of secret agents', all with the aim of undermining American supplies to Britain and France. Although his actual conduct fell far short of what was being alleged, Papen did try to blow up the Canadian Pacific Railway Line in order to stop Canadian reinforcements reaching the embarkation points for Europe, as well as having false passports made for Germans who wished to return to Europe to serve in the armed forces. Papen employed a private detective and his staff to provide security: 'As I was a complete novice in this sort of cloak-and-dagger existence, he used to give me lessons in how to avoid being shadowed.' Papen also bankrolled a munitions factory in Bridgeport, Connecticut, run by a sympathizer, which ordered huge quantities of matériel in order to prevent American firms from producing military equipment, explosives and the like for the Allies. His later insistence that he always tried to avoid acts of sabotage has to be taken with a pinch of salt. Incriminating documents somehow reached the press. Allegations and counter-allegations flew about, and the lawsuits to which they gave rise lasted well into the 1920s. Meanwhile, by December 1915, the atmosphere in the USA had become too hot for Papen and he was officially declared *persona non grata*. He returned to Germany and, his memoirs claim, tried without success to convince the Kaiser and the High Command that it would be a grievous mistake to begin unrestricted submarine warfare in the Atlantic. In January 1917, however, all restrictions were removed, and along with the publicity given to an intercepted telegram in which the German government promised the Mexican government Texas, New Mexico and Arizona if it entered the war on the German side, this prompted the United States to declare war on Germany in April 1917.[7]

After taking part in the fighting on the Western Front at Vimy Ridge and Arras, Papen was suddenly summoned to Palestine by Erich von Falkenhayn, whom he had known on the General Staff. The conflict here was between the Ottoman Turkish Army and the British Empire Forces under General Allenby. After a long campaign, the Ottoman and German forces were defeated, and armistice negotiations began, to be followed quickly by the general Armistice signed on 11 November 1918, the revolution, and the abdication of the Kaiser. Papen experienced these events as a catastrophe. 'It was the collapse of every value we had ever known. . . . It was the end of everything we had believed in for generations, the disappearance of all we had loved and fought for.' So upset was he that he repeated these sentiments several times over the following pages of his memoirs. 'The world I had known and understood had disappeared.' He had regarded the Kaiser's regime as 'permanent', but it had been replaced by a 'largely theatrical republic'. Christianity had been overthrown by atheistical Marxism. The principle on which the Weimar Republic rested – 'all power derives from the people' – was anathema to him, 'diametrically opposed to the teachings and traditions of the Roman Catholic Church', which gave ultimate power to God. The situation was made still worse by the 'grave errors and injustices' of the Treaty of Versailles. Feeling that he had no place in the new Germany as a professional soldier, he resigned his commission and leased a modest landed estate in his native Westphalia.[8]

Papen seems to have been propelled into politics by the events of March 1920, when the right-wing Kapp *putsch* in Berlin led to a left-wing uprising in the Ruhr, mounted initially to defend the Republic but then aiming to push the revolution further. The 'red army' in the Ruhr threatened the social order in Papen's part of Westphalia: 'I organized the local country people into a volunteer company to beat off the Red marauders,' he claimed later, somewhat exaggerating the importance of his activities, 'and we had to bury or hide our few valuables and reserves of food.' According to Papen's memoirs, his fellow aristocrats in the area suggested that he 'should represent their interests in the Prussian State Parliament'. Since they were all Catholics, it seemed obvious that he should join the Catholic Centre Party, especially as he felt out of sympathy with the reactionary and overwhelmingly Protestant Prussian Conservatives.[9] The Centre Party was a broad coalition of different social groups united only by the fact that they were Catholic. However, it was grounded in a solid network of social and religious institutions that underpinned the continuation of its electoral success at a time when the liberal and right-wing Protestant parties were haemorrhaging support first to small fringe parties and then, from 1929, to the Nazis. It was thus an essential participant in the coalition governments that ruled throughout the Republic's existence. Papen was on the nationalist wing of the Party, unable to convince the more liberal elements to join with parties further to the right instead of those located in the centre. In 1925, for instance, he supported Hindenburg in the Presidential elections rather than the candidate of the centrist parties, Wilhelm Marx, even though Marx was himself a leading member of the Catholic Centre. Papen considered Hindenburg entirely unpolitical, a man who would provide 'an opportunity to reawaken some of those traditions that had been lost with the collapse of the monarchy', not least 'the old Christian conception of government'. In fact, of course Hindenburg, as would emerge, was political to the core, a relic of the *Kaiserreich* and deeply imbued with its values.[10]

Papen's influence in the 1920s was enhanced by the fact that he was the owner of 47 per cent of the capital invested in the Centre Party's main national newspaper, *Germania*, founded in 1870. When he became chair of the Board of Directors, he fired the existing management, including the editor, and pushed the paper to the right, often composing leading articles himself. Behind the scenes, he also exerted influence on political affairs through his membership of the *Herrenklub*, a gentlemen's club founded in 1923 and consisting of aristocrats, businessmen and other members of the social elite. Beyond this, Papen also retained his contacts with the upper ranks of the officer corps, including in particular President Hindenburg. During the national crisis of 1923, with hyperinflation rampant, the French occupying the Ruhr, and the threat of Communist regimes taking over in parts of central Germany, Papen advocated a military coup led by General Hans von Seeckt, commander of the Reichswehr, the German Army. After Seeckt's enforced retirement in 1926, Papen was on friendly terms with another political general, Kurt von Schleicher, a close associate of Hindenburg.[11]

Just as important as all these political connections, however, was the strength of Papen's conservative Catholic faith. He was on friendly terms with the Papal Nuncio in Germany, Eugenio Pacelli, who became Cardinal Secretary of State (effectively, Foreign Minister) at the Vatican in 1930, and was elected Pope, as Pius XII, nine years later. The political position of the Catholic Church and the Vatican in the interwar years was dominated by a fear of Communism, and a willingness to see authoritarian and dictatorial governments come to power as part of the global defence of what they saw as Christian values. Papen shared this view, condemning the 'wave of decadence' that he thought was sweeping across the cultural world. 'Both literature and the visual arts sank to a level of depravity which was to a certain extent encouraged by the general denunciation of all the standards that Imperial Germany had stood for.' In 1929 he was instrumental in founding an Association for the Maintenance of Western Culture, aiming to strengthen the forces of religion against the swelling tide of rampant atheism and anticlericalism. Papen's politics were part of a widespread reactionary turn by Catholicism that resulted in the Church's Concordat with Mussolini's Fascist dictatorship in Rome in 1929, underpinned the Church's backing for the authoritarian 'clerico-fascist' regime of Engelbert Dollfuss and Kurt Schuschnigg in Austria after 1934, and fuelled its support for General Franco's Nationalists against the Republicans (and Communists) during the Spanish Civil War of 1936–39.[12]

It was in a sense, therefore, as part of a wider current of political Catholicism that Papen supported his Catholic Centre Party colleague Heinrich Brüning – like him a conservative monarchist – in ruling by decree, through Hindenburg, following the collapse of the Grand Coalition in 1930. When Chancellor Brüning was forced to resign by Hindenburg following the Presidential elections in the spring of 1932, in which he blamed Brüning for subjecting him to the humiliation of failing to win by acclamation, it was to Papen that the President and Schleicher turned, appealing to his sense of military discipline in asking him to restore order to the political chaos that was now overwhelming Germany. On 1 June 1932, somewhat to his surprise, Papen was appointed Reich Chancellor. Schleicher had already selected his entire Cabinet, which contained such a high proportion of aristocrats that it was popularly known as the 'Cabinet of Barons'. A number of them were to continue to serve in the same office under Hitler. The new government's agenda, previously agreed between the three men, was clear: a return as far as possible to the days of the ex-Kaiser, though without his participation or that of his sons; and an authoritarian political structure based (supposedly) on Christian conservative values. Papen and Schleicher were agreed that the first step was to reunite the offices of Reich Chancellor and Prussian Minister-President, as had been the practice with Bismarck. Prussia, after all, covered most of the land surface of Germany and contained the majority of its population. But Prussia was in the hands of a Social Democratic minority government that was still upholding the basic principles of democracy. Claiming that there was a danger of a 'highly treasonable' plot for the Social Democrats to stage a national coup (a mendacious claim for which there was no evidence whatsoever), Papen himself, with the help of the army, forcibly removed the Prussian government from office and imposed his own regime, a move subsequently ruled illegal by the courts. It was a devastating blow to Weimar democracy.[13]

The larger problem that confronted Schleicher, Papen and Hindenburg was to find enough support in the Reichstag to push through the constitutional changes needed to introduce an authoritarian regime. The Catholic Centre Party had broken with Papen over the ousting of Brüning and his acceptance, without its approval, of the Chancellorship. The liberal and conservative parties had lost almost all their votes to the Nazis. Only Hitler and his movement could provide the mass backing they needed. As the Nazi Party vote rocketed skywards, Papen thought that the experience of the Party in regional state elections, where the Nazis 'had to temper their programme to that of their coalition colleagues', showed that this could also be done at the national level. The campaign for Nazi support began. Papen met Hitler for the first time on 9 June 1932, just over a week after he became Reich Chancellor. As he wrote later:

> I found him curiously unimpressive. Press pictures had conveyed no idea of a dominating personality and I could detect no inner quality which might explain his extraordinary hold on the masses. He was wearing a dark blue suit and seemed the complete *petit-bourgeois*. He had an unhealthy complexion, and with his little moustache and curious hairstyle had an indefinable bohemian quality. His demeanour was modest and polite, and although I had heard much about the magnetic quality of his eyes, I do not remember being impressed by them.[14]

Following Hitler's stunning success in the July 1932 general elections, however, Papen found Hitler far more demanding. Over the following months, the Nazi leader made it clear that he would not enter a government except as its head. Papen and his Interior Minister, the arch-conservative ideologue Wilhelm von Gayl, drew up plans for changing the constitution, turning Germany into a clerico-fascist dictatorship, but the plans were pointless without Nazi support because the government required a two thirds majority in the Reichstag.[15]

Faced with a Reichstag that was unable to take any decisions, Papen got Hindenburg's approval for a dissolution. But his days as Chancellor were numbered. Hindenburg and Schleicher, in despair at the continuing impasse, effectively forced his resignation. In Papen's memoirs of this period, it was Schleicher who effectively was calling the shots. He had a power base in the army, whereas Papen himself had none. But when in December 1932 he was appointed Reich Chancellor by Hindenburg in succession to Papen, Schleicher's attempt to split the Nazi Party by co-opting Gregor Strasser into the government failed dismally. For Papen, Hindenburg, and their friends, it seemed possible for the Nazi Party to 'be neutralized by saddling it with its full share of public responsibility'.[16] Papen later asserted that the Hitler Cabinet had been appointed democratically, not least because the Nazis were still the largest party despite their losses in the November 1932 elections. In fact, of course, the new government was appointed by a clique around Hindenburg, including Papen himself, in a situation where the Reichstag was no longer functioning. Vice-Chancellor in a Cabinet packed with his political friends, Papen thought he would have no difficulty in bending Hitler and his two Nazi colleagues to his purpose: 'In two months,' he said, 'we'll have pushed Hitler into a corner so hard he'll be squeaking.'[17] Papen admitted later that he had repeatedly tried to get Hitler into government, and when he had succeeded, he had tried to 'limit him with as many securities as would be possible'.[18] In his position as Vice-Chancellor he had 'hoped to oppose radical tendencies by the application of Christian principles'. But, he later conceded: 'My own fundamental error was to underrate the dynamic power which had awakened the national and social instincts of the masses.' He had 'underrated Hitler's insatiable lust for power as an end in itself'. His own 'whole way of thinking and upbringing' had prevented him from realizing what Hitler was, and what he could do.[19] Papen's snobbery and social arrogance, in other words, self-confessedly blinded him to the possibility that a socially inferior individual such as Hitler could outmanoeuvre him.[20]

Papen and his friends had no mass following, and, as he later admitted, the power of the state, the President and the army proved insufficient as a counterweight. Papen was hostile to party politics and thought the abolition of the parties could open the way to a corporate state as established in Mussolini's Italy. But he was mistaken. If Hitler had attempted to establish a dictatorship by the sudden, violent seizure of power, there would have been serious resistance. But because he established it in stages, people, including Papen himself, were unable to pinpoint a moment when resistance was called for. When the Reichstag burned down on 27 February 1933, Papen was convinced by Hitler that it was part of a Communist plot, though he later realized it had been the work of a lone individual, Marinus van der Lubbe, a Dutch anarchist. Papen went along with the Enabling Law, but later claimed nobody could have foreseen how this would lead to a Nazi dictatorship. He played a central part in negotiating a Concordat with the Papacy, naively believing Hitler would stick to it.[21] And in a manner typical of non-Nazis who worked with Hitler, Papen claimed that he had worked hard 'to keep the anti-Jewish excesses of the Nazis within bounds'.[22] Of course, even if this were the case, events showed he had failed. But the record of debates in Cabinet over the antisemitic boycott of 1 April

1933, the law of 7 April 1933 dismissing Jews from government employment, and other, similar measures, do not mention any objections raised by Papen to these measures.²³ Papen himself delivered a speech in Gleiwitz early in 1934 criticizing what he saw to be the excessive influence of Jews on every aspect of German life, and calling for a 'defensive fight against these abuses'.²⁴ His memoirs mention the 'disorders' created by the Nazis on the streets, but concede that while Hitler often denounced them in public, 'it took some time for us to realize that although the official party attitude was to oppose these excesses, they were in fact greeted with private satisfaction' by Hitler and the leading Nazis.²⁵ In fact, Papen must have known about the violence and quite possibly witnessed instances of it himself. On 27 March 1933 the *New York Times* cited him angrily denouncing reports of 'the alleged torture of political prisoners and the maltreatment of Jews', but only to the foreign press.²⁶

Papen's speeches from the first months of 1933 show how little he disapproved of the mass brutality, tortures and murders committed against its opponents by the Nazis. He excused their violence in the coded formula of the 'unleashing of the Elemental' which, he said, was necessary to destroy the 'demon of democracy which threatened to destroy every true value'. This could not be done by the state, he confessed, but had to be accomplished by the 'great national organizations and movements', meaning the Nazis. The 'German revolution', he declared, went far beyond the victory of nationalist forces in a pluralistic democratic political system: it meant the 'total assimilation of the entire body of the people into a single will'. The religious confessions, he added, had to unite in a reconstruction of the Reich, while the federal structure of the state was 'to be coordinated for ever'. Class antagonisms and their formal institutions, such as trade unions, employers' associations and the like, had to be replaced 'by a corporate structuring of every class and profession'. Papen's profound misunderstanding of the nature of Nazism came to the fore, however, when he praised 'the real work of the leader, who is bringing the aristocratic principle to validity'. This was, Papen declared, a 'conservative revolution' that would bring about a 'conservative renewal' of the German state and its people. He had sought this during his own tenure of the Reich Chancellorship but had lacked the popular support. Now, however, the 'national uprising' was inaugurating a new historical epoch. 'We are the tools of a great spiritual transformation, which means giving the German people and Europe a new order.' Repeatedly emphasizing his own personal Catholicism, Papen thus placed himself within a broad European movement to replace democracy with an authoritarian, corporate form of government that would bring religious values to the fore.[27]

The Weimar Republic, he declared in 1933, had been characterized by defeatism and dominated by Marxism. It was time to end this chaos. Political parties had to be abolished and replaced with a unitary national political movement. The autonomy of the federated states, such as Württemberg or Bavaria, had to be curbed in the interests of national unity. Speaking on 1 March 1933, Papen said that the Communists had declared war on the German people by burning down the Reichstag, a statement that implicitly justified the use of extreme violence against them in return. Papen did not directly address the 'Jewish question', as the Nazis called it, but he did declare that 'the conservative picture of the world regards people and Reich as a biological and spiritual unity', implying that ethnic minorities and 'cosmopolitans' did not belong to the nation.[28] Papen repeatedly emphasized his credentials 'as a statesman', somewhat condescendingly talking down to the 'workers' as he urged their integration into the new national order.[29] This was all a very long way from the rabidly populist ideology of the Nazis. But it showed that conservatives like Papen put the destruction of democracy and the extirpation of 'Marxism' above any lingering concern for humanity, legality or decency.

Papen's speeches from this period show that despite the misgivings he foregrounded in his memoirs, he was an enthusiastic supporter of the destruction of democracy and of the 'national revolution'. But in 1933–34 his office became a lightning rod for expressions from members of the general public dissatisfied with the way things were going. He felt that the 'radical elements of the party were increasing the revolutionary tempo'. In December 1933 he issued in public what he later exaggeratedly called 'a violent attack on the Nazis' terror methods'. And on 17 June 1934, at the university of Marburg, he spoke out publicly against the regime's disregard for the law. The speech, written by his assistant Edgar Jung, was directed against Röhm, Goebbels and Rosenberg in particular, and criticized the 'doctrinaire fanatics' of the Nazi movement, but it was laced at the same time with extravagant declarations of loyalty to Hitler and to his 'renewal of Germany', to which Papen was 'bound with my heart's blood'.³⁰ The speech met with a good deal of approval in conservative circles, but Goebbels stopped the captive media from publicizing it, and Papen failed to capitalize on it by going to see Hindenburg to get him to intervene. Instead, he finally sought to dissociate himself from the regime by handing in his resignation. It was all too late, however. Hindenburg was raising the question of who was to succeed him. Papen's own idea, or so he claimed in his memoirs, was that the Hohenzollern monarchy should be restored, and surprisingly, he reported, Hitler had no objections, considering one of the sons of the self-styled 'Crown Prince' a suitable candidate. Reich President Hindenburg privately favoured a restoration of the monarchy after his death, and Papen also thought he had the support of Mussolini, who worked quite harmoniously with a hereditary monarch in the form of King Vittorio Emmanuele III of Italy. All of this, however, merely showed how Papen was still unable to comprehend the ruthlessness and radicalism of the Nazis. In the 'Night of the Long Knives', 30 June–1 July 1934, Himmler and Göring targeted Papen and his staff, putting the Vice-Chancellor under house arrest, while shooting dead his head of communications Herbert von Bose and Papen's speechwriter (and author of the Marburg address) Edgar Jung. Astonishingly, Papen did not protest at these murders, but even applauded Hitler for his use of political murder as a 'proclamation of the irrevocable principles of statesmanship'.³¹

The army, already penetrated by Nazi influence and won over by Hitler's rearmament programme, refused to intervene. Papen's resignation became effective, though it was not publicized. Killing him, as Hitler realized, would have been too politically damaging, so instead he offered Papen the post of ambassador to the Vatican, a demotion dramatic enough to provoke a rare outburst of anger from the former Vice-Chancellor, who curtly rejected the offer.³² Events came to the two men's rescue, however. On 25 July 1934 Austrian Nazis had assassinated the fascist dictator Engelbert Dollfuss in a botched coup attempt. Relations with Mussolini reached rock-bottom and the obvious involvement of Germany created a serious international crisis. Germany's ambassador in Vienna, Kurt Rieth, was immediately recalled and carpeted, after which he was forced into retirement. Hitler asked – according to Papen's memoirs, begged – the former Vice-Chancellor to accept an appointment as a special envoy with ministerial rank. His appointment would signal the seriousness with which the German government took the crisis, and it would also be a convenient way of removing Papen from the political scene in Berlin. Papen's conditions, including the dismissal of Theodor Habicht, the German Nazi who had coordinated the assassination, were accepted by the Reich Chancellor, but Papen also assuaged any reservations Hitler might have harboured by making clear his support for the eventual unification of Austria with Germany. His motive in accepting the position, he later claimed, was to pour oil on the troubled relationship between the two countries, patch up relations with Italy, and de-escalate a crisis which, he somewhat implausibly claimed, could have led to a European war.[33]

Over the following years, Papen worked tirelessly to build up support for the reunion of Austria and Germany, the *Anschluss*, among influential circles in Vienna. But early in 1938, Hitler abruptly radicalized the conduct of German foreign policy, replacing Foreign Minister Neurath with Joachim von Ribbentrop, sacking a number of ambassadors, and conducting a wholesale purge of the senior ranks of the army. Papen too was dismissed, on 4 February 1938, though he did manage to persuade Hitler to summon the Austrian dictator Kurt Schuschnigg to Berchtesgaden for a final attempt at a peaceful solution to the unification question. Despite his satisfaction in having negotiated a joint communiqué, Papen was forced to witness the almost immediate unravelling of the agreement, followed by the German invasion of Austria on 12 March 1938, an invasion he later claimed he had done his utmost to try and prevent. Nevertheless, as he later confessed: 'Like everyone else, I was caught up in the general enthusiasm and overwhelmed by the historical magnitude of the occasion – the union of the two German peoples.'[34]

Still basking in the glory of his Gold Medal of the Nazi Party, awarded for his services in preparing the *Anschluss*, Papen accompanied Hitler to Vienna, 'quite overcome by the extraordinary atmosphere of jubilation' as the Austrians ecstatically greeted their conquerors. His enthusiasm must surely have been confirmed by the declaration of the Austrian bishops approving the takeover.[35] But the day after the *Anschluss*, Papen was told that his long-term assistant Wilhelm von Ketteler, a close associate of Bose and Jung now based in the German Embassy in Vienna, had disappeared. Papen approached Himmler, Heydrich and even Hitler for help. Nobody provided any assistance. A few weeks later, Ketteler's body was found in the Danube at Hainburg, fifty kilometres downstream of Vienna. Traces of chloroform found in his body suggested he had been kidnapped. Later investigations revealed that the Gestapo had waylaid him, drugged him, and drowned him in his bath before throwing him into the river. He had been under surveillance ever since he had attempted personally to get Hindenburg to stop the murders being carried out during the Night of the Long Knives. There was evidence that he had been planning to assassinate Hitler by shooting him with a long-range rifle from the Viennese Embassy window as he drove past in the victory parade (Hitler would have been standing, as usual, in the front of the car, next to the driver). A spy in Papen's office had informed on Ketteler. Heydrich's agents had been spotted following him immediately before his abduction, but Himmler refused to take the matter any further. In his memoirs, Papen devoted considerable space to this episode, underlining once more his distance from the regime.[36]

Papen's final service to the Nazis was as ambassador to Turkey, a post that he had previously turned down twice. In the second week of April 1939, however, Mussolini had invaded and conquered Albania, making Germany's role in the Balkans more significant. As Papen wrote in his memoirs, when he decided to accept the post, 'many of my friends had failed to understand my decision, in view of my experiences with the Nazi régime'. He thought, however, that it offered him an opportunity to prevent a general European war from breaking out, a belief without any basis in reality. In fact, he worked hard to bring the Turks over to the German side after the outbreak of war, though the government in Ankara succeeded in playing off the Axis and Allied sides against one another until it became obvious in 1944 that Germany was losing the war. Ankara became a centre of espionage and intrigue, with the Germans employing an agent in the British Embassy (Elyesa Bazna, codename Cicero) and the Soviets launching an unsuccessful assassination attempt against Papen himself. On 2 August 1944 the Turkish government broke off relations with Germany and Papen had to return home. As late as January 1945, he continued to believe in a German victory.[37]

Papen knew some of the people involved in the 20 July 1944 bomb plot to kill Hitler, but he did not fall under suspicion, though he later claimed to have done his best to save a number of those who had been arrested and had to stand trial. Most of these claims do not stand up to scrutiny. He does not seem to have tried to help even his nephew Felix, an opponent of the regime who died in Buchenwald shortly before the end of the war.[38] A final interview with Hitler ended with the dictator handing Papen the Knight's Cross of the Military Merit Order for his services. Papen's position became increasingly difficult, especially after his country estate at Köningen was taken over by the advancing Americans. Soon after, on 9 April 1945, he was arrested by American troops and admitted his identity. He was sent to join the other senior Nazis at the Palace Hotel in Mondorf-les-Bains in Luxembourg, and from there he was sent with them for trial in Nuremberg. Like the other prisoners, Papen found the conditions he had to endure irksome and humiliating: the adjustment from being part of a social and political elite to being an inmate on remand was a difficult one. He had a low opinion of the prison psychiatrists ('few of them gave the impression of having any genuine scientific qualifications'). He was, the prison psychiatrist Gustave Gilbert commented, 'the soul of politeness and courtesy', he denounced Hitler as 'a liar and betrayer', and claimed he had tried to convince him that he was wrong in his antisemitism. Papen had, he said, stayed on in an effort to mitigate Hitler's worst features and in an attempt to preserve peace. Göring regarded these remarks as a betrayal and muttered audibly in the courtroom that Papen was a coward and a liar. Ribbentrop said: 'He should have been shot long ago.'[39]

Papen was acquitted by the International War Crimes Tribunal, but a German Denazification court then found him guilty of participating in the Nazi regime and sentenced him to eight years' hard labour, from which he was released on appeal in 1949.[40] In the remaining years of his life, until his death in 1969 at the age of eighty-nine on his family estate, he continued to defend his conduct in the years of the Third Reich, and shortly before that, in the early 1930s. Banned for a time from publishing in Germany, he launched a series of attacks on the post-war Federal Republic in newspapers published in General Franco's clerico-fascist dictatorship in Spain.

The dominant view of his character and career has been that Papen was an anachronism, a conservative in an age of revolutionary dynamism. Joachim Fest considered that he had 'a fixation with out-of-date ideas'; he was at heart a monarchist, filled with nostalgia for the *Kaiserreich* and instinctively inclined to regard the aristocracy as a class born to rule.[41] He was indeed deceived by Hitler in 1933: his sublimely condescending view that a lower-middle-class political amateur would be no match for his own inborn superiority was nullified within a few months. Yet it is too simple to see Papen merely as a dim-witted aristocratic conservative. His politics in the late 1920s and early 1930s were in fact profoundly modern, part of a widespread turn of the Catholic Church against democracy and towards the authoritarian 'corporate state' favoured by dictators like Franco, Salazar, Dollfuss and Schuschnigg. This was combined in Papen's politics with a resentful German nationalism and a strong belief, born of a lifetime's experience, in military values, which were enough to cause him to make common cause with Hitler despite repeated humiliations.

Papen was more than just a 'fellow traveller'. It is tempting to see him as an example of how easily conventional politicians can be seduced into supporting demagogues. But he was not a conventional politician: he was an enemy of democracy, a clerico-fascist, a man imbued with military and ultra-nationalist values. He salved his conscience by ignoring many of the darker aspects of Nazism. He claimed retrospectively that he knew about the concentration camps but 'always believed that the people were treated honestly there'. He blamed any atrocities committed in them on the war, equating them with the Allied bombing of Dresden.[42] He lacked the perception to realize that by serving Hitler he was not serving his country. Personal ambition, arrogance and self-importance kept him working for the Nazis in positions of decreasing importance up to the very end. His memoirs present a picture of an urbane, civilized, Christian nobleman; but it is what they leave out that is most striking. When Franz von Papen was Vice-Chancellor, the second man in the German government, nearly 200,000 Communists and Social Democrats were thrown into makeshift concentration camps, beaten, tortured and degraded; more than 600 were killed. Jews were thrown out of their jobs, their businesses boycotted, and their presence in Germany defamed in a massive and relentless propaganda campaign. During his time as ambassador to Austria, the Nuremberg race laws were passed, Jewish businesses were 'Aryanized', and antisemitic persecution intensified. As he was entering Vienna with Hitler immediately after the *Anschluss*, overwhelmed by the historic grandeur of the moment, Jews were being rounded up across the city, robbed, beaten, and forced to clean pro-independence graffiti off the walls and pavements with toothbrushes dipped in acid. Many thousands were taken off to Dachau, to be subjected to the sadism and brutality of the SS camp guards. Occupying a well-informed ambassadorial office in Ankara, he did his best to support the German war effort as millions of Jews were being shot into pits, herded into starving ghettos, and taken off to the gas chambers of Treblinka, Auschwitz and other extermination camps. None of this is even mentioned in his memoirs. But there is no way that he cannot have been aware of it.

Papen claimed to be a sincere Catholic, but sincere Catholics across Europe, including the Church hierarchy, were cheering on as dictators like Franco and Salazar imprisoned, tortured and murdered their opponents. In Germany the Catholic hierarchy did its best to accommodate itself to the regime on the basis of the Concordat negotiated by Papen in 1933. But the Nazis soon started to break the agreement, arresting Catholic priests and dissolving Catholic lay institutions. In 1936 Goebbels unleashed a violent publicity campaign against Catholic schools, flinging paedophilia charges at numerous Catholic priests who were teaching in them. As a – perhaps the – leading Catholic layman in Germany, Papen could have protested. His fellow Catholic Paul von Eltz-Rübenach, the Post and Transport Minister, demonstratively refused to accept Hitler's personal offer of the Golden Party Badge of Honour in 1937, charging him openly with suppressing the Catholic Church and its youth organizations. He was immediately dismissed from his offices but suffered no further harm. Papen, however, remained silent.[43] The mass sterilization of some 400,000 so-called 'inferior' and 'less valuable' Germans as a result of the eugenic policies of the regime was a fundamental challenge to Catholic dogma, but it called forth no condemnation from Papen, nor did the mass murder of the mentally ill and handicapped during the war, though the Catholic Bishop of Münster, Clemens von Galen, risked his life by publicly denouncing it from the pulpit. Papen was close to another bishop, the Austrian Alois von Hudal, whose attempt to counter the anti-Christian writings of Alfred Rosenberg he encouraged; but Hudal's bid to create a 'synthesis between the Christian idea and the healthy doctrines of National Socialism' made massive concessions to Nazi ideology, and he ended his career arranging for the escape of prominent surviving Nazis to Argentina after the war.[44]

As Hans Frank asked some of his fellow accused after Papen had given evidence at the Nuremberg War Crimes Trial: 'Why the devil didn't he go to the United States after January 30 [1933]? He could have come back now and still be a famous man and sit out there in the audience and laugh at us.' He was, Frank complained, 'trying to get out of the fact that he played along with the Party and was an ardent Hitler supporter all along'.[45]

11
The 'Worker': Robert Ley

Robert Ley is largely forgotten now, but in his day he was one of the most powerful and influential Nazi leaders. Head of the Labour Front, an enormous organization with some 22 million members, he commanded vast resources and carried out policies that affected the lives of almost everyone in Nazi Germany. We know about him not only from such widely available sources as his voluminous published works and his interrogation by the Nuremberg trial psychiatrists, but also through his unpublished autobiographical statement 'Bauernschicksal' ('Farmer's Fate'), written in prison in 1945 and preserved in the US National Archives. Additionally, the account of his life by his daughter, who became a university professor and was only persuaded to write about him in a book first published in 2004, casts fresh light on his origins, career, family milieu and character.[1]

Part of the reason for Ley's relative obscurity lay in the fact that he suffered under a serious speech impediment for most of his adult life. In a movement, and indeed a world, where public speaking was an essential skill, a key to political popularity and success, he stuttered, often struggling to get out the words he wanted to say. American psychiatrists, questioning him after his arrest in 1945, suggested that his stutter was the result of frontal lobe damage to his brain, sustained in an air crash during the First World War. As a young man, Ley had served as an airborne artillery observer, engaged in spotting enemy positions behind the lines. He had crashed twice, on 6 July 1917 and then again a few weeks later, on 29 July. On the first occasion the pilot had crash-landed, sustaining fatal injuries in the process. Ley survived, but he was in a coma for two hours before he came to. This did not seem to have affected his abilities, however, since he was in the air again only three days after the pilot's funeral. On the second occasion, Ley was shot in the thigh by a bullet fired from an enemy plane, and this time the pilot was forced to land behind enemy lines. It took six difficult operations to save Ley's leg from amputation, and he spent the rest of the war in a French prisoner-of-war camp. He was still on crutches when he was released in January 1920, a long time after the war was over. Examining him in his cell after his capture by the Allies in 1945, the prison psychiatrist Donald Kelley concluded that the brain injury that had caused Ley's loss of consciousness after his first crash was the cause of his speech impediment, and had also left him emotionally unstable, behaviourally uninhibited, and lacking in judgement.[2]

Whether or not this diagnosis was correct was unclear. Ley's tactlessness and undiplomatic behaviour were part of the aggressive Nazi style of leadership, rather than consequences of individual pathology. Moreover, other members of Ley's family also suffered from speech impediments, including one of his sisters and two of his children, and none of them, as far as is known, had suffered any brain damage. More importantly, perhaps, as his former secretary reported, her boss lived

> in a world removed from reality. He had little knowledge of the everyday things of life, particularly the war, and did not want to know anything about it either. When he heard about it, he would not believe it. For instance, when he was told about the bad mood of the German people as the result of the constant bombings, he refused to believe it.[3]

Ley's tendency to ignore uncomfortable realities derived not least from a social disaster that had befallen his family during his childhood. Born on 15 February 1890 in Niederbreidenbach, a village in the Bergisch Land, east of Cologne and close to Nümbrecht, Ley began his life as the seventh of eleven children of Friedrich Ley, a comfortably-off farmer and rural entrepreneur who also (through his wife Emilie) part-owned a lime quarry. Friedrich Ley's wealth was all inherited, however, and he was unused to running a business. After making a series of unwise investments, and taking out expensive loans to cover his losses, he found himself in a situation so desperate that he burned down his own farm in order to collect the insurance money. This was a dramatic and clearly carefully planned act, since most small farms were chronically underinsured, so he must have taken out insurance at least in part with his act of arson in mind. Inevitably he was discovered. Arson was not uncommon in rural communities, and the authorities treated it harshly. Friedrich

Ley was arrested, brought before a court, and sentenced to four years' imprisonment.⁴

The effect on the six-and-a-half-year-old Robert Ley was catastrophic. As his biographer Ronald Smelser comments:

> Suddenly the family was plunged into poverty. Its possessions and land were sold at auction for a fraction of their value. The older siblings scattered to find work while Robert and his youngest sister remained with their mother as she tried to eke out a living on a tiny, run-down farm in Mildsiefen which she purchased from a money-lender, who in turn demanded the maid services of one of her daughters as the first mortgage instalment. Even at a distance of more than a half century, near the end of his life, Ley could still feel the pain and humiliation of having been 'uprooted, impoverished and humiliated' at such a vulnerable age.⁵

While his brothers took on manual wage labour and his sisters went into service, Robert Ley sought compensation for the bitter experience of sudden social relegation through education, coming top of his class at elementary school and attracting the attention of his teachers, who arranged for him to be admitted to secondary school – the technical *Realschule* rather than the more elevated, middle-class *Gymnasium* – and then to take the *Abitur*, the University entrance examination, which he passed in 1910. Supporting himself throughout by tutoring and other part-time jobs, he studied successively at the universities of Jena, Bonn and Münster. In a sign of his social ambition, he joined a duelling fraternity at Jena, famous for these socially superior and snobbish institutions, describing the experience as an education in 'good breeding' and a 'sense of manhood'.⁶

Ley was a hard-working and able student, successful enough in his major subject, chemistry, to be encouraged by his professor to embark on a PhD. But just as he was about to take his final examination and begin postgraduate study, the First World War intervened. Ley enlisted in the army and spent the first two years as an artilleryman on both the Western and the Eastern Fronts, before taking to the air. After his second crash, on 29 July 1917, he spent the rest of the war in captivity. At the war's end, it took the French a long time to release him from imprisonment: 'When I returned from the War in 1920, a hero, an old soldier deserving the best of my broken Fatherland,' he wrote later, 'I found that the Jews had the best jobs and we veterans were allowed their leavings. I became convinced that the Jews were the ones who had encircled and attacked Germany.'[7] No doubt, like other ex-soldiers with similar views, he had grown up in a family permeated by casual antisemitism; and also like others, he was shocked by the fall of the Kaiser, the revolution and the creation of Weimar democracy. Unlike many others, however, he found it easy to reintegrate into civil society. His professor invited him back to complete his dissertation, which he did on 5 June 1920. Its topic, mixed glycerides in butter fat, qualified him for a job at the Bayer chemical plant in Leverkusen, situated between Cologne and Düsseldorf, not far from his former family home. He began work on 1 January 1921. A regular income enabled Ley to get married, to Elisabeth Schmidt, buy a house, and establish a family. They had one daughter, Renate Wald, born on 29 July 1922, who after World War II became a sociology professor, known for her feminist stance. Her father allowed her considerable freedom as a child, whatever his political views on education, and only beat her once when she misbehaved, she wrote. When he was around he read her bedtime stories of Germanic heroes, but he did not try to indoctrinate her. However, since he was away working for most of the week, it was her pious mother who played the most important part in her early life, even though she was often ill.[8]

The German nationalism that Ley had imbibed from his lower-middle-class upbringing, reinforcing the influence of his Protestant parents, and deepened through the war and its aftermath, was radicalized by the French occupation of the Rhineland, established under the terms of the peace treaty of 1918 and lasting until 1930. The Rhineland was the area in which Ley lived and worked, and he must have been confronted on a daily basis with the national humiliation of demilitarization and foreign occupation. Like other nationalists, Ley was outraged by the Franco-Belgian occupation, a little to the north-east, of the Ruhr, which began on 11 January 1923 and continued until 25 August 1925, confiscating coal and industrial products as reparation payments in kind. The area was convulsed during 1923 by passive resistance, strikes and unrest on the part of striking German workers, and the stirring-up of Rhenish separatism by the French, who shot no fewer than 130 German workers during the Ruhr occupation. Ley was directly affected by these events. Perhaps, too, he saw in Germany's humiliation in 1918–19 a parallel to his own, experienced through his father's imprisonment and the family's plunge into poverty before the war.

It was Hitler who offered a way out. In 1924 Ley read a report of the closing speech delivered on 27 March by Hitler at his treason trial for the unsuccessful beer-hall *putsch* of the previous year. Inspired by the Nazi leader's defiant words, Ley made his way to a Nazi Party meeting in Cologne, where he attracted attention not only by his remarks but also and above all because he was a man with a doctorate, an 'academic' among all the ordinary, lower middle-class Party members. For his part, Ley felt more comfortable with these people than he did with the social elites he had failed to join.[9]

During the confused manoeuvrings and squabbles that consumed the remnants of the Nazi Party during Hitler's absence in his fortress confinement at Landsberg and the proscription of the Party by the authorities, Ley was conspicuous by his refusal to abandon his loyalty to the Leader. This was particularly significant because he was rapidly becoming an important figure in the Nazi Party in the Rhineland, where these fissiparous tendencies were at their most pronounced. Already deputy Gauleiter, at the beginning of July 1925 he moved with Hitler's approval into the position of Gauleiter when the incumbent resigned from the post on grounds of ill-health and the demands of his position in the Reichstag, asking Ley to take his place. It has to be remembered, of course, that at this point the Nazi movement was still very small: In August 1925 the Rhenish Gau had a mere 335 members, and only managed just to double the membership by August the following year. The area had a strong Communist and Social Democratic presence among the workers, and though Ley organized violent disruptions of their meetings and assemblies, and restructured the Nazi Party there to try and make it more efficient, he was unable to make much headway. At a meeting of twenty-five Nazi functionaries in the area held in December 1925 to discuss a proposal by Gregor Strasser to replace Hitler's 25-point 1920 Party programme with a new, more left-wing one, Ley was the only person present who fully supported Hitler, who in turn rewarded him by backing him in his fight against the 'Nazi left'. As his biographer has suggested, Ley found in Hitler a father-figure who provided a powerful substitute for the disgraced and absent father of his childhood. His veneration for the Nazi leader was almost religious in its fervour from the very beginning. It was almost inevitable that he should call a book reprinting his speeches in 1937 *Wir alle helfen dem Führer* (*We All Help the Leader*).[10]

Ley's tactics as Gauleiter were typical of Nazi behaviour in the late 1920s and early 1930s: rabble-rousing speeches, campaigns against the police and the Jews in the regional Nazi paper, and the violent disruption of other parties' public meetings. At the same time, the strong-arm tactics he used in dealing with his opponents within the Nazi movement aroused fierce criticism, especially from those Ley had expelled from the Party, who accused him (inaccurately) of being Jewish and having changed his name by dropping the third letter, 'v', and (somewhat less inaccurately) of embezzlement and corruption, accusations that would dog him throughout his career. On 1 January 1928 Ley lost his job at Bayer (now part of I. G. Farben) as a result of his political activities, which were taking up more and more of his time and arousing increasingly hostile public comment. In particular, he had publicly defamed the banker Max Warburg, a Jewish member of the I. G. Farben board, and had refused to apologize when asked to do so. Hoping to ease his financial situation, he took over the regional Nazi paper, the *Westdeutscher Beobachter* (*West German Observer*) from the Gau Party organization and became its owner and publisher, taking it radically down-market. Its scandal-mongering, including frequent sex stories involving Jews ('The Jew Hirsch Seduces a Nine-Year-Old Girl' was not untypical), led to lawsuits and prosecutions, including a conviction on 21 July 1929 for incitement in an article by Ley that used the killing of a local schoolboy as the pretext for accusing the Jews of ritual murder; but such muck-raking stories did help boost circulation, which had reached 40,000 by the summer of 1928. Some local Nazis thought that turning the paper into a scandal-sheet was going too far, but Ley secured Hitler's backing and the critics were silenced.[11]

Nevertheless Ley was in deep trouble. Without a job, unable to survive on the meager income of a Gauleiter, going through his severance allowance from I. G. Farben in a very short space of time, he lost his house and had to share a small apartment with a fellow Nazi, while his wife and daughter were forced to move in with relatives. A solution came in the form of financial backing from Prince Friedrich Christian of Schaumburg-Lippe, one of many members of the aristocracy who sought in the Nazi Party a solution for their dramatic loss of status and power in the 1918 Revolution. Together, the two men set up a Nazi publishing house, and bought a large building in Cologne to refurbish as Gau headquarters. But the tortuous financial expedients that Ley employed to keep the business afloat failed to improve the poor production standards of the newspapers it published, and the business folded in March 1931. Ley had also used Party funds to support the collapsing business and incurred the wrath of Party officials in Munich for doing so.[12] Weakened by these tribulations, Ley was forced to agree to the division of his Gau into two administrative areas corresponding to Reichstag constituencies. But Hitler kept him on, valuing his loyalty. When the Party plunged into a serious internal dispute, with Gregor Strasser resigning following Hitler's refusal to abandon his insistence on entering a government only as its head, Ley, now a Reichstag deputy, once more backed the Party Leader. His reward was to receive a major government job after Hitler was appointed Reich Chancellor on 30 January 1933.[13]

For Ley, the most enticing aspect of Nazi ideology was its promise to abolish class privileges and replace them with a society based on equality of status and power, though not wealth and resources: the *Volksgemeinschaft*, the 'people's community', in which people from all walks of life would work together to build a new and harmonious nation. In this way, he could transcend the social trauma of his childhood and finally consign it to the past. Before Hitler became Reich Chancellor, Ley had been appointed Reich Organization Leader, one of two men who were in effect inspectors of Party business. With Strasser's departure, Ley was left in control of a wide range of Party institutions, including the personnel office, the organizational office, the Party training office, and a number of subsidiary departments including the National Socialist Factory Cell Organization, the Nazi organizations for teachers, students, and women. Most important of all, however, was the German Labour Front. This was created shortly after stormtroopers entered trade union premises on 2 May 1933, trashed or stole their contents, and arrested leading trade unionists. A bulwark of the moderate socialist left, the unions were regarded by Hitler as 'Marxist': in the interests of the smooth running of the rearmament programme, they were abolished and replaced by the German Labour Front, headed up by none other than Robert Ley, whose oversight over the Factory Cell Organization made him the obvious choice.[14]

The Labour Front was a huge institution, uniting all German employed people under its umbrella, and administering all the assets formerly belonging to the trade unions, from bank accounts to buildings. Leading it certainly solved all of Ley's personal financial problems, and more. He pressured the millions of members to subscribe to his periodicals and buy his books, and he had no compunction about using Labour Front funds for his personal gratification. Soon he owned villas in exclusive districts in Berlin, Munich, Bonn, and the spa town of Saarow in the Mark Brandenburg. The Labour Front paid for their upkeep and the employment of numerous servants until 1938, after which the arrangement continued on the basis of a monthly fee paid by Ley that went nowhere near covering the costs. He owned a shiny new Mercedes car and had a personal railway carriage specially fitted out for himself. When the head of the Nazi Party Court drew these excesses to Hitler's attention in 1938, the dictator took no action, and in 1940 he gifted Ley the not inconsiderable sum of a million Reichsmarks to do with what he wanted. Ley bought Rottland, a landed estate near his birthplace, and had it refurbished in grandiose style, filling it with valuable works of art. On his visits there, he ordered the staff to assemble every morning to raise the Nazi flag. At the end of the war, late in March 1945, in a striking imitation of the crime that had brought his father and his family low, he had the villa and outbuildings burned down rather than let them fall into the hands of the Allies.[15]

None of this prevented his marriage from getting into difficulties because of growing ideological differences with his pious Protestant wife, Elisabeth. Their daughter Renate recalled his deepening hostility to Christianity and his growing objections to his farming relations' employment of Jewish cattle-dealers in their business. When the family moved to Munich in 1932, the tensions in the marriage grew as Ley tried with growing insistence to wean Elisabeth away from her Evangelical faith.[16] The break came, however, as a consequence of his many extramarital affairs, one of which, with the singer Inga Spilcker, led to a divorce because she fell pregnant. (The house in Bonn was made over to his first wife and their daughter as part of the settlement; they moved there in 1938; Elisabeth lived on until 1967.) Ley married the much younger Spilcker in 1938. The couple had three children – Lore Ley, born in 1938, named as a pun on the fictional Rhineland mermaid the Loreley; Wolf, born in 1940 and named after Hitler; and Gloria, born in 1941, named in celebration of the early German victories over the Red Army in Operation Barbarossa. Inga was badly injured in 1941 when she jumped from an open carriage at Ley's country estate as the horses bolted on hearing a train whistle, leading her to take morphine for pain relief and subsequently to become dependent on the drug. Depressed, in pain, deeply unhappy with the strangeness of a rural lifestyle, upset by Ley's bad temper and verbal abuse, and at the same time desperately worried about his imminent departure for Hitler's field headquarters in East Prussia, she shot herself on 29 December 1941. She was twenty-six.[17] Ley passed the children over to her parents, and embarked on an affair with Madeleine Wanderer, an eighteen-year-old Estonian ballerina whom he had met by chance in an air-raid shelter in Berlin. (Ley was fifty-four at the time.) They had one son, named Rolf Robert; both Madeleine and her son reportedly emigrated after the war to the USA.[18]

Ley's sometimes outrageous behaviour reflected the well-known fact that he was a heavy, not to say excessive, drinker. Heinrich Himmler's Finnish masseur Felix Kersten refused to treat Ley because he was always drunk when he called on him; Himmler, however, it seems, persuaded Kersten to resume his duties because of Ley's loyalty to Hitler. On one notorious occasion, in 1937, Ley insisted on driving the Duke and Duchess of Windsor, official guests of the Labour Front, around a factory compound near Munich, crashed the car through the gates and raced it up and down, thoroughly frightening his British guests. Hitler ordered Göring to take over the management of the visit before anybody was killed, and told Ley to cut down on his drinking. In 1939 Ley did launch a campaign urging people to 'keep healthy through abstinence', but he was unable to follow this advice himself. His daughter, noting the growing stress he was under during the war, later tried to defend him from the accusation of alcoholism, but conceded that he often drank champagne, and 'when he did this, a little alcohol already had an effect'. He often, she admitted, overstepped the Party's tolerance with his drinking, and on several occasions was obliged to seek Hitler's 'absolution'.[19] Ley was in the habit of drinking a large brandy before starting to deliver a public speech, and most likely on other stressful occasions too. His former secretary told the prison psychiatrist Douglas Kelley that her boss was 'always drunk'.[20]

Despite all this, Ley remained one of the most powerful men in the Third Reich. His enormous ambition, combined with his undoubted administrative and organizational abilities, found their expression through the creation of a huge bureaucracy to run the Labour Front and the ancillary organizations that soon emerged, most notably 'Strength Through Joy', which aimed to provide leisure activities for workers, ranging from concerts and visits to the theatre to tourist trips and overseas holidays; and 'Beauty of Labour', which aimed to improve conditions in factories and other workplaces. The rapid growth in the resources of the Labour Front was fuelled by an equally rapid growth in membership, which grew from under 5 million at the beginning in May 1933 to 22 million in September 1939. Members' dues, effectively compulsory, financed the construction of housing estates, the building up of a social-security system, and the mass-production of a series of consumer goods such as a cheap domestic refrigerator, the *Volkskühlschrank*, a cheap radio, the *Volksempfänger*, and a cheap automobile, paid for by subscription – the *Volkswagen* (the 'Beetle' of post-war fame). The war intervened before the car could be mass-produced for ordinary consumers. Pushed hard by Ley, the Labour Front acquired or set up a wide variety of enterprises, including insurance firms, housing programmes, and even a publishing house, which produced a wide range of periodicals and newsletters. All of this went some way towards at least partially reconciling workers to living in the Third Reich.[21]

Ley claimed that 'National Socialism is the world of order, of adherence to the law, of discipline, of obedience'. It seemed to offer him, and by extension, the Germans, the kind of stability and certainty he felt had been so lacking under the Weimar Republic. But it also offered the opportunity for Ley to realize his ambition of 'levelling up' German society and erasing the social divisions that had been so difficult for him earlier in his life. This was indeed the primary focus of his speeches. In the Labour Front, he declared, social differences between employer and employee vanished.[22] National Socialism had abolished the class struggle through the restoration of a sense of racial pride: 'Class struggle was the outward, visible expression of a gradual racial decline', the consequence of racial mixing (his term was 'bastardization').[23] It was notable that his speeches focused overwhelmingly on the tasks that in his view lay ahead for the Labour Front and for the German people. This meant he had next to nothing to say about the Jews. But it did not mean that he had abandoned his antisemitism, which came out whenever he mentioned what he thought of as the dominance of 'Marxism' under the Weimar Republic. This, he said on one occasion, had been a time when the 'Cohns and Isidors' pretended to speak for the workers.

The feeble liberals who failed to support antisemitism, he added, were no better than the Jews themselves.[24]

Racism was at the heart of Ley's ideology. National Socialism, he declared, had brought a 'breakthrough of social honour', a society in which the true, practical and nationalist socialism of the trenches in World War I would infuse the entirety of everyday life.[25] The soldier, indeed, was the role model for the worker.[26] 'Labour means Discipline. Discipline is the expression of our race!'[27] Discipline in turn would be imposed by the new structure of labour, in which factories and other enterprises would be put in the hands of a 'leader' and the workers would be his 'retinue'. Everyone would internalize these new values of racial pride and neo-feudal honour. 'There are no more private people in National Socialist Germany. One is only a private man when one sleeps. As soon as you enter everyday life, in daily life, you are a soldier of Adolf Hitler.'[28] There could be no clearer or more radical statement of the totalitarian ideal.

But all of this rested on a series of illusions. For one thing, old and new disparities in social status and political power ensured that those who benefited from the Labour Front's schemes were above all the powerful and the rich: the 'Strength Through Joy' holiday cruises, for example, were so heavily booked by Nazi officials that they were popularly known as *Bonzenfahrten*, 'bigwigs' tours'. Many of the physical improvements to workplaces introduced by the 'Beauty of Labour' scheme had to be paid for, or put into effect, by workers themselves. The Labour Front also had to contend with the wider economic priorities of the regime, which depressed wages and increased working hours in the relentless drive for rearmament. As a result, mounting discontent on the factory floor pushed Ley to pronounce repeatedly that the Labour Front would ensure all workers received a 'just wage' for their efforts, and at a grass-roots level, the Labour Front increasingly became a vehicle for wage demands, turning it into something resembling the trade unions it had been created to replace. As the pressures exerted by the breakneck speed of rearmament bore down ever more heavily on the workforce, the Gestapo was drafted in to growing numbers of factories and workplaces to punish refractory behaviour such as go-slows, absenteeism and refusal to follow orders.[29]

Ley's energy and ambition in building this massive organizational empire were impressive.[30] But his never-ending drive to expand the remit and competence of the Labour Front increasingly ran up against opposition from other individuals and institutions. Its growing encroachment on their territory provoked counter-attacks from the Ministry of Economics, from the Gauleiter, from Chambers of Commerce, from industrialists and other employers, and above all from the Ministry of Labour. Hermann Göring's Four-Year Plan, introduced in 1936 to prepare the economy for war, brought a further rival into play. Ley proved adept at all the political and institutional infighting that ensued, and he gained considerably when the economic supremo Hjalmar Schacht was forced to resign. As a fellow 'Old Fighter', Göring proved more sympathetic to Ley than Schacht had been, but the move towards a war economy he spearheaded tended to undermine the Labour Front's role as the representative of workers' interests. Göring commented pointedly that the Labour Front should have more strength and less joy. And in 1938 four draft laws introduced by Ley that would have vastly increased the Labour Front's social, economic and institutional power and relegated the Labour and other ministries to its mere appendages were decisively rejected. With the advent of war, the Labour Front's activities were reoriented towards military purposes, the cruise liners becoming hospital ships, the housing programmes converting into the provision of emergency living quarters for bombed-out workers, the 'People's Car' retooled to become the military *Kübelwagen*.

As increasing numbers of workers were drafted into military service, they were replaced by millions of foreign workers, whose forced labour was directed by Fritz Sauckel, a 'Plenipotentiary' appointed for the purpose. Meanwhile, Heinrich Himmler's SS empire expanded almost exponentially, encroaching on many of the areas previously under the aegis of the Labour Front. Robert Ley continued to fight for the expansion of his own empire, and managed to be put in charge of emergency housing for Germans made homeless by Allied bombing raids. But this was a failure: the resources were lacking, and as Germany's situation deteriorated, Ley's plans, along with the Labour Front itself, came to exist more on paper than in reality. He had continued with his work not merely because it had been a means of accruing wealth and power to himself, but also as a vehicle for bridging and ultimately eliminating the class distinctions that had been a profound source of distress to him ever since his childhood. As this ambition was finally shattered, Ley's personality began to disintegrate.[31] After visiting Hitler in his Berlin bunker on 20 April 1945 to congratulate him on his birthday, Ley travelled south, where he was discovered on 15 May by American troops at a mountain hideout 45 miles away from Berchtesgaden. Two suicide attempts had failed – one because his pistol twice failed to go off and the other because the poison he carried with him had lost its efficacy. He had also lost a huge amount of weight (slimming down from 200 pounds to 135), was dressed in blue pyjamas, and wore a green hat. He had grown a beard and tried to palm the soldiers off with a false identity, but his long-term foe within the Nazi hierarchy, the Party Treasurer Franz Xaver Schwarz, who had tried to get Hitler to fire the Labour Front boss on many occasions because of his drunkenness and corruption, soon identified him as the former Labour Front leader.[32]

With other surviving leading Nazis, Ley was taken to a temporary holding prison at the Palace Hotel in Mondorf-les-Bains, Luxembourg. He was unrepentant. In a brief political statement written in prison, Ley praised Hitler once more 'as the shining hero of this age', who 'fought right up to the entrance to his shelter, and there, as the last one, he fell – faithful unto death'. Nobody, it seems, had been able to persuade Ley of the reality, namely that Hitler had shot himself in a squalid suicide pact with his ex-mistress, now wife, Eva Braun. Following another illusion, Ley declared his belief that there were still, amid the ruins, '80–90 million Germans who are obsessed with *one idea* – national socialism – and, whether they wish it or not, will remain so obsessed'. Friendship with America, the victor in the war, was Germany's destiny, but it could only be achieved if 'the Jewish problem in Germany is solved'. Ley seemed, or pretended, to be completely oblivious to the fact that the 'Jewish problem' had already been 'solved' by mass murder. As Donald Kelley noted, Ley might verbally condemn antisemitism as a 'mistake', but even at the end of his life he was still convinced that 'the Jews constituted a problem in Germany'. Beyond this, his conviction that the vast majority of Germans were still obsessed with National Socialism was a complete misreading of the public mood in 1945. Despite everything, he was unable to shake himself out of the mental world of the Third Reich. His failure to recognize reality was shown most profoundly in a lengthy document he wrote in July 1945 on 'Ideas on the Reconstruction of Housing in Germany', in which he clearly thought he was making an important contribution to the rebuilding of Germany's shattered cities after the war. He signed it: 'Dr. R. Ley, Reich Commissioner for Housing'. It was ignored on all sides.[33]

In his 'Political Testament', written in prison in August 1945, Ley continued to justify antisemitism as a defence against the imagined 'flooding' of Germany by 'Jews, especially from the East' (of whom there were in fact very few even before the Holocaust, making little difference to the proportion of Jews in German society, which was under one per cent in the 1920s). All his adult life, his daughter Renate Wald later admitted, he had been an extreme antisemite. Ranting on about 'the Jewish question', which he thought existed on a global scale, Ley insisted that 'Jewry must make its peace with Germany'. Hitler, he wrote, 'is too great and too noble to be tainted by a passing mistake' (meaning the Holocaust). Trivialization does not get much more extreme than this. Before his indictment, on 14 August 1945, he even wrote a long letter to his late wife Inga ('You are entering my cell again. You want to talk to me. I am willing'). In it, he imagined her telling him that rumours Hitler had suffered brain damage were 'untrue and founded on malicious reports'. She praised him for continuing to insist that Hitler was *the greatest German of all times* and lauded Nazism as having achieved 'enormously *positive things*'.[34] 'All I have done under Hitler has been simply self-defence against the Jews.' If it had been left to him, he said, he would have forced Germany's Jews to emigrate by simply denying them the right to earn their living and to own or rent somewhere to live (he forgot, of course, that the vast majority of Nazism's Jewish victims were not German). He insisted he was a patriot. 'Hitler and I were only working for the good of the people.'[35] His jailer, Colonel Andrus, said that Ley's 'fierce anti-Semitism had been surpassed only by Streicher's'.[36]

Interviewed in his cell on 23 October 1945 by the prison psychiatrist Gustave Gilbert, Ley was visibly upset by the Nuremberg court's indictment, which he had read shortly before:

'How can I prepare a defence?' he asked: 'Am I supposed to defend myself against all those crimes which I knew nothing about? – If after all the bloodshed of this war some more s-sacrifices are needed to satisfy the v-vengeance of the victors, all well and good –' (Here he placed himself against the wall, crucifix-like, and declaimed with a dramatic gesture) 'Stand us against a wall and shoot us! – All well and good – you are the victors. But why should I be brought before a Tribunal like a c-, c-, like a c-, c-?' He stammered and choked completely at the word 'criminal' until

I supplied it, then added: 'Yes, I can't even get the word out.' He repeated this trend of thought several times, pacing up and down the cell, gesticulating and stuttering in great agitation.³⁷

The following day, Ley protested that the indictment was 'so absurd and so based on propaganda' that it was obviously ridiculous. 'I am a German and a National Socialist but I am no criminal.' Conviction and imprisonment as a criminal took Ley back to 1896, when his father had been convicted as a criminal and imprisoned. Ley's attempt to escape from this humiliation had ultimately failed. The next evening, 25 October 1945, alone in his cell, he tore off the edge of a bath towel, made a noose, soaked the knots in water so they would not slip, and hanged himself from the overhead water pipe of his toilet, stuffing his mouth with rags so nobody would hear him gasping for air, and leaned forward against the noose until he had strangled himself.³⁸

After his suicide, Ley's brain was removed and taken to America for analysis, which found some frontal-lobe damage, inflicted by the aeroplane crash he had undergone in the First World War.³⁹ Colonel Andrus had him secretly buried 'in an unnamed grave in a plot only a few people could identify'.⁴⁰ As Donald Kelley recalled:

> Ley's body, after the brain had been removed, was turned over to German undertakers who hauled it away in an open box which had been lined with butcher's paper. At the cemetery, the box was dropped off beside a freshly dug grave. There Ley's nude body lay exposed for some time until a couple of aged gravediggers, bleary-eyed men with dripping noses, turned up. 'So this is the great Robert Ley, huh?' said one. The other grunted a few caustic comments on Ley and his works. Then together they tipped up the box, and the body fell into the open hole, six feet downwards, to sprawl, face buried, in the gravelly mud. Ley's only covering before the clods began to fall was a single flap of coarse butcher's paper stuck to his back. With no more comment, the two old men shoveled in the earth and flattened it over to make a concealed grave.⁴¹

12

The Schoolmaster: Julius Streicher

Those who know little about Julius Streicher except that he was the editor of the notorious antisenitic scandal-sheet *Der Stürmer* (*The Stormer*), might be surprised to learn from the late historian Robin Lenman that he was also 'devoted to the German landscape and wrote articles in favour of herbalism and Nordic fairy-tales. He composed a number of quite attractive little pre-industrial lyrics and fancied himself as a watercolour painter, a creative Germanic *Naturmensch* [nature lover].' His poems and paintings were not published, but some of them survive in his papers, including sketches made in Landsberg Prison in 1923.[1] His son Lothar described him later as a 'brown Green'. Like Hitler, Streicher was a vegetarian and a teetotaller, but he also supported homeopathy and alternative medicine with enthusiasm, and held out a utopian vision of a German 'return to nature'.[2] Among other things, he played a leading role in the annual Nazi celebration of the summer solstice at the top of the Hesselberg, an isolated mountain 2,260 feet high, the highest point in Franconia, a ceremony attended by some 100,000 people by the mid-1930s and adorned with a variety of pseudo-religious rites.[3] All of this located him in the protean movement of German *völkisch* environmentalism, and in particular its nationalist and anti-urban wing, where a host of writers celebrated the Germans' supposed rootedness in the forested landscape of medieval times, contrasting it with the imagined urban rootlessness of the Jews. These ideas had a particular appeal to German schoolteachers, who were already before the First World War, as George L. Mosse observed, 'the most outspoken advocates of the Volkish ideology, particularly in connection with the racial question'.[4]

Julius Streicher, born on 12 February 1885, was a village schoolmaster. He had no education that went beyond the elementary. The ninth son of a man who was himself a village teacher in Fleinhausen, near

Augsburg, he had left school at the age of thirteen and enrolled on a five-year teacher-training course, graduating in January 1904 at the age of eighteen with average grades and starting work immediately, first as a supply teacher. The village schools where he taught usually only had one teacher, dealing alone with all the different age-groups, so their educational level was basic enough for Streicher to cope. The huge influence wielded by the local priest on Catholic village schools was a constant source of irritation for Streicher, and there were frequent clashes, resolved in 1908 by Streicher's appointment to a permanent position at an interdenominational school in the largely Protestant city of Nuremberg on completion of his military service.[5] Streicher's social and educational level was thus a good deal lower than that of the majority of Nazi leaders, and his background, in the rural petty bourgeoisie, humbler. Tests administered by prison psychiatrists at Nuremberg found him to have the lowest intelligence quotient of any of the leading Nazis brought before the court. At 106, his IQ was only a fraction above average.[6]

Streicher's family background was Catholic, though he grew up in a largely Protestant area, and he absorbed the common-or-garden antisemitism prevalent in his social milieu. He later claimed to have become an antisemite at the age of five, when he learned from a priest that Jesus had been crucified at the behest of the Jews.[7] To begin with, however, he did not express any markedly antisemitic views, but continued his unremarkable work as a village schoolteacher. In 1913 he married a baker's daughter, Kunigunde Roth, thus remaining within the lower middle class (they had two sons, born respectively in 1915 and 1918). He began to become active in politics, campaigning against clerical influence in schools, but before he could do very much the outbreak of World War I prompted him to volunteer for the Bavarian Army. He won the Iron Cross First and Second Class on the Western Front, in Romania and in Italy. Like a number of other ex-soldiers, he was outraged by the Armistice and its unfavourable terms. He shared the most extreme version of the stab-in-the-back legend, believing that Germany's armed forces had succumbed in 1918 not to the superior strength of the Allies, but to a plot hatched against them by Jewish revolutionaries on the home front to overthrow the *Kaiserreich* and its institutions. From this point on, he was obsessed with the 'Jewish Question'. He gravitated towards the ultra-nationalist right, joining the *Deutscher Schutz- und Trutzbund* (German Protection and Defence

League) on its foundation in Bamberg, not far from Nuremberg, in February 1919. Considering it insufficiently active, however, he moved in January 1920 to another antisemitic organization, the *Deutschsozialistische Partei*, a small fringe group for which he began editing a weekly newspaper on 4 June 1920.[8]

Streicher made sure he was the registered owner of the paper, so that he could safely ignore objections from some of the party's Catholic members, whom he offended with verbal attacks on the Jesuits, and from others who were irritated by the paper's deepening antisemitism. The party's leadership, however, made its disapproval clear, so he migrated to yet another extremist organization on the far right, where he came to grief at a public meeting that was broken up by left-wing activists. In addition, his newspaper, the *Deutsche Volkswille*, was in dire financial straits.[9] Streicher had already taken note of Hitler's emergence as a significant orator of the far right, and now, in 1922, decided to hear him speak. He wrote about the occasion in his 'Political Testament' (*Mein Bekenntnis*), written at the suggestion of an American intelligence officer, Captain John Dolibois, whose job it was to look after him following his arrest at the end of World War II, but not published until 1978:[10]

> He had spoken for all, for the whole German people. It had been the last hour before midnight when his speech rang out in a solemn warning: 'Workers of brain and fist! Offer each other your hands for a German people's community of heart and deed!' ... Never before ... had the singing of the national anthem moved me so deeply, as happened in that mass demonstration in which I saw Adolf Hitler and heard him speak. I felt it: in this moment, Fate called me for a second time!! I hurried through the cheering masses over to the podium and now stood before him: 'Herr Hitler! My name is Julius Streicher! In this hour I know it: I can only be a helper. But you are a *leader*! I hereby hand over to you the people's movement in Franconia, created by me.' Quizzically he looked at me from the blue depths of his eyes. The moment was long. But then he seized my hands with great warmth: 'Streicher, I thank you!' Thus had Fate summoned me for a second time. This time it was the greatest summons of my life.[11]

In fact, Streicher had already been negotiating with the Nazi Party to bring his own organization into the movement, in a series of meetings that included at least one with Hitler in person. The main inducement for him was Hitler's offer to pay off his debts and lend him some more money. Nevertheless, there is no reason to doubt Streicher's account of their encounter, even it was not their first. From this point on, he remained one of Hitler's most devoted followers, and Hitler repaid him with many years of loyal and sometimes ill-advised support.[12]

For Julius Streicher, however, joining the Nazi Party and committing himself to Hitler was far from being an epiphany. He was already a radical antisemite, a newspaper editor, and an organizer and speaker on the extreme nationalist political right. As an orator, Streicher placed his emphasis on entertainment, offering, as the historian Robin Lenman has commented:

> ... something for everybody: utopian promises and violent threats; crude sentimentality and heroic offers of martyrdom; the emotional intensity of a revivalist meeting relieved by the jokes and repartee of a music-hall. And the object was always the same: every kind of theatrical and psychological effect – patriotic music, uniforms, the ostentatious exclusion of Jews – was employed to convert ordinary political participation into an act of total emotional commitment and to endow large numbers of anxious and excited people with a collective identity.[13]

Streicher spoke in terms aimed at the lowest common denominator among his audiences, described by some as coarse and vulgar, others as direct and straightforward. His speeches, delivered with vigour and emphasis and with the rolling 'r' typical of Franconian diction, attracted large crowds and kept him permanently in the public eye. His message, however much it was dressed up with polemics, examples, anecdotes and personal attacks on his opponents, was extremely simple: the Jews were responsible for all of Germany's ills, and as soon as they disappeared, Germany would be great again, prosperous and powerful.[14] As a newspaper columnist and editor, Streicher knew no restraint, attacking his opponents with unscrupulous and often libellous zeal; he was sued for defamation on numerous occasions by Hermann Luppe, the Mayor of Nuremberg. His allegation in 1921 that several missing children in that city had been the victim of Jews who were abducting Christian children, killing them, and using their blood for ritual purposes – a paranoid medieval 'blood-libel' for which there was of course not a shred of evidence of any kind – landed him in court, where he was fined for malicious slander. Streicher realized that drumming up local support for his paper and his movement depended on linking general questions to local issues. He demonstrated this again by calling a public meeting to protest against the verdict in a sensational court case in Nuremberg where a Jewish doctor was acquitted of poisoning two young Christian girls with an allegedly dangerous contraceptive.[15]

Streicher's views, not least on the 'Jewish Question' (a 'question', of course, entirely invented by antisemites like himself), broadly coincided with those of Hitler and the Nazis. He did not have to change or adapt ideologically: his decision to join the Nazis was an organizational one. The Nazi Party was simply the most suitable and effective vehicle for his politics, following a period of frustration and setbacks. For Hitler, Streicher's accession marked the beginning of the Party's extension beyond Munich onto a wider national stage. Yet to begin with, at least, things did not go smoothly. Streicher was embroiled in a bitter internal dispute with his successor at the helm of the *Deutsche Volkswille*, Walther Kellerbauer, who managed to secure Hitler's support in the quarrel. Streicher's response was to found yet another periodical newspaper. He called it *Der Stürmer*. Initially, it appeared irregularly, and on occasion there was very little content. In due course, however, it would become the most notorious of all the Nazis' periodicals.[16]

The Nazi Party headquarters in Munich eventually established a degree of control over the situation in Nuremberg and took over ownership of *Der Stürmer*, though Streicher continued as editor.[17] On 8 November 1923 Streicher travelled to Munich and joined the beer-hall *putsch*, delivering a series of rabble-rousing speeches in various locations before taking part in the march on the city centre. His retrospective account of the events made them seem like a mass uprising, cheered on by thousands of ordinary patriots. Streicher was arrested on the train back to his base in Nuremberg, briefly imprisoned, and suspended from his teaching post (a ban made permanent in 1928, though he kept two-thirds of his salary).[18] Now a full-time politician, Streicher plunged himself into the infighting that consumed the Nazi Party during Hitler's absence in 'fortress confinement' at Landsberg. Elected to Nuremberg city council, he spent most of his time disrupting meetings. After being ejected twice for misconduct, he avoided the meetings as far as he could: making himself and the Nazi Party noticed was his main aim, which he achieved by repeatedly insulting and defaming his opponents. The immunity from prosecution he gained after his election to the Bavarian state legislature was lifted several times, and he served a total of eight months in prison; but as the Weimar Republic entered its final phase, police and prosecutors became increasingly unwilling to bring charges against him.[19]

Julius Streicher was one of the few people permitted to address Hitler with the intimate *Du* rather than the more usual, formal *Sie*. Hitler rewarded his success in building up the Nazi Party in Nuremberg by holding the annual Party Rally there. But the two were not really on intimate terms. Streicher was simply too single-minded, too obsessed with the 'Jewish Question', and incapable of talking about the other things that interested Hitler, like music, opera, art or film. Indeed, when he visited Nuremberg, the Nazi leader tended to avoid Streicher, preferring to lunch or dine with better-educated men like Willi Liebel, a printing-house owner who had been (illegally) installed as mayor in 1933 following the ousting of the previous incumbent, Streicher's arch-enemy Hermann Luppe, and Dr Benno Martin, the new police chief, put in post by Himmler as an administrator of proven competence. For the time being, Streicher, Liebel and Martin ran Nuremberg together, but Streicher, always pugnacious and demanding, gradually alienated the other two. Installed as Gauleiter of Franconia in 1933, Streicher behaved as if Nuremberg was his personal fiefdom. Quarrelsome, refractory, uncontrollable, contemptuous of bureaucratic formalities, he was almost impossible to work with. His colleagues decided to get rid of him by gathering compromising and incriminating evidence against him. Benno Martin installed surveillance devices in Streicher's office, while Himmler allowed him to have Streicher's phone tapped. A police photographer took pictures of Streicher and a number of women as they entered and left a building the Gauleiter used for sexual assignations. It was not until the aftermath of the *Reichskristallnacht*, however, that Martin's chance came.[20]

The destruction of synagogues and trashing of Jewish shops, businesses and apartments on the night of 9–10 November provided opportunities for self-enrichment that Streicher energetically seized. However, he had already made some important enemies within the Party leadership, chief among them Hermann Göring, whom he had facetiously accused in print of having his daughter Edda conceived by artificial insemination, since he was clearly too fat to be capable of fathering a child. Incensed, Göring, informed by Benno Martin in person of further misdemeanours on Streicher's part, set up a secret tribunal in his capacity as head of the Nazi Party court, which gathered two volumes of damning evidence documenting Streicher's diversion of confiscated Jewish assets into his personal account instead of the Reich fund controlled by Göring himself. In addition there were confirmed reports of physical beatings of opponents in Nuremberg, in some cases administered by Streicher himself (he always carried a dog-whip with him), and payments to a string of girlfriends, including a salary for one of them, Anni Seitz, for a job at his daily newspaper, the *Fränkische Tageszeitung*, that was in effect little more than a sinecure. The Nuremberg Gauleiter had even had a small country house constructed for his assignations. Liebel and Martin had both already been denouncing him in letters to Hitler and Göring, but it was not until Streicher's paper offended the military by criticizing their conduct in World War I, however, that Hitler was persuaded to act.[21]

The hearings of the Party tribunal convened by Hitler and consisting of six Gauleiter sat for four days, discussed the evidence collected over the previous months, and listened to the testimony of witnesses. One of them was Benno Martin himself, who was in turn accused by Streicher of sending anonymous denunciations to Hitler about his conduct. Although the accusation was correct, Martin drew his pistol and said he would shoot Streicher if he repeated it. The chairman of the tribunal reported the incident over the phone to Göring, who told him Martin should have pulled the trigger. Hitler felt unable to ignore the tribunal's conclusion that Streicher was unfit for leadership, and ordered him to retire to his country estate at Pleikershof, outside Nuremberg, banning him from returning. On a number of occasions, Hitler expressed his regret at having had to take this action, dismissing Streicher's misdemeanours as trivial in comparison to the services he had rendered the Nazi movement.[22]

Hitler allowed Streicher to continue editing *Der Stürmer*, providing him with the necessary resources to do so. He regarded it as indispensable.[23] The magazine appeared weekly, with banner headlines, crude antisemitic cartoons penned by Philippe Rupprecht ('Fips') and, from 1930 on, photographs retouched to give them an anti-Jewish twist. Early on, it presented local scandals to its few thousand readers in Nuremberg and the surrounding area, but by the late 1920s it had extended its reach, and Streicher had turned to sensational stories of wider interest, many of them sent in by readers. As its circulation rose, from around

14,000 in 1927 to 25,000 in 1933 and then, under the Third Reich, over 100,000 towards the end of 1934, and more than half a million in 1935, it attracted increasing numbers of advertisers. Glass-fronted display cases put up beside busy streets, at bus stops, and in factory canteens, brought the paper's message to even more readers. Streicher solicited endorsements from leading figures like Himmler, to further boost circulation. In 1934 Streicher bought the paper outright following the death of the printer, who had previously held the rights, and it made him a wealthy man.[24]

In issue after issue of the paper, Streicher, his writers and his cartoonist hammered home the message that Jews were ugly, fat, hook-nosed, dirty, unshaven, greedy and depraved – a message implicitly falsified by the legal requirement, introduced by the Nazis on 1 September 1941, for everyone classified as Jewish to wear a yellow star on their clothing, to distinguish them from 'Aryans' since, presumably, it was impossible for them to be identified by their physical appearance alone. Cartoons drawn by 'Fips' equated Jews with toads, vampires, insects and bacteria. Not only were Jews dehumanized in this way, they were also robbed of their individuality by being reduced to the stereotypical and referred to in the singular ('the Jew'), as if they were all part of one vast collectivity, every one of them implicated in the alleged crimes of every other.[25] *Der Stürmer* took this as a starting point for innumerable invented stories about supposed Jewish cheats, deceivers, seducers, rapists, Satan-worshippers, paedophiles and vampires. Streicher regarded *The Protocols of the Elders of Zion* as the literal truth, despite the fact that it had repeatedly been exposed as a tissue of falsifications and plagiarisms, and he resurrected on many occasions the infamous 'blood-libel' calumny and other medieval legends. 'The Jew' was, the magazine insisted, an ever-present, all-encompassing, universal threat to Germany and the Germans. He was out to pollute German blood by using drugs, alcohol and hypnosis, or alternatively money and power, to seduce young German women. He organized the trafficking of women into brothels on a vast scale, raped German girls and beat them into sexual submission with lustful sadism. Cases of 'racial defilement' occupied an increasing amount of space in the pages of *Der Stürmer* as the 1930s went on. They operated more indirectly than directly, by innuendo and suggestion, but they were enough to earn Streicher the popular nickname of 'Reich Pornographer'. Although he had no part in drafting them, the 1935 Nuremberg

Laws provided Streicher with the opportunity to carry stories describing how Jewish men were evading them. Readers helped by sending in denunciations. 'The Jews,' declared the slogan on the paper's front page, 'are our misfortune.' They were an affront to Nature. The only way to deal with them was 'annihilation'.[26]

Many Germans, especially in the educated middle class, found *Der Stürmer* offensive, and its vulgarity and extremism prompted Hitler and Goebbels to have the display cases removed from Berlin during the Olympic Games held there in 1936. This did not, however, affect its circulation, and they were restored shortly afterwards. Moreover, *Der Stürmer* was not the only vehicle Streicher possessed for the dissemination of his extremist antisemitism. The creation of the Stürmer publishing house in 1935 allowed him to produce and sell a wide range of books, of which the best known were, and remain, antisemitic reading primers and illustrated volumes of simple verse. Among these was the twenty-one-year-old Elvira Bauer's *Trau keinem Fuchs auf grüner Heid/ Und keinem Jud bei seinem Eid* (*Trust No Fox on the Green Heath/And Trust No Jew in His Oath*), which Streicher published after several other houses had turned it down. It sold over 100,000 copies. Erika Mann, the exiled journalist daughter of the novelist Thomas Mann, described it as a book of 'sadistic crudity, demagogic mendacity, tastelessness and human depravity'. *Der Giftpilz* (*The Poisoned Mushroom*) by the leading Stürmer journalist Ernst Hiemer, was yet more distasteful; even Joseph Goebbels called it 'an awful nonsense' and expressed his surprise that Hitler had tolerated its publication. It included the verses:

> There goes a devil in the land,
> The Jew it is, known to us all,
> Race defiler, genocide,
> Bogeyman for children everywhere.
> He aims to corrupt young people,
> He wants all races to die.
> Have nothing to do with any Jew,
> Then joy and happiness'll come to you!

In addition to these activities, the Stürmer also created a physical library, inviting readers to send in Jewish publications and religious objects. It contained some pornographic shelves with restricted access. All of these programmes, however, began to wind down after Streicher's dismissal and the outbreak of war. The circulation of *Der Stürmer* also began to fall during the war, as paper restrictions reduced its size from sixteen pages to merely four, and the extermination of the Jews made it difficult to run stories on their alleged misdeeds. Streicher spent increasing amounts of his time running his farm, returning to the 'blood and soil' ideas that had animated him at the start of his career.[27]

At the end of the war, two years after the death of his first wife, Streicher married his secretary Adele Tappe. The couple decided to commit suicide, going so far as to dig a grave for themselves in the grounds of Streicher's estate at Pleikershof. They changed their minds, however. Assuming a false identity and growing a beard, Streicher made his way to Waidring, near Kitzbühel, in the Austrian Alps, where he began painting watercolours once more, in a further attempt to mislead his pursuers. When he was arrested by American soldiers, one of them joked that he looked like Julius Streicher, and, thinking this meant he had been discovered, he admitted his identity and gave himself up. He later claimed that the soldiers who took him into custody were all Black, beat him up, and forced him and his wife to parade naked in front of them.[28] Prison was therefore something of a release, though the other leading Nazis in the jail turned their backs on him in the prison canteen and refused to have anything to do with him. Only Robert Ley was prepared to shake his hand. Even the prison psychiatrist Leon Goldensohn found him unpleasant: 'He smiles constantly, the smile something between a grimace and a leer, twisting his large, thin-lipped mouth, screwing up his froggy eyes, a caricature of a lecher posing as a man of wisdom.'[29]

Bored and frustrated, Streicher apparently talked incessantly to his jailer about sexual matters and asked (in vain) for women to be brought into his cell for his pleasure. Nevertheless, a continual stream of visitors came to see him, including Erika Mann, who was in Nuremberg as a war correspondent covering the trials. When she entered Streicher's cell, dressed as usual in male attire and smoking a cigarette, he recognized her immediately. 'Ha! – So you've come to gaze at all the wild beasts in the zoo,' he said, 'and you can see everything right away!!' And, dropping his trousers, he exposed himself to her. A dyed-in-the-wool lesbian, she was not impressed, and, stubbing out her cigarette, silently made her way along the prison corridor to the next cell.[30] As the Nuremberg prison psychiatrist Gustave Gilbert noted on 15 December 1945: 'Still as unwaveringly fanatic as ever, Streicher seemed completely unaffected by the accumulation of evidence that had caused shame or at least embarrassment and defensive reactions in all the others.' The trial, Streicher declared, had been organized by the Jews. Most of the prosecutors were Jews. The US Chief Counsel Robert Jackson's real name was Jacobson. The Bolsheviks were Jews. Jewish democracy reigned in America. 'Hitler must have decided to exterminate the Jews in 1941, because I knew nothing about it.'[31]

In an extraordinary outburst at his trial, he declared:

> The democratic world is too weak and isn't fit to exist! I warned them for 25 years, but now I see that the Jews have determination and spunk. – They will still dominate the world, mark my word! – And I would be glad to help lead them to victory because they are strong and tenacious, and I know Jewry. I have spunk too! And I can stick to my guns! – And if the Jews would be willing to accept me as one of them, I would fight for them, because when I believe in a thing, I know how to fight![32]

This bizarre claim, however, made immediately after the prosecution summing-up had disabused the defendants of any remaining illusion that they would be acquitted, or at the very least receive lenient sentences, was untypical of Streicher's behaviour.[33] He was condemned to death for incitement to murder: the prosecution cited more than fifty passages both from his speeches and in the pages of *Der Stürmer* where he had called for the annihilation of the Jews.[34] He never abandoned his idolization of Hitler: 'The Leader is not dead!' he wrote in his imprisonment: 'He lives on in the creation of his near-divine spirit.'[35] Streicher refused to get dressed for his execution, but the guards managed with some difficulty to force him into his clothes. He shouted 'Heil Hitler!' and 'Purim festival 1946!' and told the officials that the Bolsheviks would hang them too one day. He was hanged on 16 October 1946. He had planned in 1933 for his body to be placed in a specially built mausoleum at the summit of the Hesselberg. Instead, his corpse was cremated and the ashes were thrown into a small river along with those of the other condemned.[36]

Streicher left behind a short letter to his son Lothar, urging him to till the fields as the only way to stop the end of Nature and thus the end of the human race.[37] Born in 1915, Lothar fully shared his father's political convictions; he had joined the SS while still at school and occasionally penned articles for *Der Stürmer*. Extracts from his diary, written during a visit to the ghetto in Zamosc, published in 1945 and used in evidence at the Nuremberg War Crimes Trials, show his deep antisemitism and his belief that the Jews should be exterminated.[38] He continued to cherish his father's memory into his eighties, insisting that Julius Streicher had always told the truth, and only wanted the Jews to emigrate.[39] During the 1980s Lothar Streicher assisted the Holocaust denier Ingrid Weckert, who lived near Nuremberg, in her planned 'revisionist' biography of his father, but the project was abandoned after he suffered a stroke.[40] His younger brother Elmar, born in 1918, underwent training at a Party school, but little is known about his subsequent life. He seems to have distanced himself from his father at Nuremberg. He was still alive in 2007, when a London newspaper interviewed him about Unity Mitford, who was (falsely) rumoured to have given birth to 'Hitler's love child'.[41]

Julius Streicher was condemned to death not because he was actively involved in the planning or execution of the Holocaust, but because he had done perhaps more than anyone else, with the possible exception of Goebbels, to stoke up the hatred of the Jews that would prepare many Germans for the Holocaust. Observing Streicher's conduct in prison after the war, Colonel Andrus noted: 'He was so obsessed with hatred that when he mentioned the word "Jew" he trembled visibly.'[42] Like Hitler, Streicher was a radical antisemite from the moment he experienced Germany's defeat in World War I as a soldier on active service and learned of what were, to him, the outrageous and unacceptable terms of the Armistice and, later, the peace settlement. He was already suffused with a deep hatred of Jews well before he met Hitler; he followed him because he saw in the Nazi movement the best vehicle for his own political beliefs. The extreme right-wing milieu in which he moved was not the military world of someone like Göring or Röhm, but rather the world of nature-worship, 'blood and soil', vegetarianism and *Lebensreform*. For Streicher, this world was threatened by the supposedly rootless, city-oriented Jews, whose extermination was the only way of preserving it. Instead, it was Streicher and the movement to which he belonged that were, in the end, annihilated.

13
The Hangman: Reinhard Heydrich

Reinhard Heydrich, head of the Gestapo and the SS Security Service (*Sicherheitsdienst*, or SD), was not a member of Hitler's immediate entourage, nor was he one of the leading decision-makers of the Nazi regime. Nevertheless, he became one of the Third Reich's most notorious figures. To contemporaries and historians alike, he was, as his deputy Werner Best called him after the war, 'the most demonic personality in the Nazi leadership'. Himmler's adjutant Karl Wolff called him 'devilish', while another SS colleague, Walter Schellenberg, likened him to a 'predatory animal'. The Swiss diplomat Carl J. Burckhardt, who met Heydrich in 1935, described him later as Nazi Germany's 'young evil God of death'. For one of his early biographers, Günther Deschner, writing in 1977, he was an amoral technocrat who threw aside all considerations of conventional humanity in his pursuit of power and perfection, in which Nazi ideology was principally a means to further his own career. After meeting Heydrich on 29 August 1939 to discuss army–SS relations in the upcoming invasion of Poland, the army's Quartermaster-General Eduard Wagner noted that Heydrich was not only 'inscrutable' but also 'particularly disagreeable'. Many other contemporaries, not least those who worked with him most closely, found Heydrich cold and suspicious. Himmler could be fatherly, warm and supportive to his subordinates when he wanted to be; Heydrich always made people feel uncomfortable. As Best noted, he 'approached people in that enquiring, distrustful way which immediately struck everyone as his dominating characteristic'. 'Everyone was afraid of Heydrich,' said his immediate subordinate Alfred Six after the war. Arthur Nebe, head of one of the SS death squads (*Einsatzgruppen*), was said to have shaken with fear when he was in Heydrich's presence.[1]

To many, including Hitler and Himmler, Heydrich seemed the perfect

Nazi: tall, blond, blue-eyed, slim, physically fit, a proficient fencer, a trained pilot, and unconditionally loyal to Hitler and the ideals of National Socialism. He drank or smoked only on the rarest of occasions (such as, for example, the conclusion of the Wannsee Conference in January 1942, when he downed a brandy to celebrate what he regarded as its outstanding success), setting an example of ascetic dedication to the cause that he expected his subordinates in the SS to follow without question. He even drew up exercise schedules for them and made sure they stuck to them by attending twice-weekly sports and physical-exercise sessions. The example he set for them included maintaining an immaculately neat and clean appearance, working long hours, and behaving 'correctly' in public. In making appointments to the SD he favoured highly educated, ideologically committed men in their early thirties, men who were physically fit and 'Aryan' in appearance, with a university education that preferably included a PhD. If Himmler's conception of the SS was as an elite, then Heydrich wanted the SD to be an elite within the elite.[2]

Yet despite his central role in anti-Jewish policy and its implementation, throughout his life Reinhard Heydrich was dogged by rumours that he was Jewish himself – perhaps not fully Jewish, but quite possibly half-Jewish. The entry in a widely used musical encyclopedia *Hugo Riemanns Musik-Lexicon* (8th edition, 1916) for his father Bruno, founder and director of the music conservatory in Halle, described him as Jewish and claimed his real name was Süss. It turned out that the claim was made by an aggrieved former pupil who had been expelled from the conservatory and sought his revenge through a relative who was a member of the encyclopedia's editorial team. Bruno Heydrich sued for defamation, and won, and the entry was corrected in subsequent editions. But the damage had been done. The rumours were strengthened by the fact that one of Reinhard Heydrich's maternal uncles was married to a Jewish woman. So current were the rumours during World War I that Reinhard's fellow pupils mocked him by using the Jewish nickname 'Isi' or 'Isidor' at school.[3] As a naval officer cadet in Kiel, he was, according to a fellow cadet, generally regarded as Jewish and called 'the white Jew' or 'white Moses'. His rivals in the Nazi Party did not scruple to make use of the rumours, and in 1932 the head of the Party organization, Gregor Strasser, when shown the entry in Riemann's musical lexicon, even felt obliged to commission the official Nazi genealogist Dr Achim Gerke to conduct an investigation. Gerke concluded there was no substance in the claim and confirmed that Bruno Heydrich was 100 per cent Aryan. Still, to lay suspicion to rest, Reinhard Heydrich himself commissioned another investigation by a member of his staff, Ernst Hoffmann; it came to the same conclusion. After the war, however, Hoffmann recalled the nervousness Heydrich displayed when they met to discuss the issue. Clearly he was worried. But he had no real cause. The rumour stemmed from the name of the second husband of Heydrich's grandmother Ernestine, a widow who in 1877 married a locksmith called Gustav Robert Süss. In fact, not only did Süss lack any trace of Jewish ancestry, but, more importantly, he was not directly related to Reinhard Heydrich, whose father Bruno was the child of Ernestine's first husband, a man who had died of tuberculosis in 1874 at the early age of thirty-seven.[4]

Some historians have nonetheless made the idea that Heydrich was half-Jewish into the key element in his character. For Joachim Fest, for instance, whether or not he had Jewish ancestors was less important than the fact that he believed he had. This was the origin of his 'deeply split personality', one side harsh and ruthless, the other side soft and artistic. Fest believed that Heydrich was driven by a desire to overcome his Jewish blood through an excess of Nazi zeal.[5] His self-hatred was expressed in a revealing incident, reported to Burckhardt by a colleague, when he came home one evening and suddenly saw his reflection in a wall mirror: whipping out his pistol, he fired two shots at it, shouting 'At last I've got you, you scum!'[6] Unfortunately, there is no way of corroborating this story, or of knowing how Burckhardt's informant obtained it, given the fact that it occurred in a very private moment, with no one else around. And the claim that both Hitler and Himmler believed that Heydrich was half-Jewish but kept this information in reserve to use in case they needed to bring him to heel is unreliable too, like Himmler's supposed assertion after Heydrich's death in 1942 that he had tried to console his tortured subordinate by mentioning 'the possibility of overcoming Jewish elements by the admixture of better German blood' – for both claims came from the dubious memoirs of Himmler's masseur Felix Kersten.[7] It is worth noting, too, that being half-Jewish was no necessary obstacle to serving the Third Reich. Erhard Milch, who was in charge of aircraft production before and during the war, made it to the rank of Field Marshal despite having a Jewish father, for example, though when his racial background came under scrutiny, his mother certified that her

Jewish husband was not the real father, and he was issued with a 'Certificate of German Blood' – which became a common practice for part-Jewish Germans who Hitler, whose signature was required on the certificate, considered behaved in an 'Aryan' manner. Considerable numbers of part-Jewish men actually served in the German armed forces even without the issue of such documents.[8] It seems doubtful, therefore, that Heydrich's character and behaviour can be explained by his need to compensate for what he feared was his Jewish ancestry.

Heydrich was no outsider, nor did he come from a poor, marginalized or uncultivated background. He was born on 7 March 1904 into a family of professional musicians: his father, Bruno, was not only founder, owner and director of the Halle music conservatory, which he built up from a small singing school into a sizeable concern, but also an accomplished tenor who sang the demanding role of Siegfried in Richard Wagner's music-dramas, as well as composing five operas of his own. He was a competent player of a variety of musical instruments, and his wife Elisabeth for a time made a living as a piano teacher. Reinhard was named after the hero of one of his father's operas; his parents gave him the second name Tristan, in homage to Wagner. They made sure he received a good musical training; he was a fine amateur pianist and an outstanding violinist, whose playing a musical acquaintance described as sensitive and romantic. Reinhard played in a string quartet at various times in his life, including during the Second World War, putting a question mark over depictions of Nazi mass murderers as 'barbarians'.

Heydrich grew up in comfortable circumstances and received a good education. His parents were pillars of local society in Halle. His father intended him to take over the conservatory when the time was ripe. But a few months after his fourteenth birthday, Reinhard Heydrich's life took a different turn with Germany's defeat in the First World War. His father, like many conventionally conservative middle-class people who supported the Kaiser's Germany and were outraged by the 1918 November Revolution, turned to the antisemitic German National People's Party. Living in the city centre, the family witnessed the turbulent events of February and March 1919, when striking workers in Halle demanded the institution of a radical socialist republic based on workers' councils just as, close by, in Weimar, the elected National Assembly was meeting to work out the details of the new parliamentary constitution.[9] The Defence Minister in the national government, Gustav Noske (a right-wing Social Democrat) ordered Major-General Georg Maercker and his heavily armed volunteer 'Free Corps' to 'restore order' in Halle. After one of his officers who had entered the city on a reconnaissance mission was spotted and lynched, the situation turned nasty, and Maercker's men took over the city, killing 29 people, wounding 67, and arresting 200 under martial-law powers. These scenes were repeated in March the following year, when workers all over Germany, including Halle, mounted a general strike to defeat a far-right coup in Berlin against the legitimate government – the so-called 'Kapp *putsch*'. The strike was successful and the coup was defeated, but the most left-wing elements among the strikers attempted to push on to a socialist revolution. Once more the government sent in 'Free Corps' troops, who again put down the uprising with considerable violence and loss of life. Heydrich later claimed to have joined the 'Free Corps' in 1919, but he was too young to play an active part. He must surely have shared the local middle class's abhorrence of the socialists, but it was to be some time before he became actively involved in politics.

When Heydrich graduated from high school in 1922, with good grades in chemistry and the sciences, he was faced with the problem of how to make a living for himself, since galloping inflation, government cutbacks, and a declining number of pupils, whose parents could now no longer afford to support them and pay their fees, were all posing a serious threat to the survival of his father's music conservatory. Like other young men of his generation, Reinhard was keen to make up for the fact that he had been too young to fight in the war. So he joined the navy, perhaps under the influence of childhood holidays spent on the Baltic coast, close to where the Imperial Navy conducted its manoeuvres, or of tales told by a family friend, Felix von Luckner, who was widely fêted as one of the few naval heroes of the war. Heydrich was a fine yachtsman, physically fit, a good swimmer and oarsman, with obvious ability and ambition, but he did not fit in to the rough milieu of the naval cadet body. His fellow cadets made fun of his habit of practising the violin on board during breaks in training, and were alienated by his lack of interest in politics. It was not this, however, that prevented him from making a career in the navy. After graduating, he became a communications officer and was promoted to first lieutenant. In 1930 he met a young woman, Lina von Osten, at a ball in Kiel. The two became engaged, and preparations were made for the wedding. However, Heydrich already had a girlfriend, and he had continued his relationship with her even after he had met his future wife. His girlfriend had assumed they were going to get married, and on hearing the news of his engagement to Lina von Osten, she had a nervous breakdown. Unfortunately for Heydrich, her father had strong connections within the higher echelons of the navy, and he wrote to Admiral Erich Raeder, commander-in-chief, complaining that Heydrich had violated the officers' code of honour by his conduct. A 'court of honour' was convened, consisting of senior officers. Rather than confessing and apologizing, however, Heydrich pleaded innocence, maintaining that his relationship with his first girlfriend had begun and continued on her initiative and he had nothing to reproach himself for. His arrogance made a very unfavourable impression on the court, and on 30 April 1931 he was dishonourably discharged from the service.[10]

Not only had his hopes of a career in the navy been brutally dashed, Heydrich was now also in deep financial trouble. His father had fallen victim to a crippling stroke, cutbacks at his conservatory had lowered standards to the point where state validation had been withdrawn, and the family of impoverished minor aristocrats to which Lina belonged was also unable to provide any financial support. The German economy was hurtling towards the deepest point of the Depression, with bank failures, business bankruptcies and mass unemployment all rising almost exponentially. It was not the lack of income that affected Heydrich most, however, or he would have accepted the job he was offered as a sailing instructor: it was the lack of a uniform. Deprived of the prospect of a military career, he turned instead to the Nazi Party; or, to put it more precisely, he was turned towards it by Lina von Osten, who stood by him in these difficult circumstances (they married on 26 December 1931). For Lina was a convinced Nazi, deeply antisemitic and xenophobic, as were her parents and her brother Hans, a Party member since April 1929. Like many aristocratic families down on their luck, the von Ostens saw in the Nazi Party the chance of restoring their status and fortunes, which had been closely linked to those of the Imperial establishment. Heydrich's own family connections helped, through his godmother Elise von Eberstein, a wealthy patron of the Halle Conservatory, whose son Karl had been his childhood friend. She secured Heydrich a job interview with Heinrich Himmler, leader of the SS.[11]

Misunderstanding the nature of Heydrich's job as naval communications expert, Elise von Eberstein had told Himmler that Heydrich had been an intelligence officer in the navy. Keen on establishing an SS intelligence agency, Himmler, despite being informed about the mistake, commissioned Heydrich to sketch out a plan for one. Perhaps he was impressed by Heydrich's impeccably Aryan appearance; perhaps, too, by the knowledge he displayed of the world of intelligence, even though it had actually only been gained from an extensive reading of detective novels and spy stories in his adolescence. In any case Himmler offered him the job. As a precondition, Heydrich joined the Nazi Party. Up to this point he had known virtually nothing about the movement, despite the nationalistic and antisemitic views he had absorbed from his family, his fellow naval cadets and his future wife. Now, however, he began to read up on Nazi ideology for the first time. Before long, he had internalized the Party's core ideas and begun to share many of Himmler's own extreme views. His unconditional loyalty to the SS chief was a major element in his success over the following years: Himmler knew he could rely on him completely, and in effect treated Heydrich as his deputy. Encouraged by the SS leader, the SD, initially intended as a kind of internal Party police, was soon gathering intelligence of all kinds. Heydrich's reading had paid off.[12]

Appointed head of the Bavarian Political Police by Himmler early in 1933, Heydrich began rounding up the Nazis' enemies and putting them in the newly opened concentration camp at Dachau, where they were beaten up, terrorized, and in some cases murdered. In April 1934 Heydrich was appointed head of the Gestapo, over which Himmler had recently gained control. He was only just thirty years of age. He supplied incriminating material on Ernst Röhm and the stormtrooper organization to justify Hitler's murderous purge on the 'Night of the Long Knives', though how decisive this information was in pushing the Nazi leader into action has been disputed.[13] As the SS grew in power, so Heydrich's position increased in importance. When Himmler finally unified all the police agencies, including the SD, within the Reich Security Head Office in 1939, he appointed Heydrich to run the new institution. What distinguished Heydrich's approach to policing was his belief that even after the Nazi seizure and consolidation of power, the Reich remained surrounded by a plethora of enemies all dedicated to its destruction. The Security Police, he wrote in 1937, 'must probe and then combat all enemy elements in order to ensure that they cannot become destructive and corrosive in the first place'. The police had to be 'hard as granite' in carrying out this task. Legal and moral considerations were to be disregarded: defending the interests of the 'Aryan' race brooked no compromise. Policing was as much preventive as reactive. The Third Reich was on a permanent war footing against its supposed internal enemies, existing in a permanent state of emergency.[14]

Up to 1935, Heydrich, and with him the Security Police, had focused on combatting Social Democracy and Communism within Germany and paid relatively little attention to the Jews. But with the deepening of Nazi antisemitism that took place that year, and under the influence of Hitler and Himmler, he came to see the Jews as the power behind all those who opposed the Third Reich. He began to deploy a range of new measures against Germany's Jews and, with the backing of Hermann Göring, became increasingly active in pressuring them to emigrate by reducing the economic basis of their existence. As well as this, and jointly with Goebbels and Himmler, Heydrich unfolded a campaign of persecution against the Catholic Church in the mid-1930s. He concocted evidence for prosecuting hundreds of priests for alleged paedophilia in order to try to discredit it as almost the only remaining institution in Germany that did not owe its allegiance to the Führer. On the night of 9–10 November 1938, Heydrich made sure that the police did not intervene against the violence unleashed by Hitler and Goebbels against Germany's Jews that became popularly known as the *Reichskristallnacht*, the 'Night of Broken Glass', from the shattered window panes that lay on the streets outside vandalized Jewish-owned businesses the next morning. It was Heydrich, dismayed by the chaotic violence of the night, who proposed in the aftermath of the pogrom that a systematic, pseudo-legal programme should be launched to secure the emigration of the Jews from the Reich. These actions brought him to the centre of what was soon to become an ever-growing nexus of mass murder. Before the Nazi invasion of Poland in September 1939, his Security Service drew up a list of 61,000 Poles to be arrested or shot, ranging from Communists to leading clerics. And he set up the SS Task Forces (*Einsatzgruppen*), armoured columns of 500 men each, who followed the German armed forces into Poland in September 1939.[15]

At the outbreak of the war, Heydrich wrote and signed a letter to his wife Lina, to be opened in the event of his death, in which he enjoined her to 'educate our children to become firm believers in the Führer and Germany; to be true to the ideas of the Nazi movement', to ensure 'that they strictly adhere to the eternal laws of the SS, that they are hard towards themselves, kind and generous towards our own people and Germany and merciless towards all internal and external enemies of the Reich'. If she remarried, it had to be to a 'real man, the kind of man I aspire to be'. Building on Heydrich's rapid ascent to high office and the rewards that came with it, the couple were now part of the elite of the Third Reich, with a three-storey house in the Berlin suburb of Schlachtensee, a specially built summer home on the Baltic island of Fehmarn, and a hunting lodge in Brandenburg, near a small concentration camp at Stolpshof which supplied prisoners to carry out renovations and improvements.[16] They mixed socially with other leading Nazis, though Lena did not get on with Margarete Himmler, and they were never part of Hitler's inner circle. Admiral Wilhelm Canaris, who had been friendly with Heydrich since his days in the navy, and was now head of German military intelligence, was a neighbour: his wife Erika played in a string quartet with Heydrich. Behind the scenes, however, not all was as harmonious as it appeared to be: Heydrich was rumoured to have conducted affairs, and Lina was suspected of a relationship with one of Heydrich's intelligence officers, Walter Schellenberg, among others. Still, to outsiders, including Hitler, the Heydrichs appeared the ideal Nazi couple.[17]

As the German forces tightened their grip on Poland in the early months of the war, Heydrich's Task Forces set to work arresting and shooting Polish professionals and intellectuals. 'The nobility, the Catholic clergy and the Jews,' he declared baldly, following the policy announced by Hitler just before the outbreak of the war, 'must be killed.' By the end of the year, over 40,000 Poles had been executed by the Task Forces and ethnic German militias. Friction with the army commanders on the ground, some of whom were appalled by the murders or alarmed by the intrusion of the SS into what they felt was a military sphere of competence, was eventually resolved as Hitler and Himmler launched their policy of ruthless ethnic cleansing and resettlement. From 22 June 1941 this was moved on to a vastly larger front with the invasion of the Soviet Union (Operation Barbarossa). This time Heydrich organized four Task Forces, eventually supplemented by others operating in the Balkans. Following Hitler's orders, he issued instructions to them to shoot Communist officials wherever they found them. All Jews in the service of the Communist Party or the state were to be 'eliminated'. The description was deliberately vague: in practice this covered all adult male Jews. Together with Himmler, Heydrich carried out tours of inspection as the Eastern Front advanced, repeatedly urging the Task Force commanders to extend their killing operations. One commander, Arthur Nebe, was forced to apologize for the fact that 'only ninety-six Jews were liquidated' by his Task Force B in the first days of its operations; he assured Heydrich that he had issued a command 'that this must be greatly intensified'.[18]

Heydrich does not seem to have been driven by an obsessive hatred of Jews, unlike, say, Alfred Rosenberg or Julius Streicher or indeed Hitler himself; nor does he seem to have blamed the Jews for setbacks he had suffered in his earlier life. He did not find in an imagined Jewish world-conspiracy the key to Germany's travails. He thought of himself as a man of action, someone who got things done; he was not an intellectual or a deep thinker. During the war he found time to escape from his everyday work as the director of the largest mass-murder programme in history to take part in fencing competitions and to fly missions as a fighter pilot, both in the Battle of Britain, flying on patrol away from the combat zone, and on the Eastern Front, where he was closer to the action, pursuing the retreating Red Army troops across the Dniestr river. On 20 July 1941 his plane was hit by flak from Soviet ground positions, however, and he had to make an emergency landing behind enemy lines. He was eventually picked up by a German infantry patrol, whose commanding officer reported that the unrecognized pilot was physically unharmed but had clearly sustained a brain injury, since he claimed to be the director of the Reich Security Head Office!

Heydrich was not personally corrupt in the sense that he sought to enrich himself at every opportunity, although he had no scruples about profiting from his position when it suited him. What drove him throughout his career was a relentless and uncompromising quest for victory, a burning desire to ensure the implementation of Nazi ideology to the fullest possible extent.[19] On 31 July 1941 Hermann Göring, the nominally responsible authority, gave Heydrich a written authorization to prepare a 'total solution of the Jewish question in the German sphere of influence in Europe', and to secure the collaboration of all other institutions whose sphere of influence was involved.[20] Over the following months, driven on by Himmler and Heydrich himself, the killing operations led by the SS in Eastern Europe intensified and expanded. Like Himmler, Heydrich was aware that these seriously violated every conventional moral norm and would be regarded by the rest of the world as criminal actions. But, as the tool of what he took to be historical necessity, he hardened himself, just as he had so often told others to be hard and unyielding. On 29 November 1941 Heydrich convened the infamous Wannsee Conference; but it was postponed from 9 December because of the imminent declaration of war on the USA. It was eventually held under his chairmanship on 20 January 1942 and brought together a variety of representatives of different German government ministries with the object of ensuring their cooperation in carrying out the largest and most horrific genocide in history. The minutes listed the number of Jews who lived in virtually every country in Europe, including those countries not, or not yet, under German control. Whatever the practical difficulties and potential delays, Heydrich made it abundantly clear to the participants in the conference that the end result would be the extermination of the entire Jewish population across the continent.[21]

The Wannsee Conference underlined Heydrich's overall responsibility for the implementation of the 'final solution of the Jewish problem in Europe'. Meanwhile, in September 1941, he had acquired significant new duties. The Munich Agreement and the final occupation of Czechoslovakia had led to the creation of a 'Reich Protectorate of Bohemia and Moravia' in what remained of the country. Under the rule of Konstantin von Neurath, a former Foreign Minister, left over from Hitler's conservative coalition partners of 1933, the focus of the occupying power had been on securing the products of Czech industry for the Reich. But growing resistance, including acts of sabotage and 'go-slow' campaigns by Czech workers, had begun to undermine this policy. Simultaneously, Hitler had decided that Jewish emigration from Germany and the Protectorate should be halted, and the Jews instead should be deported to the East. In order to smooth these processes, encouraged by Martin Bormann, and by reports from Heydrich himself on the deteriorating security situation in the Protectorate, Hitler sent Neurath on indefinite 'sick leave'. He needed someone who could be relied upon to impose the toughest measures on the occupied territory. His choice fell on Heydrich. Over the following months, now based in Prague, Heydrich introduced a regime of unrestrained terror, with thousands of arrests and executions. But he coupled this with increasing food and tobacco rations for Czech munitions workers, along with privileges such as free tickets to football matches, concerts and sports events, arguing that 'there is no point in me bludgeoning the Czech and using all efforts and police power to make him do work if he does not . . . have the physical strength required to do his work.'[22]

For Heydrich, the 'pacification' of Bohemia and Moravia was only the first step in an historic process of 'Germanizing' the entire area. 'This space,' he declared in his first official speech in Prague, on 2 October 1941, 'will once and for all be settled by Germans', so that it would form a 'bulwark of Germandom' against the East. The inhabitants would be racially screened, to see if there was a way of 'turning this Czech garbage into Germans'; those who could not be Germanized would be eliminated, along with between 30 and 45 million other 'Slavs', according to the 'General Plan for the East' devised by Nazi planners in July 1941 and adopted as official policy the following year. Heydrich thought that 'between forty and sixty per cent' of Czechs were 'Germanizable'; the rest would be deported and ultimately exterminated. An ambitious programme of racial testing began, while Heydrich started to close down Czech cultural institutions and downgrade the education system to the very basic level required for a population of manual labourers. In parallel to this policy, Heydrich built up German cultural institutions, staging a 'Cultural Week' in Prague, 'a festive manifestation of German power'.[23] At the same time, he made it clear that a 'death sentence' had been passed on the 'entirety of European Jews', and began deporting Czech Jews, whom he blamed historically for the rise and persistence of Czech nationalism. From his perspective as the director of the Reich Security Head Office, the genocide was making slow progress, particularly in France, where the German military authorities were, he thought, dragging their feet. To spur them on, he organized the bombing of seven synagogues in Paris on the night of 2–3 October 1941 by some of his men, to demonstrate, as he put it, 'that the Jews are no longer safe in their European headquarters'.[24]

Alarmed by the progress Heydrich seemed to be making in crushing the resistance and winning the mass of Czech workers over to silent toleration of his policies, the Czechoslovakian government-in-exile in London had begun in September 1941 with the help of the British Special Operations Executive (SOE) to train two agents in order to drop them into Bohemia with the aim of assassinating Heydrich, whom the SOE described as 'probably the second most dangerous man in German-occupied Europe' after Hitler. His death would be a propaganda coup both for the government-in-exile and for the SOE, and would prompt violent reprisals that would alienate the Czech people from the German occupying forces. On 27 May 1942 near Prague the assassins intercepted Heydrich, who was on his way to work in an open-top car, and struck. The bomb thrown by one of them into the car wounded him fatally, and he died in hospital on 4 June. An appalled Nazi leadership in Berlin staged an elaborate funeral, with speeches extolling him as the ideal Nazi, a man of the 'finest racial quality', 'noble', 'decent', 'feared by the sub-humans, hated and slandered by Jews and other criminals'. In private, Hitler threatened to deport millions of Czechs, though he eventually dropped the idea. Instead, he decided to annihilate the village of Lidice, which, on the flimsiest of evidence, was suspected of having helped the assassins. The village's 199 male inhabitants were all shot, along with most of the children, while the women were sent to the concentration camp at Ravensbrück. The atrocity caused outrage across the world, and towns as far away as Peru renamed themselves Lidice. More than anything else, the crime made Heydrich's name globally notorious. In London, the British government repudiated the Munich Agreement (which was long defunct anyway) and promised to support the re-creation of Czechoslovakia after the war, sanctioning the expulsion of its two million ethnic German inhabitants (which indeed began in 1944 as the German army retreated in the face of the Soviet advance). Meanwhile in Prague, a vast police operation tracked down the assassins, who died in a final shoot-out.[25]

It was inevitable that the Nazi leaders in Berlin should blame Heydrich's death on 'the Jews', although there was no evidence at all for this paranoid delusion. They subsequently intensified and speeded up the mass murder of Europe's Jewish population. The extermination programme carried out by gassing in the death camps of Belzec, Sobibór and Treblinka, already under construction, was named *Aktion Reinhard*, after Heydrich: two million Jews were murdered in the following months, mainly from the 'General Government' area of Poland. But the deterioration in the military position of the Greater German Reich, as it was now called, that began in 1942 made Heydrich's Germanization plans unworkable. His successors Kurt Daluege, a top Nazi police official, then Wilhelm Frick, former Reich Interior Minister, were obliged to focus on more immediate aims, above all mobilizing Czech industry for the ever more desperate needs of the German war economy. In Germany itself, after a brief period under Himmler, the Reich Security Head Office was taken over by the Austrian SS officer Ernst Kaltenbrunner, who failed to prevent the bomb attempt on Hitler's life on 20 July 1944. Bohemia and Moravia, two of Heydrich's principal targets for Germanization, were liberated shortly before the end of the war, amid atrocities committed by the SS and counter-measures carried out by a widespread uprising of partisan and resistance units.[26]

Heydrich's wife and children had relocated to Prague at the beginning of 1942 to be with him, and shortly afterwards moved into a large mansion outside the capital, equipped with thirty rooms and seven hectares of gardens. It had been confiscated from the Jewish industrialist and art collector Ferdinand Bloch-Bauer, who had been forced to flee to Switzerland, where he died in poverty shortly after the end of the war. The Heydrichs had installed a swimming pool in the grounds, built by prisoners from the concentration camp at Theresienstadt.[27] After Heydrich's assassination in June 1942, Hitler granted the estate to his widow and their descendants in perpetuity. The estate continued to be worked by some thirty Jewish forced labourers, whom Lina ordered to be beaten if they did not work hard enough. They were taken off to the extermination camps in January 1944 and replaced by fifteen women from the concentration camp at Ravensbrück. These were Jehovah's Witnesses, who were more racially acceptable to Lina. At the end of the war, the family, minus their eldest son, who had been killed in a car crash, fled from the imminent revenge of the Czech population to their house on Fehmarn, where Lina lived in some comfort, especially after a successful claim against the Federal German government for a pension equivalent to that of a general's widow. She denied Reinhard had ever been involved in the Holocaust and in her memoirs portrayed him as a patriot who had fallen victim to irresistible and malign historical forces. Attempts to prosecute her for her maltreatment of the slave labourers who had worked in her Bohemian estate came to nothing.[28]

In the end, as Shlomo Aronson, author of the first serious study of Heydrich, concluded, it is clear 'that Heydrich's position, although important, in no way corresponded to the common estimation in postwar literature'.[29] He only entered the SS through a series of chances, but he found there the fulfilment he had been seeking since his dismissal from the navy. From the beginning of his career there, he was 'the loyal and devoted servant of his master'. Indeed, he owed everything to Himmler:

> As apposite to his ambition as all posthumous attempts to characterise Heydrich as a 'blond God of death', or 'Himmler's brain' may be, they nevertheless fail to correspond to the truth. That was much simpler: to the end of his life, the blond colossus was bound in gratitude to the pince-nez wearing Heinrich Himmler, whose appearance was by no means as Nordic or Siegfried-like as his.[30]

Heydrich's search for power and recognition ultimately led him to order the deaths of millions, but even this was pursued within the boundaries of a policy ordained by his superiors.

14
The Bureaucrat: Adolf Eichmann

From 11 April 1961, when it began, to 15 December 1961, when it ended, the trial of Adolf Eichmann gripped viewers across the globe. Broadcast from the courtroom in Jerusalem on radio and television, reported on by legions of journalists, recounted at length in newspapers and magazines, it presented moving and harrowing testimony from some 112 surviving victims of the Holocaust, men and women who had been through the ghettos and camps and seen sadism and brutality almost beyond imagining, witnessing mass murder on a scale that almost defied comprehension. The Eichmann trial was perhaps the first occasion in which the full horror and extent of the Holocaust had been broadcast to the whole world. The defendant became notorious as the man who, more than any other, had orchestrated and organized the killing. And yet, at the end of the war, Adolf Eichmann had scarcely been known to the general public at all. Noticing his name on a draft of the judgement issued by the International Military Tribunal at Nuremberg shortly after the war, one of the judges, Francis Biddle, had scrawled next to it the words: 'who was he?'[1] Eichmann featured only incidentally in the early histories of the Nazi regime or the Holocaust.[2] He lacked entirely the kind of notoriety accorded to Himmler or Heydrich. His name cropped up in many documents, but it was always in the background, never in the glare of publicity. Even at his trial, he presented himself above all as a bureaucrat, a transportation and emigration executive, a man who never fired a shot in anger or murdered anyone with his own hands. 'I had nothing to do with killing Jews,' he told his interrogator in Jerusalem. 'I've never killed a Jew. And I've never ordered anyone to kill a Jew.'[3] The prosecution portrayed him as a new kind of killer, 'the kind that exercises his bloody craft behind a desk'.[4] But this did not satisfy the media. Early, journalistic biographies, rushed out

before the trial had even begun, argued, along the lines of other studies of Nazis at the time, that he was psychologically damaged, sexually perverted, violent and depraved. They failed to convince.[5] Nor was the prosecuting attorney's claim that he had a 'Satanic personality' in any way persuasive.[6]

In his trial, as he sat in the bullet-proof glass box that served as the dock, Eichmann did not give the impression of being a monster, a sadist, or a thug. The chief prosecutor at his trial was taken aback by his appearance: 'I almost felt like searching him for fangs and claws. For externally there was nothing to indicate his nature.' One observer at the trial thought he looked like 'everyone's next-door neighbour ... The biggest surprise was the very ordinariness of the man.' Telford Taylor, who had been lead prosecutor at the Nuremberg War Crimes Trial many years earlier, on seeing Eichmann in the courtroom in 1961, had thought he looked like a 'myopic middle-aged clerk'. The reporter Martha Gellhorn noted how, in the dock, Eichmann would sit impassively, seemingly oblivious to the testimony to which he was forced to listen, coming to life 'only when documents are submitted in evidence, when he can shift the piles of folders on his desk, sort, search for a paper, make notes ... the organization man at his chosen task'.[7] As the German-Jewish philosopher Hannah Arendt, who attended the trial as a correspondent for the *New Yorker*, noted: 'The trouble with Eichmann was precisely that so many were like him, and that the many were neither perverted not sadistic, that they were, and still are, terribly and terrifyingly normal.'[8]

What struck Arendt above all was Eichmann's seeming ordinariness as he sat in the dock. She summed it up in the subtitle to her articles on the trial when they were collected together to make a book: *A Study in the Banality of Evil*. But this phrase was widely, sometimes wilfully misunderstood. What she meant by 'the banality of evil' was not that Eichmann was a mere bureaucrat, a conscienceless pen-pusher who was only obeying orders. For Arendt, he was typical of the kind of person who, as she argued in her great study *The Origins of Totalitarianism*, were the executors of regimes like Hitler's or Stalin's: second-rate minds, lacking the faculty of independent or creative thought, men who would unquestioningly implement even the most radically evil commands. But she dismissed the claim Eichmann made in self-defence that he 'obeyed my orders without thinking, I just did as I was told. That's where I found my – how shall I say? – my fulfilment. It made no difference what the orders were.'[9] Far from being a faceless, ideologically neutral bureaucrat, he was a deep-dyed antisemite. A man of overweening ambition, he wanted not only power but also fame. He had a compulsion to 'talk big', Arendt observed, and indeed 'bragging was the vice that was Eichmann's undoing'. Neither a particularly intelligent nor a highly educated man, he assimilated the ideology and behaviour of the evil system within which he sought to achieve distinction. He admired the Third Reich not least because it allowed men from a humble background like his own – or Hitler's, for that matter – to climb to the top. He was under no compulsion to act as he did: he could have opted out at any time; all his actions were voluntary. His crimes were the crimes of a system, even a nation; as the psychologists who examined him in prison concluded, Eichmann was not personally a psychopath or a sociopath, though, as Arendt points out, he was most certainly, and frequently, a liar and a deceiver. This was the 'banality of evil'.

Arendt's book became instantly notorious because of the way it stripped Eichmann of the carapace of universal depravity with which previous writers had adorned him. The judgements Arendt offered in *Eichmann in Jerusalem* were utterly independent and totally unsparing. Time and again she raised questions that provoked and disturbed. She was highly critical of Israel, above all the intrusion of religion into its constitution. She declared that Eichmann's abduction in Buenos Aires in May 1960 by a snatch squad sent by the Israeli Secret Service had been illegal, as was his removal from Argentina to Israel. The trial was a show-trial, she observed; Eichmann's crimes were crimes against humanity, so international law rather than Israeli justice should have dealt with the case. Arendt's independence of mind was one of the most impressive features of her reporting. She wrote as a detached philosophical inquirer, not as the representative of any particular group or political tendency, let alone of a race, religion or nation. Particular outrage was caused by her condemnation of the Jewish Councils, men appointed by the Nazis to administer the ghettos into which they crowded the Jewish population of East-Central Europe before they exterminated them. And her views on Eichmann himself caused huge controversy.

The biography of Eichmann which the British-Jewish historian David Cesarani published in 2004 points out that more than 200 books and articles had been written in reaction to Arendt's account. In his view, indeed, 'this marked the birth of "Holocaust studies", an unforeseen and oblique legacy of the trial'.[10] But he was also highly critical of Arendt. Many of his objections to her book, however persuasive, were beside the point, or rested on a misrepresentation, or misunderstanding, of her concept of 'the banality of evil'. Whether or not Arendt was anti-Zionist, despised Eastern European Jews, or deplored the role of the Jewish Councils in assisting the Germans (not something in which they had much choice), had no real bearing on how she accounted for Eichmann's career as a Nazi 'desk-top murderer'. She was surely right to argue, as Cesarani noted, that 'in the topsy-turvy totalitarian universe right became wrong, and acts that were normally illegal were rendered correct'. Where he disagreed with her was in what he saw as her attempt to argue that Eichmann was a kind of everyman; anyone might have done the same in a comparably totalitarian situation. This kind of argument had a long afterlife, indeed, culminating in the American historian Christopher Browning's thesis that the police squads used alongside the SS by the Nazis to massacre thousands of Jewish men, women and children in Eastern Europe during the war consisted of 'ordinary men'.[11]

Cesarani devoted much of the last chapter of his biography to discrediting the obedience experiments carried out by the American psychologist Stanley Milgram in the 1960s, which formed the theoretical underpinning of Browning's account. According to Browning, the men of Reserve Police Battalion 101 behaved much as any men would have done under similar circumstances – as, indeed, the students in Milgram's experiment did, administering electric shocks to subjects (in fact, actors, simulating pain) when instructed to do so by their professor. Milgram's experiment was deeply flawed in a number of respects. Cesarani preferred the counter-argument of Browning's critic, the American historian Daniel Jonah Goldhagen, who argued that the policemen were driven by visceral antisemitism, built into the German sense of identity from the moment it was formed in the nineteenth century. Indeed, argued Cesarani, despite the hostility of the overwhelming majority of professional historians to his thesis, it was Goldhagen who eventually won the argument, and since the end of the twentieth century, the pendulum of scholarly opinion has swung round behind interpretations that stress the specificities of the German situation.[12]

In the meantime, the debate has moved on. Further research has pointed out that the police reservists were neither 'ordinary men' nor 'ordinary Germans'. They were, to start with, volunteers, not conscripts; they were carefully selected according to ideological criteria, including their suitability for service in the SS, which only about a quarter of applicants fulfilled; their training included heavy doses of Nazi ideology and antisemitic indoctrination; and, far from being typical members of the working class, they were mostly petty bourgeois, men with small businesses that could be managed by wives and family while they were away. As members of a police force that was actually part of the SS, and had been heavily Nazified since the mid-1930s, they found little difficulty in implementing the genocidal orders they were given.[13] At the same time, Michael Wildt and Ulrich Herbert's identification of a 'generation of the unconditional', men determined to recognize no barriers to the efficient implementation of Nazi ideology all the way up to and including genocide, men for whom ruthlessness and toughness were central to their lives, has brought us back to the central theses embodied in Arendt's concept of the 'banality of evil', properly understood.

How, then, did the commitment of Adolf Eichmann fit into this debate? Born in the industrial town of Solingen, in the Rhineland, on 19 March 1906, he was brought up in a devoutly Protestant family whose head, Adolf Karl Eichmann, was a manager in an electrical company. Well-off, comfortably middle-class, and rapidly growing, the family – eventually consisting of six boys and one girl – moved to Linz, in Austria, in 1913. Although the young Adolf Eichmann's mother died in 1916, his father was soon remarried, to another devout Protestant woman. There is no indication that young Adolf got on badly with his parents, or that he was lonely or unpopular at school, where his friends included Jewish boys as well as Christians. Like other middle-class boys, he was taught a musical instrument (the violin), learned fencing, and joined the famous *Wandervogel* youth movement, whose activities centred on hiking and communing with nature. By all accounts neither academically gifted nor hard-working, Eichmann did not do well at school, and his father took him out of the educational system and put him through a number of apprenticeships, including coalmining and electrical-goods sales. At nineteen, he obtained a well-paid job as a sales rep for the Vacuum Oil Company, an American firm closely linked to Standard Oil and specializing in lubrication oil, discovered by its founders in 1866. Eichmann owed this position to his mother's family connections, and to two senior executives in the company, both of whom happened to be Jewish. There is no indication that anything in his childhood or adolescence was unusual, or predisposed him to antisemitism.[14]

As David Cesarani pointed out, Eichmann's experience as a travelling sales rep gave him experience organizing transport, scheduling deliveries, and keeping accurate records. He worked hard, was promoted, and began an active social life, riding horses, driving a motorbike, and conversing in the coffee houses for which Austria was famous. Neither he nor his father was actively political. But as members of Austria's small Protestant minority, and with their roots in provincial Germany, they naturally identified with Protestant Germany as much as, or even more than, Catholic Austria. Attending the same school in Linz as Hitler had, though years later, Eichmann was exposed to the same kind of German-nationalist influences, including a deep-rooted contempt for 'Slavs'. Influenced by the Germanic ideology of the *Wandervogel* – a German movement more than an Austrian one – he became a member of the youth wing of a German nationalist war veterans' association. This was right-wing, antisemitic, and deeply committed to uniting 'German-Austria' – the rump state left by the hated Treaty of Versailles after Hungary, Yugoslavia and the other 'successor states' had gained their independence – with the Weimar Republic. From here the route into the Nazi Party was a relatively short one.[15]

As the Nazi Party in Austria began to emerge from obscurity, with its usual tactics of excited rallies, loud propaganda, and marches through the streets, Eichmann started to admire the order and discipline of its uniformed ranks, so different from the chaotic and poorly organized Austrian *Heimwehr* or 'Home Protection' squads, would-be fascists led by the aristocratic playboy Prince Starhemberg. In any case, the *Heimwehr* was pledged to defend Austrian independence, which Eichmann saw as a futile, un-German cause. He regarded the Nazis as the most effective opponent of the socialists, who were the dominant party in Vienna and had a strong presence in other Austrian cities. He was drawn into the movement, however, above all by personal acquaintances: Andreas Bolek, a family friend who was a regional Nazi Party leader and invited him to an election meeting held on 1 April 1932, and Ernst Kaltenbrunner, son of one of his business colleagues and an officer in the SS. The Nazi Party was already scoring some impressive election results in Germany, and raising its profile in Austria. At the meeting on

1 April, Kaltenbrunner approached Eichmann and told him, using the intimate 'Du' form of address: 'Du ... Du gehörst zu uns!', or in other words, 'You ... You belong with us!'[16]

Kaltenbrunner presented Eichmann with a membership application form and Eichmann signed it. Seven months later, he also, at Kaltenbrunner's suggestion, became a member of the SS. During his interrogation in Jerusalem, he rejected the idea that he had been motivated by antisemitism, which he said the Party was downplaying at the time because it was not electorally popular. He did not reject the Nazis' hatred of Jews, but neither did he place it, for the moment at least, at the centre of his beliefs. What motivated him was his hatred of and resentment against the Treaty of Versailles. As for the rest of the Nazi ideological package, Eichmann said later that he had read the Party programme but not *Mein Kampf*; he had imbibed Nazi ideology from the Nazi press, but he admitted he was not particularly well versed in it. Relatively well off thanks to his job with the Vacuum Oil Company, where he was promoted again by his Jewish employers, he was not beset by economic or personal problems. His activities in the Nazi Party, which included participating in meeting-hall brawls between socialists and the SS, were confined mostly to weekends.[17]

What changed matters was the Depression, which plunged the Austrian economy, like others, into the abyss of bankruptcies and mass unemployment. The crisis fuelled political radicalism on all sides. In the spring of 1933, after Hitler had come to power, the Austrian Nazis began to score spectacular election victories. Fearing that this would propel them into power in Austria, the Chancellor, Engelbert Dollfuss, head of a conservative coalition government, suspended Parliament and established a dictatorship along Italian fascist lines. When he suppressed the Austrian Nazi Party in May 1933, the Party unleashed a campaign of violence and sabotage that led to further repression, including the arrest of Party activists. The Vacuum Oil Company thought it prudent to terminate Eichmann's employment, though they gave him a generous severance package. With Kaltenbrunner's help once again, he joined an SS training centre in Bavaria, and ran a motorized patrol unit picking up fleeing Austrian Nazis and helping German activists cross the border in the other direction. His reports won him rapid promotion, but, dissatisfied with the limitations of his work, he joined Heydrich's fledgling Security Service (SD), which set him to work compiling a card index of Freemasons and preparing an exhibition about them. Impressed by his work, the head of the SD's department of Jewish affairs appointed Eichmann to his office, where he was ordered to read up systematically on the Zionist movement.[18]

Soon Eichmann had established a reputation as the SD's expert on Zionism and, more generally, Jews. A meeting with a Zionist agent led to a visit to the Middle East, authorized by Heydrich but carried out incognito (Eichmann posed as a journalist, while his companion, another SD man, posed as a student). Travelling via Haifa, the two men stayed for ten days in Cairo, where they had a variety of meetings with Jewish and Arab informants. The trip did not lead to any concrete results, but it cemented Eichmann's growing reputation as an expert on Jewish emigration – still the main aim of Nazi policy at this time. At a conference of the SD Jewish section on 1 November 1937, he delivered a speech on the Jewish world conspiracy against the Third Reich, a conspiracy he thought operated through the Unilever company, using a margarine factory as a front. Such bizarre fantasies seem to have done no harm to Eichmann's standing in the Party. When German troops marched into Austria on 12 March 1938, his time finally arrived.[19]

In preparation for the takeover, Eichmann had compiled an elaborate card index of Jews in Vienna, for arrest, expropriation and imprisonment. He set up a Jewish emigration office, forced the collaboration of Jewish institutions in facilitating its work, and ordered the vice-president of the Jewish religious community, a lawyer named Josef Löwenherz, to prepare detailed proposals. Funds to assist Jewish emigration were provided by the money Eichmann impounded from the Jewish community and from individual Jews. The lower levels of the office were staffed with Jews. Löwenherz was given targets by Eichmann. Of the 200,000 Jews in Austria, 50,000 had emigrated by the end of September 1938. This was achieved through terror: Eichmann threatened Jews with removal to a concentration camp if they did not leave, while Löwenherz was seen emerging from meetings with him 'broken and crushed'. Eichmann began to insult the Jewish representatives who came before him, resorting, as one of them said later, 'to crude barrack room language'. He had achieved total power over the Jewish community in Austria, forcing it to collaborate in its own destruction – a model that was subsequently applied to Jewish communities elsewhere in the form of the Jewish Councils.[20]

Eichmann's operation in Vienna was regarded as such a success in the leading circles of the SS and police that he was put in charge of a similar operation in Prague following the German takeover in March 1939, and then, shortly after the successful invasion of Poland in September 1939, the Central Office for Jewish Emigration from the Reich, which was based in Berlin. With this move came a dramatic change of policy. Eichmann was now responsible for organizing the deportation of Jews from the Reich, part of the far-reaching ethnic restructuring of Central Europe that the invasion inaugurated. Initially, following orders ultimately emanating from Hitler himself, he began removing Jewish men from Vienna and Katowice to a border area around the village of Nisko, chosen by himself, where he told them: 'The Führer has promised the Jews a new homeland.' There was nothing there for them, however, and no preparations had been made. And the project was abandoned by Hitler when its impracticality became obvious. The men were left to their own devices, and many died, while the rest left to join nearby Jewish communities or return home. However, the Nisko idea was regarded as a success insofar as it showed that deportations were possible, and Eichmann was now appointed to organize the deportation to the General Government of occupied Poland of some 600,000 Jews from the provinces incorporated into the Reich. Stymied by objections from Hans Frank, Governor of the General Government, who did not want such huge numbers of destitute Jews sent there, Eichmann had to accept their temporary accommodation in hastily walled-off ghettos while he began preparations for a new plan, this time hatched in the German Foreign Office, which envisaged deporting all the Jews from areas under German control to the island of Madagascar, under the rule of the collaborationist Vichy regime in France. The Jews – this time some four million in number – would have been dumped in an area without infrastructure or provision for them. But this plan also failed, because of continuing British control of the seas and the impossibility of getting together the huge number of ships that would have been required, and it was abandoned in February 1942, even before the island's occupation by the British, which happened later in the year.[21]

With the launching of Operation Barbarossa on 22 June 1941 came another step in Eichmann's career. Nazi policy evolved in the following weeks and months towards a 'final solution of the Jewish question in Europe', until sometime in August or September when Heydrich told him that 'the Führer has ordered the physical extermination of the Jews'.[22] As a consequence, Eichmann's responsibilities were extended to organizing the deportation of Jews to extermination facilities in East-Central Europe. To make sure his arrangements were working properly, Eichmann travelled around to the killing pits and gassing centres, assessing them for their capacity and witnessing the murders taking place there personally, though he had no part in devising these gruesome methods of mass murder himself. There is no reason to doubt his subsequent admission, on more than one occasion, and in private as well as during his trial, that he was sickened by what he saw. 'I was horrified,' he said later of one such event: 'My nerves aren't strong enough.'[23] Nevertheless, he neither objected to what was happening, nor tried to get the policy changed. He was also taken aback by the lack of co-ordination between the murder plan and its implementation, and by the disputes between the various agencies involved. In November, as we have seen, Heydrich convened an inter-ministerial conference that eventually met at a villa in the Berlin suburb of Wannsee on 20 January 1942.[24]

It was Eichmann who prepared the statistical briefings for Heydrich, especially on the Jewish population of the European countries envisaged for the 'Final Solution', and it was Eichmann who prepared the minutes when the conference was over, editing out 'certain over-plain talk' – 'blunt' talk of killing and 'physical annihilation', as he conceded at his trial.[25] After the conference had laid down the basic parameters of cooperation between the different agencies involved, Eichmann issued further orders for deportations to the ghettos, from where, within a short space of time, the Jews were to be sent to the killing centres at Treblinka and the other extermination camps of 'Operation Reinhard'. In the course of 1942, the 'Final Solution' reached its murderous height. Eichmann did not formulate policy, and the prosecution at his trial considerably overestimated his importance in this respect. But neither was he a mere transportation executive, as he himself maintained, though an important part of his office's responsibility did of course consist in arranging trains with the national railway service. He had constantly to negotiate details of the extermination programme with the various agencies represented at Wannsee, especially the Foreign Office, which considered itself the responsible institution regarding the Jewish populations of foreign countries. All these activities required a considerable staff, and by 1943 Eichmann was working with a team of trusted subordinates within the Reich Security Head Office.[26]

Reports of Eichmann's behaviour around this time suggest that by now he had become obsessed with carrying out the complete extermination of the Jews, which was 'necessary in order to preserve the German people in the future from the destructive intentions of the Jews', an indication that he had thoroughly internalized the paranoid fantasies of Nazi antisemitism. By late 1943 the extermination programme had largely achieved its targets and was being wound down. One last opportunity, however, came Eichmann's way with the German invasion of Hungary in March 1944, a move driven partly by fears of the country's defection to the Allies, partly by Hitler's desire to lay hands on the more than 750,000 Jews who lived there. Eichmann was sent in with a team to organize their deportation to Auschwitz. Only those few deemed capable of productive work for the German war economy were spared. With Hungarian collaboration, between 15 May and 9 July 1944 nearly 440,000 Jews were rounded up, ghettoized and sent by train to Auschwitz; some 320,000 of them were put to death in the gas chambers, while the rest were drafted as slave labourers. Eichmann was the driving force in the deportations, regarding them as a logistical problem, to be solved efficiently and without emotion. As the deportations became known in the wider world, the unfavourable publicity led the Hungarian government to stop the transports. But in October, after the fascist Arrow Cross came to power in Hungary, antisemitic persecution intensified again. Eichmann now ordered scores of thousands of Jewish men and women out of Budapest on cruel foot marches to the border, to be put to work or sent to the camps. They were without food or supplies, and no facilities were made available to them en route. Many died from exhaustion or were shot by guards if they lagged behind. Even senior SS officers who encountered them on the way were disturbed by their condition, which would surely make them useless as workers.[27]

By the end of 1944, the hopelessness of the German military situation had become apparent to many. In Budapest the Swedish Legation had already begun working to save Jews, with Raul Wallenberg, an envoy despatched from Stockholm, issuing passes and sheltering thousands of Jews in safe houses. Eichmann railed against him as a 'Jewish dog' and threatened to have him shot. A leading figure in the Jewish side of the negotiations, Joel Brand, described at Eichmann's trial how he 'approached the table ... Eichmann stood in front of it, legs astride, with his hands on his hips ... and shouted, I would say bellowed, at me. "You ... do you know who I am? I am in charge of the Aktion! In Europe Poland, Czechoslovakia, Austria, it has been completed. Now it is Hungary's turn."[28] Back in the autumn of 1944, summoned by Himmler, who was now trying to bargain with the Allies, offering to save Jewish lives in return for sparing his own, Eichmann was given a dressing-down and told he must stop the marches and transports. In any case, time was finally running out for the Nazis. The Red Army began its advance on Budapest at the end of October 1944, finally entering the city on 13 February 1945. Eichmann was already 'very nervous' in his final months in Hungary, as one of his subordinates recalled: he 'used to scream at his own officers, his own friends. He stopped smiling or laughing ... Everyone was afraid of him, really terrified.'[29]

Ordered out of Budapest by Ernst Kaltenbrunner, chief of the Reich Security Head Office, on Christmas Eve 1944, Eichmann made his way to Prague and then Berlin, where he gave a farewell speech to his subordinates. According to one of them, he said 'that the knowledge of having five million Jews on his conscience gave him such extraordinary satisfaction that he would leap into his grave laughing!' From here he went south, where Kaltenbrunner ordered him to start up a resistance movement in the Austrian Alps. But he abandoned this pointless project on Himmler's advice. He discarded his uniform, assumed a series of new identities and went north, into the German 'old Reich'.[30] Arrested and imprisoned in an American prisoner-of-war camp, he was helped to escape by the SS officers in the camp, who provided him with false papers when he revealed his true identity to them. Through SS contacts he found work as a woodcutter, then, when the forestry company that employed him was bankrupted, bred chickens, which, unlike Himmler, he did with some success. But in 1947 he learned that his real identity had been discovered as a result of the Nuremberg War Crimes investigations. Once more, with a mixture of helpers including officers of the Red Cross, who were willing to hand out identity papers to refugees and displaced persons, and (despite his Protestantism) sympathetic Catholic priests, he crossed the Alps and, reaching Genoa, boarded a ship that took him to Argentina, where the dictator Juan Perón was keen to welcome Nazi refugees who possessed useful skill sets.[31]

Arriving in 1950, he registered under the name of Ricardo Klement, native of South Tyrol, and found work as a surveyor on a hydro-electric scheme in a remote mountain district. Here he put out feelers to put his shattered family back together. During the war, Eichmann had been constantly travelling across Europe from west to east, checking on his subordinates and monitoring the progress of operations on the ground. He had seen little of his wife Veronika (Vera), whom he had married in 1935, and their three children; they had remained in Prague, where they had taken up residence during Eichmann's relatively brief tenure of office there in 1938. A faithful Catholic, she had insisted the wedding be held in church, and it is a mark of Eichmann's lack of real ideological fanaticism that he had agreed without fuss and had nothing to do with the neo-pagan side of the SS. Vera was not politically active, and during his trial Eichmann described her, somewhat contemptuously, as nothing more than a housewife. During the war he was said to have enjoyed a relatively long-term relationship with Maria Mösenbacher, an Austrian woman, though details are skimpy; in Budapest he had carried on liaisons with two different women, at the same time smoking and drinking heavily as the military situation had deteriorated. Like Heydrich, he had played in a string quartet, consisting of musical members of his office; and he was also a competent player of table tennis.[32]

But somehow his marriage held together. In 1950 he contacted Vera, who was busy telling Allied investigators that she had divorced her husband, and then that he was dead, and she joined him in Argentina with their children in July 1952. When the hydro-electric scheme fell victim to an economic recession, they moved to Buenos Aires, where Eichmann tried his hand at a number of jobs before obtaining employment as a mechanic with a branch of the Mercedes-Benz car manufacturing company which employed a number of former SS men. In Buenos Aires, as Hannah Arendt noted, Eichmann did not go underground but occupied himself with talking endlessly with members of the large ex-Nazi colony, to whom he readily admitted his identity. These conversations were recorded by a half-Dutch, half-German ex-member of the SS, Willem Sassen, and edited extracts were published anonymously, though there could be little doubt about the identity of the principal participant. The existence of the original tapes and transcripts had long been known, but until recently their poor quality has defied systematic investigation. In 2014 the German philosopher and historian Bettina Stangneth deciphered them, put them together with other, often little-known source material, and delivered a full analysis of Eichmann's ideas as he expounded them to his friends and former colleagues in exile.[33]

In the conversations he had with Sassen and others, Eichmann was completely unrepentant about the extermination of the Jews, which he saw as historically necessary, a policy he was proud to have carried out in the interests of Germany. The cynicism, inhumanity, absence of pity, and moral self-deception of the conversations is breathtaking. Ten years and more after the war's end, Eichmann's lack of realism, typical of a political exile, even persuaded him that he could make a comeback, or that Nazism could be rehabilitated in Germany. He even planned to launch a public defence of what he saw as its achievements. In one of the conversations, Eichmann described himself as a 'cautious bureaucrat' but also 'a fanatical warrior, fighting for the freedom of my blood'. He lacked any kind of moral intelligence, or any ability to judge the system for which he worked. He had assimilated Nazism so completely that he was unable as well as unwilling to escape from it years after it had completely collapsed.[34] Over nearly seven hundred pages of transcripts, Eichmann condemned himself more thoroughly than any courtroom prosecutor could hope to do. Reality finally intervened when, alerted by the German prosecutor Fritz Bauer, the Israeli secret service sent a snatch squad to Buenos Aires, kidnapped Eichmann on 11 May 1960 and smuggled him back, drugged and provided with a false identity, to Jerusalem to stand trial.[35]

At the end of his four-month trial in 1961, Adolf Eichmann was found guilty of war crimes and crimes against humanity, against the Jewish people, and against Poles, Slovenes and Gypsies, and membership of proscribed organizations, notably the SS and its Security Service. He was sentenced to death and, after an appeal against the verdict had been rejected, executed by hanging shortly after midnight on 1 June 1962. His widow, Vera, stood by him, as did their three older sons. She died in 1997. Their youngest son, Ricardo, born after the war, became a professor of archaeology; he regarded his father as a historical figure whose execution had been fully justified in view of the crimes he had committed.[36]

15
The Loudmouth: Hans Frank

Both contemporaries and historians have found Hans Frank, executed on 16 October 1946 after having been condemned to death by the International Military Tribunal at Nuremberg for war crimes and crimes against humanity, something of a puzzle. He was widely known during the war as the 'Butcher of Poland', feared for his murderous and brutal administration of what was left of the country after its conquest by the Nazis in September 1939. At the same time, the diplomat Ulrich von Hassell, a member of the German resistance, was expressing a widely held view when he described him as 'a weak character'.[1] Others, such as the legal scholar Christian Schudnagies, in his brief dissertation on Frank, found him 'deeply contradictory'.[2] For Joachim Fest, Hans Frank was an 'imitation of a man of violence', 'weak, unstable and full of contradictions . . . an insecure and vacillating character', kept loyal to the Nazi cause by his 'deeply rooted subservience' to Hitler. Fest considered, however, that it was not so much Frank's weakness of character that kept him out of the inner circle of the Nazi leadership as 'the stigma of middle-class origins' in a movement (as Fest wrongly claimed) dominated by 'petty-bourgeois prophets of violence'. If Frank preached and practised violence and brutality, it was mainly in order to win the approval of Nazi leaders and disguise his 'markedly feminine character'.[3] Curzio Malaparte, who spent a good deal of time with Frank in Poland during the war, was struck by 'the complexity of his character – a peculiar mixture of cruel intelligence, refinement, vulgarity, brutal cynicism and polished sensitiveness'. Something was missing, he felt. Listening to Frank sitting at the piano in his residence, playing a Chopin prelude, Malaparte wondered what deep subsoil of criminality was concealed beneath the veneer of civilization. As the Governor-General of Poland stopped playing, Malaparte 'looked at Frank's hands. They were small, delicate and very white. I was surprised and relieved not to see a single drop of blood on them.'[4]

Although his judgement was clouded by his snobbery and his sexism, Joachim Fest was right in one thing: Hans Frank, born on 23 May 1900 in Karlsruhe, the capital of the south-west German Grand Duchy of Baden, belonged firmly to the educated middle class. His father Karl was a lawyer, his mother Magdalena the daughter of a well-off baker. The middle child of three, Hans Frank was taught key bourgeois accomplishments in his childhood: by the time he had grown up, he had become a proficient Classical pianist, and he continued to play throughout his life. As a young man he enjoyed opera and theatre and read widely. He was, in short, outwardly civilized. In 1901 his family moved to Munich, and from 1910 to 1918 he studied at the city's most prestigious high school, the *Maximiliansgymnasium*, founded in 1849. He later said he found its teaching methods outmoded and rebelled against them. He went on to study law and economics at Munich University from 1919 to 1921, then Kiel, in Germany's far north, from 1921 to 1922, ending up at Munich again, where he passed his final examinations in 1923 and embarked on a doctorate in law. Like Reinhard Heydrich, therefore, Hans Frank was a highly educated man, steeped in the principles and practice of German culture.[5]

Despite appearances, however, all was not well with the Frank family. Unusually, Hans was the child of a religiously mixed marriage, his father a Protestant and his mother a Catholic. Moreover, both parents had affairs, and they separated when his mother left for Prague to live with a German professor with whom she had begun a sexual relationship. In 1916–17, dissatisfied with his schooling in Munich, Hans spent several months with her, following the death of his older brother Karl on 26 June 1916 in a gas attack on the Western Front. His father seems to have got into financial difficulties in this period; he was eventually convicted of embezzlement, struck off the official register of lawyers, and sent to prison for a brief period.[6] This must have been a considerable shock. The family was plunged into poverty. After the war, Frank admitted, 'it was difficult. Father was not rich and we lived on cabbages and potatoes.' His parents divorced, and his father remarried.[7] A private diary that Hans Frank kept at this time gave expression to despair at the humiliation of Germany in defeat and revolution ('Proud Germany, where has your greatness gone? Your power is destroyed. We will be the slaves of the world . . . ') and his growing conviction that he was destined in some way to 'lead the slaves' revolt'.⁸

Perhaps surprisingly, Frank conceived a strong admiration for the left-wing intellectual Kurt Eisner, who led the revolutionary government in Munich from the overthrow of the Wittelsbach monarchy in November 1918 until his assassination by an ultra-right fanatic on 21 February the following year. But this was based on a distinctly fascistic understanding of 'socialism' as a programme of uniting all Germans under the leadership of a man, as Frank wrote shortly after Eisner's murder, 'who would finally take away from humanity the curse of classes . . . People are small and weak, one man is everything!'⁹ What he wanted, in other words, was not a proletarian revolution but a 'people's community' in which some kind of universalization of bourgeois-nationalist values would be created by a great national leader. The radicalization of the revolution in Munich after Eisner's death propelled Frank decisively to the far right, as a chaotic government of anarchists who pushed the legislature aside and ruled through workers' councils gave way to a more organized regime controlled by the nascent Communist Party of Germany. Frank joined a Free Corps led by Franz Ritter von Epp in April 1919 and took part in the violent, murderous suppression of the Munich Soviet. He then signed up for the army reserve, receiving some cavalry training. In the summer he became a member of the Thule Society, a group founded in August 1918 to propagate anti-semitic conspiracy theories, pseudo-mystical Germanic racism and counter-revolutionary violence.¹⁰ His hostility to the Weimar Republic only deepened when its democratic government signed the Treaty of Versailles on 28 June 1919.¹¹

It was through membership in the Thule Society that Frank came to Nazism. Here he got to know Anton Drexler, who led him in January 1920 to join the audience at a meeting where Hitler was the main speaker. Frank was impressed by what he saw as Hitler's sincerity, his clarity and his simplicity as a speaker. The content of his speech might not have been original, Frank thought, but he communicated it directly, from heart to heart, varying his tone, pitch and volume so as to keep the audience engaged, rousing everyone to belief in the way forward to the revival of Germany's greatness. His speech was interrupted frequently by shouts of support from the audience, and at the end the applause seemed to go on without end. 'From this evening on,' Frank wrote many years later, 'I was convinced, without becoming a Party member, convinced that if any man was capable of mastering Germany's fate, it was Hitler.'¹² He joined the SA, the Brownshirts, and it was in this capacity that he took part in the beer-hall *putsch* of 8–9 November 1923, helping to set up a machine-gun post, marching on the centre of Munich, and then taking to his heels when the police opened fire.¹³

Frank escaped across the Austrian border but he was soon back, avoiding unwelcome attention from the authorities and completing his doctorate in 1926. The previous year he had bumped into Hitler by chance on a Munich street, and the Nazi leader, rebuilding the Party after his release from prison, had asked him to help in the task. Frank was hesitant about joining the Party but in October 1927 he responded to an advertisement in the Party newspaper the *Völkischer Beobachter* for a lawyer to act *pro bono* on behalf of twelve Party thugs who had thrown out all the Jewish guests from a smart Berlin restaurant then trashed the premises when the waiters refused to serve them. Their guilt was undeniable, but Frank managed to get the court to treat them leniently. When Joseph Goebbels, Gauleiter of Berlin, generated massive publicity for the case, Frank became a celebrity in Party circles. By the time the Nazis came to power in late January 1933 he had defended them in no fewer than 2,400 criminal cases and represented Hitler in court on a total of 150 occasions (mostly involving defamation suits).¹⁴ He had become the Nazi Party's top courtroom lawyer.¹⁵

Frank's courtroom tactics were unconventional, to say the least, and the language he used was often violent, coarse and brutal. He insulted the prosecuting counsel, dismissed as politically motivated criminal charges against Brownshirts and Party members for acts of violence, and shouted, pounding his fists on the table and on one occasion banging his chair on the floor to drown out the proceedings when a prosecutor referred to the accused as 'National Bolsheviks' rather than National Socialists, causing the session to be abandoned for the rest of the day. He turned trials into instruments of propaganda, his voice amplified many times over by Goebbels's Nazi media. The authorities were traitors, representing a dying system that treated upstanding patriots as pariahs, Frank thundered. In treating the courts in this way, he was not being particularly innovative: lies and abuse were the standard instruments of Nazi rhetoric, attracting (together with Nazi violence on the streets) no fewer than 40,000 prosecutions up to 1933. But he made his name in the Party with these highly publicized activities. In 1930 he was rewarded with a place on the Party's electoral list and a seat in the Reichstag.[16]

By the time the Nazis gained power in 1933, Frank was also well known as a 'demagogic and hateful speaker' – to quote a police report of a meeting he addressed in 1931. He was particularly active in Germany's universities, where the right-wing extremism of most students could guarantee him appreciative audiences. His rhetoric demonstrated time and again that while he did not, unlike many other leading Nazis, come into politics with a ready-made, pre-existing antisemitism, he had fully absorbed vicious fantasies about Jews imprinted on the movement by its leader. If a prosecuting counsel happened to be Jewish, Frank would be sure to give that fact a hostile and usually sarcastic mention. The Weimar Republic, he wrote in 1931, was dominated by 'a Jewish jurisprudence of decadence' and encouraged 'Asiatic-Marxist subhuman instincts' in public life.[17] If his antisemitism was initially superficial, no more than a tactical ploy, over time Frank nevertheless internalized it until it became second nature to him.

Frank's legal career brought him close to Hitler, since he represented him or was called as a trial witness on so many occasions. After Hitler became Reich Chancellor, Frank's services were no longer needed in this respect, since the prosecution of Party members ceased for offences of acts of murder and violence, and slanderous attacks on Nazism's opponents became official government policy. The position of Reich Minister of Justice was not available to Frank; it was occupied by Franz Gürtner, one of the most pliant and subservient of Hitler's conservative coalition partners, already in post under Hitler's two predecessors as Reich Chancellor and a particularly useful ally in getting the legal profession to accept its 'coordination' into the Nazi state. The Führer owed Gürtner a favour or two, since as Bavarian Minister of Justice in the 1920s he had been instrumental in obtaining Hitler's early release from imprisonment in Landsberg following the beer-hall *putsch* trial. Gürtner would remain in post until his death in 1941.[18] Hitler made Frank Bavarian Minister of Justice instead. Perhaps more significantly he also confirmed him as head of the National Socialist Lawyers' Association, an organization Frank himself had founded in 1928 and which now achieved official status; appointed him to lead the Academy of German Law; and charged him with the 'coordination' of Germany's legal administration, a task which involved among other things firing Jewish lawyers from their posts and depriving them of a living.[19]

Despite his unprincipled exploitation of the legal system under the Weimar Republic, however, Frank retained more than a residual attachment to basic legal norms under the new state. The transition to a full dictatorship in Germany in 1933 was a process that took many months. The 1871 Reich Criminal Code still remained in place, and murder, torture and unauthorized arrest and imprisonment remained crimes that the legal authorities still felt obliged to pursue. As prosecutors who remained in post from the days of the Weimar Republic investigated the escalating number of instances where SS men and Brownshirts were found to have beaten up suspects, interned Social Democrats and Communists without trial in makeshift concentration camps, and shot inmates 'while trying to escape', Frank began to feel that such homicidal brutality was doing the state's reputation no good. More to the point, he felt that it was undermining his position as Bavarian Minister of Justice. Right up to the end of 1933, he was responding positively to complaints from prosecutors, particularly about conditions in the concentration camp at Dachau, where murders had been taking place under a chaotic, lawless and sadistic administration. Frank was particularly upset by the fact that the SS was acting without reference to him, although he felt all matters of penal policy belonged in his sphere of competence. This was the first of many demarcation disputes with the SS leader Heinrich Himmler. It was a stand-off: Himmler persuaded Hitler to stop the prosecutions, but at the same time he reformed the camp at Dachau, replacing its disorderly commandant Hilmar Wäckerle with the SS officer Theodor Eicke, who introduced an orderly, though still extremely brutal, regimen in the camp.[20]

Frank's insistence on maintaining the appearance of some kind of legality brought him into open conflict with Hitler on the 'Night of the Long Knives' on 30 June 1934, when he visited the Brownshirt leader Ernst Röhm in prison after learning of his arrest. All revolutions, Röhm told Frank resignedly, ate their own children. When two senior SS men arrived with an order from Hitler with a list of the arrested Brownshirts who were to be shot immediately, Frank told them that since the internees were in a Bavarian state prison, for which he had responsibility as Bavarian Minister of Justice, this was not going to happen. The impasse was resolved personally by Hitler, who telephoned Frank and asked him if he wanted to be added to the list. 'The legal foundation for everything that is happening is the existence of the Reich,' he told him: 'Do you understand?' Thoroughly intimidated, Frank withdrew his objection to the executions. But he also tendered his resignation as Bavarian Justice Minister, whereupon Hitler summoned him for a talk. Brandishing the letter of resignation, Hitler told him that he was a soldier in the revolutionary battle and that he could not resign. All revolutions had to break the law, otherwise they would not be revolutions. Lawyers should not interfere. Looking back on these events later, Frank rationalized his behaviour by quoting a senior Berlin lawyer: 'The ship's doctor must surely stay on board when there's a threat of epidemics spreading through the crew.' If he stayed in office, Frank claimed he had felt, he might still be able to influence Hitler in accepting the rule of law; after all, the regime was still only in its infancy.[21]

It was a delusional rationalization, or excuse, adopted by all too many professionals in the Third Reich. Frank's attempts to reform the 1871 Criminal Code, an increasingly outdated document that the Weimar Republic had failed to replace and which owed its origins ultimately to the Prussian Criminal Code of 1851, came to nothing, even though successive drafts of a new code placed the 'protection of the race' ever more firmly at its centre, because Hitler was averse to anything that bound his regime's behaviour to a set of enforceable rules.[22] Frank might perhaps have felt some personal compensation in the fact that he was showered with important-sounding titles – *Reichsleiter* (Reich Leader), giving him high status in the Nazi order, and Reich Minister without Portfolio, a position he occupied from December 1934. This role took the place of the Bavarian Justice Ministry when the federated states were abolished, and gave him a seat in the Cabinet, though this body was also falling rapidly into irrelevance and failed to meet altogether after 5 February 1938. Empty titles were not all, however. 'Ambition!' he told the prison psychologist Gustave Gilbert after the end of the war: '... that had a lot to do with it. Just imagine – I was Minister of State in Bavaria at thirty; rode around in a limousine, had servants ...'[23] Above all, however, he was in thrall to Hitler, swept away by his charisma and by the adulation of the crowds at his public appearances, overwhelmed by his attention when they met personally and in private. Frank's hero-worship comes through clearly even in the superficially disillusioned pages of his post-war memoirs. Like a number of other leading Nazis, he paid Hitler the ultimate compliment of trying to imitate him. Unlike many of them, however, he was given the opportunity to do so, when in October 1939 the Nazi dictator appointed Frank to preside over the General Government, the part of the formerly Polish territory that had neither been occupied by the Red Army in the east under the terms of the Nazi–Soviet Pact (signed two months earlier) nor been absorbed into the German Reich in the west.[24]

As Governor-General, Frank was directly responsible to Hitler, and indeed he saw his role in his fiefdom as comparable to that of Hitler in Germany as a whole. But while Hitler regarded it as his mission to improve the status and standing of the 'Aryan' majority in the Reich, Frank's brief as far as the Poles were concerned was the exact opposite. 'Poland,' Hitler had told his generals on 22 August 1939, shortly before the invasion, 'will be depopulated and settled with Germans.' Soon, however, as the labour shortage in Germany created by mass conscription became acute, and was exacerbated by the regime's reluctance to mobilize women for the war industries, Hermann Göring, as head of the Four-Year Plan, demanded that a million Poles be drafted from the General Government to help, three-quarters of them in agriculture. Thousands volunteered in order to escape the worsening conditions there, but as news of the harsh treatment they faced in the Reich filtered back, the number of volunteers fell sharply. Frank introduced labour conscription, but this triggered the beginning of a widespread resistance movement, in which ethnic Germans were assassinated and an attempt was made on the life of the General Government's police chief. In the following months Frank had young Poles arrested and sent off to Germany in huge numbers, ordering the police to shoot anyone who resisted or tried to escape. 'Poles may only have one master – a German,' Hitler declared. 'Two masters cannot exist side by side, and this is why all members of the Polish intelligentsia must be killed.'[25]

On Frank's orders, Polish priests, professionals and intellectuals were arrested and imprisoned or shot in an effort to neutralize any potential resistance movement. On 30 May 1940 Frank had 4,000 resistance fighters and 'intellectuals' killed, along with another 3,000 Poles who had been convicted for breaching the harsh criminal code to which they were subjected. The numerous penal decrees he issued prescribed the death penalty for Poles who committed a huge range of often trivial offences, including breaching price controls or evading labour service.

Polish national identity was to be obliterated. 'The Poles,' Goebbels ordered, 'are not to be allowed wireless sets; they are to be left nothing else – there is to be no press which might express any opinions. In principle, they are to have no theatres, cinemas or cabarets, so as not to dangle before their eyes what they have lost.' At most, they were to be supplied with cheap entertainments to dull their sensibilities to the realities of their situation. Frank closed down Polish educational institutions, museums and art galleries. 'The Poles,' he said, 'do not need universities or secondary schools: the Polish lands are to be changed into an intellectual desert.' Polish books were confiscated and publicly burned. The public performance of music by Polish composers was banned.[26]

In an interview with the Nazi daily paper, the *Völkischer Beobachter*, published on 6 February 1940, Frank was asked about the differences between the Reich Protectorate of Bohemia and Moravia, established shortly before the war following the German invasion and destruction of Czechoslovakia, and the General Government of Poland. He answered in the following way:

> A solid difference, I can tell you. In Prague for example big red posters were put up, on which one could read that 7 Czechs had been shot today. And I said to myself: if I wanted to put up one poster for every seven Poles who were shot, then all the forests in Poland would not be enough to make the paper for such posters – yes, we must crack down hard![27]

Like other leading Nazis, Frank believed that 'Slavs' were incapable of acting as guardians of European culture, a mission reserved for the Germans alone. Here, according to one historian, he 'unleashed a reign of terror which put all other forms of territorial annexation by the National Socialists into the shade': 'His fanatical belief in National Socialism, in the general euphoria of a military victory limited by no kind of external restrictions, allowed him quickly to become a completely willing tool of the directives of the Leader, the executioner of a bloody terror regime that was subject to no norms of behaviour.'[28] In the weeks after Frank's appointment, the diplomat Ulrich von Hassell, later a prominent member of the conservative resistance, complained, 'Frank is behaving like a megalomaniacal pasha.'[29]

Warsaw, located in the northern part of the General Government, had been seriously damaged by German aerial bombardment and fighting in the brief war of conquest won by the Nazis in 1939, and the southern city of Cracow seemed to Frank a more appropriate location for his seat of government, so he moved into the enormous Wawel Royal Castle in the city centre and furnished it with artworks confiscated from the collections housed in many of the palaces belonging to the wealthy Polish grand aristocracy. He had a Rembrandt hung on his study wall and stolen tapestries displayed in the state rooms, while silver and other treasures adorned his private quarters. He requisitioned the noble estate of the Potocki family for his use as a country seat, furnishing it with yet more loot, and sent numerous artworks back to his old home in Bavaria: when American troops arrived there at the end of the war, they found a Leonardo, a Rembrandt, and costly religious objects taken from Cracow's cathedral. Frank tried to turn Cracow into a centre of German culture, with a German theatre and a German philharmonic orchestra among other institutions. Assembling a team of architects and designers, he embarked on an ambitious programme of construction, including housing estates, apartment blocks, and a grand hotel to accommodate visiting Nazi dignitaries. Driven around in a limousine, with an official 'guard of honour', he lived a life of conspicuous consumption and display, attending lavish banquets and receptions intended to remind everyone that he was the new King of Poland, as Goebbels called him, not without a touch of sarcasm.[30]

The reality was different. Frank might claim that Hitler regarded the General Government as the best-administered of all the territories controlled by the Reich, he might issue decrees and ordinances reconstructing its administration along what he regarded as rational lines, but the truth was that he found it difficult to staff the apparatus of government with competent German bureaucrats in sufficient numbers or of adequate ability. A posting to Poland was widely regarded as a punishment among German civil servants. The young men who landed up in Frank's administration spent much of their time drinking and gambling, and even Frank complained of their riotous lifestyle, though he was hardly renowned for setting high standards himself. In any case, Hitler's intention was to let chaos reign in the General Government, with the vast majority of its Polish population receiving no help from their German rulers in alleviating what he saw as their ingrained poverty and irredeemable backwardness. Starvation, disease, a rampant black market, and the deaths of hundreds of thousands of Poles were the results.[31]

Ten per cent of the population of pre-war Poland was Jewish by culture and religion. With the conquest of the country in 1939, some two million Jews came under German rule. Frank ordered all Jews over the age of twelve to wear a white armband with the Star of David. They were, he said, 'lice'. Their food rations were deliberately lowered to a level below what was needed for mere survival; in 1942 he abolished them altogether. 'The fact that we are sentencing 1.2 million Jews to death by starvation,' he declared on 24 August 1942, 'is only worth a marginal note.'[32] By this time, he had established sealed ghettos in the major cities into which he forced the entire Jewish population. Overcrowded, insanitary and lacking the most basic facilities, they were death-traps. Frank insisted that they should be self-administered, and he set up Jewish Councils to deal with the impossible situation in which the ghettos were placed.[33] As he told a meeting of his administrators: 'A pleasure finally to tackle the Jewish race physically. The more who die, the better . . . The Jews will realize that we've arrived.'[34]

Speaking to his officials on 16 December 1941, a few days after returning from a meeting with Hitler in Berlin where the extermination of the Jews had been discussed, Frank dealt with the subject at length:

> With the Jews – I want to say this to you quite openly – in one way or another, an end must be made . . . We want to have pity basically only with the German people, and with no one else in the world . . . We must annihilate the Jews wherever we come across them, and wherever it's in any way possible, in order to uphold the whole framework of the Reich here . . . In the General Government we have roughly 2.5, perhaps with mixed-race Jews and all that belongs to them, now 3.5 million Jews. We can't shoot these 3.5 million Jews, we can't poison them, we can still take measures that somehow lead to a successful annihilation . . .[35]

The Holocaust was already well under way, with mass shootings of Jewish men, women and children behind the Eastern Front and gas vans from the Chelmno concentration camp asphyxiating Jewish prisoners with exhaust fumes fed into the back as they drove along. In January 1942 Frank sent a representative to the Wannsee Conference. Through 1942 and on into 1943, the ghettos in the General Government were emptied as their Jewish inhabitants were transported to newly opened 'Operation Reinhard' camps at Belzec, Sobibor and Treblinka, where they were asphyxiated in gas chambers.[36] In September 1944 Frank justified the fact that, as he put it, the Jews 'are gone', in terms of security: 'If these Jews had remained in the land, the peace of this area today would have been completely destroyed.'[37]

As the Holocaust gathered momentum in the second half of 1941, Himmler, Heydrich and their top men in the General Government, Wilhelm Krüger and Odilo Globocnik, began to claim independence from Frank's civil administration in one area after another, from personnel appointments to police powers. The SS men considered themselves responsible to Himmler alone, while Frank, in a furious row with Krüger on 11 September 1941, accused the SS officer of creating 'a state within a state', and demanded that all communications with Himmler in Berlin should first be approved by his office in Cracow. Relations became so bad that Otto Wächter, a senior SS officer who was also the civilian Governor of Cracow, complained that endless disputes were making the General Government impossible to run.[38] As the SS emptied the ghettos and opened the extermination centres, Frank became increasingly upset by its encroachment on his sphere of responsibility. It was not that he was in any way trying to stop or even slow down the murders, rather the contrary. It was simply that he feared Himmler was usurping his prerogative of murder.[39]

Himmler riposted by trying to force Frank aside. He commissioned a report on corruption in the General Government. It revealed that the Governor-General, his wife and his sister had kept two warehouses filled with personal property purchased with state funds at knockdown prices, including large quantities of furs, chocolates, coffee, textiles and liquor. A good deal of these luxury items had been acquired from Jews in the Warsaw ghetto. Further goods had been shipped off to Frank's house in Bavaria. Moreover, his malfeasance encouraged corrupt practices that permeated the administration of the General Government at every level. His friend Karl Lasch, Governor of the southern Polish province of Galicia, was arrested, after a delay caused by his successful bribery of the first team of investigators, for using state funds to acquire extensive assets for himself and his father from France, where he had dispatched subordinates to purchase, among other things, four luxury automobiles, paintings, sculptures, carpets, furniture, and much more besides, smuggled into the General Government without paying duty and then in many cases sold on and the proceeds pocketed. Rather than undergo the humiliation of a trial, Lasch shot himself. Frank was left in no doubt that, unless Himmler was stopped, he would be next.[40]

Frank's response to this assault on his position was to revert to his continuing role as the head of the legal profession in Nazi Germany. In the summer of 1942 he delivered a series of lectures at German universities calling for the reassertion of the rule of law as an essential basis for the formation of the German 'people's community'. He denounced the criticism to which judges were constantly being exposed for their adherence to the letter of the law. And he attacked the arbitrariness of the 'police state' which, he said, was turning the people's community into a coercive institution. It was outrageous, he said, that people could be put into concentration camps without being given the opportunity to defend themselves in a court of law. 'We want to be humane,' he said, 'there is no state which would suffer as a result of that.' Aware of the implications of these speeches, Frank offered to resign all his offices because, as he said, he could not continue in a situation where there was no legal security and the legal profession was continually being demeaned. Not surprisingly, despite the fact that Frank had laced his speeches with constant obsequious references to Hitler's greatness, the Nazi dictator was furious. He stripped Frank of his Party offices and his presidency of the Academy of German Law, handing them over to the new Reich Justice Minister, Otto-Georg Thierack. Hitler also banned Frank from delivering any more speeches in public. But he also rejected his simultaneous offer to resign his position as Governor-General of Poland, forcing him to carry on to the end.[41]

Of course, his pleas applied only to the rule of law among German citizens; individuals who did not belong to the 'people's community', such as Jews or Poles, did not deserve the protection of the law. Frank himself had done as much as anyone to undermine legal principles by treating the law not as neutral or objective but as something to be weaponized for political purposes during the Weimar Republic. The legal code he hoped to introduce in Germany itself negated the very idea of an impartial and objective system of justice by making punishments fit not the crime but the nature of the criminal, by basing the application of the law on the criminal's supposed racial characteristics, and by turning the law into a device for the assertion of 'Aryan' racial supremacy. But the hypocrisy went much deeper than this. In reality, his speeches were a thinly veiled attempt to assert his own position in the face of the mounting power of Himmler and the SS in the General Government. Frank's own blatant corruption in administering the General Government showed how much he really cared for legality and propriety. Of course, once he had been confirmed in the office of Governor-General by Hitler, the corruption continued, as did his power struggles with Himmler and the SS. Frank scored a few successes here, eventually forcing Krüger out on 9 November 1943 (the SS officer served in a variety of capacities in the SS until he committed suicide at the end of the war).

Long before this point had been reached, mounting Polish resistance had begun to make the General Government ungovernable. German officers and administrators were assassinated in growing numbers; even Frank was targeted, narrowly surviving an attempt on his life on 29 January 1944 when a bomb went off underneath his train just outside Cracow and blew the axle off the carriage in which he was travelling. As the situation worsened, he ordered 100 Polish hostages to be shot for every German killed. But the order had no effect in dampening Polish resistance. Whole areas of the General Government began to slip out of Frank's control, as the Red Army began to advance on its territory, landing paratroopers in large numbers behind the German military lines to aid the partisans.[42] The courageous Polish uprising in Warsaw on 1 August 1944 was put down with extreme brutality by the German armed forces, but this did nothing to salvage Frank's position, and on 18 August he suggested that Hitler should close down the administration of the General Government altogether. By this time, Frank had begun to change his attitude towards the Poles, even suggesting they be allowed to join the rapidly diminishing German armed forces, offering a revival of Polish culture as an inducement.[43] But it was too late; and in any case, his radical change of tack in the autumn of 1944 looks suspiciously like an attempt, unrealistic though it was, to gather credit in preparation for the inevitable war-crimes trial once the Allies had won. On 17 January 1945 he fled with two dozen or so of his staff to Germany, taking up residence temporarily in a castle at the Prussian town of Seichau, where their drunkenness and 'unbelievable conduct' led to complaints by local people and a disapproving report sent to Martin Bormann. When they evacuated the premises on 23 January 1945 they left behind them empty bottles strewn everywhere, art objects, crates of alcohol, food, fourteen typewriters, a large Mercedes car, and pile upon pile of documents.[44]

From Seichau, Frank travelled to Neuhaus am Schliersee, in Bavaria, where he re-established the administrative centre for the now non-existent General Government. Unable to find suitable premises, he set it up in a local restaurant. His demands for cars, staff and equipment came to nothing. On 4 May he was arrested by American troops and taken to a nearby prison, where he was known as the 'Jew-butcher of Cracow' and beaten. He tried to kill himself by slashing his wrists, but failed. When he arrived at the holding centre for top Nazi criminals, in Luxembourg, he was described by its commandant as 'a pitiful wreck of a man'.[45] He was arraigned at the Nuremberg War Crimes Trials as one of the principal defendants. He had handed over his official diary, with its transcripts of meetings and speeches, perhaps in the belief that it would vindicate him. It was, however, a highly incriminating document. The prison psychiatrist Gustave Gilbert reported that in his initial interrogations, Frank had been 'surly and evasive', on one occasion leaving the interview room cursing, 'Swine!' But Frank appeared to be genuinely shocked by the atrocity films the defendants were forced to watch, and was strengthened in his determination to confess when he read that one of his father's best friends, a Jewish lawyer, had been murdered in Auschwitz. He seemed to have experienced a religious epiphany and spent much of the time in his cell at Nuremberg reading the Bible. He could, remarked Gilbert, 'curse Hitler with an amazing vehemence and literary facility . . . "If only one of us had had the courage to shoot him dead!"' Hitler, he said, was evil, a cold-blooded psychopath. Gilbert was impressed by his remorse, though he found it somewhat 'hysterical'.[46] In the dock, Frank admitted his part in the extermination of the Jews, and – to the disgust of other defendants such as Göring – associated it with that of the German people as a whole, in effect passing on the blame: 'A thousand years will pass and this guilt of Germany will not be erased.'[47]

How genuine all this was is a moot point. Frank's admiration for Hitler shone through the superficially damning verdict he passed on the dictator. The substantial volume of memoirs he wrote as he awaited execution at Nuremberg, entitled *In the Face of the Gallows*, is devoted almost entirely to Hitler rather than to its author: indeed it is subtitled 'Interpretation of Hitler and his time on the basis of personal experiences and perceptions'. Hitler, wrote Frank in conclusion, was 'intellectually an outstanding person . . . He is a masterly figure . . .' He had 'carried through tremendous achievements'. Frank even addressed him directly at the end of his book, accusing Hitler of being godless and heartless, better described as a 'demonic being' than 'as a genius in the true sense of this idea'.[48] Indeed, Frank wrote his book not least because he felt he had a unique knowledge of Hitler and wanted to share it with the German people. At the same time, his book was evasive on a number of issues, playing down his own antisemitism and his involvement in the Holocaust, which he relativized with what he supposed to be historical precedents, and minimizing the ideological elements in Hitler's drive to war. He laid stress on his commitment to the rule of law, and made no mention of his corruption and profiteering. He even claimed, referring to the final, desperate phase of his rule as Governor-General and ignoring what had gone before, that he had tried to build up Poland and Polish nationhood for the future.[49]

The Nuremberg Tribunal found Frank guilty of war crimes and crimes against humanity and condemned him to death. He was hanged on 16 October 1946. His family, unlike the families of so many other Nazis, disowned him almost entirely. His widow Brigitte was a secretary who had typed up his dissertation; they had married in 1925. They had not enjoyed an easy marriage; Frank later admitted she had turned out to be cold and distant, and he had had several affairs, all with women he had known for some time. He had asked for a divorce in 1942 in order to marry a childhood sweetheart, but Hitler had forbidden it.[50] His widow eventually committed suicide in 1981. Of their five children, only the oldest one, their daughter Sigrid, remained an unrepentant Nazi, emigrating to South Africa during apartheid, which she admired. Their son Norman dismissed his father as a womanizer and told an interviewer he was glad he had been executed. But it was their youngest child, Niklas, born in 1939, who was most hostile to his father's memory. His book *Der Vater: Eine Abrechnung* (*The Father: A Reckoning*), published in 1987, is a hate-filled tirade that in places is almost incoherent with rage at his father's crimes and deceptions. It is addressed directly to him, in language dripping with sarcasm and contempt:

> The snapping of your neck spared me a screwed-up life in which you would have poisoned my mind with your twaddle, like the silent majority of my generation, which did not have the luck to have seen their father hanged. Because of this, I am happy to be your son. How poor are other

children whose fathers churn out the same rubbish full of cowardice and deceit, full of blood-lust and inhumanity, but were not as prominent as you. There's no point in copying down their tirades, their diaries aren't listed. I'm lucky, I can cobble together the flesh-strips of your life from the archives of Europe and the USA, I can look at them undiverted by the lying family chatter. Whether I tackle them with a scalpel or a hammer, there emerges the same German monster.[51]

Niklas Frank's book is thus an indictment not merely of his father, but of twentieth-century Germans in general, and not merely one generation of them, but two.

PART IV

The Instruments

Introduction

In the mid-1960s, the German journalist Horst Krüger (1919–1999) spent many hours in the press gallery at the Frankfurt Auschwitz trials, where twenty-two former SS camp guards and lower officials were being held to account for their part in the deaths of more than a million people at the notorious concentration and extermination camp in the first half of the 1940s. Looking round the courtroom, Krüger saw only ordinary men who had built a solid and respectable existence for themselves after the war, their appalling crimes seemingly forgotten until uncovered by a courageous German state prosecutor, Fritz Bauer, and belatedly brought to justice. Here for example was Wilhelm Boger, 'an upright, reliable bookkeeper', 'a man you could depend on, who had readjusted to life, who was able to sleep at night and who certainly had colleagues and friends and a family'. And yet, the court was told, apart from participating in countless selections, gassings, mass shootings and executions, he was personally responsible for 'holding a sixty-year-old cleric in the prisoners' kitchen under water until he was dead; shooting a Polish couple with three children with a pistol from a distance of about three metres; kicking to death a Polish general who had been starved until he was practically a skeleton', and many other similar acts of sadism and brutality.

This did not mean, however, that they were 'just obeying orders', a common excuse of those who were arraigned before the courts after the war for the crimes they had committed during the Third Reich. All of them had choices; none of them was forced to do what they did. In one way or another, however, they willingly surrendered their moral autonomy to Hitler. By no means all of the individuals whose lives are recounted in this section were fanatical Nazis. But all of them subscribed to the central tenets of Nazism. This opened the door for some, like Ilse Koch or Irma Grese, to use their power – in their cases, the power of the concentration-camp commandant's wife and the camp overseer respectively – to unleash base and violent instincts against the prisoners, instincts that brought them a notoriety which far outdid that of most male camp officers and guards. Yet the flames of this notoriety were also demonstrably fanned by the perception that by taking part in the crimes of the Third Reich, such women were violating gender norms and behavioural expectations in the most radical possible way. Koch and Grese in particular were demonized to a quite extraordinary degree. Other Nazi women, notably the film star Leni Riefenstahl, director of the celebrated Nazi propaganda documentary *Triumph of the Will*, managed for a long time after the war to shake off the memory of their crimes and build new careers. While Riefenstahl distanced herself from Nazism after 1945, the so-called 'Reich Women's Leader' Gertrud Scholtz-Klink not only made no attempt to do so but continued to defend her role in the Third Reich until her dying day. Even a middle-class woman married to a man classified by the regime as a 'full Jew', such as the Hamburg schoolteacher Luise Solmitz, whose life under Nazism is analysed in the final chapter, lent her support to the regime to the extent that she even denounced her brother to the authorities for what she saw as anti-Nazi activities. In the end, however, ironically, it was precisely her roles as a woman, wife, mother and grandmother that combined to alienate Luise Solmitz from the regime.

The Third Reich was one of the most male-supremacist regimes in history, valorizing a concept of hyper-masculinity expressed through 'toughness' and 'hardness'.[1] 'The more masculine a man is,' said Hitler, 'the more effective he will be in his sphere of operation.'[2] 'Men make history!' he proclaimed on 30 January 1939. 'Great men are themselves only the strongest, most concentrated representation of a people.'[3] And, as he boasted on 24 February 1940: 'I am nothing other than a magnet, which is continually stroking the German nation and pulling the steel out of the people, and I have often explained that the time will come when whatever there is of men in Germany will stand in my camp, and whatever then does not stand in my camp, is good for nothing.'[4] Women retained the vote in Nazi Germany, but they had no independent political role, and the composition of the leading political echelons was exclusively masculine; women, after all, the Nazis believed, were incapable of decision-making or even political judgement, even though they continued to go to the polls, probably because this reinforced the impression Hitler wanted to give to the world that the entire adult population of Germany was solidly behind him and belonged to a unitary, organic 'national community'.

Such an understanding of masculinity was common to a wide range of male perpetrators. For a man like Hans Loritz, for example, who was commandant of a series of concentration camps during his career, including both Dachau and Sachsenhausen, it meant bellowing at subordinates, swearing and cursing, beating, brutalizing and humiliating prisoners, behaving in what he regarded as a military manner, and encouraging his subordinates to do the same. Loritz does not seem to have had a tendency to sadism in his youth, but in the atmosphere of Nazi Germany, and the lawless environment of the camps, he clearly was encouraged to violate every norm of human decency. In this way he sought to compensate for his loss of self-respect in 1918–19, when his career as a combat airman during the war came to an abrupt and humiliating end. His ambition and careerism brought him rapid promotion, but it also got him into trouble as his corruption became clear to his superiors. National Socialism, however, provided the underpinnings of his self-worth, and when it collapsed and he was taken into custody, he could no longer find any meaning in life, and killed himself on 31 January 1946.[5]

One of the most important sources of the Nazis' concept of masculine hegemony lay in the memory of World War I, with politics viewed as the continuation of the struggle against the enemies of the Reich. In this vision, women's only role was to look after home and family and support their menfolk on the political and military battlefronts. For the army itself, with its long tradition of military autonomy, the advent of the Nazis proved a welcome return to the readiness of the state to prepare for war and ultimately to wage it. At the same time, however, as Chapter 16 will show, the officer corps of the German army was subjected to massive interference by Hitler, who purged one general after another for not following his crude understanding of strategy and tactics, even when the conservative, anti-democratic and antisemitic culture of the generals swung them behind the regime, however reluctantly in some cases, as it implemented the Holocaust. After the war, the surviving generals insisted they had simply been professionals, a defence followed by civilians such as doctors, lawyers and university professors. Here too, for several decades there was a failure to come to terms with the Nazi past, something that was striking in its lack of moral insight.

Yet although an extreme and frequently internalized understanding of masculinity lay at the heart of Nazism, the spectrum of perpetrators ranged far beyond the power-crazed, the authoritarian and the brutal. Most Germans who belonged to the educated middle classes, the so-called *Bildungsbürgertum*, comprising people with university degrees and professional status, welcomed the coming of the Third Reich and collaborated with the Nazi regime to the end. There were numerous reasons for this. Under the Bismarckian Empire they had enjoyed a secure and respected place in a self-confident and seemingly stable society, a position they had lost with Germany's defeat in World War I, the Revolution of 1918, the creation of the Weimar Republic with its enthronement of democratic rights such as universal and equal suffrage, and the advent of the feared and hated (and largely working-class) Social Democrats to power. If relatively few of them were Nazi fanatics, the great majority still openly or tacitly supported Hitler because they saw in him the guarantor of social order, national pride, economic stability and cultural tradition, all of which had been so conspicuously absent, they thought, under the Weimar Republic. Not only medicine and the law, each of which had its own peculiarities, but also other professions followed a similar pattern. So too did the world of business, big, medium-sized and small. Nazism was not the ideology of the uneducated or the unsuccessful.

16
The General: Wilhelm Ritter Von Leeb

One of the less celebrated German generals was the army commander Wilhelm Ritter von Leeb (his noble title was granted during World War I as a military honour). Interesting precisely because he was in so many ways typical, Leeb was one of the older senior German commanders. He was one of the rare Catholics in the upper ranks of the officer corps. Less unusual was the fact that he was Bavarian, born on 5 September 1876 in Landsberg, into a family with a long military tradition.[1] But he still moved seamlessly into the Prussian-dominated ranks of the Imperial Army, up through cadet academy into the General Staff. His diaries reveal little about his personality or private affairs. His army personnel file shows that his superior officers reported through the earlier part of his career that he was a capable and energetic soldier, tough and hardworking, 'serious, not completely without humour ... Not quite of the calibre of General v. Rundstedt, but certainly a good leader in the war'. All his adult life, Leeb regarded himself as a professional soldier who took no part in politics. As an artillery officer in the Bavarian Army, he took part in the German military expedition to China, part of a punitive campaign mounted in 1900–1901 by eight nations against the anti-European uprising by the so-called 'Boxers'. After his return, he joined the Bavarian General Staff, and remained in the army throughout the Weimar Republic. Leeb did not subscribe to the 'stab-in-the-back legend', widespread in the officer corps, according to which the army had remained undefeated on the Western Front but had been fatally undermined by the Home Front, above all by the Social Democrats. His diaries show that he recognized as early as September 1918 that the war had been lost because of 'military mistakes' by Erich Ludendorff, 'who has the entire ruin of the German people on his conscience'. Ignoring Leeb's Bavarian background, the leading military figure of the Weimar

Republic, General Hans von Seeckt, ruled him out as his successor, regarding him as 'the epitome of the revolting, rigid Prussian Junker'. Still, Leeb had already signalled his disillusion with the Republic, emphasizing his distaste for the Social Democrats and pointing to the threat posed in his view by the 'Bolsheviki'; his seniority carried him into the ranks of the generals by the time the Republic was overthrown.[2]

Leeb welcomed the Nazi seizure of power, above all when the 'Day of Potsdam' on 21 March 1933 advertised what Hitler presented as his reconciliation with the old Imperial order: 'This act of state,' Leeb declared in a public address to mark the occasion, demonstrated that 'all the disunity' of the previous years would now give way to a 'strong and powerful will' that would 'include all Germans, the will to work on the rebuilding of out Fatherland'. It was noticeable, however, that he failed to mention Hitler or the Nazi Party, preferring instead to stress the leadership of the old Field Marshal Hindenburg in the resurrection of 'our old, famous black-white-red emblem', the flag of the Kaiser's Germany. That was not how Hitler saw it, of course, nor the younger generation of army officers. Leeb's misunderstanding of the real nature of National Socialism was soon to become clear.[3] To begin with, loyal military service under Hitler earned him steady promotion. As a pious Catholic, however, he turned down an invitation to a formal dinner with Alfred Rosenberg because of the latter's anti-Christian stance, and annoyed Hitler by attending Mass in full-dress uniform. Many of the older generals had misgivings about the wisdom of launching a general European war before the armed forces were ready for it. Leeb did not conceal the fact that he shared these doubts. Hitler even had him placed under Gestapo surveillance; and eventually the dictator forced him into retirement in early 1938 during the purge that followed the dismissal of Werner von Blomberg and Werner von Fritsch from the top posts in the army, along with other senior officers he considered too cautious and insufficiently committed to Nazism.[4]

Leeb's reputation for competence and efficiency led Hitler in the summer of 1938 to bring him out of retirement for the invasion of Czechoslovakia, when the dictator gave him command of the 12th Army, units of which occupied the Sudetenland when the Munich Agreement ceded it to the Nazi Reich. Leeb was closely involved in military planning for the invasion, in accordance with the terms of the

Agreement. After carrying out the occupation, Leeb retired for a second time. But once more, now well into his sixties, he was recalled to duty in September 1939, this time to command Army Group C in the southern sector of what would become the Western Front, opposite France's defensive emplacements in the Maginot Line. Leeb was still reluctant to give Hitler his full support. 'Declaration of war by England and France,' he reported in his diary on 3 September 1939, on the outbreak of World War II, adding: 'Hitler is a blind fool, a criminal!'[5] A month later, on 3 October 1939, he noted that German civilians did not support the war: 'bad mood of the population, no kind of enthusiasm, no putting out flags from houses, all expect peace. The people feel the war is unnecessary.' Despite all his misgivings, however, Leeb continued to attend planning meetings with Hitler to discuss the invasion of the Low Countries in 1940, also illegal under international law. In October 1939 he even wrote to Walther von Brauchitsch, commander-in-chief of the German Army, to warn him that:

> If Germany, by forcing the issue, should violate the neutrality of Holland, Belgium, and Luxembourg, a neutrality which has been solemnly recognized and vouched for by the German government, this action will necessarily cause even those neutral states to reverse their declared policy towards the Reich, which up till now showed some measure of sympathy for the German cause.[6]

This would, he added, be a 'crazy attack' that would 'perhaps decide the fate of our people for decades'. Nothing resulted from this outspoken missive, however, and Leeb did not act on his initial threat to resign, not least because his fellow generals, many of whom shared his opinion, decided in the end not to take any further action: such a step during wartime might after all easily be construed as mutiny; even an echo of the supposed 'stab-in-the-back' at the end of World War I. Leeb remained faithful to Hitler, despite the death of his two sons in the Polish campaign of September–October 1939.[7]

Soon after the start of the war, however, Leeb, like a number of other senior generals, was disturbed by reports that reached him of 'the behaviour of the [German] police in Poland' that was 'unworthy of a civilized nation'. The army, he wrote to the Chief of the Army General Staff, Franz Halder, was being pushed aside, demonstrating the 'dictatorship [*Alleinherrschaft*] of the SS in our people'.[8] Alarmed by the disquiet shown by Leeb and other senior generals, Halder visited his headquarters to reassure him that the reports were exaggerated and any excesses were being brought to an end. This did little to calm the older officers, however, and their alarm at the ambition of the SS only increased with Himmler's announcement on 28 October 1939 that he wanted the men of the SS to conceive children out of wedlock in order to ensure that as much as possible of their 'best blood' was passed on to a fresh generation. It was not only pious Catholics like Leeb who found this idea outrageous, but others too, including a number of leading generals, who joined him in protesting to the army leadership. In the end, relations between the army leadership and the SS deteriorated to the extent that Himmler called a meeting with Leeb and other generals on 13 March 1940, in which he praised them for the tough measures they themselves had taken to crush resistance in the occupied territories and assured them that the racial programme of the regime was necessary to ensure the future of the greater German Reich. This seemed sufficient to quell the protests.[9]

Any remaining doubts that Leeb and his fellow generals might have entertained were quelled by the rapid German conquest of France, Belgium, the Netherlands, Denmark and Norway in 1940. Along with other leading commanders in the campaign, Leeb was promoted to Field Marshal following his successful participation in the defeat of France that year, when his forces overran the French in Alsace-Lorraine. His easy victory demonstrated, he wrote, the fact that France was a 'dying land'.[10] Soon after the capitulation of France, preparations commenced for the invasion of the Soviet Union, a project about which Leeb entertained serious doubts. ('Does that have to happen as well?' he said resignedly to Walther von Brauchitsch on 31 January 1941, when informed about the plans.) Leeb's doubts were once more quelled, however, when Hitler appointed him to command Army Group C, subsequently redesignated Army Group North, which marched into Soviet-controlled Eastern Europe on 22 June 1941 as part of the huge invasion force that launched Operation Barbarossa. He had two armies at his disposal, the 16th and the 18th, together consisting of some 29 Divisions, and the 4th and 56th Panzer corps. Leeb's forces successfully subjugated Latvia, Lithuania and Estonia in the first few weeks of the campaign.[11] But his inexperience in controlling armoured brigades was demonstrated when the tank corps raced ahead, risking encirclement to the extent that they were temporarily driven back, with the loss of some 400 tanks according to one account. Leeb was under instructions to take Leningrad, but he had got into such difficulties that Hitler visited his headquarters in person on 21 July 1941 to insist that Leningrad be finished off quickly. Leeb's forces were approaching Leningrad towards the end of August, and the occupation of the city seemed only a matter of time. By mid-September he had surrounded the city, apart from a thin line of communication across Lake Ladoga, which froze over in the early winter. Leeb was overheard on the telephone asking Hitler what he should do with the starving women and children in Leningrad if the city surrendered and they started food riots. Hitler apparently told him to shoot them. Leeb refused: 'German soldiers don't shoot women and children.'[12] Disregarding this protest, Hitler privately ordered him not to accept the city's surrender. It was to be annihilated and its inhabitants exterminated.[13]

Leeb had made a reputation for himself as something of an expert on defensive warfare, even publishing a widely used book on the subject before the war.[14] But in the euphoria of the first few weeks of Operation Barbarossa, he persuaded Hitler to sanction an attempt to take the town of Tikhvin, an important transportation hub east of Leningrad, in order to link up with the forces of Germany's ally Finland. Like other sectors of Operation Barbarossa, however, this got bogged down in the autumn, and opened the way to counter-attacks by the Red Army. Leeb was also losing touch with operations on the ground, where the troops were depleted by losses and exhausted by the months of marching (one battalion commander complained that he had only sixty soldiers left out of his original 500). To make matters worse, the weather was getting colder and the troops were still in their summer uniforms. Disappointed at Leeb's slow progress, Hitler detached much of his armour and ordered it to the Moscow front.[15] Early on in the campaign, Leeb was able to preserve some freedom of action, and managed to withdraw his troops from Tikhvin when the situation became difficult, securing Hitler's approval after the event. But now that the German forces were starting to be driven back before Moscow, causing a range of top generals to suffer nervous breakdowns or even heart attacks, Hitler took over the leadership of the army himself, on 16 December 1941, and ordered uncompromising resistance to the Soviet advance.[16]

Leeb succumbed to rapidly rising levels of stress as the German advance ground to a halt, compounded by Hitler's focus on what he saw as the more important Moscow front. Complaining in his diary of frequent headaches, Leeb found himself unable to deal with the situation. Increasingly depressed by the inaction forced on him by Hitler's order not to try and take Leningrad, but simply to allow the city to starve, and despondent at the wider failure of Operation Barbarossa, Leeb suffered what was in effect a nervous breakdown. After Hitler rejected his resignation 'on health grounds' in mid-January 1942, Leeb declared flatly in a face-to-face interview that he was unable to carry out his military commands because he did not have 'sufficient new and fresh' troops to do so. He enraged Hitler by insisting that his conscience forbade him to carry out his orders under these circumstances. He had to be allowed to take his own initiative instead of being ordered repeatedly to hold the line and dig in. Hitler refused his appeal, which would have amounted to a carte blanche to make tactical withdrawals as required. This time Hitler accepted his resignation.[17] Leeb was forced to retire into the reserve on 18 January 1942, and sat out the rest of the war.[18]

Despite his reputation as an upright, independent-minded representative of the old military order, Wilhelm Ritter von Leeb was implicated in many of the crimes and atrocities committed by the Nazi regime. Unlike the generals in charge of the central and southern sectors of the Eastern Front, Leeb, as commander of Army Group North, was not confronted early on in the campaign with the problem of what to do with vast numbers of Red Army prisoners of war. By October 1941, as the campaign came to a halt before the gates of Leningrad, there was an urgent need for labour, which was met by drafting in Red Army prisoners of war, contrary to internationally agreed practice. Other sectors of the front took longer to change over to a forced-labour policy, and simply penned Soviet prisoners of war into huge enclosures behind the front, letting them starve to death – three and a half million died in this way in the months following the invasion. Only from 1943 onwards did the army and the regime more generally recognize the fact that prisoners of war and civilians under the control of the military authorities were potentially useful as forced labour, whereupon they scaled down the mass murders.[19] Starving Soviet prisoners of war was part of a wider policy: realizing that the army would have to live off the land as it advanced into Eastern Europe, well before the launching of Operation Barbarossa the Agriculture Ministry official Herbert

Backe ordered that food supplies originating in the conquered areas were to be diverted to the troops, leaving the civilian population of the region to starve.[20] Despite initial doubts, Leeb implemented this policy in full, ordering his subordinates not to allow any food supplies sent from Germany to be distributed to the troops, who had to feed themselves entirely from the occupied territory.[21]

Racist belief in the inferiority and dispensability of Slavic 'subhumans', shared by Leeb, who thought that Russians were part-Asiatic and naturally cruel, was the driver of this policy.[22] It also informed Leeb's direction of the siege of Leningrad, after he had completed the encirclement of the city on 8 September 1941. His artillery subjected it to heavy bombardment, while air raids inflicted serious damage on food supplies. Starvation spread rapidly among the population, and there were even cases of cannibalism. By the time the siege was lifted, in January 1944, more than three-quarters of a million of Leningrad's inhabitants had perished.[23] Although Leeb claimed after the war not to have followed Hitler's notorious order that all Soviet political commissars captured by German troops were immediately to be shot, there is abundant evidence to show that Army Group North followed this command just as much as any other part of the German forces.[24] Moreover, within a short space of time after the invasion, the generals on the Eastern Front, faced with the growing resistance from partisans behind the lines, were resorting increasingly to massive reprisals against civilians, and identified such resistance increasingly with Jews, though this was untrue. Leeb himself ordered his senior officers in August 1941 to combat the 'Partisans ... with drastic and draconian means against the Partisans and their helpers' helpers'.[25] A report on the actions taken by Army Security Division 281 in Rear Area 584 of Army Group North in the first week of December 1941, for instance, listed '327 Partisans shot, 23 villages burned down, 7 munitions dumps captured, 3 hospitals and 12 residential camps destroyed'. This kind of violence and destruction was going on all over the conquered parts of the East, including the rear areas behind Leeb's army, week by week, for months on end.[26] Such atrocities were the result neither of difficult military situations nor of the 'brutalization' of the troops; they were the result above all of the long-held German military doctrine of 'total war' and the deep-seated antisemitism and anti-Slav racism that had permeated the officer corps for decades and had only been strengthened by years of Nazi indoctrination.[27]

Antisemitism was widespread among the German officer corps, but it did not extend to the advocacy of genocide, at least not among the older generation. Leeb's forces were accompanied by SS Task Force A, consisting of 1,000 men under the command of Walther Stahlecker, supported by a variety of police units. They were assisted and in some cases preceded by local Latvian, Lithuanian or Estonian activists, who began rounding up the Jewish population and shooting them, or in the larger cities forcing them into ghettos, which were in turn emptied by the end of the year in the course of further shootings. By the beginning of 1942 some 300,000 Jewish inhabitants of the three Baltic states, men, women and children, had been murdered, a good number of them openly, in public scenes often attended by regular German army soldiers. Leeb made no attempt to stop any of this. 'Our German soldiers,' he noted in his diary, 'were quiet onlookers, had no orders somehow to stop the bloody judgement.' Shootings and atrocities against Jews had already caused disquiet and disapproval during the conquest of Poland in 1939, on occasion leading to protests.[28] On 8 July 1941, shortly after the beginning of Operation Barbarossa, Leeb reported in his diary a conversation with one of his officers:

> General v. Roques, commander of the rear army area, complains about the mass shootings of Jews in Kovno (thousands!) by Lithuanian militias at the instigation of the German police authorities. We have no influence on these measures. The only thing left is to stay away. Roques is no doubt right to say that the Jewish question is unlikely to be solved in this way. The surest method would be through the sterilization of all male Jews.[29]

Leeb's staff complained about these murders to Hitler's armed forces' adjutant Rudolf Schmundt when the latter paid them a visit. According to the Field Marshal's biographer Georg Meyer, Schmundt consulted Hitler, who instructed him to telephone Leeb with the instruction: 'soldiers must not be troubled with these political questions: these measures are a necessary "land clearance".'[30]

Neither Leeb nor Roques took any action to curb the shootings, although they were carried out in the areas for which they were ultimately responsible. Indeed, a senior SS officer reported to Himmler from a series of inspections he conducted locally that the cooperation between the Task Force and the army in the region had gone 'smoothly'. Both Leeb and Roques, in other words, had moral reservations about the murders, but their misgivings were not strong enough to prompt them to use their authority to try and stop them, not least given the clear instruction from Hitler to leave the matter alone. Moreover, both men accepted at the very least that there was a 'Jewish question' that was urgent enough to justify compulsory sterilization. In practice, their attitude allowed extensive cooperation between army and SS units in the murder of Jews, gypsies and the mentally ill and handicapped. Roques had also criticized the murder of Jews, but without result. All Roques could do was order that his troops were not to take part in mass shootings organized by the SS and insist that they should not act on their own initiative against the Jews in their area of responsibility.[31] Soon after the end of the war, Leeb, by now in American captivity, responded to his fellow captive Heinz Guderian, who had declared 'the fundamental principles [of the extermination of the Jews] were good': 'That is true.'[32]

Leeb's relationship with Hitler remained cordial to the end, assisted by a generous contribution of the dictator to the Field Marshal's finances – one of many examples of the widespread purchase of loyalty from military and other elites, or, better said, their corruption by the regime. On 5 September 1941 Hitler's adjutant paid Leeb another visit to convey the dictator's congratulations on the Field Marshal's sixty-fifth birthday. Discreetly, Schmundt handed Leeb a cheque for a quarter of a million Reichsmarks to mark the occasion, intended as 'capital for the purchase of a villa' or some other purpose. There is no evidence to suggest that Leeb was anything but grateful for this gift, despite the attempt of his biographer to suggest otherwise. On 16 September Leeb wrote to the head of the civil service, Hans-Heinrich Lammers, to thank him for ensuring the gift would not be subject to taxation. With the 250,000 Reichsmarks safely squirrelled away, Leeb began the search for property to spend it on. What he was looking for, he told Lammers, was 'just to acquire a wood and build a small country house in it'. It should if possible be located south of the Danube, in 'Old Bavaria', away from Allied bombing raids. But the plan encountered bureaucratic obstacles as well as the difficulty of finding someone willing to sell, and months passed without any suitable property being made available. Despite the increasingly difficult military situation, Lammers managed to find time to discuss the matter personally with Hitler, and it was agreed with the Gauleiter of Bavaria, Paul Giesler, that a state-owned property should be found. The only one to fit the bill was District XXIII of the Forestry

Office at Seestetten, near Passau, but its market value, at 660,000 Reichsmarks, far exceeded what Leeb, with a mere 250,000, could afford. Hitler and Lammers agreed to make a further donation to Leeb to cover the difference. 'I am absolutely delighted,' the Field Marshal wrote in a personal letter to Hitler on 23 November 1943, 'to be permitted to own a German wood.' Promising to take good care of it, he added that he was following the progress of the war with the keenest interest and was confident that the Red Army's resistance on the Eastern Front would soon collapse.[33]

In April 1944 the sum of 638,000 Reichsmarks was set aside for Leeb from public funds, and, when further bureaucratic hurdles had been overcome, it was paid over to him, making his total receipts 880,000 Reichsmarks. For this 'very happy news', he told Hitler in a handwritten letter dated 26 July 1944, he thanked him warmly, adding his congratulations on the dictator's 'wonderful rescue from the wicked attack' on his person attempted by Claus von Stauffenberg and his co-conspirators a few days before.[34] On 11 October the Field Marshal finally took possession of a wooded estate near Passau covering the very substantial area of 213,843 hectares. Unlike other estates gifted to leading generals and other servants of the regime, the property was safe from the Red Army, and remained in the possession of the family, though they were obliged to pay 75,000 Reichsmarks in tax on the original gift of 250,000 shortly after the end of the war. In the late 1990s investigative journalists publicized the family's continued ownership of the estate in a television programme, but Leeb's son declared he had no intention of returning the property, now worth over two million German Marks, to the state, and the conservative Bavarian government refused to take the matter any further.[35]

Leeb was in many respects typical of the military leadership of the Third Reich. We know a great deal about the military commanders who led German troops into battle during the Second World War, not least because many of them kept diaries, whether official or personal (the boundaries between the two were often, inevitably, rather fluid). Yet for a long time little use was made of this material. Individual generals were seldom mentioned by name in the post-war military histories, with a few exceptions such as Erwin Rommel, and when they were, narratives concentrated on military tactics and battles. Even Joachim C. Fest, writing on the military, preferred to indulge in sweeping generalizations about the generals' 'weakness of character' and castigate them for their failure to stand up to Hitler and the handful of committed Nazis in the upper levels of the army hierarchy.[36] Social-science approaches to history, dominant in the 1970s and 1980s, strengthened these anonymizing tendencies. Not until the second half of the 1990s did questions of individual motivation and behaviour begin to occupy the attention of military historians. Since then, there has been a growing number of critical studies of individual soldiers, mostly set in their broader historical context.[37]

The biographical approach has among other things revived questions that were largely ignored, even suppressed, from the 1950s to the 1990s. After the war, in 1948, the American authorities brought fourteen top generals, including Wilhelm Ritter von Leeb, before the last of the Nuremberg tribunals and charged them with war crimes, crimes against peace, crimes against humanity, and conspiracy to commit these crimes. The accused men all pleaded not guilty. Leeb and the others insisted that they had been unpolitical soldiers: tough, even brutal, in the face of a vile and unscrupulous Communist enemy, but always acting within the laws and conventions of warfare and under orders from above that it was impossible to escape. Such crimes as were committed, above all on the Eastern Front, were the work of ideological fanatics in the SS. These pleas were not accepted by the court, which convicted eleven of the defendants and sentenced them to often lengthy terms of imprisonment. But as the Cold War got under way, the Americans came under huge pressure from West German institutions, including the churches, politicians and numerous ordinary citizens, to rethink their judgements, and they released the other offenders. The West German establishment accepted the generals' plea that the armed forces, even under Hitler, had stayed well clear of politics, in the tradition of 'unpolitical professionalism' founded by Hans von Seeckt, the commander-in chief from 1920 to 1926.[38] In fact, of course, the army was far from unpolitical during the Weimar Republic: its allegiance remained above all to conservative nationalism, looking back to the Bismarckian empire and forward to a future in which, officers hoped, Germany would reverse the Treaty of Versailles and complete the work it had begun in 1914.[39]

The myth of the non-political army, used during and after the war to present an image of the 'clean' armed forces, convinced many historians and commentators in Britain, France and Germany. Little was known about the Eastern Front, and such testimony as there was evoked mistrust in the West because it came from the Communist authorities.[40] The overall impression created in the 1950s was reinforced by the memoirs of a range of surviving generals, which focused above all on military matters and neglected moral and ideological issues almost entirely. Typical here was Field Marshal Erich von Manstein, whose best-selling memoir, *Verlorene Siege* (*Lost Victories*), first published in Frankfurt in 1955, was perhaps the most influential propagator of this narrative.[41] Joachim Fest's condemnation of the generals for their moral weakness derived from his acceptance of the 'clean Wehrmacht' narrative of the 1950s. He thought, like most other West German commentators, that the generals adhered to a system of values that differed substantially from those of the Nazis: Prussian values of 'decency, morality, order, Christianity, all values which went together with a conservative idea of the state'. Few historians dissented from this view.

However, beginning in the 1990s, as new source material was made available following the collapse of Communism and the opening up of Eastern European archives, a new generation of historians began to uncover the involvement of the regular army and its soldiers in atrocities on the Eastern Front. A travelling exhibition on 'crimes of the *Wehrmacht*' presented visual evidence documenting the armed forces' participation in the extermination of the Jews, the mass murder of Soviet prisoners of war, and the use of terror against civilians in occupied territories. Further research by a wide range of historians has confirmed and extended its basic findings. Not only did the regular German armed forces repeatedly and deliberately ignore and violate the normal laws and customs of war on the Eastern Front, first in Poland and then, to a far greater extent, in the Soviet Union, they also did so in France and Italy, Greece and the Balkans, above all when it came to the treatment of 'partisans' and members of the armed resistance.[42]

Over the decades, the German Army's conception of warfare had come to incorporate the idea of 'total war', war waged with the aim of completely destroying not only the armed forces of the enemy but also, as General Erich Ludendorff outlined in his writings on the subject, completely annihilating the enemy nation as well. In pursuit of this aim, the traditional distinction between combatants and civilians had been obliterated.⁴³ The mechanization of warfare and the frustrations of the Western Front in the vast conflict of World War I only strengthened this doctrine.⁴⁴ Moral reservations were thrown out of the window. German soldiers had a long record of shooting civilians in occupied countries, either individuals or groups, whom they suspected of offering armed resistance, labelling them 'irregulars' (*Freischärler, Francs-tireurs*) or 'partisans'. Massacres and atrocities had taken place as far back as the war of 1870–71 in occupied France, and on a greater scale in Belgium and northern France in 1914.⁴⁵ In any case, Hitler's military successes in 1939–41 led many senior officers to abandon their independence of judgement even in the face of Hitler's genocidal drive. Interviewed by the prison psychiatrist Leon Goldensohn at Nuremberg after the war, Hermann Göring insisted that Hitler was a military genius. Now that Germany had been defeated, he said, 'the army generals are all suddenly smarter than Hitler. But when he was running things they listened to what he said and were glad of his advice.'⁴⁶ This was only too true.⁴⁷

Leeb shared this belief in the innocence of the armed forces in full. In 1945, this view was not accepted by the Allies. Leeb was arrested by American troops on 2 May 1945 at his Bavarian home, and taken through a series of prisoner-of-war camps, until he was brought to trial at Nuremberg on 18 September 1947. He did not complain about his treatment, but he insisted he had nothing to fear. Boredom was his main problem in prison; he worked in the prison garden, played patience, and even read through a railway signal instruction book he found in a cupboard to pass the time. With other high-ranking prisoners he went over the events of the war in discussions filled with recriminations, especially against the leading Nazis. His trial, along with that of other leading generals, began on 5 February 1948. He had continued to write his diary, and used it to complain that the language employed in the prosecution's opening statement 'put the way the National Socialists expressed themselves in the shadow'. As the trial proceeded, he described it as 'ever more grotesque'.⁴⁸

Leeb's defending counsel insisted that his client had not known of Nazi war crimes or transmitted criminal orders. He was an honourable soldier. The evidence had been misinterpreted: for example, Leeb's protest against the shooting of Jews was only taken as evidence that he was aware of it. Chosen by his co-defendants to present a closing statement on their behalf, Leeb presented them as victims. They had never abandoned the military virtues of loyalty, obedience, duty, unselfishness and gallantry. 'No soldier in all the world has ever yet had to fight under such a load and tragedy ... We are soldiers who have upheld their soldierly honour even in this Second World War amidst turmoil and dictatorial violence.' The demands Hitler had made of him and his fellow officers were contrary to 'their principles and natures' and their 'humane and soldierly feelings'. For the court, however, this only made their crimes worse, since despite their awareness that what Hitler was ordering them to do was wrong, they did it anyway. Or, as the court put it, 'the inescapable fact remains that in part at least, if not the whole, they permitted their consciences and opinions to become subordinate to Hitler's will and it was this which has placed such great and ineradicable shame upon the German arms'.[49] But the court dealt with Leeb leniently, finding him guilty of war crimes, crimes against humanity, and crimes against civilians, but sentencing him to no more than the three years of imprisonment he had already served:

> He was not a friend or follower of the Nazi Party. He was a soldier and engaged in a stupendous campaign with responsibility for hundreds of thousands of soldiers, and a large indigenous population spread over a vast area. It is not without significance that no criminal order has been introduced which bears his signature or the stamp of his approval.[50]

Immediately released, he retired to the Bavarian estate given him by Hitler, and lived quietly for the remainder of his life. He died peacefully on 29 April 1956, aged seventy-nine.[51]

Wilhelm Ritter von Leeb was not a particularly outstanding general, nor a particularly idiosyncratic personality. It was precisely his lack of pronounced personality traits that made him interesting. If any one individual discussed in this book could be called 'typical', it was surely Leeb, the quintessentially typical army officer. He was an almost perfect exemplar of what historians have pointed to as long-established soldierly tradition in Germany. The dominant military culture in Germany, Nuremberg prosecutor Telford Taylor concluded, was 'ripe for cooperation' with Hitler 'before the Nazis ever became a factor' in politics.[52]

17
The Professional: Karl Brandt

In the early afternoon of 15 August 1933, Hitler and several others were in a motorcade on their way to his Bavarian mountain retreat, the Berghof, after lunching at a hotel in nearby Berchtesgaden. At one point, Hitler's personal adjutant Wilhelm Brückner, in the car behind him, lost control of the steering wheel and crashed his vehicle badly, breaking a leg, fracturing his skull, and seriously damaging an eye. Luckily for him, a skilled professional surgeon who had dealt with many serious injuries while working in the mining town of Bochum was in the following car. The young doctor got out of his car and went to the rescue, administering emergency first aid to Brückner and accompanying him to the nearest hospital, where he operated on his skull, surgically removed the injured eye and mended his leg. He treated his other, less serious, injuries and stayed with him for the following six weeks until his condition began to improve. The young surgeon's name was Karl Brandt, and this chance occurrence marked a turning point in his career, bringing him within a few short years to perhaps the most influential position in the medical world of Nazi Germany. It also opened the way for Brandt to become one of the Third Reich's most notorious mass murderers.[1]

Brandt's career was an example of the sometimes haphazard process by which people were appointed to high office in the Third Reich, often irrespective of their qualifications for the job or ability to do it. But his presence in that fateful motorcade was not entirely a matter of chance. He was already a member of the Nazi Party by this time, and shared many of Hitler's views on medicine and its role in society. Born on 8 January 1904 in the Alsatian town of Mülhausen to prosperous Protestant parents, Karl Brandt seems to have had a calm and unremarkable childhood. Its tranquillity was only broken by the outbreak of World

War I in 1914 and then by the annexation of Alsace by France in 1918. Brandt's father had been taken prisoner by the French early on in the war. He did not return from captivity until 1921, and then it was to Saxony, where he found employment as a police official. Brandt and his parents surely felt a strong resentment towards the French, whom they blamed for driving them out of their home, but just as important was the influence of his mother's family, which included several doctors, most notably Brandt's uncle. While not outstandingly gifted, Brandt was hard-working and ambitious, and successfully completed his studies in medicine at a variety of German universities (Jena, Freiburg, Berlin) without difficulty. Here he must surely have been influenced by the rabidly right-wing political atmosphere among the students, and also by the hegemony of eugenicists among the professors. In Freiburg he came into close contact with Alfred Hoche, a psychiatrist who also originated in Alsace. Together with the lawyer Karl Binding, Hoche published a short tract with the title *The Legalization of the Annihilation of Life Unworthy of Life* (1920). Hoche was clearly influenced by the mass slaughter of the 'best' of Germany's youth on the battlefield during the war (his own son was killed in 1915) and advocated a eugenic rebalancing of German society. He argued for the involuntary 'euthanasia' of individuals whose life was judged to be 'ballast' for society – those who were incurably ill, or lived in a vegetative state or long-term coma, or were so mentally 'inferior' that their life had no purpose, people who could make no contribution to society and were incapable of forming an opinion as to whether they should live or die.[2]

Hoche's views were not widely shared in the German medical profession. But they clearly had an impact on the young Karl Brandt, who was confronted in his work as a surgeon in the Ruhr during the 1920s with patients in such agony from spinal injuries, crushed limbs, broken skulls and other conditions caused by mining accidents, that they pleaded with him to be put out of what he felt was their unbearable misery. Beyond this individual, personal experience, however, he had also become convinced by the eugenicist conception of German society – or the German race – as a single collective organism whose interests had to take priority over those of the individual human being. The damage done to it in World War I was such that radical surgical intervention was needed to make it good. Ever since the trauma of losing his home and, even if only temporarily, his father at a formative period in his life, coupled with the more general shock of Germany's unexpected and humiliating defeat in the war, Brandt had seemingly been in search of a leadership figure who could provide him with redemption and purpose. After a brief period of enthusiasm for the charismatic doctor Albert Schweitzer (also from Alsace), during which Brandt tried unsuccessfully to join Schweitzer's renowned clinic in French Equatorial Africa (now Gabon), he became transfixed instead by the person of Adolf Hitler.

Brandt was introduced to Hitler by his fiancée Anni Rehborn, a champion, multiple record-holding swimmer whose beauty and fame had already attracted the attention of the Nazi leader and his entourage in the mid-1920s. Anni's brother and sister also participated in the 1928 Olympic Games in Amsterdam as divers. The family fulfilled Nazi ideals of physical beauty and 'Aryan' appearance. Moreover, they were strongly nationalist and right-wing: Julius Rehborn, Anni's father, who ran the Bochum municipal swimming pool, became an active Nazi in 1932, and was joined by Anni. Brandt followed her into the Party early the following year.[3] Hitler and his immediate circle were much taken by the young couple and flattered by the social presence of a famous champion swimmer. For their part, Brandt and his fiancée were overwhelmed by their attention, especially after Hitler was appointed Reich Chancellor on 30 January 1933. The ambition of the young couple to join his circle was signalled by their decision to spend their summer holidays at Berchtesgaden in 1933 while Hitler was staying at the Berghof. It was rewarded with an invitation to lunch at a hotel in the Alpine town on 15 August; hence the couple's presence in the fateful motorcade that afternoon. In the following months, Brandt transferred his position as a surgeon specializing in head and spinal injuries to Berlin, was promoted, and in 1934 married Anni Rehborn in a ceremony attended by both Hitler and Göring. More was to come, for after the car crash in 1933, Hitler and his entourage decided it would be prudent for the dictator to be accompanied by a doctor when he travelled; it was almost inevitable that Brandt should be chosen for this role. His new function as Hitler's personal physician brought him into the Nazi leader's inner circle, and soon Brandt was spending large amounts of time on the Berghof, where he and his wife became close friends of Albert Speer, whose rise to prominence in Hitler's inner circle bore marked similarities with his own.[4]

Brandt's new position did not bring him any real political influence, except occasionally, when issues arose with respect to individual doctors or medical matters. He was not involved in the drafting of the Law for the Prevention of Hereditarily Diseased Offspring (1933), which set in motion the compulsory sterilization of nearly 400,000 German men and women over the following years for supposedly inherited conditions such as chronic alcoholism, 'feeble-mindedness', and various vaguely defined forms of social deviance. But there can be no doubt that he approved of its provisions. Similarly, Brandt not only welcomed the expulsion of Jewish doctors from the profession but also benefited from it in his own career.[5] He began to take on more responsibilities, propelled towards them by Hitler. Brandt was charged with the reorganization of surgical facilities in Berlin, and proposed a massive new building for them, using openly antisemitic language to condemn the existing arrangement as the product of Jewish influence under the Weimar Republic. Brandt accompanied Hitler on his triumphal entry into Austria following the *Anschluss* in March 1938, and in early November he was sent to Paris by the Nazi dictator to take over the treatment of Ernst vom Rath, a junior official at the German Embassy who had been shot by a young Pole in protest against the deportation of his parents from Germany; Brandt's laconic report of the official's death provided the excuse for Hitler and Goebbels to launch the nationwide pogrom known popularly as the *Reichskristallnacht* on 9–10 November 1938.[6]

Brandt must have been disappointed when, on 25 March 1939, Gerhard Wagner, a long-time Nazi who had founded the Nazi Doctors' League and been appointed 'Reich Doctors' Leader' after the seizure of power in 1933, died of cancer and Hitler did not name him as his successor, as might have been expected: the job of heading up the medical profession went instead to a man who, like Wagner, was a long-term Nazi, active since the early 1920s: the half-Swiss plastic surgeon Leonardo Conti, head of the Reich Doctors' Chamber and leader of the Nazi Doctors' League. Conti now added the title of Reich Health Leader to his portfolio, along with, a little later, State Secretary for Health in the Interior Ministry. And it was Conti to whom Hitler entrusted the realization of a new programme to exterminate mentally ill or severely handicapped children and then adults when the war broke out, to compensate, as they thought, for the loss of some of the nation's best and bravest young men that would inevitably follow. The idea went back some years, to the second half of the 1930s, when Hitler had begun to discuss it with Wagner. It was already clear to the Nazi dictator that the European war he wanted would soon begin, when in the winter of 1938–9 Hitler's private office received a request from the father of a severely mentally and physically handicapped infant in Leipzig to allow doctors to kill him. Hitler sent Brandt to ensure the request was granted, and Brandt reported at the end of July that the local doctors had ended the infant's life; he may indeed have administered the fatal injection himself, and certainly he arranged for the death certificate to be falsified. When the programme was extended to adults a few months later, it was Brandt who, together with Conti, injected the first victim with poison. But the dictator became impatient with the bureaucratic delays that the formal programme involved, particularly in the Ministry of Justice, and in October signed a written order authorizing Brandt and Philipp Bouhler, a long-time Nazi and veteran of the 1923 beer-hall *putsch* who was now head of Hitler's personal office, to begin the programme. The order was backdated to the outbreak of war on 1 September, signalling Hitler's conception of the war as one of racial renewal and extermination. It was an informal, confidential order, to be produced in case the doctors being asked to carry out the murders objected. The programme was retrospectively dubbed *Aktion T-4*, after the address of the Chancellery department from which it was run.[7]

The killings had already begun in mental institutions in occupied Poland, often with shootings of the inmates, both adults and children. In Germany itself, children were now taken from their homes to mental institutions and killed by starvation and neglect or fatal injections, or a mixture of all three. The lists included children suffering from Down's Syndrome, hydrocephaly, cerebral palsy and other afflictions, but also from more vaguely defined conditions such as 'mental deficiency'. Their ages ranged from infancy to the early teens. A conference of top officials from Hitler's office and leading medical officials, including Brandt, reached the conclusion that this was all taking too long. Gassing with carbon monoxide was the quickest way of killing the victims and reaching the entirely arbitrary target of 70,000 demanded by Hitler. Brandt himself took part in the first experiments, carried out in December 1939 in the Brandenburg penitentiary, where he administered supposedly lethal injections to a group of fifteen to twenty naked prisoners; when the injections failed to have an immediate effect, the victims were herded into a purpose-built, sealed gas chamber, and killed with carbon monoxide as Brandt and the others looked on through a peephole. Clearly, to the assembled functionaries the victims were not human at all, but mere insects or vermin. Soon *Aktion T-4* was in full swing, with thousands of hastily carried-out assessments of both adults and children being forwarded via Bouhler's office to a growing number of killing centres, located at mental hospitals well away from centres of population. If staff raised any objections, they were shown a copy of Hitler's written order. What was striking about Brandt's behaviour when observing the murders was his absolute lack of compassion. The killings were neither neat nor painless. The terror and suffering of the victims were obvious to all who witnessed them.[8]

Before long, Hitler was demanding the freeing-up of institutional capacity in hospitals to provide beds for wounded soldiers. Propaganda in posters, textbooks and even cinemas aimed to convince people that the mentally ill and handicapped were a financial burden on the German people that was holding back the war effort. The T-4 programme became more and more widely known, while the victims' families became suspicious of the lies they were fed by hospital administrators purporting to account for the sudden death of their loved ones. The victims knew what was going to happen to them when the grey buses arrived to take them away for killing, and were reported to have filled the air with screaming and shouting as they vainly tried to resist their fate. Eventually, in the summer of 1941, the Catholic Bishop of Münster, Clemens von Galen, backed by the Protestant pastor and social-welfare practitioner Friedrich von Bodelschwingh, articulated their fears and objections in an open condemnation of the killings. Who would be next in the campaign to rid the country of people who were nothing more than a burden on the economy, asked von Galen – the elderly? The war wounded? Hitler and Goebbels were furious, but did not dare move against them. T-4 was halted, and the men in charge of the gassing operations were transferred to the Eastern Front, to put their expertise into operation in the mass murder of European Jews. Meanwhile, after Hitler's target of 70,000 had been reached, the killings continued more surreptitiously, through starvation or lethal injection, eventually reaching a total approaching 200,000.[9]

In the meantime, Brandt continued to accumulate positions of power and influence, aiming, as he confessed after the war, to dislodge Conti from any position of importance in science-based medical practice. Already an officer in the SS, Brandt was promoted to the rank of *Standartenführer* (roughly, colonel) and given the title of *Generalkommissar*. In July 1942 Hitler designated him Plenipotentiary for the Health and Sanitation System. This put him in charge of relocating patients from hospitals damaged or destroyed in Allied bombing raids, and freeing up beds for soldiers wounded at the front. He consigned mental patients – for example, people suffering mental trauma or severe depression resulting from the destruction of their homes or the death of their families – to the killing centres that had been carrying out *Aktion T-4*.[10] Brandt's rejection of internationally accepted medical ethics now extended to his approval of live medical experiments on concentration-camp inmates, who were, he said quite explicitly, expendable if it helped the war effort and the development of therapies for diseases that were common in the army (for example, hepatitis, which was said to have affected between five and six million soldiers), or hypothermia, or malnutrition, or (common among civilians affected by Allied incendiary-bombing raids) serious burns. In time of war, he declared, the individual no longer counted: what mattered was the collectivity of Germans and their interests.[11] Survivors of the experiments reported after the war how the doctors who had carried them out refused to look them in the eye or call them by their name or offer any kind of reassurance, however mendacious, as they were handling them, reducing them to mere objects without human qualities. For their part, the doctors repeatedly cast doubt on the victims' post-war testimony, writing them off as 'inferior' beings incapable of rational thought or reliable memory.[12]

Karl Brandt's position in Nazi Germany was entirely dependent on the personal backing of Hitler and derived above all from his role as the Führer's personal physician. As time went on, however, his position began to be threatened by a serious rival, Dr Theo Morell, a dermatologist who had established himself as a society doctor through his treatment of prominent individuals for sexually transmitted diseases, and through his discretion and his ingratiating bedside manner. Morell was no quack, despite allegations to the contrary that have continued to the present day, and when he was introduced to Hitler by one of his patients, the Nazi leader's personal photographer, Heinrich Hoffmann, Morell and Hitler hit it off. Soon Morell was usurping Brandt's position, treating Hitler for a variety of ailments and supplying him with drugs including stimulants and aphrodisiacs (usually administered before Hitler spent a night with Eva Braun).[13] Brandt had already begun to plan an even greater expansion of his power by proposing the creation of a Reich Ministry of Health, which he himself would of course lead, as a way of engineering his final triumph over his rival Leonardo Conti, but increasingly, Conti and his fellow 'Old Fighters' Goebbels and Bormann had begun to resent his ambition and put obstacles in his way. All this meant, however, was that they would not make any effort to help Brandt when he got into difficulties with Morell. As Hitler's health deteriorated, especially in the aftermath of the July 1944 bomb plot, the rivalry between the two men reached crisis point. Brandt moved to have Morell dismissed as a quack who was poisoning the Nazi leader with strychnine in the guise of an 'anti-gas' therapy. But the move completely backfired. When Morell complained about Brandt's intrigues to Hitler, the dictator was furious. On 8 October 1944 he relieved Brandt of his duties as his personal physician, ordering him to concentrate on his administrative duties.[14]

Worse was to come. Now that he had lost Hitler's personal support, and with it direct access to the Nazi leader, Brandt was exposed to his enemies, above all Bormann and Goebbels, who began to circle around him like vultures. In the final months of the war, with the Red Army entering Germany from the east, the Western Allies invading from the west, the cities bombed out and the rail and road communications systems broken, the health system collapsed, and medical supplies dried up. When Brandt reported this to Hitler in a personal visit to his bunker in Berlin on 2 April 1945, Bormann, Goebbels and Morell accused him of defeatism. A fortnight later, Hitler ordered his arrest. The Gestapo, who had placed Brandt under surveillance some time before, had discovered that he had sent his family away to a place of safety in the Thuringian countryside that had now been taken over by the Americans. After a lengthy series of interrogations by the Gestapo chief Heinrich Müller, Brandt was taken to Goebbels's private house, where a kangaroo court of senior Nazis, including 'Reich Youth Leader' Arthur Axmann and the director of the SS Head Office Gottlob Berger, was assembled to pass judgement. Brandt was confronted with two reports he had submitted to Hitler in his defence, in the margins of which the Nazi leader had scribbled words like 'Lie, fraud, lying'. The court recommended the death penalty, which Hitler personally endorsed by signing the report.

Goebbels even had Brandt's execution announced on the radio. But by now the Reich was in a state of complete collapse. Leading Nazis were committing suicide in their hundreds rather than fall into the hands of the Allies. Himmler and Speer, thinking now about how they could save themselves, ordered a stop to Brandt's planned execution, in the belief his (in practice non-existent) contacts with the Americans might be able to help them after the defeat. So he survived – for the time being.[15]

After the war was over, Brandt surrendered to the Allied occupation forces, believing he had nothing to fear from them. But following the trial of the surviving Nazi leaders at the International Military Tribunal, the Americans decided to mount a series of further war-crimes trials in their own Zone of Occupation, as they were entitled to under Control Council Law No. 10, passed on 20 December 1945. In the first of these, held from 9 December 1946 to 20 August 1947, leading Nazi physicians were placed in the dock. The chief defendant was Karl Brandt. He was found guilty of crimes against humanity, including conducting medical experiments on live human subjects without their consent, carrying out non-consensual abortions, overseeing the mass murder by poison gas and lethal injection of prisoners of war and inmates of mental hospitals, injecting concentration-camp prisoners with malaria, jaundice and typhus bacilli, freezing prisoners to death, and engaging in painful and often fatal procedures that amounted in effect to torture and murder. He and six other doctors who had been involved in similar acts were sentenced to death, while a substantial number of other defendants were condemned to lengthy terms of imprisonment.[16]

Brandt kept a diary during his Nuremberg imprisonment, intending it to be read, above all by his wife and family, as a justification of the actions for which the prosecution demanded the death penalty. His conscience was clear, he declared. He knew nothing about the Holocaust, the mass murder of six million European Jews. The 'euthanasia' programme he had run was something entirely different, a scientifically based policy aimed solely at the improvement of the German race and the betterment of humanity. It aimed to help people by bringing an end to their suffering. The 'euthanasia' of scores of thousands of mentally ill and handicapped people was not murder; it was a form of medical treatment, aimed not at the individual but at the collective organism of the German people. People who had known Brandt under the Nazi regime testified at his trial to his professionalism, his integrity, and what they saw as his basic decency. Highly educated and qualified, he was far removed from the rough and brutal type of the 'old fighter', or the cold ideological fanaticism of the committed Nazi. He was an 'idealist'. Tall, handsome, elegant, courteous and often charming, he appeared to many of those who knew him as the epitome of the civilized professional. How could he be guilty of such crimes?[17] Yet he was perfectly aware of the fact that the killings he ordered were neither clean nor clinical, and caused enormous suffering to his victims and their families. And while Hitler may have disavowed him at the end of the Third Reich, Brandt himself never disowned Hitler or reflected critically on the nature of his regime.[18]

Brandt's crimes were not the product of some individual pathology on his part. Quite the contrary: they reflected attitudes and beliefs that were common in the overwhelming majority of the medical profession in Germany. Bolstered by the achievements of German medicine in the nineteenth and early twentieth centuries, when a whole variety of discoveries of the causes of diseases ranging from cholera to tuberculosis, above all by Robert Koch and his pupils, had transformed medical knowledge, many members of the German medical profession had come to believe they were gods, no longer subject to the dictates of the Hippocratic Oath. As students, many of them, like Brandt, were sucked into the far-right nationalism of the post-First World War university framework, putting what they regarded as the regeneration of the German nation above anything else. When the Nazis came to power, 'racial hygiene' was made a central part of medical education, training and practice in the Third Reich. Other bogus subjects were promoted as well, such as 'alternative' herbal medicine, propagated by Reich Health Leader Gerhard Wagner. One in five university teachers and researchers was dismissed or forced to resign during the Third Reich, mainly because they were Jewish, and a host of positions became available as a result, augmented by the creation of new professorships and institutes for 'racial hygiene' and related pseudo-subjects.[19] Medicine was now full of so many opportunities and such easy career paths that some older professors began to complain about the quality of their students and colleagues. And indeed, by 1939 half of all German university students were reading medicine, and 59 per cent of the Rectors of German universities were professors of medicine.[20]

Brandt's denialism was shared by the overwhelming majority of the other doctors who had survived the end of World War II. Some, like

Conti, committed suicide rather than face trial, suggesting at least some degree of realization that what they had been doing was wrong, or at least regarded as such by the overwhelming majority of the world's doctors. Most of the other doctors returned to their previous medical practice. A number of them continued to defend the involuntary 'euthanasia' programme well after the war. One, Werner Catel, who had been a major figure in setting up the child-murder operation, was appointed director of the children's clinic at Kiel University and granted immunity from prosecution because, it was concluded, he had been convinced that what he had done was legal.[21] 'Racial hygiene' and 'eugenics' were rebranded as 'genetics', and leading theorists and practitioners were reinstated in suitably redesignated university chairs. Among them was Otmar Baron von Verschuer, Director of the Kaiser Wilhelm Institute for Anthropology, Human Heredity and Eugenics, the central research body for these subjects under the Third Reich. He was supplied with material for his research on twins taken by his star PhD student, Joseph Mengele, from prisoners in Auschwitz, where Mengele carried out deadly experiments on inmates and selected candidates for the gas chambers on their arrival. In 1951 Verschuer was appointed to a chair in genetics at the University of Münster, where he stayed until his retirement in 1965. The German Doctors' Association (*Bundesärztekammer*) continued until the 1990s to be dominated by former Nazi physicians, some of whom had been involved in the forced 'euthanasia' programme. The Association now claimed that those involved in the murder of the mentally ill and handicapped, along with those who had carried out human experiments on camp inmates, had only constituted a tiny, untypical minority of the profession, a few hundred at most. When the psychologist Alexander Mitscherlich, an anti-Nazi resister appointed as an observer at the doctors' trial, published with Fred Mielke a summary of the evidence in 1947, under the title *Medizin ohne Menschlichkeit* (*Medicine without Humanity*), the entire edition of 10,000 copies, originally intended for distribution to German doctors, was secretly purchased by the German Doctors' Association and pulped. It took until 1960 for the evidence to reappear, as part of a series on Nazism by a West German publishing house, and until the 1980s for serious historical research to be undertaken on the crimes of Nazi medicine. By this time, compensating the surviving victims of Nazi medical experimentation and other crimes had become an almost impossible task.[22]

Unlike most of the doctors who had committed such terrible crimes during the Third Reich, Karl Brandt did not escape retribution. At 10.10 in the morning on 2 June 1948 a military hangman and his two assistants led Brandt across the courtyard of Landsberg Prison in Bavaria, and took him up thirteen steps to a wooden platform, where a black-painted gallows had been erected. It was raining. Standing in the courtyard were a few prison officers and journalists, who acted as witnesses. As the assistants made their preparations, Brandt delivered an impassioned denunciation of the proceedings. He was the victim of an injustice, he declared, an act of political revenge. He had done nothing wrong. The officiating power, the United States of America, had no right to condemn him, least of all after having dropped atom bombs on Hiroshima and Nagasaki. 'Justice has never existed here! Neither in general nor individually. Power is dictating. And this power wants sacrifices. We are such sacrifices. I am such a sacrifice.' As he ranted on, the executioner, who had already warned him to keep his remarks brief, lost patience and, in the middle of a sentence, put a black hood over his head, made it fast, placed a noose around his neck, tightened it, and then, stepping back, pulled hard on a lever. The trapdoor on which Brandt was standing opened, and he fell through it to his death.

Brandt's widow, Anni, lived on until 1981, believing to the end that her husband had been unjustly executed and dedicating herself above all to looking after their son, born in 1935 and named, in honour of her husband and his idol, Karl-Adolf.

18
The Killers: Paul Zapp And Egon Zill

Paul Zapp was born in 1904 in the Hessian town of Hersfeld, the son of a manufacturer, and grew up in another Hessian town, Kassel. His background was solidly middle-class, and his childhood and adolescence were marked by absorption into a typically middle-class milieu, conservative, Protestant and patriotic. Home life featured the typical bourgeois pursuits including music and literature and a veneration for German culture. Zapp was too young to fight in the First World War, but like other young men of his generation he conceived a strong admiration for the young men of the 'front-fighter generation' and a determination to fight for his ideals with coolness, toughness and the unemotional pursuit of what he thought of as Germany's interests. But his career also took an unusual form, impelled by a strong ideological commitment to some of the ideals from which Nazism emerged. After passing his school-leaving examinations, Zapp enrolled in a university, but abandoned his studies after a year. In the economically crisis-ridden Weimar years, Zapp, evidently aware of the dire job prospects of university graduates, and desperately anxious to secure an income for himself rather than live the hand-to-mouth life of a student, trained as an apprentice bookkeeper and administrator at the Deutsche Bank. After completing his training, he found employment in a number of different companies. By 1931 he had risen to the modest position of a deputy divisional executive at the Borsig engineering works in Berlin. But the Great Depression caused the company to make him redundant, and he joined the swelling ranks of the middle-class unemployed. With little or no chance of finding employment elsewhere, as the Depression deepened still further, he enrolled in Berlin University and began to study History and Philosophy. His prospects seemed as doubtful as ever.[1]

During his studies, Zapp came into contact with the theologian Jakob Wilhelm Hauer, who had served as a missionary in India and studied Sanskrit at Oxford before being appointed to a Professorship in Tübingen. Impressed by Zapp's secretarial and administrative skills, rare enough in a university but almost unheard of in a student, Hauer gave him a job as his personal secretary. In this capacity, Zapp became familiar with his employer's increasingly esoteric religious views, which included a belief in the unity of all faiths, expressed in his 'German Faith Movement' (*Deutsche Glaubensbewegung*), a synthesis of Hinduism and pseudo-Germanic paganism. Recognizing his abilities, Hauer appointed Zapp managing director and chief administrator of the organization. From his conservative, middle-class background, from his years following from the sidelines the progress of the First World War and the shattering, unexpected defeat of Germany with all its consequences for the standing of the nation in the world, and from his life in the extreme right-wing milieu of the university student body in Berlin, Zapp had absorbed many elements of radical nationalism. Now he was subjected to the esoteric ideology which was proving so influential on leading Nazis such as Heinrich Himmler; Zapp's ideological commitments were advertised in a series of books he published in the 1930s, advocating a Germanized Christmas and the replacement of Christian Confirmation with a pseudo-Germanic ritual.[2]

While Hauer's relationship with Nazism remained relatively distant, Zapp imbibed many of its central ideas and established contacts with a variety of its activists. He joined the SS in 1934, helped by his acquaintance with one of its leading officers, Werner Best. This was an obvious career move, since the German Faith Movement was by now running into trouble with Hitler, who rejected its esoteric religious ideas, and Zapp's prospects now seemed to be in doubt unless he moved away from Hauer's tutelage. So in 1936 he resigned from the movement, and found a new job working in an administrative capacity for Reinhard Heydrich's SS Security Service (SD) as an ideological instructor at the organization's training school in Bernau, a suburb of Berlin. He also, finally, became a member of the Nazi Party. Zapp's notes for his talks in these training sessions were discovered in the archive of the Soviet secret police after the fall of Communism, and were made available to historians in the 1990s. In 1939, when the war began, Zapp was transferred to occupied Poland and entrusted with training Security

Service personnel in ideological matters, winning the reputation of an expert on 'the Jewish Question', or in other words the idea of the Jewish 'world-enemy' that was supposed to lend legitimacy to the mass murders now being carried out behind the Eastern Front. All of this may have seemed academic, but the power of ideology in the SS and its ability to prompt violent, murderous action was soon to be illustrated in the most dramatic possible way.[3]

Like other men in positions of administrative and ideological responsibility in the SD, Zapp experienced no difficulty in making a seamless transition to mass murder. In 1941, put in command of a 100-strong 'special unit' (*Sonderkommando*) under Task Force D, following the German armies into south-eastern Europe in the wake of Operation Barbarossa, he took his men through eastern Romania and southern Ukraine, passing through Kherson and on to Simferopol, into the Crimea. Everywhere he went, Zapp would find a pretext for ordering the local Jewish population to present themselves, then he took them to pre-prepared pits and ordered his men to shoot them. When each row of designated victims approached the pits, they would catch sight of the blood-soaked corpses already lying there, and distressing, sometimes violent scenes would ensue. Zapp had to cajole or threaten the more reluctant of his men into carrying out the order to shoot, especially when the victims were children. On 17 July 1941 Zapp and his men shot sixty-eight 'Communist Jews' in Kishinev, then, shortly after, 551 more, including women. In mid-September 1941 his unit shot dead all 5,000 inhabitants of the Jewish community in Mikolaiv (Nikolajew), including children. More mass murders followed, including 12,000 people in Simferopol. These were anything but 'industrial' or impersonal, technical executions. As the historian Konrad Kwiet noted:

> The hours-long mass shootings, often lasting several days, made high demands of the marksmen. The burden on them was always particularly heavy when women and children were shot, when bullets tore through the bodies of the victims and bits of brain and bones mixed with blood spurted back out onto their faces, hands or uniforms, or when the ditches filled up with blood and victims who were still alive were finished off at close quarters with a *coup de grâce*.[4]

Zapp sympathized with the 'serious emotional burden' these executions placed, not however on the victims, but on his troops; he treated them to extra rations, cigarettes and schnapps, and held evening parties for them, lubricated with plentiful amounts of alcohol. By the end of the year Zapp had been supplied with a gas van to speed up the killing process. Then, following a period of leave, he went back to a desk job, ending as Inspector of the Security Police in Dresden, where he survived the Allied bombing raid of 13–14 February 1945.[5]

Paul Zapp went underground with a false name ('Friedrich Böhm') and false papers at the end of the war, living in the Hessian town of Bebra. He was finally tracked down in 1967 and put on trial in 1970. His defence was the common one of Nazi mass murderers, that he had only been following orders, that he would himself have been shot had he disobeyed them, that he tried to protect the Jews, though without success, and that he had done his best to ease their passing. These lies were rejected by the court and again on appeal, and he was sentenced to life imprisonment. Released on good behaviour in 1986, he died peacefully in Bad Arolsen in 1999. Here was somebody who served Nazism not least because it offered a way out of career problems, rescuing him from a downward spiral in his life; but without prior ideological and political commitment he would doubtless not have made the choices he did; and once committed to the regime's antisemitic ideology, internalizing its depiction of Jews as an existential threat, he had no difficulty in executing its decrees in the most murderous and brutal possible way.[6]

Further down the chain of command within the SS were the men who, day in, day out, acted as guards and overseers in the concentration-camp system, which was established at the very beginning of the Third Reich within Germany itself to incarcerate and ultimately to exterminate opponents of the regime, above all Communists and Social Democrats. The men who staffed the camps were not highly educated like Zapp. But like him, many of them were led to Nazism by downward social mobility. One typical member of the camp-guard cohort has been studied by the historian Karin Orth, a specialist on the history of the camps: the otherwise unremarkable and unimportant Egon Zill, a qualified baker born in the town of Plauen, in north-west Saxony, in 1906. Like many of his generation, Zill experienced hardship during the hyperinflation of 1922–23, but while he was unable to pursue his trade as a baker, he managed to find steady employment as a security guard in a curtain factory and retained it throughout the Great Depression of the early 1930s. Plauen was an early hotbed of Nazism, with a Party branch founded in 1923. Given his age, and his background, joining the Nazi Party was an obvious step for Zill to take.[7]

He was already socialized into the political milieu of right-wing radicalism, most probably through his father, a brewery worker and member of the Protestant lower middle class. In addition, Zill was sufficiently influenced by his girlfriend (later wife) Elfriede, who had joined the Plauen branch almost as soon as it was formed, to sign up to the Nazi Party and the Brownshirts at the age of seventeen, becoming a committed activist. He was injured in a meeting-hall brawl in 1930, and was involved in numerous acts of violence. He joined the SS, becoming the leader of its local 'storm', and in 1934 took up a position as a guard in a series of early concentration camps, undergoing training in Dachau and Buchenwald as a member of their central administration. In 1939 he was promoted to a senior position as *Erster Schutzhaftlagerführer* in Dachau. During his training he was taught to regard the inmates as dangerous enemies of the state, towards whom he was not to show any weakness. Any hint of 'softness' in his treatment of the prisoners would incur the mockery of the other SS men in the camp. New recruits were ordered to beat and kick the inmates, especially if they were Jews or homosexuals. Post-war testimony from surviving former prisoners recalled that Zill sharpened customary punishments, personally took part in beatings and torture, and ordered a prisoner to be tied to a tree while he incited dogs to savage the man's genitalia. For no particular reason, Zill told the head of a prisoner work detail to kill two of the men in his charge. The indirect, but dehumanizing, dismissive language he used in such cases ('I don't want to see these two bundles of rags again this evening') testified to the utter contempt he had for the inmates.[8]

Far from giving him a bad reputation with the SS authorities, such behaviour led to Zill's promotion to commandant of the camp at Natzweiler and then Flossenbürg during the war, but he seems to have been unequal to such senior managerial positions, and he was drafted into the Waffen-SS in 1943. He had no military training, and managed to avoid engagement in actual fighting, to the disappointment of his superiors. At the end of the war, Zill went underground, moved north, and got a job for a while as a security guard looking after the sports facilities at Hamburg University. But he was eventually tracked down and arrested in 1953. Although he denied ever having committed any crimes, the testimony of ex-prisoners in Dachau was damning, and he was sentenced to life imprisonment by a Munich court on 10 January 1955. The prison authorities reported that he not only showed no remorse for his misdeeds but also justified his Nazism and his behaviour in the camps. While he always behaved 'correctly' towards the prison officers, he was frequently involved in arguments and even physical fights with the other inmates: it was said that you could take Zill out of the camp, but you could never take the camp out of Zill. However, in 1961 his sentence was reduced on appeal, and he was released in April 1963, when he went back to his family in Dachau. He died on 23 October 1974, unchanged and unrepentant to the end.

Zill was clearly socialized into a world of violence and hatred from the very outset. But not all perpetrators at his level were like him. One of the most difficult questions to answer about the Nazi regime and its servants is how a very large number of individuals, far more than in any normal society, even in wartime, became ruthless and often sadistic killers. The victims of the Third Reich included some six million Jews, 3.3 million Soviet prisoners of war, millions of Polish and East European civilians, homosexuals, petty criminals, 'Gypsies', the mentally ill and handicapped, and many, many others. The concentration camps and extermination centres set up by the regime in Germany itself and, during the war, many other parts of Europe, above all in the East, saw the Nazis and their helpers commit numberless acts of cruelty and sadism. How can we account for this unparalleled wave of criminality, breaking every known rule and convention of warfare, politics and human decency? It is only by studying individual perpetrators that it becomes possible to reveal the mixture of motives and influences that led ordinary men to commit such acts in the service of the Nazis, and remain unrepentant even after the total collapse of the Third Reich. The mixture obviously varied from one person to another, just as individual personalities differ from one another.[9] Yet at the same time it is also possible to generalize and point to some common features.

Early post-war explanations of the conduct of perpetrators in Nazi crimes tended to focus on the pathology of individual perpetrators and regard insane or disturbed people, starting with Hitler himself and descending through the ranks to Gestapo officers and concentration-camp guards, as the ones who were principally responsible for the crimes of the regime. It was usual to demonize Nazi perpetrators, whose position in the world of National Socialism allowed them to unleash unbridled violence on their victims, putting into practice the inner sadism that in other circumstances might have remained suppressed.[10] In another view, however, the majority of members of the Gestapo or the SS had little choice but to obey the orders handed down from above – an argument used with some success by those who were brought to trial for their crimes in the early post-war years. Asked in court what would have happened had he evaded or resisted carrying out orders to kill great numbers of people, Otto Ohlendorf, the head of one of the SS killing squads, replied that 'the result would have been a court martial with a corresponding sentence'. In this argument, the totalitarianism of the Third Reich imposed an all-encompassing terror that forced obedience to criminal orders, whatever their content. At the lowest level, the perpetrators almost entirely lacked free will.[11]

By the 1960s it had become common to depict the machinery of extermination as an influence in itself, with individual Germans caught up in a vast and largely impersonal system of 'automated' or 'industrial' mass murder. Commands were issued from above, starting with Hitler and working their way down through Himmler and the SS, until they reached a mass of indoctrinated individuals, cogs in a machine who were largely deprived of individual initiative. The Gestapo and the SS were conceptually cordoned off from the rest of German society, while the mass of ordinary Germans carried on with their lives. For the perpetrators, efficiency in killing became an end in itself, irrespective of religious or moral considerations. Influences such as loyalty to one's comrades, unthinking submission to authority, and group identity and cohesion, contributed to an indifference to the suffering of others and a willingness to kill anyone designated as an enemy of the Reich. From Hannah Arendt's concept of the 'banality of evil' to Christopher Browning's depiction of a battalion of police reservists shooting 38,000 Jews behind the Eastern Front as 'ordinary men', Nazi crimes seemed to be anything but specifically German. They could have happened anywhere.[12]

Yet beginning with the trial of former SS camp guards at Frankfurt in 1963–65, at which historians from the Institute for Contemporary History in Munich provided expert testimony showing in detail how it was possible to evade orders to kill, maim or torture victims of the regime and not suffer any consequences, it became clear that the classic exculpatory claim that an offender was 'only obeying orders' had no validity. In the mid-1990s Christopher Browning's account of the massacre of Jewish men, women and children carried out by Reserve Police Battalion 101 underlined this finding with graphic testimony at a postwar trial where the commander of the unit made it clear to his men that if any of them refused to take part in the killing, they would not be punished in any way. In this sense, the men who planned, ordered and carried out the killing of Jews by shooting them into pits, letting them starve or die from disease in ghettos, or herding them into gas chambers at Auschwitz, Treblinka and elsewhere, did so out of their own free will. It followed from this that they had a good deal of room for manoeuvre, even creativity, in how they carried out their orders, if, like the overwhelming majority, they chose to follow them. At the same time, of course, they were not wholly morally and politically autonomous individuals, even if legal prosecutions of former perpetrators were based on the assumption that they were. Wider influences also impacted on their behaviour.[13]

One such influence had been suggested since the war, and became the centre of debate again in the 1990s, when the American political scientist Daniel J. Goldhagen argued that antisemitism was a central aspect of the German sense of identity which had emerged in the nineteenth century. A desire to exterminate Jews, he argued, was hard-wired into the very sense of being German. But if this was so, why did murderous antisemitism not come out into the open until the emergence of the Nazis? And how can we account for the fact that more than a third of the German electorate actively opposed antisemitism in the elections of November 1932 by voting for the Communists and Social Democrats, the two socialist mass political parties that regarded antisemitism as the bankrupt ideology of a dying petty bourgeoisie? Or the liberals who worked hard to secure equal rights for religious Jews in the nineteenth century? Goldhagen's arguments, an updated version of the wartime propaganda claim that antisemitism was part of the German 'national character', along with longing for a great leader, obedience to authority, militarism and expansionism, were not accepted by many. But they did succeed in wrenching back the discourse to the question of what it was exactly in the nature of the Third Reich that led to the extermination of millions of European Jews.[14]

Neither a concentration on individual pathology on the one hand, nor a sweeping account of national identity on the other, can explain how hundreds of thousands of Germans committed unspeakable atrocities behind the Eastern Front and elsewhere, as camp guards, SS killers, ghetto officers and others, and beyond that, remotely, sitting at their desks in Berlin. An explanation has to be found at an intermediate level between these two extremes. Studies of samples of lower-level perpetrators have shown that many of the most violent and fanatical perpetrators were relatively young men, too young to have fought in the First World War, though not so young that they had not experienced it on the home front. This was the 'generation of the unconditional', who, to follow the historian Michael Wildt's argument, took it upon themselves to avenge the German defeat of 1918 and the Treaty of Versailles by jettisoning all moral scruples and reservations in the belief that only total ruthlessness could resurrect Germany and defeat its enemies, above all the 'world-enemy', the Jew.[15] Yet a good number of lower-level perpetrators were older men, socialized already under the Kaiser, and in their forties or even fifties when the war began. Nor were they representative of German society as a whole. A good number of them had grown up in areas on the German borderlands or territory taken from Germany by the Treaty of Versailles and assigned to other countries, notably Poland. Hardly any came from a working-class or aristocratic background. The majority grew up in middle-class and most prominently lower-middle-class families, with fathers who were minor officials, artisans, or small businessmen. Former policemen and soldiers were, as one might expect, over-represented, and it was also noticeable that a significant minority came from broken families.[16]

Such men came predominantly from a right-wing familial and social milieu, in which antisemitism was common and German nationalism a given. They were hardened to extreme violence by experiencing military service in World War I, or in its glorification by the right-wing media in the 1920s, in literature, film, newspapers and magazines. A majority of them belonged in the 1920s to the Free Corps or more generally to the far-right milieu in the Weimar Republic. Some of them were very young indeed, like the young men who carried out the assassination of the liberal Foreign Minister Walther Rathenau in 1922. Most of the men in a large sample of low-level perpetrators studied by the sociologist Michael Mann had served in the Free Corps, so had already carried out acts of extreme violence against people they regarded as Communists or left-wingers in the 1920s. A majority had joined the Nazi Party in the

1920s and taken part in the political violence of the early 1930s, absorbing the movement's ideology of hatred and aggression and losing any inhibitions they might have harboured in the use of rubber truncheons, knuckledusters, knives and guns in the struggle against the paramilitary units of the Communist and Social Democratic parties. Any young Nazi or stormtrooper who had refused to use violence against the Party's opponents at the time was likely to have been expelled from the movement, while those who remained had become hardened to the sight of blood, bruises and broken limbs.[17]

The Nazi seizure of power opened up new careers to such men, solving the economic problems they encountered during the world depression and allowing them to move quickly up the ladder of promotion and income in the SS, SA or SD, organizations which valued violent and brutal backgrounds and behaviour, traits which in more normal times might have barred them from secure employment. Values such as 'toughness', 'hardness' and 'manliness' were paramount in this milieu. The training such men underwent was itself extreme in its brutality, sometimes even sadism, weeding out the 'weak' and hardening the rest.[18] Wartime service in Eastern Europe, inhabited by people the Nazi regime depicted as 'subhuman', or tools of a global conspiracy to annihilate Germany, destroyed any remaining barriers to the exercise of physical violence, while the unlimited power that SS officers possessed in 'total institutions' such as concentration camps removed inhibitions which in any case had already become weak. Time and again, in letters and diaries and in reports by observers, Nazi murderers showed that they were not just conscientiously carrying out orders, but positively enjoyed what they were doing. Within a general culture that valorized and rewarded 'brutality' and 'fanaticism', encouraged from the very top, these men found satisfaction in committing atrocities. Some were motivated originally by the hatreds and resentments of extreme antisemitism, some by conformism or careerism, some driven by their own inner impulses, released from inhibition by the encouragement of Nazi ideology and propaganda and by the situations they encountered, above all, on and behind the Eastern Front during the war. 'Comradeship', the desire not to let one's comrades down, a sense of shared responsibility and superiority over the civilian population, acted as a motor of violence, building group pressure on the individual to conform. Tough and pitiless behaviour boosted a shared sense of masculine prowess. All these men were motivated by a mixture of these different influences that varied from one perpetrator to the next.[19] Total power, whether over unarmed civilians, ghetto inhabitants, concentration-camp inmates or soldiers and partisans taken prisoner and disarmed, had its own disinhibiting influence, releasing impulses of sadism and cruelty in a situation where negotiation was impossible, victims were treated as non-human objects rather than people, and pity for or sympathy with them was out of the question.[20] Above and beyond all this, the Nazi regime itself, beginning at the very top, created a moral milieu in which hyper-masculine ideas of toughness, hardness, brutality and fanaticism – all positive terms in the language of the Third Reich – encouraged the maltreatment and dehumanization of people excluded from the national community and treated as helpless and weak, the more so if, like the Jews (among whom the Nazis included the Bolsheviks), they were regarded as a real or potential deadly threat to the future of the German race.

19
The 'Witch' and the 'Beast': Ilse Koch and Irma Grese

Few if any servants of the Third Reich were as widely or as vehemently reviled as Ilse Koch. Other Nazi women committed far more horrific crimes; Erna Petri, for example, wife of an SS officer who ran an estate in occupied Poland, told her interrogators in East Germany in 1962 that she had wanted to show her husband and his SS colleagues that she was as good as any man, so she shot four Jews and six small Jewish children in the back of the neck after taking them into a forest and standing them above a ditch, ignoring their pleas for mercy. She later retracted her account when she realized correctly that it would lead to a lengthy term of imprisonment, but it was confirmed by seventeen witnesses. Another SS wife, Liesel Willhaus, whose husband was commandant of the notorious Janowska labour and extermination camp near Lviv, was accustomed to sit on the balcony of her villa, which stood just outside the camp perimeter, and use a French parlour rifle to shoot individual prisoners for no reason at all except to show off her marksmanship.[1] A Gestapo secretary, Gertrude Segel, who worked in Drohobych, south of Lviv, was accused after the war by Jewish witnesses of having ordered the death of three housemaids, all slave labourers from the camp, and trampling a small Jewish child to death. She and her husband were also said to have shot Jewish prisoners from the balcony of their villa. Her friend Josefine Block used a riding crop to beat prisoners, and thrashed a seven-year-old Jewish girl, throwing her to the ground and stomping on her head until she was dead. But none of these women attracted such notoriety as Ilse Koch, perhaps because their crimes were committed in Eastern Europe rather than in the West, and did not involve particularly high-ranking individuals.[2]

There were very obvious reasons why Ilse Koch attracted a

notoriety denied to these women. She was married to Karl Otto Koch, a senior SS officer who was successively commandant of the concentration camps at Sachsenburg, Esterwegen, Sachsenhausen, Buchenwald and Majdanek, before being relieved of his duties following a mass prisoner breakout from Majdanek in August 1942. Ilse Koch was put on trial for a variety of offences no fewer than three times: the first, in 1944, together with her husband, by the SS itself, for corruption; the second, in 1947, by a US military court in Dachau; and the third, in 1950–51, by a West German court in Augsburg. The accusations levelled against her created a worldwide sensation. Reporting on her sentencing by an American military tribunal on 25 August 1947, *Time* magazine announced: 'Justice had caught up with the red-headed, 40-year-old Witch of Buchenwald, who had prisoners at the Nazi concentration camp flogged at her pleasure and who had made gloves and lamp shades from their skins after they died of torture.' She was 'sexually psychotic', the magazine alleged.[3] Prosecuting attorney William Denson described her as a 'sadistic pervert of monumental proportions unmatched in history'. The chief prosecutor at her trial in West Germany in 1950–51, Johann Ilkow, alleged in his concluding speech to the court that 'chased by the demon of brutality and unrestrained instincts', she had committed 'unimaginable crimes with cold-blooded composure', and had 'surrendered to her sexual instincts without shame'.[4] After her death in September 1967, the *New York Times* reported that she had ordered 'prisoners to participate in orgies involving sadism and degeneracy', while the *Washington Post* alleged she had 'sexually excited inmates' by 'striding through the camp in tight riding breeches' and 'removing her blouse'. *Newsweek* magazine was not the only media outlet to describe her as a 'nymphomaniac' as well as a 'mass murderess'. In the light of all this, it was not surprising that 1975 saw the release of a soft-porn movie entitled *Ilsa: She-Wolf of the SS* ('The most dreaded Nazi of them all: she committed crimes so terrible even the SS feared her!').[5]

So who was Ilse Koch, and why did she achieve such notoriety? Born in 1906, in Dresden, into a lower-middle-class, Protestant family, she attended elementary school in the city, then trained as a secretary. Like many other young men and women of her background, she seems to have had strongly nationalistic, right-wing views, and her secretarial work in a number of local firms evidently brought her into contact with the social circles in which members of the Dresden SS moved. In May 1932, at the age of twenty-five, she joined the Nazi Party, an unusual step for a young woman at the time. By 1934, she had entered into a relationship with one of the SS men, Karl Otto Koch. Born in 1897, Karl had served in the military during the First World War, and like many veterans found it difficult to settle back into civilian life, drifting from one small-time clerical job to another, and often spending lengthy periods of unemployment, during which he engaged in acts of petty thievery and embezzlement. His early marriage ended in divorce. Also from a lower-middle-class background – his father was a minor civil servant working in the local Registry Office – he found a solution to his troubles in March 1931 by joining the Nazi Party and then the SS, again working in a clerical capacity. In October 1934, shortly after he had met Ilse, Karl Otto Koch was transferred to the staff of the senior SS officer Theodor Eicke, who headed the Concentration Camp Inspectorate. Koch impressed his new boss with his administrative competence and his ideological commitment, and was promoted several times, before being appointed commandant of Sachsenhausen concentration camp, a new and still unfinished facility located just outside Berlin, on 1 September 1936. His frequent moves did not seem to disturb his relationship with Ilse, and on 25 May 1937 they were legally married in a nearby registry office before going through a torchlit SS wedding ritual held at midnight in an oak grove at Sachsenhausen. It was at this point that Ilse began to acquire the toxic reputation which eventually brought her into the courtroom.[6]

On 1 August 1937, Karl was appointed commandant of another, even newer concentration camp, at Buchenwald, located on a hilltop near Weimar. By the end of the year the camp held a mixture of political enemies of the Nazis and, increasingly, petty criminals, 'asocials', vagrants and deviants. Koch ran the camp with extreme and often arbitrary savagery and brutality. He put the inmates on heavy and punishing labour duties while ensuring they remained permanently undernourished. He ordered frequent executions of men who broke the rules, and tortured would-be escapees before having them shot or killed by lethal injection. On the morning after a failed attempt on Hitler's life in November 1939, by the lone socialist (and non-Jewish) carpenter Georg Elser, who had built and planted a bomb in the Munich hall (the Bürgerbräukeller) where the Nazi leader was due to speak, Koch had some twenty Jewish prisoners assembled by SS guards, who then shot each of them in the back of the neck. Deaths among the inmates were so frequent and so numerous that Koch had a crematorium built to dispose of the bodies efficiently: and indeed more than 56,000 prisoners would die at the camp between its opening in 1937 and its abandonment at the end of the war, out of a total of some 239,000.[7]

Karl Otto Koch's rule over Buchenwald was perhaps unexceptional in comparison to the control exercised by SS commandants in other concentration camps. What made him stand out from most others, however, was his brazen, uncontrolled corruption. Embezzling and diverting funds for his own use, and employing inmates as slave labourers in his villa, located outside the camp perimeter, Koch soon became rich, and Ilse began to share his ill-gotten gains; for example, he had a large hall built for her so she could ride her horse indoors in bad weather.[8] But she was also seen on a number of occasions riding through the camp. Perhaps because she was virtually the only woman they encountered, and by all accounts a relatively young and attractive one, made conspicuous by her flaming red hair, prisoners began to notice her elegant clothing and expensive jewellery and to fantasize about her private life. Stories began to circulate about how she would enter the camp and threaten to report inmates to the guards if they gave her what she regarded as lascivious glances. One prisoner, Walter Retterpath, later testified that he had seen her riding up to a gang of inmates constructing a road, then hitting one of them across the face with her riding-crop while shouting 'I dare say you are looking at my legs!' Speculation reached fever-pitch as her alleged affairs with two SS officers in the camp attracted comment, along with Karl Otto's own extramarital liaisons. Most sensationally of all, it was rumoured that she got guards to report to her if any of the regular new arrivals in the prisoner population had tattoos, and ordered them to be executed, and the tattooed skin removed and tanned and turned into lampshades.[9]

The Kochs' corruption eventually became too much for the SS leadership to take. The couple had many enemies, not least among camp officers and guards who had been subjected to abusive behaviour and disciplinary action by the commandant. Himmler generally supported Karl Otto Koch, whom he knew and valued, but thought it prudent to transfer him in September 1941 to another new concentration camp, Majdanek (near Lublin), as commandant. Here the same pattern of sadism and brutality, corruption and peculation repeated itself. It was not embezzlement however that finished Koch's career, but the fact that on the night of 14–15 July 1942 some eighty-six Red Army prisoners of war rushed the perimeter fence, put a home-made ladder up against it, clambered over and disappeared into the surrounding fields. Two were shot by camp guards during the escape, but the rest got away and were never apprehended. Koch tried to cover this up by ordering the execution of dozens of Red Army prisoners whom he (falsely) accused of participating in the break-out. Himmler immediately fired Koch, who was transferred to less senior duties elsewhere, though he retained his home in Buchenwald. Himmler now commissioned a young and ambitious SS jurist called Konrad Morgen to investigate the reports of the Kochs' corruption at Buchenwald and especially Majdanek, where Morgen found extensive evidence during many weeks of work, leading Himmler to order the arrest of Karl Otto and Ilse Koch in August 1943; according to Morgen, they always 'worked together'. It was a year before their trial began, however. Although the prosecution threw various allegations of sexual impropriety at Ilse, all she was accused of was receiving stolen goods, and at the end of the trial she was acquitted for lack of evidence and released. Her husband, however, was found guilty, and after many months in prison, he was finally executed by firing squad on 5 April 1945, little more than a month before the formal end of the war.[10]

Ilse Koch regarded her acquittal by the SS tribunal as a vindication of her protests of innocence. But her complacency did not last long. When the Americans liberated Buchenwald, they discovered more than 20,000 starving, emaciated, sick and dying inmates. Some of the prisoners, however, were well enough to be interviewed, and others presented their liberators with concrete evidence of the atrocities committed in the camp, including pieces of tattooed human skin and a lampshade allegedly made of the same material, all of them now displayed on a table for all to see. Reports began to link the preserved human skin with the former commandant's wife. In fact, the likelihood is that the samples were assembled from the corpses of prisoners on the orders of an SS doctor, Erich Wagner, who was writing a dissertation on tattoos, which he believed were linked with the criminality of those who carried them. Direct evidence of their association with Ilse Koch was lacking. One former prisoner claimed that Koch had watched newly arrived inmates from the vantage point of her private home as they were stripped naked, and 'if she saw a tattoo design ... that pleased her, she ... had him killed and the skin brought to her'. But her house was in fact located outside the prison perimeter, almost a kilometre away, so this cannot have been possible. Incriminating testimony was almost always based on hearsay or what one American investigation termed 'common knowledge' among the prisoners.[11]

The story of Ilse Koch's lampshades somehow caught the imagination of press and public as a shocking example of Nazi cruelty and disregard for human life. It became a significant part of the indictment when she was put on trial alongside thirty other defendants by the American authorities. The chief prosecutor, William Denson, impressed by repeated stories put to him by the ex-prisoners whom he interviewed, described Ilse Koch as 'a sexy-looking depraved woman who beat prisoners, reported them for beatings, and trafficked in human skin'. She could not enter the already customary plea that she had 'only been following orders' since she did not hold any formal position in the Nazi hierarchy. Her description by Denson as the 'commandeuse' of the camp was an invention. The discovery just before the trial began that she was three months' pregnant convinced prosecutors and press that the description of her as a 'nymphomaniac' was all too accurate. At the trial itself, the newspapers reported her presence in strongly sexualized language, noting her 'voluptuous body' and calling her the 'sex-hungry witch of Buchenwald'. Yet the testimony of former inmates often fell apart under cross-examination. Nobody, not even Konrad Morgen, had in fact discovered any lampshades made of skin or provided proof that the tattooed skin had been taken from living subjects or collected on her orders. There was no first-hand evidence to underpin the allegation that prisoners had been killed on her instruction. Called as a witness, Ilse Koch denied everything and pointed out that she had been pregnant for much of her time at Buchenwald; but her blanket protestation that she had not known anything about what went on in the camp was exposed as a lie when Denson pointed out that she had employed prisoners as slave labourers in her house and garden. At the end of the trial, she was sentenced to life imprisonment; the points made by her defence attorney were largely disregarded by the court, but her pregnancy probably saved her from the noose.[12]

A review of the court's sentences, however, while confirming the death penalty for a number of the defendants, reduced Koch's life imprisonment to four years on the grounds that much of the supposed evidence was 'of doubtful veracity' and her conduct had not resulted in any deaths or serious injuries. Nor had she borne any responsibility for the overall operation of the camp. The outcry in the American press was immediate and immense. So great was the public outrage at the perceived leniency of the army court that President Truman intervened, and a Senate sub-committee launched an investigation, heavily criticizing the review body and its recommendations. This prompted the US authorities to escape from the controversy by passing the case over to the West German judiciary. The German prosecutor described Ilse Koch as a monster. She was 'cruel in a manner rarely found in women'. She was 'not even a good mother' but had been a heavy drinker and was 'always running around with married men'. The prosecution revived the discredited allegation that she was the 'commandeuse' of Buchenwald, and Karl Otto Koch was 'her devoted slave in everything'. She was 'tickled by the terrible sight' of the cruel punishments visited on refractory inmates. On no fewer than twenty-five occasions she had incited guards to murder, and had been present at some of the killings she had ordered. She had 'surrendered to her sexual instincts without shame'. The prosecutor repeated the previously rejected lampshade allegations.

On 27 November 1950 her fresh trial began in Augsburg, where Ilse Koch once more denied everything. 'I am a normal woman,' she insisted. Over the following six weeks, no fewer than 241 witnesses gave their testimony to the court. Although much of this testimony was hearsay, a good portion of it sounded convincing. Alfred Risser, a Catholic clergyman, testified that he had personally seen Ilse Koch single out an inmate for punishment, after which an SS man had lifted a heavy stone and smashed the prisoner's head with it. Another clergyman, Alfred Berchtold, informed the court he had also seen Ilse Koch report a man who was in a column of prisoners to an SS guard, after which the man had been taken away and murdered. Ilse Koch rejected these allegations outright, thus claiming implicitly that the priests were deliberately lying. For her part, her statement that she had never even entered the camp was patently untrue. Particularly telling was documentary evidence that proved her membership of the Nazi Party, although she had always denied this. Under extreme pressure, Ilse Koch suffered a breakdown, and for several periods of time the proceedings continued without her presence. In the end, the court sentenced her to life imprisonment (the death penalty having been abolished in West Germany in 1949). The judgement convicted her for incitement to murder, rejecting some of the most *outré* accusations levelled at her. The court found her offences, in effect, were aggravated by her violation of the gender norms of the day. She had, it declared, 'consciously suppressed any feeling of compassion and pity she had as a woman'. She had 'wilfully closed herself to any better insight and to adjusting her behaviour accordingly, whereas feelings of pity and empathy would have been especially obvious for every woman'. The West German press enthusiastically endorsed the verdict. Her complete rejection of the charges brought against her, her lies, and her lack of remorse, had all reinforced these sentiments. The liberal weekly *Die Zeit* spoke for many when it described her as a 'perverted, nymphomaniacal, hysterical, power-obsessed' woman.[13]

Despite submitting innumerable petitions for clemency, Ilse Koch was never released from the women's prison of Aichach. She always rejected all the allegations brought against her. In despair, she hanged herself with bedsheets in her cell on 2 September 1967. She had certainly been guilty of profiting from her husband's corruption in a variety of ways. The testimony from some former inmates that she had incited SS guards to murder was convincing. She shared fully in the Nazi world view: the 'hate propaganda' against her, she charged, 'was orchestrated against me mainly by Jews', although the witnesses who testified against her, like the journalists who vilified her in the press, were overwhelmingly not Jewish. She did herself no favours by refusing to recognize that she had done anything wrong. Her defiance was unrepentantly Nazi: when she was arrested in Germany, she is reported to have said that the West German 'regime' would be short-lived, the Third Reich would return, and those who were prosecuting her 'will see what will happen to them'. Not only in America but above all in West Germany, a tendency to ascribe crimes of Nazism to a perverted, psychopathic individual provided a convenient excuse for the vast numbers of ordinary Germans who had brought Nazism to power, sustained it there, and participated in its crimes. Both West Germans and Americans could claim that by bringing the 'Witch of Buchenwald' to justice, they had demonstrated their willingness to punish Nazi criminals, whereas in fact hundreds of men who had carried out murder and cruelty on an industrial scale escaped with far more lenient sentences or avoided retribution altogether.[14]

Among those who were brought to justice were relatively few women, unsurprisingly in view of the extreme masculinist nature of the Nazi regime. Some attracted a good deal of notoriety, though few as much as Ilse Koch. Prominent among them was Irma Grese, dubbed by the press as the 'beautiful beast of Belsen', 'Queen of the Belsen gang', a 'blonde monster' and 'Satan's woman'.[15] 'She was one of the most beautiful women I have ever seen,' testified an inmate camp doctor in Auschwitz, Gisella Perl: 'Her body was perfect in every line, her face clear and angelic, and her blue eyes the gayest, the most innocent eyes one can imagine. And yet Irma Grese was the most depraved, cruel, imaginative pervert I ever came across.'[16]

Grese figured prominently among the accused at the trial of guards and officials of the Bergen-Belsen concentration camp, whose discovery by British forces on 15 April 1945 caused shock and horror across the world. Some 60,000 starving and disease-ridden inmates were found inside, with another 13,000 lying dead and unburied around them; 14,000 of the survivors were so weak that they died within a few weeks of liberation.[17] Grese had stayed on in the camp, seemingly unaware that she had anything to fear from the representatives of the Allies. But two days after their arrival, she was arrested. After being made to assist in the burial of the dead, she was transferred to a prison in the town of Celle, where she was held until she was brought to trial at a British military court in Lüneburg, along with the camp commandant Josef Kramer and forty-three others. Some 200 journalists and observers were in attendance as the charges were read out, accusing all of them of willing participation in a 'system of murder, brutality, cruelty or criminal neglect'. Many of them, including Grese, had previously served at Auschwitz and had been evacuated to Belsen as the Red Army approached.[18]

On the witness stand, Grese admitted to having forced inmates to stand for hours on early-morning roll calls, and confessed she had carried a horse-whip with her at Auschwitz, which she had used on prisoners. 'It was a very light whip,' she told the court, 'but if I hit somebody with it, it would hurt.' Although the camp commandant had expressly forbidden it, she used the whip if she found a prisoner stealing something, or if her orders were ignored. She confessed she had also carried a gun, and had beaten prisoners with a walking stick and with her gloved hand. Former prisoners testified they had seen her shoot a thirty-year-old Hungarian Jewish woman at Auschwitz without provocation. Another witness told the court that Grese's 'favourite occupation was beating them and kicking them with her heavy boots after they fell over onto the ground'. A Polish former inmate described how Grese had cycled on her bike with a work detail, accompanied by a dog, as the prisoners marched some sixteen kilometres outside the camp to collect herbs for the camp kitchen. Some of the prisoners had collapsed on the way, too weak and malnourished to go on, and Grese had set her dog on them. Although she claimed under cross-examination never to have had a dog, she did admit to having forced a work-detail to run around the camp as 'sport' as punishment for the theft, by persons unknown, of some meat from the camp kitchen. Several of them had collapsed from exhaustion, though Grese denied any of them had died. In Auschwitz, she had also assisted the camp doctor Josef Mengele in selecting prisoners for the gas chamber, which she knew was awaiting them. 'If one ran away,' the prosecuting attorney put to her, 'you brought her back and gave her a beating'. 'Yes,' she answered. Asked whether she made prisoners kneel if they misbehaved at the morning roll call, she said yes, she had.[19]

Irma Grese's crimes were no more serious than those of many male SS camp guards. What attracted the attention of the overwhelmingly male media corps at her trial were her youth and beauty. Born on 7 October 1923 in rural Mecklenburg, she had a troubled family background; her mother committed suicide in 1936, apparently because of marital difficulties. After leaving school at the age of fourteen, Grese had done labour service on a farm, before working as an auxiliary nurse in the SS sports sanatorium at Hohenlychen. This led her to join the SS and take up a position as a guard in Ravensbrück women's concentration camp, a decision that caused her father to break off relations with her. In March 1943 she was transferred to Auschwitz-Birkenau, where she was put in charge of work details until the camp was evacuated on 18 January 1945. Although still a teenager when she arrived at Auschwitz, this was nothing unusual: two-thirds of the female guards in Ravensbrück in 1943–44 were twenty-five or younger.[20] By early March 1945, after a brief spell in Ravensbrück, Grese was moved to Belsen. Most of the testimony against her was given, therefore, by prisoners she had supervised in Birkenau. It was sufficient for the court to convict her, and she was hanged on 13 December. The British executioner, Albert Pierrepoint, thought she was 'as bonny a girl as one could ever wish to meet'.[21]

Grese continued to the end to believe she had done nothing wrong. At one point during her cross-examination, she lost her temper and shouted at the prosecuting counsel, banging her fist on the witness stand as she did so. 'For the first time during the trial,' reported the *Daily Herald*, 'blonde Irma Grese was looking frightened, probably for the first time in her life.'[22] Otherwise, her lack of emotion, and the coolness and lack of contrition with which she described her crimes, were deeply shocking to observers. 'Irma Shows her Claws' was the headline in one British newspaper over a report of her response to cross-examination.[23] Press reporting of the whole trial was dominated by accounts of her behaviour: finally, the mask of denial that had covered the testimonies of the other accused had slipped. The papers charged her with crimes she had consistently denied, and even crimes with which she was not confronted by any of the prosecution witnesses. The *Daily Herald* managed to turn her testimony in court into an orgiastic experience: 'Shouting answers in a harsh voice, it was Irma Grese, the S.S. guard, who spoke. The climax came when, laughing derisively, she demonstrated to the court how she used a whip.'[24] One report alleged she had ordered the legs of women prisoners tied together during childbirth, causing them to die in agony. She was, reported the *Sunday Telegraph*, 'the woman whose cruelty probably exceeds that of any other in history', a 'murderer and sadist' according to a German paper, 'a devil in disguise' as another put it. The American historian Daniel Patrick Brown even described her as notorious in Auschwitz 'for her late-night affairs with female inmates (whom she later dispatched to the gas chambers)'.[25] Even some former camp inmates gave testimonies that reflected the stereotype she had become, more than the reality they had experienced. The inmate doctor Gisella Perl claimed Grese had selected pretty women from among the prisoners, and beaten their breasts with a jewelled whip, her body writhing in orgasmic spasms.[26]

Perl recalled how Grese came along to watch her operate on the breast of a young female prisoner, which, she said, had become infected after being cut open by Grese's whip. The operation was performed without anaesthetic, and 'my patient screamed with pain' throughout. Grese, she reported:

... watched me plunge my knife into the infected breast which spurted blood and pus in every direction. I happened to look up and encountered the most horrible sight I have ever seen, the memory of which will haunt me for the rest of my life. Irma Grese was enjoying the sight of this human suffering. Her tense body swung back and forth in a revealing, rhythmical motion. Her cheeks were flushed and her wide-open eyes had the rigid, staring look of complete sexual paroxysm.

Yet these accounts raise a good deal of suspicion. Grese came across to more rational observers as a rather immature, simple young woman who had little idea of why she was being demonized, and could not even understand why she was being tried in a British military court. The letters she wrote from her condemned cell to her family reveal her to have retained in full the illusions of Nazism. 'I shall never lose my honour,' she told them, using the words of the motto of the SS, 'for this is called: loyalty!' Her conscience was unsullied, she insisted. She was dying for her beloved Fatherland. She remained loyal to it unto death, she wrote.[27]

The selection criteria for female guards focused on ideological commitment, physical fitness and mental toughness. Only a minority of candidates were accepted, with staff shortages leading to a relaxing of these criteria later in the war.[28] Altogether in January 1945 there were 546 female guards in the women's camp at Ravensbrück and twelve in Bergen-Belsen. Overall there were almost 3,500 female concentration-camp guards by this time, many of them drafted in from factories and labour exchanges.[29] After the war, very few were prosecuted, perhaps reflecting 'a disbelief among the Allies that women could have committed atrocities, and from Germany's desire to rehabilitate its men by asserting the normalcy of its women', as one historian has argued.[30] Surviving former guards universally denied their culpability, even presenting themselves as victims, often for many decades afterwards.[31] Such trials as did occur tended to minimize the freedom of action of female guards, and play down the personal responsibility of all but a very few, stressing instead their subordination to male authority.[32] Only a small number were singled out because of what was taken as their dramatic violation of the norms of feminine character, behaviour or appearance, sensationalized, and pilloried as beasts or monsters in the media, thus uncoupling their cases from what was generally understood to be normal.[33] But in fact, female normality in the Third Reich encompassed a huge variety of behaviours, and the conduct of perpetrators such as Ilse Koch and Irma Grese, greatly though the two women differed from one another, was by no means as exceptional as their demonization would seem to have suggested. It did not require any deep-seated psychopathic personality disorder for an ordinary woman to become a killer, let alone assisting in the crimes of Nazism or facilitating them.

20

The Mother: Gertrud Scholtz-Klink

Writing in 1946, the American historian Mary Ritter Beard portrayed a hitherto little-known figure in the Nazi hierarchy, Gertrud Scholtz-Klink, as a female Hitler, a Nazi dictator for the female sex:

> By 1941 she was governing some thirty million German women and tightening her grip on some twenty million other women in lands occupied by German troops. The dictatorial authority of this Lady *Führer über Alles* was vividly described by Peter Engelmann ... 'Frau Klink,' wrote Engelmann, 'rules the lives of women in all things. She tells them how many children they must have, and when; what they shall wear, what they shall cook and how. What they shall say, laughing to their husbands and sons marching to war. How they shall behave, smiling, when their men are killed. Here is the responsibility for the home spirit, the core of national morale.'[1]

Interviewing Scholtz-Klink in Germany some years after Beard wrote, another American historian, Claudia Koonz, presented her as 'the woman who bore the major responsibility for creating a separate female sphere in Nazi society', establishing a 'massive organization that indoctrinated a generation of young women and girls' into the ideology of Nazism. Scholtz-Klink had been instrumental in the formation of one-half of 'an orderly world dominated by men and a gentle world of love preserved by women'.[2] The latter indeed was what made the former possible: 'Mothers and wives ... made a vital contribution to Nazi power by preserving the illusion of love in an environment of hatred.'[3] What would be her attitude to her role in the Third Reich now, Koonz wondered, more than three and a half decades after it had come to its violent and catastrophic end?

To her surprise, Scholtz-Klink proved utterly unrepentant about her

time as the 'Reich Women's Leader' in Nazi Germany. 'My own women's division,' she said, '... formed almost a state within a state. In my ministry I directed departments of economics, education, colonial issues, consumer affairs and health, education and welfare. No man ever interfered with us; we did as we pleased.' They were 'one big happy family'. Scholtz-Klink claimed (falsely, as it turned out) that she had enjoyed frequent informal contacts with Hitler, Himmler, Göring, Rosenberg and the other Nazi leaders. They had listened to what she had said and followed her advice. 'Our job (and we did it well) was to infuse the daily life of all German women – even in the tiniest villages – with Nazi ideals.' She had 'unified all German women' in the people's community.

How, then, had she become interested in Nazism? In the 1920s, Scholtz-Klink said, she had just been a housewife and mother. Of course, she had supported the political activities of her first husband, 'an ardent SA man'. But one day he had suffered a fatal heart attack while attending a demonstration. Instead of blaming the Nazi movement for his death, however, she blamed its enemies, although there was no evidence that her husband had been involved in street-fighting or any other kind of violence. He had just died of over-excitement. 'I wanted to replace him,' she said, 'to devote myself to the movement for which he had been martyred.' She offered immediately to help the Party, and was set the task of organizing Nazi women in Baden, where she lived. She accomplished this with energy and ruthlessness. When the Nazis came to power in 1933, she swung into action. In February and March Hitler took the first crucial steps in establishing his dictatorship, and on 27 April Scholtz-Klink felt confident enough to declare the umbrella organization of the liberal feminist societies, the Federation of German Women's Associations, dissolved in Baden. The hapless feminists reacted with surprise and dismay, and protested to the Reich Minister of the Interior, but it got them nowhere. Scholtz-Klink's declaration that she was assuming the leadership of all women's activities in Baden was repeated by other Nazi women in every other part of Germany. As the process of *Gleichschaltung*, 'coordination', was getting under way across the Reich, affecting all parts of civil society except the Churches, it became clear that women's organizations were no exception. Faced with the threat, on a national level, of being forcibly shut down, the Federation dissolved itself on 15 May 1933.[4]

The Nazi Party had long dismissed the feminist movement in

Germany as a subversive organization, dedicated to undermining the German family, and ripping the German woman away from her biologically ordained role as housewife and mother. Feminism, leading Nazis declared, was a Jewish doctrine, and the feminist movement was inspired and led by Jews (in fact, there were relatively few Jewish women in its ranks, since most of them enrolled in the entirely separate Jewish Women's League). Nazi ideas about women's place in society were a mixture of the traditional, emphasizing for example separate male and female spheres in society, and the radical, stressing the need to dispense with Christian morality in the drive to produce more children for the Reich. Hitler himself declared in 1935 that women's highest honour was to bear children for the nation. He repeatedly declared that women had no place in politics.[5] 'Women's equality exists in the fact that she receives the high estimation which belongs to her in the areas of life that nature determines for her ... Man and woman represent two completely different kinds of being. In the man, understanding is dominant, in the woman feeling.'[6] Speaking directly to Scholtz-Klink, he said: 'You have really brilliantly understood how to avoid making the organization of women into the polar opposite of men's, and by contrast, making the women's organization into a complement of men's fighting organization.'[7]

Talking to Claudia Koonz in 1981, Scholtz-Klink tried however to foreground her own feminist, or, better said, pseudo-feminist credentials. At first, she claimed, the leading men in the Nazi movement had only wanted the Nazi women's organization to act as a subordinate, auxiliary movement: but, she said, 'I was determined to create a dignified and independent women's organization. To really accomplish something.' Her work, she went on, had essentially been non-political. 'Next to the dominant motif of male brutality,' Koonz concluded, 'Gertrud Scholtz-Klink and millions of followers created the social side of tyranny. Busily administering welfare services, educational programs, leisure activities, ideological indoctrination, and consumer organization, Nazi women mended while Nazi men marched.' Utterly unrepentant, Scholtz-Klink defended what she had done in the Third Reich, even producing a book of essays shot through with nostalgic vindication of her glory days as 'Reich Women's Leader'.[8]

How did Scholtz-Klink reach her position at the head of the Nazi women's organization? The path there was far from smooth; and she needed a lot of male patronage and assistance along the way. Born on 9

February 1902 in Adelsheim, a picturesque small town in the southwest German state of Baden, she was the daughter of a minor state official who died when she was only eight years of age. After completing her school-leaving examinations, she did not go on to study for the *Abitur*, the examination that would have qualified her for university entrance, but stayed at home to help her mother manage the family household, which also included two younger brothers. At the age of nineteen, she married the secondary-school teacher Eugen Klink, with whom she had two daughters and three sons, the youngest of whom died in infancy. Klink had served as an army officer in the First World War, and like many such veterans, he gravitated towards far-right politics during the Weimar Republic. After his sudden death in March 1930, she fell under the patronage of the Nazi Regional Leader (Gauleiter) in Baden, Robert Wagner, a veteran of the Party's early days and participant in the beer-hall *putsch* of 1923. It was Wagner, a friend of her late husband, who ensured that she was appointed leader of the Nazi women's organization in Baden. Meanwhile she had lost no time in finding a substitute for Klink, marrying Günther Scholtz, a rural doctor and local Nazi official, in 1932, and adding his name to her first husband's.[9]

The coming of the Third Reich propelled Scholtz-Klink onto the national stage. But it also landed her in a complicated political situation, and presented her with serious domestic difficulties. When she moved to Berlin in 1934, Scholtz-Klink persuaded her husband to leave his medical practice and accompany her with the rest of the family, to which two more children had now been added. But things did not work out. After only a year, Scholtz tired of his new life as a house-husband and returned to Baden, ending the marriage, which was formally terminated by a legal divorce in 1937.[10] Gertrud's political activism had put him in the shade, in a striking reversal of the roles the regime expected husbands and wives to play. Yet she was anything but a strident or self-assertive feminist. The secret of her success lay in a combination of steely determination on the one hand, and a discreet and tactful display of adherence to conservative gender roles on the other. Only in this way was she able to deal with the paradox of engaging in a political world that denied women the right to engage in politics. On a national level, the organization of women members of the Nazi Party – a tiny minority, only about 5 per cent of the overall membership – had been bedevilled by personal rivalries and political rows. The two leading figures, Paula

Siber and Lydia Gottschewski, were notably assertive, tactless and headstrong. Their rivalry was destroying the careful organizational restructuring of the Nazi women's movement achieved by Gregor Strasser in 1931. Moreover, Gottschewski's speeches sounded suspiciously like feminist propaganda to the Party leadership. Accusations and counter-accusations began to fly. Financial irregularities were exposed, and the Party hierarchy banned Siber from speaking in public.[11]

While Siber and Gottschewski were engaging in theoretical disputes about the proper role of women in National Socialism and rallying their supporters in the struggle for power within the movement, Scholtz-Klink, after her decisive action in destroying the feminist movement in Baden, focused her attention on welfare and social work, and refrained from making grand statements or launching political initiatives. Gauleiter Robert Wagner was fulsome in his praise, and as his stock rose within the Party, so too did hers. This attracted the support of Erich Hilgenfeldt, head of the National Socialist People's Welfare organization, the NSV, who saw in his patronage of Scholtz-Klink a way of stealing a march on his own rivals such as Reich Minister Wilhelm Frick, who had backed Siber. There were rumours of an affair between Hilgenfeldt and Scholtz-Klink, and certainly their respective marriages were both in deep trouble, with Hilgenfeldt separating from his wife in 1935 and divorcing her five years later. Whatever the truth of these allegations, the solution of the disputes within the Nazi women's movement – the appointment of a man, Gottfried Krummacher, a conservative local administrator whose nomination came from the Protestant Church – was clearly no more than a temporary expedient. But in a short space of time, Krummacher reorganized the movement, establishing a twofold division of labour between an umbrella organization, the *Deutsches Frauenwerk*, and a more elite club of Nazi Party members and activists, the *NS-Frauenschaft*. With the support of Reich Labour Minister Robert Ley and the Deputy Leader of the Party and head of the Nazi Party's administration, Rudolf Hess, Krummacher brought in Hilgenfeldt to sort out the remaining problems.[12]

With the backing of these significant figures, the search began for a permanent appointment to lead the Nazi women. With her combination of unobtrusiveness, loyalty and administrative efficiency, Scholtz-Klink was the obvious choice. She was appointed to head all the major women's organizations in the course of 1934, including the Women's Labour

Service, culminating in her official designation in November as Reich Women's Leader (*Reichsfrauenführerin*). This made her indisputably the most senior woman in the Third Reich. Although her title and position conformed outwardly to the 'leadership principle' which had dominated Nazism since the mid-1920s, however, the idea that she was some kind of dictator, a female equivalent of Hitler, was a gross exaggeration. It was not Scholtz-Klink who told German women how many children to bear, what kind of clothes to buy, what sort of meals to cook, or how to behave when their menfolk perished in battle. The Nazi *Frauenschaft* was closely bound into the social welfare institutions of the Labour Front and the National Socialist People's Welfare organization. Its members knitted clothes and prepared meals for Party members at meetings, set up classes for pregnant women and new mothers, lectured women on matters of health and personal hygiene, and joined with the Labour Front in organizing outings and cultural trips for working women. They also taught classes on the ideas and purposes of the Nazi movement, and were commissioned by the SS to set up instruction courses for the approved future wives of its members. During the war, the competences of the *Frauenschaft* grew, especially in areas such as rescue work after bombing raids.[13]

These were all low-level activities that were clearly subordinate to the overall leadership of the Labour Front and the welfare organization of the Nazi Party. The subordinate position of the *Frauenschaft* remained clear: in handbooks of the Nazi movement, for example, it always appeared at the very end of any list of the Party's constituent and associated organizations. Scholtz-Klink never succeeded in obtaining an audience with Hitler after 1933. She remained dependent on the patronage of powerful men in the regime, and got into trouble when this was withdrawn. In 1937 she clashed with Robert Ley over the issue of who should be responsible for female apprenticeships, and despite a provisional if limited agreement between the two over the demarcation of responsibilities, Ley criticized her for using the title *Leiterinnen* ('leaders') for some of her functionaries, accusing her of promoting the emancipation of women and endangering the unity of the Party. Scholtz-Klink was rescued by Hess, who announced that Hitler was entirely satisfied with what she was doing, but after Hess's deranged attempt to broker an Anglo-German peace treaty by flying unannounced to Scotland on 10 May 1941, his successor, Martin Bormann, was far less sympathetic, and in cooperation with Ley, prevented Scholtz-Klink from merging the *Frauenschaft* with the *Frauenwerk* on the grounds that this would challenge the authority of the Labour Front on the welfare scene.[14]

Conscious of her precarious and subordinate position in the Nazi hierarchy, Scholtz-Klink was careful not to venture too far outside her allotted sphere. She spoke fairly frequently to public audiences, but usually on women's issues. She was active in the 'yes' campaign in the plebiscite on the annexation of Austria in 1938, for example, and in a similar campaign in the Sudetenland, though the plebiscite there was never held. She surrounded herself with a loyal group of highly educated women, including some with PhDs and others with professional qualifications, notably in teaching, who took on much of the administrative burden of running the various women's organizations over which Scholtz-Klink held sway. But she had virtually no influence over the policies of the Labour Front towards women, and key issues such as family policy, birth control, contraception, education, admission to professional qualifications and much more besides remained beyond her control. The campaign to entice more women into the workforce during the war was run by the Labour Front, not by Scholtz-Klink. Moreover, she completely failed to gather even a majority of adult German women into the *Deutsches Frauenwerk*: indeed, her proposal to merge it with the more elite *NS-Frauenschaft* was an admission of her failure to establish it as an effective mass organization on its own terms. Unlike other Nazi institutions, such as the Reich Culture Chamber or professional associations, the *Frauenwerk* had no instruments of coercion available to force women to join. German housewives and mothers could not be threatened with dismissal from their jobs, and denying them welfare support would undermine the regime's purpose of persuading them to stay at home and raise children. Indeed, so generous was this support that women paid little attention to the campaign to get them to work in munitions factories and other industries when the drafting of men into the war effort created growing labour shortages from 1939 onwards, forcing the regime to recruit foreign workers, who numbered no fewer than seven million by 1944. The *Deutsches Frauenwerk* remained marginal to women's lives, and the *NS-Frauenschaft* failed altogether to acquire real political clout.[15]

German women, the historian Jill Stephenson concluded, were

'peculiarly resistant' to the appeal of Nazism because they were difficult to politicize, and they were tied to the Church to a far greater extent than men were. Some 90 per cent of women were uninterested in Nazi organizations. Most of them 'wished simply to remain private, unorganized citizens'. And many of those who joined did so for purely instrumental reasons, taking Nazi ideology as a given but failing to buy into it.[16] The argument that the *NS-Frauenschaft* developed its own ideology independently of that of the Nazi Party has failed to convince historians; all Scholtz-Klink did was to parrot the clichés of Nazi conceptions of gender roles, which indeed was a major reason why she could obtain and keep the position she occupied.[17] Moreover, the oft-proclaimed aim of the Nazi Party to create wholly separate spheres for men and women in the Third Reich could never be achieved. Politics did indeed become a male preserve, and Nazi propaganda constantly emphasized the need for men to be courageous and women to be motherly. Yet Claudia Koonz's portrayal of women as indirect perpetrators whose peaceful domesticity sustained men's violent barbarism oversimplifies the issue. Just as problematic, however, is the opposing view that women were overwhelmingly victims of Nazi male supremacism and misogyny. These two diametrically opposed visions of women's place in Nazi Germany led to a fierce controversy in the late 1980s and early 1990s.[18] But historical research has moved on since then, particularly in the study of female perpetrators. It has uncovered not just the activities of women concentration-camp guards, female secretaries and administrators, and doctors and nurses involved in medical experiments on concentration-camp inmates or in *Aktion T-4*, the murder of the mentally ill and handicapped, including children, but also many others who, less dramatically, denounced their fellow citizens to the Gestapo for offences of various kinds, or volunteered for service in 'Germanizing' occupied Poland, taking part in the SS-led expulsion of Polish families from their farms to make way for incoming German settlers and looting Polish property unashamedly in the process.[19] Moreover, women were deeply involved in many aspects of the regime, even if they did not engage directly in its crimes. As wives and mothers, they knew, and for the most part tolerated or approved of, and sometimes even assisted in, the crimes of their menfolk. The range of their activities in support of the Third Reich was vast.[20]

By the time war broke out, Gertrud Scholtz-Klink had found a new partner following her divorce from Günther Scholtz. This was August Heissmeyer, an *Obergruppenführer* (Senior Group Leader) in the SS. They married on 6 December 1940 – no doubt not coincidentally the day before the man said to have been her lover, Erich Hilgenfeldt, married his second wife. Since 1936, Heissmeyer had been Inspector of the National Political Educational Institutions, or *Napolas*, elite Nazi institutions whose emphasis was on physical courage and military discipline. Heissmeyer brought with him no fewer than six children from his first marriage, bringing the total in Gertrud Scholtz-Klink's family up to ten in all, an example to every Nazi wife and mother. Heissmeyer was not just an educationalist, however. A Nazi since the mid-1920s, he was also the Higher SS and Police Leader for Berlin, and for a brief time in 1939–40 Acting Inspector of Concentration Camps, filling the post after it had been vacated by Theodor Eicke, the creator of the camp regime, before it was taken up by Richard Glücks. Heissmeyer was thus in the top echelon of SS officials. Among other things, he commanded a military unit in the final stage of the war, in the capacity of general in the Waffen-SS. His influence helped ensure that his nephew Kurt, a doctor specializing in tuberculosis, obtained permission in 1944 to conduct experiments on twenty Jewish children under the age of twelve sent to him in the concentration camp at Neuengamme from Auschwitz by Dr Josef Mengele. Kurt Heissmeyer had them injected with tuberculosis bacilli as part of an experiment designed to contribute to his second doctorate and thereby his appointment as a professor. After they had been infected, he had their axillary lymph nodes surgically removed for analysis, leaving them in considerable pain. The 'research' was scientifically useless, based as it was on fraudulent Nazi assumptions about the different medical constitutions of Jews and others. As British troops advanced on Hamburg in April 1945, the children were taken to a sub-camp on Bullenhuser Damm, in Hamburg, and hanged in an attempted cover-up. In 1948, August Heissmeyer was arrested by the French authorities, tried and imprisoned. Following his release in 1952, he worked as director of the Coca-Cola bottling plant in Schwäbisch Hall until his retirement, dying in 1979, aged eighty-two. Kurt Heissmeyer returned to medical practice in Magdeburg after the war but was tracked down and put on trial in 1963, dying in prison four years later.[21]

Scholtz-Klink was therefore deeply implicated in the most criminal aspects of the Nazi regime, or at the very least must have been fully aware of them. She signalled her independence and status by refusing to take August Heissmeyer's name when she married him. But there could be no doubt that her new relationship was a genuine one and not merely a marriage of political convenience. In 1944 she gave birth to a son, bringing the total number of her children by birth or marriage to eleven. The relationship brought her into close contact with the darkest side of Nazism – the SS, the camps, the inhumane medical experiments, the brutal murders, the extermination of the Jews. What, Claudia Koonz asked Scholtz-Klink during their conversation in 1981, was her view of all this now? She had, she conceded, 'grown up in an anti-Semitic family, so the ideas did not seem unusual.' 'Of course,' she said, 'we never intended that so many Jews would disappear.' The statement is worth a close reading, from the euphemism 'disappear' to the unexplained 'we' – did she perhaps mean 'women' as opposed to men? 'We,' she continued, referring to the Nazi women's organizations she led, were focused on 'welfare programmes to help German people.' Not Jews, then; and indeed Jews were banned both from joining the organizations she led, and from receiving any help from them. As for the concentration camps, she conceded, she did know about them and even visited one near Berlin because 'some of my women worked there as social workers'. Life there was 'normal'. And in any case: 'After the inmates had been re-educated, they would be released to return to productive roles in society.' Concentration camps could on occasion be smartened up for presentation to visitors or even to journalists. On 23 August 1940, for example, August Heissmeyer visited the women's concentration camp at Ravensbrück together with Scholtz-Klink. Conditions in the camp were not quite as dire as in the men's camps, at least at this stage, but the degrading and inhuman rituals of admission and everyday discipline still obtained. In 1981, Scholtz-Klink had not revised her position since the days of the Third Reich: the inmates of the camps were criminals who needed to be 're-educated', not political opponents of the Nazis, or 'asocials', who failed to participate in the construction of the supposed 'national community'. Nor did she reveal what 're-education' actually involved, or betray what she must have known, that huge numbers of inmates died in the camps, or were never released.[22]

Later in life, Gertrud Scholtz-Klink presented the war, the camps and the extermination of the Jews as impersonal acts of fate for which Nazism was not really to blame. They should not have been allowed in her view to obliterate the memory of the good side of Nazism that she in particular represented.[23] But at the end of the war, she was conscious enough that she and her husband would be regarded as criminals by the victorious Allies, so they decided to go underground. At the beginning of May 1945, they were still in Berlin, but as the news of Hitler's death reached them over the radio, they left the capital, narrowly evading the soldiers of the Red Army as the couple became involved in a gun battle in which Scholtz-Klink was lightly wounded. By now in disguise, their papers burned and their weapons thrown away, they were arrested at Red Army checkpoints on more than one occasion, but managed to escape. Under the names 'Heinrich and Maria Stuckenbrock', the couple made their way south, and with the assistance of Pauline Princess zu Wied, daughter of the last King of Württemberg and a functionary of the German Red Cross, they obtained false papers and settled in the town of Bebenhausen located in Baden-Württemberg, in the French occupation zone, after they had left their children with Heissmeyer's mother. Here they lived quietly, earning their living, Gertrud from domestic work, August from farm labour, until the French occupation authorities, tipped off by someone who had noticed the princess's frequent visits to one of Scholtz-Klink's close female associates, eventually tracked them down through this woman and had them arrested on the night of 28–29 February 1948.[24]

Scholtz-Klink, whose name was sufficiently notorious for her now to change it to Heissmeyer, was jailed for eighteen months for using a false name, and then, like millions of other Germans, made to fill out a lengthy and detailed questionnaire about her activities during the Nazi period, which led to her classification by the denazification authorities as 'implicated' (*belastet*), the second-highest category below the guilty. This barred her from voting or engaging in professional work, including teaching, for five years. In August 1949 she went on trial. She justified her involvement by presenting the war as a conflict between Europe and the East. She still admired Hitler, she said, and had believed up to the end that Germany would win the war. She denied any involvement in 'men's politics' and whatever crimes it might have led to. Her lack of any repentance, and the evidence presented against her, persuaded the court to classify her as a 'Principal Culprit' (*Hauptschuldige*), the highest level of involvement in Nazism. The period of the restrictions already imposed on her activities was doubled, and she was sentenced to eighteen months' imprisonment, which the court declared she had already served, even though this was for a different offence. An appeal was granted and she was sentenced to two and a half years in jail, without counting the term she had previously served. In July 1950, however, she successfully applied to the President of the State of Württemberg-Hohenzollern for a commutation because she had to care for eleven children, and the sentence was lifted.[25] From this time on, she lived privately as a housewife, while her husband, similarly classified, convicted and then released after his sentence was commuted, entered the world of business through the Coca-Cola company. Scholtz-Klink published a self-exculpatory book on women in Nazi Germany and continued to maintain that the regime had been basically a good thing, especially for women. She eventually died in 1999, at the age of ninety-seven, unrepentant to the very end.[26]

Nazi Germany was full of people who bore grand-sounding but basically empty titles, so much so that a whole genre of humour developed making fun of them. *Reichsfrauenführerin*, Reich Women's Leader, was one such. As Claudia Koonz observed, 'Scholtz-Klink obeyed her superiors' orders without participating in any of the high-level discussions at which those orders were debated.' But this did not seem to worry her. 'It was the outward show of status that impressed her', as Koonz concluded.[27] Yet around half of the victims who were subjected by the regime to compulsory sterilization were women, while the other half, to state the obvious, were men, and they suffered just as much as women. Men and women could be victims in different, gendered ways, just as they could behave differently to one another as perpetrators. But the fact that the Third Reich was, at every level, even more male-supremacist than the society that gave rise to it did not mean that men were simply perpetrators and women simply victims.[28]

Gertrud Scholtz-Klink did not physically kill or torture anybody, nor did she commit acts of violence or preside over criminal institutions. She played no direct part in the formulation of the policies of genocide and warfare pursued by her masters. But, as the War Crimes Tribunal recognized, she was nonetheless a significant figure in the regime, helping to present it to millions of women, and, indirectly, through them, to men, as a benign social and political system whose negative side only affected a tiny minority of the population – Jews, Socialists, Communists, 'asocials', Gypsies, petty criminals and the like. Women's lives were not separate from those of men in Nazi Germany, nor did they provide their menfolk with an emotionally warm and supportive environment that allowed them to commit acts of violence based on a creed of hatred. The vast majority of women carried on with their lives, not just as guardians of the home but also in a whole range of roles in the world of work and, as the war progressed, the world of warfare as well. By 1944, some 450,000 young women were enrolled in the anti-aircraft defence system, and towards the end of the war, they were being armed and taught how to shoot. More prosaically, Scholtz-Klink and her organizations aimed above all to sustain the regime, popularize its policies, and support it to the end in its futile efforts to win the war. The image Scholtz-Klink purveyed after the war was a false one, covering up women's close involvement in the regime and effectively denying both its crimes and women's involvement in them.

21

The Star: Leni Riefenstahl

On 10 September 1939 the celebrated film star and director Leni Riefenstahl found herself in the Polish town of Lublinitz, shortly after it had been overrun by German troops. She had brought with her an officially authorized movie-camera unit. She was following Hitler with the intention of recording his first great military triumphs of World War II for a documentary along the lines of the films that had made her world-famous – *Triumph of the Will*, on the 1934 Nazi Party Rally in Nuremberg, and *Olympia*, on the 1936 Olympic Games in Berlin. The regional military commander in the area, General Erich von Manstein, was not best pleased. Some years later, in his memoirs, he described her arrival in the area, looking 'nice and dashing ... somewhat like an elegant Partisan, who might have obtained her costume from the rue de Rivoli in Paris ... She wore a kind of tunic, breeches and high, soft boots. From the leather belt that girded her hips there hung a pistol. The equipment for close combat was augmented by a knife sheathed in Bavarian fashion in her boot.' Despite his advice not to venture any further, she said she was under Hitler's orders to film at the front, and expressed a wish to continue with her film crew to Konskie, which Hitler himself had visited shortly before (hence her arrival in the town). Manstein felt it imprudent to refuse her request.[1] She arrived there on 11 September, just after German troops had found the dead bodies of a senior German police officer, three policemen and two German soldiers nearby. The German military put the blame for the killings on the local Jews, whom they rounded up on the market square the following day, ordering them to begin digging graves and attacking them with kicks and blows. Although the graves were intended for the assassinated Germans, the Jews were afraid they were for themselves, and became restive. When the army officer in command, Bruno Kleinmichel, fired a warning

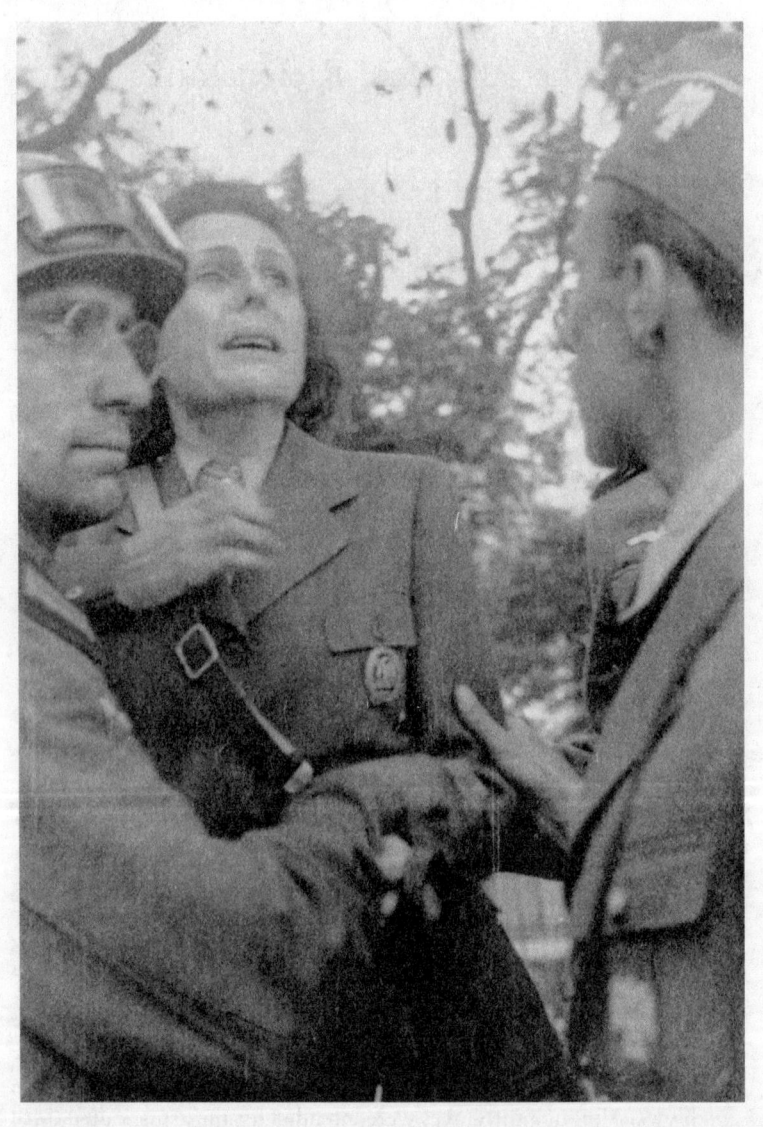

shot above their heads, the German soldiers panicked and fired indiscriminately into the mass of Jewish prisoners, killing nineteen and wounding many more.[2]

Leni Riefenstahl and her film crew always denied having witnessed this atrocity. But in the late 1940s a photograph emerged showing her with an anguished expression on her face, surrounded by soldiers on the town square, clearly upset by the brutal, senseless massacre. When confronted with the photo, she claimed it was taken as the soldiers were threatening her because she had protested against their manhandling of the Jewish prisoners. She claimed she had only heard the shots from afar. But the soldier in the photo is facing away from her, with a clearly concerned expression on his face. Another photo shows soldiers standing very close to her, in a position from which they could in no way have been threatening to shoot her. Manstein's memoirs confirmed her presence on the town square, so she had not heard the shots 'from afar'.[3] Similar evidence was provided by one of Manstein's staff officers at the general's trial in November 1949. At the time, indeed, Riefenstahl was sufficiently shocked at the killings to lodge a protest with the troops' commanding officer, General von Reichenau, who, as Manstein confirmed, sentenced Kleinmichel to two years in prison and degradation to the ranks. What Riefenstahl did not say, however, was that he was released only days later, following a general amnesty issued by Hitler on 4 October 1939, covering all antisemitic atrocities committed during the invasion of Poland. Nor did she mention in her memoirs the fact that the victims of the massacre were Jews; she only called them Poles. Finally, her claim to have been so shocked that she immediately abandoned her film project is undermined by evidence that she was still working on it at the end of September 1939. Only after this did it become clear to her that the material she had collected was in no way up to the challenge of making a film to match her earlier, triumphant projects of the 1930s.[4]

Riefenstahl's denial was part of a much broader undertaking, a determined and consistent attempt to distance herself from Nazism and convince the world that she was unpolitical, naïve perhaps, but no ideologue or fanatic. Born on 22 August 1902, she died over a century later, on 8 September 2003, so that the Nazi years only counted for a very small part of her very long life. She never formally joined the Nazi Party, and never took part in its political activities, hardly a surprising fact when one remembers the extent to which Hitler's movement was an expression of male supremacy and exclusivity. Her role was confined to her own field of technical expertise, movie-making, and did not stray beyond it. Subject to denazification proceedings after the war, she was classified, like so many others, as a 'fellow-traveller'. Interviewed late in life for a BBC documentary, she equated her life with that of the vast majority of ordinary Germans in the 1930s and early 1940s: 'I am one of millions who thought Hitler had all the answers. We saw only the good things, we didn't know bad things were to come.' This exculpatory pseudo-confession was itself a lie: even in 1933 the bad things were not just 'to come': Hitler's stormtroopers were already murdering Communists, Socialists and Jews on the streets of Berlin and other German cities, concentration-camp commandants and guards were already carrying out their brutal and sadistic business, Hitler was already shutting down democratic and civil freedoms, and preparations for the most destructive war in history were already under way. Dishonest in a different way was her claim that meeting Hitler 'was the biggest catastrophe of my life'. At the time, it did not seem like that: her encounter with Hitler made her one of the very few women to achieve a position of real prominence in the Third Reich.[5]

Riefenstahl first came into contact with Hitler on 27 February 1932, after the sight of posters plastered on walls and advertising columns all over Berlin advertising a speech he was to give at the Sportpalast to launch his campaign for the national Presidency prompted her 'spontaneously' to attend. After Hitler had kept the packed hall waiting for what seemed an age, the Nazi Party leader finally appeared. The audience sprang to their feet with shouts of 'Heil! Heil! Heil!' as he walked to the podium. Once the pandemonium had subsided, Hitler began to speak, addressing his listeners as 'racial comrades' (*'Volksgenossen, Volksgenossinen'*). And then, as Riefenstahl reported in her memoirs:

> Remarkably in the same moment I had an almost apocalyptic vision that I could never forget. It was as if the surface of the earth spread out before me – like a half-globe that suddenly split in the middle and from which an enormous stream of water poured out, so powerful that it touched the heavens and shook the earth. I was as if paralyzed ... No doubt, I was infected. Unexpected new thoughts shot through my head.[6]

It was the force of his personality rather than his intellectual or political message that penetrated Riefenstahl's emotional core and won her over to his cause, much in the way in which he had portrayed the relationship between the leader and the masses in *Mein Kampf*: 'The people are in their overwhelming majority so feminine in their disposition and inclination,' he declared, following a widespread contemporary belief in the essentially emotional mental constitution of the female sex, 'that their thought and action are less determined by sober reflection than by emotional feeling.'[7] He believed that in speaking to a crowd, he was manipulating a feminine collective body. 'Hitler,' his biographer Ian Kershaw has remarked, 'needed the orgasmic excitement which only the ecstatic masses could give him.'[8]

Riefenstahl always insisted that what had bowled her over was the man rather than his message. Claiming to be an unpolitical innocent, she had many Jewish friends, she said, and rejected the racist core of Hitler's ideology. What was decisive for her was his promise to end unemployment. His ideology she wrote off as an electoral ploy.[9] But like so much else in her memoirs, this was a deception. Harry R. Sokal, a Romanian-born producer with whom she worked on a number of films in the previous three years, starting in 1929, recalled many years later that one of them, *Das blaue Licht* (*The Blue Light*, 1932), had run into some harsh criticism from reviewers in the left-wing press, and 'Riefenstahl blamed Jewish film critics for ruining her career.' Angrily throwing the objectionable newspapers onto Sokal's desk, she shouted:

> How has it come to pass that I have allowed my work to be destroyed by these strangers, who can't understand our mentality or the life of our soul? Thank God, that won't last much longer! As soon as the Leader comes to power, these newspapers will only be permitted to write for their own people. They will appear in Hebrew!

She based this prophecy on Hitler's *Mein Kampf*, which according to Sokal she had already read before shooting for *Das blaue Licht* had begun, or in other words a year before she admitted in her memoirs that she had read it. In 1938 she managed to obtain a re-release of the movie, which was greeted by the now official Nazi press as a vindication of 'German' filmmaking over the carping reviews that had appeared in 1932 ('except for the few Aryan exceptions among the critics'). The name of her co-director, Béla Balász, a Jewish-Hungarian poet and filmmaker, was removed from the credits, as was that of Sokal himself, also Jewish.[10]

Riefenstahl came from the kind of conservative, Protestant, lower-middle-class background where antisemitism was a commonplace. Her father, Alfred, and his family were craftsmen and small businessmen, sober and hard-working, and the building boom around the turn of the century allowed his domestic-heating and ventilation company to prosper. The family moved upwards from the working-class Berlin district of Wedding into increasingly bourgeois locations, and were able to buy a small summer-house in rural Brandenburg, on the shores of a lake where the father spent a good deal of time fishing. In this milieu, the family could relax, far from the hustle and bustle of the big city, and, more importantly, from the irritable authoritarianism of the father. For Leni Riefenstahl herself, nature became a means of escape, providing time to think and, she recalled in her memoirs, dream. Her father's veneration of the early nineteenth-century nationalist, Friedrich Jahn, who saw in gymnastics a way to unite the nation and train it physically and spiritually for unity and independence, opened the way for her to learn to swim and to spend time in physical activities including roller-skating, ice-skating, swimming and of course gymnastics itself.[11] Alfred Riefenstahl's conservative German nationalism made him susceptible to the blandishments of Nazi ideology. In April 1933 he joined the Nazi Party, with immediately beneficial effects on his now failing business, new contracts, and later on official commissions from the state to build prisoner-of-war camps, for which he managed to recruit forced labourers from areas under German occupation. By this time, too, the family had moved house to a fashionable district in the western part of Berlin, sealing the rise through the ranks of society that had already begun before Leni Riefenstahl's birth.[12]

Her own ascent had been far more spectacular. Roller-skating led to an enthusiasm for dancing, and at the age of seventeen she enrolled in a ballet school, persisting in her ambition to become a professional dancer against the outraged objections of her father, who considered it far from respectable. Having begun her training when she was too old by the standards of classical ballet, she began to earn a living in modern dance, moving out of the family home into a Berlin apartment. With her earliest solo performances she won widespread acclaim from the press, and went on tour with a programme she put together herself, using only her own choreography.[13] Her career as a dancer came to an end after a short time as a result of a knee injury, but she quickly moved from one modern cultural milieu, the 'dancing craze' of the 1920s, into another – the movie industry, now expanding with breathtaking rapidity and constantly on the lookout for new talent. She had already been approached by Sokal, who was for a brief time her lover and rented an apartment in the same block as hers in Berlin. Soon she was acting in silent films, not the arthouse movies that made Weimar cinema famous across the globe, but romantic dramas set in the Alps, the specifically German genre of the *Bergfilm* (mountain film). Shot on location, foregrounding the natural environment, and featuring actors engaged in demanding activities such as skiing and climbing, they were the creations of the director Arnold Fanck. These films made an overwhelming impression on Riefenstahl when she first saw them in the cinema. Here was nature on a vastly grander scale than anything to be found in the environs of Berlin. Riefenstahl visited the Dolomites with Sokal, and introduced herself to Luis Trenker, the lead actor in *Berg des Schicksals* (*Mountain of Fate*), who was staying in the same hotel. To his astonishment, she announced that she would star in Fanck's next mountain movie.[14]

Women had so far hardly featured in the genre but, undaunted, Riefenstahl telephoned Fanck once she was back in Berlin, and succeeded in obtaining an interview with him. Impressed by the 'most beautiful woman in Europe', as he called her in a letter to Trenker, he offered her the part, most likely a condition of an offer from Sokal to cover a quarter of the production costs if he gave Riefenstahl star billing. Grasping at the opportunity, she had her knee operated on successfully, travelled to the Dolomites, and learned how to ski and climb. Not only did she fracture her ankle during training, there were other injuries in the team too, and the main financial backer, the UFA (*Universum Film-Aktien Gesellschaft*), Germany's biggest movie concern, threatened to pull out. While Fanck was in Berlin trying to persuade the company to change its mind, Riefenstahl resumed shooting, operating the camera herself, and sent the rushes to Berlin. UFA executives were persuaded, and *Der heilige Berg* (*The Holy Mountain*) was released in December 1926, with Riefenstahl playing the central character, the dancer and *femme fatale* Diotima, using her specially composed choreography and performing her own stunts. It was a public sensation. She shot to stardom overnight. A string of further *Bergfilme* followed. The world of moviemakers and critics continued, however, to regard Riefenstahl as a sportswoman, incorporating modern values of female independence and assertiveness, not as an actress capable of adapting her performance to the varied demands of different roles.[15]

Aware of these limitations, and conscious that the viewing public was becoming familiar enough with depictions of the Alps on the silver screen to find their repetition increasingly tedious, Riefenstahl decided to begin directing movies, after mastering the necessary techniques of filming, cutting, editing and all the rest through her years of close collaboration with Arnold Fanck. Her first film, *Das blaue Licht*, released on 24 March 1932, followed the *Bergfilm* genre but added a strong dose of mysticism. Filmed on location once more in the Dolomites, it centres on a supposed witch, played by Riefenstahl, who alone is able to climb a mountain and enter a mysterious grotto, while all the men who have tried have met their death in the attempt. When a man finally reaches the grotto, it is destroyed, and the witch leaps to her death. To portray the local peasants and craftsmen, Riefenstahl won the confidence and cooperation of the initially suspicious villagers in the area where she was shooting. Fanck played a significant part in editing the film, but whereas in his own movies he had done little more than present the *Bergfilm* as a synthesis of romantic love and physical adventure, Riefenstahl introduced the idea of nature as a source of ecstasy, a concept that had not only a personal meaning for her but also a wider significance that dovetailed with the Nazi ideology of 'blood and soil'. Hitler, who saw the film, particularly appreciated the use of supposedly unspoilt peasants as characters.[16]

It was this, and his knowledge that Riefenstahl was a well-known film star whose support would resonate strongly with the German public, that no doubt prompted Hitler to agree to see her, much to her surprise, when she wrote to him on 18 May 1932 to say how impressed she had been by his speech and the audience reaction in the Sportpalast a few weeks earlier, and asking if she could meet him. But Hitler was an enthusiast for movies, and an admirer of the film star ('the most beautiful thing I've ever seen in a film,' he had told a member of his staff even before her letter had arrived in his postbox, 'was Riefenstahl's dance by the sea in *The Holy Mountain*'). They met in Wilhelmshaven on 22–23 May 1932 and got on so well that Hitler, according to Riefenstahl's memoirs, said to her: '"Once we come to power, then you have to make my films."'[17] After her return from a lengthy shoot in Greenland for Fanck's new film *SOS Eisberg* (*SOS Iceberg*), she got in touch with

Hitler again, and soon she was his regular guest at public and private social occasions in Berlin. Now part of his inner circle, she made the acquaintance of leading Nazis such as Göring and Goebbels, and was a sympathetic listener when Hitler gave vent to his rage and despair at his 'betrayal' by Gregor Strasser when he resigned from his Party offices in December 1932. Soon it began to be rumoured that Hitler and Riefenstahl had embarked on an affair.[18]

In her memoirs, Riefenstahl sought to portray her relationship with Hitler as distant and professional. Her meeting with him had been 'fateful'. When she met him again it was 'through a coincidence'. If she got to know Goebbels and his wife, it was because they cultivated her. At one encounter, Goebbels even declared his love for her on bended knee. After Riefenstahl had turned him down (like Hitler, he was not exactly the kind of muscular, sporty man she favoured), Goebbels did his best to bring her together with his Party boss, but this too came to nothing. According to Riefenstahl's memoirs, Hitler tried to kiss her as they were walking together one evening, but like so much in her memoirs, however, these and other details about their relationship were very far from convincing. Riefenstahl's version was contradicted by a number of Hitler's acquaintances, including his Munich housekeeper, his manservant, and his secretary, all of whom recognized the hero-worship in her eyes as she gazed adoringly at him on private social occasions. However, all of them denied that their relationship was anything other than 'platonic'. Although they met privately far more frequently than Riefenstahl later admitted, they did not become sufficiently intimate to call each other by the second-person singular, *Du*, instead of the more formal plural, *Sie*, as Hitler did, for instance, with Winifred Wagner, the daughter-in-law of his favourite composer and manager of the Wagnerian shrine at Bayreuth. For Hitler, Riefenstahl functioned as part of the circle of cultural icons with which he liked to surround himself in a vicarious fulfilment of his early, frustrated wish to make a name for himself as an artist.[19]

Although her friendship with the Nazi leader was more than simply instrumental on her part – she used a period of illness following her return from Greenland to read *Mein Kampf*, and declared her enthusiasm for it – there was no doubt that it helped her career as a film director. Hitler appreciated that while her mountain movies were works of fiction, the fact that – unlike the overwhelming majority of films at the time – they were shot outside, on location, made her almost uniquely suited to create a documentary on a matching scale, vastly greater than that of the usual newsreel reports, carefully crafted to convey images that were overwhelming in their beauty and power. So he asked Riefenstahl to make a film of the Nazi Party rally, to be held in Nuremberg in the autumn of 1933, the first after the seizure of power. Despite the initial reluctance she described at length (and somewhat unconvincingly) in her memoirs, she eventually allowed Hitler's passionate entreaties to convince her. She was the only person, he said, capable of making a work of art of events, something the newsreels and the Ministry of Propaganda could never do. In addition, any film made of the 1933 Rally would be a 'talkie', the first to give Hitler's rhetorical talents their full due. With a small team of cameramen and technicians, Riefenstahl recorded the main events of the Rally, spending three months on editing her material into a coherent whole, and presented it to the public at a gala premiere on 1 December 1933 in Berlin, attended by Hitler, Goebbels and other prominent figures in the regime. *Sieg des Glaubens* (*Victory of Faith*) was a triumph, not least because of technical novelties such as the use of moving cameras, or the many close-ups of Hitler. But within a few months, all copies were withdrawn from circulation and destroyed: the 'Night of the Long Knives' on 30 June–1 July 1934 turned Ernst Röhm, who featured prominently in the film's action, almost as co-ruler with Hitler, into an unperson, to be deleted from the record as Stalin deleted Trotsky from his, while the emphasis on the supposed bond between the Nazi Party and the German people seemed to take the focus away from the personal dictatorship of the Führer solemnized after Hindenburg's death in August 1934. A copy of *Sieg des Glaubens* was only rediscovered in East Germany after the fall of the Berlin Wall in 1989.[20]

Riefenstahl was one of a number of cultural figures, like Albert Speer or Winifred Wagner, whom Hitler co-opted into his private circle, bypassing the elaborate monopoly created by Goebbels through the Reich Chamber of Culture. Goebbels was not best pleased, especially since his preference was for propaganda films that adopted a softly-softly approach rather than the direct, 'in-your-face' style of Riefenstahl's film. In her memoirs, she built this difference of opinion into an antagonism far greater than it really was, ascribing Goebbels's alleged hostility to the fact that she had rebuffed his advances some time before the

Nazis came to power. But there is no independent evidence by which this claim can be supported, while Goebbels must have recognized early on that Riefenstahl enjoyed Hitler's full backing, and the concept of propaganda that her films embodied was fundamentally his. In fact, Goebbels's diaries reveal strong support for her project going back to May 1933, and it was through him that she came to enter Hitler's inner circle. A more genuine obstacle was the irritation of established documentary filmmakers, who objected to the fact that Riefenstahl was a woman muscling in on what they saw as the masculine world of Nazi propaganda. Hints were spread that she was Jewish, and it was even rumoured that her life was in danger from enemies among the Brownshirts. Hitler's support, however, trumped all these (real or supposed) threats and ensured her bid to make the replacement film, centred on the Nuremberg Party Rally of 1934, was successful.[21]

Riefenstahl was conscious that the relatively meagre resources devoted to her film of the 1933 Party Rally meant that it had failed at many points to live up to her expectations. She secured from Hitler almost limitless resources to make the new one – from Nazi Party funds rather than from more conventional movie-industry sources. Preparations for filming went hand in hand with preparations for the Rally itself. Special cameras were installed at key points, and a small electric elevator was attached to one of the 38-metre-high flagpoles on the parade ground so that a cameraman could film the events from above. The crew of 170 included 36 cameramen, 17 lighting operatives, and 9 men for aerial shots. Hitler himself picked the title – *Triumph des Willens* (*Triumph of the Will*), denoting both his willpower and the German people's, claimed by Rudolf Hess at the film's climax to be identical with one another – but otherwise left Riefenstahl to get on with things. It took Riefenstahl and her team many months to edit the 128,000 metres of film collected in the week-long Rally down to the 2,000 metres needed for the final two-hour movie. A few interior shots were unsatisfactory, so at Riefenstahl's request Hitler ordered them to be repeated in the studio, including even some of the speeches. Released on 28 March 1935, the film portrayed the apotheosis of Hitler as Führer, striding alone along a broad alley between massive, anonymous blocks of stormtroopers and SS men, or shot in isolation from below, against a backdrop of clouds, as he worked himself up into an emotional climax in his final speech, or, at the beginning, descending in an aircraft onto Nuremberg like a god coming down from Heaven. The film was a huge success, winning not only, predictably enough, the German National Film Prize but also top prizes at the Venice film festival and the Paris World Exposition (accompanied by street demonstrations against the choice).[22]

The often breathtaking technical and directorial innovations on display in *Triumph of the Will*, as well as her own reputation as a sportswoman, made Riefenstahl the obvious choice to film the 1936 Olympic Games, which the International Olympic Committee had decided five years before – or in other words, still under the Weimar Republic – would be held in Berlin. Initially hesitant, Hitler had eventually realized that the Games could offer an unparalleled opportunity to advertise the new Germany across the world. Antisemitic signs, advertisements and newspapers were banished from the city, vagrants and the down-and-out were taken off the streets, and a couple of half-Jewish *Mischlinge* were even found to represent Germany in the events.[23] Although Riefenstahl later claimed to have been commissioned by the International Olympic Committee, which in 1932 had introduced a requirement for the host country to film the Games, and to have been financed independently, in fact this was another of her inventions, for she was commissioned personally by Hitler, with the support of Goebbels, and was financed by the Reich. Given the enormous costs involved – 2.8 million Reichsmarks – it could hardly be otherwise. Hitler gave Riefenstahl carte blanche to make the film as she wished, and forbade any third-party interference. Her team grew to over 300 people, who undertook preparations over a period of several months, experimenting with new kinds of film, filters, lighting and other equipment. She had trenches and towers built to create fresh camera angles, tracks along which moving cameras were propelled, and airships, including the famous *Hindenburg*, for aerial photography. Other innovations included slow-motion and underwater filming. Everything was tried and tested, prepared for unforeseen eventualities such as rainstorms, and adapted to the peculiarities of each of the 136 different kinds of sport on display, thoroughly researched in advance by Riefenstahl and her team.[24]

The film stressed, not least through its extended opening sequence, the links between the twentieth-century Games and their model in Ancient Greece, implicitly claiming that the Nazi ideals of physical strength and beauty were rooted in antiquity, incorporating what the Third Reich proclaimed to be the supreme racial type. Scenes featuring mass gymnastics suggested a society perfectly regimented and coordinated.[25] It was for the 1936 Olympics that the idea of lighting the Olympic Flame at the site of the original Games with sunlight focused through a lens and having it carried to the modern venue was invented, and Riefenstahl made sure this was filmed as well. But while it was far less overtly propagandistic than *Triumph of the Will*, there is no doubt that *Olympia* also served the purposes of the Nazi regime, not least by purporting to show a Germany that was peaceful, well organized, efficient, and friendly to all nations and races. Hitler even used the fact that the film was made by a woman to claim in an interview with a foreign journalist that women had equal rights in the Third Reich.[26] *Olympia* made no distinction between races, indeed, and Riefenstahl insisted (over Goebbels's objections) on showing the Black American sprinter Jesse Owens winning his four Gold Medals. Nevertheless, the filming did not pass off without controversy, as officials and athletes complained about the obtrusiveness of some of the enormous cameras and the distractions they caused, while Riefenstahl's peremptory demands of the press corps, to stay seated during some of the filming, or to avoid breaching her exclusive right to film the events, caused a good deal of irritation, as did the prominence the director gave herself in the process (she even appeared as a dancer in the opening sequence). Goebbels was outraged by the length of time she claimed for the editing process – two full years – and in the end she had to call in Hitler to put an end to his interference. Once she had completed the gargantuan task of editing more than 400,000 metres of film down to 6,000, to be shown in two parts, Riefenstahl won Hitler's approval for the premiere to take place on his birthday, 20 April 1938. A few weeks earlier, German forces had invaded Austria, and Hitler had incorporated the country into the Reich, sealing the *Anschluss* with a plebiscitary 'yes' vote on 10 April, for which Riefenstahl offered her enthusiastic and very public support.[27]

Olympia was an enormous triumph, even more so than the more overtly political *Triumph des Willens*. The huge sums of money invested in it were quickly earned back. It was the high point of her career. She embarked on a tour of America to promote the film. But no sooner had she begun her tour than the murderous and destructive antisemitic pogrom popularly known as the *Reichskristallnacht* broke out across the Reich, on 9–10 November 1938. Regarded as Hitler's cultural ambassador, Riefenstahl was boycotted in America and her film could not be shown there. It was the beginning of a sharp decline in her fortunes. With the coming of the war, Hitler had little time for her any more. Her intention of making a documentary focusing on Hitler and the war came to nothing. She began making a new movie, first mooted as far back as 1934, this time fiction rather than documentary: *Tiefland* (*Lowlands*), despite its title another *Bergfilm*. It built on an obscure opera much prized by Hitler, but the film could not be finished until after the war, when it got into trouble because of Riefenstahl's use of gypsy (Sinti and Roma) prisoners from a concentration camp as extras. Later, she denied knowing that they were ultimately destined to be gassed in Auschwitz; indeed, she denied knowing about the atrocities committed in the camps altogether. On its release in 1954 *Tiefland* was criticized as out of date – the *Bergfilme* belonged now to a fairly remote past – and Riefenstahl herself, playing the main female protagonist, was widely seen as too old for the part. Attempts to portray the film as a coded act of resistance to Nazism were neither borne out by Riefenstahl's past career nor by the film itself.[28]

Riefenstahl was subjected after the war to a series of denazification investigations, but was classified merely as a 'fellow-traveller'. She had never joined the Nazi Party. She found it impossible to accept that Hitler, a man she thought she had known well, was responsible for the Holocaust. To the end of her days she portrayed herself as a political innocent, just a filmmaker, free from ideological ties and commitments. *Sieg des Glaubens*, *Triumph des Willens* and *Olympia*, she declared, were unpolitical documentaries, movies that did nothing more than chronicle and observe the events they were recording. She had always remained entirely independent as an artist.[29] In the 1960s she became widely known again for a series of spectacular photographic studies in which she recorded the way of life of the Nuba, a tribe living in a remote part of Sudan, people she regarded as part of the natural world, without history or politics.[30] Later still, she turned to underwater filming, recording the beauty of coral reefs and their colourful inhabitants. These new projects increasingly seemed to relativize her close involvement with the Third Reich, and underpinned a renewed interest in her work, focusing on her undoubted technical achievements, drawing attention away from the services they had rendered to Nazi ideology, and laying the groundwork for acceptance of her self-presentation as no more than a professional documentary filmmaker. To many, her survival into extreme old age rendered the work she had done in her thirties increasingly remote, criticism of it increasingly pointless in the light of her later, supposedly less political projects. To those who took an interest in her early films, she presented a heavily doctored account that wrote Jewish members of her team back into the story after she had carefully written them out during the Nazi years.[31]

This process of rehabilitation was rudely interrupted by the American critic Susan Sontag in a brilliant essay published on 6 February 1974 in the *New York Review of Books* under the title 'Fascinating Fascism'. Sontag saw Riefenstahl's entire corpus of work as a single example of fascist aesthetics in action. The *Bergfilme* were 'an anthology of proto-Nazi sentiments', focusing on a wild, primitive creature (the central figure in *Das blaue Licht*) who alone could scale a mountain that in Sontag's interpretation symbolized the nation. In this movie, and in the later *Tiefland*, the mountains, with their clear light and pure white snow, threw into sharp relief the corrupt civilization of the lowlands. The condemnation of modern civilization central to these movies resurfaced in the glorification of physical strength in her work on the 'primitive' Nuba, who, like Hitler's SS, Riefenstahl wrote, 'look upon death as simply a matter of fate'. Celebrating physical perfection here and in her Nazi documentaries, Riefenstahl pushed the sick, the ill and the old, not to mention the female sex, out of the picture, just as Hitler marginalized them all in Nazi society. Sontag even drew a line from the black-clad SS soldiers whose marching dominates the closing scenes of *Triumph of the Will* to the fetishization of Nazism in the underworld of sadomasochistic sex. What she drew out above all, however, were the continuities in Riefenstahl's work, from the 1920s through to the end of the century, exploding the myth that her portrayal of a black African tribe somehow constituted a kind of expiation for her earlier portrayal of Nazi rituals in the Nuremberg Party Rallies.[32]

Leni Riefenstahl was a complex and ambivalent figure. She was more than just an example of a German politically seduced by Hitler; she was more, indeed, than an amoral careerist who focused on getting to the top of her chosen profession and didn't care how she did it. She was obsessive about her art, but her art was itself highly political, serving the interests and purposes of the regime in the 1930s and purveying a message after 1945 that would not have been out of place in the Third

Reich were it not for the fact that the Nuba project focused on Black men, whom the Nazis wrote off as subhuman: Hitler, indeed, would have been horrified. Riefenstahl was not a fanatical Nazi, but she willingly served those who were. And her persistent, retrospective editing of her life and career after 1945 to make it seem harmless and unpolitical fails to convince. Yet perhaps Sontag went too far in claiming Riefenstahl's work was all 'fascist'; what was striking was how much of it, including the great Nazi propaganda films, was the product of Riefenstahl's own independent aesthetic judgement. From start to finish, over an extraordinarily long period, her work had a striking consistency, reflecting cultural attitudes towards the natural world, the human body, physical prowess, the mystical celebration of masculinity in the individual and the group, that fitted effortlessly into the ideology of the Nazi Party.

22
The Denunciator: Luise Solmitz

Nazism succeeded not least because it appealed to wide sectors of German society. Not all Germans by any means bought into the whole range of its ideas, promises and practices. But enough of them did to ensure that the Third Reich continued for well over a decade in power. Thanks to the pioneering researches of Ian Kershaw and many others, we know a great deal about the nature of Hitler's appeal, how it differed from one sector of society to another, and how it changed over time.[1] To focus on those who remained 'Hitler's true believers' from start to finish may give a misleading impression. In particular, there were many Germans who were not fanatical Nazis but supported Nazism because it put into practice a sufficient range of their desires and aspirations for them to discount the other aspects of its ideology for which they felt less enthusiasm. Conservative nationalists from Franz von Papen downwards supported Hitler and his regime despite the numerous reservations they held about them. The stability of the Third Reich indeed depended on this broad range of support from outside the Nazi Party, as well as on the regime's ruthless repression of real and potential opposition. At the same time, many sectors of society, both at the time and afterwards, did not see themselves as 'perpetrators' or supporters of Hitler. This final chapter focuses on one such individual, a conservative nationalist who represented millions of such silent supporters, people who were prepared on occasion to assist Hitler and his people in sustaining the dictator's rule, if necessary by joining in its repression of dissent and opposition. One such was Luise Solmitz, a Hamburg schoolteacher, born in 1889. Her story illustrates some of the complexities and contradictions of ordinary middle-class Germans in the period of the Third Reich, their willingness to go along with the regime for most of its period, and some of the reasons for their

eventual disillusion with it. They too were perpetrators in a sense. Luise Solmitz kept a diary from 1905 onwards, filling one 700-page notebook with closely spaced lines of tiny, crabbed handwriting every year. She continued to write at the same pace and intensity throughout the following decades, making her diaries one of the most voluminous and detailed sources we have for everyday life in Germany in the first half of the twentieth century, rivalling the comparable, though very different diaries of Joseph Goebbels or Victor Klemperer in scope and scale. In December 1953 Luise donated her diaries to the Hamburg State Archive as an historical record, but a year later she found that she could not bear to be without them and retrieved them for her private use. She donated them again in 1967, but took them back home once more three months later, keeping them until her death in 1973 at the age of eighty-four. In the 1960s the Research Centre for the History of National Socialism in Hamburg secured her agreement to come in every day and dictate from the diaries for 1918–45 to a shorthand typist, since they were virtually illegible to anyone apart from herself. The transcripts form only a relatively small selection from the huge archive: the then director of the Research Centre, Werner Jochmann, published some passages in a book of documents on the Nazi seizure of power in Hamburg, and some have also appeared in anthologies of diary extracts. All the transcripts contain omissions and amendments, often with the aim of toning down some of Solmitz's originally more emotional and enthusiastic endorsements of Nazism. Recent research, above all by Beate Meyer, has helped uncover these changes and direct attention back to the original text.[2]

Luise Solmitz (née Stephan) was born on 25 May 1889 on the border between Hamburg and the contiguous urban community of Altona. Her parents were successful traders in household goods, with enough money to send her for a year to a boarding school in England and another in France, giving her a broader experience than most people of her background and class. The family frequently discussed politics at home, and while Luise imbibed the conservative-nationalist and antisemitic views of her father, her younger brother Werner (born in 1895) gravitated towards left-wing liberalism, becoming a prominent spokesperson for the German Democratic Party during the Weimar Republic. Luise was educated in a *Höhere Tochterschule*, a kind of elevated finishing school, then trained as a teacher. In 1912 she met Friedrich Solmitz, a military engineer, born in 1877. The two fell in love and began an affair which survived his war service and produced a child, Gisela, born in 1920. Friedrich, however, refused to marry Luise, and she moved to Berlin to stay with her brother for a year, away from the prying eyes of friends, family and neighbours in Altona. Shortly after returning home, she married a well-off acquaintance, Oskar Zipperling, in order to legitimize and provide for her daughter, since returning to her professional life as a teacher was out of the question. However, her relationship with Friedrich Solmitz continued, and when he pressed for recognition of his paternal rights over Gisela, she obtained a divorce from Zipperling, helped once more by her brother Werner, and married Friedrich Solmitz on 23 April 1925.[3]

This unconventional behaviour was largely a consequence of the fact that Friedrich Solmitz was concealing a secret: he was Jewish, his mother and brother having converted to Christianity shortly after his father's death in 1881 and joined the Protestant Evangelical Church. Conservative and nationalist in politics, Friedrich had refused to propose to Luise because he did not want to saddle his children with the burden of Jewish ancestry. He had not even informed Luise of his background, but Gisela's birth made this reservation redundant. Friedrich had joined the German air force in the war, but was badly wounded in a plane crash, from which he only slowly recovered. After the war, now a decorated ex-officer, he became a freelance engineering consultant, making enough money for the family to live comfortably and even to employ a maid-of-all-work at home. They built a social circle that included numerous conservative nationalists, and joined a range of right-wing voluntary associations including a society for the protection of the German language, in whose name Friedrich frequently wrote letters to the press complaining about the use of non-German words in articles and reports.

With this background, it is not surprising that Luise became a supporter of Hitler as he rose to prominence. Her diaries for the final years of the Weimar Republic show in dramatic detail how Hitler and the Nazis were able to overcome the initial doubts and hesitations of the German middle classes and win them over to their cause. An admirer of Hindenburg, the embodiment of Prussian, Protestant and military values, she was strongly critical of Catholic Centre Party politicians like Reich Chancellor Heinrich Brüning. She was concerned both by the Nazis' street violence in the early 1930s, and by what she saw as their 'socialist' tendencies. Temperamentally inclined to vote for the German National People's Party, she was nonetheless swept away by Hitler's rhetoric when she went to hear him at a rally in Hamburg in April 1932, and overjoyed when he was appointed head of a conservative-dominated coalition Cabinet on 30 January 1933. Nationalists of all hues had joined together to restore national pride, she thought. 'Nat(ional) soc(ialist) élan, Ger(man) nat(ionalist) reason, the unpolitical Steel Helmets, a(nd) Papen, unforgotten by us.'[4] Taking part in a torchlit parade on 6 February 1933, she confessed herself 'as if drunk with enthusiasm'. She recorded the massed ranks of uniformed Nazi stormtroopers chanting 'The Republic is shit'. She took Gisela along so that 'she would and had to feel for once what Fatherland means'. '"Juda, perish!," was also shouted out, amid songs about Jewish blood that must spurt from the knife.' 'Who took that seriously then?', she added as she dictated the entry decades later.[5]

As the Nazis consolidated their power, Luise continued to record her approval, welcoming the emergence of Hitler as a 'strongman' and applauding the dictatorial measures taken in the wake of the Reichstag fire on 27 February 1933, which she agreed – following Nazi propaganda – had been part of a Communist plot to bring about a Soviet Germany by violent revolution. Her reaction to the elaborate ceremonial of the 'Day of Potsdam' on 21 March 1933, as Hitler offered a symbolic obeisance to the Prussian monarchical tradition, was little short of ecstatic ('The great, unforgettably beautiful German day!'); she wept with joy as she contemplated the spectacle.[6] More than this, she so disapproved of her brother Werner's liberalism that she decided to denounce him to the authorities out of a feeling of loyalty to the regime and duty as a citizen. She copied politically incriminating extracts from his letters to her into a dossier which she handed to the *Fichte-Bund*, a Hamburg-based organization engaged in propaganda against foreign criticism of Germany – both Luise and Friedrich Solmitz were members before it was incorporated into the Propaganda Ministry by Joseph Goebbels. She showed no sympathy for Werner's situation as the prospect of his continuing to work under the new regime was clearly endangered, preferring, as she wrote in her diary, to betray her brother rather than betray Hitler, who was the absolute incarnation of Germany. Werner had after all been engaged in stirring up anti-Nazi sentiment abroad. She felt extremely guilty about her actions, and agonized about them in the privacy of her diary. Denunciations were common enough, and often led to serious consequences for those who were denounced, but fortunately for all involved, her dossier did not go any further. Had she sent in her denunciation to the Gestapo, as many people did, the results would have been different, since the police always followed up on the information they received. Werner was so prized as a skilled and experienced propagandist in any case that Goebbels kept him in his position, now working for the Propaganda Ministry rather than against it, until the very end. People had many reasons for denouncing their fellow citizens to the authorities, and they did not necessarily include approval of the regime – they were commonly enough purely personal in nature. Indeed, Luise Solmitz was somewhat unusual in the ideological reasons for her behaviour. It showed, however, that even people who were not active Nazis could feel an approval of the regime that was strong enough for them to betray their own close relatives, with consequences that might have included arrest, beating, confinement to a concentration camp or even death.[7]

Yet Luise Solmitz was not entirely uncritical of the Nazi regime. She thought the antisemitic violence of the stormtroopers was excessive and unnecessary – by this time, she was fully aware of her husband's Jewish ancestry. Her worries about the 'socialist' tendencies of the regime, typical of Germany's conservative nationalist elites, came to the fore again when it began to confiscate the assets of Jews like Albert Einstein who had emigrated: it undermined the concept of private property, she thought, fearing there would be 'Bolshevism without it'. By contrast, she had no reservations about Hitler's violent assault on the leadership of the stormtroopers, and on various former rivals with whom he had scores to settle, in the 'Night of the Long Knives' on 30 June 1934, when dozens were shot in cold blood without so much as a semblance of legality – though such a semblance was quickly supplied retrospectively. She implicitly believed Hitler's declaration that the victims had been plotting a violent revolution, and was shocked by the revelation that some of them had been homosexuals. Hitler's 'personal courage . . . decisiveness and effectiveness' were unique, she gushed, worthy of Frederick the Great or Napoleon. Like many other middle-class Germans, she was willing to accept almost any measure taken by the Nazis if it could be justified in terms of maintaining order and warding off the threat of revolution.

Luise never joined the Nazi Party, but she did show her enthusiasm for the regime in a number of ways. Nazism, she wrote on 27 April 1933, meant 'no more class struggle, or Marxism, religious antagonisms – only Germany – in Hitler'. Her support intensified still further as Hitler began to chalk up major foreign-policy successes that restored Germany, in her view, to its former international greatness. Hitler's announcement that he was reintroducing military conscription was the source of enormous satisfaction to Luise. As she wrote on 16 March 1935, this was 'the day that we have longed for since the disgrace of 1918'. When the announcement came over the radio, she reported, 'I rose to my feet. It overcame me, the moment was too great. I had to listen standing.' A year later, on 7 March 1936, she was 'completely overpowered' with emotion as German troops marched into the Rhineland to reclaim it for Germany after years of formal demilitarization imposed by the Treaty of Versailles. She was 'delighted by . . . the greatness of Hitler and the power of his language, the force of this man.' He was, she wrote in a series of jubilant entries on 11–13 March 1938 following the German annexation of Austria, 'a man who fears nothing, knows no compromises, hindrances or difficulties'. She filled page after page of her diary with a blow-by-blow narrative of events as they unfolded, recording 'world history, the fulfilment of my old German dream, a truly united Germany . . . It's all like a dream, one is completely torn away from one's own world and from oneself.'

Luise and her war veteran husband were keen to play their part in the new Germany. From 1935, for instance, as the regime began to encourage people to use Germanic names for the months of the year instead of the traditional Latinate ones, Luise began to record her diary entries under headings such as *Julmond*, *Brechmond* and so on. Already in 1933, when the regime set up the new post of Air Raid Protection League Block Warden, Friedrich volunteered at once, and soon found himself touring the houses and apartments blocks in his locality getting the inhabitants to make preparations and carry out exercises for the bombing raids which the Nazis feared might come at some future date, when the European war they were working towards had begun. Before long, however, he found himself in difficulties. The 'Aryan Paragraph' to which all such organizations had to subscribe forbade Jews from taking office in them, and Friedrich conscientiously applied it in relation to others, despite the fact that, unknown to his fellow members of the Air

Raid Protection League, he himself did not qualify for membership. But it proved impossible to keep his Jewish ancestry secret, given that a certificate of Aryan descent was required for many different purposes in the Third Reich. Showing complete incomprehension of the situation, Friedrich even complained in a letter to the local Nazi Party chief, copied into the pages of his wife's manuscript diary for 1934, that he had to encounter persistent and open hostility from the other members of the Air Raid Protection League, to such a degree that he eventually felt he had no option but to resign.

Neither Friedrich nor Luise Solmitz felt any affinity with Germany's Jewish community at all: as she wrote in her diary on 15 September 1935, 'most people, or many, still reject Jewry, like I do; they have no relation to that side, and they don't want any. Have never had any, don't know any Jewish people.' Luise, indeed, approved of the Nazi government's measures restricting the rights of *Ostjuden*' (Jewish immigrants from Eastern Europe). The couple were classified under the Nuremberg Laws as living in a 'privileged mixed marriage', because Luise was not Jewish and they were bringing their daughter Gisela up in the Christian faith. Nevertheless, Friedrich, much to his chagrin, was excluded from membership of the Nazi Officers' Association and the Steel Helmets veterans' movement, he lost his citizenship rights, and he and his wife were obliged to lower the Nazi flag they had proudly raised above their residence in 1933. Their daughter was classified as 'mixed-race of the first degree' and was not allowed to marry a non-Jewish German, matriculate at a university, or do many of the other things that young middle-class German girls of her age expected to be able to do. The family were particularly bitter about the fact that she could not join the League of German Girls, the Nazi youth organization to which virtually every non-Jewish German girl of her age belonged.

So outraged were the Solmitzes at being treated in this way that on 8–9 March 1936 they wrote a personal letter of protest to Hitler himself. On 17 September they received a reply from a junior official: no exceptions could be made to the law, not even in their case. Worse was to come. On 10 November 1938, the morning after the nationwide orgy of antisemitic violence known in popular parlance as *Reichskristallnacht*, the 'Night of Broken Glass', the Solmitzes were visited by two Gestapo officers, following up on Hitler's personal order to arrest 30,000 Jewish men and take them off to concentration camps until they promised to emigrate. The retired major silently showed them his gallantry medals from the First World War, and the officers relented. All Jews had to surrender any weapons they might possess, however, so with great reluctance Friedrich handed them his sword ('touched in honour, surrendered in shame'). To add insult to injury, the Nazi authorities levied a huge fine on Germany's Jewish community to pay for the damage caused by rampaging stormtroopers in the pogrom. Here too, however, Friedrich's military record came to his aid. Did he not wish to emigrate? he was asked. 'I am an old officer, born in Germany, and will die in Germany too,' he replied. Impressed at his steadfast demeanour, the Nazi finance officials suggested that he make over all his assets to his non-Jewish wife, thus allowing them to evade the levy and escape the expropriation that was now looming over the property of other German Jews. From 1 January 1939 Friedrich's official identity papers had to carry the additional first name *Israel*, as did those of all German Jews – 'the dishonouring, depressing additional name', as Luise called it in her diary on 14 September 1938, not long after the measure had been announced. None of this, astonishingly enough, prevented Friedrich from volunteering for military service during the Munich crisis in 1938, an offer that was brusquely declined by an unsympathetic official.[8]

Gradually Luise's anger and fear at her husband and daughter's worsening situation began to cast a shadow over her enthusiasm for the Third Reich. Her own life was made more difficult by the fact that the couple were no longer permitted to employ an 'Aryan' servant. Their social circle began to shrink as non-Jewish citizens were either banned from mixing with them or backed away voluntarily. In March 1938, amid the excitement of the *Anschluss* of Austria, she found it difficult to 'recall that one is excluded from the people's community oneself like a criminal or degraded person'. Now her concern about the prospect of war began to underpin her increasingly critical stance. Like many other Germans, perhaps even the majority, the Solmitzes were deeply worried about the possible effects on Germany of a general European war, and, as one loomed, so they became ever more anxious. The spectre of mass bombing raids on German cities was particularly horrifying. Luise's admiration for Hitler was based not least on the fact that all his foreign-policy successes up to 1939 had been carried off without bloodshed. Now, on 29 August 1939, as it became clear that a general war was going to break out over the imminent German invasion of Poland, she asked despairingly: 'Who is going to help tortured humanity away from war to peace? Easy to answer: Nothing and no one.' They were entering a time, she felt, 'in comparison to which the 30 Years' War was a Sunday School outing'.

Yet after a few months, during which air-raid warnings were more an inconvenience than anything else, German military successes in East and West brought back her old nationalist pride and confidence once more. A high point was reached with the defeat of France: 'A grand, grand day for the German people,' she wrote in her diary on 17 June 1940 on hearing the announcement that the French leader Marshal Pétain was suing for peace: 'We were all exhilarated by happiness and enthusiasm.' The victory was 'an unbelievably great national change of fortune, the fulfilment of long-held nationalist dreams'. In comparison with this, the daily cares of wartime, which had dominated her diary up to this point, faded into the background. Only when she remembered the petty persecution to which her Jewish husband Friedrich and their daughter Gisela were subject, did she pause for thought: 'The successes are so tremendous that the shadow cast by this light is becoming ever darker and more threatening.'

She had reached a point where her nationalist euphoria at Hitler's success seemed almost perfectly balanced by her gloom and despondency about the effects of his antisemitic policies on her family. From this moment onwards, indeed, as the regime ratcheted up its persecution of the Jews, the negative aspects of living in Hitler's Germany began to occupy more and more space in Luise's diary. From September 1941, Jews in Germany were obliged by law to wear the 'Jewish star', black against a yellow cloth background, on their clothing when they were in public. Friedrich's privileged status as the war-decorated husband of a non-Jew, and as someone who was bringing up a daughter as a Christian meant, however, that he was spared this indignity. Luise recorded bitterly on 13 September 1941: 'Our luck is now negative – everything that doesn't affect us.' They had no sympathy with the Jewish community as it underwent ever greater privations: they continued to think that there was no reason why they, as patriotic Germans, should share them. When the regime pushed discrimination a stage further by ordering Jews to share accommodation with each other – a halfway house to ghettoization – the Solmitzes secured a ruling from the Gestapo that people in privileged mixed marriages such as theirs were not obliged to provide accommodation to any Jews. They breathed another sigh of relief.[9]

Cuts in pensions, benefits and rations they shared with other Germans. Otherwise they lived much as they had done before, though necessarily more privately, since Friedrich was effectively barred from taking part in the social life of the non-Jewish circles in which they had previously moved. As the Gestapo began to deport Germany's remaining Jews to the East, to ghettos and eventually to extermination camps, however, Luise was not without a degree of sympathy when recording the very public round-ups in Hamburg's streets. 'The whole of Hamburg is filled with the deportation or the removal even of the oldest people,' she noted. An acquaintance reported that 'whooping children had accompanied the removal' of one group of Jews, although Luise herself had never witnessed such behaviour. 'Once more, Jews have gone to Warsaw,' she reported on 14 July 1942: 'I found confirmation of this in the rubbish-bins outside their home, which were full to the brim with the miserable remains of their few possessions, with coloured tin cans, old bedside lamps, torn handbags. Children were rummaging about in them, cheering, making an indescribable mess.' Fear that the same fate might befall her husband must surely have been a factor in stimulating the interest in the deportations that led her to record them in her diary.

The family's situation deteriorated steadily as the war went on. Luise and her husband gradually lost weight as food supplies became shorter. By 21 December 1942 she weighed 96 pounds. Yet her worry about changes in rationing arrangements was not so much that their diet would become even more restricted, but that she would for some reason be banned from collecting the family's ration cards, thus obliging Friedrich to go to the ration office himself as a Jew, with his 'evil, impossible epithet' imposed by the government ('Israel'), and queue 'amidst all the people who one has never had anything to do with', or in other words Hamburg's remaining, old, poor and virtually destitute population of Jews. Her concern for the safety of her half-Jewish daughter Gisela grew as rumours circulated that people classified as mixed-race were to be deported. 'We are already the playthings of dark and malicious powers,' Luise recorded gloomily in her diary on 24 November 1942.

Only once did Friedrich Solmitz fall foul of the police. The shortage of labour in the German war economy, caused not least by the repeated call-ups of workers to serve at the front, led to rapidly increasing numbers of foreign workers being drafted in, voluntarily at first, then by force, to work in Germany's factories and mines. There were so many foreign workers in Hamburg by the summer of 1943, Luise noted in her diary, that there was 'a confused babel of languages wherever you hear people speaking':

> In the meantime, Fr.[iedrich] saw a miserable procession of foreign workers in the Ostmark Street: blonde girls, young people, amongst them unmistakeable Asiatics, old people, staggering under their burden, without an Eastern smile, loaded down with their meagre possessions, close to dying from exhaustion. 'Get down off the pavement, you bandits!'

Such sympathy was not unknown, even though, as Luise's reference to 'Asiatics' suggests, German people frequently felt a sense of racial superiority over Soviet prisoners and forced labourers. When, a few months later, he gave some food to a starving forced labourer, Friedrich Solmitz was denounced anonymously to the police and arrested by the Gestapo; but, perhaps once more thanks to his military bearing and background, he escaped with nothing more than a warning.

The presence of foreign labourers in Germany had a far more direct effect on the Solmitz family, however, when Gisela fell in love with a Belgian man working as a volunteer in a Hamburg factory and they decided to marry. At the Registry Office, an official told Luise that the Reich Ministry of Justice had turned down the couple's application to marry, adding:

> 'Do the young man's parents know that your daughter is a half-breed of the first grade? I'm sure they've given their consent, but do they know that?' – 'Belgium doesn't recognize such laws or such views.' – 'What do you mean, "Belgium"? Today we don't even use the term "Germany". We think: "Europe". No Jew is to remain in Europe. This is my personal view – not the official one, but I notice it from signs that the Jews will be dealt with even more severely than before.' He said that to me twice. And there I sat, defenceless. 'Look,' he continued to lecture me, 'at what the Jews have done in Russia, in America. Now we're noticing it for the first time.'

When Luise made so bold as to mention her Jewish husband, the official was thoroughly taken aback. 'Your husband is still here?!' he exclaimed in disbelief.[10]

The bombing raids that the Solmitzes had so feared at the outbreak of war in 1939 were beginning to have a real impact on everyday life by the middle of 1942. Hamburg was within relatively easy range of British bombers, and as Germany's second city, with dockyards, shipbuilding facilities and munitions factories, an obvious target. The first major raids carried out were aimed at the nearby Hanseatic town of Lübeck, with its narrow streets and combustible wooden buildings. Luise recorded the raid impersonally in her diary, as if this was a natural disaster or an act of God. 'We are no longer in control of our fate, we are forced to allow ourselves to be driven by it and to take what comes without confidence or hope,' she wrote resignedly on 8 September 1942. The destruction of Lübeck saddened her, but at the same time she also recorded with horror, and a characteristic piece of racial reasoning, the bombing of York and Norwich in the revenge 'Baedeker raids' carried out by the German Air Force in retaliation: 'a terrible pity about all those Germanic cultural possessions . . . Suffering and annihilation everywhere'. It was not until the massive and devastating raids on Hamburg itself, carried out in July and August 1943, however, that the destruction really came home to the Solmitzes. During the most intense of the raids, the whole centre of the city was engulfed in a vast firestorm; entire street blocks were incinerated, and some 40,000 of the city's inhabitants were killed.

The raids so shocked Luise that she was unable to find words to describe them. When she and her husband ventured out of doors onto the streets of the city at the beginning of August 1943, they saw 'nothing but rubble, rubble in our path'. In horror and fascination she observed the slowness with which the superheated buildings gradually cooled:

> During the daytime the air was shimmering with heat. The coal bunker at Rebienhaus on the corner finally, finally burnt out. A fantastic drama. The shops [on top of the bunker] destroyed, glowing red and rosy-red. I went into the cellar staircase, it was irresponsibility to do it; the enormous house loomed steeply above me, all destroyed, and down below I could see the lonely, blazing hell, filled with flames raging with their own life. Later only the bunker shafts were aglow, the shops were black, dead caves. At the end the flame was burning blue.

Yet in the air-raid shelters, attempts to fan the flames of hatred against the British frequently met with rebuffs. 'Almost 3 hours in the bunker,'

Luise reported on a subsequent occasion: '"The Londoners have to sit in their bunkers for 120 hours. I hope they never get out – they deserve not to!" – "They've got to do what their government wants. What else are they to do?"' said a woman's voice. 'Despite everything,' Luise wrote later, 'that we have suffered in the attacks, there's not much hatred in Hamburg for the "enemy".'

Under the impact of defeat and retreat, and worn out by the constant bombing raids on her home city of Hamburg, Luise at last began to lose her faith in Hitler, though she was too cautious to say so too explicitly even in the privacy of her diary. Gathering together her thoughts about the Germans and their current situation on 8 September 1942, she had written:

> For me, a great man is only one who knows how to moderate himself, because there is not just a present time in which revenge can be tasted, but also a future in which retribution will come. Bismarck could restrain himself, one of the few who resisted being swept away by the power of success, a man who opposed his own internal law to the kind of law of nature that carried the conqueror away. The inescapable fate of most conquerors is self-destruction.

But it was not until her daughter Gisela, who had married her Belgian fiancé in his home country, left her newborn son Richard in the safekeeping of his grandparents, fearing the effects of the coming Allied invasion, that Luise really turned against Hitler. It was bad enough to think that she and her husband Friedrich might die in the bombing, but the threat it posed to their baby grandchild, the innocent carrier of Germany's future, appalled her.

Now she had only 'hate' und 'curses' for Hitler. 'I got into the habit of accompanying every bomb with a "Let Hitler die a miserable death" when we were amongst ourselves,' she wrote. The family started to refer to the Nazis as 'Herr Jaspers', allowing them to discuss the decline and the coming end of the Nazi system without fear of being arrested if anyone overheard them. Every time Goebbels or another leading Nazi came onto the radio, they rushed across the room to switch it off. Luise's attitude to the Third Reich was now being driven by her role as a mother and grandmother; a role that mingled with her disillusion at the state to which Hitler's policies had brought Germany to produce a diametrical reversal of the adulation she had felt a decade before.

For the latter part of the war, she spent much of her time simply trying to keep her family alive. Although she was a non-smoker, she applied for a cigarette ration card because, as she noted, 'cigarettes are currency, hard currency'. Thus she was able to exchange them for food rations for her infant grandson. The gas connection to her home had been broken in the massive air raids at the end of July 1943 and was not restored until January 1944; but by early 1945 both gas and electricity supplies were being regularly shut off again for so-called 'Gas-saving days' and 'current-saving days'. By this time, too, four-week ration cards were having to last for five weeks. At the end of 1944, official food rations began to be cut to levels on which nobody could survive. The country's infrastructure was crumbling rapidly 'I'm at the end of my strength, my will; completely exhausted and finished,' she wrote despairingly on 9 April 1945.

In Hamburg on 30 April 1945, hearing of Hitler's death, which she believed to have been caused by his having poisoned himself, Luise at last felt free to release the hatred that she had been building up for him over the previous months. He was, she wrote in her diary, 'the shabbiest failure in world history'. He was 'uncompromising, unbridled, irresponsible', qualities that had at first brought him success but then led to catastrophe. 'National Socialism,' she now thought, 'brought together all the crimes and depravities of all the centuries.' Twelve years previously she had thought very differently, but 'Hitler turned me from a meek and mild being into an opponent of war.' Goebbels was also dead: but 'no death can expunge such crimes'. As for Hitler: 'Now that we hopefully have his unimaginable crimes, lies, meannesses behind us, his botch-ups and his incompetence, his 5 years and 8 months of war, most Germans are saying: the best day of our life!' She noted: 'Hitler's promise: "Give me 10 years and you'll see what I've made out of Germany" has for months been his most often-quoted, out of bitterness.' On 5 May 1945 the Solmitzes burned the Nazi flag that they had so resented having been forced to lower ten years before. But it was not just Nazism that was defeated. 'Never has a people supported such a bad cause with such enthusiasm,' she wrote on 8 May 1945, perhaps thinking of her own earlier attitudes, 'never so impelled itself to self-annihilation.' The Germans were 'lemmings' rushing to self-destruction. Not only the Nazis, but also the Germans, had lost.

The journey recorded in Luise Solmitz's diaries, from love and admiration of Hitler to hatred and contempt, from the conviction that he was Germany's saviour to the belief that he was Germany's nemesis, was also a journey from Protestant middle-class typicality to a more individual political stance, impelled not just by reactions to the big events and impressions of the war years but also by more personal factors. Luise's ambivalence about Nazism in the early 1930s, her mistrust of its 'socialist' element, her relief that when Hitler was appointed as Reich Chancellor he was surrounded by a Cabinet of sound conservatives who would surely have a restraining influence on his radicalism, was shared by the great majority of Germans of her background and her class. There was nothing unusual, either, in the speed with which she dispensed with these reservations, nor in the reasons why she came to admire Hitler so rapidly and so unreservedly. For the German middle classes, the Nazi restoration of order and stability after the violence and upheavals of the Weimar years was enough to outweigh any lingering fears about their intentions; and soon Hitler's foreign-policy successes turned enthusiasm into euphoria. That euphoria reached its height with the stunning victories achieved by the German armed forces in Western Europe in 1940 and above all with the crushing defeat of the traditional enemy, the architect of the hated Treaty of Versailles, France. Here too Luise's reaction was entirely typical, this time not just of the German bourgeoisie but also of the vast majority of Germans in all stations of life.

The German popular consensus behind Hitler's foreign and military policy achieved in 1940 already began to fall apart the following year, however. With 13 million men under arms, Germany had become a society that on the home front was dominated by women, at least in terms of numbers. Increasingly, it was their experience that Luise's diaries recorded. Although she was always keenly interested in politics, the diaries have relatively little to say about the progress of the war on the battlefronts of Europe. It was not so much the defeat of the German armies at Stalingrad early in 1942 as the devastating effects of Allied bombing on daily life in Germany's towns and cities, which began to be felt later the same year, that convinced her that Hitler had overreached himself.

Here the war came home to Germany itself, and here increasing numbers of German women began to feel its direct effects. Added to this was another common reaction – anger and despair among middle-class nationalists like Luise Solmitz at the destruction of Germany's cultural heritage. The men at the front whose field-post letters have survived in their millions had other concerns, of which simply staying alive was an increasingly prominent one. Here already, Luise's diaries were starting to reflect concerns that were necessarily more gender-specific than they had been in the early 1930s. Gender-specific, too, was their reaction to the Allied bombing and the devastation it caused: while the criticisms of Britain and America recorded in her diary were all uttered by men, the general view among women seems to have been a more fatalistic one, in which nobody was to blame for what was simply an act of war; or if anyone was, then it was Hermann Göring's Luftwaffe, which had failed to defend Germany's towns and cities.

What gave Luise's diaries an added critical edge and drove them across the borderline from disillusion with Hitler and the Third Reich, a feeling shared by millions of Germans by 1943, to hatred, an emotion still felt by relatively few even in April 1945, were two influences that were not only gender-specific but also peculiar to Luise's role as a wife and mother: her concern for her infant grandson and the almost unbearable fear that the baby's life might be ended almost before it had begun, because of Hitler's folly in bringing about a war that Germany could not win. Alongside this was a second and more long-standing influence: Luise's situation as the non-Jewish wife of a German Jew. Living as he did in a 'privileged mixed marriage', Friedrich Solmitz was not going to be deported and killed, but he was subjected to growing discrimination and privation, and Luise felt just as keenly the legal, social and educational marginalization of their 'mixed-race' daughter Gisela.

Yet what the diaries do not say is perhaps as significant as what they do. Luise did not record any pressure by the Gestapo, such as was exerted on other 'Aryan' spouses of German Jews, to obtain a divorce, nor did she ever display any doubts about the wisdom of staying married to Friedrich. This was, perhaps, not least because she never really thought of him as Jewish; the family never mixed with the Jewish community in Hamburg, and Luise's diaries betray no more than the merest hint of sympathy with its fate. Indeed, it is clear that the transcripts from which historians have worked to date were edited by Luise in some places as she dictated them to the transcriber, toning down or even omitting altogether the antisemitic sentiments she had imbibed from her father and expressed at intervals throughout the diary.[11] As far as she was concerned the Solmitzes were German, and even after everything that had happened, it was to Germany that they still owed their exclusive national allegiance, even in 1945: Hitler's ultimate crime indeed in her view was that he betrayed Germany.

When, ironically, Gisela sought a way out of her situation by marrying a foreigner and leaving Germany for Belgium, Luise does not seem to have raised any objections. Together with Friedrich, she made a valiant, if unrealistic, attempt to have the marriage allowed in Germany itself. By this time, her attitude to Hitler and the Nazis had come to be governed by factors almost exclusively specific to herself: there cannot have been many families living in a 'privileged mixed marriage' that ran up against a hostile and alienating Nazi officialdom by trying to win approval for their 'mixed-race' daughter to marry a foreigner at a late stage of the war. When the war ended, the depth of Luise's hatred for Hitler was far from typical: emotional reactions among Germans to his death and their country's defeat varied wildly, from a despair so radical that it led to suicide, to resentment of the Jews who (in the view of some) had conspired to bring about the defeat, to regret at the destruction, to puzzlement, or indifference. Perhaps most widespread of all was a pervasive feeling of guilt that had been growing steadily in many sectors of the population for some time: guilt at the atrocities carried out by the German forces and the SS in the East, guilt at the persecution and extermination of the Jews. Guilt did not figure in Luise's diaries, however, perhaps because after all she did feel herself to be one of the persecuted minority as well as one of the German majority, at one and the same time. Her sympathy with the Jewish victims of Nazi persecution remained strictly limited. When at the end of the war the British Occupation authorities billeted Jewish refugees returning from Belgium with the Solmitz family, Friedrich and Luise sent the authorities protest after protest until the refugees were removed.[12] Like Luise Solmitz, the vast majority of Germans retained a wide range of the attitudes and beliefs with which they had lived through the Third Reich. What they did not retain was their faith in Hitler. He had brought only death and destruction. After 1945 there was to be no resistance to the occupying powers, and no revival of Nazism.

Conclusion

As individuals, the perpetrators whose lives are recounted in this book were not psychopaths; nor were they deranged, or perverted, or insane, despite the portrayal of many of them as such in the media and the historical literature. They were not gangsters or hoodlums who took over the German state purely or even principally in order to enrich themselves or gain fame and power, though when opportunity knocked many of them did not hesitate to take advantage of it. Apart from flying in the face of the evidence, thinking of them as depraved, deviant or degenerate puts them outside the bounds of normal humanity and so serves as a form of exculpation for the rest of us, past, present and future. Nor were they people who existed on the margins of society, or grew up beyond the social mainstream. In most of their life, they were completely normal by the standards of the day. They came overwhelmingly from a middle-class background; there was not a single manual labourer among them. Many of them shared the conventional cultural attributes of the German bourgeoisie, were well-read, or played a musical instrument with some proficiency, or painted, or wrote fiction or poetry. But they all had in common the shattering emotional experience of a sharp and shocking loss of status and self-worth at an early point of their lives. For a number of them, Germany's sudden and unexpected defeat in World War I was a traumatic event, bringing a promising career to an end and mocking the sacrifice that they and their families had offered, sometimes in blood. In some instances, an economic disaster – the hyperinflation, or the Great Depression – had a comparable effect.

Hitler offered them a way out of their feelings of inferiority, linking their fate – and his own – to what he depicted as the modern historical trajectory of Germany as a whole, from defeat and humiliation to regeneration and resurgence, above all through overcoming seemingly unbridgeable political, economic and social divisions and antagonisms by creating a genuine, unitary people's community such as supposedly had brought the nation together at the outbreak of World War I in August 1914 and shattered under the impact of defeat just over four years later. Most of them grew up socialized into a bourgeois milieu of strong German nationalism and conservatism; converts from Socialism or Communism or even conventional liberalism were rare in the extreme. The step from here to the more radical form of nationalism represented by the Nazis was only a short one.

The experience of World War I had a hugely divisive effect on German political life. During and after the conflict, the militarization of society became more pronounced. Uniforms permeated public life and were to be seen everywhere on the streets. Yet it would be wrong to claim that the experience of war brutalized an entire generation. The majority of men who fought in the war were, by definition, drawn from the working classes, and when the war ended they returned to civilian life as Social Democrats, committed to the creation and preservation of Weimar democracy, or, especially if they were young, newly created parties further to the left, above all, following the initial, chaotic post-war years, the Communists. German nationalists were already convinced even before the war that the Social Democrats – the largest single party in the Reichstag from 1912 on – were traitors, hell-bent on dividing and undermining Germany. For many on the nationalist right, they were steered from behind by a Jewish conspiracy, a paranoid fantasy that offered an even more powerful pseudo-explanation of the international Communist movement. The fragile stability achieved by the Weimar Republic after the hyperinflation came to an end in 1924 only papered over the gaping cracks in the fabric of society. For more than a third of the electorate, the subsequent Great Depression and the disintegration of the political world came as the last straw. If they were not stupid, then, others have suggested, the vast majority of Germans were simply ignorant of the realities of Nazism. Only a small minority of fanatics lent themselves to the ideas and practices of Nazism; the rest knew nothing about them. Such exculpatory explanations reached into the highest echelons of the Nazi leadership: indeed, Hitler's architect and Minister of Munitions, Albert Speer, somehow persuaded the judges at the International Military Tribunal held in Nuremberg after the war that he had been unaware of Nazism's crimes, and remained ignorant of Auschwitz and the Holocaust all the way up to Germany's defeat. His self-serving memoirs repeated this claim; they were a bestseller, and not just in Germany, when they were published in the 1960s; they provided a persuasive excuse for millions of Germans who had lived under the Third Reich.

A great deal of research has appeared in the past few years, however, the cumulative effect of which has been to explode for good these convenient myths. Nearly all Germans had the opportunity to observe for themselves the murderous violence of the Nazis, or to learn about the mass shootings and gassings of the Jews at Auschwitz and elsewhere from reports sent home by soldiers from the Eastern Front, or brought back to Germany by soldiers on leave. It was easier to find out about mass shootings, carried out in the open, than about the gas chambers, often operated in conveniently out-of-the-way extermination camps, but even here, news filtered back to Germany. The Jewish diarist Victor Klemperer, for example, was already recording stories of Auschwitz, 'a swift-working slaughterhouse', by the autumn of 1942. The publication of a comprehensive collection of secret Nazi reports on popular attitudes to the Jews from 1933 to 1945 in a 1,000-page English translation in 2010 showed just how widespread knowledge was of the fate of the Jews, and also underlines the extent to which the 'deportation' of Jews from Germany met with popular approval from non-Jewish Germans, despite the misgivings of a minority.[1]

This does not mean, however, as some historians have argued, beginning with Allied wartime propaganda writers, that exterminatory antisemitism, subservience to authority, lust for conquest, militarism and similar characteristics, were hard-wired into the Germans' sense of national identity since the beginning or even further back.[2] Some historians have argued that Hitler and the Nazis came to power with overwhelming popular approval, ruled largely by consent, and only targeted small, unpopular, deviant social, racial and political minorities with their violence, to the satisfaction of the vast majority of ordinary Germans.[3] Most recently, a number of historians have put forward the view that the twelve years of Nazi Germany constituted a chapter in Germany's long 'affair' with democracy, and that Hitler's regime is best classified as an 'illiberal democracy', to borrow a term used by the authoritarian populist politician Viktor Orbán to describe his own rule over Hungary.[4]

These arguments seriously underestimate the depth and breadth of

CONCLUSION

coercion and violence used by the Nazis to bring Germans into line. Votes of 99 per cent for Hitler and his policies, such as the regime regularly obtained in elections and plebiscites held from 1933 onwards in order to impress foreign governments with the scale of Hitler's domestic support, were only obtained by the massive use of intimidation, manipulation and falsification. The publicity given to the early concentration camps was not a sign that they won the approval of the majority of the population, but a crude advertisement of what would happen to those who showed signs of dissent or opposition. Pointing to the fact that only about 4,000 prisoners were held in the concentration camps by 1935 ignores the far more significant fact that the task of repression had been passed to the regular courts and the state prisons and penitentiaries, which held some 23,000 inmates for offences classified as political at the same time. A huge range of other sanctions was used by the Nazis against refractory citizens, including dismissal from state employment and withdrawal of benefits. Surveillance and control, especially over former Communists and Social Democrats, was exercised not just by the Gestapo but, more importantly, by officials such as the 'Block Wardens', more than two million of whom were supervising their respective street blocks in Germany's towns and cities by the time the war broke out. The Nazis did not come to power peacefully; those who opposed them, above all Social Democrats and Communists, were not marginal or deviant groups; together, these two parties had won more votes and gained more seats in the Reichstag than the Nazis had in the last free elections of the Weimar Republic, held in November 1932. Indeed, Hitler and the Nazis never managed to win the votes of more than around 37 per cent of the electorate in any free national election, and even under the coercive and intimidatory conditions of the elections of March 1933, when other parties were prevented from campaigning, but before the Nazis had established full control, they still failed to win a majority.[5]

The Third Reich was not an 'illiberal' or any other kind of democracy. As Peter Longerich has concluded in a discussion of Hitler's 'charisma':

> First and foremost, Hitler's was in fact a dictatorship. Basic rights had been abolished since February 1933; anyone was liable to be dragged off to a concentration camp for an unspecified length of time, without due process of law and without any verifiable reason, and was therefore at the

mercy of the guards. Torture, torments of all kinds, and the murder of prisoners were part of this system, and were not prosecuted... The concentration camps were one part of a comprehensive system of repression that from 1936 had been unified and centralized under Himmler's direction; other branches of it were the Gestapo, the criminal police, the uniformed order police, the SS with its own intelligence service (SD), as well as armed organizations.[6]

Hitler's 'charisma' was exercised within the framework of this all-encompassing system of surveillance and control, and produced by unceasing, all-pervading propaganda projections of his power. There was no free press, no independent judiciary, no political alternative, no free-acting local government, no other institution apart from the Nazi Party, with the increasingly compromised exceptions of the Churches and the armed forces. The Nazi regime was not a dictatorship produced and sustained by popular endorsement; it was not a 'consensual dictatorship', since consent cannot be consent unless it is given freely and can just as freely be rescinded or withdrawn.[7] Nor was it a 'people's dictatorship': it was Hitler's dictatorship, in which the cult of Hitler's personality and power extended even to the enforced substitution of 'Good morning' or 'Yours sincerely' by 'Heil Hitler!' as the standard form of greeting.[8]

But the twelve years of the Third Reich were not enough to remould German society from top to bottom. Despite the constant rhetoric of social egalitarianism, differences of income, property, class and status remained. Industrial workers reacted to worsening conditions in the factories and mines as the rearmament economy overheated in the run-up to war by pressuring the Labour Front into action to try and improve their situation. Deep-seated religious beliefs were not extirpated by coercion and propaganda, and sparked courageous acts of public protest from time to time, for example when the Nazis tried to replace crucifixes on classroom walls in Catholic schools with pictures of Hitler, or when popular religious objections to the mass murder of mentally ill and handicapped citizens prompted public condemnation from Clemens von Galen, Bishop of Münster, during the war, driving the 'euthanasia' campaign underground. The regime's concern not to damage popular wartime morale led to more backtracking, for example when the wives of Jewish men arrested en masse by the Gestapo gathered in Berlin's Rosenstrasse to demonstrate for days until they were released, or when Himmler called a pause to deportations to Auschwitz from Berlin in November 1941 for fear that they would spark resistance from the remaining Jewish population in the capital. But these remained relatively isolated incidents, and did not involve any generalized hostility to the regime, let alone any intention to overthrow it: it was 'opposition', as it has been called by historians, rather than 'resistance'.[9] None of this means that the Third Reich was not a dictatorship, or that its rule was not imposed by violence and the threat of violence alongside propaganda and the mobilization of opinion: the two went together, as the boundaries of the 'People's Community' were marked on all sides by force and coercion.[10]

Indeed, the idea of the Third Reich as a generally accepted 'People's Community' fails to differentiate between social groups. It was more popular and more widely accepted among the young, influenced by school, Hitler Youth, and the Nazi permeation of social institutions, than the middle-aged and the elderly, for example, who had formed their values and social identity before 1933. Nazi violence and intimidation reached their first climax in 1933 as the initially insecure Nazi regime arrested and imprisoned up to 200,000 of its opponents in the newly opened concentration camps, declined for some time as the state took over the main task of political control, then increased again as popular disillusion and discontent began to grow again with the failing fortunes of Hitler's war and the collapse of what was left of the 'People's Community'. Middle-class support was proportionately greater than working-class, rural more than urban, Protestant more than Catholic. Over time, levels of support for the regime varied greatly, remaining limited until the mid-1930s, growing to a climax after the rapid victory over France in the summer of 1940, then plummeting once again as the German armed forces began to experience defeat on the Eastern Front and, especially from 1942, as Allied bombing raids started to inflict serious damage on German cities.[11]

And yet, despite all this, the idea of a national or people's community, transcending differences of class, income, politics, religion and social identity, still exerted a powerful emotional appeal in the 1930s and early 1940s.[12] It meshed with existing feelings of patriotism that similarly reached across these boundaries, even encompassing committed former Social Democrats and Communists, and grew more important during the war. It formed a significant part of Hitler's appeal even before

CONCLUSION

1933; after the seizure of power that year, he became a unifying symbol for many Germans, a concept he placed at the centre of his rhetorical strategy. Personal economic interests and opportunities undoubtedly played a part in bringing many Germans to join, support or tolerate Nazism and its policies, but it would be wrong to ascribe support for the regime to economic factors, given the length of time it took the economy to recover from the Depression of the early 1930s, and the transition to a war economy of increasing privation and sacrifice well before the actual outbreak of the war itself.

In terms of cultural practices and everyday behaviour, the psychological and cultural impact of the constantly reiterated concept of the 'People's Community' was undeniable. Germans from many walks of life found it attractive, while those who were excluded from the community – the mentally handicapped and mentally ill, homosexuals, petty criminals, 'Gypsies' (Roma and Sinti), cultural modernists, and above all those whom the regime classified as 'Jews' – were driven out, silenced by being forced into exile, sentenced to imprisonment, placed under surveillance, or eventually murdered.[13] Prominent among such 'enemies of the Reich' were the members and followers of the Social Democrats and the Communists, overwhelmingly working class. Cowed into submission by the unbridled mass Nazi violence of 1933 and the vast apparatus of surveillance and control exercised by the regime thereafter, they lapsed into political quiescence, and became the objects of its unceasing efforts to incorporate them as workers in a conflict-free national community – a community that claimed not to abolish class differences but to reconcile them in the name of the national interest.[14] At the same time, the idea of the 'national community' was in a state of constant change and flux over time, especially during the war, when it ran into increasing trouble. Economic prosperity, welfarism and full employment, major reasons for reconciling the working class, former Communists and Social Democrats, to the idea of the 'national community', began to fade under the harsh impact of war and privation. People began to tell jokes about Hitler more freely and frequently than before.[15] After Stalingrad, the idea of the organic national community began to lose its power for the overwhelming majority of people to whom it had appealed. Terror and coercion began to take its place, though they had never entirely disappeared from the scene.[16]

CONCLUSION

The Nazi regime created a framework that encouraged its followers, especially during the war, to commit acts that would have been unimaginable in other circumstances. The regime first dehumanized whole categories of people, including the mentally ill and handicapped, Slavs, Gypsies, petty criminals, the 'asocial' and the 'work-shy', and above all, of course, Jews, then placed at the disposal of its followers means of violence normally beyond the reach of most people. Upending the moral restraints common to all human societies in normal times, the regime made murder, cruelty, even sadism and torture legitimate, even desirable, attributes of those who worked for it. When normal moral values and behaviour were restored after 1945, therefore, perpetrators found no difficulty in settling back into peacetime society. Individual psychology might in part explain why some of them engaged in violence and destruction with greater enthusiasm than others, or deployed a particular kind or degree of sadism in doing so, but it does not explain why hardly any perpetrators refused to take part in mass killings, even though there was demonstrably no risk of incurring sanctions such as imprisonment or death for the tiny minority who followed this path.

Opinion surveys conducted among soldiers captured by the Americans, or conversations recorded between ex-members of the armed forces interned by the Allies, showed that at every level they were united in their admiration for Hitler, even in the final months of the war. Their indoctrination demonstrated a continuing majority approval of the acquisition of living-space and the 'struggle against Bolshevism' as fundamental reasons why they were fighting. A strong minority – well over a third – also voiced the belief that they were fighting against the Jews, whom they made responsible for the outbreak of the war in the first place. The willingness of ordinary Germans, members of the armed forces and the SS to engage in mass killing was strengthened by a sense of loyalty towards their comrades and the knowledge that what they were doing was approved, indeed, desired by the state they served, so that what they knew to be a transgression of the moral norms approved by the rest of the world would receive absolution. When Himmler described the mass killings as 'a glorious chapter in our history' that would never be written, he was confessing that the world would regard them as crimes, but simultaneously asserting the right of Germany and the Germans to commit them in the overriding interest of their own survival. Germans, the Nazis believed, were victims, above all of the Jewish world-conspiracy to destroy the 'Aryan' race, but more generally of the great powers that emerged victorious from the First World War, as well as Soviet Russia. Overcoming the trauma of defeat required the suspension of conventional morality and the assertion of the principle that any means necessary could and should be used to achieve this end.[17]

It is none the less striking how Nazis and other perpetrators, in the army or the professions or the world of business, failed after the war to realize that they had committed gross violations of human decency and morality or, if they were put on trial, understand why they were in the dock. Many if not most of them knew, like Himmler in his Posen speech of 1943, that they were breaking the legal and moral norms accepted by most societies across the globe, but like him, they felt deeply that they were doing this in the service of a higher necessity – the future of the human race and its protection from the evil machinations of the Jews. Those who went on trial sought to reconcile their status as defendants with the self-understanding produced by a dozen years or more spent in the all-encompassing moral environment generated by the Nazis, where they had internalized the upending of conventional morality, with words such as 'fanatical', 'ruthless', 'annihilation' and 'pitiless', turned from negatives into positives, by drawing the conclusion that the Jews had defeated them. By denying the humanity of the Jews from the beginning, forcing them out of society and reducing to a minimum their contact with the non-Jewish majority in Germany, the Third Reich opened the door to treating them as what Hitler repeatedly said they were: 'vermin', 'lice', or 'bacilli'.[18]

In the course of the 1930s and the early 1940s, the triumphs and conquests of the Nazi regime released the demons of antisemitism, cruelty and aggression in one European country after another, as dictatorships established themselves across Europe. Given the space in which to do so, with the overall hegemony of the Nazis and the removal of political and institutional obstacles, regimes like the Vichy government in unoccupied France, or the Antonescu dictatorship in Romania, unleashed their own particular forms of hatred and violence on their populations, without any direct encouragement from Berlin. The Holocaust was also a European event, and extended even to parts of North Africa that were under temporary German occupation following the military successes of Rommel and the Afrika Korps. It was not just the

CONCLUSION

puppet regimes established under Nazi occupation that persecuted and murdered the Jews. As the historian Dan Stone has pointed out in his recent history of the Holocaust:

> Although the persecution of the Jews that led to the Holocaust was a German project – a point which cannot be overemphasized – it chimed with the programmes of many European fascist and authoritarian regimes. Without the Germans' umbrella project, the Holocaust in Europe would not have happened. Nor were its allies as obsessed with the 'world-historical threat' posed by the Jews as the Germans were, although some came close, especially certain figures in the Croatian, Romanian and French leadership strata, but without the willing participation of so many collaborators across Europe, the Germans would have found it much harder to kill so many Jews.[19]

Yet in the end, it was the rise, triumph and rule of Nazism in Germany that was key to it all. That is why it is important above all to examine the mentalities and the motives of the people who were responsible for it. As the psephologist Jürgen Falter recently concluded, despite all the pressures on them, Germans who lived in the 1920s, 1930s and early 1940s exercised their own individual will when making the decisions they took.[20]

At the same time, however, the historian Mary Fulbrook has reminded us that: 'It is not individual motivation or specific personality aberrations that explain how many people became active participants in state-sanctioned persecution ... These are collective, social phenomena that need to be looked at in larger contexts.'[21] Only by situating the biographies of individual Nazi perpetrators, with all their idiosyncracies and peculiarities, in these larger contexts, can we begin to understand how Nazism exerted its baleful influence. By doing this, we can perhaps start to recognize the threats that democracy and the assertion of human rights are facing in our own time, and take action to counter them.

Epilogue: The Lady On The Train

Sometime in late September 1977, I forget exactly when, I finished a fairly lengthy research stay in Hamburg, packed my bags, made my way to the central train station, climbed onto the Copenhagen to Paris express, and found the 'through-coach to the Hook of Holland'. In those days before cheap flights from Britain to the Continent, I regularly took the ferry to Harwich and so back to Norwich, where term was about to start at the University of East Anglia, my base at the time. I found a compartment on the train, stowed my case on the overhead rack, and sat down by the window. Sitting opposite me was a neatly dressed, rosy-cheeked, white-haired, elderly lady, knitting.

This was the time of the 'German Autumn', when a series of attacks carried out by the Baader-Meinhof terrorist group had created an atmosphere among the German public that bordered on hysteria. In every German town, the police had put up posters with mugshots of two dozen or so wanted terrorists, and gathered in front of every poster were crowds of people trying to memorize the faces of the wanted men and women so they would know who they were if they came across them. As a casually dressed young man with longish hair, I was often asked by older Germans with whom I fell into conversation what I thought of terrorism, so I had prepared an answer something along the lines of 'It's terrible, but I think the Germans are making too much of it.' And so it was on the Copenhagen to Paris express on the through-coach to the Hook of Holland.

'What do you think of terrorism?' the elderly lady asked me, after we had established that she was German, though living in Copenhagen, and I was British (we spoke in German). I gave my usual answer, 'It's terrible, but I think the Germans are making too much of it.' Her

EPILOGUE: THE LADY ON THE TRAIN

response was a surprising one, to say the least. 'Yes,' she replied, 'they are making too much of it. *It's all the fault of the upper ten thousand. They should all be shot!*'

The 'upper ten thousand', she went on, meaning the wealthy elites who she believed had ruled Germany since the 1930s and were still in charge, at least of its western part – these were the days of the division of the country into a Communist East and a capitalist West – were stirring up hatred and fear by stoking the hysteria against the so-called terrorists. She was fortunate to be living in Denmark.

How had this harmless old lady come to hold beliefs that were so strikingly similar to those of the Baader-Meinhof group? I began to ask her about her life story. It turned out that she had been born in Hamburg before the Nazis came to power, and as a young woman had obtained a job as personal secretary to a Jewish businessman. Her employer had been exceptionally kind to her, invited her to his home to eat with his wife and children, and generally treated her as one of the family. She had found it all the more shocking, then, when the Nazis began to impose restrictions on his civil rights, 'Aryanized' his business in the mid-1930s, and then arrested her employer during the nationwide pogrom of the *Reichskristallnacht* in November 1938, putting him into a concentration camp for several weeks, one of 30,000 Jewish men who suffered the same fate. When he returned home after his release, having promised to leave the country, he was covered in bruises and scarcely recognizable.

His secretary was so outraged that she decided she couldn't stay in Germany any longer. 'I took the train to Copenhagen,' she told me, 'found a job there, though I didn't speak any Danish at the time, and started looking for a husband.' Under international law at the time, a woman who married a man from another country automatically took on the nationality of her husband, and this was her aim. She wanted nothing more to do with Germany and the Germans. 'I was quite pretty in those days,' she said, with a touch of vanity, 'so it wasn't too difficult. Then,' she laughed, 'I eventually found a man I really liked, got a divorce, and married him.'

She evidently found nothing exceptional in any of this, and, encouraged by my interest in her life story, she started showing me photos of her grandchildren, one of whom she was on her way to meet in the Netherlands. I quickly became bored, but it was clear she didn't want to

EPILOGUE: THE LADY ON THE TRAIN

carry on talking about the 1930s. She had concluded that the 'upper ten thousand' were responsible for Nazism, and hadn't changed her mind over the intervening decades. What more was there to say about it? She eventually returned to her knitting, and we said goodbye when she got off the train.

The encounter has haunted me ever since. For if a very ordinary, not particularly intelligent or intellectual or politically engaged young woman had seen what was morally wrong about Nazism and the Third Reich, and taken drastic action as a consequence, why couldn't other Germans have done the same?

Notes

Preface

1. See the illuminating brief discussion of the allergic reaction of many late twentieth-century historians to the biographical approach, by Ernst Piper, *Alfred Rosenberg: Hitlers Chefideologe* (Munich, 2005), 9–17; also, at greater length, Ian Kershaw, *Hitler I 1889–1936: Hubris* (London, 1998), xi–xx; and Hans Mommsen, 'Keine Katharsis blieb aus. Joachim Fests sorgfältige Biographie von Albert Speer', *Frankfurter Rundschau*, 13 October 1999 (cited in Piper, *Alfred Rosenberg*, 16).
2. Klaus-Michael Mallmann and Gerhard Paul (eds.), *Karrieren der Gewalt. Nationalsozialistische Täterbiographien* (Darmstadt, 2004); see also the discussion of the 'return of biography' in Martin Dröge, *Männlichkeit und 'Volksgemeinschaft': Der westfälische Landeshauptmann Karl Friedrih Kolbow (1899–1945: Biographie eine NS-Täters)* (Paderborn, 2015), 19–33.
3. For a recent collection of thoughtful biographical explorations of the relationship between the individual and his (or in one case – Margaret Thatcher – her) historical context, see Ian Kershaw, *Personality and Power: Builders and Destroyers of Modern Europe* (London, 2022). Previous collections of biographical essays of leading Nazis include Anthony Read, *The Devil's Disciples: The Lives and Times of Hitler's Inner Circle* (London, 2003), framed as a narrative history of the Nazi Party; Guido Knopp, *Hitler's Hitmen* (Stroud, 2002), containing six brief biographies; and *The Nazi Elite*, edited by Ronald Smelser and Rainer Zitelmann (London, 1993).
4. *Cosmopolitan Islanders* (2009); *Altered Pasts* (2014); *The Pursuit of Power* (2016); *Eric Hobsbawm: A Life in History* (2019); *The Hitler Conspiracies* (2021).

Part I

Introduction

1. Konrad Heiden, *Adolf Hitler. Das Zeitalter der Verantwortungslosigkeit. Eine Biographie* (Zurich, 1936); idem, *Adolf Hitler. Ein Mann gegen Europa* (Zurich, 1937); idem, *Der Führer – Hitler's Rise to Power* (London, 1944).
2. Alan Bullock, *Hitler: A Study in Tyranny* (London, 1952); Hermann Rauschning, *Die Revolution des Nihilismus. Kulisse und Wirklichkeit im Dritten Reich* (Zurich, 1938); idem, *Germany's Revolution of Destruction* (London, 1939); Hugh Trevor-Roper, 'The Mind of Adolf Hitler', in *Hitler's Table Talk 1941–1944* (London, 1953). For an account of their differences, based on interviews with the two historians, see Ron Rosenbaum, *Explaining Hitler: The Search for the Origins of his Evil* (New York, 1998), 63–98.
3. Eberhard Jäckel, *Hitlers Weltanschauung. Entwurf einer Herrschaft* (Tübingen, 1969); idem, *Hitler's Weltanschauung: A Blueprint for Power* (Middletown, CT, 1972).
4. Rosenbaum, *Explaining Hitler*, loc. cit.; Alan Bullock, *Hitler and Stalin: Parallel Lives* (London, 1991).
5. Joachim C. Fest, *Hitler: Eine Biographie* (Frankfurt, 1973); idem, *Hitler* (London, 1974).
6. Hermann Graml, 'Probleme einer Hitler-Biographie. Kritische Bemerkungen zu Joachim C. Fest', *Vierteljahrshefte für Zeitgeschichte*, vol. 22 (1974), 76–92; Volker Ullrich, 'Speers Erfindung', *Die Zeit* 19 (4 May 2005).
7. For the 'seduction' thesis, see for example Rainer Zitelmann, *Hitler: The Politics of Seduction* (London, 1999), first published as *Hitler: Selbstverständnis eines Revolutionärs* (Hamburg, 1987, new edition 2017). Kershaw's biography appeared in two volumes: Ian Kershaw, *Hitler*, published in 1998 and 2000. Kershaw's approach is spelled out with great clarity in his *Hitler* (Longmans Profiles in Power, Harlow, 1991). The idea of 'working towards the Führer' was put forward by the civil servant Werner Willikens: first quoted and discussed by Jeremy Noakes in idem, and Geoffrey Pridham (eds.), *Nazism 1919–1945: A Documentary Reader*, 2nd edn (Exeter, 2000 [1984]), II: *State, Economy and Society 1933–1939*, 13–17.
8. Peter Longerich, *Goebbels: A Biography* (London, 2015); idem, *Heinrich Himmler* (Oxford, 2012).
9. Peter Longerich, *Hitler: Biographie* (Munich, 2015), 12–13; idem, *Hitler: A Life* (Oxford, 2019), 4–5. Longerich simultaneously presents a Hitler who is a 'nobody', a man whose conduct as dictator 'cannot be explained by the first three decades of his life', and a Hitler whose conduct is heavily influenced by 'personality factors' (ibid, 6).
10. Dust-jacket text of German edition; the English edition modifies this bald statement by introducing the word 'sometimes', not there in the original.

11. Klaus Hildebrand, 'Nichts Neues über Hitler. Ian Kershaws zünftige Biographie über den deutschen Diktator', *Historische Zeitschrift* 270 (2000), 389–97.
12. Volker Ullrich, *Adolf Hitler. Biographie*: I: *Die Jahre des Aufstiegs* (Frankfurt am Main, 2013), 11–12. Kershaw outlines his approach in *Hitler* I, xix–xxx.
13. Volker Ullrich, *Adolf Hitler. Biographie*: II: *Die Jahre des Untergangs 1939–1945* (Frankfurt am Main, 2018).
14. Heiden, *Adolf Hitler. Ein Mann gegen Europa*, 213.
15. Kershaw, *Hitler* I, 46.
16. Longerich, *Hitler: A Life*, 357; see also 163, 364.
17. Fest, *Hitler. Eine Biographie*, 448, 718.
18. Ulrich, *Adolf Hitler* I, 307.
19. Hans-Joachim Neumann and Henrik Eberle, *Was Hitler Ill?* (London, 2013) [*War Hitler krank?* (Cologne, 2009)], 37, 86, 88–89.
20. Ullrich, *Adolf Hitler* I, 18–19. For a fuller critical survey of earlier biographies of Hitler, see Kershaw, *Hitler* I, 598–601. Longerich, *Hitler: A Life*, 968–69 n.17, disposes of attempts to psychoanalyse Hitler, all of which lack plausibility because in the absence of evidence about his childhood they are almost entirely speculative.
21. Max Domarus (ed.), *Hitler. Reden und Proklamationen 1932–1945. Kommentiert von einem deutschen Zeitgenossen*, 4 vols. (Munich, 1962–1973); Domarus collected this material personally during the 1930s, and much of it is still indispensable. There is also an English edition.
22. Eberhard Jäckel and Axel Kuhn (eds.), *Hitler. Sämtliche Aufzeichnungen 1905–1923* (Stuttgart, 1980); 76 of the documents reprinted in this volume, almost all very short and unimportant, were later revealed to have been forged by Konrad Kujau, the author of the 'Hitler Diaries' – see Eberhard Jäckel and Axel Kühn, 'Neue Erkenntnisse zur Fälschung von Hitler-Dokumenten', *Vierteljahrshefte für Zeitgeschichte*, vol. 32, no. 1 (1984), 163–69, and Robert Harris, *Selling Hitler: The Story of the Hitler Diaries* (London, 1986), 152–53. Hitler's speeches and other writings before the period covered by Domarus are printed in Clemens Vollnhals *et al.* (eds.), *Hitler. Reden, Schriften, Anordnungen Februar 1925 bis Januar 1933*, 12 vols. (Munich, 1992–2003). See also Christian Hartmann *et al.* (eds.), *Hitler, Mein Kampf. Eine kritische Edition*, 2 vols. (Munich, 2016); Elke Fröhlich (ed.), *Die Tagebücher von Joseph Goebbels: Sämtliche Fragmente*, 4 vols. (Munich, 1987); eadem (ed.), *Die Tagebücher von Joseph Goebbels*, 32 vols. (Munich, 1993–2008); Jürgen Matthäus and Frank Bajohr (eds.), *Alfred Rosenberg: Die Tagebücher von 1934 bis 1944* (Frankfurt am Main, 2015); Peter Witte *et al.* (eds.), *Der Dienstkalender Heinrich Himmlers 1941/42* (Hamburg, 1999); Matthias Uhl *et al.* (eds.), *Die Organisation des Terrors: Der Dienstkalender Heinrich Himmlers 1943–1945* (Munich, 2020).

23. Werner Jochmann (ed.), *Adolf Hitler. Monologe im Führerhauptquartier 1941–1944. Aufgezeichnet von Heinrich Heim* (Hamburg, 1980; the edition used here was published in Munich in 2000); Henry Picker, *Hitlers Tischgespräche im Führerhauptquartier* (Stuttgart, 1976).
24. Jochmann's introduction (7–34) has a source-critical discussion. See also Mikael Nilsson, *Hitler Redux: The Incredible History of Hitler's So-Called Table Talks* (London, 2021), 1–57, and the careful discussion in Ian Kershaw, *Hitler II 1936–1945: Nemesis* (London, 2000), 1,024–25 n.121.
25. These are not the only conversations recorded from memory in modern historical documents. In the 1890s and early 1900s, for example, the political police in Hamburg sent agents dressed as workers into Social Democratic pubs and bars to keep tabs on the conversations that went on there, with a view to assessing the political views of the Social Democratic rank and file; the agents then returned to their station and wrote up what they overheard. Over time, they developed an ear for the more striking and significant phrases they heard, so that the workers' authentic voices often come through the bland official summaries. This was even more likely to be the case with Heim's reports of the Führer's precious words. See Richard J. Evans (ed.), *Kneipengespräche im Kaiserreich. Stimmungsberichte der Hamburger Politischen Polizei 1892–1914* (Reinbek bei Hamburg, 1989).
26. See among other recent publications Elizabeth Harvey and Johannes Hürter (eds.), *Hitler – New Research* (German Yearbook of Contemporary History, vol. 3, Munich, 2018). Despite its title, this useful collection includes English versions of German articles published over the past decades in the *Vierteljahrshefte für Zeitgeschichte*.

1. The Dictator

1. Speculation about Hitler's alleged Jewish ancestry, for instance, lacks any foundation in the evidence: see Ullrich, *Adolf Hitler* I, 23–25. For Hitler's family background, including his father's decision to change his name from Schicklgruber in order to receive a legacy, see Kershaw, *Hitler* I, 3–11; Wolfgang Zdral, *Die Hitlers. Die unbekannte Familie des Führers* (Bergisch Gladbach, 2008); and the older but still valuable study by Bradley F. Smith, *Adolf Hitler: His Family, Childhood, and Youth* (Stanford, CA, 1967).
2. Hartmann et al. (eds.), *Hitler, Mein Kampf*, I, 102 n.30.
3. Ibid, 104 n.32, 108 n.38.
4. Ullrich, *Adolf Hitler* I, 23–40; August Kubizek, *Adolf Hitler. Mein Jugendfreund* (Göttingen, 1953), translated as *Young Hitler: The Story of Our Friendship* (Maidstone, 1954). See also Franz Jetzinger, *Hitlers Jugend. Phantasien, Lügen und Wahrheit* (Vienna, 1956); and Kershaw, *Hitler* I, 11–24. Documentary extracts, including school reports ('Fleiß: ungleichmäßig'), in

Ernst Deuerlein (ed.), *Der Aufstieg der NSDAP in Augenzeugenberichten* (Munich, 1974), 62–76 (also with Hitler's family tree).

5. Hitler's claims were first critically investigated by Brigitte Hamann, *Hitler's Vienna: A Dictator's Apprenticeship* (Oxford, 1999); see also Hartmann et al. (eds.), *Hitler, Mein Kampf*, I, 136 n.35, 142 n.46, 166 n.84, 262 n.73, 362 n.264, 368 n.278. He also claimed to have read the antisemitic tract *Handbuch der Judenfrage* by Theodor Fritsch as a young man in Vienna: see Vollnhals et al. (eds.), *Hitler*, IV/1, 133 (Hitler to Fritsch, 28 November 1930). Kubizek's claim that Hitler was already a radical antisemite before 1914 is not to be trusted.
6. Kubizek, *Adolf Hitler*, 18–41, 72–84. Kubizek's report that Hitler became obsessed with politics and consumed by antisemitism while in Vienna is uncorroborated.
7. Thomas Weber, *Hitler's First War: Adolf Hitler, the Men of the List Regiment, and the First World War* (Oxford, 2010), esp. 95–106; Ullrich, *Adolf Hitler* I, 63–74; Kershaw, *Hitler* I, 87–97. The doubt thrown on the authenticity of the photograph of Hitler in the crowd at the Odeonsplatz by Sven Felix Kellerhoff, 'Berühmtes Hitler-Foto möglicherweise gefälscht', *Die Welt*, 14 October 2010, does not convince. For the misleading account of Hitler's enrolment in the Bavarian army given in *Mein Kampf*, see Hartmann et al. (eds.), *Hitler, Mein Kampf*, 55–56. The memoirs of Fritz Wiedemann, his commanding officer and later his adjutant, are particularly valuable: *Der Mann, der Feldherr werden wollte. Erlebnisse und Erfahrungen des Vorgesetzten Hitlers im 1. Weltkrieg und seines späteren Persönlichen Adjutanten* (Velbert und Kettwig, 1964).
8. Ullrich, *Adolf Hitler* I, 75–89; Longerich, *Hitler: A Life*, 33–45. Hitler's blindness was most likely genuine, caused by a severe inflammation of the eyelids as a result of the gas attack; see Neumann and Eberle, *Was Hitler Ill?*, 21–27. There is little convincing evidence that it was hysterical or psychosomatic. (The discussion in Hartmann et al. [eds.], *Hitler, Mein Kampf*, 548 n.79, equivocates; Kershaw, *Hitler* I, 101–5, is more persuasive.) The thesis that Hitler was homosexual, put forward by the ex-Marxist German historian Lothar Machtan, rests on a mixture of baseless speculation and testimony from highly unreliable witnesses, including one particularly untrustworthy fellow soldier from his army years: ibid, 32–36; Weber, *Hitler's First War*, 137–39.
9. Ullrich, *Adolf Hitler* I, 89–100; Longerich, *Hitler: A Life*, 49–57. For more detail, see Othmar Plöckinger, *Unter Soldaten und Agitatoren. Hitlers prägende Jahre im deutschen Militär 1918–1920* (Paderborn, 2013), and Anton Joachimsthaler, *Hitlers Weg begann in München 1913–1923* (Munich, 2000), also for the following period. For the late emergence of Hitler's antisemitism, compare his wartime correspondence with his post-war letters in Jäckel and Kuhn (eds.), *Hitler*, nos. 24–30 and 61; Hartmann et al. (eds.),

Hitler, Mein Kampf, 556 n.97 ('Für ihn war die Politik die Fortsetzung des Krieges mit anderen Mitteln').

10. Ullrich, *Adolf Hitler* II, 101–3; Kershaw, *Hitler* I, 109–28. Quotations in Jäckel and Kuhn (eds.), *Hitler*, 88–90 and 648. Gemlich letter in ibid, 88–90, and Deuerlein (ed.), *Der Aufstieg*, 91–94. For the overpowering antisemitism of the far right in Munich at this time, see ibid, 52–53, and Longerich, *Hitler: A Life*, 52–57. For antisemitism in the army, see ibid, 57–62, and Plöckinger, *Unter Soldaten*, 181–93, 210–17. Thomas Weber, *Becoming Hitler: The Making of a Nazi* (Oxford, 2017), emphasizes the gradual coalescence of Hitler's central ideological tenets over the period 1919 to 1925.
11. Vollnhals et al. (eds.), *Hitler*, IV/2, 115, 75. See also Werner Reichelt, *Das braune Evangelium. Hitler und die NS-Liturgie* (Wuppertal, 1990).
12. Ernst Hanfstaengl, *Zwischen Weissem und Braunem Haus. Memoiren eines politischen Aussenseiters* (Munich, 1970), 38.
13. Kershaw, *Hitler* I, 149–53; Ullrich, *Adolf Hitler* I, 113–16; Longerich, *Hitler: A Life*, 63–79, 164–72. For examples, see Reginald H. Phelps, 'Hitler als Parteiredner im Jahre 1920', *Vierteljahrshefte für Zeitgeschichte*, vol. 11 (1961), 274–330; idem, 'Hitlers "grundlegende" Rede über den Antisemitismus', *Vierteljahrshefte für Zeitgeschichte*, vol. 16 (1968), 390–420; Jäckel and Kuhn (eds.), *Hitler*. See also Deuerlein (ed.), *Der Aufstieg*, and idem, 'Hitlers Eintritt in die Politik und die Reichswehr', *Vierteljahrshefte für Zeitgeschichte*, vol. 7 (1959), 177–227; and Vollnhals et al. (eds.), *Hitler*, vol. I, xvi–xvii; also the older Georg Franz-Willing, *Ursprung der Hitler-Bewegung* (Preussisch Oldendorf, 1974 [1962]). Examples of Hitler's notes for speeches are printed in Jäckel and Kuhn (eds.), *Hitler*, 356–61, 486–90, 626–29, 714–15, etc. Hitler devoted an entire chapter of *Mein Kampf* to the art of public speaking: Hartmann et al. (eds.), *Hitler, Mein Kampf*, 1,175–213.
14. For Hitler's vague but directly anti-Marxist, and especially anti-Communist and anti-Social Democratic, idea of 'socialism', see Robert Gellately, 'Das sozialistische Versprechen des Nationalsozialismus und die Doppelkrise des Kapitalismus und der Demokratie', in Weber (ed.), *als die Demokratie starb*, 75–88; at greater length in idem, *Hitler's True Believers*, 13–40, on Hitler's early ideological development. The antecedents of Nazi 'socialism' can be found in the 'German-social' ideals of the late nineteenth-century antisemitic parties: see Peter G. J. Pulzer's classic, *The Rise of Political Anti-Semitism in Germany and Austria* (London, 1964).
15. Ullrich, *Adolf Hitler* I, 100–109; Kershaw, *Hitler* I, 131–56; Longerich, *Hitler: A Life*, 80–97; Vollnhals et al. (eds.), *Hitler* I, 24 and III/3, 460, *Sunday Express* (28 September 1930), for 'socialism'; for the swastika, see Karl-Heinz Weissmann, *Das Hakenkreuz. Symbol eines Jahrhunderts* (Schnellrode, 2006), 61; more generally, Deuerlein, *Der Aufstieg*, 56–61. For the milieu, see Anthony J. Nicholls, 'Hitler and the Bavarian Background to National Socialism', in idem, and Erich Matthias (eds.), *German Democracy and the*

Triumph of Hitler: Essays on Recent German History (London, 1971), 129–59; Hartmann et al. (eds.), *Hitler, Mein Kampf*, 582 n. 1, 984 n. 46, 1,224–25 and nn.24–27; ibid, II, 1,246–53, and notes for the flag.

16. The greeting '*Heil!*' originated with the followers of the pan-German antisemite Georg Ritter von Schönerer, in Austria, before 1914: Kershaw, *Hitler I*, 156–65, 169–75; Albrecht Tyrell, *Vom 'Trommler zum 'Führer'. Der Wandel von Hitlers Selbstverständnis zwischen 1919 und 1924 und die Entwicklung der NSDAP* (Munich, 1975); idem (ed.), *Führer befiehl ... Selbstzeugnisse aus der 'Kampfzeit' der NSDAP* (Düsseldorf, 1969), 11–67; Tilman Allert, *The Nazi Salute: On the Meaning of a Gesture* (New York, 2008); Richard J. Evans, *The Third Reich in History and Memory* (London, 2015), 119–23; Ullrich, *Adolf Hitler I*, 110–52; Deuerlein (ed.), *Der Aufstieg*, 135–41; Ludolf Herbst, *Hitlers Charisma. Die Erfindung eines deutschen Messias* (Frankfurt am Main, 2010); for Hitler's immediate circle of subordinates, see the following chapters of the present book. Eckart died in December 1923; Feder was sidelined as too left-wing; Drexler, an alcoholic, left the Nazi Party after Hitler's takeover. Hitler's account of the prehistory of the Nazi Party is in Hartmann et al. (eds.), *Hitler, Mein Kampf*, 1,487–509.

17. Deuerlein (ed.), *Der Aufstieg*, 142–83; Sven Reichardt, *Faschistische Kampfbünde. Gewalt und Gemeinschaft im italienischen Squadrismus und in der deutschen SA* (Vienna, 2002); also Daniel Siemens, *Stormtroopers: A New History of Hitler's Brownshirts* (London, 2017). For post-war conflict in Europe, see Robert Gerwarth, *The Vanquished: Why the First World War Failed to End, 1917–1923* (London, 2016).

18. Franz-Willing, *Ursprung*, 126–27; idem, *Krisenjahr der Hitlerbewegung 1923* (Preussisch Oldendorf, 1975); Kershaw, *Hitler I*, 175–200; Harold J. Gordon, *Hitler and the Beer-Hall Putsch* (Princeton, NJ, 1972), Part I; Stefan Ihrig, *Atatürk in the Nazi Imagination* (Cambridge, MA, 2014).

19. Ullrich, *Adolf Hitler I*, 153–78; Kershaw, *Hitler I*, 200–12; Longerich, *Hitler: A Life*, 98–119; Gordon, *Hitler and the Beer-Hall Putsch*, 270–409; Franz-Willing, *Ursprung*, 66–141; Ernst Deuerlein (ed.), *Der Hitler-Putsch: Bayerische Dokumente zum 8./9. November 1923* (Stuttgart, 1962), 308–417, 487–515; idem (ed.), *Der Aufstieg*, 184–208; proclamation in Jäckel and Kuhn (eds.), *Hitler*, 1,056–57. Most recently, see Mark Jones, *1923: The Crisis of German Democracy in the Year of Hitler's Putsch* (London, 2023), and Volker Ullrich, *Germany 1923: Hyperinflation, Hitler's Putsch, and Democracy in Crisis* (New York, 2023).

20. Ullrich, *Adolf Hitler I*, 179–87; Kershaw, *Hitler I*, 212–19; Longerich, *Hitler: A Life*, 120–40. Transcript and full details of the trial can be found in Lothar Gruchmann et al. (eds.), *Der Hitler-Prozess*, 4 vols. (Munich, 1997). See also Otto Gritschneder, *Der Hitler-Prozess und sein Richter Georg Neithardt. Skandalurteil von 1924 ebnet Hitler den Weg* (Munich, 2001), esp. 79–83,

and Bernhard Huber, 'Georg Neithardt – nur ein unpolitischer Richter?', in Marita Kraus (ed.), *Rechte Karrieren in München. Von der Weimarer Zeit bis in die Nachkriegsjahre* (Munich, 2010), 95–113.

21. Sabine Behrenbeck, *Der Kult um die toten Helden. Nationalsozialistische Mythen, Riten und Symbole 1923 bis 1945* (Vierow bei Greifswald, 1996), 299–313; Jay W. Baird, *To Die for Germany: Heroes in the Nazi Pantheon* (Bloomington, IN, 1990), 41–72. Hitler's lengthy speeches from the dock are reprinted in Jäckel and Kuhn (eds.), *Hitler*, 1,061–227 (quotes on 1,226–27). See also Longerich, *Hitler: A Life*, 120–26.

22. Peter Fleischmann (ed.), *Hitler als Häftling in Landsberg am Lech 1923/24: Der Gefangenen-Personalakt Hitler nebst weiteren Quellen aus der Schutzhaft-, Untersuchungshaft- und Festungshaftanstalt Landsberg am Lech*, 3rd edn (Neustadt an der Aisch, 2018); Hartmann et al. (eds.), *Hitler, Mein Kampf*, 13–14; Ullrich, *Adolf Hitler* I, 188–97 (quote on 191); see also the floor plan of the south-west wing of the prison, where Hitler's cell was located, in Hartmann et al. (eds.), *Hitler, Mein Kampf*, II, 1,749.

23. Hartmann et al. (eds.), *Hitler, Mein Kampf*, 15–20; Ullrich, *Adolf Hitler* I, 197–210; Sven Felix Kellerhoff, *'Mein Kampf'. Die Karriere eines deutschen Buches* (Stuttgart, 2015), 51–64; detailed account in Othmar Plöckinger, *Geschichte eines Buches: Adolf Hitlers 'Mein Kampf' 1922–1945* (Munich, 2006), 11–164; documents reprinted in Othmar Plöckinger (ed.), *Quellen und Dokumente zur Geschichte von 'Mein Kampf' 1924–1945* (Stuttgart, 2016), 23–133.

24. Hartmann et al. (eds.), *Hitler, Mein Kampf*, 21–24. The first, and still important, analysis of Hitler's language, and that of Nazism more generally, was delivered by Viktor Klemperer, a Jewish professor of French literature who survived the Third Reich because he had a non-Jewish wife: *LTI. Notizbuch eines Philologen* (Leipzig, 1975 [1946]; 'LTI' stands for *Lingua Tertii Imperii*, the language of the Third Reich). See esp. 62–67 ('fanatisch'), 228–37 ('Der Fluch des Superlativs').

25. Hartmann et al. (eds.), *Hitler, Mein Kampf*, 771–859, for the main section on 'the Jew'.

26. Ibid, 1,719 and n.73 (not a concrete plan, rather an expression of the murderous nature of Hitler's antisemitism); for Hitler's self-belief, see ibid, 1,474 n.13.

27. Hartmann et al. (eds.), *Hitler, Mein Kampf*, I, 487–513, 879; ibid, II, 1,472 n.11. The idea itself was far from new: see more generally George L. Mosse, *The Nationalisation of the Masses: Political Symbolism and Mass Movements in Germany from the Napoleonic Wars Through the Third Reich* (New York, 1975).

28. Hartmann et al. (eds.), *Hitler, Mein Kampf*, I, 25–53, 64, 478 n.83; II, 1041–47 and notes; II, 1,070–975 and notes; II, 1,228–43 and notes; 1,272–77 and

notes; 1,286 n.10; 1,382–99 and notes (Coburg). For a brief survey of contemporary reviews, see Kellerhoff, 'Mein Kampf', 131–58, 225–42, 261–88; for a comprehensive discussion of the book's reception in Germany and abroad, see Plöckinger, *Geschichte eines Buches*, 203–578; for its limited impact in Germany before 1933, ibid, 448. The reviews and commentaries are reprinted in Plöckinger (ed.), *Quellen*, 163–304. There is a useful brief discussion in Emma Smith, *Portable Magic: A History of Books and their Readers* (London, 2022), 189–204.

29. Hartmann et al. (eds.), *Hitler, Mein Kampf*, I, 9; II, 1,584 n.107.
30. For Hitler's early royalty statements from the publisher, see Plöckinger (ed.), *Quellen*, 137–60.
31. Ullrich, *Adolf Hitler* I, 203–5; Kershaw, *Hitler* I, 240–53; Plöckinger, *Geschichte eines Buches*, 225–47, 443–44. For the claim that the book provided a blueprint for the Third Reich, see Jäckel, *Hitlers Weltanschauung*, passim; for a rebuttal, see Hartmann et al. (eds.), *Hitler, Mein Kampf*, I, 64–67, 882 n.59, also II, 1,465–1,466.
32. Ullrich, *Adolf Hitler* I, 197; Hartmann et al. (eds.), *Hitler, Mein Kampf*, II, 1,288 n.11.
33. Hartmann et al. (eds.), *Hitler, Mein Kampf*, II, 1,279 and 1,286 n.10.
34. For the difficulties of the Nazi Party in the years after the *putsch*, see Deuerlein (ed.), *Der Aufstieg*, 231–302; for Hitler's reconstruction of the party, see Kershaw, *Hitler* I, 223–34, 257–311, Longerich, *Hitler: A Life*, 164–86, and Vollnhals et al. (eds.), *Hitler*, I, 4–9; for Otto Strasser, see Kershaw, *Hitler* I, 325–29.
35. See, in general, Eric D. Weitz, *Weimar Germany: Promise and Tragedy* (Princeton, NJ, 2007); the useful collection of documents on the reconstruction of the Nazi Party after 1923 in Tyrell (ed.), *Führer befiehl...*, 68–268; and the narrative in Longerich, *Hitler: A Life*, 143–69. For Hitler's attempt to put a positive spin on the election result, see Vollnhals et al. (eds.), *Hitler*, II/2, 847–48 (20 May 1928).
36. Overviews in Harold James, *The German Slump: Politics and Economics 1924–1936* (Oxford, 1986); Charles P. Kindleberger, *The World in Depression 1929–1939* (Berkeley, 1987 [1973], new edn 2013); Barry Eichengreen, *Golden Fetters: The Gold Standard and the Great Depression, 1919–1939* (Oxford, 1992); more recently, see also Tobias Straumann, *1931: Debt, Crisis, and the Rise of Hitler* (Oxford, 2019).
37. Heinrich August Winkler, *Der Schein der Normalität. Arbeiter und Arbeiterbewegung in der Weimarer Republik 1924 bis 1930* (Bonn, 1985), 661–823; idem, *Der Weg in die Katastrophe. Arbeiter und Arbeiterbewegung in der Weimarer Republik 1930 bis 1933* (Bonn, 1987), 19–99, 123–88; overview in Richard J. Evans, *The Coming of the Third Reich* (London, 2003), 232–55. For the Communists, see Eric D. Weitz, *Creating German Communism*,

1890–1990: From Popular Protests to Socialist State (Princeton, 1997), 131, 60–87, 233–79; Winkler, *Der Weg in die Katastrophe*, 231–36, 591–602, 765–73, 848–49; Eve Rosenhaft, 'Beating the Fascists'? *The German Communists and Political Violence 1929–1933* (Cambridge, 1983); Vollnhals et al. (eds.), *Hitler*, II/I, 347–366 ('Marxisten, warum habt ihr den Arbeiter Hirschmann ermordet?', 9 June 1927); ibid, III/3, 11–15 (11 January 1930), III/3, 120–23 ('Tatsächlich existiert nur *ein* Marxismus', 8 March 1930), etc.; more generally, see Klaus-Michael Mallmann, *Kommunisten in der Weimarer Republik. Sozialgeschichte einer revolutionären Bewegung* (Darmstadt, 1996).
38. Longerich, *Hitler: A Life*, 178–96; Vollnhals et al. (eds.), *Hitler*, III/3, 58–64, and Noakes and Pridham (eds.), *Nazism 1919–1945*, I, 115–20, for Hitler's appeal to rural voters.
39. Ullrich, *Adolf Hitler* I, 250–55.
40. Ibid, 257–65; Evans, *The Coming of the Third Reich*, 255–65; Jürgen W. Falter et al., *Wahlen und Abstimmungen in der Weimarer Republik. Materialien zum Wahlverhalten 1919–1933* (Munich, 2009), 41, 92; Longerich, *Hitler: A Life*, 200–208.
41. Falter et al., *Wahlen*, 86–113.
42. Ibid, 46; Karl Dietrich Bracher, *Die Auflösung der Weimarer Republik. Eine Studie zum Problem des Machtverfalls in der Demokratie* (Villingen/Schwarzwald, 1955), 443–80; Vollnhals et al. (eds.), *Hitler*, IV/3, 153–64, 174–85.
43. Falter et al., *Wahlen*, 41; Deuerlein (ed.), *Der Aufstieg*, 371–82; Bracher, *Die Auflösung*, 481–526; Longerich, *Hitler: A Life*, 224–53.
44. Domarus, *Hitler*, 96. At the last-named event the Nazi press implausibly estimated an attendance of 180,000 (ibid, 277, doc. 150, n.1). For the recording, see Domarus, *Hitler*, 115.
45. Vollnhals et al. (eds.), *Hitler*, III/3, 111–14 (1 March 1930) and 268–69 (6 July 1930); ibid, V/I, 274–77 (27 July 1932), for examples.
46. Domarus, *Hitler*, 293–95 (2 August 1930) for one example among many.
47. Vollnhals et al. (eds.), *Hitler*, III/3, 219–21 (6 June 1930), repeated in following speeches (226–36).
48. Henry Ashby Turner, Jr., *German Big Business and the Rise of Hitler* (Oxford, 1985), 47–59, 111–42, 191–203; Ullrich, *Adolf Hitler* I, 136–46; Kershaw, *Hitler* I, 186–91, 299–300, 356–60; Longerich, *Hitler: A Life*, 103–5, 211–14, 233–35; for the Hamburg speech, see ibid, 167, and Vollnhals et al. (eds.), *Hitler*, I, 297–330; for the Düsseldorf speech, Vollnhals et al. (eds.), *Hitler*, IV/3, 74–110; Günter Brakelmann, *Zwischen Mitschuld und Widerstand: Fritz Thyssen und der Nationalsozialismus* (Essen, 2010).
49. Gerhard Paul, *Aufstand der Bilder. NS-Propaganda vor 1933* (Bonn, 1990); Kershaw, *Hitler* I, 329–33; Vollnhals (ed.), *Hitler*, I, xvii; II/1 for frequent libel cases, in which Hitler was often obliged to appear as a witness. See ibid,

117–19, for an example of Hitler's antisemitic claims ('German poverty and the way to liberation from slavery, shame and mass misery, from Jewish-capitalist and Marxist servitude', 11 January 1927). For the downplaying of antisemitism, see Longerich, *Hitler: A Life*, 177–78; for reasons why people voted Nazi, ibid, 204–7.

50. The appeal of the 'Crown Prince' is reprinted in Domarus, *Hitler*, 103.
51. Kershaw, *Hitler* I, 333–40; Jürgen W. Falter, *Hitlers Wähler* (Munich, 1991), esp. 364–74; also Thomas Childers, *The Nazi Voter: The Social Foundations of Fascism in Germany, 1919–1933* (Chapel Hill, NC, 1981). On the family of ex-Kaiser Wilhelm II, especially his son, the self-styled 'Crown Prince' Wilhelm, and their role in persuading monarchists and conservatives to support Hitler, see Stephan Malinowski, *Die Hohenzollern und die Nazis: Geschichte einer Kollaboration* (Berlin, 2021), esp. 241–331. Numerous speeches denouncing the Young Plan can be found in Vollnhals et al. (eds.), *Hitler*, III/3; the promise of national unity in ibid, IV/1, 76–88, 90–106, etc.; on the 'Bolshevism/Nazism' choice, ibid, V/2, 131 (30 October 1932). The best overall account of the reparations question is in Bruce Kent, *The Spoils of War: The Politics, Economics, and Diplomacy of Reparations, 1918–1932* (Oxford, 1989), 288–321.
52. Ullrich, *Adolf Hitler* I, 254–57, 282–86; Longerich, *Hitler: A Life*, 173–74, 196–200, 218–19; Kershaw, *Hitler* I, 325–29; Günter Bartsch, *Zwischen drei Stühle: Otto Strasser. Eine Biographie* (Koblenz, 1990).
53. Deuerlein, *Der Aufstieg*, 337–38; Vollnhals et al. (eds.), *Hitler*, III/1, 434–51, and III/2, 72–100; Longerich, *Hitler: A Life*, 207–8; Kershaw, *Hitler* I, 337–38; Peter Bucher, *Der Reichswehrprozess. Der Hochverrat der Ulmer Reichswehroffiziere 1929/30* (Boppard am Rhein, 1967).
54. Deuerlein (ed.), *Der Aufstieg*, 361–63; Bracher, *Die Auflösung*, 431–35; Tyrell (ed.), *Führer befiehl...*, 269–351; Kershaw, *Hitler* I, 337–38, 346–51, 365–67; Ullrich, *Adolf Hitler* I, 270–78; Longerich, *Hitler: A Life*, 230–31; Vollnhals et al. (eds.), III/3, 434–51, and IV/2, 231–33. Hitler's warning that the measures outlined by Best would be necessary in the event of a Communist uprising experienced a kind of fulfilment in the Reichstag Fire Decree of 28 February 1933.
55. Bracher, *Die Auflösung*, 482–90, 545–52.
56. Vollnhals et al. (eds.), *Hitler*, IV/2, 233 ('Pressekonferenz in Berlin, 4. Dezember 1931').
57. Kershaw, *Hitler* I, 361–63, 368; Ullrich, *Adolf Hitler* I, 271–77, 293–98; Longerich, *Hitler: A Life*, 202–4, 216–18; Paul Kluke, 'Der Fall Potempa', *Vierteljahrshefte für Zeitgeschichte*, vol. 5 (1957), 279–97; Richard Bessel, 'The Potempa Murder', *Central European History*, vol. 10 (1977), 241–54; Deuerlein (ed.), *Der Aufstieg*, 383–95; Daniel Siemens, *The Making of a Nazi Hero: The Murder and Myth of Horst Wesssel* (London, 2013 [Munich,

2009]); Rosenhaft, *'Beating the Fascists'?*, 6–8; eadem, 'Working-Class Life and Working-Class Politics; Communists, Nazis and the State in the Battle for the Streets, Berlin 1928–1932', in Richard Bessel and Edgar Feuchtwanger (eds.), *Social Change and Political Development in Weimar Germany* (London, 1981), 207–40; James M. Diehl, *Paramilitary Politics in Weimar Germany* (Bloomington, IN, 1977); Karl Rohe, *Das Reichsbanner Schwarz-Rot-Gold: Ein Beitrag zur Geschichte und Struktur der politischen Jampfverbände zur Zeit der Weimarer Republik* (Düsseldorf, 1966). On Altona, see Anthony McElligott, *Contested City: Municipal Politics and the Rise of Nazism in Altona, 1917–1937* (Ann Arbor, MI, 1998). For the Papen coup in Prussia, carried out by the *Reichswehr*, see Bracher, *Die Auflösung*, 559–600. Hitler's call to the SA to be loyal and disciplined and avoid random violence is printed in Vollnhals *et al.* (eds.), *Hitler*, IV/1, 277–81 (9 April 1931); his angry insistence, in the face of persistent and penetrating cross-examination from the Communist lawyer Hans Litten, that he was not responsible for SA violence, can be found in ibid, IV/I, 360–70 (trial of four stormtroopers for violence against Communists) and IV/2, 51–57. Hitler lied persistently in his testimony, claiming for example that 'The S. A. is unarmed'. See also Benjamin Carter Hett, *Crossing Hitler: The Man Who Put the Nazis on the Witness Stand* (New York, 2008). For Hitler's speech at Horst Wessel's grave, with its call to carry on his violent work, see Vollnhals *et al.* (eds.), *Hitler*, V/2, 389–93. More details of Nazi violence in Gellately, *Hitler's True Believers*, chs. 4–7.

58. Vollnhals *et al.* (eds.), *Hitler*, V/1, 304–9 (16 August 1932).
59. Thomas Mergel, *Parlamentarische Kultur in der Weimarer Republik: Politische Kommunikation, symbolische Politik und Öffentlichkeit im Reichstag* (Düsseldorf, 2002), 179–81; Bracher, *Die Auflösung*, 377–88 ('Selbstausschaltung des Reichstags'); Ullrich, *Adolf Hitler* I, 289–96.
60. Kershaw, *Hitler* I, 396–400; Domarus, *Hitler*, 164–65. The best study of these events remains Bracher, *Die Auflösung*, updated in the much briefer and more limited study by Henry Ashby Turner, *Hitler's Thirty Days to Power: January 1933* (London, 1996); see also, more generally, Winkler, *Der Weg*, and idem, *Die Weimarer Republik 1918–1933: Die Geschichte der ersten deutschen Demokratie* (Munich, 1993).
61. Falter *et al.*, *Wahlen*, 43–44.
62. Bracher, *Die Auflösung*, 644–85.
63. Ibid, 686–732; Kershaw, *Hitler* I, 379–427; Longerich, *Hitler: A Life*, 191–275; Ullrich, *Adolf Hitler* I, 324–420; Domarus, *Hitler*, 182–85. For the many commentators who underestimated Hitler at this time, see Ullrich, *Adolf Hitler* I, 265–70. For Papen, see below, pp. 255–74.
64. For gossip and fantasy, or avoidance and denial, about Hitler's sex life, spread by Ernst Hanfstaengl, Lothar Machtan, Joachim Fest and many

others, see Ullrich, *Adolf Hitler* I, 299–306; for Geli Raubal, see ibid, 306–18. Longerich, *Hitler: A Life*, 159–63, insists that Hitler's life was asexual, blocked by 'arrested emotional development'. Hitler's reaction to Geli Raubal's suicide is in Vollnhals *et al.* (eds.), *Hitler*, IV/2, 109–10 (letter to the newspaper *Münchener Post* on its report on the affair, 21 September 1931, and notes).

65. Ullrich, *Adolf Hitler* I, 306–23; Heike B. Görtemaker, *Eva Braun: Life with Hitler* (London, 2011 (German edn 2010)); Evans, *The Third Reich in History and Memory*, 150–63; Longerich, *Hitler: A Life*, 220–23.
66. Richard Overy (ed.), *Interrogations: The Nazi Elite in Allied Hands, 1945* (London, 2001), 101–9; Kershaw, *Hitler* I, 329–51.
67. Ullrich, *Adolf Hitler* I, 421–57, presents a rounded portrait, building on a large number of personal testimonies of those who knew him.
68. For the Reichstag Fire and the various implausible and unprovable conspiracy theories surrounding it, see Richard J. Evans, *The Hitler Conspiracies: The Third Reich and the Paranoid Imagination* (London, 2020), 85–119. For the wider context, Kershaw, *Hitler* I, 431–62, and Ullrich, *Adolf Hitler* I, 468–72.
69. Rudolf Diels, *Lucifer ante Portas . . . es spricht der erste Chef der Gestapo* (Stuttgart, 1950), 193–95 (in Noakes and Pridham, *Nazism*, I, 140). For the 'Day of Potsdam' see Ullrich, *Adolf Hitler* I, 480–84; Klaus Scheel, *Der Tag von Potsdam* (Berlin, 1993); Malinowski, *Die Hohenzollern*, 343–72; Werner Freitag, 'Nationale Mythen und kirchliches Heil: Der 'Tag von Potsdam'', *Westfälische Forschungen*, vol. 41 (1991), 379–439; Kershaw, *Hitler* I, 464–65; and Karl Dietrich Bracher, *Die nationalsozialistische Machtergreifung: Studien zur Errichtung des totalitären Herrschaftssystems in Deutschland 1933/34*, I: *Stufen der Machtergreifung* (Cologne, 1960), 202–13.
70. Bracher, *Stufen*, 213–36; Ullrich, *Adolf Hitler* I, 484–88; Longerich, *Hitler: A Life*, 289–332; Rudolf Morsey (ed.), *Das 'Ermächtigungsgesetz' vom 24. März 1933. Quellen zur Geschichte und Interpretation des 'Gesetzes zur Behebung der Not von Volk und Reich'*, 2nd edn (Düsseldorf, 2010); Michael Frehse, *Ermächtigungsgesetzgebung im Deutschen Reich, 1914–1933* (Pfaffenweiler, 1985); Domarus, *Hitler*, 237–47.
71. Hermann Beck, *The Fateful Alliance: German Conservatives and Nazis in 1933. The 'Machtergreifung' in a New Light* (Oxford, 2008); Josef Becker, 'Zentrum und Ermächtigungsgesetz 1933: Dokumentation', *Vierteljahrshefte für Zeitgeschichte*, vol. 9 (1961), 195–210.
72. Ullrich, *Adolf Hitler* I, 498–500; Kershaw, *Hitler* II, 429–95; Bracher, *Stufen*, 237–306; above all, the still essential collection by Erich Matthias and Rudolf Morsey (eds.), *Das Ende der Parteien 1933* (Düsseldorf, 1960), with extended articles on each of the major parties; summary narrative in Evans, *The Coming of the Third Reich*, 355–74; more recently the synoptic surveys

by Larry Eugene Jones, *The German Right, 1918–1930: Political Parties, Organized Interests, and Patriotic Associations in the Struggle against Weimar Democracy* (new ed., Cambridge, 2016), and *German Liberalism and the Dissolution of the Weimar Party System, 1918–1933* (Chapel Hill, NC, 1988), among many other studies.

73. Ullrich, *Adolf Hitler* I, 493–506; Winkler, *Der Weg*, 867–954, for the end of the labour movement; also Michael Schneider, *Unterm Hakenkreuz. Arbeiter und Arbeiterbewegung 1933 bis 1939* (Bonn, 1999).
74. For details, see Evans, *The Coming of the Third Reich*, 342–61; see also Gellately, *Hitler's True Believers*, ch. 6.
75. Ullrich, *Adolf Hitler* I, 462–63; Thilo Vogelsang, 'Neue Dokumente zur Geschichte der Reichswehr 1930–1933', *Vierteljahrshefte für Zeitgeschichte*, vol. 2 (1954), 397–439, and Andreas Wirsching, "Man kann nur Boden germanisieren'. Eine neue Quelle zu Hitlers Rede vor den Spitzen der Reichswehr am 3. Februar 1933', *Vierteljahrshefte für Zeitgeschicthe*, vol. 49 (2001), 517–50.
76. Ullrich, *Adolf Hitler* I, 466; Turner, *Big Business*, 328–32; Dirk Stegmann, 'Zum Verhältnis von Grossindustrie und Nationalsozialismus 1930–1933', *Archiv für Sozialgeschichte*, vol. 13 (1973), 351–432 (for a more critical view of the role of big business in the triumph of Nazism); Henry A. Turner, 'Grossunternehmertum und Nationalsozialismus, 1930–33', *Historische Zeitschrift*, vol. 221 (1975), 18–68; and Dirk Stegmann, 'Antiquierte Personalisiserung oder sozialökonomische Faschismus-Analyse? Eine Antwort auf H. A. Turners Kritik an meinen Thesen zum Verhältnis von Nationalsozialismus und Grossindustrie for 1933', *Archiv für Sozialgeschichte*, vol. 17 (1977), 175–296.
77. Domarus, *Hitler*, 286–91, 305, 355.
78. Ibid, 485.
79. Ibid, 328, 338, 355, etc.
80. Ibid, 259–64, 281–86.
81. Kershaw, *Hitler* I, 499–526; Ullrich, *Adolf Hitler* I, 507–27; Daniel Siemens, *Stormtroopers: A New History of Hitler's Brownshirts* (London, 2017), 157–79; Heinz Höhne, *Mordsache Röhm, Hitlers Durchbruch zur Alleinherrschaft 1933–1934* (Reinbek bei Hamburg, 1984); Eleanor Hancock, 'The Purge of the SA Reconsidered: "An Old Putschist Trick"', *Central European History*, vol. 44 (2011), 669–83; see also below, pp. 149–62.
82. For Röhm and Papen, see respectively chapters 4 and 10 below.
83. Longerich, *Hitler: A Life*, 368–414.
84. Domarus, *Hitler*, 315–16. Hitler denounced 'rootless Jewish-international wandering scholars' as a source of internal division and disorder on other occasions (e.g. Domarus, *Hitler*, 526).
85. Ibid, 527–29 (11 September 1935, speech on laying the foundation stone for the new Congress Hall in Nuremberg); ibid, 705–10 (speech on opening the *Haus der deutschen Kunst* in Munich, 19 July 1937); also ibid, 718–19, 871, 877–78. See also Alan E. Steinweis, *Art, Ideology, and Economics in Nazi*

NOTES TO PP. 53-4

Germany: The Reich Chambers of Music, Theater, and the Visual Arts (Chapel Hill, NC, 1993); Joan L. Clinefelter, *Artists for the Reich: Culture and Race from Weimar to Nazi Germany* (Oxford, 2005); Paul B. Jaskot, *The Architecture of Oppression: The SS, Forced Labor, and the Nazi Monumental Building Economy* (London, 2000); and Ernst Klee, *Das Kulturlexikon zum Dritten Reich. Wer war was vor und nach 1945* (Frankfurt, 2009).

86. Domarus, *Hitler*, 765, 1,031-36; Gellately, *Hitler's True Believers*, 213-37.
87. Domarus, *Hitler*, 642 (12 September 1936); similarly ibid, 778-79 (22 January 1938), and 1,218-19 (16 July 1939); Ullrich, *Adolf Hitler I*, 660-72; Longerich, *Hitler: A Life*, 477-99; Evans, *The Third Reich in Power*, 164-86; idem, *The Third Reich at War*, 585-92.
88. Reinhard Merker, *Die bildenden Künste im Nationalsozialismus; Kulturideologie, Kulturpolitik, Kulturproduktion* (Cologne, 1983), 148-52; Peter Adam, *The Arts in the Third Reich* (London, 1992).
89. Domarus, *Hitler*, 717; Robert N. Proctor, *Racial Hygiene: Medicine under the Nazis* (London, 1988); Hans-Walter Schmuhl, *Rassenhygiene, Nationalsozialismus, Euthanasie: Von der Verhütung zur Vernichting 'lebensunwerten Lebens'* (Göttingen, 1987); Jeremy Noakes, 'Nazism and Eugenics: The Background to the Nazi Sterilization Law of 14 July 1933', in Roger Bullen et al. (eds.), *Ideas into Politics: Aspects of European History 1850-1930* (London, 1984), 75-94. See also Ernst Klee, *Euthanasie im Dritten Reich: Die 'Vernichting lebensunwerten Lebens'* (Frankfurt, 2010), and *Dokumente zur 'Euthanasie' im NS-Staat* (Frankfurt, 1985); for an appreciation of Klee's pioneering work, see Richard J. Evans, 'Ernst Klee obituary', *The Guardian* (21 May 2013).
90. Domarus, *Hitler*, 637-38; Longerich, *Hitler: A Life*, 447-76. The Table Talk records Hitler admitting he did not understand financial matters (Jochmann, *Monologe*, 291).
91. Domarus, *Hitler*, 649-50, 666.
92. John Weitz, *Hitler's Banker: Hjalmar Horace Greeley Schacht* (Boston, MA, 1997).
93. Domarus, *Hitler*, 891; Adam Tooze, *The Wages of Destruction: The Making and Breaking of the Nazi Economy* (London, 2006); Evans, *The Third Reich in Power*, 322-411; idem, *The Third Reich in History and Memory*, 167-90.
94. Peter Hayes, *Industry and Ideology: I.G. Farben in the Nazi Era* (Cambridge, 1987).
95. Norbert Frei et al., *Flick. Der Konzern, die Familie, die Macht* (Munich, 2009), esp. 326-442; Ulrich Herbert, *Hitler's Foreign Workers: Enforced Foreign Labour in Germany Under the Third Reich* (Cambridge, 1997); Kim Christian Priemel, *Flick. Eine Konzerngeschichte vom Kaiserreich bis zur Bundesrepublik* (Göttingen, 2007), esp. 470-507, 616-50, 761-90.

96. Domarus, *Hitler*, 208–9, 867–68, 1,081–83; Evans, *The Third Reich in Power*, 322–50; Bernhard Rieger, *The People's Car: A Global History of the Volkswagen Beetle* (Cambridge, MA, 2013); Evans, *The Third Reich in History and Memory*, 167–90.
97. Domarus, *Hitler*, 369–71; also 574–79 and 680–81; more generally, Tooze, *The Wages of Destruction*.
98. Michael Wildt, *Volksgemeinschaft als Selbstermächtigung. Gewalt gegen Juden in der deutschen Provinz 1919 bis 1939* (Hamburg, 2007), 107–16; Kulka and Jäckel (eds.), *The Jews in the Secret Nazi Reports*, 3–8.
99. Ullrich, *Adolf Hitler* I, 489–92; Hannah Ahlheim, '*Deutsche, kauft nicht bei Juden!' Antisemitischer Boycott in Deutschland 1924 bis 1935* (Göttingen, 2011).
100. Ullrich, *Adolf Hitler* I, 492–93; Longerich, *Hitler: A Life*, 329–437; Saul Friedländer, *Nazi Germany and the Jews: The Years of Persecution 1933–39* (London, 1997), 9–39; Gellately, *Hitler's True Believers*, 239–63; Hermann Beck, *Before the Holocaust: Antisemitic Violence and the Reaction of German Elites and Institutions during the Nazi Takeover* (Oxford, 2022). Hitler's proclamation is in Domarus, *Hitler*, 247–52.
101. Domarus, *Hitler*, 574; Gellately, *Hitler's True Believers*, 239–63.
102. Domarus, *Hitler*, 899.
103. Ibid, 1,057–58.
104. Ibid, 1,663–829.
105. Martin Hirsch et al. (eds.), *Recht, Verwaltung und Justiz im Nationalsozialismus* (Cologne, 1984); Lothar Gruchmann, *Justiz im Dritten Reich. Anpassung und Unterwerfung in der Ära Gürtner* (Munich, 1988); Evans, *The Third Reich in Power*, 536–79; Alan B. Steinweis and Robert Rachlin (eds.), *The Law in Nazi Germany: Ideology, Opportunism and the Perversion of Justice* (Oxford, 2015).
106. Evans, *The Third Reich in Power*, 580–602; Kershaw, *Hitler* II, 129–53; Longerich, *Hitler: A Life*, 589–97. For recent work, see Wolf Gruner and Steven J. Ross (eds.), *New Perspectives on Kristallnacht: After 80 Years, the Nazi Pogrom in Global Comparison* (West Lafayette, IN, 2019); Wolfgang Benz, *Gewalt im November 1938. Die 'Reichskristallnacht'. Initial zum Holocaust* (Berlin, 2018); Raphael Gross, *November 1938. Die Katastrophe vor der Katastrophe* (Munich, 2013); and esp. Alan E. Steinweis, *Kristallnacht 1938* (Harvard, MA, 2009).
107. Nikolaus Wachsmann, *Hitler's Prisons: Legal Terror in Nazi Germany* (London, 2004), 66–226; Richard J. Evans, *Rituals of Retribution: Capital Punishment in Germany 1600–1997* (Oxford, 1996), 613–737.
108. Domarus, *Hitler*, 522–24, 1,924; Geoffrey Giles, 'The Persecution of Gay Men and Lesbians during the Third Reich', Jonathan C. Friedman (ed.), *The Routledge History of the Holocaust* (London, 2011), 385–96, is a reliable brief guide.

109. Domarus, *Hitler*, 745.
110. Ibid, 1,058–65; see also the report of Ribbentrop's audience with Pope Pius XII on 10 March 1940, ibid, 1,480–81; Kershaw, *Hitler* II, 39–42; also Evans, *The Third Reich in Power*, 220–60; and Evans, *The Third Reich at War*, 546–53, both with references to the large literature on the 'Church struggle'. For Hitler's rejection of occultism, see also Richard J. Evans, 'Nuts about the Occult', *London Review of Books*, vol. 40, no. 15 (2 August 2018).
111. Domarus, *Hitler*, 892–94.
112. Ibid, 1,469; similarly on 8 November 1943 (Domarus, *Hitler*, 2,057–58).
113. Jochmann (ed.), *Adolf Hitler*, 67, 83–84, 103, 135, 150, 286, 301–3.
114. Vollnhals *et al.* (eds.), *Hitler*, IV//1, 53. While Hitler was here referring to Germany's failure (as he saw it) to gain more than a handful of overseas territories in the 'Scramble for Africa' of the 1880s, the recovery of the German colonies confiscated in the peace settlement of 1919 was not one of his major foreign-policy objectives. See also Jochen Thies, *Hitler's Plans for Global Domination: Nazi Architecture and Ultimate War Aims* (Oxford, 2012).
115. Longerich, *Hitler: A Life*, 334.
116. Domarus, *Hitler*, 237–38.
117. Ibid, 475; Kershaw, *Hitler* I, 490–95.
118. Longerich, *Hitler: A Life*, 525.
119. Succinct surveys of foreign policy to 1939 in Longerich, *Hitler: A Life*, 415, 333–67, 415–24, 438–76, 527–647.
120. Ibid, 334.
121. Domarus, *Hitler*, 476.
122. Ibid, 269–79 (quote on 279), 306–15, 496–97.
123. Longerich, *Hitler: A Life*, 334; Kershaw, *Hitler* I, 522–24.
124. Longerich, *Hitler: A Life*, 134–38; Domarus, *Hitler*, 472–74 (Saar).
125. Domarus, *Hitler*, 580–614.
126. Ibid, 317–22, 356–57; Christian Leitz, *Nazi Foreign Policy, 1933–1941: The Road to Global War* (London, 2004); Kershaw, *Hitler* I, 542–58.
127. Domarus, *Hitler*, 760.
128. Ibid, 745, information given to Domarus by one of the participants in the meeting, Waldemar Vogt.
129. Ibid, 743. The Polish Corridor was a broad strip of land taken from Germany by the Treaty of Versailles, and given to the newly created state of Poland in order to provide it with an outlet to the Baltic Sea.
130. Ibid, 745–56.
131. Evans, *The Third Reich in Power*, 642–46; Domarus, *Hitler*, 880–86 (sceptical of the generals' seriousness).
132. See below, pp. 183–202.
133. Domarus, *Hitler*, 755–59, 784–85, 796–800.
134. Ibid, 796 (20 February 1938).

135. Kershaw, *Hitler* II, 3–125; Ullrich, *Adolf Hitler* I, 734–838.
136. Domarus, *Hitler*, 483; for the personnel changes, see ibid, 764.
137. Zara Steiner, *The Triumph of the Dark: European International History 1933–1939* (Oxford, 2011), 311–18, 360–64, 551–53; Domarus, *Hitler*, 1,065, 1,202, 1,383, 1,386, 1,490.
138. Evans, *The Third Reich in Power*, 646–52; Kershaw, *Hitler* II, 63–72; Stefan Martens, 'Die Rolle Hermann Görings in der deutschen Aussenpolitik 1937/38', in Franz Knipping and Klaus-Jürgen Müller (eds.), *Machtbewusstsein in Deutschland am Vorabend des Zweiten Weltkrieges* (Paderborn, 1984), 75–82; more generally, Gerhard Botz, *Der 13. März und die Anschluss-Bewegung: Selbstaufgabe, Okkupation und Selbstfindung Österreichs 1918–1945* (Vienna, 1978), esp. 5–12; Domarus, *Hitler*, 788–91; Kershaw, *Hitler* II, 9–86.
139. Domarus, *Hitler*, 851–52, 868–70.
140. Ibid, 888–90, 901–56; Kershaw, *Hitler* II, 87–125. Among many studies from a variety of perspectives, see most recently Tim Bouverie, *Appeasing Hitler: Chamberlain, Churchill and the Road to War* (London, 2019).
141. Domarus, *Hitler*, 963–69.
142. Ibid, 974.
143. Evans, *The Third Reich in Power*, 704.
144. Domarus, *Hitler*, 727 (13 September 1937, Nuremberg Party Rally).
145. Ibid, 729–31.
146. Ibid, 1,089–90, 1,154–56.
147. Ibid, 1,047–55, 1,121–23, 1,143–45, 1,443 (1 January 1940).
148. Ibid, 1,255–338.
149. Ibid, 1,196–201; Kershaw, *Hitler* II, 97–230.
150. Kershaw, *Hitler* II, 189–217; Geoffrey Roberts, 'The Soviet Decision for a Pact with Nazi Germany', *Soviet Studies* 55 (1992), 57–78; Roger Moorhouse, *The Devils' Alliance: Hitler's Pact with Stalin 1939–41* (London, 2016); see however my article 'Was Stalinism Worse than Nazism?', *The Guardian* (9 August 2014), Review Section, 6. For the general background, see Gerhard L. Weinberg, *The Foreign Policy of Hitler's Germany*, 2 vols. (London, 1970, 1980); and Kershaw, *Hitler* II, 200–30.
151. Evans, *The Third Reich in Power*, 699–700.
152. Domarus, *Hitler*, 1,336–43.
153. Ibid, 1,332–35; Longerich, *Hitler: A Life*, 652–762, for the opening stages of the war, up to Operation Barbarossa.
154. Domarus, *Hitler*, 1,405–14; similarly on 30 January 1940 (ibid, 1,452–61).
155. Ibid, 1,405–18; Anton Hoch, 'Das Attentat auf Hitler im Münchner Bürgerbräukeller 1939', *Vierteljahrshefte für Zeitgeschichte* 17 (1969), 383–413; Kershaw, *Hitler* II, 271–75.
156. Domarus, *Hitler*, 1,180–83, 1,207.

157. Ibid, 1,237–40; Alexander B. Rossino, *Hitler Strikes Poland: Blitzkrieg, Ideology, and Atrocity* (Lawrence, KS, 2003).
158. Jochmann (ed.), *Adolf Hitler*, 48, 90–91, 137; Kershaw, *Hitler* II, 400–407; Evans, *The Third Reich at War*, 170–73.
159. Ibid, 62, 331, 440, 453; Picker, *Hitlers Tischgespräche*, 214–17, 247, 284–87.
160. Kershaw, *Hitler* II, 233–52; Evans, *The Third Reich at War*, 28–47, with further references.
161. Evans, *The Third Reich at War*, 112–36.
162. Domarus, *Hitler*, 1,487–99.
163. Ibid, 1,528–33; Kershaw, *Hitler* II, 283–337; Longerich, *Hitler: A Life*, 653–762.
164. Domarus, *Hitler*, 1,501, 1,519; for Frank, see below, pp. 335–51.
165. Saul Friedländer, *The Years of Extermination: Nazi Germany and the Jews, 1939–45* (New York, 2007), Part 1 (3–196).
166. Domarus, *Hitler*, 503.
167. Ibid, 1,421–27; Kershaw, *Hitler* II, 281–338.
168. Domarus, *Hitler*, 1,525.
169. Ibid, 1,520–22.
170. Ibid, 1,533, 1,547.
171. Ibid, 1,534.
172. Ibid, 1,535; Walther Hubatsch (ed.), *Hitlers Weisungen für die Kriegführung 1939–1945. Dokumente des Oberkommandos der Wehrmacht* (Frankfurt, 11 August 1940), 66 (16 July 1942, 2), 61–66, 71 (12 November 1940).
173. Domarus, *Hitler*, 1,540–1,559.
174. Ibid, 1,575–83.
175. Ibid, 1,564–67, 1,583–86, 1,652–53; Kershaw, *Hitler* II, 309–10; Richard Overy, *The Battle of Britain: Myth and Reality* (London, 2001).
176. Domarus, *Hitler*, 1,635–38; Hubatsch (ed.), *Hitlers Weisungen*, 84–88 (18 December 1940); Kershaw, *Hitler* II, 339–89.
177. Domarus, *Hitler*, 1,659–64.
178. Kershaw, *Hitler* II, 524–26; Hubatsch (ed.), *Hitlers Weisungen*, 96–100 (January–February 1941), 106–29 (March–September 1941).
179. Domarus, *Hitler*, 1,725–32; also 1,752 ('thus Jewish capitalism and Bolshevism have united in a world that is hostile to us today', 24 September 1941).
180. Ibid, 1,004–8, 1,071–72.
181. Ibid, 1,041, 1,447, 1,913.
182. Ibid, 1,753.
183. Traudl Junge, *Bis zur letzten Stunde. Hitlers Sekretärin erzählt ihr Leben* (unter Mitarbeit von Melissa Müller, Munich, 2002), 123.
184. Evans, *The Third Reich at War*, 167–90.
185. Friedländer, *The Years of Extermination*, Parts II–III (197–663), is still the best account; for a succinct narrative, see Longerich, *Hitler: A Life*, 763–76.

186. Richard J. Evans, 'The Decision to Exterminate the Jews of Europe', in Larissa Allwork and Rachel Pistol (eds.), *The Jews, the Holocaust, and the Public: The Legacies of David Cesarani* (Palgrave Macmillan, London, 2019), 117–44.
187. Domarus, *Hitler*, 1,758–67.
188. Ibid, 1,769–81.
189. Kershaw, *Hitler* II, 393–457.
190. Hubatsch (ed.), *Hitlers Weisungen*, 171–74 (8 December 1941).
191. Domarus, *Hitler*, 1,815.
192. Ibid, 1,785–91, 1,812–13.
193. Evans, *The Third Reich at War*, 191–214.
194. Domarus, *Hitler*, 1,794–811; Kershaw, *Hitler* II, 442–46.
195. Domarus, *Hitler*, 1,822; Ian Kershaw, *Fateful Choices: Ten Decisions that Changed the World, 1940–1941* (London, 2008), Chapter 9, for a full analysis.
196. Domarus, *Hitler*, 1,826–34.
197. Ibid, 1,909.
198. Ibid, 2,035–39; Kershaw, *Hitler* II, 534, 538–39.
199. Domarus, *Hitler*, 1,935; Kershaw, *Hitler* II, 543–45.
200. Domarus, *Hitler*, 1,983; Antony Beevor, *Stalingrad* (London, 2007); Kershaw, *Hitler* II, 544–46.
201. Domarus, *Hitler*, 1,996; for another example of Hitler's refusal to listen to military advice, see ibid, 2,077–78.
202. Ibid, 2,011 (7 May 1943).
203. Kershaw, *Hitler* II, 649–50.
204. Domarus, *Hitler*, 1,991 (24 February 1943).
205. Ibid, 2,001 (21 March 1943).
206. Ibid, 2,052, 2,056, 2,058, 2,061, 2,071.
207. For the Obersalzberg, see Kershaw, *Hitler* I, 282–86, and Ernst Hanisch, *Der Obersalzberg: das Kehlsteinhaus und Adolf Hitler* (Berchtesgaden, 1995); for the July plot, see Peter Hoffmann, *The History of the German Resistance, 1933–1945* (London, 1977); updated in subsequent German editions; good brief account in Joachim C. Fest, *Plotting Hitler's Death: The German Resistance to Hitler* (London, 1996).
208. Linda von Keyserlingk-Rehbein, *'Nur eine ganz kleine Clique': Die NS-Ermittlungen über das Netzwerk vom 20. Juli 1944* (Berlin, 2018); Domarus, *Hitler*, 2,123–31.
209. Domarus, *Hitler*, 1,058.
210. Jochmann, *Monologe*, 106. See also the discussion in Richard J. Evans, *Telling Lies About Hitler: The Holocaust, History and the David Irving Trial* (London, 2002), 78–79. The marshes were too shallow to cause the Jews to drown.
211. Domarus, *Hitler*, 1,866–69; also 1,978 ('Die Verschwörung vom internationalen Kapitalismus und Bolschewismus', 30 January 1943); similarly

on 24 February 1943 (Domarus, *Hitler*, 1,992, referring to an 'alliance between . . . the Jewish bank houses of New York, the Jewish-plutocratic leadership stratum in London and the Jews of the Kremlin in Moscow'); see also ibid, 2,002 (21 March 1943).
212. Kershaw, *Hitler* II, 459–95.
213. Jochmann (ed.), *Adolf Hitler*, 229 (no. 110, 25 January 1942).
214. Domarus, *Hitler*, 1,920; see also Jochmann (ed.), *Adolf Hitler*, 293, 340, 400, 422, 456.
215. Picker, *Hitlers Tischgespräche*, 340, 388.
216. Domarus, *Hitler*, 2005, also in Andreas Hillgruber (ed.), *Staatsmänner und Diplomaten bei Hitler* (Frankfurt, 1970), II, 256–57.
217. Domarus, *Hitler*, 2,051, 2,083, 2,160–67.
218. Ibid, 2,083–85; Kershaw, *Hitler* II, 473.
219. Junge, *Bis zur letzten Stunde*, 159–61.
220. Ullrich, *Adolf Hitler* II, 588–90; Junge, *Bis zur letzten Stunde*, 144–52; Christa Schroeder, *Er war mein Chef. Aus dem Nachlass der Sekretärin von Adolf Hitler*, 2nd edn (Munich, 1985), 19; Albert Speer, *Inside the Third Reich* (London, 1970), 629; Evans, *The Third Reich in History and Memory*, 142–49; Fritz Redlich, *Hitler: Diagnosis of a Destructive Prophet* (New York, 1998); Neumann and Eberle, *Was Hitler Ill?* Hitler's sweet tooth is described in Hanfstaengl, *Zwischen Weissem und Braunen Haus*, 45. For the myth of Hitler's drug addiction, see Richard J. Evans, '*Blitzed: Drugs in Nazi Germany* by Norman Ohler review – A Crass and Dangerously Inaccurate Account', *The Guardian* (6 November 2016), and Kershaw, *Hitler* II, 870–71. Hugh Trevor-Roper, *The Last Days of Hitler* (London, 1947), 105–13, relies mainly on Speer and Brandt and presents a correspondingly negative portrait of Morell. See also Joachimsthaler, *Hitlers Ende*, 98–200, for a detailed narrative.
221. Junge, *Bis zur letzten Stunde*, 140.
222. Alexandra Richie, *Warsaw 1944: The Fateful Uprising* (London, 2013).
223. Evans, *The Third Reich at War*, 616–18, 653–55; Ullrich, *Adolf Hitler* II, 543–47, 556–7; Domarus, *Hitler*, 2,151, 2,156–57.
224. Evans, *The Third Reich at War*, 660–75; Fritz Hahn, *Waffen und Geheimwaffen des deutschen Heeres, 1933–1945*, 2 vols. (Koblenz, 1986–1987); Junge, *Bis zur letzten Stunde*, 154–56; Below, *Als Hitlers Adjutant*, 403; Domarus, *Hitler*, 2,107; Kershaw, *Hitler* II, 641–45.
225. David Welch, *Propaganda and the German Cinema, 1933–1945* (Oxford, 1983), 221–37; Rolf Giesen, *Nazi Propaganda Films: A History and Filmography* (Jefferson, NC, 2003), 163–84; and Felix Moeller, *Der Filmminister: Goebbels und der Film im Dritten Reich* (Berlin, 1998), 295–99, 309–12; Bill Niven, *Hitler and Film: The Führer's Hidden Passion* (London, 2018), 221–25; Domarus, *Hitler*, 2,150.

226. Klaus Mammach, *Der Volkssturm: Bestandteil des totalen Kriegseinsatzes der deutschen Bevölkerung 1944/45* (Berlin, 1981); Franz Seidler, *'Deutscher Volkssturm': Der letzte Aufgebot 1944/45* (Munich, 1989); Speer, *Inside the Third Reich*, 560–61.
227. Domarus, *Hitler*, 2,171.
228. Below, *Als Hitlers Adjutant*, 398; Ullrich, *Adolf Hitler* II, 560–73; Junge, *Bis zur letzten Stunde*, 139–40; Domarus, *Hitler*, 2,172–75; Kershaw, *Hitler* II, 737–47.
229. Overy (ed.), *Interrogations*, 101–9.
230. Domarus, *Hitler*, 2,179–88; Ullrich, *Adolf Hitler* II, 574–85.
231. Ullrich, *Adolf Hitler* II, 570–71; Toby Thacker, *Joseph Goebbels: Life and Death* (London, 2009), 287; Domarus, *Hitler*, 2,195–98, 2,203–6; similarly in his proclamations of 11 March and 13 April (Domarus, *Hitler*, 2,212, 2,223).
232. Trevor-Roper, *The Last Days of Hitler*, 89; Fröhlich (ed.), *Die Tagebücher*, 17 March 1945, 7 April 1945; Domarus, *Hitler*, 2,191.
233. Jochmann (ed.), *Adolf Hitler*, 366.
234. Hubatsch (ed.), *Hitlers Weisungen*, 303 (19 March 1945).
235. Speer, *Inside the Third Reich*, 586–88; Below, *Als Hitlers Adjutant*, 404–5, 417; Goebbels, *Tagebuch* (17 March 1945); Domarus, *Hitler*, 2,214–2,257. The *Table Talk* recorded him already saying on 27 January 1942: 'If the German people is not prepared to commit itself to its preservation, very good. Then it should, vanish.' (Jochmann, *Monologe*, 239).
236. Joachimsthaler, *Hitlers Ende*, 41–97.
237. Kershaw, *Hitler* II, 901–2; Ullrich, *Adolf Hitler*, II, 630–33.
238. Junge, *Bis zur letzten Stunde*, 176–78; Trevor-Roper, *The Last Days of Hitler*, 89–90; Kershaw, *Hitler* II, 926–28; Below, *Als Hitlers Adjutant*, 408–11.
239. Hubatsch (ed.), *Hitlers Weisungen*, 310–11 (15 April 1945). For the road to Germany's defeat, see Longerich, *Hitler: A Life*, 868–965.
240. Junge, *Bis zur letzten Stunde*, 179–88; Ullrich, *Adolf Hitler*, II, 633–41; Kershaw, *Hitler* II, 802–7; Domarus, *Hitler*, 2,226–28.
241. Junge, *Bis zur letzten Stunde*, 193; Below, *Als Hitlers Adjutant*, 411.
242. Junge, *Bis zur letzten Stunde*, 197–99; Below, *Als Hitlers Adjutant*, 412–15; Ullrich, *Adolf Hitler*, II, 643–50; Kershaw, *Hitler* II, 804–19; Domarus, *Hitler*, 2,228–234.
243. Junge, *Bis zur letzten Stunde*, 195–96; Kershaw, *Hitler* II, 953.
244. Ullrich, *Adolf Hitler* II, 652–53; Kershaw, *Hitler* II, 820–24. These documents must be distinguished from the spurious 'Political Testament', an alleged record of a conversation between Hitler and Bormann first published in French in 1959 (Nilsson, *Hitler Redux*, 278–339).
245. Domarus, *Hitler*, 570 (30 January 1936)

246. Junge, *Bis zur letzten Stunde*, 194; Below, *Als Hitlers Adjutant*, illustration opposite 401, and 416; Ullrich, *Hitler* II, 651–54; Domarus, *Hitler*, 2, 236–42.
247. Junge, *Bis zur letzten Stunde*, 206–7. Junge claimed that the fatal shot was heard throughout the bunker.
248. Ullrich, *Adolf Hitler*, II, 656–60; Anton Joachimsthaler, *The Last Days of Hitler: Legend, Evidence and Truth* (London, 2000), 288–383.
249. Junge, *Bis zur letzten Stunde*, 208; Kershaw, *Hitler* II, 827–31; Anton Joachimsthaler, *Hitlers Ende*, 201–87. For the Soviet investigation into the circumstances of Hitler's death, kept under wraps until after the fall of Communism, see Henrik Eberle and Matthias Uhl (eds.), *The Hitler Book: The Secret Dossier Prepared for Stalin* (London, 2005), 268–74, following the testimony of Günsche and Linge in Soviet captivity. For the many conspiracy theories alleging Hitler's survival, all of them completely unfounded, see Evans, *The Hitler Conspiracies*, 165–211.
250. Kershaw, *Hitler* II, 831–41.
251. Ibid, xxvii.
252. Jochmann, *Monologe*, 321, 333, 378.
253. See the summary by Kershaw, *Personality and Power*, 83–114.

Part II

Introduction

1. Christoph Klessmann, 'Der Generalgouverneur Hans Frank', *Vierteljahrshefte für Zeitgeschichte*, vol. 19 (1971), 45–260, at 246.
2. Burton C. Andrus, *The Infamous of Nuremberg* (London, 1969), 92–111; Douglas R. Kelley, *22 Cells in Nuremberg: A Psychiatrist Examines the Nazi Criminals* (London, 1947), 30, 118, 129–30.
3. The reference is to Act 5, Scene 1 of William Shakespeare's *The Tempest*, where the servant Caliban expresses his disillusion with Stephano: 'thrice-double ass' means a supersized donkey, an animal synonymous at the time with stupidity. 'Ashcan' and 'Dustbin' were nicknames for Allied detention centres.
4. Richard Overy (ed.), *Interrogations: The Nazi Elite in Allied Hands, 1945* (London, 2001), 3–26.
5. Bosley Crowther, 'Varnished Truth: "The Hitler Gang" Gives Evidence of an Incomplete Political Analysis', *New York Times* (14 May 1944), X, 3.
6. Trevor-Roper, *The Last Days of Hitler*. As an undergraduate in Oxford, I attended Trevor-Roper's lectures on Gibbon, for whom he had an entirely uncritical admiration.

7. Heike B. Görtemaker, *Hitlers Hofstaat. Der innere Kreis im Dritten Reich und danach* (Munich, 2019).
8. C. Wright Mills, *The Power Elite* (Oxford, 1956).

2. The 'Iron Man: Hermann Göring

1. Mark Felton, 'Hermann Goering's Pet Lions' (https://www.youtube.com/watch?v=gzDK4RVfARs); Emmy Goering, *My Life with Goering* (London, 1972), 1 (in general, a vapid and uninformative work). For the context, see Gary Bruce, *Through the Lion Gate: A History of Berlin Zoo* (New York, 2017); Jan Mohnhaupt, *Tiere im Nationalsozialismus* (Munich, 2020).
2. Uwe Neumärker, 'Wo die braunen Hirsche röhrten', *Der Spiegel* (online), 5 May 2008. See also the photographs in the authorized biography by Erich Gritzbach, *Hermann Goering: The Man and His Work* (London, 1939), 48–49, 64–65.
3. Quoted in Richard Overy, *Goering: The Iron Man*, 2nd edn (London, 2021), 269. New College, despite its name, is one of the oldest Colleges in the University of Oxford.
4. Kenneth D. Alford, *Hermann Göring and the Nazi Art Collection: The Looting of Europe's Art Treasures and Their Dispersal After World War II* (Jefferson, NC, 2012), 15–16, 126, 183–249; Günther Haase, *Die Kunstsammlung des Reichsmarschalls Hermann Göring: eine Dokumentation* (Berlin, 2000); Nikola Doll, *Mäzenentum und Kunstförderung im Nationalsozialismus: Werner Peiner und Hermann Göring* (Weimar, 2009); Hanns Christian Löhr, *Der eiserner Sammler: die Kollektion Hermann Göring: Kunst und Korruption im 'Dritten Reich'* (Berlin, 2009); Roger Manvell and Heinrich Fraenkel, *Hermann Göring* (London, 1962), 265–79; Gritzbach, *Hermann Goering*, 2, 14–251 ('The Man and the Artist'), for the public image.
5. François Kersaudy, *Hermann Goering: Le deuxième homme du IIIe Reich* (Paris, 2009), 13–21; Asher Lee, *Goering: Air Leader* (London, 1972), 11–13; Manvell and Fraenkel, *Hermann Göring*, 1–2.
6. Lee, *Goering*, 13–16; 13–25; Kersaudy, *Hermann Goering*, 22–26; Stefan Martens, *Hermann Göring. 'Erster Paladin des Führers' und 'Zweiter Mann im Reich'* (Paderborn, 1985), 15–20; Manvell and Fraenkel, *Hermann Göring*, 3–9 (with unconvincing psychological speculations).
7. Norman Franks and Hal Giblin, *Under the Guns of the German Aces Immelmann, Voss, Göring, Lothar von Richthofen: The Complete Record of their Victories and Victims* (London, 1997), 41–64.
8. Lee, *Goering*, 17–21; Franks and Giblin *Under the Guns*, 41–64; Manvell and Fraenkel, *Hermann Göring*, 9–15.
9. Peter Fritzsche, *A Nation of Fliers: German Aviation and the Popular Imagination* (Cambridge, MA, 1992), 59–102.

10. Lee, *Goering*, 21–24; Kersaudy, *Hermann Goering*, 22–42; Manvell and Fraenkel, *Hermann Göring*, 15–19.
11. Lee, *Goering*, 22–25; Björn Fontander, *Göring och Sverige* (Kristjanstad, 1984), 13–50; Kersaudy, *Hermann Goering*, 43–58; Manvell and Fraenkel, *Hermann Göring*, 19–24.
12. Jack El-Hai, *The Nazi and the Psychiatrist: Hermann Göring, Dr. Douglas M. Kelley, and a Fatal Meeting of Minds at the End of WWII* (New York, 2013), 11–12; Manvell and Fraenkel, *Hermann Göring*, 24–25.
13. Siemens, *Stormtroopers*, 10, 18–19; Alfred Kube, *Pour le mérite und Hakenkreuz. Hermann Göring im Dritten Reich* (Munich 1986), 11; Kersaudy, *Hermann Goering*, 43–87; Manvell and Fraenkel, *Hermann Göring*, 26–36; Leon Goldensohn, *The Nuremberg Interviews: An American Psychiatrist's Conversations with the Defendants and Witnesses*, ed. Robert Gellately (New York, 2005), 132.
14. Alford, *Hermann Göring*, 6 (quoting from Carin's letters, held in the US Army Military History Institute, Carlisle, Pennsylvania); Kersaudy, *Hermann Goering*, 73–87; Manvell and Fraenkel, *Hermann Göring*, 37–42, 142–43.
15. Fontander, *Göring och Sverige*, 58–110 (quoting medical reports); Lee, *Goering*, 26–34; Kersaudy, *Hermann Goering*, 88–139 (with a map of his travels in 1923–24 on 97); Alford, *Hermann Göring*, 7; Manvell and Fraenkel, *Hermann Göring*, 42–43.
16. Kube, *Pour le mérite*, 1–15; Manvell and Fraenkel, *Hermann Göring*, 44–57.
17. Lee, *Goering*, 35–39; Kube, *Pour le mérite*, 15–21; Manvell and Fraenkel, *Hermann Göring*, 57–72.
18. Manvell and Fraenkel, *Hermann Göring*, 80–88.
19. Kube, *Pour le mérite*, 22–27; Evans, *The Third Reich in Power*, 27–38; Kersaudy, *Hermann Goering*, 140–76; Manvell and Fraenkel, *Hermann Göring*, 73–120.
20. Kube, *Pour le mérite*, 27–29.
21. Kersaudy, *Hermann Goering*, 177–257; Manvell and Fraenkel, *Hermann Göring*, 133–36, 149–51.
22. Overy, *Goering*, 72–86.
23. Quoted in ibid, ix.
24. Hermann Goering, *Germany Reborn* (London, 1934), 27, 124–31; idem, *Reden und Aufsätze*, 2nd edn (Munich, 1938).
25. Noakes and Pridham, *Nazism 1919–1945*, vol. II, 558–65; Kersaudy, *Hermann Goering*, 258–64; Manvell and Fraenkel, *Hermann Göring*, 171–77.
26. Kube, *Pour le mérite*, 29–30; Kersaudy, *Hermann Goering*, 206–7; Emmy Goering, *My Life with Goering*, 8–19, 41.
27. Kube, *Pour le mérite*, 265–78, 303–13; Kersaudy, *Hermann Goering*, 258–319, also for the following; Manvell and Fraenkel, *Hermann Göring*,

93, 144–72, 185–86, 192. Wolfgang Paul's popular biography, *Hermann Göring: Hitler Paladin or Puppet?* (London, 1998), 7–23, 182–97, emphasizes Göring's attempts to negotiate with the British government in 1939. The dissertation by Martens, *Hermann Göring, passim*, focuses on Göring's foreign-policy ambitions and activities.
28. Kube, *Pour le mérite*, 313–23; Emmy Goering, *My Life with Goering*, 5–6; Manvell and Fraenkel, *Hermann Göring*, 189–92, 198–213.
29. Kube, *Pour le mérite*, 323–35; Kersaudy, *Hermann Goering*, 320–442, 497–581; Overy, *Goering*, 187–233; Manvell and Fraenkel, *Hermann Göring*, 214–56.
30. Gustave Gilbert, *Nuremberg Diary* (London, 1948), 78; Martens, *Hermann Göring*, 223–41, 259–60.
31. Overy, *Goering*, 157–86.
32. Ibid, 234–62.
33. Noakes and Pridham, *Nazism*, vol. III, 451, 503.
34. Lee, *Goering*, 141, 148–49.
35. Overy, *Goering*, 187–233.
36. Lee, *Goering*, 211; Kersaudy, *Hermann Goering*, 443–96.
37. El-Hai, *The Nazi and the Psychiatrist*, 14–15; Manvell and Fraenkel, *Hermann Göring*, 280–96.
38. Trevor-Roper, *The Last Days of Hitler*, 66.
39. Ibid, 130 n.; Manvell and Fraenkel, *Hermann Göring*, 258–59.
40. Ibid, 161, 168–70, 176–79, 187–89, 210, 215; Evans, *The Third Reich at War*, 728; Kersaudy, *Hermann Goering*, 582–647; Manvell and Fraenkel, *Hermann Göring*, 297–314; Overy (ed.), *Interrogations*, 145–47.
41. Andrus, *The Infamous*, 29.
42. Kelley, *22 Cells*, 47–49.
43. Andrus, *The Infamous*, 40, 46–47.
44. Manvell and Fraenkel, *Hermann Göring*, xiv.
45. Papen, *Memoirs*, 554–55.
46. Goldensohn, *The Nuremberg Interviews*, 111.
47. Gilbert, *Nuremberg Diary*, 162, 205–7, 79, 400–402, 79–80; Overy (ed.), *Interrogations*, 144–53; Kersaudy, *Hermann Goering*, 648–745; Manvell and Fraenkel, *Hermann Göring*, 315–79; Goldensohn, *The Nuremberg Interviews*, 101–34; Andrus, *The Infamous*, 190–91. See also testimonies of participants in the Nuremberg trials, such as interpreters, secretaries, etc., in Hilary Gaskin, *Eyewitnesses at Nuremberg* (London, 1990), esp. 77–84, on Göring's aggression in the dock towards witnesses.
48. Ben E. Swearingen, *The Mystery of Hermann Goering's Suicide* (London, 1985), 210–14; Andrus, *The Infamous*, 199–201.
49. James Wyllie, *Nazi Wives: The Women at the Top of Hitler's Germany* (Cheltenham, 2019); Harris, *Selling Hitler*, 64–67; Manvell and Fraenkel, *Hermann Göring*, xii.

50. James Wyllie, *The Warlord and the Renegade; The Story of Hermann and Albert Goering* (Stroud, 2006).
51. For this argument, see Alfred Kube, 'Hermann Goering: Second Man in the Third Reich', in Ronald Smelser and Rainer Zitelmann (eds.), *The Nazi Elite* (London, 1993), 62–73.
52. Overy (ed.), *Interrogations*, 144.
53. Overy, *Göring*, 264–67.

3. The Propagandist: Joseph Goebbels

1. Michael Tracey, *A Variety of Lives: A Biography of Sir Hugh Greene* (London, 1983), 45–55; for the context, see Christian Goeschel, *Mussolini and Hitler: The Forging of the Fascist Alliance* (London, 2018), 111. At 5 foot 5 inches, Goebbels was in fact fourteen inches shorter than Greene. Greene's report on page 17 of the following day's *Daily Telegraph* presented a more discreet version of the story.
2. Hans-Jochen Gamm, *Der Flüsterwitz im Dritten Reich* (Hamburg, 1964), 84–94.
3. Fröhlich (ed.), *Die Tagebücher*, 4 April and 30 June 1931, quoted in Longerich, *Goebbels*, 147, 151.
4. Longerich, *Goebbels*, 3–27; Ralf Georg Reuth, *Goebbels. Eine Biographie* (1995), 11–55.
5. Longerich, *Goebbels*, 28–46; Reuth, *Goebbels*, 57–75.
6. Fröhlich (ed.), *Die Tagebücher*, 22 March 1924; Longerich, *Goebbels*, 37; Reuth, *Goebbels*, 37–41, 83–91.
7. Fröhlich (ed.), *Die Tagebücher*, 16 May 1924; Longerich, *Goebbels*, 41.
8. Fröhlich (ed.), *Die Tagebücher*, 13 October 1925; Longerich, *Goebbels*, 63; Reuth, *Goebbels*, 76–107.
9. Fröhlich (ed.), *Die Tagebücher*, 15 February 1926; Longerich, *Goebbels*, 56; Reuth, *Goebbels*, 94–99.
10. Fröhlich (ed.), *Die Tagebücher*, 24 July 1926; Reuth, *Goebbels*, 100–107; Longerich, *Goebbels*, 62–72.
11. Longerich, *Goebbels*, 73–92; Reuth, *Goebbels*, 108–37; Dietz Bering, *Kampf um Namen. Bernhard Weiss gegen Joseph Goebbels* (Stuttgart, 1991).
12. Longerich, *Goebbels*, 93–104; Reuth, *Goebbels*, 138–62; Daniel Siemens, *Horst Wessel. Tod und Verklärung eines Nationalsozialisten* (Berlin, 2009); more generally, Behrenbeck, *Der Kult*.
13. Longerich, *Goebbels*, 151–57; Reuth, *Goebbels*, 196–98.
14. Longerich, *Goebbels*, 157–60, quoting Fröhlich (ed.), *Die Tagebücher*, 14–16 September 1931; Reuth, *Goebbels*, 196–98, 235, 310, 334, 382, 462.
15. Evans, *The Coming of the Third Reich*, 289–308; Longerich, *Goebbels*, 190–201; Reuth, *Goebbels*, 210–55.

16. Longerich, *Goebbels*, 205–15; Reuth, *Goebbels*, 267–71.
17. Evans, *The Third Reich in Power*, 120–218; Reuth, *Goebbels*, 270–81.
18. Longerich, *Goebbels*, 328–57; Reuth, *Goebbels*, 291, 364–69.
19. Walther Gehl (ed.), *Die nationalsozialistische Revolution: Tatsachen und Urkunden, Reden und Schilderungen, 1. August 1914 bis 1. Mai 1933* (Breslau, 1933), 277; Fröhlich (ed.), *Die Tagebücher*, 11 May 1933; Reuth, *Goebbels*, 281–86.
20. Longerich, *Goebbels*, 301–6; Reuth, *Goebbels*, 368–70, 686–87, n. 137 (Fröhlich [ed.)], *Die Tagebücher*, 11 February 1937).
21. Longerich, *Goebbels*, 262–70; Reuth, *Goebbels*, 313–19.
22. Longerich, *Goebbels*, 375.
23. Longerich, *Goebbels*, 315–18, 322–25, 358–64, 405–6; Reuth, *Goebbels*, 290–92, 385–86, 415–41, 462–63.
24. Longerich, *Goebbels*, 246–47, 315–18, 324, 363, 392–96, 404–6; Reuth, *Goebbels*, 348–52, 363–64, 378, 382–83, 388–90.
25. Longerich, *Goebbels*, 382–83, 396–402 (quotes on 383, 398); Reuth, *Goebbels*, 395–400.
26. Jürgen Runzheimer, 'Der Überfall auf den Sender Gleiwitz im Jahre 1939', *Vierteljahrshefte für Zeitgeschichte*, vol. 10 (1962), 408–26.
27. Longerich, *Goebbels*, 433–55 (quoting Fröhlich [ed.], *Die Tagebücher*, 7 July 1940); Reuth, *Goebbels*, 468–70.
28. Longerich, *Goebbels*, 468–70, 479; David Welch, *Propaganda and the German Cinema, 1933–1945* (Oxford, 1983), esp. 221–37, 271–306; Niven, *Hitler and Film*, 163–83.
29. Evans, *The Third Reich at War*, 256–70; Longerich, *Goebbels*, 514–15, 547–48.
30. Longerich, *Goebbels*, 508–20, 549–62; Reuth, *Goebbels*, 515–24.
31. Longerich, *Goebbels*, 569–79, 637–47.
32. Longerich, *Goebbels*, 675 (for quote), 683–87, ix–xii; Reuth, *Goebbels*, 613–14. The order was officially called the *Decree Concerning Demolitions in the Reich Territory*.
33. Evans, *The Third Reich at War*, 727.
34. Reuth, *Goebbels*, 615–16 (and photograph, 385); Longerich, *Goebbels*, x–xi.
35. Longerich, *Goebbels*, xvi–xvii, 3–4, 9–10, 194–95, 340, 533, 691–92.
36. Reuth, *Goebbels*, 341; Longerich, *Goebbels*, 195.
37. Evans, *The Coming of the Third Reich*, 395–99; Longerich, *Goebbels*, 689–708.

4. The Soldier: Ernst Röhm

1. Eleanor Hancock, *Ernst Röhm: Hitler's SA Chief of Staff* (New York, 2008), 95–96; eadem, 'Ernst Röhm versus General Hans Kundt in Bolivia,

1929–30? The Curious Incident', *Journal of Contemporary History*, vol. 47, no. 4 (2012), 691–708, also for the following paragraph; and Len E. Bieber, 'La política militar alemana en Bolivia, 1900–1935', *Latin American Research Review*, vol. 29 (1994), 1, 85–106. See also John P. Fox, 'Max Bauer: Chiang Kai-shek's First German Military Adviser', *Journal of Contemporary History*, vol. 5, no. 4 (1970), 21–44.
2. As n. 1; see also Robert Brockmann, *El general y sus presidentes: vida y tiempos de Hans Kundt, Ernst Röhm y siete presidentes en la historia de Bolivia, 1911–1939* (La Paz, 2007), 385–448 (largely based on secondary sources).
3. Hancock, *Ernst Röhm*, 1–13 (quotes on 9, 13); Peter Longerich, *Die braunen Bataillone. Geschichte der SA* (Munich, 1989), 17. See also Ernst Röhm, *Die Geschichte eines Hochverräters* (Volksausgabe, Munich, 1933; first pub. 1928), 15–28; the reissue of 1933 contains new material added by Röhm, for example on his stay in Bolivia (357–64). An English edition appeared in 2020 with a Foreword by Eleanor Hancock. Ernst Röhm, *Die Memoiren des Stabschefs Röhm* (Munich, 1934), is heavily expurgated and contains material not written by Röhm: see Heinrich Bennecke, 'Die Memoiren des Ernst Röhm. Ein Vergleich der verschiedenen Ausgaben und Auflagen', *Politische Studien*, vol. 14, no. 1 (1963), 179–88. Marcus Mühle, *Ernst Röhm. Eine biographische Skizze* (Berlin, 2016), is a brief introductory account that adds little to Hancock's well-researched biography.
4. Hancock, *Ernst Röhm*, 14–26; eadem, 'Ernst Röhm and the Experience of World War I', *Journal of Military History*, vol. 60, no. 1 (1996), 39–60; Röhm, *Die Geschichte*, 28–86.
5. Hancock, *Ernst Röhm*, 27–35; Longerich, *Die braunen Bataillone*, 18; Röhm, *Die Geschichte*, 91.
6. Hancock, *Ernst Röhm*, 36–51.
7. Ibid, 40–41.
8. Ibid, 52–70; Röhm, *Die Geschichte*, 233–58.
9. Hancock, *Ernst Röhm*, 71–85, 92–93; Siemens, *Stormtroopers*, 3–61; Longerich, *Die braunen Bataillone*, 45–52; Röhm, *Die Geschichte*, 233–77; Hartmann et al. (eds.), *Hitler, Mein Kampf*, I, 1,068 n. 193.
10. Hancock, *Ernst Röhm*, 105–9.
11. Siemens, *Stormtroopers*, 58–74; Hancock, *Ernst Röhm*, 105–19; Andreas Dornheim, *Röhms Mann fürs Ausland: Politik und Ermordung des SA-Agenten Georg Bell* (Münster, 1998), 77 (a detailed account of Röhm's attempts to raise funds from abroad for the SA); Bruce Campbell, *The SA Generals and the Rise of Nazism* (Lexington, KY, 1998), 105–10; Heinrich Bennecke, *Hitler und die SA* (Munich, 1972), 160; Mathilde Jamin, *Zwischen den Klassen: Zur Sozialstruktur der SA-Führerschaft* (Wuppertal, 1984); Hitler's order for a purge in Vollnhals et al. (eds.), *Hitler*, IV/1,

246–48 and 248–58 ('Adolf Hitlers Abrechnung mit den Rebellen', 4 April 1931, and following documents).
12. Siemens, *Stormtroopers*, 56–57.
13. Quoted in ibid, 53; see also Longerich, *Die braunen Bataillone*, 109–78.
14. Hancock, *Ernst Röhm*, 119–40; Siemens, *Stormtroopers*, 117–56.
15. Ullrich, *Adolf Hitler* I, 507.
16. Ibid, 510–11.
17. Viktor Lutze, who was to succeed Röhm as head of the SA, claimed to have overheard Röhm saying privately after the other participants had left: 'What the ridiculous corporal explained doesn't hold for us. Hitler is faithless and must at least take some leave. We'll do the job without Hitler if necessary' (as quoted in Helmut Krausnick, 'Der 30. Juni 1934: Bedeutung – Hintergründe – Verlauf', *Aus Politik und Zeitgeschichte: Beilage zur Wochenzeitung 'Das Parlament'*, 30 June 1954, 319). But this does not fit with either Röhm's much-documented loyalty to Hitler, or his public statements, and Lutze had every reason to make it up in order to justify his own position.
18. Hancock, *Ernst Röhm*, 131–51; Longerich, *Die braunen Bataillone*, 164–206.
19. Kershaw, *Hitler* I, 505–26; Hancock, *Ernst Röhm*, 153–66; Ullrich, *Adolf Hitler* I, 507–27. Höhne, *Mordsache Röhm*, presents Röhm as part of a broader attempt by the 'Nazi left' to push on to a 'second revolution'. Other accounts include Charles Bloch, *Die SA und die Krise des NS-Regimes 1934* (Frankfurt, 1970); Max Gallo, *La nuit des longs couteaux: 30 juin 1934* (Paris, 1970); Longerich, *Die braunen Bataillone*, 206–19; and Otto Gritschneider, *'Der Führer hat Sie zum Tode verurteilt . . .' Hitlers 'Röhm-Putsch' Morde vor Gericht* (Munich, 1993).
20. Evans, *The Coming of the Third Reich*, 183.
21. Fest, *The Face of the Third Reich*, 207.
22. Röhm, *Die Geschichte*, 363.
23. As noted by Siemens, *Stormtroopers*, 25, and Hancock, *Ernst Röhm*, 171–72.
24. Röhm, *Die Geschichte*, 281. See also Ihrig, *Atatürk*.
25. Richard Bessel, *Political Violence and the Rise of Nazism: The Storm Troopers in Eastern Germany 1925–1934* (London, 1984), 123.
26. Röhm, *Die Geschichte*, 9.
27. Ibid, 363–66.
28. Quoted in Hancock, *Ernst Röhm*, 87.
29. Longerich, *Goebbels*, 267.
30. George L. Mosse, *Nationalism and Sexuality: Respectable and Abnormal Sexuality in Modern Europe* (New York, 1997); see also the reissue (Madison, WI, 2020) with a critical introduction by Mary Louise Roberts; and the same author's *The Image of Man: The Creation of Modern Masculinity*

(New York, 1996); and Susanne Zur Nieden (ed.), *Homosexualität und Staatsräson: Männlichkeit, Homophobie und Politik in Deutschland 1900– 1945* (Frankfurt am Main, 2005).

31. Susanne Zur Nieden, *Aufstieg und Fall des viril Männerhelden – Der Skandal um Ernst Röhm und seine Ermordung* (Frankfurt am Main, 2005), 156.
32. Sefton Delmer, *Trail Sinister: An Autobiography* (London, 1961), 123; see also Karen Bayer, *'How Dead is Hitler?' Der britische Starreporter Sefton Delmer und die Deutschen* (Mainz, 2008).
33. Eleanor Hancock, '"Only the Real, the True, the Masculine Held Its Value": Ernst Röhm, Masculinity, and Male Homosexuality', *Journal of the History of Sexuality*, vol. 8, no. 4 (1998), 616–41; Hitler's directive of 3 February 1931 in Vollnhals *et al.* (eds.), *Hitler*, IV/1, 183.
34. Wilfried U. Eissler, *Arbeiterparteien und Homosexuellenfrage. Zur Sexualpolitik von SPD und KPD in der Weimarer Republik* (Berlin, 1980).
35. Zur Nieden, *Aufstieg und Fall*, 148–57; Herbert Linder, *Von der NSDAP zur SPD Der politische Lebensweg des D. Helmuth Klotz (1894–1943)* (Konstanz, 1998), 168–89.
36. Hancock, *Ernst Röhm*, 88–90, 111–15.
37. Matthäus and Bajohr (eds.), *Alfred Rosenberg*, 141–46.
38. Jürgen Reulecke *'Ich möchte einer werden, so wie die . . .' Männerbünde im 20. Jahrhundert* (Frankfurt, 2001); George L. Mosse, *The Crisis of German Ideology: Intellectual Origins of the Third Reich* (London, 1964); Zur Nieden, *Aufstieg und Fall*; Alexander Zinn, *Die soziale Konstruktion des homosexuellen Nationalsozialisten. Zur Genese und Etablierung eines Stereotyps* (Frankfurt am Main, 1997); Claudia Bruns, 'Der homosexuelle Staatsfreund: Von der Konstruktion des erotischen Männerbunds bei Hans Blüher', in Zur Nieden (ed.), *Homosexualität und Staatsräson*, 100–17; and Chandak Sengoopta, *Otto Weininger: Sex, Science, and Self in Imperial Vienna* (Chicago, IL, 2000). For the pre-war scandal, see Norman Domeier, *The Eulenburg Affair: A Cultural History of Politics in the German Empire* (Rochester, NY, 2015). More generally, see Burkhard Jellonek, *Homosexuelle unterm Hakenkreuz* (Paderborn, 1990).
39. For the view that Röhm wanted to bring about a 'second revolution', see Conan Fischer, 'Ernst Julius Röhm: Chief of Staff of the SA and Indispensable Outsider', in Smelser and Zitelman (eds.), *The Nazi Elite*, 173–82; also Otis C. Mitchell, *Hitler's Stormtroopers and the Attack on the German Republic, 1919–1933* (Jefferson, NC, 2008), 160–70.
40. Hancock, *Ernst Röhm*, 86.
41. Röhm, *Die Geschichte*, 366.
42. Ibid, 9.

5. The Policeman: Heinrich Himmler

1. Himmler's visit to the sauna on the day in question is documented in Peter Witte et al. (eds.), *Der Dienstkalender Heinrich Himmlers 1941/42* (Hamburg, 1999), 504. The full story is told in Curzio Malaparte, *Kaputt* (New York, 2005 [1944]), 336–42, also for the following.
2. For Himmler's favourable views on the health benefits of saunas in general, which caused him to order saunas to be built, using Russian prisoners of war as slave labour, in SS barracks, see Bradley F. Smith and Agnes F. Peterson (eds.), *Heinrich Himmler Geheimreden 1933 bis 1945 und andere Ansprachen* (Frankfurt, 1974), 194 (1942).
3. William B. Cohen and Jörgen Svensson, 'Finland and the Holocaust', *Holocaust and Genocide Studies*, vol. 9 (1995), 70–93; Antero Holmila, 'Finland and the Holocaust: A Reassessment', *Holocaust and Genocide Studies*, vol. 23 (2009), 413–40.
4. Fest, *The Face*, 171–73.
5. Trevor-Roper, *The Last Days of Hitler*, 68–69.
6. Bracher, *The German Dictatorship*, 356.
7. Richard Breitman, *The Architect of Genocide: Himmler and the Final Solution* (London, 1991), 5.
8. Peter Longerich, *Heinrich Himmler: Biographie* (Munich, 2008).
9. Ibid, 717; Witte et al. (eds.), *Der Dienstkalender*; Matthias Uhl et al. (eds.), *Die Organisation des Terrors: Der Dienstkalender Heinrich Himmlers 1943–1945* (Munich, 2020); Katrin Himmler and Michael Wildt (eds), *Himmler privat. Briefe eines Massenmörders* (Munich, 2014).
10. Katrin Himmler, *Die Brüder Himmler. Eine deutsche Familiengeschichte* (Frankfurt am Main, 2005), 29–54; Lion Feuchtwanger, *The Oppermanns* (London, 2020; first published as *Die Geschwister Oppermann*, 1934); Witte et al., *Der Dienstkalender* (Introduction), 19–20.
11. Longerich, *Heinrich Himmler*, 1–19; Himmler's social background in the *Bildungsbürgertum* is correctly noted for example in Breitman, *The Architect of Genocide*, 9–12, and Helmut Heiber (ed.), *Reichsführer! Briefe an und von Himmler* (Munich, 1970), 10. See also Bradley F. Smith, *Heinrich Himmler: A Nazi in the Making 1900–1926* (Stanford, CA, 1971).
12. Longerich, *Heinrich Himmler*, 1–19; Michael Wildt, *Generation des Unbedingten. Das Fürhungskorps des Reichssicherheitshauptamtes* (Hamburg, 2003).
13. Longerich, *Heinrich Himmler*, 19–32, quote on 32.
14. Ibid, 32–69; Katrin Himmler, *Die Brüder Himmler*, 88–103.
15. Himmler and Wildt (eds.), *Himmler privat*, 7–16.
16. Longerich, *Heinrich Himmler*, 70–139.
17. Ibid, 140–47.
18. Ibid, 147–79.

19. Ibid, 197.
20. Wachsmann, *Hitler's Prisons*; idem, *KL: A History of the Nazi Concentration Camps* (New York, 2015), esp. 23–78. Longerich, *Heinrich Himmler*, 179–201, misunderstands this process and so presents the misleading paradox that increased Gestapo powers and activities seem in his narrative to lead to reduced numbers of prisoners in the camps.
21. Longerich, *Heinrich Himmler*, 239.
22. Evans, *The Third Reich in Power*, 533.
23. Longerich, *Heinrich Himmler*, 239.
24. Ibid, 251.
25. Tom Neuhaus, *Tibet in the Western Imagination* (London, 2012).
26. Ibid, 255–98; Michael Kater, *Das 'Ahnenerbe' der SS 1935–1945. Ein Beitrag zur Kulturpolitik des Dritten Reiches*, 4th edn (Munich, 2006). Mosse, *The Crisis*, is the classic study of the intellectual milieu from which such ideas emerged. For the *Lebensborn*, see Georg Lilienthal, *Der 'Lebensborn e.V.' Ein Instrument nationalsozialistischer Rassenpolitik* (Stuttgart, 1985).
27. Heiber (ed.), *Reichsführer!*, 291.
28. Ibid, 36–41.
29. Ibid, 28.
30. Ibid, 346.
31. Ibid, 163.
32. Witte et al., *Der Dienstkalender* (Introduction), 19–20.
33. International Military Tribunal, *Der Nürnberger Prozess gegen die Hauptskriegsverbrecher vom 14. November 1945 bis 1. Oktober 1946: Urkunden und anderes Beweismaterial* (Nuremberg, 1948), vol. XXIX, 1919-PS.
34. Robert L. Koehl, *RKFDV: German Resettlement and Population Policy 1939–1945: A History of the Reich Commission for the Strengthening of Germandom* (Cambridge, MA, 1957); Mechthild Rössler and Sabine Schleiermacher (eds.), *Der 'Generalplan Ost'. Hauptlinien der nationalsozialistischen Planungs-und Vernichtungspolitik* (Berlin, 1993).
35. Smith and Peterson (eds.), *Himmler: Geheimreden*, 169–70 and 200–205; see also Noakes and Pridham (eds.), *Nazism*, III, 614–27.
36. Quotes in Longerich, *Heinrich Himmler*, 609.
37. Witte et al. (eds.), *Der Dienstkalender*, 294.
38. Heiber (ed.), *Reichsführer!*, 130.
39. Ibid, 193.
40. Uhl et al., *Die Organisation des Terrors*, 843–44 (14 August 1944). Thälmann was shot in Buchenwald four days later.
41. Ibid, 12–15.
42. Longerich, *Heinrich Himmler*, 696–731.
43. Ibid, 1–3, 719–48.
44. Katrin Himmler, *Die Brüder Himmler*, 237.
45. Ibid, 233–44.

46. Himmler and Wildt (eds.), *Himmler privat*, 17–23.
47. Katrin Himmler, *Die Brüder Himmler*, passim.

6. The Diplomat: Joachim von Ribbentrop

1. Fest, *The Face*, 268–69.
2. Trevor-Roper, *The Last Days of Hitler*, 121; Wolfgang Michalka, 'Joachim von Ribbentrop: From Wine Merchant to Foreign Minister', in Smelser and Zitelman (eds.), *The Nazi Elite*, 165–72; John Weitz, *Joachim von Ribbentrop: Hitler's Diplomat* (London, 1992), 'The Champagne Salesman', 21–41; Turner. Jr., *Hitler's Thirty Days*, 70 ('a champagne salesman').
3. Gabriel Gorodestky (ed.), *The Maisky Diaries: Red Ambassador to the Court of St James's 1932–1943* (London, 2015), 40, 115.
4. Quoted from interviews in Laurence Rees, *The Nazis: A Warning from History* (London, 1997), 93.
5. Papen, *Memoirs*, 552.
6. Michael Bloch, *Ribbentrop* (London, 1992; 2nd ed., London, 2003), 185–86.
7. Quoted in ibid, 460.
8. Gilbert, *Nuremberg Diary*, 132–40.
9. Kelley, *22 Cells*, 93.
10. Joachim von Ribbentrop, *Zwischen London und Moskau. Erinnerungen und letzte Aufzeichnungen*, ed. Annelies von Ribbentrop (Leoni am Starnberger See, 1954), 7–12; Bloch, *Ribbentrop*, 1–6. Ribbentrop's memoirs can only be trusted up to a point and are most useful for details of his life before he joined the Nazi Party. Stefan Scheil, *Ribbentrop. Oder: Die Verlockung des nationalen Aufbruchs. Eine politische Biographie* (Berlin, 2013), was written by an historian who is also an active politician of the far-right *Alternative für Deutschland* and it puts forward many disputable contentions while omitting a good deal. Bloch, *Ribbentrop*, is the best biography.
11. Martin Kitchen, *The German Officer Corps 1890–1914* (Oxford, 1968); see also Gordon A. Craig, *The Politics of the Prussian Army 1640–1945* (Oxford, 1955), and Karl Demeter, *Das deutsche Offizierskorps in Gesellschaft und Staat 1650–1945* (Frankfurt am Main, 1962).
12. Ribbentrop, *Zwischen London und Moskau*, 12–13.
13. Ibid. His teacher, wife of the later State Secretary Otto Meissner, later described Ribbentrop as 'the shallowest' or 'most vapid' pupil in her class (Hanfstaengl, *Zwischen Weissem und Braunem Haus*, 320).
14. Ribbentrop, *Zwischen London und Moskau*, 13–15. For his mother's tuberculosis, see Weitz, *Joachim von Ribbentrop*, 4; Charles Spicer, *Coffee with Hitler: The British Amateurs who Tried to Civilise the Nazis* (London, 2022), 20.

15. Domeier, *The Eulenburg Affair*.
16. Ribbentrop, *Zwischen London und Moskau*, 14, claims that his father resigned his commission voluntarily, but this was clearly not the case: his statement that his father renounced the right to wear his uniform of his own volition is implausible in the extreme.
17. Ibid, 15–17; Weitz, *Hitler's Diplomat*, 7–8.
18. Ribbentrop, *Zwischen London und Moskau*, 17–23; Weitz, *Hitler's Diplomat*, 9–13; Bloch, *Ribbentrop*, 6–8; Robert Lawson, 'Ribbentrop in Canada 1910 to 1914: A Note', *International History Review*, vol. 29, no. 4 (2007), 821–32.
19. Weitz, *Hitler's Diplomat*, 13–17; Ribbentrop, *Zwischen London und Moskau*, 23–26; Bloch, *Ribbentrop*, 7–8 and nn. 19 and 23. The *Potsdam* was later converted into a whaling ship. For his brother Lothar's tuberculosis, from which he died four years later, see Weitz, *Hitler's Diplomat*, 5–7. Douglas Glen, *Von Ribbentrop Is Still Dangerous* (London, 1941), is a fantastic concoction of unsubstantiated speculations alleging Ribbentrop was a spy in Canada and the USA during the war.
20. Ribbentrop, *Zwischen London und Moskau*, 27–30; Bloch, *Ribbentrop*, 9–12; quote in Evans, *The Hitler Conspiracies*, 73. For the original, see Ernst von Wrisberg, 'Über die Angriffe gegen die Offiziersstande', *Militär-Wochenschrift für die deutsche Wehrmacht*, 25 March 1919, 262. Ribbentrop later falsely claimed to have been attached to the German delegation at the Paris Peace Conference, though there is no evidence for his attendance (Bloch, *Ribbentrop*, 10–11).
21. Bloch, *Ribbentrop*, 12–17.
22. Ribbentrop, *Zwischen London und Moskau*, 31–35; Weitz, *Hitler's Diplomat*, 7–8, 21–41; Bloch, *Ribbentrop*, 17–21. Gertrud's father was Quartermaster-General in the Prussian Army and had been ennobled in 1884. Since her branch of the family would otherwise have died out, Ribbentrop could plausibly claim that his adoption was intended to stop this happening, a widely accepted reason in the 1920s. However, when he ceased to pay her pension, Gertrud took him to court to force him to resume the payments (Bloch, *Ribbentrop*, 19).
23. Ribbentrop, *Zwischen London und Moskau*, 34–35.
24. Bloch, *Ribbentrop*, 24–29.
25. Quoted in ibid, 28. Ribbentrop's memoirs misdate this dinner to 1933 (ibid, 27, note).
26. Bloch, *Ribbentrop*, 29–30; Ribbentrop, *Zwischen London und Moskau*, 36–37. His claim that this was the first time he had met Hitler was inaccurate (Bloch, *Ribbentrop*, 25–26).
27. Weitz, *Hitler's Diplomat*, 47; Hans-Jürgen Döscher, *Das Auswärtige Amt im Dritten Reich. Diplomatie im Schatten der 'Endlösung'* (Berlin, 1987), 148.

28. Turner, *Hitler's Thirty Days*, 112–17; Bloch, *Ribbentrop*, 31–36; Bracher, *Die Auflösung*, 707–32; Weitz, *Hitler's Diplomat*, 51–56; Ribbentrop, *Zwischen London und Moskau*, 38–42 (printing extracts from diary notes made at the time by Ribbentrop and his wife). Such was the secrecy in which these discussions were held that when Hitler arrived by car at Ribbentrop's house, he got out in the garage and made his way into the house through the garden, returning by the same route.
29. Ribbentrop, *Zwischen London und Moskau*, 47.
30. Wolfgang Michalka, *Ribbentrop und die deutsche Weltpolitik 1933–1940. Aussenpolitische Konzeptionen und Entscheidungsprozesse im Dritten Reich* (Munich, 1980), 50–109, also for the following.
31. Weitz, *Hitler's Diplomat*, 59–111; Eckart Conze et al., *Das Amt und die Vergangenheit. Deutsche Diplomaten im Dritten Reich und in der Bundesrepublik* (Munich, 2010), 61–64; Hans-Adolf Jacobsen, *Nationalsozialistische Aussenpolitik 1933–1939* (Frankfurt, 1968), 252–318.
32. Weitz, *Hitler's Diplomat*, 101–3.
33. Ian Kershaw, *Making Friends with Hitler: Lord Londonderry and Britain's Road to War* (London, 2004), 157–66, for a vivid description of the visit.
34. Bloch, *Ribbentrop*, 131–36.
35. Ibid, 122–45; Weitz, *Hitler's Diplomat*, 103–38.
36. Interview, quoted in Rees, *The Nazis*, 93.
37. Weitz, *Hitler's Diplomat*, 133–61; Bloch, *Ribbentrop*, 175–80. For the willing participation of the Foreign Office and its staff in Hitler's policies, see Conze et al. (eds.), *Das Amt*, 25–294; but also Evans, *The Third Reich in History and Memory*, 262–93.
38. Bloch, *Ribbentrop*, 167–74.
39. Ibid, 253–71; Michalka, *Ribbentrop*, 247–94.
40. Gorodetsky (ed.), *The Maisky Diaries*, 115–16.
41. Bloch, *Ribbentrop*, 190–214, 219.
42. Ibid, 255–99.
43. Ibid, 384–89; Christopher Browning, *The Final Solution and the German Foreign Office: A Study of Referat D III of Abteilung Deutschland 1940–43* (New York, 1978), 1–34.
44. Bloch, *Ribbentrop*, 221–24.
45. Ibid, 389–90; Browning, *The German Foreign Office*, 35–146.
46. Hillgruber (ed.), *Staatsmänner*, vol. 2, 256–57.
47. Bloch, *Ribbentrop*, 432–43, 449–51; Browning, *The German Foreign Office*, 147–77; Conze et al. (eds.), *Das Amt*, 260–67.
48. Kelley, *22 Cells*, 92.
49. Gellately, *The Nuremberg Interviews*, 184–85.
50. Gilbert, *Nuremberg Diary*, 133–40.
51. Gellately, *The Nuremberg Interviews*, 184.

52. Ibid, 189–94.
53. Bloch, *Ribbentrop*, 448–98; Overy (ed.), *Interrogations*, 35.
54. Richard Sandomir, 'Rudolf von Ribbentrop, Son of Top Nazi Diplomat, Dies at 98', *New York Times* (6 June 2019); Rudolf von Ribbentrop, *Mein Vater Joachim von Ribbentrop. Erlebnisse und Erinnerungen* (Graz, 2008), esp. 445.

7. The Philosopher: Alfred Rosenberg

1. Ernst Piper, *Alfred Rosenberg: Hitlers Chefideologe* (Munich, 2005), 19. 'Rosenberg' was a Jewish name, but also common among people of non-Jewish descent, and rumours that there was a Jewish element in Alfred Rosenberg's ancestry were without foundation.
2. Idem, *Alfred Rosenberg*, 19–29.
3. Brendan McGeever, *Antisemitism and the Russian Revolution* (Cambridge, 2019). More generally, see Michael Kellogg, *The Russian Roots of Nazism: White Émigrés and the Making of National Socialism, 1917–1945* (Cambridge, 2005).
4. Piper, *Alfred Rosenberg*, 45. In prison at Nuremberg after the war, Rosenberg sought to play down his admiration for Hitler at this point.
5. Ibid, 43–69.
6. Ibid, 70–75; Evans, *The Hitler Conspiracies*, ch. 1.
7. Jochmann (ed.), *Adolf Hitler*, 356–57 (21 August 1942).
8. Piper, *Alfred Rosenberg*, 76–126; Alfred Rosenberg, *Der Mythus des 20. Jahrhunderts. Eine Wertung der seelisch-geistigen Gestaltenkämpfe unserer Zeit*, 24th edn (Munich, 1934).
9. Alfred Rosenberg, *Der Sumpf. Querschnitte durch das 'Geistes'-leben der November-Demokratie* (Munich, 1930), esp. 5, 29, 31–36, 41.
10. Piper, *Alfred Rosenberg*, 179–231.
11. Fest, *Face*, 247–64, quotes in particular from the post-war memoirs of the former *Gauleiter* of Hamburg, Albert Krebs, *Tendenzen und Gestalten der NSDAP: Erinnerungen an die Frühzeit der Partei* (Stuttgart, 1974), and Rosenberg's own writings, especially *Letzte Aufzeichnungen: Ideale und Idole der nationalsozialistischen Revolution* (Göttingen, 1946).
12. Picker (ed.), *Hitlers Tischgespräche*, 213 (11 April 1942).
13. IMG, vol. 14, p. 494. Quoted in Reinhard Bollmus, 'Alfred Rosenberg: National Socialism's 'Chief Ideologue?'', in Smelser and Zitelmann (eds.), *The Nazi Elite*, 183–92, at 187.
14. Selections from the book, and other writings, are available in English in Robert Pois (ed.), *Alfred Rosenberg: Selected Writings* (London, 1970).
15. Picker (ed.), *Hitlers Tischgespräche*, 416 (4 July 1942).

16. Alfred Rosenberg, *Die Tagebücher*, 205–6 (17 September 1936); Evans, *The Third Reich in Power*, 220–60.
17. Piper, *Alfred Rosenberg*, 399–422.
18. Ibid, 179–231.
19. Rosenberg, *Die Tagebücher*, 226 (11 December 1936).
20. Ibid, 190 (11 August 1936).
21. Ibid, 294 (5 October 1939).
22. Guenter Lewy, *Harmful and Undesirable: Book Censorship in Nazi Germany* (New York, 2016), esp. 74–81; Piper, *Alfred Rosenberg*, 323–68; Jan-Pieter Barbian, *Literaturpolitik in 'Dritten Reich'. Institutionen, Kompetenzen, Betätigungsfelder* (Munich, 1995), for the wider context.
23. Jan Björn Potthast, *Das jüdische Zentralmuseum der SS in Prag. Gegnerforschung und Völkermord im Nationalsozialismus* (Frankfurt, 2002); Piper, *Alfred Rosenberg*, 462–77.
24. Rosenberg, *Die Tagebücher*, 367 (28 March 1941).
25. Ibid, 472–73 (2 February 1943); Piper, *Alfred Rosenberg*, 486–508.
26. Hanns Christian Löhr, *Der Einsatzstab Reichsleiter Rosenberg. Ideologie und Kunstraub im 'Dritten Reich'* (Berlin, 2018), esp. 167–71.
27. Rosenberg, *Die Tagebücher*, 336 (6 September 1940).
28. Ibid, 363 (2 February 1941); Piper, *Alfred Rosenberg*, 477–86.
29. Piper, *Alfred Rosenberg*, 168–275; Reinhard Bollmus: *Das Amt Rosenberg und seine Gegner. Studien zum Machtkampf im nationalsozialistischen Herrschaftssystem* (Stuttgart, 1970; 2nd ed., Munich, 2006).
30. Rosenberg, *Die Tagebücher*, 133 (5 June 1934), 185 (end of July 1936), etc.
31. Thomas Mathieu, *Kunstauffassungen und Kulturpolitik im Nationalsozialismus. Studien zu Adolf Hitler – Joseph Goebbels – Alfred Rosenberg – Baldur von Schirach – Heinrich Himmler – Albert Speer – Wilhelm Frick* (Saarbrücken, 1997), 164–243, and esp. 303; Rosenberg, *Die Tagebücher*, 240–42 (20 July 1937).
32. Evans, *The Third Reich in Power*, 252, 158, 165–66, 193–200; Piper, *Alfred Rosenberg*, 369–99.
33. Piper, *Alfred Rosenberg*, 127–67.
34. Alfred Rosenberg, *Der Zukunftsweg einer deutschen Aussenpolitik* (Munich, 1927), 142–44.
35. Rosenberg, *Die Tagebücher*, 124 (15 May 1934).
36. Ibid, 119 (14 May 1934), 219 (15 November 1936), 276–77 (21 May 1939).
37. Ibid, 279 (22 August 1939).
38. Ibid, 286–87 (retrospective entry, 24 September 1939); Piper, *Alfred Rosenberg*, 285–322; Jacobsen, *Nationalsozialistische Aussenpolitik*, 45–89.
39. Piper, *Alfred Rosenberg*, 275–84.
40. Bollmus, 'Alfred Rosenberg', in Smelser and Zitelmann (eds.), *The Nazi Elite*, 183–92; Rosenberg, *Die Tagebücher*, 305 (14 December 1939), 313 (27 January 1940), etc.

41. Rosenberg, *Die Tagebücher*, 375 (9 April 1941).
42. Ibid, 372–73 (28 March 1941), 379–81 (20 April 1941).
43. Ibid, 399 (1 June 1941).
44. Ibid, 393 (20 July 1941).
45. Ibid, 403 (1 September 1941).
46. Ibid, 515 (26 October 1944).
47. Christian Gerlach, *Kalkulierte Morde. Die deutsche Wirtschafts- und Vernichiungspolitik in Weissrussland 1941 bis 1944* (Hamburg, 1999), 361–62.
48. Andreas Zellhuber, '*Unsere Verwaltung treibt einer Katastrophe zu . . .*': *das Reichsministerium für die besetzten Ostgebiete und die deutsche Besatzungsherrschaf in der Sowjetunion 1941–1945* (Munich, 2006); Piper, *Alfred Rosenberg*, 509–77.
49. Rosenberg, *Die Tagebücher*, 514 (22 October 1944).
50. Ibid, 507 (29 July 1944).
51. Ibid, 509 (30 July 1944).
52. Ibid, 511 (27 August 1944).
53. Ibid, 335 (10 May 1940), 469 (25/26 January 1943).
54. Ibid, 484 (7 August 1943).
55. Ibid, 485 (7 August 1943).
56. Ibid, 486 (7 August 1943).
57. Piper, *Alfred Rosenberg*, 565.
58. Ibid, 423–34; Rosenberg, *Die Tagebücher*, 199 (23 August 1936).
59. Ibid.
60. Piper, *Alfred Rosenberg*, 435–48; Magnus Brechtken, '*Madagaskar für die Juden'. Antisemitische Idee und politische Praxis 1885–1945* (Munich, 1997), 287.
61. Rosenberg, *Die Tagebücher*, 410 (14 September 1941).
62. Ibid, 408 (12 September 1941). The figure of 400,000 was in fact a considerable underestimate.
63. Quoted in Piper, *Alfred Roseneberg*, 589 (Rosenberg, 'Vermerk über eine Unterredung beim Führer am 14.12.1941 vom 16.12.1941', document 1517-PS in volume 27 of the International Military Tribunal proceedings from 1946).
64. Quoted in Piper, *Alfred Rosenberg*, 594 (Führertagung 4 May 1943, in Rosenberg's personal file in the Berlin Document Center).
65. Goldensohn, *The Nuremberg Interviews*, 197–99.
66. Alfred Rosenberg, *Letzte Aufzeichnungen. Nürnberg 1945/46* (Uelzen, 1996 [1955]), 316–43.
67. Rosenberg, *Die Tagebücher*, 440 (14 July 1942).
68. Rosenberg, *Letzte Aufzeichnungen*, 343.
69. Piper, *Alfred Rosenberg*, 82.
70. Kelley, *22 cells*, 39.

8. The Architect: Albert Speer

1. Richard J. Evans, *Rereading German History: From Unification to Reunification 1800–1996* (London, 1997), 199–203; Gitta Sereny, *Albert Speer: His Battle with Truth* (London, 1995); Magnus Brechtken, *Albert Speer. Eine deutsche Karriere* (Munich, 2017), 385–493.
2. Trevor-Roper, *The Last Days of Hitler*, 269.
3. Speer, *Inside the Third Reich*.
4. Brechtken, *Albert Speer*, 398.
5. Ibid, 385–493.
6. Ibid, 19–30.
7. Michael H. Kater, *Studentenschaft und Rechtsradikalismus in Deutschland 1918–1933: Eine sozialgeschichtliche Studie zur Bildungskrise in der Weimarer Republik* (Hamburg, 1975).
8. Brechtken, *Albert Speer*, 31–37.
9. Ibid, 69.
10. Ibid, 38–59; Shelley Baranowski, *Strength Through Joy: Consumerism and Mass Tourism in the Third Reich* (New York, 2004), esp. 75–227.
11. Brechtken, *Albert Speer*, 47–98, 124; Wachsmann, *KL*, 162.
12. Brechtken, *Albert Speer*, 99–101.
13. Ibid, 102–10, 130–36, 141–42, 148–49; Susanne Willems, *Der entsiedelte Jude. Albert Speers Wohnungsmarktpolitik für den Berliner Hauptstadtbau* (Berlin, 2000); Janin Reif et al., *Schwanenwerder. Ein Inselparadies in Berlin* (Berlin, 2000).
14. Brechtken, *Albert Speer*, 111–24.
15. Ibid, 139–52. See also Gernot Schaulinski and Dagmar Thorau (eds.), *Mythos Germania. Vision und Verbrechen* (Berlin, 2014), and Jaskot, *The Architecture of Oppression*.
16. Brechtken, *Albert Speer*, 111–29.
17. There is no evidence to support speculation that the crash was engineered by Hitler because he found Todt excessively pessimistic about Germany's military prospects; had he wished to rid himself of the Munitions Minister, he would most likely simply have retired him on 'health grounds'. Still less is there even a shred of evidence to suggest that Speer was involved.
18. Brechtken, *Albert Speer*, 155–64.
19. Ibid, 164–84.
20. Ibid, 185–207.
21. Speer, *Inside the Third Reich*, 281–320.
22. Quoted in Brechtken, *Albert Speer*, 209.
23. Evans, *The Third Reich at War*, 332; Jonas Scherner and Jochen Streb, 'Das Ende eines Mythos? Albert Speer und das sogenannte Rüstungswunder', *Vierteljahrschrift für Sozial- und Wirtschaftsgeschichte*, 93/2 (2006), 172–96.
24. Evans, *The Third Reich at War*, 664–65.

25. Evans, *The Third Reich at War*, 272–74; Brechtken, *Albert Speer*, 208–66.
26. Rüdiger Overmans, *Deutsche militärische Verluste im Zweiten Weltkriege* (Munich, 1999); Evans, *The Third Reich at War*, 682–83.
27. Brechtken, *Albert Speer*, 275–90; Overy (ed.), *Interrogations*, 132–35.
28. Brechtken, *Albert Speer*, 291–92.
29. Overy (ed.), *Interrogations*, 128–40.
30. Brechtken, *Albert Speer*, 295–310.
31. Matthias Schmidt, *Albert Speer. Das Ende eines Mythos. Speers wahre Rolle im Dritten Reich* (Munich, 1982; English edn, *Albert Speer: The End of a Myth*, London, 1985).
32. Brechtken, *Albert Speer*, 537–79.

Part III
Introduction

1. Guenter Lewy, *Perpetrators: The World of the Holocaust Killers* (New York, 2017), 118–21; Theodor W. Adorno *et al.*, *The Authoritarian Personality* (New York, 1950); George C. Browder, 'Perpetrator Character and Motivation: An Emerging Consensus', *Holocaust and Genocide Studies*, 17 (2003), 480–97.
2. Alex J. Kay, *Empire of Destruction: A History of Nazi Mass Killing* (London, 2021), 286.
3. For the 'ordinary men' argument, see Christopher Browning, *Ordinary Men: Reserve Police Battalion 101 and the Final Solution in Poland* (New York, 1992); Mark W. Hornburg *et al.* (eds.), *Beyond 'Ordinary Men': Christopher R. Browning and Holocaust Historiography* (Paderborn, 2019), updates the debate.

9. The Deputy: Rudolf Hess

1. J. Bryan Lowder, 'The One-Eyed Man Is King: How Did the Monocle Become a Symbol of Wealth?', *Slate*, 27 December 2012.
2. Klara Hess to Rudolf Hess, 4 March 1914, in Rudolf Hess, *Briefe 1909–1933*, ed. Wolf Rüdiger Hess (Munich, 1987), 74.
3. Kurt Pätzold and Manfred Weissbecker, *Rudolf Hess. Der Mann an Hitlers Seite* (Leipzig, 1999), 12–17; Fest, *The Face of the Third Reich*, 283–86; for the notion of Hitler as a substitute father, see Kelley, 22 *Cells*, 15–31.
4. Päztold and Weissbecker, *Rudolf Hess*, 19–20.
5. Hess, *Briefe*, 84.
6. Päztold and Weissbecker, *Rudolf Hess*, 22–23, discounting Hess's later statement that his father did not want him to enlist.

7. Ibid, 21–22.
8. Rudolf to Klara and Fritz Hess, 1 November 1918, in Hess, *Briefe*, 228–29.
9. Rudolf to Klara and Fritz Hess, 29 October and 1 November 1918, in Hess, *Briefe*, 226–29.
10. Rudolf to Klara and Fritz Hess, 14 November 1918, in Hess, *Briefe*, 236. For Hess's early life, see now Manfred Görtemaker, *Rudolf Hess: Der Stellvertreter. Eine Biographie* (Munich, 2023), 23–96. For the 'stab-in-the-back' legend, see Evans, *The Hitler Conspiracies*, 47–84.
11. Päztold and Weissbecker, *Rudolf Hess*, 22–30; Matthias Berg, *Karl Alexander von Müller: Historiker für den Nationalsozialismus* (Munich, 2014).
12. Päztold and Weissbecker, *Rudolf Hess*, 31–32.
13. Rudolf Hess to Karl Haushofer, 6 October 1923, in Hans-Adolf Jacobsen, *Karl Haushofer: Leben und Werk*, 2 vols. (Boppard, 1979), vol. II, 25; Rudolf to Klara Hess, 10 June 1920, and Rudolf Hess to Ilse Pröhl, 29 November 1923, 18 June 1924, in Hess, *Briefe*, 259, 314, 338, etc.
14. Päztold and Weissbecker, *Rudolf Hess*, 32–34; Rudolf to Klara and Fritz Hess, 25 June 1919 and 24 March 1920, in Hess, *Briefe*, 243, 251.
15. Rudolf to Klara and Fritz Hess, 25 June 1919, in Hess, *Briefe*, 243.
16. Rudolf to Klara and Fritz Hess, 8 and 24 March 1920, n.d., and 18 May 1919, in Hess, *Briefe*, 249, 251–52, 241; Klaus Theweleit, *Männerphantasien*, 2 vols. (Frankfurt am Main, 1977).
17. Päztold and Weissbecker, *Rudolf Hess*, 34–37.
18. Jacobsen, *Karl Haushofer*, vol. II, 23: Hess to Haushofer, 6 October 1923.
19. Päztold and Weissbecker, *Rudolf Hess*, 37–47; Görtemaker, *Rudolf Hess*, 97–153.
20. Ibid, 47–56; Rudolf to Fritz and Klara Hess, 8/16 November 1923, 4 December 1923, and Rudolf to Klara Hess, 11 May 1924, in Hess, *Briefe*, 311–13, 322.
21. Hess, *Briefe*, 323–59; Hartmann et al. (eds.), *Hitler: Mein Kampf*, vol. 1, 13–20; Päztold and Weissbecker, *Rudolf Hess*, 57.
22. Rudolf to Klara and Fritz Hess, 24 April 1925, in Hess, *Briefe*, 366–68.
23. Päztold and Weissbecker, *Rudolf Hess*, 57–79.
24. Ibid, 79–94; Görtemaker, *Rudolf Hess*, 158–259.
25. Norman Goda, *Tales from Spandau: Nazi Criminals and the Cold War* (Cambridge, 2007), 226.
26. Peter Longerich, *Hitlers Stellvertreter. Führung der Partei und Kontrolle des Staatsapparates durch den Stab Hess und die Partei-Kanzlei Bormann* (Munich, 1992), 109–18.
27. Päztold and Weissbecker, *Rudolf Hess*, 95–222.
28. Hanfstaengl, *Zwischen Weissem und Braunem Haus*, 324.
29. Matthäus and Bajohr (eds.), *Alfred Rosenberg*, 288, 384–87.
30. Wulf Schwarzwäller, *Rudolf Hess. Der Stellvertreter* (Munich, 1987), 160. Görtemaker, *Rudolf Hess*, 260–362, argues unconvincingly for Hess's continued importance.

31. Kelley, 22 *Cells*, 15–31.
32. Roy Conyers Nesbit and Georges Van Acker, *The Flight of Rudolf Hess: Myths and Reality* (Stroud, 1999), is the most accurate account of these events, also for the following. For Hamilton, see Spicer, *Coffee with Hitler*.
33. For the numerous fanciful conspiracy theories attached to these events, see Evans, *The Hitler Conspiracies*, 121–64.
34. Daniel Pick, *The Pursuit of the Nazi Mind: Hitler, Hess and the Analysts* (Oxford, 2012); see also Kelley, 22 *Days*, 25, speculating that Hess was at least partly pretending when he showed signs of amnesia. See also Overy (ed.), *Interrogations*, 118–27; Andrus, *The Infamous of Nuremberg*, 72–73, 119, 123; and Gaskin, *Eyewitnesses at Nuremberg*, 83.
35. Quoted in Overy (ed.), *Interrogations*, 126, 577 n. 24.
36. Papen, *Memoirs*, 553–54; balanced assessment in Görtemaker, *Rudolf Hess*, 517–86.

10. The Collaborator: Franz von Papen

1. Joachim Petzold, *Franz von Papen. Ein deutsches Verhängnis* (Munich, 1995), 7–14; quotes in Franz Müller, *Ein Rechtskatholik zwischen Kreuz und Hakenkreuz: Franz von Papen als Sonderbevollmächtiger in Wien 1934–1938* (Frankfurt am Main, 1990), 375.
2. Biographies include Petzold, *Franz von Papen*, 15–21; Richard W. Rolfs, *The Sorcerer's Apprentice: The Life of Franz von Papen* (Lanham, MD, 1996), 1–4 (incorporating archival research, but marred by numerous minor errors and misprints); Reiner Möckelmann, *Franz von Papen: Hitlers ewiger Vassall* (Darmstadt, 2016), 1–11 (well-researched and critical biography by a former diplomat); see also the contemporary accounts by the Central Europe correspondent of the *Daily Telegraph*, Hugh W. Blood-Ryan, *Franz von Papen: His Life and Times* (London, 1938); by the Hungarian journalist Tibor Kövés, *Satan in a Top Hat: The Biography of Franz von Papen* (New York, 1941); and Otto Erich Deutsch, an Austrian journalist, one of whose books was publicly burned by the Nazis in 1933, after which he lived in exile in the UK. He published a number of critical books on Nazism under a pseudonym – see Oswald Dutch, *The Errant Diplomat: The Life of Franz von Papen* (London, 1940). A more sympathetic account is provided by two friends of the Papens, Henry M. and Robin K. Adams, *Rebel Patriot: A Biography of Franz von Papen* (Santa Barbara, CA, 1987). Petzold, *Franz von Papen*, 292 n. 11, provides a list of uncritical and critical biographical essays on Papen. For a critical review of *Rebel Patriot*, a biography that largely follows Papen's own self-presentation in Franz von Papen, *Memoirs*, trans. Brian Connell (London, 1952), see George O. Kent, 'Problems and Pitfalls of a Papen Biography', *Central European History*, vol. 20 (1987), 191–97.

3. Papen, *Memoirs*, 4–6 (for a list of the numerous critical reviews of this book by German historians, see Petzold, *Franz von Papen*, 291, n. 7). A later volume by Papen, *Vom Scheitern einer Demokratie 1930–1933* (Mainz, 1968), goes over much the same ground as the relevant part of the memoirs.
4. Rolfs, *The Sorcerer's Apprentice*, 1–4; Papen, *Memoirs*, 4–6, 7–8; Petzold, *Franz von Papen*, 15–25, gives a brisk summary of Papen's life before he entered politics.
5. Rolfs, *The Sorcerer's Apprentice*, 4–5; Papen, *Memoirs*, 8–14.
6. Papen, *Memoirs*, 13–28.
7. Ibid, 29–65; Rolfs, *The Sorcerer's Apprentice*, 6–19 ('Apprenticeship in Intrigue').
8. Papen, *Memoirs*, 66–96; Rolfs, *The Sorcerer's Apprentice*, 31–35.
9. Papen, *Memoirs*, 97.
10. Ibid, 98–108.
11. Ibid, 109–24; Petzold, *Franz von Papen*, 25–62.
12. Papen, *Memoirs*, 125–30; Matthew Feldman *et al.* (eds.), *Clerical Fascism in Interwar Europe* (London, 2013).
13. Papen, *Memoirs*, 180–97; Rolfs, *The Sorcerer's Apprentice*, 77–162; Petzold, *Franz von Papen*, 61–118; Ulrike Hörster-Philipps, *Konservative Politik in der Endphase der Weimarer Republik: Die Regierung Franz von Papen* (Cologne, 1982), provides a narrative from a left-wing point of view.
14. Papen, *Memoirs*, 162.
15. Kershaw, *Hitler* I, 372; see above all the classic and still important analysis by Bracher, *Die Auflösung*, 529–643.
16. Papen, *Memoirs*, 251.
17. Ewald von Kleist-Schmenzin, 'Die letzte Möglichkeit: Zur Ernennung Hitlers zum Reichskanzler am 30. Januar 1933', *Politische Studien*, vol. 10 (1959), 90–106, quoted in Rolfs, *The Sorcerer's Apprentice*, 252.
18. Overy (ed.), *Interrogations*, 426.
19. Papen, *Memoirs*, 251–63; Rolfs, *The Sorcerer's Apprentice*, 163–249.
20. Petzold, *Franz von Papen*, 119–62.
21. Möckelmann, *Franz von Papen*, 26–27, 290–307; Thomas Brechenmacher (ed.), *Das Reichskonkordat 1933. Forschungsstand, Kontroversen, Dokumente* (Paderborn, 2007); and for the controversy on the relationship between the Konkordat and the Catholic Centre Party's vote in favour of the Enabling Act, Hubert Wolf, 'Reichskonkordat für Ermächtigungsgesetz? Zur Historisierung der Scholder-Repgen-Kontroverse über das Verhältnis des Vatikans zum Nationalsozialismus', *Vierteljahrshefte für Zeitgeschichte*, vol. 60 (2012), 169–200.
22. Papen, *Memoirs*, 287, for quote, and more generally for the early months of Hitler's coalition cabinet, 264–75; Rolfs, *The Sorcerer's Apprentice*, 251–52.

23. Möckelmann, *Franz von Papen*, 441.
24. Ibid, 364–65.
25. Papen, *Memoirs*, 284–95.
26. Möckelmann, *Franz von Papen*, 364–67; more generally, see Rolfs, *The Sorcerer's Apprentice*, 251–86.
27. Franz von Papen, *Appell an das deutsche Gewissen. Reden zur nationalen Revolution* (Oldenburg, 1933), 7–42.
28. Ibid, 43–44, 63, 77.
29. Ibid, 80–104.
30. Möckelmann, *Franz von Papen*, 254; Petzold, *Franz von Papen*, 206–22.
31. Quoted in Möckelmann, *Franz von Papen*, 23–25; also ibid, 255–59; Petzold, *Franz von Papen*, 222–30 ('Der moralische Tiefpunkt').
32. Papen, *Memoirs*, 296–336.
33. Rolfs, *The Sorcerer's Apprentice*, 286–311; Petzold, *Franz von Papen*, 230–62; Müller, *Ein 'Rechtskatholik'*, for a detailed account.
34. Papen, *Memoirs*, 337–430; Rolfs, *The Sorcerer's Apprentice*, 313–79.
35. Papen, *Memoirs*, 430–32; Rolfs, *The Sorcerer's Apprentice*, 368.
36. Papen, *Memoirs*, 433–37.
37. Ibid, 436–533; Möckelmann, *Franz von Papen*, 43–246; Rolfs, *The Sorcerer's Apprentice*, 381–425.
38. Möckelmann, *Franz von Papen*, 261–89.
39. Gilbert, *Nuremberg Diary*, 29, 120, 385.
40. Hans Rein, *Franz von Papen im Zwielicht der Geschichte. Sein letzter Prozess* (Baden-Baden, 1979).
41. Fest, *The Face*, 227–46.
42. Overy (ed.), *Interrogations*, 431, 433–34, 437, 442; Papen, *Memoirs*, 538–40.
43. Möckelmann, *Franz von Papen*, 29–34; Evans, *The Third Reich in Power*, 234–53.
44. Möckelmann, *Franz von Papen*, 321–31; Alois Hudal, *Die Grundlagen des Nationalsozialismus: Eine ideengeschichtliche Untersuchung* (Leipzig, 1937); Gerald Steinacher, *Nazis on the Run: How Hitler's Henchmen Fled Justice* (New York, 2011), *passim*.
45. Gilbert, *Nuremberg Diary*, 29, 120, 385. Papen's granddaughter Patricia went some way towards making amends by taking a History degree and writing a dissertation on academic antisemitism in the Weimar Republic.

11. The 'Worker': Robert Ley

1. Ronald Smelser, *Robert Ley: Hitler's Labor Front Leader* (Oxford, 1988), makes full use of the prison memoir; Renate Wald, *Mein Vater Robert Ley. Meine Erinnerungen und Vaters Geschichte* (Nümbrecht, 2004). 'Ley' is

pronounced like the English 'Lie'. There is no satisfactory recent biography, and Smelser's study remains the standard work. Karl Schröder, *Aufstieg und Fall des Robert Ley* (Siegburg, 2008), adds little of note.

2. Smelser, *Robert Ley*, 15–16; Kelley, *22 Cells*, 126–27; Wald, *Mein Vater*, 26–27.
3. Kelley, *22 Cells*, 129, 140.
4. Smelser, *Robert Ley*, 7–8; Wald, *Mein Vater*, 21–22. For the wider context, see Regina Schulte, 'Feuer im Dorf', in Heinz Reif (ed.), *Räuber, Volk und Obrigkeit. Studien zur Geschichte der Kriminalität in Deutschland seit dem 18. Jahrhundert* (Frankfurt am Main, 1984), 100–52; Richard J. Evans, *The Pursuit of Power: Europe 1815–1914* (London, 2016), 372–74.
5. Smelser, *Robert Ley*, 8–9; Wald, *Mein Vater*, 15–18 (drawing on her father's unpublished memoirs, along with family memories).
6. Smelser, *Robert Ley*, 6–10; Wald, *Mein Vater*, 21–25.
7. Kelley, *22 Cells*, 140.
8. Wald, *Mein Vater*, 35–55.
9. Smelser, *Robert Ley*, 32–33; for the political position of the Ley family, see Wald, *Mein Vater*, 37–38.
10. Ibid, 34–47; Robert Ley, *Wir alle helfen dem Führer. Deutschland braucht jeden Deutschen*, 4th edn (Munich, 1939 [1937]), 11–21.
11. Smelser, *Robert Ley*, 47–65; Wald, *Mein Vater*, 52.
12. Smelser, *Robert Ley*, 65–69; more generally, see Stephan Malinowski, *Nazis and Nobles: The History of a Misalliance* (Oxford, 2020). Schaumburg-Lippe, who continued to defend the Third Reich after the war, gave his own account of his relationship with Ley in his memoir *Zwischen Krone und Kerker* (Wiesbaden, 1952).
13. Smelser, *Robert Ley*, 67–97.
14. Ibid, 98–108.
15. Ibid, 108–16; Wald, *Mein Vater*, 83–95. Wald describes as a legend the claim that her father had the staff line up to greet him when he arrived at the house from a journey (91). She insisted that her father was not corrupt and that the family lived a comparatively modest lifestyle (93–95).
16. Wald, *Mein Vater*, 76–81.
17. Smelser, *Robert Ley*, 56–62, 83–102; Wald, *Mein Vater*, 147–48. Stories that Ley had a portrait of her naked from the waist up displayed in his Berlin home for visitors to admire, or that he tore her clothes off at a reception in his house so that his guests could admire her youthful body, seem to be later inventions. See Richard Grunberger, *A Social History of the Third Reich* (London, 1971), 93–94; Glenn Enfield, *Hitler's Secret Life* (New York, 1979), 114; Achim Besgen, *Der stille Befehl. Medizinalrat Kersten, Himmler und das Dritte Reich* (Munich, 1960), 183.
18. Smelser, *Robert Ley*, 109–12; Wald, *Mein Vater*, 107–16.

19. Smelser, *Robert Ley*, 114; Wald, *Mein Vater*, 56–62, 105–7.
20. Wald, *Mein Vater*, 27–28, 130–32; Kelley, *22 Cells*, 129, 140.
21. Smelser, *Robert Ley*, 117–79.
22. Robert Ley, 'Sieg des Glaubens', speech delivered at the Nuremberg Party Rally on 12 September 1936, reprinted in idem, *Wir alle helfen dem Führer*, 11–21, quote at 12.
23. Robert Ley, *Durchbruch der sozialen Ehre. Reden und Gedanken für das schaffende Deutschland* (Berlin, 1935), 69 (speech delivered on 17 January 1934).
24. Robert Ley, *Soldaten der Arbeit* (Leipzig, 1938), 145–47 (speech to construction workers in March 1937).
25. Robert Ley, 'Wirtschaftsführung in Dritten Reich', in idem, *Durchbruch der sozialen Ehre*, 130 (speech to Rhenish industry leaders on 14 April 1934).
26. Ibid, *passim*.
27. Ley, *Durchbruch der sozialen Ehre*, 205.
28. Ley, *Soldaten der Arbeit*, 125 (speech delivered in March 1937). In *Das dritte Reich des Traums* (Frankfurt am Main, 1966), the Jewish writer Charlotte Beradt analysed fifty dreams she collected from unsuspecting friends and acquaintances in the 1930s, showing that the Third Reich appeared, often threateningly, to people while they slept as well.
29. Evans, *The Third Reich in Power*, 455–503; Timothy W. Mason, *Social Policy in the Third Reich: The Working Class and the 'National Community'* (Providence, RI, 1993); Shelley Baranowski, *Strength Through Joy: Consumerism and Mass Tourism in the Third Reich* (New York, 2004); Smelser, *Robert Ley*, 180–217.
30. Wald, *Mein Vater*, 62–63.
31. Smelser, *Robert Ley*, 218–91.
32. Ibid, 292–93.
33. Robert Ley, 'Life or Fame? A Political Analysis', printed in Kelley, *22 Cells*, 130–38; 'Rebuilding the Reich', in Overy (ed.), *Interrogations*, 538–46.
34. Overy (ed.), *Interrogations*, 487–90.
35. Kelley, *22 Cells*, 140; Wald, *Mein Vater*, 109–11, 150 n. 6.
36. Andrus, *The Infamous of Nuremberg*, 88.
37. Gustave Gilbert, *Nuremberg Diary* (New York 1947), 8; similar account in Kelley, *22 Cells*, 140–41.
38. Kelley, *22 Cells*, 141; Overy (ed.), *Interrogations*, 491–98; Wald, *Mein Vater*, 143–44; Andrus, *The Infamous of Nuremberg*, 88.
39. Kelley, *22 Cells*, 141.
40. Andrus, *The Infamous of Nuremberg*, 90–91.
41. Kelley, *22 Cells*, 141–42.

12. The Schoolmaster: Julius Streicher

1. Robin Lenman, 'Julius Streicher and the Origins of the NSDAP in Nuremberg, 1919–1923', in Nicholls and Matthias (eds.), *German Democracy and the Triumph of Hitler*, 129–60, at 133.
2. 'Julius Streicher – der Frankenführer' (film by Medienwerkstatt Franken, Nuremberg, 1995, with interviews with family members and former staff): https://vimeo.com/57370281, accessed 11 August 2021.
3. Thomas Greif, *Frankens braune Wallfahrt. Der Hesselberg im Dritten Reich* (Ansbach, 2007); Frank Baumeister (ed.), *Hesselbergland. Land und Leute in Ehingen, Dambach und Lentersheim* (Gunzenhausen, 1991).
4. Mosse, *The Crisis*, 18–20, 253–57; Raymond H. Dominick III, *The Environmental Movement in Germany: Prophets and Pioneers, 1871–1971* (New York, 1992). See also Franco Ruault, *Tödliche Maskeraden: Julius Streicher und die 'Lösung der Judenfrage'* (Frankfurt am Main, 2009), 65–104.
5. Randall L. Bytwerk, *Julius Streicher: Nazi Editor of the Notorious Anti-Semitic Newspaper* Der Stürmer (New York, 2001 [1983]), 1–4, superseding an earlier biography, William Varga, *The Number One Nazi Jew Baiter* (New York, 1981); Dennis E. Showalter, *Little Man, What Now? Der Stürmer in the Weimar Republic* (Hamden, CT, 1982), 20–21; Greif, *Frankens braune Wallfahrt*, 71–127. Daniel Roos, *Julius Streicher und 'Der Stürmer' 1923–1945* (Paderborn, 2014), is the most recent and most thorough study. For Streicher's career as a teacher, see Franz Poggeler, *Der Lehrer Julius Streicher. Zur Personalgeschichte des Nationalsozialismus* (Frankfurt am Main, 1991).
6. Bytwerk, *Julius Streicher*, 46–47. Roos, *Julius Streicher*, 477–78, for the IQ – he claims (n. 50, 478) that when adjusted for age Streicher's IQ was actually 15–20 points lower on the Wechsler-Bellevue Intelligence Scale for adults. Kelley, *22 Cells*, 117–25, and Edward N. Peterson, *The Limits of Hitler's Power* (Princeton, NJ, 1969), 225, quote an IQ of 100 and 102 respectively. The correct score was 106.
7. Jay W. Baird, 'Das politische Testament Julius Streichers. Ein Dokument aus den Papieren des Hauptmanns Dolibois', *Vierteljahrshefte für Zeitgeschichte*, vol. 26, no. 4 (1978), 660–95, at 670.
8. Bytwerk, *Julius Streicher*, 5–11; Baird, 'Das politische Testament', 661–80; Showalter, *Little Man*, 21–27; Roos, *Julius Streicher*, 29–46.
9. Lenman, 'Julius Streicher', 129–45.
10. Baird, 'Das politische Testament', 671–81.
11. Ibid, 682–83. Streicher also wrote a longer autobiography in 1943–44 at his farm in Pleikershof, and another set of reflections entitled 'Wie ich zur Politik kam' ('How I came to politics'), while in Allied custody after the end of the war.
12. Bytwerk, *Julius Streicher*, 15–16; Roos, *Julius Streicher*, 47–70; Hartmann et al. (eds.), *Hitler, Mein Kampf*, II, 1,296 n. 27.

13. Lenman, 'Julius Streicher', 143; Bytwerk, *Julius Streicher*, 22–29.
14. Bytwerk, *Julius Streicher*, 24–33.
15. Lenman, 'Julius Streicher', 140–44. See also Hermann Hanschel, *Oberbürgermeister Hermann Luppe: Nürnberger Kommunalpolitik in der Weimarer Republik* (Nuremberg, 1977).
16. Bytwerk, *Julius Streicher*, 15–16; Lenman, 'Julius Streicher', 145–46; Showalter, *Little Man*, 27–41; Randall L. Bytwerk, 'Julius Streicher and the Early History of "Der Stürmer", 1923–1933', *Journalism History*, vol. 5 (1978), 74–79.
17. Lenman, 'Julius Streicher', 147–59. See also Rainer Hambrecht, *Der Aufstieg der NSDAP in Mittel- und Oberfranken (1925–1933)* (Nuremberg, 1976).
18. Baird, 'Das politische Testament', 684–87.
19. Bytwerk, *Julius Streicher*, 17–32; Showalter, *Little Man*, 200–32; Hambrecht, *Der Aufstieg der NSDAP*, 12–194, 309–403; Roos, *Julius Streicher*, 47–232, for a detailed narrative.
20. Bytwerk, *Julius Streicher*, 33–37; Utho Grieser, *Himmlers Mann in Nürnberg. Der Fall Benno Martin: Eine Studie zur Struktur des Dritten Reiches in der 'Stadt der Reichsparteitage'* (Nuremberg, 1974), 61–95; Peterson, *The Limits of Hitler's Power*, 224–68.
21. Bytwerk, *Julius Streicher*, 38–41; Roos, *Julius Streicher*, 233–349.
22. Bytwerk, *Julius Streicher*, 40–41; Grieser, *Himmlers Mann*, 101–8, 162–212; Peterson, *The Limits of Hitler's Power*, 269–85.
23. For the contrary view, see Showalter, *Little Man*, 235.
24. Bytwerk, *Julius Streicher*, 41–63; Roos, *Julius Streicher*, 398–433.
25. Bytwerk, *Julius Streicher*, 101–17; Showalter, *Little Man*, 49–172. For Streicher's obsession with *Rassenschande* ('racial pollution'), see Franco Ruault, *'Neuschöpfer des deutschen Volkes': Julius Streicher im Kampf gegen 'Rassenschande'* (Frankfurt am Main, 2006), a rather speculative analysis.
26. Bytwerk, *Julius Streicher*, 119–70; see also Fred Hahn, *Lieber 'Stürmer'. Leserbriefe an das NS-Kampfblatt 1924 bis 1945* (Stuttgart, 1978); John L. Cahill, 'Dear Herr Streicher: Letters to the Third Reich's Foremost Anti-Semite', in Otis C. Mitchell (ed.), *Nazism and the Common Man* (Washington DC, 1981), 139–57; Ruault, *Tödliche Maskeraden*, 149–200; Showalter, *Little Man*, 82–199.
27. Roos, *Julius Streicher*, 434–66, including quotations; Goebbels, *Tagebuch*, vol. 5, 323 (29 May 1938).
28. Baird, 'Das politische Testament', 662; Roos, *Julius Streicher*, 467–72; Overy (ed.), *Interrogations*, 33–34; Andrus, *The Infamous of Nuremberg*, 53.
29. Gellately, *The Nuremberg Interviews*, 252.
30. Baird, 'Das politische Testament', 663–64, based on an interview of the author with Captain Dolibois. Streicher dictated his memoir to the son of the Nazi Party Treasurer Franz Xaver Schwarz, in the presence of Dolibois.
31. Goldensohn, *The Nuremberg Interviews*, 257.

32. Gilbert, *Nuremberg Diary*, 419. See also Overy (ed.), *Interrogations*, 185–87.
33. Gilbert, *Nuremberg Diary*, 73, 125, 9–10.
34. Bytwerk, *Julius Streicher*, 44.
35. Baird, 'Das politische Testament', 695.
36. Bytwerk, *Julius Streicher*, 1; Roos, *Julius Streicher*, 483–500; Greif, *Frankens braune Wallfahrt*, 126–27; Joseph Kingsbury-Smith, 'Die Hinrichtung der Nazi-Kriegsverbrecher am 16. Oktober 1946', in Steffen Radlmaier (ed.), *Der Nürnberger Lernprozess. Von Kriegsverbrechern und Starreportern* (Frankfurt am Main, 2001), 339–48; Andrus, *The Infamous of Nuremberg*, 197 (refuting claims that Streicher went to the gallows dressed only in his underpants).
37. 'Julius Streicher – der Frankenführer'.
38. US Holocaust Memorial Museum, Photograph Number: 95309.
39. 'Julius Streicher – der Frankenführer'.
40. Greif, *Frankens braune Wallfahrt*, 74.
41. Roos, *Julius Streicher*, 479–82; Tony Rennell, 'The Truth About Hitler's British Love Child', *Daily Mail*, 13 December 2007.
42. Andrus, *The Infamous of Nuremberg*, 39.

13. The Hangman: Reinhard Heydrich

1. Gerwarth, *Hitler's Hangman*, xiv–xv, 136, 73. See also ibid, 308, n. 89, where the author claims that Nebe wrote this 'after the war', although Nebe was executed in March 1945 for his part in the 20 July bomb plot. For postwar attempts to characterize Heydrich, see Charles Whiting, *Heydrich: Henchman of Death* (Barnsley, 1999), Charles Wighton, *Heydrich: Hitler's Most Evil Henchman* (London, 1962), and Mario Diederichs, *Heydrich: The Face of Evil* (London, 2006), all emphasizing what they regard as Heydrich's evil nature. Günther Deschner, *Heydrich: The Pursuit of Total Power* (London, 1981), portrays him as a conscienceless bureaucratic careerist. A biography by the forger and fabulist Edouard Calic, *Reinhard Heydrich: The Chilling Story of the Man Who Masterminded the Nazi Death Camps* (New York 1985), is not to be taken seriously: see Evans, *The Hitler Conspiracies*, 97–100.
2. Gerwarth, *Hitler's Hangman*, 71–75.
3. Ibid, 26–27, 36–37, 61–62.
4. Ibid, 15. For more detail, see Karin Flachowsky, 'Neue Quellen zur Abstammung Reinhard Heydrichs', *Vierteljahrshefte für Zeitgeschichte*, vol. 48 (2000), 319–27.
5. Fest, *The Face*, 152–70.
6. Carl J. Burckhardt, *Meine Danziger Mission 1937–1939* (Munich, 1960), 57; Heinz Höhne, *The Order of the Death's Head: The Story of Hitler's SS*

(London, 1969), 148–50, citing a conversation between Burckhardt and 'some SS men', unnamed.
7. Felix Kersten, *The Kersten Memoirs 1940–1945* (London, 1957). Hugh Trevor-Roper provided an introduction, in which he incautiously accepted Kersten's claim that Heydrich was Jewish.
8. Bryan Rigg, *Hitler's Jewish Soldiers: The Untold Story of Nazi Racial Laws and Men of Jewish Descent in the German Military* (Lawrence, KS, 2002).
9. Gerwarth, *Hitler's Executioner*, 14–30; Shlomo Aronson, *Reinhard Heydrich und die Frühgeschichte von Gestapo und SD* (Stuttgart, 1971), 11–25.
10. Gerwarth, *Hitler's Executioner*, 31–45; Aronson, *Reinhard Heydrich*, 25–38. See also Nancy Dougherty, *The Man with the Iron Heart: The Definitive Biography of Reinhard Heydrich, Architect of the Holocaust*, ed. Christopher Lehmann-Haupt (London, 2022); original title *The Hangman and his Wife: The Life and Death of Reinhard Heydrich*), based in particular on a series of interviews with Lina Heydrich.
11. Gerwarth, *Hitler's Executioner*, 46–49.
12. Ibid, 50–78; Aronson, *Reinhard Heydrich*, 39–65; George C. Browder, *Hitler's Enforcers: The Gestapo and the SS Security Service in the Nazi Revolution* (Oxford, 1996), 103–29.
13. For the view that Heydrich was the moving force behind the purge (almost certainly an exaggeration), see Höhne, *The Order of the Death's Head*, 89–99.
14. Gerwarth, *Hitler's Hangman*, 79–92.
15. Ibid, 93–144.
16. Quoted in ibid, 139.
17. Ibid, 109–15.
18. Ibid, 145–93; Helmut Krausnick, *Hitlers Einsatzgruppen. Die Truppen des Weltanschauungskrieges 1928–1942* (Frankfurt am Main, 1985).
19. Höhne, *The Order*, 147–66, for an extended character sketch.
20. Gerwarth, *Hitler's Hangman*, 194–98.
21. Ibid, 194–217.
22. Quoted in ibid, 235; more generally, 218–237. See also Chad Bryant, *Prague in Black: Nazi Rule and Czech Nationalism* (Cambridge, MA, 2007).
23. Gerwarth, *Hitler's Hangman*, 238–70.
24. Ibid, 271–77.
25. Ibid, 1–13, 278–84.
26. Ibid, 285–89.
27. Ibid, 231–34.
28. Ibid, 235–94; Dougherty, *The Man with the Iron Heart*, 549–80.
29. Aronson, *Reinhard Heydrich*, 244.
30. Ibid, 254.

14. The Bureaucrat: Adolf Eichmann

1. David Cesarani, *Eichmann: His Life and Crimes* (London, 2004), 1.
2. Lord Russell's sensationalist *The Scourge of the Swastika* (London, 1954), gives him no more than a mention (167), as does the first edition of Gerald Reitlinger, *The Final Solution* (London, 1953), 27, a deficit made good in the second edition (1961).
3. Jochen von Lang (ed.), *Eichmann Interrogated: Transcripts from the Archives of the Israeli Police* (London, 1983), 102.
4. Quoted in ibid, 3.
5. Comer Clarke, *Eichmann: The Savage Truth* (London, 1960); John Donovan, *Eichmann: Man of Slaughter* (New York, 1960); Quentin Reynolds (with Ephraim Katz and Zwy Aldouby), *Minister of Death: The Adolf Eichmann Story* (London, 1961).
6. Quoted in Cesarani, *Eichmann*, 3.
7. All quoted in ibid, 256–57 and 326–28.
8. Hannah Arendt, *Eichmann in Jerusalem* (London, rev. ed., 1964), 276, also, more generally, for the following.
9. Lang (ed.), *Eichmann Interrogated*, 157.
10. Cesarani, *Eichmann*, 325.
11. Christopher Browning, *Ordinary Men: Reserve Police Battalion 101 and the Final Solution in Poland* (London, 1992); Cesarani, *Eichmann*, 347.
12. Cesarani, *Eichmann*, 324–56; Daniel Jonah Goldhagen, *Hitler's Willing Executioners: Ordinary Germans and the Holocaust* (London, 1996).
13. Helmut Fangmann et al., *'Parteisoldaten': Die Hamburger Polizei im '3. Reich'* (Hamburg, 1987); Jürgen Matthäus et al., *Ausbildungsziel Judenmord? 'Weltanschauliche Erziehung' von SS, Polizei und Waffen-SS im Rahmen der 'Endlösung'* (Frankfurt am Main, 2003); Peter Longerich, *Politik der Vernichtung: Eine Gesamtdarstellung der nationalsoialistischen Judenverfolgung* (Munich, 1998), 303–10.
14. Cesarani, *Eichmannn*, 18–23; Lang (ed.), *Eichmann Interrogated*, 4–13.
15. Cesarani, *Eichmann*, 24–30.
16. Ibid, 31–35, also for the following paragraph; Lang (ed.), *Eichmann Interrogated*, 13–17.
17. Lang (ed.), *Eichmann Interrogated*, 37.
18. Cesarani, *Eichmann*, 36–54; Lang (ed.), *Eichmann Interrogated*, 18–30. The Nazis considered Freemasonry to be part of a global Jewish conspiracy, as suggested in *The Protocols of the Elders of Zion*.
19. Cesarani, *Eichmann*, 55–62; Lang (ed.), *Eichmann Interrogated*, 41–47.
20. Cesarani, *Eichmann*, 63–77; Lang (ed.), *Eichmann Interrogated*, 49–62. Here, as elsewhere, Eichmann minimized the degree of coercion he had applied, and exaggerated the freedom of action of the Jews and their representatives such as Löwenherz.

21. Ibid, 78–90; Brechtken, 'Madagaskar für die Juden'; Lang (ed.), *Eichmann Interrogated*, 65–69; Hans Safrian, *Die Eichmann-Männer* (Vienna, 1993), esp. 23–67 (the 'Vienna Model') and 68–86 (Nisko).
22. Lang (ed.), *Eichmann Interrogated*, 75.
23. Ibid, 76–78.
24. Ibid, 79–89; Cesarani, *Eichmann*, 91–160.
25. Mark Roseman, *The Wannsee Conference and the Final Solution: A Reconsideration* (New York, 2002), 144.
26. Cesarani, *Eichmann*, 112–29; Lang (ed.), *Eichmann Interrogated*, 98–200, recording in detail Eichmann's responsibilities, which he repeatedly declared were all about transportation, not about killing.
27. Cesarani, *Eichmann*, 159–92; Wachsmann, *KL*, 457–60.
28. Quoted in Cesarani, *Eichmann*, 159.
29. Ibid, 195.
30. Ibid, 188–203.
31. Ibid, 204–10. For the general background, see Steinacher, *Nazis on the Run*.
32. Cesarani, *Eichmann*, 43–45, 129–30.
33. Bettina Stangneth, *Eichmann before Jerusalem: The Unexamined Life of a Mass Murderer* (New York, 2014); Cesarani, *Eichmann*, 211–17.
34. Irmtrud Wojak, *Eichmanns Memoiren. Ein kritischer Essay* (Frankfurt am Main, 2002).
35. Neal Bascomb, *Hunting Eichmann: How a Band of Survivors and a Young Spy Agency Chased Down the World's Most Notorious Nazi* (Boston, MA, 2009).
36. Deborah E. Lipstadt, *The Eichmann Trial* (New York, 2011).

15. The Loudmouth: Hans Frank

1. Quoted in Ulrich von Hassell, *The von Hassell Diaries: The Story of the Forces against Hitler inside Germany 1938–1944* (Boulder, CO, 1994), 15 February 1942.
2. Christian Schudnagies, *Hans Frank. Aufstieg und Fall des NS-Juristen und Generalgouverneurs* (Frankfurt am Main, 1989), 97.
3. Fest, *The Face*, 315–17.
4. Malaparte, *Kaputt*, 149, 154.
5. Martyn Housden, *Hans Frank: Lebensraum and the Holocaust* (Basingstoke, 2003), 13–17; Christoph Klessmann, 'Hans Frank: Party Jurist and Governor-General in Poland', in Smelser and Zitelmann (eds.), *The Nazi Elite*, 39–47; Goldensohn, *The Nuremberg Interviews*, 20–21.
6. Housden, *Hans Frank*, 13–15.
7. Goldensohn, *The Nuremberg Interviews*, 22–23, 37–38.
8. Housden, *Hans Frank*, 15, quoting manuscript diary entries for 3 January and 4 March 1919, and 16–19; Dieter Schenk, *Hans Frank. Hitlers Kronjurist und Generalgouverneur* (Frankfurt am Main, 2006), 19–30.

9. Quoted in Klessmann, 'Der Generalgouverneur', 248.
10. Reginald G. Phelps, 'Before Hitler Came: Thule Society and Germanen Orden', *Journal of Modern History*, vol. 35 (1963), 245–61; Hermann Gilbhard, *Die Thule-Gesellschaft. Vom okkulten Mummenschanz zum Hakenkreuz*, 2nd edn (Munich, 2015); Frank Jacob, *Die Thule-Gesellschaft* (Berlin, 2010).
11. Housden, *Hans Frank*, 18–21; Schenk, *Hans Frank*, 29–45.
12. Hans Frank, *Im Angesicht des Galgens. Deutung Hitlers und seiner Zeit auf Grund eigener Erlebnisse und Erkenntnisse. Geschrieben im Nürnberger Justizgefängnis* (Munich, 1953), 31–42.
13. Housden, *Hans Frank*, 21–23; Schenk, *Hans Frank*, 46–56.
14. Schudnagies, *Hans Frank*, 18–19.
15. Schenk, *Hans Frank*, 57–66.
16. Ibid, 66–80; Housden, *Hans Frank*, 24–31.
17. Housden, *Hans Frank*, 31–33.
18. Lothar Gruchmann, *Justiz im Dritten Reich 1933–1940*.
19. Housden, *Hans Frank*, 34–35; Schenk, *Hans Frank*, 86–103.
20. Housden, *Hans Frank*, 36–39; Schenk, *Hans Frank*, 103–17.
21. Frank, *Im Angesicht*, 193–95; Schenk, *Hans Frank*, 117–31.
22. Housden, *Hans Frank*, 40–70; Evans, *Rituals*, 632–35.
23. Gustave M. Gilbert, *The Psychology of Dictatorship* (New York, 1950), 147, quoted in Housden, *Hans Frank*, 30. Housden points out that Frank was actually thirty-two when he was appointed to the Bavarian Ministry of Justice.
24. Schenk, *Hans Frank*, 143–70.
25. Evans, *The Third Reich at War*, 3–22; Schenk, *Hans Frank*, 117–28.
26. Housden, *Hans Frank*, 71–82; Schenk, *Hans Frank*, 181–91; Evans, *The Third Reich at War*, 23–40.
27. Werner Präg and Wolfgang Jacobmeyer (eds.), *Das Diensttagebuch des deutschen Generalgouverneurs in Polen 1939–1945* (Quellen und Darstellungen zur Zeitgeschichte, vol. 20, Stuttgart, 1975), 104.
28. Klessmann, 'Hans Frank', 41; idem, 'Der Generalgouverneur Hans Frank', 252.
29. Hassell, *The von Hassell Diaries*, 100.
30. Housden, *Hans Frank*, 83–89; Schenk, *Hans Frank*, 170–81, 191–97, 236–53.
31. Housden, *Hans Frank*, 211–16; Schenk, *Hans Frank*, 293–325.
32. Präg and Jacobmeyer (eds.), *Das Diensttagebuch*, 55; Housden, *Hans Frank*, 145–48.
33. Housden, *Hans Frank*, 126–28.
34. Quoted in Safrian, *Die Eichmann-Männer*, 88; Housden, *Hans Frank*, 145.
35. Präg and Jacobmeyer (eds.), *Das Diensttagebuch*, 450–59.
36. Auschwitz was in the part of Poland annexed by the German Reich, and so not under Frank's suzerainty. For Operation Reinhard, see Peter Longerich, *Holocaust: The Nazi Persecution and Murder of the Jews* (Oxford, 2010),

277–345; Evans, *The Third Reich at War*, 260–318. For Frank's part in the Holocaust, see Schenk, *Hans Frank*, 300–14.
37. Präg and Jacobmeyer (eds.), *Das Diensttagebuch*, 914; Schenk, *Hans Frank*, 221–35.
38. Housden, *Hans Frank*, 154–59.
39. Schenk, *Hans Frank*, 254–68, also for the following.
40. Housden, *Hans Frank*, 160–69.
41. Ibid, 154–76; Schenk, *Hans Frank*, 268–80.
42. Schenk, *Hans Frank*, 281–99.
43. Ibid, 315–22.
44. Housden, *Hans Frank*, 209–13; Schenk. *Hans Frank*, 340–71.
45. Housden, *Hans Frank*, 214–19.
46. Gilbert, *Nuremberg Diary*, 19–22.
47. Ibid, 276, 280; Schenk, *Hans Frank*, 372–402.
48. Frank, *Im Angesicht*, 430–31.
49. Housden, *Hans Frank*, 220–38.
50. Goldensohn, *The Nuremberg Interviews*, 30–35.
51. Niklas Frank, *Der Vater. Eine Abrechnung* (Munich, 1987), 19.

Part IV

Introduction

1. Catherine Epstein, *Model Nazi: Arthur Greiser and the Occupation of Western Poland* (Oxford, 2010). Unfortunately the order of the text and notes, running heads and pagination become extremely confused towards the end of the book.
2. Domarus, *Hitler*, 721 (10 September 1937).
3. Ibid, 1,063.
4. Ibid, 1,467.
5. Dirk Riedel, *Ordnungshüter und Massenmörder im Dienst der 'Volksgemeinschaft': Der KZ-Kommandant Hans Loritz* (Berlin, 2010).

16. The General: Wilhelm Ritter von Leeb

1. Johannes Hürter, *Hitlers Heerführer. Die deutschen Oberbefehlshaber im Krieg gegen die Sowjetunion 1941/42* (Munich, 2007), 28, 30.
2. Ibid, 86–87, 102–3.
3. Ibid, 127–28, 135.
4. Gene Mueller, 'Generalfeldmarschall Wilhelm Ritter von Leeb', in Gerd R. Ueberschär (ed.), *Hitlers militärische Elite*, vol. I (Darmstadt, 1998), 146–53;

NOTES TO PP. 362–6

Hürter, *Hitlers Heerführer*, 58–73; Samuel Mitcham, Jr., and Gene Mueller, *Hitler's Commanders* (London, 1992), 48.
5. Georg Meyer (ed.), *Generalfeldmarschall Wilhelm Ritter von Leeb. Tagebuchaufzeichnungen und Lagebeurteilungen aus zwei Weltkriegen* (Stuttgart, 1976), 172.
6. Quoted in Valerie G. Hébert, *Hitler's Generals on Trial: The Last War Crimes Tribunal at Nuremberg* (Lawrence, KS, 2020), 76.
7. Meyer (ed.), *Generalfeldmarschall*, 51, 177; Hürter, *Hitlers Heerführer*, 165; Mueller, 'Generalfeldmarschall'.
8. Hürter, *Hitlers Heerführer*, 185.
9. Ibid, 187–88.
10. Ibid, 171–73.
11. Harrison E. Salisbury, *The 900 Days: The Siege of Leningrad* (London, 1969), 94–95.
12. Meyer (ed.), *Generalfeldmarschall*, 373–74 n. 484; Mitcham and Mueller, *Hitler's Commanders*, 48.
13. Meyer (ed.), *Generalfeldmarschall*, 188–89, 330–31; Hürter, *Hitlers Heerführer*, 296, 499.
14. Wilhelm Ritter von Leeb, *Defence* (Great Military Classics, Pentagon Press, New Delhi, 2017). It seems an exaggeration, however, to describe Leeb as 'a thinker and an intellectual' (Mitcham and Mueller, *Hitler's Commanders*, 45).
15. Meyer (ed.), *Generalfeldmarschall*, 307–8; Salisbury, *900 Days*, 348–49.
16. Hürter, *Hitlers Heerführer*, 340–41; Geoffrey Megargee, *Insider Hitler's High Command* (Lawrence, KS, 2000), 143–49.
17. Meyer (ed.), *Generalfeldmarschall*, 71–74, 436–41; quote on 72 n. 174.
18. Megargee, *Inside Hitler's High Command*, 172. Leeb's later claim that he resigned because of his opposition to the whole policy of Nazism, both domestic and foreign, has to be taken with a pinch of salt (Hürter, *Hitlers Heerführer*, 354–55 n. 377).
19. Dieter Pohl, *Die Herrschaft der Wehrmacht. Deutsche Militärbesatzung und einheimische Bevölkerung in der Sowjetunion 1941–1944* (Munich, 2008), 201–42.
20. Hürter, *Hitlers Heerführer*, 243; Wigbert Benz, *Der Hungerplan im 'Unternehmen Barbarossa' 1941* (Berlin, 2011); Gesine Gerhard, 'Food and Genocide: Nazi Agrarian Politics in the Occupied Territories of the Soviet Union', *Contemporary European History*, 18 (1) (2009), 45–65; Alex J. Kay, *Exploitation, Resettlement, Mass Murder: Political and Economic Planning for German Occupation Policy in the Soviet Union, 1940–1941* (Oxford, 2006); idem, 'Germany's *Staatssekretäre*, Mass Starvation and the Meeting of 2 May 1941', *Journal of Contemporary History*, 41 (4) (2006), 685–700. See also Klaus Gerbet (ed.), *Generalfeldmarschall Fedor von Bock: Zwischen Pflicht und Verweigerung. Das Kriegstagebuch* (Munich, 1995), 298.

21. Hürter, *Hitlers Heerführer*, 504.
22. Christian Streit, *Keine Kameraden. Die Wehrmacht und die sowjetischen Kriegsgefangenen 1941–45* (Stuttgart, 1978). See also Hannes Heer (ed.), '*Stets zu erschiessen sind Frauen, die in der Roten Armee dienen*'. *Geständnisse deutscher Kriegsgefangener über ihren Einsatz an der Ostfront* (Hamburg, 1995).
23. Anna Reid, *Leningrad: Tragedy of a City under Siege, 1941–44* (London, 2011), 134–35; John Barber and Andrei Dzeniskevich, *Life and Death in Besieged Leningrad, 1941–44* (New York, 2005).
24. Hürter, *Hitlers Heerführer*, 395–96; Hans-Adolf Jacobsen, 'The Kommissarbefehl and Mass Executions of Soviet Russian Prisoners of War', in Helmut Krausnick et al., *Anatomy of the SS State* (London, 1965), 505–30.
25. Hürter, *Hitlers Heerführer*, 414–15.
26. Manfred Oldenburg, *Ideologie und militärisches Kalkül. Die Besatzungspolitik der Wehrmacht in der Sowjetunion 1942* (Cologne, 1942), 308–23.
27. Jochen Böhler, 'Intention oder Situation? Soldaten der Wehrmacht und die Anfänge des Vernichtungskrieges in Polen', in Timm C. Richter (ed.), *Krieg und Verbrechen. Situation und Intention: Fallbeispiele* (Munich, 2006), 165–72; Alexander Hill, *The War Behind the Eastern Front: The Soviet Partisan Movement in North-West Russia 1941–1944* (London, 2005). For the 'brutalization' thesis, see Omer Bartov, *The Eastern Front 1941–45: German Troops and the Barbarisation of Warfare* (Oxford, 1985). For German army atrocities in other theatres of war from 1939 to 1945, see Ben Shepherd, *Terror in the Balkans: German Armies and Partisan Warfare* (Cambridge, MA, 2012), 222–23; see also idem and Juliette Pattinson (eds.), *War in a Twilight World: Partisan and Anti-Partisan Warfare in Eastern Europe, 1939–45* (London, 2010), esp. 189–256. For atrocities and mass shootings of civilians in Greece, see Hermann Frank Meyer, *Blutiges Edelweiss. Die 1. Gebirgs-Division im Zweiten Weltkrieg* (Berlin, 2008), esp. 463–556. For Italy, see Carlo Gentile, *Wehrmacht und Waffen-SS im Partisanenkrieg: Italien 1943–1945* (Paderborn, 2012), 406–7. For the tradition of harsh reprisals aimed at supposed 'Partisans', see John Horne and Alan Kramer, *German Atrocities 1914: A History of Denial* (London, 2001).
28. Hürter, *Hitlers Heerführer*, 513, 539 note 97.
29. Meyer (ed.), *Generalfeldmarschall*, 62–63 and n. 146. See also Helmut Krausnick, *Hitlers Einsatzgruppen. Die Truppen des Weltanschauungskrieges 1938–1942* (Frankfurt, 1985), 181, confirming the authenticity of Hitler's warning and suggesting that the idea of sterilization was influenced by the typically mendacious propaganda campaign by Goebbels centred on the alleged American plan to sterilize the Germans suggested by the Jewish writer Theodore Kaufman (see Evans, *The Third Reich at War*, 245–46).
30. Kriegstagebuch der Heeresgruppe Nord, 2.7.41, quoted in Krausnick, *Hitlers Einsatzgruppen*, 182. See also Hürter, *Hitlers Heerführer*, 540–41. Both

these sources make it clear that post-war attempts to suggest that Leeb's doubts amounted to a full-scale protest are unconvincing.

31. Krausnick, *Hitlers Einsatzgruppen*, 227–45; Jörn Hasenclever, *Wehrmacht und Besatzungspolitik in der Sowjetunion. Die Befehlshaber der rückwärtigen Heeresgebiete 1941–1943* (Paderborn, 2010), 527–42; Pohl, *Die Herrschaft der Wehrmacht*, 340–49.
32. Hürter, *Hitlers Heerführer*, 599.
33. Norman Goda, 'Black Marks: Hitler's Bribery of his Senior Officers During World War II', *The Journal of Modern History*, 72 (2000), 413–52; Gerd R. Ueberschär and Winfried Vogel, *Dienen und Verdienen. Hitlers Geschenke an seine Eliten* (Frankfurt, 2000), 151–55.
34. Ueberschär and Vogel, *Dienen und Verdienen*, 156.
35. Ibid, 156–57; Gerhard L. Weinberg, 'Zur Dotation Hitlers an Generalfeldmarschall Ritter von Leeb', 2, *Militärgeschichtliche Mitteilungen*, 1979, 97–99.
36. Fest, *The Face of the Third Reich*, 355–75.
37. Christian Hartmann (ed.), *Von Feldherren und Gefreiten. Zur biographischen Dimension des Zweiten Weltkriegs* (Munich, 2008), 7–9.
38. Hans Meier-Welcker, *Seeckt* (Frankfurt am Main, 1967); Claus Guske, *Das politische Denken des Generals von Seeckt. Zur Diskussion des Verhältnisses Seeckt – Reichswehr – Republik* (Lübeck, 1971).
39. See above all the classic and still valuable work by Francis L. Carsten, *The Reichswehr and Politics 1918–1933* (Oxford, 1966). See also Robert J. O'Neill, *The German Army and the Nazi Party 1933–1939* (London, 1966), still in many ways the standard work in English. Also valuable, above all for the author's personal knowledge of some of the participants in the process, is John W. Wheeler-Bennett, *The Nemesis of Power: The German Army in Politics 1918–1945* (London, 2005 [first ed., 1971]). The most recent general account, extending the focus to the rank-and-file troops, is Ben H. Shepherd, *Hitler's Soldiers: The German Army in the Third Reich* (London, 2016), esp. 521–24.
40. Hébert, *Hitler's Generals on Trial*, includes a discussion of the myth of the 'clean' *Wehrmacht*.
41. Alex J. Kay et al., 'Introduction', in idem (eds.), *Nazi Policy on the Eastern Front, 1941: Total War, Genocide, and Radicalization* (Rochester, NY, 2012), 1–18 (with full bibliographical references). See also Jens Westemeier (ed.), *'So war der deutsche Landser': Das populäre Bild der Wehrmacht* (Paderborn, 2019).
42. Wolfram Wette, *Die Wehrmacht: Feindbilder, Vernichtungskrieg, Legenden* (Frankfurt, 2005), esp. 197–270. The exhibition caused outrage among Germans – mainly of the older generation – who still clung to the belief that the armed forces had behaved honourably towards the enemy during the war. In 1997 some 5,000 demonstrators, mainly neo-Nazis, staged a march through the streets of Munich condemning the exhibition. Critics alleged

that many of the photos presented in the exhibition were in fact pictures of atrocities carried out by the Red Army and the NKVD, or the SS and SD, not the regular German armed forces. The exhibition was temporarily withdrawn while a committee of experts examined its contents. Eventually it was discovered that only 20 of the 1,400 photos were wrongly identified, along with inaccuracies in some of the exhibition's captions. It was revised and displayed again in 2001; altogether it received well over a million visitors.

43. Kay *et al.*, 'Introduction'; Erich Ludendorff, *Der totale Krieg* (Munich, 1935).
44. Michael Geyer, 'German Strategy in the Age of Machine Warfare, 1914–1945', in Peter Paret (ed.), *Makers of Modern Strategy: From Machiavelli to the Nuclear Age* (Princeton, NJ, 1986), 543–72.
45. Horne and Kramer, *German Atrocities 1914*.
46. Goldensohn, *The Nuremberg Interviews*, 111.
47. Bernhard R. Kroener, 'Gibt es ein richtiges Leben im falschen? Biographischen Deutungen im Zeitalter zusammenbrechender Werte und Welten', in Hartmann (ed.), *Von Feldherren und Gefreiten*, 113–26.
48. Meyer (ed.), *Generalfeldmarschall*, 76–78.
49. Ibid, 57–58, 64, 68, 70–77, 88, 93, 97, 102–5, 126–27, 146–47.
50. Ibid, 147.
51. Ibid, 76–78.
52. Megargee, *Inside Hitler's High Command*, 231; see also Isabel Hull, *Absolute Destruction: Military Culture and the Practices of War in Imperial Germany* (Ithaca, NY, 2004); and Telford Taylor, *Sword and Swastika: Generals and Nazis in the Third Reich* (New York, 1952).

17. The Professional: Karl Brandt

1. Ulf Schmidt, *Hitlers Arzt Karl Brandt. Medizin und Macht im Dritten Reich* (Berlin, 2007), 93. Brandt was a highly qualified and expert surgeon, not, as the historian Dan Stone has suggested, 'a charlatan as a medic' (Stone, *The Holocaust*, 85).
2. Schmidt, *Hitlers Arzt*, 335–76; Karl Binding and Alfred Hoche, *Die Freigabe der Vernichtung lebensunwerten Lebens. Ihr Mass und Ihr Form* (Leipzig, 1920); Klaus-Dietmar Henke (ed.), *Tödliche Medizin im Nationalsozialismus. Von der Rassenhygiene zum Massenmord* (Cologne, 2008); Proctor, *Racial Hygiene*, esp. ch. 7; Michael Burleigh, *Death and Deliverance: 'Euthanasia' in Germany 1900–1945* (Cambridge, 1994); Udo Benzenhöfer, *Euthanasia in Germany Before and During the Third Reich* (Münster, 2010).
3. Schmidt, *Hitlers Arzt*, 77–92.
4. Ibid, 93–126.

5. Ibid, 127–31; Schmuhl, *Rassenhygiene*.
6. Schmidt, *Hitlers Arzt*, 157–74; Evans, *The Third Reich in Power*, 580–610.
7. Henry Friedlander, *The Origins of Nazi Genocide: From Euthanasia to the Final Solution* (Chapel Hill, NC, 1995); Burleigh, *Death and Deliverance*; Evans, *The Third Reich at War*, 75–85, also for the following.
8. Burleigh, *Death and Deliverance*, 230–80.
9. Friedlander, *The Origins*, describes this transfer; for Brandt's role, see Schmidt, *Hitlers Arzt*, 177–267; and Robert Jay Lifton, *The Nazi Doctors: A Study of the Psychology of Evil* (London, 1986), 71–72. See also Beth A. Griech-Polelle, *Bishop von Galen: German Catholicism and National Socialism* (New Haven, CT, 2002).
10. Burleigh, *Death and Deliverance*, 259.
11. Lifton, *The Nazi Doctors*, 269–302; Schmidt, *Hitlers Arzt*, 268–465.
12. Angelika Ebbinghaus, 'Zwei Welten. Die Opfer und die Täter der kriegschirurgischen Experimente', in eadem and Klaus Dörner (eds.), *Vernichten und Heilen. Der Nürnberger Ärzteprozess und seine Folgen* (Berlin, 2001), 219–40.
13. Evans, *The Third Reich in History and Memory*, 142–49; Eberle and Neumann, *Was Hitler Ill?*; Redlich, *Hitler*, who confirm the orthodoxy of Morell's therapies.
14. Schmidt, *Hitlers Arzt*, 466–69.
15. Schmidt, *Hitlers Arzt*, 466–507.
16. Ibid, 612–14. The trial records are available in an English-language microfiche edition edited by Klaus Dörner, Angelika Ebbinghaus and Karsten Linne (*The Nuremberg Medical Trial 1946/4,7*, Munich, 2001). For the originals see *Trials of War Criminals Before the Nuernberg Military Tribunals under Control Council Law No. 10: The Medical Case*, 2 vols. (Washington DC, 1950). See also Paul Weindling, *Nazi Medicine and the Nuremberg Trials: From Medical War Crimes to Informed Consent* (London, 2004), and Ebbinghaus and Dörner (eds.), *Vernichten und Heilen*, esp. 331–438.
17. Ibid, 13–34.
18. Lifton, *The Nazi Doctors*, 114–17.
19. Michael Grüttner, 'The Expulsion of Academic Teaching Staff from Germa Universities, 1933–1945', *Journal of Contemporary History*, 57/3 (July 2022), 513–33.
20. Kater, *Doctors under Hitler*, 22–25, 111–26, 147, 172–73; Proctor, *Racial Hygiene*, 295–97.
21. Theresa Maria Duckwitz and Dominik Gross, 'Searching for Motives: Suicides of Doctors and Dentists in the Third Reich and the Postwar Period, 1933–1939', *Endeavour*, 45/2 (December 2021); Proctor, *Racial Hygiene*, 299; more generally, Christian Goeschel, *Suicide in Nazi Germany* (Oxford, 2009).
22. Christian Pross, 'Breaking Through the Postwar Cover-Up of Nazi Doctors in Germany', *Journal of Medical Ethics*, 17 (1991), Supplement, 13–16; Proctor,

Racial Hygiene, 309–12; Kater, *Doctors*, 222–40; Weindling, *Nazi Medicine*, 333–43. More generally, see Ernst Klee, *Auschwitz, die Medizin und ihre Opfer* (Frankfurt, 1997); idem, *Deutsche Medizin im Dritten Reich: Karrieren vor und nach 1945* (Frankfurt, 2001); and Henke (ed.), *Tödliche Medizin*.

18. The Killers: Paul Zapp and Egon Zill

1. Konrad Kwiet, 'Paul Zapp – Vordenker und Vollstrecker der Judenvernichtung', in Mallmann and Paul (eds.), *Karrieren der Gewalt*, 252–63; Horst Jünginger, 'Tübinger Exekutoren der Endlösung', *Schwäbishes Tagblatt* (18 June 2003), 'Audimax Spezial'.
2. Karla Poewe and Irving Hexham, 'Jakob Wilhelm Hauer's New Religion and National Socialism', *Journal of Contemporary Religion*, 20 (2005), 195–215; Mosse, *The Crisis of German Ideology*, passim; Paul Zapp, *Germanisch-deutsche Weihnacht* (Stuttgart, 1934), *Religiöser Zerfall und deutscher Glaube* (Eisenach, 1935), and *Deutsche Weihestunden* (Berlin, 1936). See also Wolfgang Dierker, *Himmlers Glaubenskrieger. Der Sicherheitsdienst der SS und seine Religionspolitik 1933–1941* (Paderborn, 2002).
3. Schaul Baumann, *Die Deutsche Glaubensbewegung und ihr Gründer Jakob Wilhelm Hauer (1881–1962)* (Marburg, 2005).
4. Kwiet, 'Paul Zapp', 260.
5. Carsten Schreiber, *Elite im Verborgenen: Ideologie und regionale Herrschaftspraxis des Sicherheitsdienstes der SS und seines Netzwerks am Beispiel Sachsens* (München, 2008).
6. Ibid, 258–62; see also Andrej Angrick, *Besatzungspolitik und Massenmord. Die Einsatzgruppe D in der südlichen Sowjetunion 1941–1943* (Hamburg, 2003); summary in idem, 'The Men of Einsatzgruppe D: An Inside View of a State-Sanctioned Killing Group in the "Third Reich"', in Jensen and Szejnmann (eds.), *Ordinary People*, 78–96; more generally, see Krausnick and Wilhelm, *Die Truppe*; and Peter Klein (ed.), *Die Einsatzgruppen in der besetzten Sowjetunion 1941/42: Die Tätigkeits-und Lageberichte des Chefs der Sicherheitspolizei und des SD* (Berlin, 1997).
7. For the background, see Claus-Christian W. Szejnmann, *Nazism in Central Germany: The Brownshirts in Red Saxony* (Oxford, 1999).
8. Karin Orth, 'Egon Zill – ein typischer Vertreter der Konzentrationslager-SS', in Mallmann and Paul (eds.), *Karrieren der Gewalt*, 264–73, also for the following. See also Stanislav Zámecnik, *Das war Dachau* (Frankfurt 2007), 128–29, and Christopher Dillon, *Dachau and the SS: A Schooling in Violence* (Oxford, 2015), 114–15.
9. Donald Bloxham, 'Motivation und Umfeld. Vergleichende Anmerkungen zu den Ursachen genozidaler Täterschaft', in Martin Cüppers *et al.* (eds.), *Naziverbrechen. Täter, Taten, Bewältigungsversuche* (Darmstadt, 2013), 62–74.

10. Gerhard Paul, 'Von Psychopathen, Technokraten des Terrors und 'ganz gewöhnlichen' Deutschen. Die Täter der Shoah im Spiegel der Forschung', in idem (ed.), *Die Täter der Shoah. Fanatische Nationalsozialisten oder ganz normale Deutsche?* (Göttingen, 2002), 13–90, here at 13–20; Gerhard Paul and Klaus-Michael Mallmann, 'Sozialisation, Milieu und Gewalt. Fortschritte und Probleme der neueren Täterforschung', in idem (eds.), *Karrieren der Gewalt*, 1–32, here at 2.
11. Paul and Mallmann, 'Sozialisation, Milieu und Gewalt', 3–4.
12. Claus-Christian W. Szejnmann, 'Perpetrators of the Holocaust: A Historiography', in Olaf Jensen and Claus-Christian Szejnmann (eds.), *Ordinary People as Mass Murderers: Perpetrators in Comparative Perspective* (London, 2008), 25–54 (Ohlendorf quote on 29); see also Ulrich Herbert, 'Extermination Policy: New Answers and Questions about the History of the "Holocaust" in German Historiography', in idem (ed.), *National Socialist Extermination Policies: Contemporary German Perspectives and Controversies* (Oxford, 2000), 1–52; Paul, 'Von Psychopathen', 20–33.
13. Alf Lüdtke, '"Fehlrgreifen in der Wahl der Mittel". Optionen im Alltag militärischen Handelns', *Mittelweg*, 36:12 (2003), 61–75; Hans Mommsen, 'Die Grenzen der Biografie. Prozesse und Entscheidungen: Ein Sammelband über die "Täter der Shoah" wirft die Frage nach dem Verhältnis von Individuum und Struktur im Nationalsozialismus auf', *Frankfurter Rundschau* (26 November 2002); Dillon, *Dachau*, 63–69. There are many more examples of refusal or reluctance to obey orders to kill civilians, e.g. Thomas Kühne, 'Male Bonding and Shame Culture: Hitler's Soldiers and the Moral Basis of Genocidal Warfare', in Szejnmann and Jensen (ed.), *Ordinary People*, 55–77; Klaus-Michael Mallmann, 'Dr. Jekyll & Mr. Hyde. Der Täterdiskurs in Wissenschaft und Gesellschaft', in idem, and Andrej Angrick (eds.), *Die Gestapo nach 1945. Karrieren, Konflikte, Konstruktionen* (Darmstadt, 2009), 292–318. More generally, see Paul, 'Von Psychopathen', 33–43.
14. Szejnmann, 'Perpetrators', 37–38, 44–45; Goldhagen, *Hitler's Willing Executioners*; Tom Stammers and Simon Taylor, *An Analysis of Daniel Jonah Goldhagen's 'Hitler's Willing Executioners': Ordinary Germans and the Holocaust* (London, 2017); Johannes Heil and Rainer Erb (eds.), *Geschichtswissenschaft und Öffentlichkeit: der Streit um Daniel J. Goldhagen* (Frankfurt, 1998); Robert R. Shandley (ed.), *Unwilling Germans? The Goldhagen Debate* (Minneapolis, MN, 1998); Geoff Eley (ed.), *The 'Goldhagen Effect': History, Memory, Nazism – Facing the German Past* (Ann Arbor, MI 2000); Julius Schoeps (ed.), *Ein Volk von Mördern? Die Dokumentation zur Goldhagen-Kontroverse um die Rolle der Deutschen im Holocaust* (Hamburg, 1996); for antisemitism and the left, see Rosemarie Leuschen-Seppel, *Sozialdemokratie und Antisemitismus im Kaiserreich. Die Auseinandersetzungen der Partei mit den konsevativen und völkischen Strömungen des Antisemitismus 1871–1914* (Bonn, 1978).

15. Wildt, *Generation des Unbedingten*.
16. Paul and Mallmann, 'Sozialisation', 6–9; Paul, 'Von Psychopathen', 43–61; see also Michael Mann, 'Were the Perpetrators of Genocide "Ordinary Men" or "Real Nazis"? Results from Fifteen Hundred Biographies', *Holocaust and Genocide Studies*, 14 (2000), 331–66.
17. Mann, 'Were the Perpetrators'; Paul and Mallmann, 'Sozialisation', 15–16.
18. Hans Buchheim, 'Command and Compliance', in Helmut Krausnick *et al.*, *Anatomy of the SS State* (London, 1968), 303–96; Dillon, *Dachau*, 80–82.
19. Paul and Mallmann, 'Sozialisation', 17–18; Ernst Klee *et al.* (eds.), *'Those Were the Days': The Holocaust as Seen by the Perpetrators and Bystanders* (London, 1991); Kühne, 'Male Bonding', 74–75; Dillon, *Dachau*, 179–217.
20. Wolfgang Sofsky, *Die Ordnung des Terrors: Das Konzentrationslager* (Frankfurt, 1993), 229–324.

19. The 'Witch' and the 'Beast': Ilse Koch and Irma Grese

1. Philip Friedman, *Roads to Extinction: Essays on the Holocaust* (Melrose Park, PA, 1980), 311.
2. Wendy Lower, *Hitler's Furies: German Women in the Nazi Killing Fields* (London, 2013), 120–44. Only Petri was tried, after the war, and sentenced to life imprisonment; see Gudrun Schwarz, *Eine Frau an seiner Seite. Ehefrauen in der 'SS-Sippengemeinschaft'* (Hamburg, 1997).
3. Quoted in Tomaz Jardim, *Ilse Koch on Trial: Making the 'Bitch of Buchenwald'* (London, 2023), 143.
4. Ibid, 159, 174, 251.
5. Ibid, 164, 289–91.
6. Ibid, 11–20.
7. Ibid, 21–33; Walter Bartel, *Buchenwald: Mahnung und Verpflichtung, Dokumente und Berichte* (East Berlin, 1983).
8. Wachsmann, *KL*, 197–98.
9. Jardim, *Ilse Koch*, 31–40.
10. Ibid, 41–77; Wachsmann, *KL*, 383–91.
11. Jardim, *Ilse Koch*, 77–91.
12. Ibid, 91–146. Koch already had three children, of whom one died in infancy. The father of her fourth was unknown, and the baby was taken into care.
13. Ibid, 147–259.
14. Ibid, 260–94, 217. See also Alexandra Przyrembel, 'Der Bann eines Bildes. Ilse Koch, die "Kommandeuse von Buchenwald"', in Insa Eschenbach *et al.* (eds.), *Gedächtnis und Geschlecht. Deutungsmuster in Darstellungen des nationalsozialistischen Genozids* (Frankfurt, 2002), 245–67.

15. John Cramer, *Belsen Trial 1945. Der Lüneburger Prozess gegen Wachpersonal der Konzentrationslager Auschwitz und Bergen–Belsen* (Göttingen, 2011), 287.
16. Gisella Perl, *I Was a Doctor in Auschwitz* (reprint, London, 2019).
17. Joanne Reilley, *Belsen: The Liberation of a Concentration Camp* (London, 1998); Ben Shepherd, *After Daybreak: The Liberation of Bergen-Belsen, 1945* (New York, 2007).
18. Claudia Taake, *Angeklagt: SS-Frauen vor Gericht* (Oldenburg, 1998), 49–66.
19. Raymond Phillips (ed.), *Trial of Josef Kramer and Forty-Four Others (The Belsen Trial)* (London, 1949), 248–60, 615–16. For the duties and equipment of female camp guards, who were usually trained to use firearms, see Kathrin Kompisch, *Täterinnen. Frauen im Nationalsozialismus* (Cologne, 2008), 155–202.
20. Anette Kretzer, *NS-Täterschaft und Geschlecht. Der erste britische Ravensbrück-Prozess 1946/47 in Hamburg* (Berlin, 2009), 243; Bernhard Strebel, *Das KZ Ravensbrück. Geschichte eines Lagerkomplexes* (Paderborn, 2003), 78.
21. Albert Pierrepoint, *Executioner: Pierrepoint* (London, 1974), 148.
22. Quoted in Cramer, *Belsen Trial*, 281.
23. Quoted in ibid, 288.
24. Quoted in ibid, 294.
25. Daniel P. Brown, *The Camp Women: The Female Auxiliaries Who Assisted the SS in Running the Nazi Concentration Camp System* (Atglen, PA, 2002), 12; see also idem, *The Beautiful Beast: The Life and Crimes of SS-Aufseherin Irma Grese* (San Marino, CA, 2004).
26. Perl, *I Was a Doctor*, 45, also for the following.
27. Quoted in Taake, *Angeklagt*, 135–41.
28. Gudrun Schwarz, 'Frauen in Konzentrationslagern – Täterinnen und Zuschauerinnen', in Ulrich Herbert *et al.* (eds.), *Die nationalsozialistischen Konzentrationslager* (Frankfurt, 2002), 800–21; eadem, "'... möchte ich nochmals um meine Einberufung als SS-Aufseherin bitten." Wärterinnen in den nationalsozialistischen Konzentrationslagern', in Barbara Distel (ed.), *Frauen im Holocaust* (Gerlingen, 2001), 331–52.
29. Kompisch, *Täterinnen*, 30–36; also Ino Arndt, *Das Frauenkonzentrationslager Ravensbrück* (Munich, 1993); Claus Füllberg-Stollberg (ed.), *Frauen in Konzentrationslagern: Bergen-Belsen und Ravensbrück* (Bremen, 1994); Sarah Helm, *Ravensbrück: Life and Death in Hitler's Concentration Camp for Women* (New York, 2014); Wachsmann, *KL*, 468; and Strebel, *Das KZ Ravensbrück*.
30. Susannah Heschel, 'Does Atrocity Have a Gender? Feminist Interpretations of Women in the SS', in Jeffrey M. Diefendorf (ed.), *Lessons and Legacies* VI: *New Currents in Holocaust Research* (Evanston, IL, 2004), 300–21, at 318.

31. Lavern Wolfram, 'Margot Pietzners autobiografische Aufzeichnungen "Schuldig oder Opfer?" Selbstwahrnehmung einer ehemaligen SS-Aufseherin in ihren Selbstzeugnissen', in Viola Schubert-Lehnhardt and Sylvia Korch (eds.), *Frauen als Täterinnen und Mittäterinnen im Nationalsozialismus. Gestaltungsspielräume und Handlungsmöglichkeiten* (Halle, 2006), 115–32; Jeanette Toussaint, 'Die Auseinandersetzung mit der nationalsozialistischen Vergangenheit. Interviews mit ehemaligen SS-Aufseherinnen und ihren Töchtern', in ibid, 147–60.
32. Irmtrud Heike, 'Female Concentration Camp Guards as Perpetrators: Three Case Studies', in Jensen and Szejnmann (eds.), *Ordinary People*, 120–42; more generally, Johannes Schwartz, 'Weibliche Angelegenheiten'. *Handlungsräume von KZ-Aufseherinnen in Ravensbrück und Neubrandenburg* (Hamburg, 2018).
33. Ljiljana Heise, *KZ-Aufseherinnen vor Gericht. Grete Bösel – 'another of those brutal types of women'?* (Frankfurt, 2009), esp. 101; Simone Erpel, 'Im Gefolge der SS. Aufseherinnen des Frauen-Konzentrationslagers Ravensbrück', in Marita Krauss (ed.), *Sie waren dabei. Mitläuferinnen, Nutzniesserinnen, Täterinnen im Nationalsozialismus* (Göttingen, 2008), 166–84.

20. The Mother: Gertrud Scholtz-Klink

1. Mary R. Beard, *Woman as a Force in History: A Study in Traditions and Realities* (New York, 1946), 23, cited in Claudia Koonz, *Mothers in the Fatherland: Women, the Family and Nazi Politics* (London, 1987), xvii. Peter Engelmann was a German newspaper editor exiled by the Nazis. He had also interviewed Scholtz-Klink.
2. Koonz, *Mothers*, xx–xxi.
3. Ibid, 17.
4. Richard J. Evans, *The Feminist Movement in Germany, 1894–1933* (London, 1976), 236–57.
5. As reported in Picker (ed.), *Tischgespräche*, 145; Jochmann (ed.), *Adolf Hitler*, 235, 316.
6. Domarus, *Hitler*, 531.
7. Ibid, 721 (10 September 1937).
8. Koonz, *Mothers*, xxiii–xxxiii.
9. Christiane Berger, 'Die Reichsfrauenführerin Gertrud Scholtz-Klink', in Krauss (ed.), *Sie waren dabei*, 103–26.
10. Berger, 'Reichsfrauenführerin', 104–5; eadem, *'Reichsfrauenführerin' Gertrud Scholtz-Klink. Eine nationalsozialistische Frauenkarriere in Verlauf, Retrospektive und Gegenwart* (Saarbrücken 2007), 21–22.
11. Ibid; Jill Stephenson, *The Nazi Organisation of Women* (London, 1981), is still the standard work on these conflicts. See also Michael Kater, 'Frauen in der NS-Bewegung', *Vierteljahrshefte für Zeitgeschichte*, 31 (1983), 202–41.

12. Stephenson, *The Nazi Organisation of Women*, 75–117.
13. Kater, 'Frauen in der NS-Bewegung', 222–24.
14. Ibid, 224–28; Stephenson, *The Nazi Organisation of Women*, 113–25.
15. Stephenson, *The Nazi Organisation of Women*, 18–19, 122–24; see also Andrea Böltken, *Führerinnen im 'Führerstaat': Gertrud Scholtz-Klink, Trude Mohr, Jutta Rüdiger und Inge Viermetz* (Pfaffenweiler, 1995), 60.
16. Kater, 'Frauen in der NS-Bewegung'; also Jill Stephenson, *Women in Nazi Society* (London, 1975), *passim*.
17. Berger, 'Reichsfrauenführerin', 117; for the argument that Scholtz-Klink was ideologically autonomous, see Massimiliano Livi, *Gertrud Scholtz-Klink: Die Reichsfrauenführerin* (Münster, 2005), 180–95.
18. Gisela Bock, 'Die Frauen und der Nationalsozialismus. Bemerkungen zu einem Buch von Claudia Koonz', *Geschichte und Gesellschaft*, vol. 15, no. 4 (1989), 563–79; Claudia Koonz, 'Erwiderung auf Gisela Bocks Rezension von "Mothers in the Fatherland"', *Geschichte und Gesellschaft*, vol. 18, no. 3 (1992), 394–99; Gisela Bock, *Zwangssterilisation im Nationalsozialismus: Studien zur Rassenpolitik und Frauenpolitik* (Opladen, 1986); Christina Herkommer, 'Women under National Socialism: Women's Scope for Action and the Issue of Gender', in Jensen and Szejnmann (eds.), *Ordinary People*, 99–119.
19. Kompisch, *Täterinnen*; Christoph Thonfeld, 'Frauen und Denunziation. Anmerkungen aus geschlechterhistorischer Perspektive', in Krauss (ed.), *Sie waren dabei*, 127–47; Elizabeth Harvey, *Women in the Nazi East: Agents and Witnesses of Germanization* (London, 2003); Vandana Joshi, *Gender and Power in the Third Reich: Female Denouncers and the Gestapo, 1933–1945* (London, 2003); overview in Christina Herkommer, *Die Rolle von Frauen im Spiegel des Diskurses der Frauen- und Geschlechterforschung* (Frankfurt am Main, 2005); Adelheid von Saldern, 'Victims or Perpetrators? Controversies about the Role of Women in the Nazi State', in David F. Crew (ed.), *Nazism and German Society, 1933–1945* (London, 1994), 141–65.
20. Kompisch, *Täterinnen*, *passim*; for a comprehensive account, see Lower, *Hitler's Furies*.
21. Michael Kater, *Doctors under Hitler* (Chapel Hill, NC, 1989), 124–25; Fritz Bringmann, *Kindermord am Bullenhuser Damm. SS-Verbrechen in Hamburg 1945, Menschenversuche an Kindern* (Frankfurt, 1978).
22. Wachsmann, *KL*, 226–29; Koonz, *Mothers*, xxviii–xxxii.
23. Livi, '*Reichsfrauenführerin*', 102–33.
24. Ibid, 199–205.
25. Ibid, 205–19.
26. Berger, 'Reichsfrauenführerin', 120–23; Gertrud Scholtz-Klink, *Die Frau im Dritten Reich* (Tübingen, 1978).
27. Koonz, *Mothers*, 181.
28. For a general historiographical overview, see Herkommer, 'Women under National Socialism', 99–119.

21. The Star: Leni Riefenstahl

1. Erich von Manstein, *Verlorene Siege* (Frankfurt am Main, 1955), 43–44.
2. Jürgen Trimborn, *Riefenstahl. Eine deutsche Karriere. Biographie* (Berlin, 2002), 292–317, also for the following.
3. Manstein, *Verlorene Siege*, 44. See also Karin Wieland, *Dietrich und Riefenstahl. Der Traum von der neuen Frau* (Munich, 2011), 353–62.
4. Leni Riefenstahl, *Memoiren 1902–1945* (Berlin, 1987), 349–52; Trimborn, *Riefenstahl*, 292–317; Rainer Rother, *Leni Riefenstahl: Die Verführung des Talents* (Berlin, 2000), 140–45; Steven Bach, *Leni: The Life and Work of Leni Riefenstahl* (London, 2007), 187–92.
5. See Nick Higham, 'The Five Lives of Leni Riefenstahl', http://news.bbc.co.uk/1/hi/entertainment/986528.stm, accessed 13 July 2021; also 'Her Films Glorified Hitler: Now Leni Riefenstahl's Own Story Hits the Screen', *The Scotsman* (12 June 2012), accessed 13 July 2021.
6. Riefenstahl, *Memoiren*, 152. For the speech, see Domarus, *Hitler*, 119–20.
7. Hartmann et al. (eds.), *Hitler. Mein Kampf*, I, 507 and n. 41.
8. Kershaw, *Hitler* I, 133.
9. Riefenstahl, *Memoiren*, 153.
10. Harry R. Sokal, 'Über Nacht Antisemitin geworden?', *Der Spiegel*, 46 (8 November 1976); Leni Riefenstahl, in a reader's letter published in the same magazine on 15 November 1976, dismissed Sokal's testimony as a pack of lies. For their relationship, see Wieland, *Dietrich und Riefenstahl*, 18–39.
11. Trimborn, *Riefenstahl*, 21–33.
12. Ibid, 276.
13. Rother, *Leni Riefenstahl*, 21–29; Wieland, *Dietrich und Riefenstahl*, 104–18.
14. Trimborn, *Riefenstahl*, 34–67.
15. Ibid, 69–85; Wieland, *Dietrich und Riefenstahl*, 117–54.
16. Trimborn, 86–119; Wieland, *Dietrich und Riefenstahl*, 155–75.
17. Riefenstahl, *Memoiren*, 152–60.
18. Trimborn, *Riefenstahl*, 120–43; Wieland, *Dietrich und Riefenstahl*, 176–83.
19. Trimborn, 143–55; Riefenstahl, *Memoiren*, 161–203 (also for her filming in Greenland); Niven, *Hitler and Film*, 53–58.
20. Trimborn, *Leni Riefenstahl*, 156–97, also for the following paragraph; Riefenstahl, *Memoiren*, 204–16; Rother, *Leni Riefenstahl*, 52–66; Niven, *Hitler and Film*, 61–65; Wieland, *Dietrich und Riefenstahl*, 292–328. For Riefenstahl's reading of *Mein Kampf*, see Ernst Sorge, *Mit Flugzeug, Faltboot und Filmkamera in den Eisfjorden Grönlands* (Berlin, 1933), 157, quoted in Wieland, *Dietrich und Riefenstahl*, 181.
21. Niven, *Hitler and Film*, 71–81.
22. Trimborn, *Leni Riefenstahl*, 198–237; Riefenstahl, *Memoiren*, 220–34; Rother, *Leni Riefenstahl*, 67–86; Welch, *Propaganda*, 147–259; Niven, *Hitler and Film*, 71–81.

23. David Clay Large, *Nazi Games: The Olympics of 1936* (New York, 2007).
24. Trimborn, *Leni Riefenstahl*, 238–49; Rother, *Leni Riefenstahl*, 87–101; Wieland, *Dietrich und Riefenstahl*, 329–51.
25. Welch, *Propaganda*, 112–21.
26. Domarus, *Hitler*, 567.
27. Trimborn, *Leni Riefenstahl*, 250–65; Riefenstahl, *Memoiren*, 235–41, 249–53, 265–88, 298–99, 303–22; Niven, *Hitler and Film*, 84–95. Cooper C. Graham, *Leni Riefenstahl and Olympia* (London, 1986), like Welch, underlines the propagandistic nature of the film.
28. Trimborn, *Leni Riefenstahl*, 266–361; Riefenstahl, *Memoiren*, 216–20, 322–32, 336–38, 399–400; Rother, *Leni Riefenstahl*, 118–40; Wieland, *Dietrich und Riefenstahl*, 364–79. For Riefenstahl's use of concentration-camp inmates as extras, see Nina Gladitz, *Leni Riefenstahl. Karriere einer Täterin* (Zurich, 2020), esp. 257–342. Gladitz's attempt to argue that Riefenstahl's visit to Poland in 1939 was really about the 'euthanasia' action (ibid, 230–55) does not convince. For Gladitz's obsessive campaign against Riefenstahl, see Kate Connolly, 'Burying Leni Riefenstahl', *The Guardian*, G2 supplement (Thursday, 9 December 2021), 5–8. For an accurate account of the 'euthanasia' meeting in occupied Poland, see Schmidt, *Karl Brandt, the Nazi Doctor* 117–28.
29. Riefenstahl, *Memoiren*, 410–20; Wieland, *Dietrich und Riefenstahl*, 444–62.
30. Rother, *Leni Riefenstahl*, 154–60.
31. Ibid, 180–98; Trimborn, *Leni Riefenstahl*, 484–505; Wieland, *Dietrich und Riefenstahl*, 463–81, 544–50.
32. Wieland, *Dietrich und Riefenstahl*, 550–55; Susan Sontag, *Under the Sign of Saturn* (New York, 1980), 73–108.

22. The Denunciator: Luise Solmitz

An earlier version of this chapter appeared in 2008 in *Sisters of Subversion: Histories of Women, Tales of Gender*, ed. Willem de Blécourt (Amsterdam, 2008).

1. Ian Kershaw, *Popular Opinion and Political Dissent in the Third Reich: Bavaria 1933–1945* (Oxford 1983); idem, *The Hitler Myth: Image and Reality in the Third Reich* (Oxford, 1989).
2. Beate Meyer, 'Zwischen Begeisterung und Skepsis. Die Wandlung der Luise Solmitz im Spiegel ihrer Tagebücher', in Frank Bajohr *et al.* (eds.), *Bedrohung, Hoffnung, Skepsis. Vier Tagebücher des Jahres 1933* (Göttingen, 2013), 127–42, and diary excerpts, 142–270; Daniel Führer, *Alltagssorgen und Gemeinschaftssehnsüchte. Tagebücher der Weimarer Republik (1913–1934)* (Stuttgart, 2020), 70–93; Werner Jochmann, *Nationalsozialismus und Revolution. Ursprung und Geschichte der NSDAP in Hamburg 1922–1933*.

Dokumente (Frankfurt, 1962), 400–32; Beate Meyer, '"Ich schlüpfe ungeachtet wie eine graue Motte mit durch." Die Wandlungen der Louise Solmitz zwischen 1933 und 1945 im Spiegel ihrer Tagebücher', in Frank Bajohr and Sibylle Steinbacher (eds.), '... *Zeugnis ablegen bis zum Letzten'. Tagebücher und persönliche Zeugnisse aus der Zeit des Nationalsozialismus und des Holocaust* (Göttingen, 2015), 61–80. The original manuscript diaries are held in the Solmitz Family Archive (622-1/40) in the Staatsarchiv der Freien- und Hansestadt Hamburg. The transcripts are held in the Forschungsstelle für Zeitgeschichte Hamburg.

3. Meyer, 'Zwischen Begeisterung und Skepsis', 127–32; Werner Stephan, *Acht Jahrzehnte erlebtes Deutschland. Ein Liberaler in vier Epochen* (Düsseldorf, 1983), 7–23.
4. Tagebuch Solmitz, 30 January 1933 (Meyer, 'Zwischen Begeisterung und Skepsis', 152).
5. Meyer, 'Zwischen Begeisterung und Skepsis', 133–35, 155–56; Jochmann, *Nationalsozialismus und Revolution*, 423.
6. Meyer, 'Zwischen Begeisterung und Skepsis', 162–79.
7. Ibid, 133–35. For denunciation more generally see Robert Gellately, *The Gestapo and German Society: Enforcing Racial Policy, 1933–1945* (Oxford, 1990); Gisela Diewald-Kerkmann, *Politische Denunziation im NS-Regime oder die kleine Macht der 'Volksgenossen'* (Bonn, 1995); and Rita Wolters, *Verrat für die Volksgemeinschaft. Denunziantinnen im Dritten Reich* (Pfaffenweiler, 1996). Women could sometimes use their power of denunciation to free themselves from a difficult personal situation in a society where divorce was particularly difficult in wartime: see Vandana Joshi, *Gender and Power in the Third Reich: Female Denouncers and the Gestapo (1939–1945)* (London, 2003).
8. Meyer, 'Zwischen Begeisterung und Skepsis', 136–39. More generally, see Beate Meyer (ed.), *Die Verfolgung und Ermordung der Hamburger Juden. Geschichte, Zeugnis, Erinnerung* (Göttingen, 2006), 42–78.
9. Meyer, 'Zwischen Begeisterung und Skepsis', 140–42.
10. See Beate Meyer, *'Jüdische Mischlinge'. Rassenpolitik und Verfolgungserfahrung 1933–1945* (Hamburg, 1999), 29–67, 166–84.
11. Michael Wildt, 'Die Tagebücher der Luise Solmitz – Zwei Originale', in Thomas Grossbölting and Kirsten Heinsohn (eds.), *Zeitgeschichte in Hamburg 2021* (Hamburg, 2022), 139–48.
12. Meyer, 'Zwischen Begeisterung und Skepsis', 77–78.

Conclusion

1. Ian Kershaw, *Hitler, the Germans, and the Final Solution* (London, 2008); Peter Longerich, *'Davon haben wir nichts gewusst!': Die Deutschen und die Judenverfolgung 1933–1945* (London, 2009); Frank Bajohr and Dieter Pohl,

Der Holocaust als offenes Geheimnis: die Deutschen, die NS-Führung und die Alliierten (Munich, 2006); David Bankier, *The Germans and the Final Solution: Public Opinion Under Nazism* (Cambridge, 1992); Sarah Gordon, *Hitler, Germans, and the Jewish Question* (Princeton, NJ, 1984); Victor Klemperer, *To the Bitter End: The Diaries of Victor Klemperer 1942–1945* (London, 1999), 148 (17 October 1942); Otto Dov Kulka and Eberhard Jäckel (eds.), *The Jews in the Secret Nazi Reports on Popular Opinion in Germany, 1933–1945* (London, 2010), xxv–lxiv (with further references, esp. to older research).

2. For wartime Allied propaganda, see for example Fossey J. C. Hearnshaw, *Germany the Aggressor Throughout the Ages* (London, 1940), or Rohan d'Olier Butler, *The Roots of National Socialism* (London, 1941).

3. Robert Gellately, *Backing Hitler: Consent and Coercion in Nazi Germany* (Oxford, 2002); Eric A. Johnson and Karl-Heinz Reuband, *What We Knew: Terror, Mass Murder, and Everyday Life in Nazi Germany* (New York, 2005); Götz Aly, *Hitler's Beneficiaries: Plunder, Racial War, and the Nazi Welfare State* (New York, 2007); Peter Fritzsche, *Hitler's First Hundred Days: When Germans Embraced the Third Reich* (New York: 2020). Gellately's later, excellent book, *Hitler's True Believers: How Ordinary People Became Nazis* (New York, 2020), however, gives full weight to the violence and coercion that lay at the heart of the Nazi seizure of power, though it still, inexplicably, excludes the millions who supported and voted for the Communist Party from the category of 'ordinary people'. For a thoughtful discussion of these issues, see Mary Fulbrook, *Bystander Society: Conformity and Complicity in Nazi Germany and the Holocaust* (Oxford, 2023).

4. Thomas Weber (ed.), *Als die Demokratie starb. Die Machtergreifung der Nationalsozialisten – Geschichte und Gegenwart* (Freiburg, 2022).

5. Evans, *The Third Reich in History and Memory*, 87–141 ('Coercion and Consent' and 'The People's Community'); for 'democracy' arguments, see Weber (ed.), *Als die Demokratie starb*, esp. ch. 4 (Thomas Weber, 'Nationalsozialistische illiberale Demokratie') and ch. 5 (Hedwig Richter, 'Wahlen im Nationalsozialismus: Eine dunkle Seite der Demokratiegeschichte'; at greater length also eadem, *Demokratie. Eine deutsche Affäre* [Munich, 2020]). The concept of an 'illiberal democracy' was devised by the Hungarian strongman Viktor Orbán, who remains subject to removal in a multi-party system characterized by elections that are still (more or less) free.

6. Longerich, *Hitler*, 516–17.

7. Claudia Koonz, *The Nazi Conscience* (London, 2003), 273.

8. Alan E. Steinweis, *The People's Dictatorship: A History of Nazi Germany* (Cambridge, 2023), despite the title now the best one-volume history of Nazi Germany available in English, along with Jane Caplan's *Nazi Germany: A Very Short Introduction* (Oxford, 2019).

9. Jeremy Noakes, 'The Oldenburg Crucifix Struggle of November 1936: A Case Study of Opposition in the Third Reich', in Peter D. Stachura (ed.), *The Shaping of the Nazi State* (London, 1978), 210–33; Longerich, *Heinrich Himmler*, 550; Evans, *The Third Reich at War*, 90–101 (with further references); Nathan Stoltzfus, *Resistance of the Heart: Intermarriage and the Rosenstrasse Protest in Nazi Germany* (New York, 1996); see also Wolf D. Gruner, *Widerstand in der Rosenstrasse: Die Fabrik-Aktion und die Verfolgung der Mischehen 1943* (Frankfurt, 2005), for a less dramatic interpretation of the Rosenstrasse events. In his often vehement reply to critics, *Hitler's Compromises: Coercion and Consensus in Nazi Germany* (New Haven, CT, 2016), and in an important collection of essays co-edited with Birgit Maier-Katkin, *Protest in Hitler's 'National Community': Popular Unrest and the Nazi Response* (Oxford, 2015), Stoltzfus has argued that widespread and frequent public protest against the Third Reich's policies and actions forced Hitler and his subordinates to compromise on a whole range of issues, limiting the regime's power in the process. But this is neither a new nor an original insight, and a recognition of the importance of coercion in establishing and sustaining the Third Reich is not the same as advancing the claim that every aspect of life under it was regimented and controlled: see also the older works of Peterson, *The Limits*; Detlev Peukert and Jürgen Reulecke (eds.), *Die Reihen fast geschlossen: Beiträge zur Geschichte des Alltags unterm Nationalsozialismus* (Wuppertal, 1981); Mason, *Social Policy*; and many other social-historical studies.
10. Nicholas Stargardt, 'Beyond "Consent" or "Terror": Wartime Crises in Nazi Germany', *History Workshop Journal*, 72 (2011), 190–204; and Steber and Gotto (eds.), *Visions of Community*, 15–16.
11. See the essays by Ian Kershaw (29–42) and Ulrich Herbert (60–72) in Steber and Gotto (eds.), *Visions of Community*. The polemical essay by Rudolf Tschirbs, *Das Phantom der Volksgemeinschaft* (Düsseldorf, 2015), defends the idea of the Third Reich as a class society.
12. Michael Wildt, '*Volksgemeinschaft*: A Modern Perspective on National Socialist Society', in Steber and Gotto (eds.), *Visions of Community*, 60–72.
13. Detlev Peukert, *Volksgenossen und Gemeinschaftsfremde: Anpassung, Ausmerze und Aufbegehren unter dem Nationalsozialismus* (Cologne, 1982; English version *Inside Nazi Germany: Conformity, Opposition and Racism in Everyday Life*, London, 1987); Armin Nolzen, 'Inklusion und Exklusion im "Dritten Reich". Das Beispiel der NSDAP', in Frank Bajohr and Michael Wildt (eds.), *Volksgemeinschaft. Neue Forschungen zur Gesellschaft des Nationalsozialismus* (Frankfurt, 2009), 60–77.
14. Peukert, *Volksgenossen und Gemeinschaftsfremde*; Frank Bajohr, '"Community of Action and Diversity of Attitudes: Reflections on Mechanisms of Social Integration in National Socialist Germany 1933–45', in Steber and

Gotto (eds.), *Visions of Community*, 187–99; Rüdiger Hachtmann, 'Volksgemeinschaftliche Dienstleister? Anmerkungen zu Selbstverständnis und Funktion der Deutschen Arbeitsfront und der NS-Gemeinschaft "Kraft durch Freude"', in Detlef Schmiechen-Ackermann (ed.), *'Volksgemeinschaft': Mythos, wirkungsmächtige soziale Verheissung oder soziale Realität im 'Dritten Reich'* (Paderborn, 2012), 111–31.

15. Frank Bajohr, '"Volksgemeinschaft" von außen betrachtet. Gemeinschaftsutopien und soziale Praxis in Berichten ausländischer Diplomaten und des sozialdemokratischen Exils 1933–45', in Dietmar von Reeken and Malte Thiessen (eds.), *'Volksgemeinschaft' als soziale Prazis: Neue Forschungen zur NS-Gesellschaft vor Ort* (Paderborn, 2013), 79–96. For more detail, see Bernd Stöver, *Volksgemeinschaft im Dritten Reich: Die Konsensbereitschaft der Deutschen aus der Sicht sozialdemokratischer Exilberichte* (Düsseldorf, 1993).
16. Sven Keller, *Volksgemeinshaft am Ende. Gesellschaft und Gewalt 1944/45* (Munich, 2013).
17. Ibid, 287–93.
18. Harald Welzer, *Täter. Wie aus ganz normalen Menschen Massenmörder werden* (Frankfurt am Main, 2005), 246–68.
19. Dan Stone, *The Holocaust: An Unfinished History* (London, 2023), xviii.
20. Jürgen Falter (ed.), *Junge Kämpfer, alte Opportunisten. Die Mitglieder der NSDAP 1919–1945* (Frankfurt, 2016), 475.
21. Mary Fulbrook, *Reckonings: Legacies of Nazi Persecution and the Quest for Social Justice* (Oxford, 2018), 538.

Bibliography

Adam, Peter, *The Arts in the Third Reich* (London, 1992)
Adams, Henry M. and Robin K., *Rebel Patriot: A Biography of Franz von Papen* (Santa Barbara, CA, 1987)
Adorno, Theodor W. et al., *The Authoritarian Personality* (New York, 1950)
Ahlheim, Hannah, *'Deutsche, kauft nicht bei Juden!' Antisemitischer Boycott in Deutschland 1924 bis 1935* (Göttingen, 2011)
Alford, Kenneth D., *Hermann Göring and the Nazi Art Collection: The Looting of Europe's Art Treasures and Their Dispersal After World War II* (Jefferson, NC, 2012)
Allert, Tilman, *The Nazi Salute: On the Meaning of a Gesture* (New York, 2008)
Aly, Götz, *Hitler's Beneficiaries: Plunder, Racial War, and the Nazi Welfare State* (New York, 2007)
—, and Susanne Heim, *Architects of Annihilation: Auschwitz and the Logic of Destruction* (Princeton, NJ, 2002)
Andrus, Burton C., *The Infamous of Nuremberg* (London, 1969)
Angrick, Andrej, *Besatzungspolitik und Massenmord. Die Einsatzgruppe D in der südlichen Sowjetunion 1941–1943* (Hamburg, 2003)
—, 'The Men of *Einsatzgruppe D*: An Inside View of a State-Sanctioned Killing Group in the "Third Reich"', in Olaf Jensen and Claus-Christian W. Szejnmann (eds.), *Ordinary People as Mass Murderers: Perpetrators in Comparative Perspective* (London, 2008), 78–96
Arndt, Ino, *Das Frauenkonzentrationslager Ravensbrück* (Munich, 1993)
Aronson, Shlomo, *Reinhard Heydrich und die Frühgeschichte von Gestapo und SD* (Stuttgart, 1971)
Bach, Steven, *Leni: The Life and Work of Leni Riefenstahl* (London, 2007)
Baird, Jay W., *To Die for Germany: Heroes in the Nazi Pantheon* (Bloomington, IN, 1990)
Bajohr, Frank, *Parvenüs und Profiteure. Korruption in der NS-Zeit* (Frankfurt, 2001)
—, and Dieter Pohl, *Der Holocaust als offenes Geheimnis: Die Deutschen, die NS-Führung und die Alliierten* (Munich, 2006)

BIBLIOGRAPHY

—, '"Volkegsmeinschaft" von aussen betrachtet. Gemeinschaftsutopien und soziale Praxis in Berichten ausländischer Diplomaten und des sozialdemokratischen Exils 1933–45', in Dietmar von Reeken and Malte Thiessen (eds.), *'Volksgemeinschaft' als soziale Prazis: Neue Forschungen zur NS-Gesellschaft vor Ort* (Paderborn, 2013), 79–96

Bankier, David, *The Germans and the Final Solution: Public Opinion Under Nazism* (Cambridge, 1992)

Baranowski, Shelley, *Strength Through Joy: Consumerism and Mass Tourism in the Third Reich* (New York, 2004)

Barber, John, and Andrei Dzeniskevich, *Life and Death in Besieged Leningrad, 1941–44* (New York, 2005)

Barbian, Jan-Pieter, *Literaturpolitik in 'Dritten Reich'. Institutionen, Kompetenaen, Betätigungsfelder* (Munich, 1995)

Bartel, Walter, *Buchenwald: Mahnung und Verpflichtung, Dokumente und Berichte* (East Berlin, 1983)

Bartov, Omer, *The Eastern Front 1941–45: German Troops and the Barbarisation of Warfare* (Oxford, 1985)

Bartsch, Günter, *Zwischen drei Stühle: Otto Strasser. Eine Biographie* (Koblenz, 1990)

Bascomb, Neal, *Hunting Eichmann: How a Band of Survivors and a Young Spy Agency Chased Down the World's Most Notorious Nazi* (Boston, MA, 2009)

Baumann, Schaul, *Die Deutsche Glaubensbewegung und ihr Gründer Jakob Wilhelm Hauer (1881–1962)* (Marburg, 2005)

Baumeister, Frank (ed.), *Hesselbergland. Land und Leute in Ehingen, Dambach und Lentersheim* (Gunzenhausen, 1991)

Bayer, Karen, *'How Dead is Hitler?' Der britische Starreporter Sefton Delmer und die Deutschen* (Mainz, 2008)

Beard, Mary R., *Woman as a Force in History: A Study in Traditions and Realities* (New York, 1971)

Beck, Hermann, *The Fateful Alliance: German Conservatives and Nazis in 1933. The 'Machtergreifung' in a New Light* (Oxford, 2008)

—, *Before the Holocaust: Antisemitic Violence and the Reaction of German Elites and Institutions during the Nazi Takeover* (Oxford, 2022)

Becker, Josef, 'Zentrum und Ermächtigungsgesetz 1933: Dokumentation', *Vierteljahrshefte für Zeitgeschichte*, vol. 9 (1961), 195–210

Beevor, Antony, *Stalingrad* (London, 2007)

Behrenbeck, Sabine, *Der Kult um die toten Helden. Nationalsozialistische Mythen, Riten und Symbole 1923 bis 1945* (Vierow bei Greifswald, 1996)

Below, Nicolaus von, *Als Hitlers Adjutant 1939–45* (Mainz, 1980)

Bennecke, Heinrich, 'Die Memoiren des Ernst Röhm. Ein Vergleich der verschiedenen Ausgaben und Auflagen', *Politische Studien*, vol. 14, no. 1 (1963), 179–88

—, *Hitler und die SA* (Munich, 1972)

Benz, Wigbert, *Der Hungerplan im 'Unternehmen Barbarossa' 1941* (Berlin, 2011)

Benz, Wolfgang, *Gewalt im November 1938. Die 'Reichskristallnacht'. Initial zum Holocaust* (Berlin, 2018)
Benzenhöfer, Udo, *Euthanasia in Germany Before and During the Third Reich* (Münster, 2010)
Beorn, Waitman Wade, *Marching into Darkness: Local Participation of the Wehrmacht in the Holocaust, 1941–1942* (Cambridge, MA, 2014)
Beradt, Charlotte, *Das dritte Reich des Traums* (Frankfurt, 1966)
Berg, Matthias, *Karl Alexander von Müller: Historiker für den Nationalsozialismus* (Munich, 2014)
Berger, Christiane, *'Reichsfrauenführerin' Gertrud Scholtz-Klink. Eine nationalsozialistische Frauenkarriere in Verlauf, Retrospektive und Gegenwart* (Saarbrücken, 2007)
—, 'Die Reichsfrauenführerin Gertrud Scholtz-Klink', in Marita Krauss (ed.), *Sie waren dabei. Mitläuferinnen, Nutzniesserinnen, Täterinnen im Nationalsozialismus* (Göttingen, 2008), 103–26
Bering, Dietz, *Kampf um Namen. Bernhard Weiss gegen Joseph Goebbels* (Stuttgart, 1991)
Besgen, Achim, *Der stille Befehl. Medizinalrat Kersten, Himmler und das Dritte Reich* (Munich, 1960)
Bessel, Richard, 'The Potempa Murder', *Central European History*, vol. 10 (1977), 241–54
—, *Political Violence and the Rise of Nazism: The Storm Troopers in Eastern Germany 1925–1934* (London, 1984)
Bieber, Len E., 'La política militar alemana en Bolivia, 1900–1935', *Latin American Research Review*, vol. 29, no. 1 (1994), 85–106
Binding, Karl, and Alfred Hoche, *Die Freigabe der Vernichtung lebensunwerten Lebens. Ihr Mass und Ihr Form* (Leipzig, 1920)
Bloch, Charles, *Die SA und die Krise des NS-Regimes 1934* (Frankfurt, 1970)
Bloch, Michael, *Ribbentrop* (London, 1992; 2nd ed., London 2003)
Blood-Ryan, Hugh W., *Franz von Papen: His Life and Times* (London, 1938)
Bloxham, Donald, 'Motivation und Umfeld. Vergleichende Anmerkungen zu den Ursachen genozidaler Täterschaft', in Martin Cüppers *et al.* (eds.), *Naziverbrechen. Täter, Taten, Bewältigungsversuche* (Darmstadt, 2013), 62–74
Bock, Gisela, *Zwangssterilisation im Nationalsozialismus: Studien zur Rassenpolitik und Frauenpolitik* (Opladen, 1986)
—, 'Die Frauen und der Nationalsozialismus. Bemerkungen zu einem Buch von Claudia Koonz', *Geschichte und Gesellschaft*, vol. 15, no. 4 (1989), 563–79
Böhler, Jochen, *Auftakt zum Vernichtungskrieg: Die Wehrmacht in Polen 1939* (Frankfurt, 2006)
—, 'Intention oder Situation? Soldaten der Wehrmacht und die Anfänge des Vernichtungskrieges in Polen', in Timm C. Richter (ed.), *Krieg und Verbrechen. Situation und Intention: Fallbeispiele* (Munich, 2006), 165–72

BIBLIOGRAPHY

Bollmus, Reinhard, *Das Amt Rosenberg und seine Gegner. Studien zum Machtkampf im nationalsozialistischen Herrschaftssystem* (Stuttgart, 1970; 2nd ed., Munich, 2006)

Böltken, Andrea, *Führerinnen im "Führerstaat": Gertrud Scholtz-Klink, Trude Mohr, Jutta Rüdiger und Inge Viermetz* (Pfaffenweiler, 1995)

Botz, Gerhard, *Der 13. März und die Anschluss-Bewegung: Selbstaufgabe, Okkupation und Selbstfindung Österreichs 1918–1945* (Vienna, 1978)

Bouverie, Tim, *Appeasing Hitler: Chamberlain, Churchill and the Road to War* (London, 2019)

Bracher, Karl Dietrich, *Die Auflösung der Weimarer Republik. Eine Studie zum Problem des Machtverfalls in der Demokratie* (Villingen/Schwarzwald, 1955)

—, *Die nationalsozialistische Machtergreifung: Studien zur Errichtung des totalitären Herrschaftssystems in Deutschland 1933/34*, I: *Stufen der Machtergreifung* (Cologne, 1960)

Brakelmann, Günter, *Zwischen Mitschuld und Widerstand: Fritz Thyssen und der Nationalsozialismus* (Essen, 2010)

Brechenmacher, Thomas (ed.), *Das Reichskonkordat 1933. Forschungsstand, Kontroversen, Dokumente* (Paderborn, 2007)

Brechtken, Magnus, *'Madagaskar für die Juden'. Antisemitische Idee und politische Praxis 1885–1945* (Munich, 1997)

—, *Albert Speer. Eine deutsche Karriere* (Munich, 2017)

Breitman, Richard, *The Architect of Genocide: Himmler and the Final Solution* (London, 1991)

Bringmann, Fritz, *Kindermord am Bullenhuser Damm. SS-Verbrechen in Hamburg 1945, Menschenversuche an Kindern* (Frankfurt, 1978)

Brockmann, Robert, *El general y sus presidentes: vida y tiempos de Hans Kundt, Ernst Röhm e siete presidentes en la historia de Bolivia, 1911–1939* (La Paz, 2007)

Browder, George C., *Hitler's Enforcers: The Gestapo and the SS Security Service in the Nazi Revolution* (Oxford, 1996)

—, 'Perpetrator Character and Motivation: An Emerging Consensus', *Holocaust and Genocide Studies*, 17 (2003), 480–97

Brown, Daniel P., *The Camp Women: The Female Auxiliaries Who Assisted the SS in Running the Nazi Concentration Camp System* (Atglen, PA, 2002)

—, *The Beautiful Beast: The Life and Crimes of SS-Aufseherin Irma Grese* (San Marino, CA, 2004)

Browning, Christopher, *The Final Solution and the German Foreign Office: A Study of Referat D III of Abteilung Deutschland 1940–43* (New York, 1978)

—, *Ordinary Men: Reserve Police Battalion 101 and the Final Solution in Poland* (New York, 1992)

Bruce, Gary, *Through the Lion Gate: A History of Berlin Zoo* (New York, 2017)

Bryant, Chad, *Prague in Black: Nazi Rule and Czech Nationalism* (Cambridge, MA, 2007)

BIBLIOGRAPHY

Bucher, Peter, *Der Reichswehrprozess. Der Hochverrat der Ulmer Reichswehroffiziere 1929/30* (Boppard am Rhein, 1967)

Buchheim, Hans, 'Command and Compliance', in Helmut Krausnick *et al.*, *Anatomy of the SS State* (London, 1968), 303–96

Bullock, Alan, *Hitler: A Study in Tyranny* (London, 1952)

—, *Hitler and Stalin: Parallel Lives* (London, 1991)

Burckhardt, Carl J., *Meine Danziger Mission 1937–1939* (Munich, 1960)

Burleigh, Michael, *Germany Turns Eastwards: A Study of Ostforschung in the Third Reich* (Cambridge, 1988)

—, *Death and Deliverance: 'Euthanasia' in Germany 1900–1945* (Cambridge, 1994)

Butler, Rohan d'Olier, *The Roots of National Socialism* (London, 1941)

Bytwerk, Randall F., 'Julius Streicher and the Early History of "Der Stürmer"', *Journalism History*, vol. 5 (1978), 74–79

—, *Julius Streicher: Nazi Editor of the Notorious Anti-Semitic Newspaper* Der Stürmer (New York, 2001 [1983])

Cahill, John L., 'Dear Herr Streicher: Letters to the Third Reich's Foremost Anti-Semite', in Otis C. Mitchell (ed.), *Nazism and the Common Man* (Washington DC, 1981), 139–57

Calic, Edouard, *Reinhard Heydrich: The Chilling Story of the Man Who Masterminded the Nazi Death Camps* (New York, 1985)

Campbell, Bruce, *The SA Generals and the Rise of Nazism* (Lexington, KY, 1998)

Caplan, Jane, *Nazi Germany: A Very Short Introduction* (Oxford, 2019)

Carsten, Francis L., *The Reichswehr and Politics 1918–1933* (Oxford, 1966)

Childers, Thomas, *The Nazi Voter: The Social Foundations of Fascism in Germany, 1919–1933* (Chapel Hill, NC, 1981)

Christensen, Claus Bundgård, *et al.*, *War, Genocide and Cultural Memory: The Waffen-SS, 1933 to Today* (London, 2023) 225–70

Clarke, Comer, *Eichmann: The Savage Truth* (London, 1960)

Clinefelter, Joan L., *Artists for the Reich: Culture and Race from Weimar to Nazi Germany* (Oxford, 2005)

Cohen, William B., and Jörgen Svensson, 'Finland and the Holocaust', *Holocaust and Genocide Studies*, vol. 9 (1995), 70–93

Connolly, Kate, 'Burying Leni Riefenstahl', *The Guardian*, G2 supplement (Thursday, 9 December 2021), 5–8

Conze, Eckart, *et al.*, *Das Amt und die Vergangenheit. Deutsche Diplomaten im Dritten Reich und in der Bundesrepublik* (Munich, 2010)

Craig, Gordon A., *The Politics of the Prussian Army 1640–1945* (Oxford, 1955)

Cramer, John, *Belsen Trial 1945. Der Lüneburger Prozess gegen Wachpersonal der Konzentrationslager Auschwitz und Bergen-Belsen* (Göttingen, 2011)

Crowther, Bosley, 'Varnished Truth: "The Hitler Gang" Gives Evidence of an Incomplete Political Analysis', *New York Times* (14 May 1944), Section X, 3

BIBLIOGRAPHY

Delmer, Sefton, *Trail Sinister: An Autobiography* (London, 1961)
Demeter, Karl, *Das deutsche Offizierskorps in Gesellschaft und Staat 1650–1945* (Frankfurt am Main, 1962)
Deschner, Günther, *Heydrich: The Pursuit of Total Power* (London, 1981)
Deuerlein, Ernst, 'Hitlers Eintritt in die Politik und die Reichswehr', *Vierteljahrshefte für Zeitgeschichte*, vol. 7 (1959), 177–227
—(ed.), *Der Hitler-Putsch: Bayerische Dokumente zum 8./9. November 1923* (Stuttgart, 1962)
—(ed.), *Der Aufstieg der NSDAP in Augenzeugenberichten*, 4th edn (Munich, 1980)
Diederichs, Mario, *Heydrich: The Face of Evil* (London, 2006)
Diehl, James M., *Paramilitary Politics in Weimar Germany* (Bloomington, IN, 1977)
Diels, Rudolf, *Lucifer ante Portas . . . es spricht der erste Chef der Gestapo* (Stuttgart, 1950)
Dierker, Wolfgang, *Himmlers Glaubenskrieger. Der Sicherheitsdienst der SS und seine Religionspolitik 1933–1941* (Paderborn, 2002)
Diewald-Kerkmann, Gisela, *Politische Denunziation im NS-Regime oder die kleine Macht der 'Volksgenossen'* (Bonn, 1995)
Dillon, Christopher, *Dachau and the SS: A Schooling in Violence* (Oxford, 2015)
Dougherty, Nancy, *The Man with the Iron Heart: The Definitive Biography of Reinhard Heydrich, Architect of the Holocaust*, ed. Christopher Lehmann-Haupt (London, 2022)
Doll, Nikola, *Mäzenentum und Kunstförderung im Nationalsozialismus: Werner Peiner und Hermann Göring* (Weimar, 2009)
Domarus, Max (ed.), *Hitler. Reden und Proklamationen 1932–1945. Kommentiert von einem deutschen Zeitgenossen*, 4 vols. (Munich, 1962–73)
Domeier, Norman, *The Eulenburg Affair: A Cultural History of Politics in the German Empire* (Rochester, NY, 2015)
Dominick, Raymond H. III, *The Environmental Movement in Germany: Prophets and Pioneers, 1871–1971* (New York, 1992)
Dörner, Klaus, et al., *The Nuremberg Medical Trial 1946/47* (Munich, 2001)
Dornheim, Andreas, *Röhms Mann fürs Ausland: Politik und Ermordung des SA-Agenten Georg Bell* (Münster, 1998)
Döscher, Hans-Jürgen, *Das Auswärtige Amt im Dritten Reich. Diplomatie im Schatten der 'Endlösung'* (Berlin, 1987)
Dröge, Martin, *Männlichkeit und 'Volksgemeinschaft': Der westfälische Landeshauptmann Karl Friedrich Kolbow (1899–1945): Biographie eine NS-Täters* (Paderborn, 2015)
Duckwitz, Theresa Maria, and Dominik Gross, 'Searching for Motives: Suicides of Doctors and Dentists in the Third Reich and the Postwar Period, 1933–1939', *Endeavour*, vol. 45, no. 2 (December 2021)

Dutch, Oswald (pseud. i.e., Otto Erich Deutsch), *The Errant Diplomat: The Life of Franz von Papen* (London, 1940)

Ebbinghaus, Angelika, 'Zwei Welten. Die Opfer und die Täter der kriegschirurgischen Experimente', in eadem and Klaus Dörner (eds.), *Vernichten und Heilen. Der Nürnberger Ärzteprozess und seine Folgen* (Berlin, 2001), 219–40

Eberle, Henrik, and Hans-Joachim Neumann, *Was Hitler Ill? A Final Diagnosis* (Cambridge, 2012)

Eichengreen, Barry, *Golden Fetters: The Gold Standard and the Great Depression, 1919–1939* (Oxford, 1992)

Eissler, Wilfried U., *Arbeiterparteien und Homosexuellenfrage. Zur Sexualpolitik von SPD und KPD in der Weimarer Republik* (Berlin, 1980)

Eley, Geoff (ed.), *The 'Goldhagen Effect': History, Memory, Nazism – Facing the German Past* (Ann Arbor, MI, 2000)

El-Hai, Jack, *The Nazi and the Psychiatrist: Hermann Göring, Dr. Douglas M. Kelley, and a Fatal Meeting of Minds at the End of WWII* (New York, 2013)

Enfield, Glenn, *Hitler's Secret Life* (New York, 1979)

Epstein, Catherine, *Model Nazi: Arthur Greiser and the Occupation of Western Poland* (Oxford, 2010)

Evans, Richard J., *The Feminist Movement in Germany, 1894–1933* (London, 1976)

—(ed.), *Kneipengespräche im Kaiserreich. Stimmungsberichte der Hamburger Politischen Polizei 1892–1914* (Reinbek bei Hamburg, 1989)

—, *Rituals of Retribution: Capital Punishment in Germany 1600–1997* (Oxford, 1996)

—, *Rereading German History: From Unification to Reunification 1800–1996* (London, 1997)

—, *Telling Lies About Hitler. The Holocaust, History and the David Irving Trial* (London, 2002)

—, 'Ernst Klee Obituary', *The Guardian* (21 May 2013)

—, 'Was Stalinism Worse than Nazism?', *The Guardian* (9 August 2014), Review Section, 6

—, 'Blitzed: Drugs in Nazi Germany by Norman Ohler, Review – A Crass and Dangerously Inaccurate Account', *The Guardian* (6 November 2016)

—, 'Nuts about the Occult', *London Review of Books*, vol. 40 no. 15 (2 August 2018)

—, 'The Decision to Exterminate the Jews of Europe', in Larissa Allwork and Rachel Pistol (eds.), *The Jews, the Holocaust, and the Public: The Legacies of David Cesarani* (London, 2019), 117–44

—, *The Hitler Conspiracies: The Third Reich and the Paranoid Imagination* (London, 2020)

Falter, Jürgen W., *Hitlers Wähler* (Munich, 1991)

—et al., *Wahlen und Abstimmungen in der Weimarer Republik. Materialien zum Wahlverhalten 1919–1933* (Munich, 2009)

—(ed.), *Junge Kämpfer, alte Opportunisten. Die Mitglieder der NSDAP 1919–1945* (Frankfurt, 2016)

Fangmann, Helmut, et al., *'Parteisoldaten': Die Hamburger Polizei im '3. Reich'* (Hamburg, 1987)

Feldman, Matthew et al. (eds.), *Clerical Fascism in Interwar Europe* (London, 2013)

Felton, Mark, 'Hermann Goering's Pet Lions' (https://www.youtube.com/watch?v=gzDK4RVfARs)

Fest, Joachim C., *The Face of the Third Reich* (London, 1961)

—, *Hitler: Eine Biographie* (Frankfurt, 1973; English edn *Hitler*, London, 1974)

—, *Plotting Hitler's Death: The German Resistance to Hitler* (London, 1996)

Feuchtwanger, Lion, *The Oppermanns* (London, 2020; first published as *Die Geschwister Oppermann*, 1934)

Flachowsky, Karin, 'Neue Quellen zur Abstammung Reinhard Heydrichs', *Vierteljahrshefte für Zeitgeschichte*, vol. 48 (2000), 319–27

Fleischmann, Peter (ed.), *Hitler als Häftling in Landsberg am Lech 1923/24: Der Gefangenen-Personalakt Hitler nebst weiteren Quellen aus der Schutzhaft-, Untersuchungshaft- und Festungshaftanstalt Landsberg am Lech*, 3rd edn (Neustadt an der Aisch, 2018)

Fontander, Björn, *Göring och Sverige* (Kristjanstad, 1984)

Förster, Jürgen, 'Operation Barbarossa as a War of Conquest and Annihilation', in Horst Boog et al. (eds.), *Germany and the Second World War*, vol. 4 (Oxford, 1998), 413–50

Förster, Michael, *Jurist im Dienst des Unrechts: Leben und Werk des ehemaligen Staatssekretärs im Reichsjustizministerium, Franz Schlegelberger, 1876–1970* (Baden-Baden, 1995)

Fox, John P., 'Max Bauer: Chiang Kai-shek's First German Military Adviser', *Journal of Contemporary History*, vol. 5, no. 4 (1970), 21–44

Frank, Hans, *Im Angesicht des Galgens. Deutung Hitlers und seiner Zeit auf Grund eigener Erlebnisse und Erkenntnisse. Geschrieben im Nürnberger Justizgefängnis* (Munich, 1953)

Frank, Niklas, *Der Vater. Eine Abrechnung* (Munich, 1987)

Franks, Norman, and Hal Giblin, *Under the Guns of the German Aces. Immelmann, Voss, Göring, Lothar von Richthofen: The Complete Record of their Victories and Victims* (London, 1997)

Franz-Willing, Georg, *Ursprung der Hitler-Bewegung* (Preussisch Oldendorf, 1974 [1962])

Frehse, Michael, *Ermächtigungsgesetzgebung im Deutschen Reich, 1914–1933* (Pfaffenweiler, 1985)

Frei, Norbert et al., *Flick. Der Konzern, die Familie, die Macht* (Munich, 2009)

BIBLIOGRAPHY

Freitag, Werner, 'Nationale Mythen und kirchliches Heil: Der "Tag von Potsdam"', *Westfälische Forschungen*, vol. 41 (1991), 379–439

Friedlander, Henry, *The Origins of Nazi Genocide: From Euthanasia to the Final Solution* (Chapel Hill, NC, 1995)

Friedländer, Saul, *Nazi Germany and the Jews: The Years of Persecution 1933–39* (London, 1997)

—, *The Years of Extermination: Nazi Germany and the Jews, 1939–45* (New York, 2007)

Friedman, Philip, *Roads to Extinction: Essays on the Holocaust* (Melrose Park, PA, 1980)

Friedrichs, Axel (ed.), *Die nationalsozialistische Revolution 1933 (Dokumente der deutschen Politik*, I, Berlin, 1933)

Fritzsche, Peter, *A Nation of Fliers: German Aviation and the Popular Imagination* (Cambridge, MA, 1992)

—, *Hitler's First Hundred Days: When Germans Embraced the Third Reich* (New York, 2020)

Fröhlich, Elke (ed.), *Die Tagebücher von Joseph Goebbels: Sämtliche Fragmente*, 4 vols. (Munich, 1987)

—(ed.), *Die Tagebücher von Joseph Goebbels*, 32 vols. (Munich, 1993–2008)

Führer, Daniel, *Alltagssorgen und Gemeinschaftssehnsüchte. Tagebücher der Weimarer Republik (1913–1934)* (Stuttgart, 2020)

Fulbrook, Mary, *Reckonings: Legacies of Nazi Persecution and the Quest for Social Justice* (Oxford, 2018)

—, *Bystander Society: Conformity and Complicity in Nazi Germany and the Holocaust* (Oxford, 2023)

Füllberg-Stollberg, Claus (ed.), *Frauen in Konzentrationslagern: Bergen-Belsen und Ravensbrück* (Bremen, 1994)

Gallo, Max, *La nuit des longs couteaux: 30 juin 1934* (Paris, 1970)

Gamm, Hans-Jochen, *Der Flüsterwitz im Dritten Reich* (1964)

Gaskin, Hilary, *Eyewitnesses at Nuremberg* (London, 1990)

Gehl, Walther (ed.), *Die nationalsozialistische Revolution: Tatsachen und Urkunden, Reden und Schilderungen, 1. August 1914 bis 1. Mai 933* (Breslau, 1933)

Gellately, Robert, *The Gestapo and German Society: Enforcing Racial Policy, 1933–1945* (Oxford, 1990)

—, *Backing Hitler: Consent and Coercion in Nazi Germany* (Oxford, 2002)

—, *Hitler's True Believers: How Ordinary People Became Nazis* (New York, 2020)

Gentile, Carlo, *Wehrmacht und Waffen-SS im Partisanenkrieg: Italien 1943–1945* (Paderborn, 2012)

Gerbet, Klaus (ed.), *Generalfeldmarschall Fedor von Bock: Zwischen Pflicht und Verweigerung. Das Kriegstagebuch* (Munich, 1995)

BIBLIOGRAPHY

Gerhard, Gesine, 'Food and Genocide: Nazi Agrarian Politics in the Occupied Territories of the Soviet Union', *Contemporary European History*, vol. 18, no. 1 (2009), 45–65

Gerlach, Christian, *Kalkulierte Morde. Die deutsche Wirtschafts- und Vernichtungspolitik in Weissrussland 1941 bis 1944* (Hamburg, 1999)

Gerwarth, Robert, *The Vanquished: Why the First World War Failed to End, 1917–1923* (London, 2016)

Geyer, Michael, 'German Strategy in the Age of Machine Warfare, 1914–1945', in Peter Paret (ed.), *Makers of Modern Strategy: From Machiavelli to the Nuclear Age* (Princeton, NJ, 1986), 543–72

Giesen, Rolf, *Nazi Propaganda Films: A History and Filmography* (Jefferson, NC, 2003)

Gilbert, Gustave M., *The Psychology of Dictatorship* (New York, 1950)

Gilbhard, Hermann, *Die Thule-Gesellschaft. Vom okkulten Mummenschanz zum Hakenkreuz*, 2nd edn (Munich, 2015)

Giles, Geoffrey, 'The Persecution of Gay Men and Lesbians during the Third Reich', in Jonathan C. Friedman (ed.), *The Routledge History of the Holocaust* (London, 2011), 385–96

Gladitz, Nina, *Leni Riefenstahl. Karriere einer Täterin* (Zurich, 2020)

Glen, Douglas, *Von Ribbentrop Is Still Dangerous* (London, 1941)

Goda, Norman, 'Black Marks: Hitler's Bribery of his Senior Officers During World War II', *Journal of Modern History*, vol. 72 (2000), 413–52

—, *Tales from Spandau: Nazi Criminals and the Cold War* (Cambridge, 2007)

Goering, Emmy, *My Life with Goering* (London, 1972)

Goering, Hermann, *Germany Reborn* (London, 1934)

—, *Reden und Aufsätze*, 2nd edn (Munich, 1938)

Goeschel, Christian, *Suicide in Nazi Germany* (Oxford, 2009)

—, *Mussolini and Hitler: The Forging of the Fascist Alliance* (London, 2018)

Goldensohn, Leon, *The Nuremberg Interviews: An American Psychiatrist's Conversations with the Defendants and Witnesses*, ed. Robert Gellately (New York, 2005)

Goldhagen, Daniel Jonah, *Hitler's Willing Executioners: Ordinary Germans and the Holocaust* (London, 1996)

Gordon, Harold J., *Hitler and the Beer-Hall Putsch* (Princeton, NJ, 1972)

Gordon, Sarah, *Hitler, Germans, and the Jewish Question* (Princeton, NJ, 1984)

Gorodetsky, Gabriel (ed.), *The Maisky Diaries: Red Ambassador to the Court of St. James's 1932–1943* (London, 2015)

Görtemaker, Heike B., *Eva Braun: Life with Hitler* (London, 2011)

—, *Hitlers Hofstaat. Der innere Kreis im Dritten Reich und danach* (Munich, 2019)

Görtemaker, Manfred, *Rudolf Hess. Der Stellvertreter. Eine Biographie* (Munich, 2023)

Graham, Cooper C., *Leni Riefenstahl and Olympia* (London, 1986)

BIBLIOGRAPHY

Graml, Hermann, 'Probleme einer Hitler-Biographie. Kritische Bemerkungen zu Joachim C. Fest', *Vierteljahrshefte für Zeitgeschichte*, vol. 22 (1974), 76–92
Greif, Thomas, *Frankens braune Wallfahrt. Der Hesselberg im Dritten Reich* (Ansbach, 2007)
Griech-Polelle, Beth A., *Bishop von Galen: German Catholicism and National Socialism* (New Haven, CT, 2002).
Grieser, Utho, *Himmlers Mann in Nürnberg. Der Fall Benno Martin: Eine Studie zur Struktur des Dritten Reiches in der 'Stadt der Reichsparteitage'* (Nuremberg, 1974)
Gritschneder, Otto, *'Der Führer hat Sie zum Tode verurteilt...' Hitlers 'Röhm-Putsch' Morde vor Gericht* (Munich, 1993)
—, *Der Hitler-Prozess und sein Richter Georg Neithardt. Skandalurteil von 1924 ebnet Hitler den Weg* (Munich, 2001)
Gritzbach, Erich, *Hermann Goering: The Man and His Work* (London, 1939)
Gross, Raphael, *November 1938. Die Katastrophe vor der Katastrophe* (Munich, 2013)
Gruchmann, Lothar, *Justiz im Dritten Reich 1933–1940. Anpassung und Unterwerfung in der Ära Gürtner* (Munich, 1988)
—, et al. (eds.), *Der Hitler-Prozess*, 4 vols. (Munich, 1997)
Grunberger, Richard, *A Social History of the Third Reich* (London, 1971)
Gruner, Wolf D. *Widerstand in der Rosenstrasse: Die Fabrik-Aktion und Verfolgun, der Mischehen 1943* (Frankfurt, 2005)
—, and Steven J. Ross (eds.), *New Perspectives on Kristallnacht: After 80 Years, the Nazi Pogrom in Global Comparison* (West Lafayette, IN, 2019)
Grüttner, Michael, 'The Expulsion of Academic Teaching Staff from German Universities, 1933–1945', *Journal of Contemporary History*, vol. 57, no. 3 (July 2022), 513–33
Guske, Claus, *Das politische Denken des Generals von Seeckt. Zur Diskussion des Verhältnisses Seeckt – Reichswehr – Republik* (Lübeck, 1971)
Haar, Ingo, and Michael Fahlbusch, *German Scholars and Ethnic Cleansing 1919–1945* (Oxford, 2006)
Haase, Günther, *Die Kunstsammlung des Reichsmarschalls Hermann Göring: eine Dokumentation* (Berlin, 2000)
Hachtmann, Rüdiger, '"Volksgemeinschaftliche Dienstleister"? Anmerkungen zu Selbstverständnis und Funktion der Deutschen Arbeitsfront und der NS-Gemeinschaft "Kraft durch Freude"', in Detlef Schmiechen-Ackermann (ed.), *'Volksgemeinschaft': Mythos, wirkungsmächtige soziale Verheissung oder soziale Realität im 'Dritten Reich'* (Paderborn, 2012), 111–31
Hahn, Fred, *Lieber 'Stürmer'. Leserbriefe an das NS-Kampfblatt 1924 bis 1945* (Stuttgart, 1978)
Hahn, Fritz, *Waffen und Geheimwaffen des deutschen Heeres, 1933–1945*, 2 vols. (Koblenz, 1986–87)

BIBLIOGRAPHY

Halder, Franz (ed. Hans-Adolf Jacobsen), *Kriegstagebuch: tägliche Aufzeichnungen des Chefs des Generalstabes des Heeres, 1939–1942*, 3 vols. (Stuttgart, 1962)
Hamann, Brigitte, *Hitler's Vienna: A Dictator's Apprenticeship* (Oxford, 1999)
Hambrecht, Rainer, *Der Aufstieg der NSDAP in Mittel- und Oberfranken (1925–1933)* (Nuremberg, 1976)
Hancock, Eleanor, 'Ernst Röhm and the Experience of World War I', *Journal of Military History*, vol. 60, no. 1 (1996), 39–60
—, '"Only the Real, the True, the Masculine Held Its Value": Ernst Röhm, Masculinity, and Male Homosexuality', *Journal of the History of Sexuality*, vol. 8, no. 4 (1998), 616–41
—, *Ernst Röhm: Hitler's SA Chief of Staff* (New York, 2008)
—, 'The Purge of the SA Reconsidered: "An Old Putschist Trick"', *Central European History*, vol. 44 (2011), 669–83
—, 'Ernst Röhm versus General Hans Kundt in Bolivia, 1929–30? The Curious Incident', *Journal of Contemporary History*, vol. 47, no. 4 (2012), 691–708
Hanfstaengl, Ernst, *Zwischen Weissem und Braunem Haus. Memoiren eines politischen Aussenseiters* (Munich, 1970)
Hanisch, Ernst, *Der Obersalzberg: das Kehlsteinhaus und Adolf Hitler* (Berchtesgaden, 1995)
Hanschel, Hermann, *Oberbürgermeister Hermann Luppe: Nürnverger Kommunalpolitik in der Weimarer Republik* (Nuremberg, 1977)
Harris, Robert, *Selling Hitler: The Story of the Hitler Diaries* (London, 1986)
Hartmann, Christian (ed.), *Von Feldherren und Gefreiten. Zur biographischen Dimension des Zweiten Weltkriegs* (Munich, 2008)
—et al. (eds.), *Hitler, Mein Kampf. Eine kritische Edition*, 2 vols. (Munich, 2016)
Harvey, Elizabeth, *Women in the Nazi East: Agents and Witnesses of Germanization* (London, 2003)
—, and Johannes Hürter (eds.), *Hitler – New Research* (German Yearbook of Contemporary History, vol. 3, Munich, 2018)
Hasenclever, Jörn, *Wehrmacht und Besatzungspolitik in der Sowjetunion. Die Befehlshaber der rückwärtigen Heeresgebiete 1941–1943* (Paderborn, 2010)
Hassell, Ulrich von, *The von Hassell Diaries: The Story of the Forces against Hitler inside Germany 1938–1944* (Boulder, CO, 1994)
Hayes, Peter, *Industry and Ideology: I. G. Farben in the Nazi Era* (Cambridge, 1987)
Hearnshaw, Fossey J. C., *Germany the Aggressor Throughout the Ages* (London, 1940)
Hébert, Valerie G., *Hitler's Generals on Trial: The Last War Crimes Tribunal at Nuremberg* (Lawrence, KS, 2020)
Heer, Hannes (ed.), *'Stets zu erschiessen sind Frauen, die in der Roten Armee dienen'. Geständnisse deutscher Kriegsgefangener über ihren Einsatz an der Ostfront* (Hamburg, 1995)

Heiber, Helmut (ed.), *Reichsführer! Briefe an und von Himmler* (Munich, 1970)
Heiden, Konrad, *Adolf Hitler. Das Zeitalter der Verantwortungslosigkeit. Eine Biographie* (Zurich, 1936)
—, *Adolf Hitler. Ein Mann gegen Europa* (Zurich, 1937)
—, *Der Führer – Hitler's Rise to Power* (London, 1944)
Heike, Irmtrud, 'Female Concentration Camp Guards as Perpetrators: Three Case Studies', in Olaf Jensen and Claus-Christian W. Szejnmann (eds.), *Ordinary People as Mass Murderers: Perpetrators in Comparative Perspective* (London, 2008), 120–42
Heil, Johannes, and Rainer Erb (eds.), *Geschichtswissenschaft und Öffentlichkeit: der Streit um Daniel J. Goldhagen* (Frankfurt, 1998)
Helm, Sarah, *Ravensbrück: Life and Death in Hitler's Concentration Camp for Women* (New York, 2014)
Henke, Klaus-Dietmar (ed.), *Tödliche Medizin im Nationalsozialismus. Von der Rassenhygiene zum Massenmord* (Cologne, 2008)
Herbert, Ulrich, *Hitler's Foreign Workers: Enforced Foreign Labour in Germany Under the Third Reich* (Cambridge, 1997)
—, 'Extermination Policy: New Answers and Questions about the History of the "Holocaust" in German Historiography', in idem (ed.), *National Socialist Extermination Policies: Contemporary German Perspectives and Controversies* (Oxford, 2000), 1–52
Herbst, Ludolf, *Hitlers Charisma. Die Erfindung eines deutschen Messias* (Frankfurt, 2010)
Herkommer, Christina, *Die Rolle von Frauen im Spiegel des Diskurses der Frauen- und Geschlechterforschung* (Frankfurt, 2005)
—, 'Women under National Socialism: Women's Scope for Action and the Issue of Gender', in Olaf Jensen and Claus-Christian W. Szejnmann (eds.), *Ordinary People as Mass Murderers: Perpetrators in Comparative Perspective* (London, 2008), 99–119
Heschel, Susanne, 'Does Atrocity Have a Gender? Feminist Interpretations of Women in the SS', in Jeffrey M. Diefendorf (ed.), *Lessons and Legacies* VI: *New Currents in Holocaust Research* (Evanston, IL, 2004), 300–21
Hess, Rudolf, *Briefe 1909–1933*, ed. Wolf Rüdiger Hess (Munich, 1987)
Hett, Benjamin Carter, *Crossing Hitler: The Man Who Put the Nazis on the Witness Stand* (New York, 2008)
Higham, Nick, 'The Five Lives of Leni Riefenstahl', http://news.bbc.co.uk/1/hi/entertainment/986528.stm
Hildebrand, Klaus, 'Nichts Neues über Hitler. Ian Kershaws zünftige Biographie über den deutschen Diktator', *Historische Zeitschrift*, no. 270 (2000), 389–97
Hilger, Andreas, *Deutsche Kriegsgefangene in der Sowjetunion, 1941–1956: Kriegsgefangenenpolitik, Lageralltag und Erinnerung* (Essen, 2000)

Hill, Alexander, *The War Behind the Eastern Front: The Soviet Partisan Movement in North-West Russia 1941–1944* (London, 2005)

Hillgruber, Andreas, (ed.), *Staatsmänner und Diplomaten bei Hitler*, 2 vols. (Frankfurt, 1970)

Himmler, Katrin, *Die Brüder Himmler. Eine deutsche Familiengeschichte* (Frankfurt am Main, 2005)

—, and Michael Wildt (eds.), *Himmler privat. Briefe eines Massenmörders* (Munich, 2014)

Hirsch, Martin, *et al.* (eds.), *Recht, Verwaltung und Justiz im Nationalsozialismus* (Cologne, 1984)

Hoch, Anton, 'Das Attentat auf Hitler im Münchner Bürgerbräukeller 1939', *Vierteljahrshefte für Zeitgeschichte*, vol. 17 (1969), 383–413

Höhne, Heinz, *The Order of the Death's Head: The Story of Hitler's SS* (London, 1969)

—, *Mordsache Röhm, Hitlers Durchbruch zur Alleinherrschaft 1933–1934* (Reinbek bei Hamburg, 1984)

Holmila, Antero, 'Finland and the Holocaust: A Reassessment', *Holocaust and Genocide Studies*, vol. 23 (2009), 413–44

Hornburg, Mark W., *et al.* (eds.), *Beyond 'Ordinary Men': Christopher R. Browning and Holocaust Historiography* (Paderborn, 2019)

Horne, John, and Alan Kramer, *German Atrocities 1914: A History of Denial* (London, 2001)

Hörster-Philipps, Ulrike, *Konservative Politik in der Endphase der Weimerer Republik: Die Regierung Franz von Papen* (Cologne, 1982)

Housden, Martyn, *Hans Frank: Lebensraum and the Holocaust* (Basingstoke, 2003)

Hubatsch, Walther (ed.), *Hitlers Weisungen für die Kriegführung 1939–1945. Dokumente des Oberkommandos der Wehrmacht* (Frankfurt, 1962)

Huber, Bernhard, 'Georg Neithardt – nur ein unpolitischer Richter?', in Marita Kraus (ed.), *Rechte Karrieren in München. Von der Weimarer Zeit bis in die Nachkriegsjahre* (Munich, 2010), 95–113

Hudal, Alois, *Die Grundlagen des Nationalsozialismus: Eine ideengeschichtliche Untersuchung* (Leipzig, 1937)

Hull, Isabel, *Absolute Destruction: Military Culture and the Practices of War in Imperial Germany* (Ithaca, NY, 2004)

Hürter, Johannes, *Hitlers Heerführer. Die deutschen Oberbefehlshaber im Krieg gegen die Sowjetunion 1941/42* (Munich, 2007)

Ihrig, Stefan, *Atatürk in the Nazi Imagination* (Cambridge, MA, 2014)

International Military Tribunal, *Der Nürnberger Prozess gegen die Hauptskriegsverbrecher vom 14. November 1945 bis 1. Oktober 1946: Urkunden und anderes Beweismaterial* (Nuremberg, 1948)

Jäckel, Eberhard, *Hitlers Weltanschauung. Entwurf einer Herrschaft* (Tübingen, 1969; English trans., *Hitler's Weltanschauung: A Blueprint for Power*, Middletown, CT, 1972)

—, and Axel Kuhn (eds.), *Hitler. Sämtliche Aufzeichnungen 1905–1923* (Stuttgart, 1980)
—, and Axel Kühn, 'Neue Erkenntnisse zur Fälschung von Hitler-Dokumenten', *Vierteljahrshefte für Zeitgeschichte*, vol. 32, no. 1 (1984), 162–69
Jacob, Frank, *Die Thule-Gesellschaft* (Berlin, 2010)
Jacobsen, Hans-Adolf, *Nationalsozialistische Aussenpolitik 1933–1939* (Frankfurt, 1968)
—, *Karl Haushofer: Leben und Werk*, 2 vols. (Boppard, 1979)
James, Harold, *The German Slump: Politics and Economics 1924–1936* (Oxford, 1986)
Jamin, Mathilde, *Zwischen den Klassen: Zur Sozialstruktur der SA-Führerschaft* (Wuppertal, 1984)
Janssen, Karl-Heinz, and Fritz Tobias, *Der Sturz der Generäle. Hitler und die Blomberg-Fritsch Krise 1938* (Munich, 1994)
Jarausch, Konrad, *The Unfree Professions: German Lawyers, Teachers, and Engineers, 1900–1950* (Chapel Hill, NC, 1990)
Jardim, Tomaz, *Ilse Koch on Trial: Making the 'Bitch of Buchenwald'* (London, 2023)
Jaskot, Paul B., *The Architecture of Oppression: The SS, Forced Labor, and the Nazi Monumental Building Economy* (London, 2000)
Jellonek, Burkhard, *Homosexuelle unterm Hakenkreuz* (Paderborn, 1990)
Jetzinger, Franz, *Hitlers Jugend. Phantasien, Lügen und Wahrheit* (Vienna, 1956)
Joachimsthaler, Anton, *Hitlers Weg begann in München 1913–1923* (Munich, 2000)
—, *The Last Days of Hitler: Legend, Evidence and Truth* (London, 2000)
—, *Hitlers Ende* (Munich, 1995)
Jochmann, Werner, *Nationalsozialismus und Revolution. Ursprung und Geschichte der NSDAP in Hamburg 1922–1933. Dokumente* (Frankfurt, 1962)
—(ed.), *Adolf Hitler. Monologe im Führerhauptquartier 1941–1944. Aufgezeichnet von Heinrich Heim* (Hamburg, 1980)
Johnson, Eric A., and Karl-Heinz Reuband, *What We Knew: Terror, Mass Murder, and Everyday Life in Nazi Germany* (New York, 2005)
Jones, Larry Eugene, *German Liberalism and the Dissolution of the Weimar Party System, 1918–1933* (Chapel Hill, NC, 1988)
—, *The German Right, 1918–1930: Political Parties, Organized Interests, and Patriotic Associations in the Struggle against Weimar Democracy* (new ed., Cambridge, 2016)
Jones, Mark, *1923: The Crisis of German Democracy in the Year of Hitler's Putsch* (London, 2023)
Joshi, Vandana, *Gender and Power in the Third Reich: Female Denouncers and the Gestapo (1939–1945)* (London, 2003)
Junge, Traudl, *Bis zur letzten Stunde. Hitlers Sekretärin erzählt ihr Leben* (unter Mitarbeit von Melissa Müller, Munich, 2002)

Jünginger, Horst, 'Tübinger Exekutoren der Endlösung', *Schwäbishes Tagblatt* (18 June 2003), 'Audimax Spezial'
Kater, Michael H., *Studentenschaft und Rechtsradikalismus in Deutschland 1918–1933: Eine sozialgeschichtliche Studie zur Bildungskrise in der Weimarer Republik* (Hamburg, 1975)
—, 'Frauen in der NS-Bewegung', *Vierteljahrshefte für Zeitgeschichte*, vol. 31 (1983), 202–41
—, *Doctors under Hitler* (Chapel Hill, NC, 1989)
—, *Das 'Ahnenerbe' der SS 1935–1945. Ein Beitrag zur Kulturpolitik des Dritten Reiches*, 4th edn (Munich, 2006)
Kay, Alex J., *Exploitation, Resettlement, Mass Murder: Political and Economic Planning for German Occupation Policy in the Soviet Union, 1940–1941* (Oxford, 2006)
—, 'Germany's *Staatssekretäre*, Mass Starvation and the Meeting of 2 May 1941', *Journal of Contemporary History*, vol. 41, no. 4 (2006), 685–700
—et al., 'Introduction', in idem (eds.), *Nazi Policy on the Eastern Front, 1941: Total War, Genocide, and Radicalization* (Rochester, NY, 2012)
—, *Empire of Destruction: A History of Nazi Mass Killing* (London, 2021)
Keller, Sven, *Volksgemeinshaft am Ende. Gesellschaft und Gewalt 1944/45* (Munich, 2013)
Kellerhoff, Sven Felix, 'Berühmtes Hitler-Foto möglicherweise gefälscht', *Die Welt* (14 October 2010)
—, *'Mein Kampf'. Die Karriere eines deutschan Buches* (Stuttgart, 2015)
Kelley, Douglas R., *22 Cells in Nuremberg: A Psychiatrist Examines the Nazi Criminals* (London, 1947)
Kellogg, Michael, *The Russian Roots of Nazism: White Émigrés and the Making of National Socialism, 1917–1945* (Cambridge, 2005)
Kent, Bruce, *The Spoils of War: The Politics, Economics, and Diplomacy of Reparations, 1918–1932* (Oxford, 1989)
Kent, George O., 'Problems and Pitfalls of a Papen Biography', *Central European History*, vol. 20 (1987), 191–97
Kersaudy, François, *Hermann Goering: Le deuxième homme du IIIe Reich* (Paris, 2009)
Kershaw, Ian, *Popular Opinion and Political Dissent in the Third Reich: Bavaria 1933–1945* (Oxford 1983)
—, *The Hitler Myth: Image and Reality in the Third Reich* (Oxford, 1989)
—, *Hitler* (Harlow, 1991)
—, *Hitler I 1889–1936: Hubris* (London, 1998)
—, *Hitler II 1936–1945: Nemesis* (London, 2000)
—, *Making Friends with Hitler: Lord Londonderry and Britain's Road to War* (London, 2004)

—, *Fateful Choices: Ten Decisions that Changed the World, 1940–1941* (London, 2008)
—, *Hitler, the Germans, and the Final Solution* (London, 2008)
—, *Personality and Power: Builders and Destroyers of Modern Europe* (London, 2022)
Kersten, Felix, *The Kersten Memoirs 1940–1945* (London, 1957)
Keyserlingk-Rehbein, Linda von, *'Nur eine ganz kleine Clique': Die NS-Ermittlungen über das Netzwerk vom 20. Juli 1944* (Berlin, 2018)
Kindleberger, Charles P., *The World in Depression 1929–1939* (Berkeley, CA, 1987 [1973], new edn 2013)
Kingsbury-Smith, Joseph, 'Die Hinrichtung der Nazi-Kriegsverbrecher am 16. Oktober 1946', in Steffen Radlmaier (ed.), *Der Nürnberger Lernprozess. Von Kriegsverbrechern und Starreportern* (Frankfurt, 2001), 339–48
Kitchen, Martin, *The German Officer Corps 1890–1914* (Oxford, 1968)
Klee, Ernst (ed.), *Dokumente zur 'Euthanasie' im NS-Staat* (Frankfurt, 1985)
—et al. (eds.), *'Those Were the Days': The Holocaust as Seen by the Perpetrators and Bystanders* (London, 1991)
—, *Auschwitz, die Medizin und ihre Opfer* (Frankfurt, 1997)
—, *Deutsche Medizin im Dritten Reich: Karrieren vor und nach 1945* (Frankfurt, 2001)
—, *Das Kulturlexikon zum Dritten Reich. Wer war was vor und nach 1945* (Frankfurt, 2009)
—, *Euthanasie im Dritten Reich: Die 'Vernichtung lebensunwerten Lebens'* (Frankfurt, 2010)
Klein, Peter (ed.), *Die Einsatzgruppen in der besetzten Sowjetunion 1941/42: Die Tätigkeits-und Lageberichte des Chefs der Sicherheitspolizei und des SD* (Berlin, 1997)
Kleist-Schmenzin, Ewald von, 'Die letzte Möglichkeit: Zur Ernennung Hitlers zum Reichskanzler am 30. Januar 1933', *Politische Studien*, vol. 10 (1959), 90–106
Klemperer, Viktor, *LTI. Notizbuch eines Philologen* (Leipzig, 1975 [1946])
—, *To the Bitter End: The Diaries of Victor Klemperer 1942–1945* (London, 1999)
Klessmann, Christoph, 'Der Generalgouverneur Hans Frank', *Vierteljahrshefte für Zeitgeschichte*, vol. 19 (1971), 45–60
Kluke, Paul, 'Der Fall Potempa', *Vierteljahrshefte für Zeitgeschichte*, vol. 5 (1957), 279–97
Knopp, Guido, *Hitler's Hitmen* (Stroud, 2002)
Koehl, Robert L., *RKFDV: German Resettlement and Population Policy 1939–1945: A History of the Reich Commission for the Strengthening of Germandom* (Cambridge, MA, 1957)

BIBLIOGRAPHY

Kompisch, Kathrin, *Täterinnen. Frauen im Nationalsozialismus* (Vienna, 2008)
Koonz, Claudia, *Mothers in the Fatherland: Women, the Family and Nazi Politics* (London, 1987)
—, 'Erwiderung auf Gisela Bocks Rezension von "Mothers in the Fatherland"', *Geschichte und Gesellschaft*, vol. 18, no. 3 (1992), 394–99
—, *The Nazi Conscience* (London, 2003)
Kövés, Tibor, *Satan in a Top Hat: The Biography of Franz von Papen* (New York, 1941)
Krausnick, Helmut, 'Der 30. Juni 1934: Bedeutung – Hintergründe – Verlauf', *Aus Politik und Zeitgeschichte: Beilage zur Wochenzeitung 'Das Parlament'* (30 June 1954)
—, *Hitlers Einsatzgruppen. Die Truppen des Weltanschauungskrieges 1938– 1942* (Frankfurt, 1985)
Krauss, Marita, *Sie waren dabei. Mitläuferinnen, Nutzniesserinnen, Täterinnen im Nationalsozialismus* (Göttingen, 2008)
Krebs, Albert, *Tendenzen und Gestalten der NSDAP: Erinnerungen an die Frühzeit der Partei* (Stuttgart, 1974)
Kroener, Bernhard, R., 'Gibt es ein richtiges Leben im falschen? Biographische Deutungen im Zeitalter zusammenbrechender Werte und Welten', in Christian Hartmann (ed.), *Von Feldherren und Gefreiten. Zur biographischen Dimension des Zweiten Weltkriegs* (Munich, 2008), 113–26
Kube, Alfred, *Pour le mérite und Hakenkreuz. Hermann Göring im Dritten Reich* (Munich, 1986)
Kubizek, August, *Adolf Hitler. Mein Jugendfreund* (Göttingen, 1953, English trans., *Young Hitler: The Story of Our Friendship*, Maidstone, 1954)
Kulka, Otto Dov, and Eberhard Jäckel (eds.), *The Jews in the Secret Nazi Reports on Popular Opinion in Germany, 1933–1945* (London, 2010)
Kwiet, Konrad, 'Paul Zapp – Vordenker und Vollstrecker der Judenvernichtung', in Klaus-Michael Mallmann and Gerhard Paul (eds.), *Karrieren der Gewalt. Nationalsozialistische Täterbiographien* (Darmstadt, 2004), 252–63
Large, David Clay, *Nazi Games: The Olympics of 1936* (New York, 2007)
Lawson, Robert, 'Ribbentrop in Canada 1910 to 1914: A Note', *International History Review*, vol. 29, no. 4 (2007), 821–32
Lee, Asher, *Goering: Air Leader* (London, 1972)
Leeb, Wilhelm Ritter von, *Defence* (New Delhi, 2017)
Leitz, Christian, *Nazi Foreign Policy, 1933–1941: The Road to Global War* (London, 2004)
Lenman, Robin, 'Julius Streicher and the Origins of the NSDAP in Nuremberg, 1919–1933', in Anthony J. Nicholls and Erich Matthias (eds.), *German Democracy and the Triumph of Hitler: Essays on Recent German History* (London, 1971), 129–60

BIBLIOGRAPHY

Leuschen-Seppel, Rosemarie, *Sozialdemokratie und Antisemitismus im Kaiserreich. Die Auseinandersetzungen der Partei mit den konsevativen und völkischen Strömungen des Antisemitismus 1871–1914* (Bonn, 1978)

Lewy, Guenter, *Harmful and Undesirable: Book Censorship in Nazi Germany* (New York, 2016)

—, *Perpetrators: The World of the Holocaust Killers* (New York, 2017)

Ley, Robert, *Durchbruch der Sozialen Ehre. Reden und Gedanken für das schaffende Deutschland* (Berlin, 1935)

—, *Wir alle helfen dem Führer. Deutschland braucht jeden Deutschen*, 4th edn (Munich, 1939 [1937])

—, *Soldaten der Arbeit* (Leipzig, 1938)

Lieb, Peter, *Konventioneller Krieg oder NS-Weltanschauungskrieg? Kriegführung und Partisanenbekämpfung in Frankreich 1943/44* (Munich, 2007)

—, 'Generalleutnant Harald von Hirschfeld. Eine nationalsozialistische Karriere in der Wehrmacht', in Christian Hartmann (ed.), *Von Feldherren und Gefreiten. Zur biographischen Dimension des Zweiten Weltkriegs* (Munich, 2008), 45–54

—, 'Militärische Elite? Die Panzerdivisionen von Waffen-SS und Wehrmacht in der Normandie 1944 im Vergleich', in Jan-Erik Schulte et al. (eds.), *Die Waffen-SS. Neue Forschungen* (Paderborn, 2014), 336–56

Lifton, Robert Jay, *The Nazi Doctors: A Study of the Psychology of Evil* (London, 1986)

Lilienthal, Georg, *Der 'Lebensborn e.v.' Ein Instrument nationalsozialistischer Rassenpolitik* (Stuttgart, 1985)

Linder, Herbert, *Von der NSDAP zur SPD Der politische Lebensweg des D. Helmuth Klotz (1894–1943)* (Konstanz, 1998)

Liulevicius, Gabriel, *War Land on the Eastern Front: Culture, National Identity, and German Occupation in World War I* (Cambridge, 2000)

Livi, Massimiliano, *Gertrud Scholtz-Klink: Die Reichsfrauenführerin* (Münster, 2005), 180–95

Löhr, Hanns Christian, *Der eiserner Sammler: die Kollektion Hermann Göring: Kunst und Korruption im 'Dritten Reich'* (Berlin, 2009)

—, *Der Einsatzstab Reichsleiter Rosenberg. Ideologie und Kunstraub im 'Dritten Reich'* (Berlin, 2018)

Longerich, Peter, *Die braunen Bataillone. Geschichte der SA* (Munich, 1989)

—, *Hitlers Stellvertreter. Führung der Partei und Kontrolle des Staatsapparates durch den Stab Hess und die Partei-Kanzlei Bormann* (Munich, 1992)

—, *'Davon haben wir nichts gewusst!': Die Deutschen und die Judenverfolgung 1933–1945* (London, 2009)

—, *Politik der Vernichtung: Eine Gesamtdarstellung der nationalsozialistischen Judenverfolgung* (Munich, 1998; English trans., *Holocaust: The Nazi Persecution and Murder of the Jews* (Oxford, 2010)

—, *Heinrich Himmler: Biographie* (Munich, 2008; English edn, *Heinrich Himmler*, Oxford, 2012)
—, *Goebbels: A Biography* (London, 2015)
—, *Hitler: Biographie* (Munich, 2015; English edn, *Hitler: A Life*, Oxford, 2019)
Lowder, J. Bryan, 'The One-Eyed Man Is King. How Did the Monocle Become a Symbol of Wealth?', *Slate* (27 December 2012)
Lower, Wendy, *Hitler's Furies: German Women in the Nazi Killing Fields* (London, 2013)
Ludendorff, Erich, *Der totale Krieg* (Munich, 1935)
Lüdtke, Alf, '"Fehlrgreifen in der Wahl der Mittel". Optionen im Alltag militärischen Handelns', *Mittelweg*, vol. 36, no. 12 (2003), 61–75
Madajczyk, Czeslaw (ed.), *Vom Generalplan Ost zum Generalsiedlungsplan: Dokumente* (Berlin, 1994)
Malaparte, Curzio, *Kaputt* (New York, 2005 [1944])
Malinowski, Stephan, *Nazis and Nobles: The History of a Misalliance* (Oxford, 2020)
—, *Die Hohenzollern und die Nazis: Geschichte einer Kollaboration* (Berlin, 2021)
Mallmann, Klaus-Michael, *Kommunisten in der Weimarer Republik. Sozialgeschichte einer revolutionären Bewegung* (Darmstadt, 1996)
—, and Gerhard, Paul (eds.), *Karrieren der Gewalt. Nationalsozialistische Täterbiographien* (Darmstadt, 2004)
—, 'Dr. Jekyll & Mr. Hyde. Der Täterdiskurs in Wissenschaft und Gesellschaft', in idem, and Andrej Angrick (eds.), *Die Gestapo nach 1945. Karrieren, Konflikte, Konstruktionen* (Darmstadt, 2009), 292–318
Mammach, Klaus, *Der Volkssturm: Bestandteil des totalen Kriegseinsatzes der deutschen Bevölkerung 1944/45* (Berlin, 1981)
Mann, Michael, 'Were the Perpetrators of Genocide "Ordinary Men" or "Real Nazis"? Results from Fifteen Hundred Biographies', *Holocaust and Genocide Studies*, vol. 14 (2000), 331–66
Manoschek, Walter (ed.), *'Es gibt nur Eines für das Judentum: Vernichtung'. Das Judenbild in deutschen Soldatenbriefen 1939–1941* (Hamburg, 1997)
Manstein, Erich von, *Verlorene Siege* (Frankfurt am Main, 1955)
Manvell, Roger, and Heinrich Fraenkel, *Hermann Göring* (London, 1962)
Martens, Stefan, 'Die Rolle Hermann Görings in der deutschen Aussenpolitik 1937/38', in Franz Knipping and Klaus-Jürgen Müller (eds.), *Machtbewusstsein in Deutschland am Vorabend des Zweiten Weltkrieges* (Paderborn, 1984)
—, *Hermann Göring. 'Erster Paladin des Führers' und 'Zweiter Mann im Reich'* (Paderborn, 1985)
Mason, Timothy W., *Social Policy in the Third Reich: The Working Class and the 'National Community'* (Providence, RI, 1993)

BIBLIOGRAPHY

Mathieu, Thomas, *Kunstauffassungen und Kulturpolitik im Nationalsozialismus. Studien zu Adolf Hitler – Joseph Goebbels – Alfred Rosenberg – Baldur von Schirach – Heinrich Himmler – Albert Speer – Wilhelm Frick* (Saarbrücken, 1997)

Matthäus, Jürgen, et al., *Ausbildungsziel Judenmord? 'Weltanschauliche Erziehung' von SS, Polizei und Waffen-SS im Rahmen der 'Endlösung'* (Frankfurt am Main, 2003)

—, and Frank Bajohr (eds.), *Alfred Rosenberg: Die Tagebücher von 1934 bis 1944* (Frankfurt am Main, 2015)

Matthias, Erich, and Rudolf Morsey (eds.), *Das Ende der Parteien 1933* (Düsseldorf, 1960)

McElligott, Anthony, *Contested City: Municipal Politics and the Rise of Nazism in Altona, 1917–1937* (Ann Arbor, MI, 1998)

McGeever, Brendan, *Antisemitism and the Russian Revolution* (Cambridge, 2019)

Megargee, Geoffrey P., *Inside Hitler's High Command* (Lawrence, KS, 2000)

Meier-Welcker, Hans, *Seeckt* (Frankfurt am Main, 1967)

Mergel, Thomas, *Parlamentarische Kultur in der Weimarer Republik: Politische Kommunikation, symbolische Politik und Öffentlichkeit im Reichstag* (Düsseldorf, 2002)

Merker, Reinhard, *Die bildenden Künste im Nationalsozialismus; Kulturideologie, Kulturpolitik, Kulturproduktion* (Cologne, 1983)

Messerschmidt, Manfred, and Fritz Wüllner, *Die Wehrmachtjustiz im Dienste des Nationalsozialismus: Zerstörung einer Legende* (Baden-Baden, 1987)

Meyer, Beate, *'Jüdische Mischlinge'. Rassenpolitik und Verfolgungserfahrung 1933–1945* (Hamburg, 1999)

—(ed.), *Die Verfolgung und Ermordung der Hamburger Juden. Geschichte, Zeugnis, Erinnerung* (Göttingen, 2006)

—, 'Zwischen Begeisterung und Skepsis. Die Wandlung der Luise Solmitz im Spiegel ihrer Tagebücher', in Frank Bajohr et al. (eds.), *Bedrohung, Hoffnung, Skepsis. Vier Tagebücher des Jahres 1933* (Göttingen, 2013), 127–42

—, '"Ich schlüpfe ungeachtet wie eine graue Motte mit durch." Die Wandlungen der Louise Solmitz zwischen 1933 und 1945 im Spiegel ihrer Tagebücher', in Frank Bajohr and Sibylle Steinbacher (eds.), *'...Zeugnis ablegen bis zum Letzten'. Tagebücher und persönliche Zeugnisse aus der Zeit des Nationalsozialismus und des Holocaust* (Göttingen, 2015), 61–80

Meyer, Georg (ed.), *Generalfeldmarschall Wilhelm Ritter von Leeb. Tagebuchaufzeichnungen und Lagebeurteilungen aus zwei Weltkriegen* (Stuttgart, 1976)

Meyer, Hermann Frank, *Blutiges Edelweiss. Die 1. Gebirgs-Division im Zweiten Weltkrieg* (Berlin, 2008)

BIBLIOGRAPHY

Michalka, Wolfgang, *Ribbentrop und die deutsche Weltpolitik 1933–1940. Aussenpolitische Konzeptionen und Entscheidungsprozesse im Dritten Reich* (Munich, 1980)

Mills, C. Wright, *The Power Elite* (Oxford, 1956)

Mitcham, Samuel Jr., and Gene Mueller, *Hitler's Commanders* (London, 1992)

Mitchell, Otis C., *Hitler's Stormtroopers and the Attack on the German Republic, 1919–1933* (Jefferson, NC, 2008)

Möckelmann, Reiner, *Franz von Papen: Hitlers ewiger Vassall* (Darmstadt, 2016)

Moeller, Felix, *Der Filmminister: Goebbels und der Film im Dritten Reich* (Berlin, 1998)

Mohnhaupt, Jan, *Tiere im Nationalsozialismus* (Munich, 2020)

Mommsen, Hans, 'Keine Katharsis blieb aus. Joachim Fests sorgfältige Biographie von Albert Speer', *Frankfurter Rundschau* (13 October 1999)

—, 'Die Grenzen der Biografie. Prozesse und Entscheidungen: Ein Sammelband über die "Täter der Shoah" wirft die Frage nach dem Verhältnis von Individuum und Struktur im Nationalsozialismus auf', *Frankfurter Rundschau* (26 November 2002)

Moorhouse, Roger, *The Devils' Alliance: Hitler's Pact with Stalin 1939–41* (London, 2016)

Morsey, Rudolf (ed.), *Das 'Ermächtigungsgesetz' vom 24. März 1933. Quellen zur Geschichte und Interpretation des 'Gesetzes zur Behebung der Not von Volk und Reich'*, 2nd edn (Düsseldorf, 2010)

Mosse, George L., *The Crisis of German Ideology: Intellectual Origins of the Third Reich* (London, 1964)

—, *The Nationalisation of the Masses: Political Symbolism and Mass Movements in Germany from the Napoleonic Wars Through the Third Reich* (New York, 1975)

—, *The Image of Man: The Creation of Modern Masculinity* (New York, 1996)

—, *Nationalism and Sexuality: Respectable and Abnormal Sexuality in Modern Europe* (New York, 1997)

Mueller, Gene, 'Generalfeldmarschall Wilhelm Ritter von Leeb', in Gerd R. Ueberschär (ed.), *Hitlers militärische Elite*, vol. I (Darmstadt, 1998), 146–53

Mühle, Eduard, *Für Volk und deutschen Osten. Der Historiker Hermann Aubin und die deutsche Ostforschung* (Düsseldorf, 2005)

Mühle, Marcus, *Ernst Röhm. Eine biographische Skizze* (Berlin, 2016)

Müller, Franz, *Ein Rechtskatholik zwischen Kreuz und Hakenkreuz: Franz von Papen als Sonderbevollmächtiger in Wien 1934–1938* (Frankfurt am Main, 1990)

Nathans, Eli, *Franz Schlegelberger* (Baden-Baden, 1990)

—, 'Legal Order as Motive and Mask: Franz Schlegelberger and the Nazi Administration of Justice', *Law and History Review*, vol. 18, no. 2 (2000), 281–304

Neitzel, Sönke, *Abgehört. Deutsche Generäle in britischer Kriegsgefangenschaft 1942–1945* (Berlin, 2007 [2005])
Nesbit, Roy Conyers, and Georges Van Acker, *The Flight of Rudolf Hess: Myths and Reality* (Stroud, 1999)
Neuhaus, Tom, *Tibet in the Western Imagination* (London, 2012)
Neumann, Hans-Joachim, and Henrik Eberle, *Was Hitler Ill?* (London, 2013) [*War Hitler krank?* (Cologne, 2009)]
Neumärker, Uwe, 'Wo die braunen Hirsche röhrten', *Der Spiegel* (online) (5 May 2008)
Nicholls, Anthony J., 'Hitler and the Bavarian Background to National Socialism', in idem, and Erich Matthias (eds.), *German Democracy and the Triumph of Hitler: Essays on Recent German History* (London, 1971), 129–59
Nilsson, Mikael, *Hitler Redux: The Incredible History of Hitler's So-Called Table Talks* (London, 2022)
Niven, Bill, *Hitler and Film: The Führer's Hidden Passion* (London, 2018)
Noakes, Jeremy, 'The Oldenburg Crucifix Struggle of November 1936: A Case Study of Opposition in the Third Reich', in Peter D. Stachura (ed.), *The Shaping of the Nazi State* (London, 1978), 210–33
—, 'Nazism and Eugenics: The Background to the Nazi Sterilization Law of 14 July 1933', in Roger Bullen *et al.* (eds.), *Ideas into Politics: Aspects of European History 1850–1930* (London, 1984), 75–94
—, and Geoffrey Pridham (eds.), *Nazism 1919–1945: A Documentary Reader*, 4 vols., 2nd edn (Exeter, 2000 [1984])
Nolzen, Armin, 'Inklusion und Exklusion im "Dritten Reich". Das Beispiel der NSDAP', in Frank Bajohr and Michael Wildt (eds.), *Volksgemeinschaft. Neue Forschungen zur Gesellschaft des Nationalsozialismus* (Frankfurt, 2009), 60–77
Oldenburg, Manfred, *Ideologie und militärisches Kalkül. Die Besatzungspolitik der Wehrmacht in der Sowjetunion 1942* (Cologne, 1942)
O'Neill, Robert J., *The German Army and the Nazi Party 1933–1939* (London, 1966)
Orth, Karin, 'Egon Zill – ein typischer Vertreter der Konzentrationslager-SS', in Klaus-Michael Mallmann and Gerhard Paul (eds.), *Karrieren der Gewalt. Nationalsozialistische Täterbiographien* (Darmstadt, 2004), 264–73
Ortner, Helmut, *Der Hinrichter. Roland Freisler, Mörder im Dienste Hitlers* (Vienna, 1993)
Overmans, Rüdiger, *Deutsche militärische Verluste im Zweiten Weltkriege* (Munich, 1999)
Overy, Richard, *The Battle of Britain: Myth and Reality* (London, 2001)
—(ed.), *Interrogations: The Nazi Elite in Allied Hands, 1945* (London, 2001)
—, *Goering: The Iron Man*, 2nd edn (London, 2021)
Papen, Franz von, *Appell an das deutsche Gewissen. Reden zur nationalen Revolution* (Oldenburg, 1933)

—, *Memoirs* (trans. Brian Connell, London, 1952)
—, *Vom Scheitern einer Demokratie 1930–1933* (Mainz, 1968)
Pätzold, Kurt, and Manfred Weissbecker, *Rudolf Hess. Der Mann an Hitlers Seite* (Leipzig, 1999)
Paul, Gerhard, *Aufstand der Bilder. NS-Propaganda vor 1933* (Bonn, 1990)
—, 'Von Psychopathen, Technokraten des Terrors und "ganz gewöhnlichen" Deutschen. Die Täter der Shoah im Spiegel der Forschung', in idem (ed.), *Die Täter der Shoah. Fanatische Nationalsozialisten oder ganz normale Deutsche?* (Göttingen, 2002), 13–90
—, and Klaus-Michael Mallmann, 'Sozialisation, Milieu und Gewalt. Fortschritte und Probleme der neueren Täterforschung', in idem (eds.), *Karrieren der Gewalt*, 1–32
Paul, Wolfgang, *Hermann Göring: Hitler Paladin or Puppet?* (London, 1998)
Perl, Gisella, *I Was a Doctor in Auschwitz* (Madison, CT, 1948, reprinted London, 2019)
Peterson, Edward N., *The Limits of Hitler's Power* (Princeton, NJ, 1969)
Petzold, Joachim, *Franz von Papen. Ein deutsches Verhängnis* (Munich, 1995)
Peukert, Detlev, and Jürgen Reulecke (eds.), *Die Reihen fast geschlossen: Beiträge zur Geschichte des Alltags unterm Nationalsozialismus* (Wuppertal, 1981)
—, *Volksgenossen und Gemeinschaftsfremde: Anpassung, Ausmerze und Aufbegehren unter dem Nationalsozialismus* (Cologne, 1982, English version, *Inside Nazi Germany: Conformity, Opposition and Racism in Everyday Life*, London, 1987)
Phelps, Reginald H., 'Hitler als Parteiredner im Jahre 1920', *Vierteljahrshefte für Zeitgeschichte*, vol. 11 (1961), 274–330
—, 'Before Hitler Came: Thule Society and Germanen Orden', *Journal of Modern History*, vol. 35 (1963), 245–61
—, 'Hitlers "grundlegende" Rede über den Antisemitismus', *Vierteljahrshefte für Zeitgeschichte*, vol. 16 (1968), 390–420
Pick, Daniel, *The Pursuit of the Nazi Mind: Hitler, Hess and the Analysts* (Oxford, 2012)
Picker, Henry (ed.), *Hitlers Tischgespräche im Führerhauptquartier* (Stuttgart, 1976)
Pierrepoint, Albert, *Executioner: Pierrepoint* (London, 1974)
Piper, Ernst, *Alfred Rosenberg: Hitlers Chefideologe* (Munich, 2005)
Plöckinger, Othmar, *Geschichte eines Buches: Adolf Hitlers 'Mein Kampf', 1922–1945* (Munich, 2006)
—, *Unter Soldaten und Agitatoren. Hitlers prägende Jahre im deutschen Militär 1918–1920* (Paderborn, 2013)
—(ed.), *Quellen und Dokumente zur Geschichte von 'Mein Kampf', 1924–1945* (Stuttgart, 2016)

Poewe, Karla, and Irving Hexham, 'Jakob Wilhelm Heuer's New Religion and National Socialism', *Journal of Contemporary Religion*, vol. 20 (2005), 195–215
Poggeler, Franz, *Der Lehrer Julius Streicher. Zur Personalgeschichte des Nationalsozialismus* (Frankfurt am Main, 1991)
Pohl, Dieter, *Die Herrschaft der Wehrmacht. Deutsche Militärbesatzung und einheimische Bevölkerung in der Sowjetunion 1941–1944* (Munich, 2008)
Pois, Robert (ed.), *Alfred Rosenberg: Selected Writings* (London, 1970)
Potthast, Jan Björn, *Das jüdische Zentralmuseum der SS in Prag. Gegnerforschung und Völkermord im Nationalsozialismus* (Frankfurt, 2002)
Präg, Werner, and Wolfgang Jacobmeyer (eds.), *Das Diensttagebuch des deutschen Generalgouverneurs in Polen 1939–1945* (Stuttgart, 1975)
Priemel, Kim Christian, *Flick. Eine Konzerngeschichte vom Kaiserreich bis zur Bundesrepublik* (Göttingen, 2007)
Proctor, Robert N., *Racial Hygiene: Medicine under the Nazis* (London, 1988)
Pross, Christian, 'Breaking Through the Postwar Cover-Up of Nazi Doctors in Germany', *Journal of Medical Ethics*, vol. 17 (1991), Supplement, 13–16
Przyrembel, Alexandra, 'Der Bann eines Bildes. Ilse Koch, die "Kommandeuse von Buchenwald"', in Insa Eschenbach et al. (eds.), *Gedächtnis und Geschlecht. Deutungsmuster in Darstellungen des nationalsozialistischen Genozids* (Frankfurt, 2002), 245–67
Pulzer, Peter G. J., *The Rise of Political Anti-Semitism in Germany and Austria* (London, 1964)
Rauschning, Hermann, *Die Revolution des Nihilismus. Kulisse und Wirklichkeit im Dritten Reich* (Zurich, 1938; English edn, *Germany's Revolution of Destruction*, London, 1939)
Read, Anthony, *The Devil's Disciples: The Lives and Times of Hitler's Inner Circle* (London, 2003)
Redlich, Fritz, *Hitler: Diagnosis of a Destructive Prophet* (New York, 1998)
Rees, Laurence, *The Nazis: A Warning from History* (London, 1997)
Reichardt, Sven, *Faschistische Kampfbünde. Gewalt und Gemeinschaft im italienischen Squadrismus und in der deutschen SA* (Vienna, 2002)
Reichelt, Werner, *Das braune Evangelium. Hitler und die NS-Liturgie* (Wuppertal, 1990)
Reid, Anna, *Leningrad: Tragedy of a City under Siege, 1941–44* (London, 2011)
Reif, Janin, et al., *Schwanenwerder. Ein Inselparadies in Berlin* (Berlin, 2000)
Reilly, Joanne, *Belsen: The Liberation of a Concentration Camp* (London, 1998)
Rein, Hans, *Franz von Papen im Zwielicht der Geschichte. Sein letzter Prozess* (Baden-Baden, 1979)
Rennell, Tony, 'The Truth About Hitler's British Love Child', *Daily Mail* (13 December 2007)
Reulecke, Jürgen, '*Ich möchte einer werden, so wie die* . . .'. *Männerbünde im 20. Jahrhundert* (Frankfurt, 2001)
Reuth, Ralf Georg, *Goebbels. Eine Biographie* (1995)

Reynolds, Quentin et al., *Minister of Death: The Adolf Eichmann Story* (London, 1961)

Ribbentrop, Joachim von, *Zwischen London und Moskau. Erinnerungen und letzte Aufzeichnungen* (ed. Annelies von Ribbentrop, Leoni am Starnberger See, 1954)

Ribbentrop, Rudolf von, *Mein Vater Joachim von Ribbentrop. Erlebnisse und Erinnerungen* (Graz, 2008)

Richie, Alexandra, *Warsaw 1944: The Fateful Uprising* (London, 2013)

Riedel, Dirk, *Ordnungshüter und Massenmörder im Dienst der 'Volksgemeinschaft': Der KZ-Kommandant Hans Loritz* (Berlin, 2010)

Riefenstahl, Leni, *Memoiren 1902–1945* (Berlin, 1987)

Rieger, Bernhard, *The People's Car: A Global History of the Volkswagen Beetle* (Cambridge, MA, 2013)

Rigg, Bryan, *Hitler's Jewish Soldiers: The Untold Story of Nazi Racial Laws and Men of Jewish Descent in the German Military* (Lawrence, KS, 2002)

Roberts, Geoffrey, 'The Soviet Decision for a Pact with Nazi Germany', *Soviet Studies*, vol. 55 (1992), 57–78

Rohe, Karl, *Das Reichsbanner Schwarz-Rot-Gold: Ein Beitrag zur Geschichte und Struktur der politischen Kampfverbände zur Zeit der Weimarer Republik* (Düsseldorf, 1966)

Röhm, Ernst, *Die Geschichte eines Hochverräters* (Munich, 1933; first pub. 1928)

—, *Die Memoiren des Stabschefs Röhm* (Munich, 1934)

Rolfs, Richard W., *The Sorcerer's Apprentice: The Life of Franz von Papen* (Lanham, MD, 1996)

Römer, Felix, *Kameraden. Die Wehrmacht von innen* (Munich, 2012)

Roos, Daniel, *Julius Streicher und 'Der Stürmer' 1923–1945* (Paderborn, 2014)

Roseman, Mark, *The Wannsee Conference and the Final Solution: A Reconsideration* (New York, 2002)

Rosenbaum, Ron, *Explaining Hitler: The Search for the Origins of his Evil* (New York, 1998)

Rosenberg, Alfred, *Der Zukunftsweg einer deutschen Aussenpolitik* (Munich, 1927)

—, *Der Sumpf. Querschnitte durch das 'Geistes'-leben der November-Demokratie* (Munich, 1930)

—, *Der Mythus des 20. Jahrhunderts. Eine Wertung der seelisch-geistigen Gestaltenkämpfe unserer Zeit*, 24th edn (Munich, 1934)

—, *Letzte Aufzeichnungen: Ideale und Idole der nationalsozialistischen Revolution* (Göttingen, 1946)

Rosenhaft, Eve, 'Working-Class Life and Working-Class Politics: Communists, Nazis and the State in the Battle for the Streets, Berlin 1928–1932', in Richard Bessel and Edgar Feuchtwanger (eds.), *Social Change and Political Development in Weimar Germany* (London, 1981), 207–40

—, *'Beating the Fascists'? The German Communists and Political Violence 1929–1933* (Cambridge, 1983)

Rossino, Alexander B., *Hitler Strikes Poland: Blitzkrieg, Ideology, and Atrocity* (Lawrence, KS, 2003)

Rössler, Mechthild, and Sabine Schleiermacher (eds.), *Der 'Generalplan Ost' Hauptlinien der nationalsozialistischen Planungs- und Vernichtungspolitik* (Berlin, 1993)

Rother, Rainer, *Leni Riefenstahl: Die Verführung des Talents* (Berlin, 2000)

Ruault, Franco, *'Neuschöpfer des deutschen Volkes': Julius Streicher im Kampf gegen 'Rassenschande'* (Frankfurt, 2006)

—, *Tödliche Maskeraden: Julius Streicher und die 'Lösung der Judenfrage'* (Frankfurt am Main, 2009)

Runzheimer, Jürgen, 'Der Überfall auf den Sender Gleiwitz im Jahre 1939', *Vierteljahrshefte für Zeitgeschichte*, vol. 10 (1962), 408–26

Russell, (Lord) Edward, *The Scourge of the Swastika: A Short History of Nazi War Crimes* (London, 1954)

Safrian, Hans, *Die Eichmann-Männer* (Vienna, 1993)

Saldern, Adelheid von, 'Victims or Perpetrators? Controversies about the Role of Women in the Nazi State', in David F. Crew (ed.), *Nazism and German Society, 1933–1945* (London, 1994), 141–65.

Sandomir, Richard, 'Rudolf von Ribbentrop, Son of Top Nazi Diplomat, Dies at 98', *New York Times* (6 June 2019)

Schaulinski, Gerlot, and Dagmar Thorau (eds.), *Mythos Germania. Vision und Verbrechen* (Berlin, 2014)

Schaumburg-Lippe, Christian Fürst von, *Zwischen Krone und Kerker* (Wiesbaden, 1952)

Scheel, Klaus, *Der Tag von Potsdam* (Berlin, 1993)

Scheil, Stefan, *Ribbentrop. Oder: Die Verlockung des nationalen Aufbruchs. Eine politische Biographie* (Berlin, 2013)

Schenk, Dieter, *Hans Frank. Hitlers Kronjurist und Generalgouverneur* (Frankfurt, 2006)

Scherner, Jonas, and Jochen Streb, 'Das Ende eines Mythos? Albert Speer und das sogenannte Rüstungswunder', *Vierteljahrschrift für Sozial- und Wirtschaftsgeschichte*, vol. 93, no. 2 (2006), 172–96

Schmidt, Matthias, *Albert Speer. Das Ende eines Mythos. Speers wahre Rolle im Dritten Reich* (Munich, 1982; English edn, *Albert Speer: The End of a Myth*, London, 1985)

Schmidt, Ulf, *Hitlers Arzt Karl Brandt. Medizin und Macht im Dritten Reich* (Berlin, 2007)

Schmuhl, Hans-Walter, *Rassenhygiene, Nationalsozialismus, Euthanasie: Von der Verhütung zur Vernichtung 'lebensunwerten Lebens'* (Göttingen, 1987)

Schneider, Michael, *Unterm Hakenkreuz. Arbeiter und Arbeiterbewegung 1933 bis 1939* (Bonn, 1999)

Schoeps, Julius (ed.), *Ein Volk von Mördern? Die Dokumentation zur Goldhagen-Kontroverse um die Rolle der Deutschen im Holocaust* (Hamburg, 1996)

Scholtz-Klink, Gertrud, *Die Frau im Dritten Reich* (Tübingen, 1978)

Schreiber, Carsten, *Elite im Verborgenen: Ideologie und regionale Herrschaftspraxis des Sicherheitsdienstes der SS und seines Netzwerks am Beispiel Sachsens* (Munich 2008)

Schröder, Karl, *Aufstieg und Fall des Robert Ley* (Siegburg, 2008)

Schroeder, Christa, *Er war mein Chef. Aus dem Nachlass der Sekretärin von Adolf Hitler,* 2nd edn (Munich, 1985)

Schudnagies, Christian, *Hans Frank. Aufstieg und Fall des NS-Juristen und Generalgouverneurs* (Frankfurt am Main, 1989)

Schulte, Regine, 'Feuer im Dorf', in Heinz Reif (ed.), *Räuber, Volk und Obrigkeit. Studien zur Geschichte der Kriminalität in Deutschland seit dem 18. Jahrhundert* (Frankfurt, 1984), 100–52

Schulte, Theo, *The German Army and Nazi Policies in Occupied Russia* (Oxford, 1988)

Schwartz, Johannes, *'Weibliche Angelegenheiten'. Handlungsräume von KZ-Aufseherinnen in Ravensbrück und Neubrandenburg* (Hamburg, 2018)

Schwarz, Gudrun, *Eine Frau an seiner Seite. Ehefrauen in der 'SS-Sippengemeinschaft'* (Hamburg, 1997)

—, "'. . . möchte ich nochmals um meine Einberufung als SS-Aufseherin bitten." Wärterinnen in den nationalsozialistischen Konzentrationslagern', in Barbara Distel (ed.), *Frauen im Holocaust* (Gerlingen 2001), 331–52

—, 'Frauen in Konzentrationslagern – Täterinnen und Zuschauerinnen', in Ulrich Herbert et al. (eds.), *Die nationalsozialistischen Konzentrationslager* (Frankfurt, 2002), 800–21

Schwarzwäller, Wulf, *Rudolf Hess. Der Stellvertreter* (Munich, 1987)

Scotsman Newsroom, 'Her Films Glorified Hitler: Now Leni Riefenstahl's Own Story Hits the Screen', *The Scotsman* (12 June 2012)

Seibt, Gustav, 'Hans-Ulrich Wehlers erstaunlich sanfte Worte über Theodor Schieders Karriere im Dritten Reich: Kritisches Goldrähmchen', *Berliner Zeitung* (11 December 1998)

Seidler, Franz, *'Deutscher Volkssturm': Der letzte Aufgebot 1944/45* (Munich, 1989)

Sengoopta, Chandak, *Otto Weininger: Sex, Science, and Self in Imperial Vienna* (Chicago, 2000)

Sereny, Gitta, *Albert Speer: His Battle with Truth* (London, 1995)

Shandley, Robert R. (ed.), *Unwilling Germans? The Goldhagen Debate* (Minneapolis, MN, 1998)

Shepherd, Ben, *War in the Wild East: The German Army and Soviet Partisans* (Cambridge, 2004)

—, *After Daybreak: The Liberation of Bergen-Belsen, 1945* (New York, 2007)

—, and Juliette Pattinson (eds.), *War in a Twilight World: Partisan and Anti-Partisan Warfare in Eastern Europe, 1939–45* (London, 2010)
—, *Terror in the Balkans: German Armies and Partisan Warfare* (Cambridge, MA, 2012)
—, *Hitler's Soldiers: The German Army in the Third Reich* (London, 2016)
Showalter, Dennis E., *Little Man, What Now? Der Stürmer in the Weimar Republic* (Hamden, CT, 1982)
Siemens, Daniel, *Horst Wessel. Tod und Verklärung eines Nationalsozialisten* (Berlin, 2009; English edn, *The Making of a Nazi Hero: The Murder and Myth of Horst Wesssel*, London, 2013)
—, *Stormtroopers: A New History of Hitler's Brownshirts* (London, 2017)
Smelser, Ronald, *Robert Ley: Hitler's Labor Front Leader* (Oxford, 1988)
—, and Rainer Zitelmann (eds.), *The Nazi Elite* (London, 1993)
—, and Edward J. Davies, *The Myth of the Eastern Front: The Nazi-Soviet War in American Popular Culture* (Cambridge, 2008)
Smith, Bradley F., *Adolf Hitler: His Family, Childhood, and Youth* (Stanford, CA, 1967)
—, *Heinrich Himmler: A Nazi in the Making 1900–1926* (Stanford, CA, 1971)
—, and Agnes F. Peterson (eds.), *Heinrich Himmler Geheimreden 1933 bis 1945 und andere Ansprachen* (Frankfurt, 1974)
Smith, Emma, *Portable Magic: A History of Books and their Readers* (London, 2022)
Sofsky, Wolfgang, *Die Ordnung des Terrors: Das Konzentrationslager* (Frankfurt, 1993)
Sokal, Harry, 'Über Nacht Antisemitin geworden?', *Der Spiegel*, 46 (8 November 1976)
Sontag, Susan, *Under the Sign of Saturn* (New York, 1980)
Sorge, Ernst, *Mit Flugzeug, Faltboot und Filmkamera in den Eisfjorden Grönlands* (Berlin, 1933)
Speer, Albert, *Inside the Third Reich* (London, 1970)
Spicer, Charles, *Coffee with Hitler: The British Amateurs Who Tried to Civilise the Nazis* (London, 2022)
Stammers, Tom, and Simon Taylor, *An Analysis of Daniel Jonah Goldhagen's 'Hitler's Willing Executioners': Ordinary Germans and the Holocaust* (London, 2017)
Stangneth, Bettina, *Eichmann Before Jerusalem: The Unexamined Life of a Mass Murderer* (New York, 2014)
Stargardt, Nicholas, 'Beyond "Consent" or "Terror": Wartime Crises in Nazi Germany', *History Workshop Journal*, vol. 72 (2011), 190–204
Stegmann, Dirk, 'Zum Verhältnis von Grossindustrie und Nationalsozialismus 1930–1933', *Archiv für Sozialgeschichte*, vol. 13 (1973), 351–432
—, 'Antiquierte Personalisierung oder sozialökonomische Faschismus-Analyse? Eine Antwort auf H. A. Turners Kritik an meinen Thesen zum Verhältnis von

Nationalsozialismus und Grossindustrie for 1933', *Archiv für Sozialgeschichte*, vol. 17 (1977), 175–296

Steinacher, Gerald, *Nazis on the Run: How Hitler's Henchmen Fled Justice* (New York, 2011)

Steiner, Zara, *The Triumph of the Dark: European International History 1933–1939* (Oxford, 2011)

Steinweis, Alan E., *Art, Ideology, and Economics in Nazi Germany: The Reich Chambers of Music, Theater, and the Visual Arts* (Chapel Hill, NC, 1993)

—, *Kristallnacht 1938* (Cambridge, MA, 2009)

—, *The People's Dictatorship: A History of Nazi Germany* (Cambridge, 2023)

—, and Robert Rachlin (eds.), *The Law in Nazi Germany: Ideology, Opportunism and the Perversion of Justice* (Oxford, 2015)

Stephan, Werner, *Acht Jahrzehnte erlebtes Deutschland. Ein Liberaler in view Epochen* (Düsseldorf, 1983)

Stephenson, Jill, *Women in Nazi Society* (London, 1975)

—, *The Nazi Organisation of Women* (London, 1981)

Stoltzfus, Nathan, *Resistance of the Heart: Intermarriage and the Rosenstrasse Protest in Nazi Germany* (New York, 1996)

—, *Hitler's Compromises: Coercion and Consensus in Nazi Germany* (New Haven, 2016)

—, and Birgit Maier-Katkin, *Protest in Hitler's 'National Community': Popular Unrest and the Nazi Response* (Oxford, 2015)

Stone, Dan, *The Holocaust: An Unfinished History* (London, 2023)

Stöver, Bernd, *Volksgemeinschaft im Dritten Reich: Die Konsensbereitschaft der Deutschen aus der Sicht sozialdemokratischer Exilberichte* (Düsseldorf, 1993)

Straumann, Tobias, *1931: Debt, Crisis, and the Rise of Hitler* (Oxford, 2019)

Strebel, Berhard, *Das KZ Ravensbrück. Geschichte eines Lagerkomplexes* (Paderborn, 2003)

Streit, Christian, *Keine Kameraden. Die Wehrmacht und die sowjetischen Kriegsgefangenen 1941–45* (Stuttgart, 1978)

Swearingen, Ben E., *The Mystery of Hermann Goering's Suicide* (London, 1985)

Szejnmann, Claus-Christian W., *Nazism in Central Germany: The Brownshirts in 'Red' Saxony* (Oxford, 1999)

—, 'Perpetrators of the Holocaust: A Historiography', in Olaf Jensen and Claus-Christian Szejnmann (eds.), *Ordinary People as Mass Murderers: Perpetrators in Comparative Perspective* (London, 2008), 25–54

Taylor, Telford, *Sword and Swastika: Generals and Nazis in the Third Reich* (New York, 1952)

Thacker, Toby, *Joseph Goebbels: Life and Death* (London, 2009)

Theweleit, Klaus, *Männerphantasien*, 2 vols. (Frankfurt, 1977)

Thies, Jochen, *Hitler's Plans for Global Domination: Nazi Architecture and Ultimate War Aims* (Oxford, 2012)

BIBLIOGRAPHY

Thyssen, Fritz, *I Paid Hitler* (London, 1941)
Tooze, Adam, *The Wages of Destruction: The Making and Breaking of the Nazi Economy* (London, 2006)
Toussaint, Jeanette, 'Die Auseinandersetzung mit der nationalsozialistischen Vergangenheit. Interviews mit ehemaligen SS-Aufseherinnen und ihren Töchtern', in Viola Schubert-Lehnhardt and Sylvia Korch (eds.), *Frauen als Täterinnen und Mittäterinnen im Nationalsozialismus. Gestaltungsspielräume und Handlungsmöglichkeiten* (Halle, 2006), 147–60
Tracey, Michael, *A Variety of Lives: A Biography of Sir Hugh Greene* (London, 1983)
Trevor-Roper, Hugh, *The Last Days of Hitler* (London, 1947)
—, 'The Mind of Adolf Hitler', in *Hitler's Table Talk, 1941–1944* (London, 1953)
Trials of War Criminals Before the Nuremberg Military Tribunals under Control Council Law No. 10: The Medical Case, 2 vols. (Washington DC, 1950)
Trimborn, Jürgen, *Riefenstahl. Eine deutsche Karriere. Biographie* (Berlin, 2002)
Tschirbs, Rudolf, *Das Phantom der Volksgemeinschaft* (Düsseldorf, 2015)
Turner, Henry Ashby Jr., 'Grossunternehmertum und Nationalsozialismus, 1930–33', *Historische Zeitschrift*, vol. 221 (1975), 18–68
—, *German Big Business and the Rise of Hitler* (Oxford, 1985)
—, *Hitler's Thirty Days to Power: January 1933* (London, 1996)
Tyrell, Albrecht (ed.), *Führer befiehl . . . Selbstzeugnisse aus der 'Kampfzeit' der NSDAP* (Düsseldorf, 1969)
—, *Vom 'Trommler zum 'Führer'. Der Wandel von Hitlers Selbstverständnis zwischen 1919 und 1924 und die Entwicklung der NSDAP* (Munich, 1975)
Ueberschär, Gerd R., and Winfried Vogel, *Dienen und Verdienen: Hitlers Geschenke an seine Eliten* (Frankfurt, 1999)
Uhl, Matthias et al. (eds.), *Die Organisation des Terrors: Der Dienstkalender Heinrich Himmlers 1943–1945* (Munich, 2020)
Ullrich, Volker, 'Speers Erfindung', *Die Zeit*, 19 (4 May 2005)
—, *Adolf Hitler. Biographie*: I: *Die Jahre des Aufstiegs* (Frankfurt am Main, 2013)
—, *Adolf Hitler. Biographie*: II: *Die Jahre des Untergangs 1939–1945* (Frankfurt am Main, 2018)
—, *Germany 1923: Hyperinflation, Hitler's Putsch, and Democracy in Crisis* (New York, 2023)
Varga, William, *The Number One Nazi Jew Baiter* (New York, 1981)
Vogelsang, Thilo, 'Neue Dokumente zur Geschichte der Reichswehr 1930–1933', *Vierteljahrshefte für Zeitgeschichte*, vol. 2 (1954), 397–439
Vollnhals, Clemens et al. (eds.), *Hitler. Reden, Schriften, Anordnungen Februar 1925 bis Januar 1933*, 12 vols. (Munich, 1992–2003)
Wachsmann, Nikolaus, *Hitler's Prisons: Legal Terror in Nazi Germany* (New Haven, CT, 2004)
—, *KL: A History of the Nazi Concentration Camps* (New York, 2015)

Wald, Renate, *Mein Vater Robert Ley. Meine Erinnerungen und Vaters Geschichte* (Nümbrecht, 2004)
Weber, Thomas, *Hitler's First War: Adolf Hitler, the Men of the List Regiment, and the First World War* (Oxford, 2010)
—, *Becoming Hitler: The Making of a Nazi* (Oxford, 2017)
—(ed.), *Als die Demokratie starb. Die Machtergreifung der Nationalsozialisten – Geschichte und Gegenwart* (Freiburg, 2022)
Weinberg, Gerhard L., *The Foreign Policy of Hitler's Germany*, 2 vols. (London, 1970, 1980)
Weindling, Paul, *Nazi Medicine and the Nuremberg Trials: From Medical War Crimes to Informed Consent* (London, 2004)
Weissmann, Karl-Heinz, *Das Hakenkreuz. Symbol eines Jahrhunderts* (Schnellrode, 2006)
Weitz, Eric D., *Joachim von Ribbentrop: Hitler's Diplomat* (London, 1992)
—, *Creating German Communism, 1890–1990: From Popular Protests to Socialist State* (Princeton, NJ, 1997)
—, *Weimar Germany: Promise and Tragedy* (Princeton, NJ, 2007)
Weitz, John, *Hitler's Banker: Hjalmar Horace Greeley Schacht* (Boston, MA, 1997)
Welch, David, *Propaganda and the German Cinema, 1933–1945* (Oxford, 1983)
Welzer, Harald, *Täter. Wie aus ganz normalen Menschen Massenmörder werden* (Frankfurt am Main, 2005)
Wette, Wolfram, *Die Wehrmacht: Feindbilder, Vernichtungskrieg, Legenden* (Frankfurt, 2005)
Wheeler-Bennett, John W., *The Nemesis of Power: The German Army in Politics 1918–1945* (London, 1953)
Whiting, Charles, *Heydrich: Henchman of Death* (Barnsley, 1999)
Wiedemann, Fritz, *Der Mann, der Feldherr werden wollte. Erlebnisse und Erfahrungen des Vorgesetzten Hitlers im 1. Weltkrieg und seines späteren Persönlichen Adjutanten* (Velbert und Kettwig, 1964)
Wieland, Karin, *Dietrich und Riefenstahl. Der Traum von der neuen Frau* (Munich, 2011)
Wighton, Charles, *Heydrich: Hitler's Most Evil Henchman* (London, 1962)
Wildt, Michael, *Generation des Unbedingten. Das Führungskorps des Reichssicherheitshauptamtes* (Hamburg, 2003)
—, *Volksgemeinschaft als Selbstermächtigung. Gewalt gegen Juden in der deutschen Provinz 1919 bis 1939* (Hamburg, 2007)
—, 'Die Tagebücher der Luise Solmitz – Zwei Originale', in Thomas Grossbölting and Kirsten Heinsohn (eds.), *Zeitgeschichte in Hamburg 2021* (Hamburg, 2022), 139–48
Willems, Susanne, *Der entsiedelte Jude. Albert Speers Wohnungsmarktpolitik für den Berliner Hauptstadtbau* (Berlin, 2000)

Winkler, Heinrich August, *Der Schein der Normalität. Arbeiter und Arbeiterbewegung in der Weimarer Republik 1924 bis 1930* (Bonn, 1985)
—, *Der Weg in die Katastrophe. Arbeiter und Arbeiterbewegung in der Weimarer Republik 1930 bis 1933* (Bonn, 1987)
—, *Die Weimarer Republik 1918–1933: Die Geschichte der ersten deutschen Demokratie* (Munich, 1993)
Wirsching, Andreas, '"Man kann nur Boden germanisieren". Eine neue Quelle zu Hitlers Rede vor den Spitzen der Reichswehr am 3. Februar 1933', *Vierteljahrshefte für Zeitgeschichte*, vol. 49 (2001), 517–50
Witte, Peter, et al. (eds.), *Der Dienstkalender Heinrich Himmlers 1941/42* (Hamburg, 1999)
Wojak, Irmtrud, *Eichmanns Memoiren. Ein kritischer Essay* (Frankfurt, 2002)
Wolf, Hubert, 'Reichskonkordat für Ermächtigungsgesetz? Zur Historisierung der Scholder-Repgen-Kontroverse über das Verhältnis des Vatikans zum Nationalsozialismus', *Vierteljahrshefte für Zeitgeschichte*, vol. 60 (2012), 169–200
Wolfram, Lavern, 'Margot Pietzners autobiografische Aufzeichnungen "Schuldig oder Opfer?" Selbstwahrnehmung einer ehemaligen SS-Aufseherin in ihren Selbstzeugnissen', in Viola Schubert-Lehnhardt and Sylvia Korch (eds.), *Frauen als Täterinnen und Mittäterinnen im Nationalsozialismus. Gestaltungsspielräume und Handlungsmöglichkeiten* (Halle, 2006), 115–32
Wolters, Rita, *Verrat für die Volksgemeinschaft. Denunziantinnen im Dritten Reich* (Pfaffenweiler, 1996)
Wrisberg, Ernst von, 'Über die Angriffe gegen die Offiziersstande', *Militär-Wochenschrift für die deutsche Wehrmacht* (25 March 1919), 262
Wulff, Arne, *Staatssekretär Professor Dr. Dr. h.c. Franz Schlegelberger, 1876–1970* (Frankfurt am Main, 1991)
Wyllie, James, *The Warlord and the Renegade: The Story of Hermann and Albert Goering* (Stroud, 2006)
—, *Nazi Wives: The Women at the Top of Hitler's Germany* (Cheltenham, 2019)
Zámecnik, Stanislav, *Das war Dachau* (Frankfurt, 2007)
Zapp, Paul, *Germanisch-deutsche Weihnacht* (Stuttgart, 1934)
—, *Religiöser Zerfall und deutscher Glaube* (Eisenach, 1935)
—, *Deutsche Weihestunden* (Berlin, 1936)
Zdral, Wolfgang, *Die Hitlers. Die unbekannte Familie des Führers* (Bergisch Gladbach, 2008)
Zellhuber, Andreas, '*Unsere Verwaltung treibt einer Katastrophe zu*' – *das Reichsministerium für die besetzten Ostgebiete und die deutsche Besatzungsherrschaft in der Sowjetunion 1941–1945* (Munich, 2006)
Zinn, Alexander, *Die soziale Konstruktion des homosexuellen Nationalsozialisten. Zur Genese und Etablierung eines Stereotyps* (Frankfurt am Main, 1997)

BIBLIOGRAPHY

Zitelmann, Rainer, *Hitler: The Politics of Seduction* (London, 1999, first published as *Hitler: Selbstverständnis eines Revolutionärs* (Hamburg, 1987, new ed., 2017)

Zur Nieden, Susanne, *Aufstieg und Fall des viril Männerhelden – Der Skandal um Ernst Röhm und seine Ermordung* (Frankfurt am Main, 2005)

—(ed.), *Homosexualität und Staatsräson: Männlichkeit, Homophobie und Politik in Deutschland 1900–1945* (Frankfurt, 2005)

Index

Abetz, Otto, 197
Aga Khan, visits Hitler (1937), 63
Amann, Max, 140, 146, 209
Andrus, Colonel, 128, 129, 253, 288, 289, 302
Anglo-German Naval Agreement (1935), 65
Angriff, Der (newspaper), 137, 141
antisemitism: in *Mein Kampf*, 25–6; in Hitler's election campaign (1932), 32; Jewish ghettos, 72–3; and communism, 32, 76, 77, 85, 87, 94, 145, 171, 204, 462; driving force for Hitler, 55–9; and German humiliation in the First World War, 237–8; and German identity, 395; anti-Jewish conspiracy theories, 16, 85, 469; Rosenberg's influence on, 205–6; and socialism, 246
Arendt, Hannah, 'banality of evil', 394; on Adolf Eichmann, 321–3, 332
Argentina, Eichmann in, 331–2
Aronson, Shlomo, 317
Atatürk, Kemal (Mustafa Kemal Pasha), 21, 157
Auschwitz-Birkenau: Finnish Jews deported to, 165; gas chambers, 78, 96; Hungarian Jews deported to, 89, 199, 330; Irma Grese's abuses at, 408–10; Italian Jews deported to, 177; medical experiments at, 422; prisoner testimony, xxi–xxiv; public knowledge of, 463; Speer denies knowledge of, 231, 462–3; Speer supplies materials and finance for, 227 *see also* Frankfurt Auschwitz trials (1960s)
Austria: failed German coup (1934), 62; *Anschluss* (1938), 62, 122, 268, 271, 327–8, 378, 439
Austrian Nazi Party, 325–6
Axmann, Arthur, 382

Baader-Meinhof group, 471–2
Baarová, Lida, 142
Backe, Herbert, 365–6
Balász, Béla, 431
Baldwin, Stanley, 64–5
Baltic Germans, 203
Barlach, Ernst, 211
Battle of Britain (1940), 74
'Battle of the Bulge' (1944–45), 90
Bauer, Max, 149
Bauer, Elvira, 299
Bauer, Fritz, 333, 355
Bavaria, 15–16, 19
Bayreuth Festival, 40
Bazna, Elyesa, 269
Beard, Mary Ritter, 413
'Beauty of Labour' scheme, 284, 285

581

INDEX

Bechstein, Edwin, 32
Bechstein, Helene, 32, 40, 107
beer-hall *putsch* (1923), 21–2, 116, 135, 152–3, 206, 248, 338
Belgium, German invasion (1940), 71
Below, Nicolaus von, 90, 96, 107
Belzec extermination camp, 77–8, 316, 346
Berchtesgaden, 84, 127, 191, 268, 375, 377
Berchtold, Alfred, 406
Bergen-Belsen concentration camp, 408, 411
Berger, Gottlob, 382
Berlin Olympics (1936), 100–101, 141, 299, 439
Bernadotte, Folke, 179, 183
Bernhardi, Friedrich von, 247
Best, Werner, 35, 303, 389
Biddle, Francis, 319
Binding, Karl, 376
Birkett, Lord, 128
Bismarck, Otto von, 185
Bloch-Bauer, Ferdinand, 317
Block, Josefine, 399
'Block Wardens', 464
Blomberg, Werner von, 48, 64, 122, 156
Blüher, Hans, 161
Bock, Fedor von, 77
Bodelschwingh, Friedrich von, 380
Boden, Margarete (Marga), 169
Boger, Wilhelm, 355
Bolek, Andreas, 325
Bolivia, German military mission in, 149–50
Bolshevik Revolution, 20, 204
Bolz, Eugen, 48
Bormann, Martin, 7–8, 84, 95, 96, 97, 127, 215, 226, 252
Bose, Herbert von, 267
Bouhler, Philip, 379

Bracher, Karl Dietrich, *The German Dictatorship*, 165
Brand, Joel, 330–31
Brandt, Anni, (*née* Rehborn), 107, 377
Brandt, Karl: background and medical training, 375–6; Hitler's personal physician, 107, 377–8, 381–2; role in euthanasia of mentally ill patients, 379–80, 383–4; approves medical experiments on concentration camp inmates, 381; Nazi death sentence and reprieval, 382–3; tried for war crimes and receives death penalty, 383; execution, 386
Brauchitsch, Walther von, 362, 363
Braun, Eva, 41, 96, 97, 107
Braunau, Austria, 11
Brechtken, Magnus, 221, 232
Breitman, Richard, 165
Breker, Arno, 74
Breloer, Heinrich, 232
Britain: Munich Agreement (1938), 66; guarantees to Poland, 68; Dunkirk evacuation, 72; Hitler's planned invasion, 74
British Special Operations Executive (SOE), 315–16
Broszat, Martin, 4
Brown, Daniel Patrick, 410
Browning, Christopher, 323, 394, 395
Brownshirts (stormtroopers), 35–6, 55, 118, 138, 154–7
Bruckmann, Hugo and Elsa, 32, 107
Brückner, Wilhelm, 375
Brüning, Heinrich, 29–31, 36, 118, 262
Buchenwald concentration camp, 401, 402–3
Bullock, Alan, 219; *Hitler: A Study in Tyranny*, 3–4, 7
Burckhardt, Carl J., 303, 306

INDEX

Canaris, Admiral Wilhelm, 312
Catel, Werner, 385
Catholic Centre Party, 14, 15, 31, 37, 45–6, 47, 260, 262
Catholics, in Nazi Germany, 59
Cesarani, David, 322–3, 325
Chamberlain, Neville, 64, 65, 66, 68, 183
Chelmno extermination camp, 77, 345, 346
Christian churches, and the Nazi regime, 59–60
Churchill, Winston, 66, 74, 105, 253
Ciano, Galeazzo, 70, 196
Communism: emergence in 1918, 20; and Jewish conspiracy theories, 18, 29, 57, 87, 205; Vatican's fear of, 46, 60, 261
Communist Party (German), 29, 31, 36, 37, 43–4, 47, 337
concentration camps: and forced labour, 125, 224; guards, 391–5; Himmler's control of, 172, 175–6; homosexuals and Catholic priests incarcerated in, 59; Jews sent to, 58, 143; medical experiments at, 383; Nazi opponents sent to (1930s), 47, 155, 340, 464; SS unlimited power in, 397; political opponents sent to during Hitler's seizure of power, 464; used for 'preventive detention', 172 *see also* extermination camps; individual camps
consumer goods, mass-produced in Germany, 284
Conti, Leonardo, 378–9, 382, 385
Craig, Gordan A., 219
Crete, 75
Crowther, Bosley, 106
Czechoslovakia, annexation (1938–39), 65–8, 361–2

Dachau concentration camp, 44, 129, 170–71, 310, 340, 392
Dahlerus, Birger, 123
Daluege, Kurt, 316–17
Darré, Richard Walther, 46
'degenerate' art, 140–41
Delmer, Sefton, 43, 159
'denazification', 98
Denmark: non-aggressive pact with Germany, 65; German invasion (1940), 71
Denson, William, 401, 405
Deschner, Günther, 303
Nationalsozialistische Frauenschaft (Nazi women's organization), 418, 419–21
Diels, Rudolf, 43
Dietl, General Eduard, 163
Dietrich, Otto, 140
Dimitrov, Georgii, 118–19
Dirksen, Herbert von, 195
Dolibois, Captain John, 293
Dollfuss, Engelbert, 62, 261, 267, 326
Domaus, Max, 7
Dönitz, Karl, 96, 97, 107, 179, 199
Drexler, Anton, 18, 19, 107, 245, 337

Eberstein, Elise von, 309–10
Eckart, Dietrich, 19, 107, 245
Edward VIII, King *see* Windsor, Duke of
Ehrhardt, Hermann, 116
Eichmann, Adolf: background, 324–5; joins the Nazi Party and the SS, 325–6; in the Security Service (SD), 326–7; incognito visit to Middle East, 327; in the Central Office for Jewish Emigration, 328; role in Jewish emigration from Austria, 327; role in implementation of the 'Final Solution', 329–30; organises deportation of Hungarian Jews to

Eichmann, Adolf – *cont'd.*
  Auschwitz, 330–31; arrested and escapes to Argentina, 331–2; eventual trial of (1961), 319–22, 333; character and ideology, 333
Eichmann, Veronika, 332
Eicke, Theodor, 156–7, 171, 340, 402
Einsatzgruppen (death squads), 311, 312
Einstein, Albert, 448
Eisenhower, General, 127–8
Eismann, Hans-Georg, 165
Eisner, Kurt, 15, 16, 245, 337
El Alamein, German defeat (1942), 80–81
Elser, Georg, 70, 402
Eltz-Rübenach, Paul von, 272
Enabling Act (1933), 45–6
Engel, Gerhard, 107
Epp, Franz Ritter von, 337
Eppenstein, Hermann, 112, 130
Esser, Hermann, 107
Estonia, independence after Bolshevik revolution, 203
Eternal Jew, The (propaganda film, 1940), 143–4
eugenics, 376, 385
euthanasia programmes, 378–80, 383–5
extermination camps, 77–8, 96, 272, 329, 391, 393

Falkenhayn, Erich von, 259
Fallada, Hans, 211
Falter, Jürgen, 470
Fanck, Arnold, 433–4
Farrow, John, 106
Fechenbach, Felix, 48
Feder, Gottfried, 19, 27, 245
Federation of German Women's Associations, 415
Fegelein, Hermann, 95

Fest, Joachim C.: on Alfred Rosenberg, 207; on Ernest Röhm, 157; on Franz von Papen, 270; on German Generals, 369–70, 371; on Hans Frank, 335–6; on Himmler, 165; on Reinhard Heydrich, 306; on Ribbentrop, 183; on Rudolf Hess, 241; and Speer's memoirs, 221, 232, 463; *The Face of the Third Reich*, xviii, xix; *Hitler*, 4, 5
Feuchtwanger, Lion, 166
Fighting League for German Culture, 211
'Final Solution' policy, 177, 197–9, 314, 328–30
First World War: Hitler's service in, 13–14; militarization of German society, 462
Flensburg, Germany, 97
France: German invasion via the Ardennes (1940), 71–2; German occupation, 81; Allied liberation of Paris, 83
Franco, Francisco, 261
Frank, Brigitte, 350
Frank, Hans: background, family and education, 336; member of Thule Society, 245, 337; takes part in beer-hall *putsch*, 338; provides legal defence for Nazis, 338–9; Bavarian Minister of Justice, 339–41; head of German legal administration, 339–40; disputes with Himmler, 340; conflict with Hitler over 'Night of the Long Knives', 340–41; Governor-General in Poland, 328, 342–8; reign of terror in Poland, 342–4; requisition of artworks and property in Poland, 344; establishes Jewish ghettos, 345; deportation of Jews to extermination camps, 346; lectures calling for return to rule of law, 347; Hitler strips of his Party

offices, 347; flees Poland, 348–9;
arrested and stands trial at
Nuremberg, 349–50; admiration for
Hitler, 337–8, 341–2; antisemitism,
339; contradictory character,
335–6; on Franz von Papen, 272–3;
psychological assessment, 105; on
Ribbentrop, 183; *In the Face of the
Gallows* (memoir), 349–50
Frank, Niklas, 350–51
Frank, Norman, 350
Frank, Sigrid, 350
Frankfurt Auschwitz trials (1960s),
355, 394
Frederick the Great, 94
Frick, Wilhelm, 39, 171, 317, 418
Friedrich Christian of Schaumburg-
Lippe, Prince, 280
Fritsch, Werner von, 64, 241
Fröhlich, Elke, 147
Fulbrook, Mary, 470
Funk, Walther, 227

Galen, Clemens von, 272, 380, 465
gas chambers, 77–8, 96, 330
Gayl, Wilhelm von, 263
Gellhorn, Martha, 321
Gemlich, Adolf, 16
George VI, King, 193
Gerke, Dr Achim, 305–6
German army, morals and politics in,
370–72
'German Autumn' (1970s), 471
German Doctors' Association, Nazi
members in, 385
'German Faith Movement', 389
German Labour Front, 281–5
German National People's Party
(DNVP), 33, 37, 38, 307
German Workers' Party, 18
Gestapo, 84, 171–2, 285
Gieseler, Hermann, 226
Giesler, Paul, 368

Gilbert, Gustave, 128, 131, 183, 200,
270, 288, 300–1, 341, 349
Glauer, Adam, 245
Globocnik, Odilo, 346
Glücks, Richard, 422
Goebbels, Joseph: background and
family, 134–5; appointed Gauleiter
of Berlin, 137; propaganda
methods, 137, 140, 143–5; elected
as Reichstag deputy (1928), 137–8;
and the Kristallnacht pogroms, 58,
143; departure on state visit to
Italy (1938), 133; marriage to
Magda Quandt (1931), 41, 138–9;
appointed head of Propaganda
Ministry, 46, 139–40; creates Reich
Chamber of Culture, 48, 140;
organises 'degenerate' art
exhibition (1937), 52, 140;
antisemitic measures, 140–41,
143–4; releases *Kolberg*
(propaganda movie), 89–90, 145;
attends book-burnings, 141;
campaign to send clothes to
German soldiers in Russia, 79,
144; appointed 'Plenipotentiary
for Total War', 145; excluded
from key decision-making, 141–2;
and Stauffenberg's attempted
assassination of Hitler, 84;
substantial income, 142; joins
Hitler in the bunker, 94–5, 146;
witnesses Hitler's marriage to
Eva Braun, 96; at Hitler's death,
97; commits suicide after
murdering his children, 146–7;
deformity and limp, 134–5;
dependence on Hitler's approval,
134, 138; devotion to Hitler,
136–7, 145–7; diaries, 146–7;
responsibility for extermination of
the Jews, 147; and Riefenstahl's
films, 436–7

585

INDEX

Goebbels, Magda (*formerly* Quandt), 41, 42, 95, 122, 138–9, 142, 146
Goga, Octavian, 213
Goldensohn, Leon, 120, 300, 372
Goldhagen, Daniel J., 323, 395
Göring, Albert, 130
Göring, Edda, 122, 130
Göring, Franziska, 112
Göring, Hermann: background and family, 112–13; pilot in the First World War, 113–15; joins Nazi party, 115–16; Hitler appoints as head of Storm Division, 116; injured in the beer-hall *putsch*, 116; confined to mental hospital in Sweden, 117; drug addiction, 116–17; Prussian Minister of the Interior, 39, 44, 118–19; passing of the Enabling Act, 45, 118; role in 'Night of the Long Knives', 119, 128–9; nominated as Hitler's successor, 119; emissary to Italy, 119; appointed Air Reich Minister, 119–20; placed in charge of Four-Year Plan, 120, 342; antisemitic policies, 120–21; insatiable appetite for power, 121; fails to be appointed as War Minister, 122; attempts to avoid war, 122, 123; loss of influence and prestige, 122–3, 124–5, 126; presses annexation of Austria, 65, 122; failure of Luftwaffe in Battle of Britain, 124; signs order for 'final solution', 125; surrenders to the Allies, 127; at the Nuremberg Trials, 128–9; commits suicide, 129; art collection, 111–12, 126–7; drug addiction, 126, 128; hunting activities, 109–11; lions kept on country estate, 109; obesity, 116, 128; psychological assessment, 105; on Ribbentrop, 183; voluptuous tastes, 127

Gottschewski, Lydia, 418
Great Depression, 118, 326, 462
'Great German Art Exhibition' (1934), 211
Greene, Hugh Carleton, 133
Grese, Irma, 356, 408–11
Gruhn, Erna, 64
Grzesinski, Albert, 155
Guderian, Heinz, 71, 82, 90, 368
Günsche, Otto, 97
Gürtner, Franz, 107, 339

Habicht, Theodor, 268
Halder, Franz, 77, 78, 80, 81, 362–3
Halle, 305, 307–8
Hamburg, bombing of, 218, 455–6
Hamilton, Duke of, 252–3
Hamilton-Ewing, Catherine, 187
Hancock, Eleanor, 157, 159, 161
Hanfstaengl, Ernst 'Putzi', 17, 32, 107, 252
Harden, Maximilian, 186
Harzburg Front (political coalition), 37
Hassell, Ulrich von, 335, 343
Hauer, Jakob Wilhelm, 389
Haushofer, Albrecht, 252
Haushofer, Karl, 246–7, 249, 252
Heck, Dr Lutz, 109
Heidemann, Gerd, 130
Heiden, Konrad, 3, 5, 7
Heim, Heinrich, 7–8
Heimsoth, Karl-Günther, 160–61
Heissmeyer, August, 422, 423
Heissmeyer, Kurt, 422
Helldorf, Wolf-Heinrich Graf von, 189, 190
Henderson, Sir Nevile, 196
Herbert, Ulrich, 324
Hermann-Göring-Werke (steel conglomerate), 120
Hertwig, Johanne Sophia, 184–5
Hess, Fritz, 241

586

INDEX

Hess, Ilse (*née* Pröhl), 24, 250, 253
Hess, Johann Christian, 241
Hess, Klara (*née* Münch), 239, 241
Hess, Rudolf, background and family, 241–2; imprisoned with Hitler, 23; on Hitler's identification with Germany, 41, 147; service in First World War, 242–4; Hitler's amanuensis, 24; member of the Thule Society, 244–5; joins the Nazi Party, 247; closeness to Hitler, 247–9; takes part in beer-hall *putsch*, 248; in Landsberg Prison with Hitler, 249; private secretary to Hitler, 249–50; nominated Deputy Leader after Hitler's seizure of power, 251; limitations and loss of power, 252; flight to England, 252–3; at the Nuremberg Trials, 253; suicide in Spandau Prison, 253; antisemitism, 246, 251; monocle-wearing, 239; psychological assessment, 105, 253–4
Hess, Wolf-Rüdiger, 250, 253
Heydrich, Bruno, 305–6, 307
Heydrich, Lina (*née* Osten), 308–9, 312, 317
Heydrich, Reinhard: background and family, 307; dishonourably discharged from the navy, 309; offered job by Himmler, 309–10; head of the Gestapo, 310; sets up *Einsatzgruppen* (SS Task Forces), 311–13; elite status in the Third Reich, 312; on flying missions as fighter pilot, 313; responsibility for implementing the 'final solution', 313–14; convenes the Wannsee Conference (1942), 314; 'Operation Reinhard', 77–8, 329; regime of terror in Czechoslovakia, 314–15; organises bombing of synagogues in Paris, 315; assassinated in Prague (1942), 316; character and appearance, 303–5; loyalty to Himmler, 310, 318; notoriety, 303; rumours that he was Jewish, 305–7
Hiemer, Ernst, 299
Hilgenfeldt, Erich, 418, 422
Himmler, Ernst, 181
Himmler, Gebhard (HH's brother), 168, 181
Himmler, Gebhard (HH's father), 166, 174
Himmler, Gebhard (HH's son), 180
Himmler, Gudrun, 180
Himmler, Heinrich: background, family and education, 166–7; enrols in army, 167; political radicalization, 168–9; takes part in beer-hall *putsch*, 168; marriage to Margarete Boden, 169, 180–81; Reich leader of the SS, 169–70; Pripet Marshes massacre, 85; sets up concentration camp in Dachau, 44, 170–71; supplies forced labour on Speer's building projects, 224–5; appointed head of Gestapo, 171–2; extends role of concentration camps, 172; Posen speech, 175–6, 229, 469; appointed Reich Minister of the Interior, 177; role in the Holocaust, 165, 176–8; and Stauffenberg's attempted assassination of Hitler, 177–8; attempts to liaise with Western Allies, 95, 178–9; Hitler dismisses from all posts, 95, 179; arrested by British troops and commits suicide, 179–80; belief in 'decency', 175–6; close relationship with Hitler, 177–8; diaries and letters, 165, 166, 167; historians' views of, 165–6; obsessive

587

Himmler, Heinrich – *cont'd.*
  antisemitism, 165; phobias, prejudices and passions, 172–4; promotion of Germanic religious cults, 60, 173; racial ideology, 174–7, 181; relationship with Hedwig Potthast, 180–81; sadism, 174
Himmler, Katrin, 166, 181
Hindemith, Paul, 211
Hindenburg, Oskar, 38, 191
Hindenburg, Paul von: Reich President, 29, 30–31, 36; brings Hitler into government, 38–40, 44–5; support for Franz von Papen, 260–63, 267; protection of Jews who fought in the First World War, 56; decline and death, 50–51
Hinkel, Hans, 211
Hitler, Adolf: birth and childhood, 11; interest in art and architecture, 12; moves to Munich, 13; rejected for military service, 13; serves in the First World War, 13–14; enters politics, 15–16; embraces rabid antisemitism, 16–17; discovers talent for public speaking, 17–18; transforms German Workers' Party into National Socialist Party, 18–19; assumes leadership of Nazi Party, 19–20; arrested after the beer-hall *putsch*, 21–2; contemplates suicide, 22; imprisoned for role in beer-hall *putsch*, 22–4; writes *Mein Kampf*, 24–8; re-founds and extends Nazi Party, 27; rhetorical appeal in election campaign (1932), 31–4; support for use of violence, 37, 48, 49; intent on destruction of Weimar Republic, 37; appointed Reich Chancellor, 39–40, 43, 139; relationships with women, 40–41, 138–9; charismatic leadership, 41–3; capitalizes on burning of the Reichstag, 43–4; introduces Enabling Act, 45–6; appoints Nazis to the Reich Cabinet, 46; gains support of army, 48; abolishes post of President on Hindenburg's death, 51; attempts to curb personality cult, 51; censorship of Modern art, 51–3; introduces compulsory sterilization, 53; weakness in economics, 53–4; promotion of the motor-vehicle and other consumer goods, 55; visceral hatred for Jews, 55–9, 67, 75–6, 78, 85–7, 91–2, 96, 100; attacks on Christianity, 59–60; belief in Nazism as scientific movement, 60; ambition for global hegemony, 60–61; conceals ambition in foreign policy, 61–4; profession of friendship with England, 63; disregard for international agreements, 64–5; frustration at 'appeasement', 66; invasion of Czechoslovakia, 67–8; invasion of Poland, 68–71; blames Britain for outbreak of war, 69–70; first assassination attempt (1939), 70; genocidal intentions, 70–71; triumph at France's surrender, 72; vanity and narcissism, 73–4; belief in willpower, 73, 81; visits Napoleon's tomb in Paris, 74; planned invasion of Britain, 74; Operation Barbarossa, 75–6, 79; rhetorical speeches decline in number, 76; takes over as commander-in-chief of the army, 79; declares war on USA, 80; escalation in war against Jews, 77–8; ignores all military advice, 82; Stauffenberg assassination attempt, 83–5, 88, 214; health declines, 87–8; effects of

INDEX

Parkinson's disease, 88; refusal to accept defeat, 88–90; launches fresh offensive on Western Front, 90; acknowledges war is lost, 90; last radio broadcasts, 91–2; refusal to surrender, 92; 'Nero order' for destruction of Germany's economic resources, 93, 145, 230–31; contempt for German people, 93, 97; retreats to bunker, 93–4; celebrates 56th birthday, 93; loses touch with reality, 94; dismisses Himmler, 95; marries Eva Braun, 96; dictates personal and political testaments, 96–7; commits suicide, 97; body burned in Reich Chancellery garden, 97; biographies of, 3–9; 'charisma', 464–5; on masculinity, 356; *Mein Kampf*, 11, 12, 13, 24–8, 51, 136, 249, 431; *Table-Talk*, 7–8, 58, 60, 71, 85, 86
Hitler, Alois (Hitler's father), 11
Hitler, Klara (Hitler's mother), 11
'Hitler diaries' (1983), 130
Hitler Gang, The (film, 1944), 106
Hoche, Alfred, 376
Hoffmann, Ernst, 306
Hoffmann, Heinrich, 40, 41, 42, 107
Hoffmann, Henriette, 40
Hoffmann, Johannes, 16
Hofweber, Max Eduard, 244
Holocaust, 77–8, 86, 176–8, 319, 345–6, 469–70
"Holocaust studies", 323
homosexuality: in the Kaiser's circle, 186; Nazi attitudes to, 159–61
homosexuals, imprisoned in concentration camps, 59, 161, 172
Horthy, Miklós, 86–7, 89, 198–9
Hösch, Leopold von, 193
Hudal, Alois von, 272
Hugenberg, Alfred, 34, 46

Hungary: Hitler orders military takeover (1944), 89; deportation of Jews, 198–9, 330
hyperinflation (1920s), 20, 152, 168, 261, 461, 462
hyper-masculinity, and Nazism, 356–8

Ilkow, Johann, 401
Israel secret service, kidnap of Eichmann, 333
Italy: North African campaign, 75; German conquest of, 81

Jäckel, Eberhard, 4, 232
Jackson, Robert, 301
Janowska extermination camp, 399
Janssen, Karl-Heinz, 232
Japan, bomb Pearl Harbour (1941), 79–80
Jewish Councils, 322, 323, 327, 345
Jewish pograms (1930s), 55–9
Jewish Women's League, 416
Jews: 'blood-libel', 294, 298; dehumanized in *Der Stürmer*, 298–9; deportation from Hungary, 89, 198–9; deported from Finland, 165; forced emigration from Austria, 327–8; looting of books and cultural artefacts, 210; mass emigration (1930s), 57; massacres in Eastern Europe, 77, 395; murdered in extermination camps, 77–8, 316, 328; persecution in 1930s Germany, 55–8, 121, 225; plans to evacuate to Madagascar, 216, 328; Polish ghettos, 72–3; Pripet Marshes massacre, 85; required to wear yellow star, 298; widespread knowledge of persecution of, 463
Jochmann, Werner, 445
Johst, Hanns, *Schlageter*, 111
Jud Süss (propaganda film, 1940), 143

589

INDEX

Jung, Edgar, 266, 267
Junge, Traudl, 77, 95, 96–7

Kahle, Hubert, 117
Kahr, Gustav Ritter von, 19
Kaltenbrunner, Ernst, 317, 325–6, 331
Kammler, Hans, 229
Kantzow, Carin von, 115, 116–17, 122
Kantzow, Nils von, 115
Kapp *putsch* (1920), 152, 245, 260, 308
Kay, Alex J., 236–7
Kehrl, Hans, 228
Keitel, Wilhelm, 196
Kellerbauer, Walther, 295
Kelley, Douglas M., 105, 128, 218, 276, 283, 287, 289
Kempke, Erich, 107
Kershaw, Ian, 4–5, 98, 431, 443
Kersten, Felix, 283, 306
Ketteler, Wilhelm von, 268–9
Kleinmichel, Bruno, 427, 429
Klemperer, Victor, 463
Klessmann, Christoph, 105
Klink, Eugen, 417
Klintzsch, Hans Ulrich, 20, 116
Klotz, Helmuth, 160
Koch, Erich, 214
Koch, Ilse: background and marriage to Karl Koch, 401–2; corruption and conduct in Buchenwald, 403; arrest and acquittal by SS tribunal, 404; unsubstantiated story of using human skin to make lampshades, 404–5; tried and sentenced by American authorities, 405–6; the 'Witch of Buchenwald', 401, 405; fresh trial in Augsburg, 406–7; commits suicide in prison, 407; notoriety, 356, 399–401
Koch, Karl Otto, 401, 402–4
Koch, Robert, 384

Kolberg (propaganda film, 1945), 145
Koonz, Claudia, 413, 416, 423, 425
Köpenick, Germany, 48
Kramer, Josef, 408
Kristallnacht (Night of Broken Glass, 1938), 58, 121, 296, 311, 378, 439–40, 450–51
Kropp, Robert, 128
Krosigk, Lutz Schwerin von, 96
Krüger, Horst, 355
Krüger, Wilhelm, 346, 348
Krummacher, Gottfried, 418
Kubizek, August, 12
Kundt, Hans, 149–50
Kunz, Helmut, 146
Kursk, battle of (1943), 83
Kwiet, Konrad, 390

Lammers, Hans-Heinrich, 368–9
Landsberg Prison, Nazi members in, 22–4
Lasch, Karl, 346–7
Lausanne, Treaty of (1923), 21
League of Nations, 61
Lebensraum ('living-space'), 4, 32, 48, 63, 68, 70, 247, 249
Leeb, Wilhelm Ritter von: military career, 359–61; role in invasion of Czechoslovakia, 361–2; reluctant support of Hitler, 362–3; promoted to Field-Marshal, 363; role in Operation Barbarossa, 363–5; resignation, 365; and the siege of Leningrad, 364, 366; buys estate at Passau with financial aid from Hitler, 368–9; at the Nuremberg trials, 370, 372–3; belief in innocence of the armed forces, 372; crimes and atrocities, 365–8; racist beliefs, 366–8
Leningrad, siege lifted (1944), 92
Lenman, Robin, 291, 294
Leviné, Eugen, 16

INDEX

Ley, Elisabeth (*née* Schmidt), 278, 282
Ley, Friedrich, 276–7
Ley, Robert, 105, 223; background and childhood, 276–7; service in First World War, 275–6, 276–7; marriages and children, 278, 282–3; Gauleiter of the Rhineland, 279–81; attempted suicides and delusional beliefs, 287; runs Nazi publishing house, 280–81; Head of German Labour Front, 281–6; Political Testament', 288; Nuremberg court indictment, 288–9; commits suicide, 289; political ideology, 284–5; psychological assessment, 275–6; 'Bauernschicksal' ('Farmer's Fate'), 275
Lidice, massacre at (1942), 316
Liebel, Willi, 296–7
Linge, Heinz, 97
Loerzer, Bruno, 113
Londonderry, Lord, 193
Longerich, Peter, 4–5, 61, 166, 173, 464–5
Loritz, Hans, 357
Lowder, J. Bryan, 239
Löwenherz, Josef, 327
Lubbe, Marinus van der, 43, 118, 264
Lübeck, bombing of, 455
Luckner, Felix von, 308
Ludendorff, Erich, 21, 22, 23, 27, 241, 243–4, 247, 371
Luftwaffe, 119–20, 124
Luppe, Hermann, 294, 296
Luther, Martin (subordinate of Ribbentrop), 197–8

Madagascar, plan to deport Jews to, 316, 328
Maercker, Georg, 308
Maisky, Ivan, 183
Majdanek extermination camp, 200, 401, 403–4
Malaparte, Curzio, 163–5, 335–6
Mann, Erika, 299, 300
Mann, Michael, 396
Mannerheim, Marshal, 75
Manstein, Erich von, 71, 371, 427, 429
Martin, Benno, 296–7
Marx, Wilhelm, 260
Maurice, Emil, 107
Mauthausen concentration camp, 225, 227
May, Karl, 12
medical experiments, on concentration camp inmates, 174, 381, 383, 385, 421, 422–3
Meissner, Otto, 38, 39, 191
Mengele, Joseph, 385, 409, 422
Messerschmitt Me262 (fighter plane), 89
Meyer, Beate, 445
Meyer, Georg, 367
Mielke, Fred, 385
Mikolaiv (Nikolajew), Crimea, 390
Milch, Erhard, 228, 306–7
Milgram, Stanley, 323
Mills, C. Wright, 108
Milward, Alan, 219
Mitford, Unity, 302
Mitscherlich, Alexander, 385
Molotov, Vyacheslav, 69, 196
Mommsen, Hans, xvi
Morell, Theo, 87, 107, 381–2
Morgen, Konrad, 401, 404
Mösenbacher, Maria, 332
Mosse, George L., 159, 219, 291
Müller, Hermann, 28, 118, 382
Müller, Karl Alexander von, 244
Munich, 13, 18, 21, 152–3, 337
Munich Agreement (1938), 66, 122
Mussolini, Benito, 20, 70, 75, 81, 95, 157, 196, 261

Natzweiler-Struthof concentration camp, 225
Nazi crimes, theories and explanations for, 393–8
Nazi Doctors' League, 378
Nazi ideology, 235–8
Nazi Party (National Socialists): Hitler renames, 18; use of physical violence, 20, 35–7, 44–7; members in Landsberg Prison, 23; increased representation in Reichstag, 29–31, 138; election campaign (1932), 31–4; propaganda, 33, 137, 139; rapid growth, 34–5, 45; Brownshirts, 35–6, 44; elections (1933), 44; seizure of power, 46–51; and the Storm Division (SA), 116; use of violence and intimidation in the 1930s, 463–4; and women's role in society, 415–16
Nazi women, demonization of, 356
Nazi–Soviet Pact (1939), 65, 69, 195–6, 213
Nebe, Arthur, 303, 313
Neithardt, Georg, 22
Netherlands, German invasion (1940), 71
Neurath, Konstantin von, 61, 64, 122, 191, 192, 193, 194–5, 314
'Night of the Long Knives' (1934), 50, 119, 156–7, 267, 340, 436, 448
Nisko, 328
Nolde, Emil, 140
Normandy landings (1944), 83
Norway, German invasion, 71–2, 213
Noske, Gustav, 307–8
November 1918 revolution (Germany), 14, 16, 151, 259, 307
Nuremberg race laws, 57, 141, 251
Nuremberg trials, 97–8, 105, 183, 207, 217, 219, 231, 319

Obersalzberg, Bavaria, 41, 84
Ohlendorf, Otto, 394
Ohm Kruger (propaganda film, 1941), 143
Olympia (Nazi documentary of 1936 Olympics), 427, 438–9
Operation Barbarossa, 75–6, 79, 125, 197, 311, 328, 363
'Operation Reinhard', 78, 329, 346
Orbán, Viktor, 147, 463
Orth, Karin, 391
Osten, Hans von, 309
Owens, Jesse, 439

Papen, Franz von: background and military training, 255–8; military attaché in Washington, 258–9; serves in First World War, 259; part ownership of *Germania* (newspaper), 260–61; Catholic faith, 261; Reich Chancellor, 31, 36, 38–40, 190–91, 262–3; underestimation of Hitler, 263–4; misunderstanding of Nazism, 265–7; Marburg address (1934), 266–7; targeted in the 'Night of the Long Knives', 267; special envoy to Austria, 267–9; ambassador to Turkey, 269; arrested and tried at Nuremberg, 270; sentenced by German Denazification court, 270; antisemitism, 264–5; Concordat with Vatican, 272; on Hermann Göring, 128; historians and contemporaries' contempt for, 255; political ideas and allegiances, 270–72; on Ribbentrop, 183–4
Papen, Martha von (*née* Boch-Galhau), 257–8
Paris: shooting of German embassy official, 58; Hitler visits after German victory, 74; liberated (1944), 92

INDEX

Paris World Exposition (1937), 224
Pauline, Princess zu Wied, 424
Paulus, Friedrich, 82
Pearl Harbour, Japanese bombing (1941), 79–80
'People's Community', appeal of, 466–7
Perl, Gisella, 408, 410–11
Péron, Juan, 331
Petacci, Clara, 95
Petri, Erna, 399
Pfeffer von Salomon, Franz, 154
Philipp of Eulenburg, Prince, 160
Phipps, Sir Eric, 111, 192
Picker, Henry, 7–8
Pierrepoint, Albert, 410
Pius XII, Pope (*formerly* Eugenio Pacelli), 261
Plauen, Saxony, 391
Poland: non-aggressive pact with Germany (1934), 62; Germany invades (1939), 69; rounding up of Jews into ghettos, 72–3, 345; Hans Frank's reign of terror, 342–4; Jews deported from, 346; euthanasia in mental institutions, 379; atrocities against Jews, 427, 429
political violence, in the 1920s, 20
Porsche, Ferdinand, 55
Potthast, Hedwig, 180
Prittwitz und Gaffron, Olga-Margarete von, 185
Protocols of the Elders of Zion, 205, 298

Quandt, Günther, 138
Quandt, Harald, 138, 146
Quisling, Vidkun, 213

'racial hygiene', 53, 384, 385
Raeder, Erich, 309
Rath, Ernst vom, 378
Rathenau, Walther, 168, 396
Ratzel, Friedrich, 247
Raubal, Angela ('Geli'), 40
Rauschning, Hermann, 4
Ravensbrück concentration camp, 316, 317, 423
Reeves, Elmer, 33
Rehborn, Julius, 377
Reich Chancellery, and Hitler's bunker, 93
Reich Criminal Code, 340, 341
Reich Security Head Office, 310, 317
Reichenau, General von, 429
Reichstag: elections (1928), 28, 137; Communists win seats in, 29, 38; elections (1932), 30–31, 38–9, 118, 139; Nazi deputies attend in uniform, 35; stalemate in (1930s), 37–9; Hitler appointed Chancellor, 39–40; burned down, 43, 118, 264; elections (1933), 44; passes Enabling Act, 45–6; Reichstag Fire Decree, 46, 139; ceases to meet (1942), 76
Reiter, Maria, 40
Remnitz, Gustav von, 195
Residents' Defence League (*Einwohnerwehr*), 152
Retterpath, Walter, 403
Reval (Tallinn), Estonia, 203
Rhineland, French occupation, 135, 278
Ribbentrop, Annelies von (*née* Henkell), 189, 200
Ribbentrop, Joachim von: background and family, 184–6; work in Canada, 186–7; returns to Europe on the *Potsdam*, 187–8; serves in First World War, 188; wine-selling business, 189–90; joins Nazi Party, 191; role in Hitler's appointment as chancellor, 191; foreign policy missions for Hitler, 191–2; in London to negotiate Anglo-German

INDEX

Ribbentrop, Joachim von – *cont'd*.
Naval Agreement, 192; German Ambassador to Britain, 193–4; role as Foreign Minister, 64, 122, 194–7; signs Nazi–Soviet Pact, 69, 195–6; role in deportation of Hungarian Jews, 198–9; attempt to broker peace with Soviets, 199; arrested by the British, 199; at the Nuremberg trials, 199–200; command of foreign languages, 186, 191–2; gaffes and errors, 194, 196–7; historians and contemporaries' contempt for, 183–4; numerous grand residences, 195; psychological assessment, 105

Ribbentrop, Richard, 184–6

Ribbentrop, Rudolf von, 200–1

Richthofen, Baron Manfred von, 114

Riefenstahl, Leni, background and career as dancer, 432–3; won over by Hitler to Nazism, 430–31; film star and movie-making, 433–4; part of Hitler's inner circle, 434–5, 436–7; makes Nazi propaganda films, 436; witnesses killing of Jews in Poland, 427–9; antisemitism, 431; artistic and cultural attitudes, 441–2; attempts to distance herself from Nazis, 429–30, 440; classed as 'fellow-traveller' in denazification investigations, 440; Goebbels hostility to, 436–7; post-war film work, 356, 440–41; Susan Sontag's essay on, 441; *Das blaue Licht* (*The Blue Light*, film, 1932), 431, 434, 441; *Olympia* (Nazi documentary of 1936 Olympics), 438–9; *Sieg des Glaubens* (*Victory of Faith*, film, 1933), 436; *Tiefland* (*Lowlands*, film, 1954), 440, 441; *Triumph des Willens* (*Triumph of the Will*, Nazi propaganda film, 1934), 41–2, 437–8

Rieth, Kurt, 267

Risser, Alfred, 406

Ritter von Epp, Franz, 151–2

Ritter von Kahr, Gustav, 50, 247

Röhm, Ernst: background and military training, 150–51; wounded in First World War, 151; joins Free Corps after the war, 151–2; friendship with Hitler, 23, 152; at the beer-hall *putsch*, 152–3; joins German military mission in Bolivia, 149–50, 153; leadership of the stormtroopers (SA), 50, 154–7, 161; Minister and member of Reichstag cabinet, 155; arrested and shot dead in the 'Night of the Long Knives', 156–7; character and motivations, 157–8; cultural interests, 161–2; homosexuality, 158–60; member of Thule Society, 245; military character, 150, 158

Rolff, Robert, 283

Rommel, Erwin, 75, 80–81

Roosevelt, Franklin D., 80, 94

Roques, General von, 367–8

Rosen, Eric von, 115

Rosenberg, Alfred: Baltic German heritage, 203–4; witnesses Bolshevik revolution, 203–4; antisemitic writings, 205–8, 216; acting leader of the Nazi Party, 206–7; in charge of Nazi political education and censorship, 209; looting of Jewish books and art, 210; plans for Institute for Research on the Jewish Question, 210–11; 'Fighting League for German Culture', 140, 211; influence in foreign policy, 211–13; Reich Minister for Occupied Eastern Territories, 214–15; mass shootings of Jews in Eastern territories, 216–17; at the Nuremberg trials, 217;

autobiography, 217; lack of humanity, 218; member of Thule Society, 245; on Nazi opposition to homosexuality, 160; psychological assessment in Nuremberg, 105, 217–18; visceral antisemitism, 216; *The Myth of the 20th Century*, 207–9

Roth, Kunigunde, 292

Ruhr: Communist uprising (1920), 152, 246, 260; French occupation, 20–21, 261, 278

Rupprecht, Philippe, 297

Rupprecht of Bavaria, 'Crown Prince', 153, 157

Saarland, reintegration into Germany (1935), 62

Sachsenhausen concentration camp, 224, 401, 402

Sassen, Wilhelm, 332–3

Sauckel, Fritz, 227, 231–2, 286

Schacht, Hjalmar, 54, 64, 120, 183, 286

Schaub, Julius, 41, 107

Schellenberg, Walter, 303, 312

Schirach, Baldur von, 105, 208

Schleicher, Kurt von, 31, 38–9, 48, 50–51, 118, 119, 191, 261, 262, 263

Schmidt, Matthias, 232

Schmundt, Rudolf, 367, 368

Scholtz, Günther, 417

Scholtz-Klink, Gertrud: background and rise in Nazi movement, 416–18; 'Reich Women's Leader', 413–16, 419–20; marriage to August Heissmeyer, 422–3; antisemitism, 423; imprisonment and later life, 424; role in Nazi regime, 425–6; interview with Claudia Koonz, 356, 413, 416, 432

Schönerer, Georg Ritter von, 12

Schröder, Kurt von, 39

Schroeder, Christa, 88

Schudnagies, Christian, 335

Schuschnigg, Kurt, 65, 261, 268

Schwarz, Franz Xaver, 287

Schweitzer, Albert, 377

Schwerin von Krosigk, Lutz Graf, 107

Seeckt, Hans von, 239, 261, 361, 370

Segel, Gertrude, 399

Seitz, Anni, 297

Sereny, Gitta, 219

Seyss-Inquart, Arthur, 65, 199

Shakespeare, William, Hitler quotes from, 25

Siber, Paula, 417–18

Siedler, Wolf Jobst, 221, 232

Siles, Hernando (President of Bolivia), 150

Simferopol, Ukraine, 390

Six, Alfred, 303

Sobibór extermination camp, 78, 316

Social Democrats, 14–15, 36, 45, 48, 467

Sokal, Harry R., 431, 433

Solmitz, Friedrich, 445–6, 449–54, 459

Solmitz, Gisela, 446, 447, 450, 454, 456, 460

Solmitz, Luise: background, 445–6; support for Hitler, 446–7; criticism of the Nazi regime, 448; enthusiasm for Nazi regime, 449; in 'privileged mixed marriage', 450, 452–3, 459; persecution of Jewish husband and daughter, 450–51, 454; pride at German military successes, 452; on the bombing of Hamburg, 455–6; turns against Hitler, 456–60; diaries, 445, 446

Sonnemann, Emmy (*later* Göring), 122, 129–30

Sontag, Susan, essay on Leni Riefenstahl's work, 441

INDEX

Soviet Union: Nazi–Soviet Pact (1939), 69; Germany invades (1941), 75–6; successfully repels Operation Barbarossa, 78–9; battle of Stalingrad, 80–81; Red Army advances towards Germany, 88–9; *Einsatzgruppen* operating in, 312–13

Speer, Albert: background and education, 221–2; takes commissions from the Nazi Party, 223; designs Nazi Party rally site, 223; directs 'Beauty of Labour' programme, 223–4; contract for Reich Chancellery, 224; urban plan for Berlin, 224–6; use of forced labour on building projects, 224–5, 227, 229; construction projects for the armed forces, 225; German pavilion at Paris World Exposition (1937), 224; accompanies Hitler to Paris, 74, 225; appointed Minister of Munitions, 226–9; takes control of war economy, 125, 226–30; supplies finance and materials to extend Auschwitz, 227; present at Himmler's 'Final Solution' speech, 229; claims plan to assassinate Hitler, 230–31; ignores Hitler's 'Nero' order, 93, 230–31; at the Nuremberg trials, 219, 229, 231; imprisoned in Spandau Prison, 232; sanitized reputation, 219–20, 232; claims of innocence, 462–3; on Hermann Göring, 126; on Hitler's charisma, 42; on Hitler's declining health, 88; *Inside the Third Reich* (memoir), 4, 219–20, 227–8, 463

Speer, Margarete (*née* Weber), 222, 232

Spilcker, Inga, 282–3

Spitzy, Reinhard, 183, 194

SS Security Service (SD), 303, 305, 389–90

'stab-in-the-back' myth, 188, 292

Stahlecker, Walther, 367

Stalin, Josef: Nazi–Soviet Pact (1939), 69; encourages resistance to Germans, 78; refusal to help the Poles, 89; ethnic cleansing of Germans, 216

Stalingrad, German defeat at, 81–2, 144–5

Stangneth, Bettina, 332

Stauffenberg, Claus von, attempt to assassinate Hitler, 84, 177, 214

Steiner, Felix, 94

Stelling, Johannes, 48

Stennes, Walter, 35, 154

Stephan, Werner, 445, 447–8

Stephenson, Jill, 420–21

sterilization programme, 378

Stolpshof concentration camp, 312

Stolzing-Cerny, Josef, 24

Stone, Dan, 470

Stormtroopers (*Sturmabteilung*; SA), 49–50, 116, 118, 119

Strasser, Gregor, 27, 38, 50, 119, 137, 139, 169, 251, 263, 281, 305, 418

Strasser, Otto, 34–5, 137

Strauss, Richard, 211

Streicher, Elmar, 302

Streicher, Julius: modest background, 291–2; service in First World War, 292; joins Nazi Party, 294–5; edits *Der Stürmer* (newspaper), 297–9; joins the beer-hall *putsch*, 295; on Nuremberg city council, 295–6; Gauleiter of Franconia, 296; dismissed by Hitler for misdemeanours, 297; founds Stürmer publishing house, 299;

arrested and imprisoned, 300; at the Nuremberg trials, 301; convicted and hanged, 301; alternative lifestyle, 291; devotion to Hitler, 293–4; extreme antisemitism, 292–5, 296, 298–300, 301, 302; oratory, 294; poems and paintings, 291; 'Political Testament', 293; psychological assessment, 105, 292; sexual obsessiveness, 300
Streicher, Lothar, 291, 301
'Strength Through Joy' scheme, 284, 285
Stresemann, Gustav, 21
Stumpfegger, Ludwig, 146
Stürmer, Der (newspaper), 295, 297–300, 301
Swedish Legation, works to save Jews in Budapest, 330

Tappe, Adele, 300
Taylor, Telford, 321, 373
Tessenow, Heinrich, 222
Thälmann, Ernst, 172, 178
Theresienstadt concentration camp, 317
Theweleit, Klaus, *Männerphantasien (Male Fantasies)*, 246, 250
Thierack, Otto-Georg, 347
Third Reich: established, 43, 51; command economy, 54; dictatorship, 464–6
Thule Society (*Thule-Gesellschaft*), 244–5, 337
Thyssen, Fritz, 33
Times, The, 36
Todt, Fritz, 125, 226, 228
Toller, Ernst, 16
Treblinka extermination camp, 78, 316, 346
Treitschke, Heinrich, 246
Trenker, Luis, 433

Trevor-Roper, Hugh, 4, 106–7, 127, 165, 219
Triumph of the Will (Nazi propaganda film, 1934), 356, 427, 437–8
Troost, Paul Ludwig, 224
Truman, President, 406
Trump, Donald, 147
Tukhachevsky, Marshal, 82
Turkey, establishment of Republic (1923), 21

Ukraine, German atrocities in, 78, 214
Ullrich, Volker, 4–5, 232
Ulm officers' trial, 35
United States of America: supply Allies with military aid, 77; Atlantic Charter, 77, 79–80; bombing of Pearl Harbour, 78–9

Vaillant-Couturier, Marie-Claude, xxi–xxiv
Vatican: Reich Concordat with, 59; support of authoritarian regimes, 46
Versailles, Treaty of, 15, 21, 62, 63, 66, 115
Verschuer, Otmar Baron von, 385
Vienna, Academy of Fine Arts, 11, 12
Vienna Settlement (1815), 255
Völkischer Beobachter (newspaper), 205–6, 343
Volkish ideology, 291
Volkssturm ('People' Storm'), 89–90
Volkswagen car, 55

Wächter, Otto, 346
Wäckerle, Hilmar, 340
Wagner, Eduard, 303
Wagner, Gerhard, 378, 379, 384
Wagner, Richard, 12, 307
Wagner, Robert, 417, 418
Wagner, Winifred, 40, 42, 107, 435

Wald, Renate, 278, 282, 288
Wall Street crash (1929), 28, 28–9
Wallenberg, Raul, 330
Wanderer, Madeleine, 283
Wannsee Conference (1942), 197, 217, 305, 314, 329, 345
war reparations (after First World War), 15, 20–21, 29, 34
Warburg, Max, 280
Warsaw: destruction of, 88–9; evacuated by the Germans, 92
Wecker, Ingrid, 302
Weimar Republic, 15, 19, 28, 30, 37, 51, 152
Weininger, Otto, 161
Welles, Sumner, 197
Wels, Otto, 45
Wessel, Horst, 36, 138
Wiedemann, Fritz, 107, 133
Wildt, Michael, 166, 324, 396
Wilhelm, 'Crown Prince', support for Hitler, 33–4
Wilhelm, ex-Kaiser, 117, 160, 185–6
Willhaus, Liesel, 399
Windsor, Duke of (*formerly* Edward VIII), 193, 197, 283
Wolff, Karl, 303

women: concentration camp guards, 411–12; convicted of Nazi crimes, 408; experience of war in Germany, 458–9; Nazi attitudes to, 415–16; role in Nazi regime, 421, 426
Workers' and Soldiers' Councils, 14, 15, 151
World at War, The (TV series), 221
Wrisberg, Ernst von, 188

Yugoslavia, 75

Zapp, Paul: ideological background, 387–90; mass killings of Jews in Eastern Europe, 390–91; eventual trial and imprisonment, 391
Zeitzler, Kurt, 81–2
Zhukov, Georgy, 79
Zill, Egon, as concentration camp guard, 391–3
Zill, Elfriede, 392
Zipperling, Oskar, 446
Zörgiebel, Karl, 137
Zyklon-B, 78

ALSO AVAILABLE

THE COMING OF THE THIRD REICH

There is no story in twentieth-century history more important to understand than Hitler's rise to power and the collapse of civilization in Nazi Germany. With *The Coming of the Third Reich*, historian Richard J. Evans restores drama and contingency to the rise to power of Hitler and the Nazis, even as it shows how ready Germany was by the early 1930s for such a takeover to occur. *The Coming of the Third Reich* is a masterwork of the historian's art and the book by which all others on the subject will be judged.

THE THIRD REICH IN POWER

By 1933, the democracy of the Weimar Republic had been transformed into the police state of the Third Reich, mobilized around the cult of the leader, Adolf Hitler. Evans chronicles the incredible story of Germany's radical reshaping under Nazi rule. As the Holocaust began, Hitler's drive to prepare Germany for the war that he saw as its destiny reached its fateful hour in September 1939. This is the fullest and most authoritative account yet written of how, in six years, Germany was brought to the edge of that terrible abyss.

THE PURSUIT OF POWER

Richard J. Evans returns with an addition to the acclaimed Penguin History of Europe series, covering the period from the fall of Napoleon to the outbreak of World War I. Among the great themes it discusses are the rise of secular science and medicine; the journey of art, music, and literature from Romanticism to Modernism; and the emergence of industrial society. The first single-volume history of the century, this comprehensive account gives the reader a magnificently human picture of Europe in the age when it dominated the rest of the globe.

Ready to find your next great read? Let us help. Visit prh.com/nextread